Written by the TeeJay Writing Group

HODDER
GIBSON
AN HACHETTE UK COMPANY

Acknowledgements

Every effort has been made to trace all copyright holders, but if any have been inadvertently overlooked, the Publishers will be pleased to make the necessary arrangements at the first opportunity.

Although every effort has been made to ensure that website addresses are correct at time of going to press, Hodder Gibson cannot be held responsible for the content of any website mentioned in this book. It is sometimes possible to find a relocated web page by typing in the address of the home page for a website in the URL window of your browser.

Hachette UK's policy is to use papers that are natural, renewable and recyclable products and made from wood grown in well-managed forests and other controlled sources. The logging and manufacturing processes are expected to conform to the environmental regulations of the country of origin.

Orders

Orders: please contact Hachette UK Distribution, Hely Hutchinson Centre, Milton Road, Didcot, Oxfordshire, OX11 7HH. Telephone: +44 (0)1235 827827. Email education@hachette.co.uk

Lines are open from 9 a.m. to 5 p.m., Monday to Friday. You can also order through our website:

www.hoddergibson.co.uk

If you have queries or questions that aren't about an order you can contact us at hoddergibson@hodder.co.uk

Higher Textbook

This book covers the entire contents of the **Higher** course in depth, assuming students have completed **National 5**, (see TeeJay's Books **CfE4+** and **N5**), or equivalent and the book will also provide a firm foundation for those students who wish to continue on to Advanced Higher Mathematics.

- The teaching panels provide an explanation of the topic with full notes and worked examples.

- Students should have obtained a **National 5** qualification, or equivalent, before using this book.

- This **TeeJay** book covers the **Scottish Higher Course** in its entirety, with what we feel is just the right number of questions accompanying each exercise, thus providing adequate practice at each topic, and including challenging questions where appropriate.

- Students who cope well with the content of the course will be well prepared to sit the SQA Higher Exam at the end of the course.

- The book begins with a **Chapter Zero**, which primarily revises all necessary algebraic and numeric skills from National 5, covered in TeeJay's Books 4^+ and **N5**.

- Several chapters begin with a **Recall** exercise for extra revision.

- Each chapter ends with an **Exam Practice Exercise**, containing exam type questions, similar to those used in the last 20 years of Higher Maths Papers.

- Every three chapters are followed by a **Cumulative Home Exercise** allowing recall skills to be assessed.

- The book may be used as a free standing resource for students returning in S5 or S6 who intend to sit the **Higher** examination.

- It includes a **Specimen Higher Exam Paper 1 and Paper 2**.

- Answers for Home Exercises and Specimen Exam Papers can be found at www.hoddergibson.co.uk/teejay-maths-higher-answers

- Higher Support Material will be developed by TeeJay to provide extra practice resources.

We make no apologies for the multiplicity of colours used throughout the book, both for text and in diagrams - we feel it helps brighten up the pages !!

T Strang, J Geddes, J Cairns

(July 2018)

Contents

TeeJay Higher Maths

Introduction

The following examples revise the important topics from the Algebraic/Numeric content of the National 5 course.
The Higher Course will assume you understand and are confident in the use of most of this material.

As much as 60% of the Higher Course relies on algebraic manipulation so it is imperative you work your way though the examples in this Chapter Zero, and seek help in overcoming any early problems.

1. Expand and simplify :-

   (a) $(3a + 5b)(a - 2b)$ (b) $(2x - 7)^2$

   (c) $(x - 3)^3$ (d) $(x + 5)^2 - (x - 5)^2$

   (e) $(3x - 1)^2 - (2x + 1)(3x - 2)$

   (f) $2(5t - 1)^2 - (6t + 1)^2$.

2. The diagram shows a rectangle measuring $(3x + 2)$ centimetres by $(x + 3)$ centimetres.

   A smaller rectangle measuring $(x + 4)$ centimetres by $(x + 1)$ centimetres has been removed.

   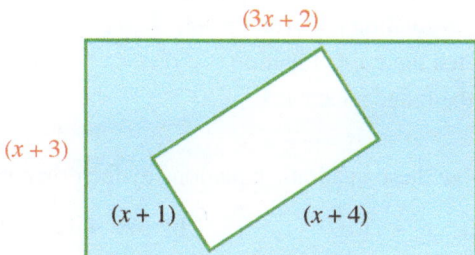

   Calculate the blue area in terms of x.

3. Calculate :-

   (a) $2\frac{1}{4} + 3\frac{1}{2}$ (b) $5\frac{5}{6} - \frac{2}{3}$

   (c) $\frac{5}{6} - \frac{2}{5}$ (d) $6\frac{1}{2} + 2\frac{7}{8}$

   (e) $3\frac{3}{4} + 7\frac{2}{3}$ (f) $8\frac{9}{10} - 8\frac{2}{5}$

   (g) $4\frac{1}{4} - 2\frac{2}{3}$ (h) $6 - 2\frac{5}{9}$.

4. Calculate :-

   (a) $\frac{9}{10} \times \frac{2}{3}$ (b) $\frac{3}{5} \times \frac{7}{12}$

   (c) $3\frac{3}{4} \times 2\frac{1}{5}$ (d) $4\frac{1}{2} \times 1\frac{1}{6}$

   (e) $\frac{5}{6} \div \frac{2}{3}$ (f) $\frac{5}{12} \div \frac{3}{4}$

   (g) $3\frac{2}{3} \div 1\frac{1}{6}$ (h) $\frac{2}{3}$ of $(5\frac{1}{4} \div 3\frac{1}{2})$.

5. Factorise fully :-

   (a) $8x^2 + 6x$ (b) $ab^2c - 2abc^2$

   (c) $x^2 + 3x - 28$ (d) $x^2 - 8x + 16$

   (e) $x^2 - 2x - 63$ (f) $x^2 + 2xy - 15y^2$

   (g) $3x^2 - 75$ (h) $2px^2 - 18p$

   (i) $2x^2 - 5x - 12$ (j) $6x^2 + 28x - 10$

   (k) $10a^2 - 29ab + 10b^2$ (l) $20 - x - x^2$.

6. Simplify :-

   (a) $\frac{1}{x} - \frac{1}{y}$ (b) $\frac{3}{x} + \frac{2}{3x}$

   (c) $\frac{2}{x} + \frac{1}{x - 1}$ (d) $\frac{3}{x - 2} - \frac{2}{x + 2}$

   (e) $\frac{2}{x^2} - \frac{5}{x}$ (f) $\frac{3}{x(x - 1)} + \frac{1}{x(x + 3)}$

   (g) $\frac{3}{(x + 2)(x - 1)} + \frac{2}{(x + 2)(x + 1)}$

   (h) $\frac{2}{x(x - 3)} - \frac{4}{x(x + 5)}$

   (i) $\frac{1}{x^2 - 1} + \frac{1}{x^2 + x}$.

7. Simplify :-

   (a) $\frac{x - 3}{x(x - 3)}$ (b) $\frac{(x + 2)(x - 2)}{x(x + 2)}$

   (c) $\frac{x - 5}{x^2 - 5x}$ (d) $\frac{x^2 - 16}{x^2 - 4x}$

   (e) $\frac{x^2 + 5x + 6}{x^2 + 6x + 8}$ (f) $\frac{x^2 - 36}{x^2 + 8x + 12}$.

8. Change the subject each time to the variable shown in brackets.

   (a) $y = mx + c$ (x) (b) $C = 3(a - b)$ (b)

   (c) $V = \frac{1}{3}\pi r^2 h$ (h) (d) $V = \frac{1}{3}\pi r^2 h$ (r)

   continued ....

8. .... continued

(e) $mx + n = px + r$ (x) (f) $T = \dfrac{3g}{2h}$ (h)

(g) $\sqrt{2M - n} = 3q$ (M) (h) $\dfrac{w - 2a}{w - 2b} = 4.$ (w)

9. Solve the following pairs of simultaneous equations :-

(a) $5x - 2y = 7$
$x + 4y = 19$

(b) $4x + 3y = 1$
$3x + 7y = -4$

(c) $1·5x - y = 0$
$3x + 2·5y = 27$

(d) $y = x - 4$
$3y - 2x + 6 = 0.$

10. Simplify :-

(a) $\sqrt{50}$

(b) $\sqrt{300}$

(c) $5\sqrt{8} + 8\sqrt{8}$

(d) $\sqrt{50} + \sqrt{50}$

(e) $3\sqrt{2} \times 5$

(f) $2\sqrt{5} \times 5\sqrt{2}$

(g) $\sqrt{2} + 2\sqrt{8} - \sqrt{18}$

(h) $3\sqrt{6} \times 4\sqrt{6}$

(i) $4\sqrt{10} \times 3\sqrt{5}$

(j) $4\sqrt{3}(5\sqrt{3} - 1)$

(k) $2\sqrt{12}(\sqrt{12} - \sqrt{3})$

(l) $(3\sqrt{7} + 1)(2\sqrt{7} - 1)$

(m) $(4\sqrt{3} - 2\sqrt{5})^2.$

11. Simplify :-

(a) $4x^3 \times 5x^2$

(b) $\dfrac{10p^5}{2p^{-1}}$

(c) $(4m^2)^3$

(d) $(3r^2s^3)^4$

(e) $(3x + \frac{1}{x})^2$

(f) $2h^{\frac{1}{2}}(3h^{\frac{5}{2}} - 5h^{-\frac{1}{2}})$

(g) $(x^{\frac{1}{2}} - x^{-\frac{1}{2}})^2$

(h) $(8m^{\frac{3}{2}})^{\frac{2}{3}}$

(i) $2b^2 \times (b^2)^3$

(j) $\frac{1}{n^3} \times (n^2)^5$

(k) $\dfrac{4w^3 \times 3w^{-2}}{6w}$

(l) $(15t^{-2} \div 3t^{-1})^{-1}$

(m) $3a^2b^{-2} \times 4a^{-1}b^3$

(n) $\dfrac{20p^3q^{-2}}{4p^{-1}q^{-3}}$.

12. Evaluate :-

(a) $36^{\frac{1}{2}}$

(b) $8^{\frac{2}{3}}$

(c) $4^{-\frac{3}{2}}$

(d) $7^0 + 2^{-1}$

(e) $10000^{\frac{1}{4}}$

(f) $64^{-\frac{1}{3}}$

(g) $27^{\frac{2}{3}} \times 4^{-\frac{1}{2}}$

(h) $64^{\frac{1}{2}} \div 8^{-\frac{1}{3}}.$

13. Express with a rational denominator :-
(*in its simplest form*)

(a) $\dfrac{3}{\sqrt{6}}$

(b) $\dfrac{\sqrt{20}}{\sqrt{4}}$

(c) $\dfrac{3\sqrt{6}}{6\sqrt{3}}$

(d) $\sqrt{6} + \dfrac{8}{\sqrt{6}}.$

14. (a) Given $f(x) = x^2 - 3x + 5$, find $f(4)$.

(b) Evaluate $f(-3)$, given $f(m) = m^3 - 2m^2$.

(c) Given $g(y) = 5y^2 - 7y$, find $g(-1)$.

(d) Evaluate $h(5)$, given $h(x) = \sqrt{x^2 + 2x + 1}.$

(e) Given $g(x) = x^3 - x^2 + 1$, find $g(2p)$.

(f) If $f(x) = 4x - 3$, find m given that $f(m) = 17$.

(g) If a function is defined as $f(x) = x^2 - \frac{1}{2}$, find w, given $f(w) = \frac{17}{2}$. (*Hint :- there are 2 answers*).

(h) A function is defined as $f(x) = 2x(x - 5)$. Find c given $f(c) = 12$.

(i) Given $f(x) = 2x - 7$ and $g(x) = 5 - x$, find z, if $f(z) = -g(z)$.

15. By evaluating $f(x)$, for $x = $ -3, -2, -1, ... 2, 3, sketch the **cubic** function :- $f(x) = x^3 - 4x$, in the range $-3 \le x \le 3$.

16. Solve these quadratic equations by factorising :-

(a) $x^2 - 7x = 0$

(b) $4x^2 + 12x = 0$

(c) $10x^2 - 5x = 0$

(d) $x^2 - 16 = 0$

(e) $2x^2 - 50 = 0$

(f) $25 - 36x^2 = 0$

(g) $x^2 + 7x + 12 = 0$

(h) $x^2 - 4x - 21 = 0$

(i) $40 - 3x - x^2 = 0$

(j) $3x(2x - 5) = 9$

(k) $6x^2 + 11x - 10 = 0$

(l) $(x - 3)^2 = 25.$

17. Find the coordinates of points P, Q, R, S, T, U, V and W for the following 3 parabolas :-

(a)

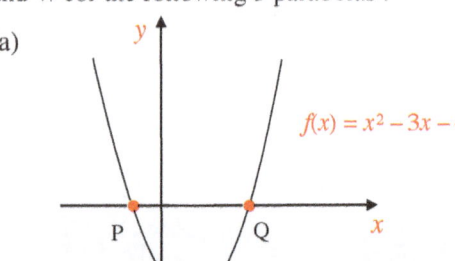

$f(x) = x^2 - 3x - 4$

continued ....

17. (b)

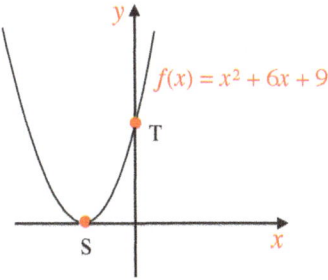

$f(x) = x^2 + 6x + 9$

(c)

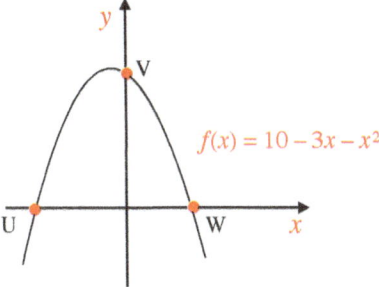

$f(x) = 10 - 3x - x^2$

18. Write each equation in **completed square form**, showing each stage of your working :-

(a) $y = x^2 - 4x + 3$ (b) $y = x^2 + 10x + 20$.

(c) $y = x^2 + 3x - 1$ (d) $y = x^2 - 6x$

(e) $y = 8 + 4x - x^2$ (f) $y = 12x - x^2$.

19. Solve, to 1 decimal place :-

(a) $x^2 + 6x + 3 = 0$ (b) $x^2 - 5x + 2 = 0$

(c) $x^2 - 7x - 1 = 0$ (d) $2x^2 + 7x + 4 = 0$

(e) $4x^2 = 7 - x$ (f) $(x - 1)^2 - 5 = 0$.

20. Each parabola is of the form :-

$y = (x - a)^2 + b$ or $y = b - (x - a)^2$.

For each parabola, find :-

(i) the values of a and b.

(ii) the equation of the **axis of symmetry**.

(iii) the coordinates of the point where the parabola crosses the y-axis.

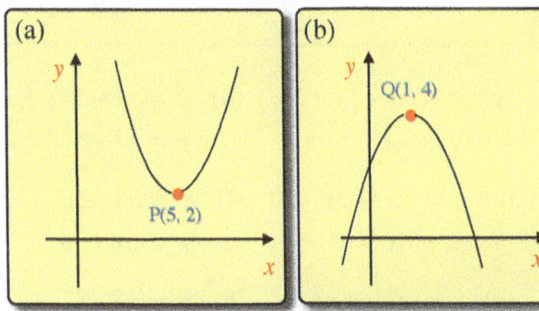

(a)

P(5, 2)

(b)

Q(1, 4)

(c)

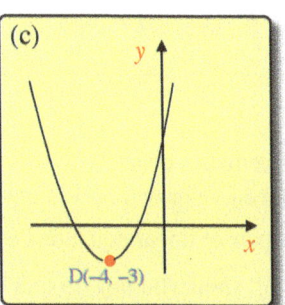

D(-4, -3)

(d)

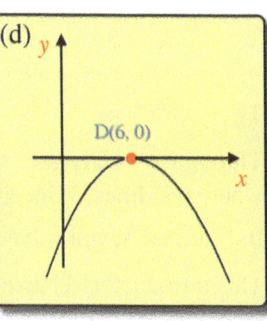

D(6, 0)

21. The following two parabolas are of the form $y = kx^2$, where k may be positive or negative.

Find the equation of each parabola.

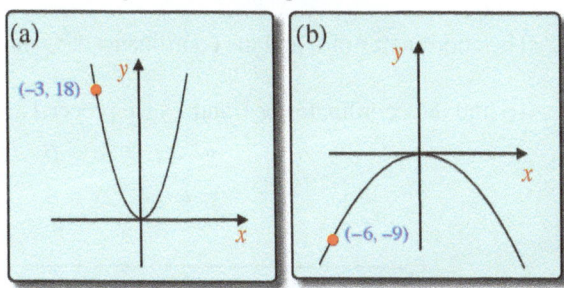

(a)

(-3, 18)

(b)

(-6, -9)

22. Calculate the **discriminant** for each of these and use it to determine the **nature** of the roots :-

(a) $x^2 + 6x + 3 = 0$ (b) $x^2 + 2x + 5 = 0$

(c) $2x^2 + 6x - 1 = 0$ (d) $5x^2 - 10x + 5 = 0$.

23. $x^2 + ax + 9 = 0$ has 1 root. Find two values for a.

24. $bx^2 + 4x + 2 = 0$ has two real distinct roots.
Set up an inequality in b, and solve for b.

25. $px^2 - 10x + p = 0$ has 1 root. Find two values for p.

26. Shown below is the graph of the function :-

$f(x) = 2x^2 - 3x - 1$.

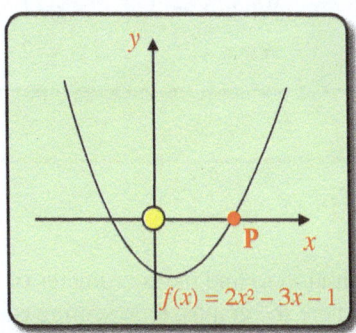

$f(x) = 2x^2 - 3x - 1$

P

Determine the coordinates of the point **P**.
Give your answer to two decimal places.

Introduction

Throughout the Higher mathematics course you will be required, on many occasions, to find the point(s) where two lines, a line and a curve or two curves meet.

In National 5, you solved a pair of linear equations using the **simultaneous equations** method.

This introductory chapter will show you how to quickly and efficiently use the "**substitution method**".

Example 1 :- The diagram shows the graphs of two functions :-

    (1)   The line $y - x + 5 = 0$

    (2)   The parabola $y = x^2 - 2x - 3$.

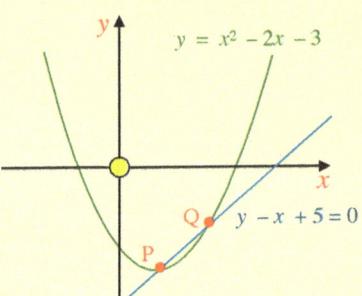

The coordinates of P and the coordinates of Q must satisfy both equations.

To find the coordinates of P and Q, we proceed as follows :-

$$y - x + 5 = 0 \qquad - \quad \textbf{(1)}$$
$$y = x^2 - 2x - 3 \qquad - \quad \textbf{(2)}$$

Step 1 :-   Consider the simpler equation, (the line here), and arrange it to obtain letter y (or x) by itself.

            =>   from **(1)**   => $y = x - 5$

Step 2 :-   Now look at the 2nd equation, and where the letter y appears, **substitute** $y = x - 5$ instead.

$$y = x^2 - 2x - 3 \qquad - \quad \textbf{(2)}$$
$$(x - 5) = x^2 - 2x - 3$$

(rearrange this) $x^2 - 2x - 3 - x + 5 = 0$ (we've eliminated y)

(tidy it up) $x^2 - 3x + 2 = 0$,   *(which we can solve by factorising)*

                 $(x - 1)(x - 2) = 0$

                 $x = 1$ or $x = 2$.

Step 3 :-   Now substitute $x = 1$ and $x = 2$ into **(1)** in order to find the values of y.

      When $x = 1$ $y = 1 - 5 = $ -4 => **P(1, -4)**

      When $x = 2$ $y = 2 - 5 = $ -3 => **Q(2, -3)**.

Exercise H1·1

1.   Use substitution to find the coordinates of the point(s) where the graphs, representing each pairs of curves, meet.

    (a) $y = x^2 - 2x - 8$ (b) $y = 2x^2 + 3x - 7$
           $y = 2x - 11$ $y = 3x + 1$

    (c) $y = x^2 + 5x - 2$ (d) $y = x^2 + 5x + 3$
           $y = 4x$ $y = x^2 + 8$

    (e) $y = 2x^2 - 3x - 10$ (f) $y = x^2 - 2x$
           $y - 5x = 0$ $y = 3x + 14$

    (g) $y = x^2 - x - 6$ (h) $y = x^2 - 8$
           $y = 3x - x^2$ $y = 10 - x^2$.

Lines and Circles etc.

Later in the course you will meet various curves :-

cubics, circles, ellipses, quartics, hyperbolas etc.

The substitution method is used to find where any two curves intersect.

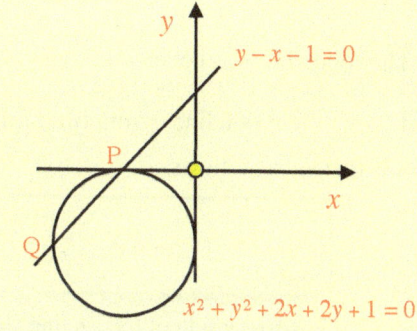

Example 2 :- Find where the line and circle intersect :-

The line $y - x - 1 = 0$ –   **(1)**

The circle* $x^2 + y^2 + 2x + 2y + 1 = 0$ –   **(2)**

Step 1 :-   Rearrange equation **(1)** to become $y = x + 1$

Step 2 :-   Substitute $(x + 1)$ for y in equation **(2)**.

$$x^2 + y^2 + 2x + 2y + 1 = 0$$

$$x^2 + (x + 1)^2 + 2x + 2(x + 1) + 1 = 0 \qquad (\textit{we have eliminated } y)$$

$$x^2 + x^2 + 2x + 1 + 2x + 2x + 2 + 1 = 0$$

$$2x^2 + 6x + 4 = 0$$

$$x^2 + 3x + 2 = 0$$

$$(x + 1)(x + 2) = 0 \quad => \quad x = \text{-1 or -2.}$$

Step 3 :-   Substitute $x = \text{-1}$ in   **(1)**, $y = \text{-1} + 1 = 0$,   **P(-1, 0)**

Substitute $x = \text{-2}$ in   **(1)** $y = \text{-2} + 1 = \text{-1}$,   **Q(-2, -1).**

* You will meet the equation of a circle in Chapter 9.

Exercise H1·2

1.   Use the substitution method to find the coordinates of the points where each pair of curves meet :-

(a) $x^2 + y^2 = 16$
    $y = x - 4$

(b) $x^2 + 2y^2 = 11$
    $y = x - 2$

(c) $x^2 - 2y^2 = 1$
    $y = x - 1$

(d) $4y^2 - 3x^2 - 1 = 0$
    $x - 2y - 1 = 0$

(e) $y = x - 4$
    $y^2 = 26 - x^2$

(f) $y = \dfrac{12}{x}$
    $y = 2x - 2$

(g) $y = \sqrt{x}$
    $x^2 - y^2 = 12$
    (careful with answer)

(h) $x = y^2 - 5$
    $x^2 + y^2 = 25.$
    (careful with answer)

2.   Find the coordinates of the points where the line

$$y + 3x + 1 = 0$$

and the circle

$$x^2 + y^2 + 24x + 10y - 1 = 0$$

meet.

3.   If a line and a circle meet at only one point, then the line is a **tangent** to the circle.

(a)   Show that the line $y = 3x + 10$ is a tangent to the circle $x^2 + y^2 - 8x - 4y - 20 = 0.$

(b)   Find the point of intersection.

A Summary of National 5 Line Work

The following was covered in **National 5** :-

The **gradient** of a line is simply a measure of how **steep** the line is.
It is defined as follows :-

$$\text{gradient} = m_{AB} = \frac{vertical}{horizontal} = \frac{BC}{AC} = \frac{y_2 - y_1}{x_2 - x_1}$$

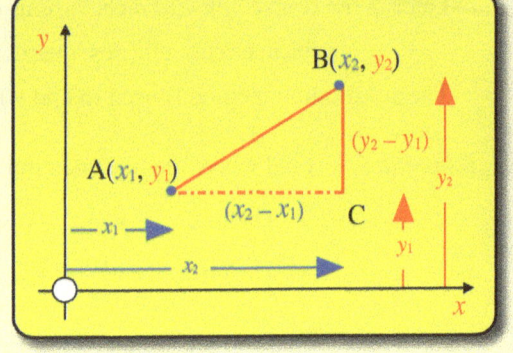

Positive gradient means line slopes up from left to right.
Negative gradient means line slopes down from left to right.

Example 1 :-   Find the gradient of the line joining
P(-3, 10) to Q(3, 0).

Here, $x_1 = -3$, $x_2 = 3$, $y_1 = 10$, $y_2 = 0$.

$$m = \frac{y_2 - y_1}{x_2 - x_1} = \frac{0 - 10}{3 - (-3)} = \frac{-10}{6} = -\frac{5}{3}$$

A line, with gradient *m*, intersecting the *y*-axis at (0, *c*) has equation

$$y = mx + c.$$

Example 2 :-   The line through (0, -1) with gradient $\frac{1}{2}$.
is $y = \frac{1}{2}x - 1$

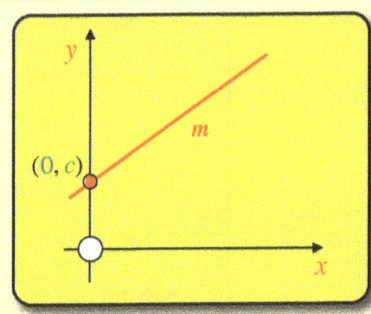

A line, with gradient *m*, passing through any point P(*a*, *b*) has equation

$$y - b = m(x - a).$$

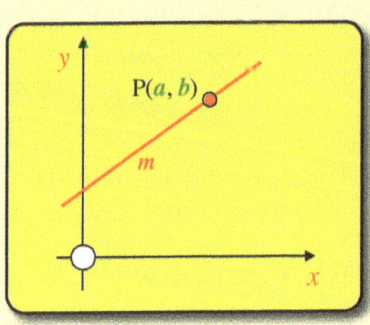

Example 3 :-   Find the equation of the line through
the points (-2, 7) and (1, -2).

Gradient $m = \frac{y_2 - y_1}{x_2 - x_1} = \frac{-2 - 7}{1 - (-2)} = -3$

Use either point e.g. (1, -2)

=> $y - (-2) = -3(x - 1)$

=> $y = -3x + 1$

Any equation of the form $Ax + By + C = 0$ represents a line, provided that *A* and *B* are not **both** 0.

This is called the **General Equation** of the line.

Example 4 :-   Express the equation $3x + 2y - 6 = 0$ in
the form $y = mx + c$ and find *m* and *c*.

$3x + 2y - 6 = 0$

$2y = -3x + 6$

$y = -\frac{3}{2}x + 3$

gradient, $m = -\frac{3}{2}$ and $c = 3$.

Exercise H2·1

1. Calculate the gradient of the line joining L(-3, 1) to N(1, 9). (i.e. find m_{LN}.)

2. Use the gradient formula shown in **Example 1** to determine the gradients of the lines joining each pair of points :-

   (a) P(3, 2), Q(9, 4)   (b) R(-2, 1), S(8, 6)

   (c) T(2, -2), U(4, 4)   (d) V(-3, 0), W(0, 7).

3. Draw a new diagram and plot the two points B(3, -2) and C(3, 5).

   Calculate the gradient of the line BC.

   (note :- it is **NOT** zero ! - Use your calculator if you are not sure of the value).

   > (We say that the gradient of a vertical line is "infinite" or more commonly, it is said to be **undefined** - too steep to be measured).

4. Two points have coordinates A(-1, -2) and B(3, p). The gradient $m_{AB} = 3$.

   Set up an equation and find the value of p.

5. Draw a Cartesian diagram and plot the 4 points P(-4, 2), Q(4, 3), R(6, 0) and S(-2, -1).

   (a) Show that $m_{QR} = m_{PS}$.

   (b) Show also that $m_{PQ} = m_{RS}$.

   (c) What kind of quadrilateral does this prove PQRS is ?

6. State the **gradient** and **y-intercept** in each of these equations :-

   (a) $y = 4x + 1$ (b) $y = 6x - 4$

   (c) $y = -3x + 6$ (d) $y = \frac{1}{2}x + 5$

   (e) $y = -\frac{1}{3}x - 7$ (f) $y = 10 - 2x$.

7. State the **equation** of each of these lines :-

   (a) $m = 2$, and the y-intercept is (0, 1).

   (b) $m = -3$, and the y-intercept is (0, 5).

   (c) gradient is $-\frac{1}{2}$, passing through (0, 4).

8. For each of the lines shown at the top of the next column :-

   (i) calculate the gradient,

   (ii) state the coordinates of the y-intercept,

   (iii) write the equation of the line.

8. (a) 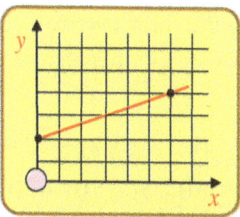 (b)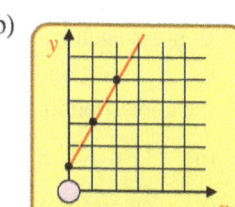

   (c) 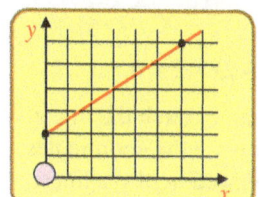 (d)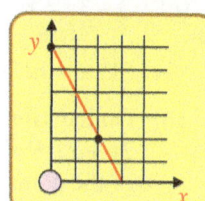

9. The line shown has equation $y = mx + c$.

   (a) What is the value of c ?

   (b) Calculate the gradient.

   (c) State the **equation** of the line.

   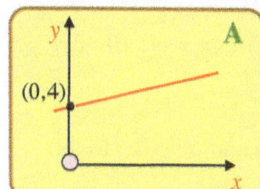

10. Match each equation to its corresponding graph :-

    (a) $y = 4x$ (b) $y = 3x - 2$

    (c) $y = -3x$ (d) $y = -x - 4$

    (e) $y = \frac{1}{2}x + 4$ (f) $y = -3$.

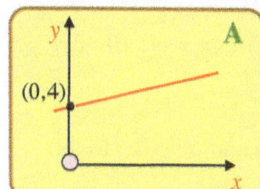
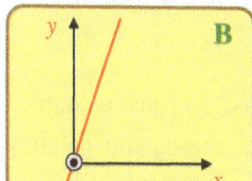
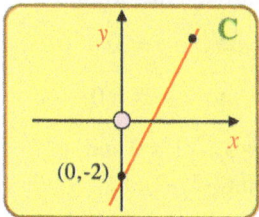
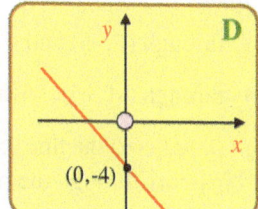
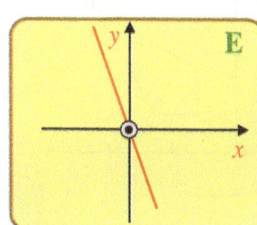
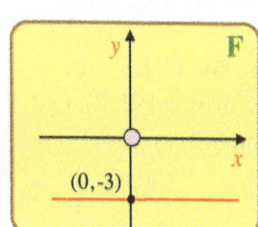

11. Express each equation in the form $y = mx + c$, state the **gradient** and the **y-intercept** of each and **sketch** the corresponding line.

    (a) $3x + 4y + 8 = 0$ (b) $3x - 2y - 12 = 0$

    (c) $2y - 2x + 3 = 0$ (d) $5y - 10x + 20 = 0$

    (e) $3 - 3y = x$ (f) $y + 3 = x$.

12. (a) Sketch the line $y - 2x - 2 = 0$.

    (b) On the same diagram, sketch the line given by $2y + x - 9 = 0$ and write the coordinates of the point of intersection of the lines.

13. Re-arrange each set of equations where necessary and use **simultaneous equations** methods to solve each set :-

    (a) $x + y = 3$ (b) $3y + x + 4 = 0$
          $y - x = -3$ $2y + x - 6 = 0$

    (c) $3y - x - 21 = 0$ (d) $2x - y + 2 = 0$
          $y - 2x + 3 = 0$ $x - 4y + 8 = 0$.

14. Given that $(p, -1)$ lies on the line $3y - 2x = -1$, find the value of p.

15. Find the equation of each line given the gradient and a point on the line.

    (a) $m = 5$, $(1, 2)$ (b) $m = 2$, $(3, 2)$

    (c) $m = 4$, $(-3, 4)$ (d) $m = 1$, $(-1, -2)$

    (e) $m = -2$, $(5, 8)$ (f) $m = -4$, $(0, -3)$.

16. Find the equation of the line :-

    (a) through the point $(4, 5)$ and **parallel** to the line $y = 5x - 1$.

    (b) **parallel** to $y + x = 10$ through the origin.

    (c) through $(3, -5)$ and **parallel** to $y = 3x - 1$.

    (d) through $(-1, -5)$, **parallel** to $y + 2x = 0$.

    (e) **parallel** to the line $2x + 3y - 1 = 0$ and passing through the point $(-3, -2)$.

17. The line $y = x$ is the **axis of symmetry** of the kite PQRS with vertices at P(2, 2), Q(4, 2), and S(2, 4).

    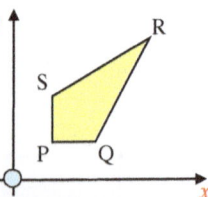

    SR has equation $3y - 2x - 8 = 0$.

    Find the coordinates of the vertex R.

18. Find the equation of the line which passes through each pair of points :-

    (a) $(1, 6)$, $(2, 8)$ (b) $(2, 5)$, $(4, 9)$

    (c) $(3, 3)$, $(4, 4)$ (d) $(2, 6)$, $(6, 2)$

    (e) $(-2, 1)$, $(4, 7)$ (f) $(-5, 1)$, $(-1, -1)$.

19. A parallelogram JKLM has vertices at J(3, 5), K(1, -2), L(-3, -5) and M(-1, 2).

    (a) Find the equations of the diagonals of the parallelogram.

    (b) Find the coordinates of the point where the diagonals meet.

20. A line passing through P(-2, 2) and T(6, t) has its equation $2y - x - 6 = 0$.

    Find the value of t.

21. Triangle ABC has vertices A(-6, 0) and B(8, 0).

    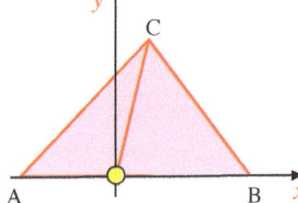

    The line OC has equation $y = 7x$.

    The line AC has equation $y = x + 6$.

    (a) Determine the coordinates of C.

    (b) Find the equation of the line CB.

22. An **isosceles** triangle STV has its base ST along the x-axis.
    The triangle has an axis of symmetry with equation $x = 7$.

    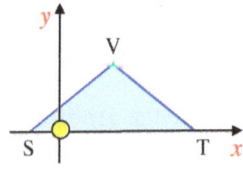

    S is the point $(-1, 0)$, and the line SV has equation $4y - 3x - 3 = 0$.

    (a) Find the coordinates of T and V.

    (b) Find the equation of the line VT.

    (c) Find the sizes of angles STV and SVT.

23. An **equilateral** triangle OPQ has vertices at the origin and at Q(10, 0).

    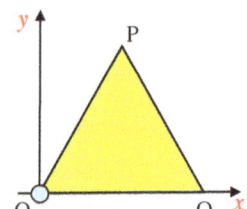

    (a) Show that the vertex at P is $(5, 5\sqrt{3})$.

    (b) Find the equation of the line PQ.

Collinear Points

If three or more points lie on a straight line, they are said in mathematics to be **collinear**.

Three points, A, B and C are collinear if :-

> • m_{AB} and m_{BC} are equal.
>
> • the lines AB and BC have a point (B) in common.

This proves the points are **collinear**.

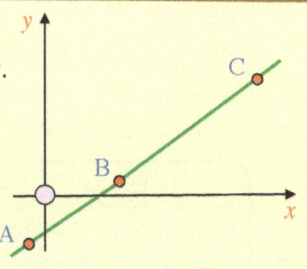

Example :-   Prove that the points A(-1, -2), B(5, 1) and C(13, 5) are collinear.

$$m_{AB} = \frac{1-(-2)}{5-(-1)} = \frac{1}{2}, \qquad m_{BC} = \frac{5-1}{13-5} = \frac{1}{2}$$

They have equal gradients, with point B in common.

Points A, B and C are **collinear**.

Exercise H2·2

1. A(-4, 5), B(2, 3) and C(5, 2).

    (a) Find the gradient m_{AB} and m_{BC}.

    (b) Because B is a common point, what does this prove about the points A, B and C ?

    (c) Plot the three points on a coordinate diagram and check this out.

2. Prove that the three points U(-4, 6), V(2, 3) and W(10, -1) are **collinear**.

3. Prove that each set of three points are collinear :-

    (a) F(3, 1), G(5, 3) and H(8, 6).

    (b) R(-1, 8), S(5, 5) and T(9, 3).

    (c) D(-5, -15), E(-3, -12) and F(5, 0).

4. Three points, F, G and H **are** collinear.

    F is the point with coordinates (-3, 7), G is the point (-1, 3) and H has coordinates (2, p).

    Determine the value of p.

5. L(8, 2), M(2, t) and N(-1, -1) are collinear.

    Find the value of t.

The Angle between a Line and the x-axis

Since $m_{AB} = \dfrac{y_2 - y_1}{x_2 - x_1}$, we can see from the diagram that :-

> $$\tan\theta = \frac{y_2 - y_1}{x_2 - x_1} = m_{AB}$$

since $\tan = \dfrac{\text{opposite}}{\text{adjacent}}$

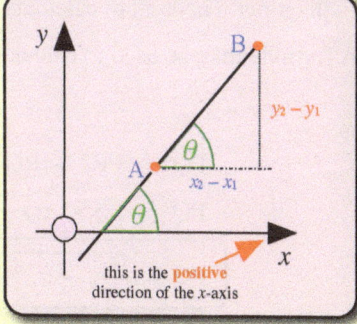

> If you put the **gradient** of a line into your calculator and press "Inverse - Tangent" (or tan^{-1}), you will obtain the **angle** between the **line** and the **positive** direction of the *x*-axis.

Example 1 :-   Calculate the size of the angle the line through A(2, -1) and B(8, 3) makes with the positive direction of the *x*-axis.

$$m_{AB} = \frac{y_2 - y_1}{x_2 - x_1} = \frac{3-(-1)}{8-2} = \frac{4}{6} = 0·6666..$$

$$\theta = \tan^{-1}(0·6666..) = \mathbf{33·7°}$$

Example 2 :-   A line makes an angle of 76° with the *x*-axis.

Calculate the gradient of the line.

The angle the line makes is 76°.

gradient = tan 76°.

gradient = **4·0**

1. Copy and complete to determine the angle the line through P(1, 3) and Q(8, 5) makes with the positive direction of the x-axis :-

$$m_{PQ} = \frac{y_2 - y_1}{x_2 - x_1} = \frac{5 - 3}{8 - ...} = \frac{2}{...} = 0·2....$$

$$\Rightarrow \theta = ...°$$

2. Calculate the size of the angle between the line joining each pair of points and the positive direction of the x-axis :-

(a) E(8, 2) and F(10, 7)

(b) M(0, 3) and N(5, 5)

(c) U(-1, -4) and T(5, -1)

(d) C(0, -5) and D(7, -4).

3. The line through points A(1, 8) and B(7, 5) has a **negative** gradient.

Calculate the size of the angle this line makes with the **positive** direction of the x-axis.

(*Hint - the **obtuse** angle*).

4. Calculate the size of the **obtuse** angle between the line joining each pair of points and the x-axis :-

(a) C(10, 2) and D(8, 7)

(b) M(0, 3) and N(5, -5).

5. A line makes an angle of 63·4° with the **positive** direction of the x-axis.

Calculate its **gradient**.

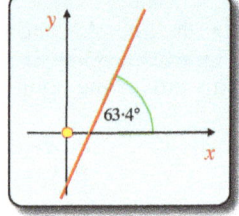

6. Calculate the gradient of the line which makes an angle of 71·5° with the positive direction of the x-axis.

7. Calculate the gradient of the line which makes an angle of 14° with the positive direction of the x-axis, to 2 decimal places.

8. Calculate the gradient of the line which makes an angle of 116·6° with the positive direction of the x-axis.

The Distance Formula

Given the coordinates of any two points P(x_1, y_1) and Q(x_2, y_2), you can construct a right angled triangle, (as shown), and use Pythagoras' Theorem to calculate the distance from P to Q.

A formula may be used to calculate the distance between the two points.

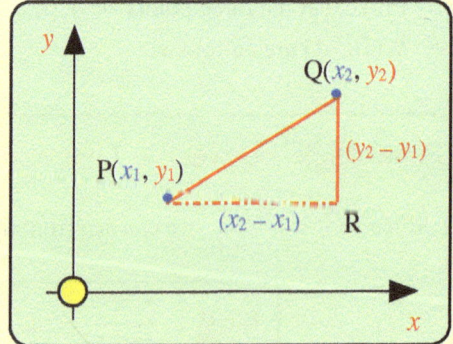

$$PQ^2 = PR^2 + RQ^2$$

$$PQ^2 = (x_2 - x_1)^2 + (y_2 - y_1)^2$$

$$PQ = \sqrt{(x_2 - x_1)^2 + (y_2 - y_1)^2}$$

This is called the **distance formula**.

Example :- Calculate the length of the line AB, between points A(-2, -3) and B(6, 4).

$$AB = \sqrt{(x_2 - x_1)^2 + (y_2 - y_1)^2}$$

$$\Rightarrow \quad AB = \sqrt{(6 - (-2))^2 + (4 - (-3))^2}$$

$$\Rightarrow \quad AB = \sqrt{8^2 + 7^2} = \sqrt{113} = \textbf{10·6}$$

to 1 d.p.

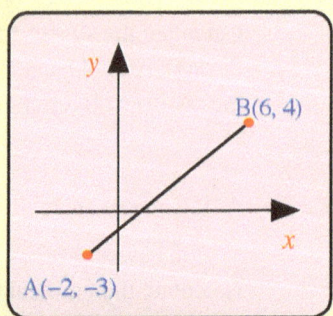

Exercise H2·4

1. Calculate the length of the line RS where R(3, -1) and S(5, 7). **Copy** and complete :-

$$RS = \sqrt{(x_2 - x_1)^2 + (y_2 - y_1)^2}$$
$$RS = \sqrt{(5 - \ldots)^2 + (\ldots - (-1))^2}$$
$$RS = \sqrt{2^2 + \ldots^2} = \sqrt{\ldots} = \ldots$$

2. Calculate the length of the line joining each pair of points :-

   (a) D(2, 1) and E(6, 5)

   (b) P(5, 0) and Q(1, 8)

   (c) F(-1, 2) and G(5, 3)

   (d) U(-2, 5) and V(1, -3).

3. For the four points J(-1, 4), K(5, -3), L(4, -3) and M(0, 5), determine which is longer - the line JL or the line KM.

4. Plot the points C(2, 7), D(5, 3) and E(-2, 4) on a coordinate diagram.

   (a) Calculate the length of the line CD.

   (b) Calculate the length of the line CE.

   (c) What kind of triangle is CDE ?

5. Prove that the three points A(5, 1), B(-2, 2) and C(-3, -5) lie on the **circumference** of a circle with centre P(1, -2).

6. Plot the following three points :-

   R(-2, 5), S(6, -1) and T(3, -5).

   (a) Calculate the lengths of the three sides RS, ST and RT.

   (b) Use the converse of Pythagoras' Theorem to prove that RST is a right angled triangle.

Perpendicular Lines

Two lines are **perpendicular** if they intersect at **right angles**.

The figure shows the point **P(a, b)** under a rotation of +90° about O.

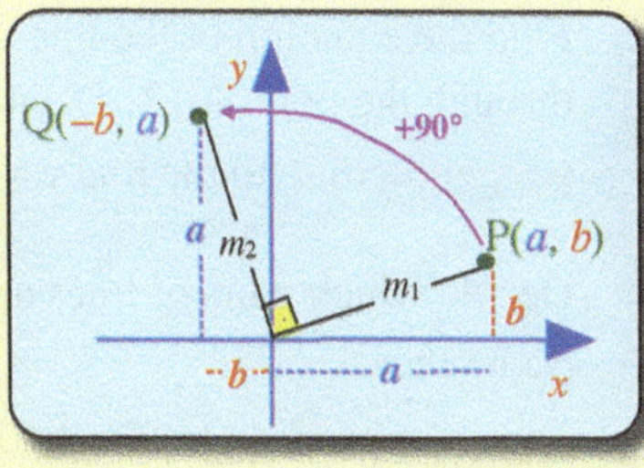

From the diagram, we see that :-

$$P(a, b) \longrightarrow Q(-b, a).$$

Let the gradient of OP = m_1 and the gradient of OQ = m_2.

Then $m_1 = \dfrac{b}{a}$ and $m_2 = \dfrac{a}{-b}$, and hence $m_1 \times m_2 = \dfrac{b}{a} \times \dfrac{a}{-b} = -1$, $\quad a \neq 0, b \neq 0$.

If OQ is **perpendicular** to OP, then $m_1 \times m_2 = -1$.

The **converse** is also true :-

If $m_1 \times m_2 = -1$, then OQ is **perpendicular** to OP.

NOTE :- this is <u>not</u> true for lines parallel to the x and the y-axes.

Example 1 :- Find the equation of the line through the point (-3, 1) which is **perpendicular** to the line with equation :-
$$2x + 4y - 12 = 0.$$

$2x + 4y - 12 = 0$ rearranges to $y = -\frac{1}{2}x + 3$.

The gradient of the given line is $-\frac{1}{2}$ and the gradient of the perpendicular line is 2, (since $m_1 \times m_2 = -1$)

Using $y - b = m(x - a)$ gives .....

$$y - 1 = 2(x + 3)$$

i.e. $\quad y = 2x + 7$

Example 2 :- Prove that the line with equation $x + 3y + 6 = 0$ is **perpendicular** to the line $y = 3x - 1$.

$x + 3y + 6 = 0$ rearranges to

$y = -\frac{1}{3}x - 2$. Hence $m_1 = -\frac{1}{3}$

For $y = 3x - 1$, $m_2 = 3$.

Since $m_1 \times m_2 = -\frac{1}{3} \times 3 = -1$,

the lines are **perpendicular**.

Exercise H2·5

1. Which of the following pairs of gradients represent those of **perpendicular** lines :-

   (a) 5 and $\frac{1}{5}$

   (b) 4 and $-\frac{1}{4}$

   (c) $\frac{2}{5}$ and $\frac{5}{2}$

   (d) $\frac{5}{4}$ and $-\frac{4}{5}$

   (e) 0·3 and -3

   (f) 0·375 and $-\frac{8}{3}$

   (g) $-1\frac{1}{2}$ and $\frac{2}{3}$

   (h) 1·6 and -0·625 ?

2. Find the **gradient** of each line, **perpendicular** to the line with gradient :-

   (a) $\frac{1}{2}$

   (b) -3

   (c) 7

   (d) $-\frac{7}{2}$

   (e) -1

   (f) $\frac{5}{9}$

   (g) -5·5

   (h) $2\frac{1}{3}$

   (i) 0.

3. Find the equation of the line which is **perpendicular** to the line with equation $y = 5x$, passing through the point $(0, 4)$.

4. Find the equation of the line which passes through the point A(-2, 3), and which is **perpendicular** to the line $y = \frac{2}{3}x - 2$.

5. Decide which pairs of lines are perpendicular to each other.

   (a) $y = 2x + 4$ and $y = -\frac{1}{2}x - 1$

   (b) $y = -3x + 6$ and $y = \frac{1}{3}x - 2$

   (c) $2x + y = 5$ and $x - 2y = 3$

   (d) $3x - y - 2 = 0$ and $3y - x + 7 = 0$.

6. Determine the equation of the line through the point $(5, 2)$, perpendicular to the line with equation $2y - 5x + 6 = 0$.

7. Find the equations of the lines through the **origin**, perpendicular to each line :-

   (a) $x - 5y = 1$

   (b) $5x - 3y + 1 = 0$.

8. Find the equation of the line perpendicular to the line $2y + x - 4 = 0$, passing through the point $(2, -4)$.

9. The equation of the line through $(2, 1)$, perpendicular to the line $y - px - 7 = 0$ is $y = -\frac{1}{2}x + q$. Determine the value of p and then q.

"Vertical" and "Horizontal" Lines

Lines running **parallel** to the **x-axis** have equation

$$y = (a\ constant)$$

Lines running **parallel** to the **y-axis** have equation

$$x = (a\ constant)$$

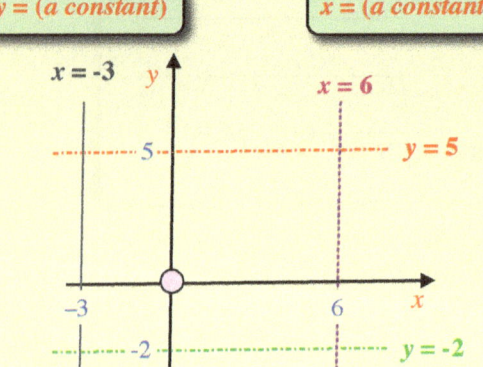

The **red** line has equation $y = 5$ ($m = 0$).

The **green** line has equation $y = -2$ ($m = 0$).

The **purple** line has equation $x = 6$ (m is undefined).

The **grey** line has equation $x = -3$ (m is undefined).

10. Determine the equation of the line **parallel** to :-

    (a) the y-axis, passing through the point $(3, 1)$

    (b) the x-axis, passing through the point $(-2, 4)$

    (c) the y-axis, passing through the point $(-1, 5)$.

11. Find the equation of the line perpendicular to :-

    (a) the line $x = 5$, through the point $(7, -2)$

    (b) the line $y = -2$, through the point $(4, 6)$

    (c) the line $x = 0$, through the point $(-4, 8)$.

12. P is the point $(-4, 3)$, Q$(-6, -3)$ and R$(2, -1)$. Find the equation of the line through :-

    (a) P, parallel to QR

    (b) P, perpendicular to QR

    (c) Q, parallel to PR

    (d) Q, perpendicular to PR.

13. K is $(1, 2)$, L$(3, -4)$, M$(-5, -1)$ and N$(1, k)$. Find k, given that KL is perpendicular to MN.

14. P is $(8, 1)$, Q$(-7, 3)$, R$(-6, -6)$ and S$(-3, -5)$. Prove that line PR is perpendicular to line QS.

15. Prove that the lines with equations :-
    $$px + qy + r = 0 \text{ and } qx - py + s = 0, (p, q \neq 0),$$
    are perpendicular to each other.

16. AB makes an angle of 63·5° with the positive direction of the x-axis. RT is perpendicular to AB. Find m_{RT}.

Lines within Triangles :- Medians, Altitudes and Perpendicular Bisectors

Median

In triangle DEF, R is the mid-point of DF.

The line ER is known as the **median** from point E to the side DF.

In any triangle, there are three medians joining each vertex to the mid-point of the opposite side.

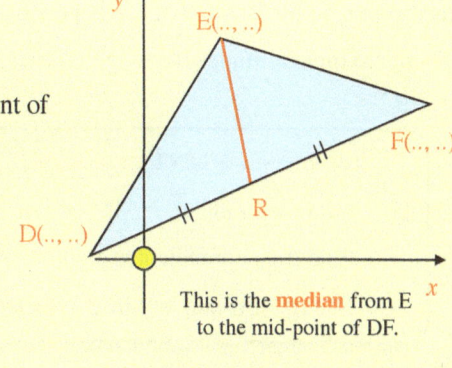

This is the **median** from E to the mid-point of DF.

To find the equation of a median, ER :-

- Find R, the mid-point of DF, using $\left(\dfrac{x_1 + x_2}{2}, \dfrac{y_1 + y_2}{2} \right)$.

- Use R and point E to find the gradient of ER, m_{ER}.

- Use either E or R, along with m, in $y - b = m(x - a)$.

Example :-   Find the equation of the **median** from A to BC.

Midpoint of BC = E$(4\tfrac{1}{4}, 6\tfrac{1}{4})$

$$m_{AE} = \frac{6\tfrac{1}{4} - (-5)}{4\tfrac{1}{4} - (-7)} = 1$$

Using point A, and $y - b = m(x - a)$, the median is

$$y + 5 = 1(x + 7) \quad \Rightarrow \quad \boxed{y = x + 2}$$

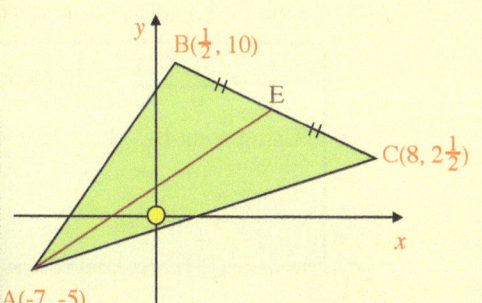

If the medians in a triangle are drawn, it is found that they meet at a single point. This point **P** is called the **centroid** of the triangle.

- The centroid divides each of the 3 medians in the ratio 1 : 2
- The centroid is at the centre of gravity of the triangle.
  (the point you could place the tip of a pencil on and the triangle would balance).

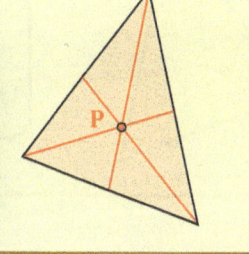

Exercise H2·6   *Hint :- Where there is no diagram, it is **advisable** to make a sketch.*

1. A, B and C are the points (6, -3), (-2, 5) and (-2, -1) respectively.

   Find the equation of the **median** from C to AB.

2. Find the equation of the **median** from P to QR in triangle PQR where the coordinates of P, Q and R are (-2, 5), (-3, -4) and (5, 2) respectively.

3. The diagram shows a triangle KLM with vertices K(6, 5), L(8, 3) and M(0 -1).

   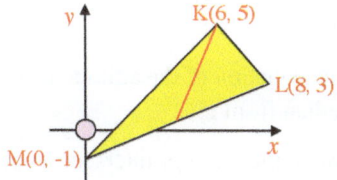

   Find the equation of the **median** through K.

4. The vertices of a triangle are J(-6, -1), T(4, 5) and G(8, -3).

   (a) Find the equation of the **median** from J to TG.

   (b) Find the equation of the **median** from T to JG.

   (c) Find the coordinates of the point of intersection of the two **medians**.

   (d) Prove that the three **medians** of triangle JTG are **concurrent** (i.e. they all meet at the same point), by showing that the point of intersection lies on the third **median** from G to JT. Write down the coordinates of the **centroid** of triangle JTG.

5. Prove that the **medians** of triangle ABC, with points A(-1, 3), B(3, 7) and C(5, -3) are concurrent.

Altitude

In triangle ABC, the line CT is known as the **altitude** from the point C to the line AB, if CT is perpendicular to AB.

There are three altitudes in any given triangle.

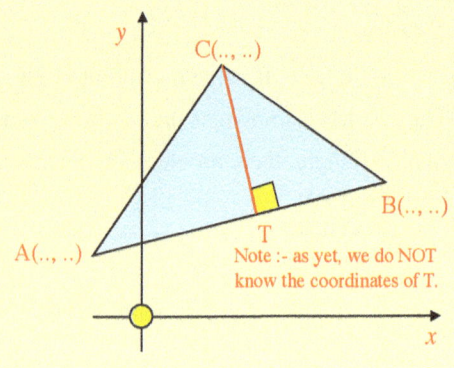

Shown here is the **altitude** from C to AB.

> **To find the equation of an altitude**, CT :-
> - Find the gradient of AB. (m_{AB}).
> - Find the perpendicular gradient, m_{CT}, (using $m_1 \times m_2 = -1$).
> - Use point C and m_{CT} in $y - b = m(x - a)$.

Note :- as yet, we do NOT know the coordinates of T.

Example :- Find the equation of the **altitude** from B to AC.

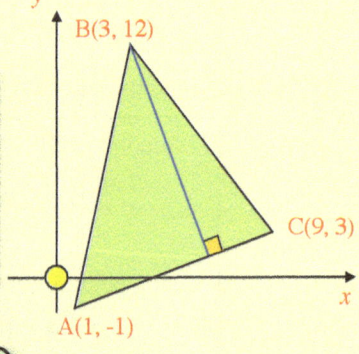

$$m_{AC} = \frac{3-(-1)}{9-1} = \frac{1}{2}. \text{ Hence } m_{perp} = -2 \ (\text{since } m_1 \times m_2 = -1)$$

Using point B(3, 12), the equation of the altitude is

$$y - 12 = -2(x - 3)$$

$$\boxed{y = -2x + 18}$$

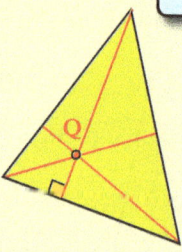

> When the altitudes in a triangle are drawn, we find that they meet at a single point.
>
> This point **Q** is called the **orthocentre** of the triangle.

Exercise H2·7

1. P(-6, 5), Q(-4, -2) and R(2, 1) are the vertices of triangle PQR.

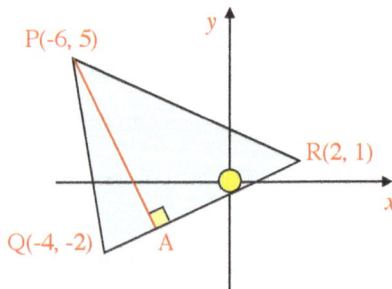

   Find the equation of PA, the **altitude** from P.

2. Triangle ABC has vertices A(-1, -1), B(2, 1) and C(-6, 2).

   Find the equation of the **altitude** of triangle ABC, drawn from A.

3. H is the point (6, 6), R is (-3, 0) and G is (0, -3) in triangle HRG.

   (a) Find the equation of the **altitude** from H to RG.

   (b) Find the equation of the **altitude** from R to HG.

   (c) Find the equation of the third altitude.

   (d) Prove that the three **altitudes** of triangle HRG are **concurrent** by showing that the point of intersection lies on the third **altitude**, and write the coordinates of the **orthocentre** of triangle HRG.

4. The coordinates of three points are D(-2, 0), E(7, 8) and F(4, -3).

   (a) Find the equation of the altitude from E and the median from F.

   (b) Determine the point of intersection of these two lines.

Perpendicular Bisector

In triangle JKL, the **perpendicular bisector** of KL is shown in the diagram.
The Perpendicular Bisector cuts KL at right angles through its mid-point, S.
(There are three perpendicular bisectors in any triangle).

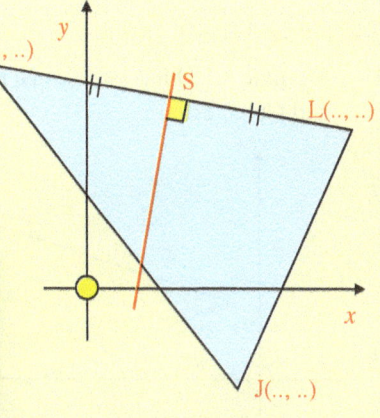

To find the equation of a perpendicular bisector, KL :-

- Find the coordinates of S, the mid-point of KL using $\left(\dfrac{x_1 + x_2}{2}, \dfrac{y_1 + y_2}{2}\right)$

- Find the gradient of line KL, m_{KL}.

- Find the perpendicular gradient, m_{perp}, (using $m_1 \times m_2 = -1$).

- Use m_{perp} and point S to find the equation using $y - b = m(x - a)$.

Note :- in a triangle, a
perpendicular bisector need
not go through any of the vertices.

Example :-   Find the equation of the perpendicular bisector of PQ if P is (3, -2) and Q is (-5, 4).

It will make the question easier if you **make a sketch** first.

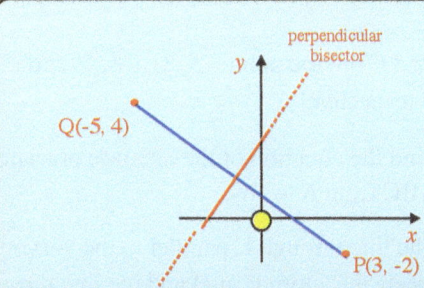

Midpoint of PQ = $\left(\dfrac{-5 + 3}{2}, \dfrac{4 + (-2)}{2}\right)$ = (-1, 1)

$m_{PQ} = \dfrac{4 - (-2)}{-5 - 3} = -\dfrac{6}{8} = -\dfrac{3}{4}$. Hence $m_{perp} = \dfrac{4}{3}$ (since $m_1 \times m_2 = -1$)

Using (-1, 1) and $m = \dfrac{4}{3}$, the equation of the perpendicular
bisector is $y - 1 = \dfrac{4}{3}(x + 1)$, which simplifies to :-

$$y = \tfrac{4}{3}x + \tfrac{7}{3}.$$

Exercise H2·8

1. Find the equation of the **perpendicular bisector** of the line joining M(2, -1) and N(8, 3).

2. N(-2, 1), T(-4, 3) and L(8, 1) are the vertices of triangle NTL.

   Find the equation of the **perpendicular bisectors** of both the line NT and the line TL.

3. F is the point (-3, 1), K is (5, 5) and Q is (6, -2) in triangle FKQ.

   (a) Find the equation of the **perpendicular bisector** of the line FK.

   (b) Find the equation of the **perpendicular bisector** of the line FQ.

   (c) Find the coordinates of the point of intersection of these two **perpendicular bisectors**.

   (d) Prove that the three **perpendicular bisectors** of triangle FKQ are **concurrent**.

If the three perpendicular bisectors are drawn, it is found that they meet at a single point.

This point **R** is called the **circumcentre** of the triangle.

It is the centre of the circle drawn through the three vertices of the triangle.

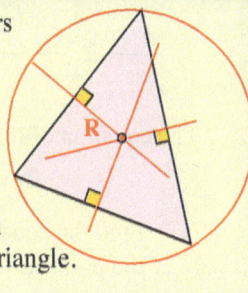

4. Triangle ABC has vertices A(-6, -3), B(2, -7) and C(5, 9).

   (a) Find the equation of the **perpendicular bisector** of the line AB.

   (b) Prove that C lies on this **perpendicular bisector**.

   (c) What kind of triangle must ABC be ?

Exercise H2·9   Mixed Exercise

1. Triangle NUQ has vertices N(1, 3), U(9, -1) and Q(13, 7).

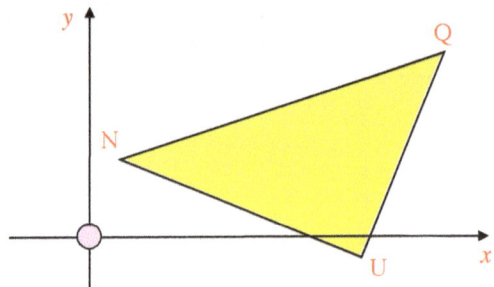

(a) Determine the equation of the **perpendicular bisector** of NU.

(b) Find the equation of the **perpendicular bisector** of NQ.

(c) Find the coordinates of the **circumcentre** of triangle NUQ.

2. Triangle DRP has coordinates D(1, 1), R(3, 15) and P(11, 5).

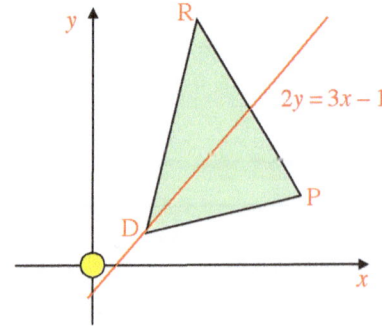

The equation of the **median** from D to RP is
$$2y = 3x - 1.$$

(a) Find the equation of the **median** through the point R.

(b) Determine the coordinates of the **centroid** of triangle DPR.

(c) Find the equation of the **altitude** through P.

3. Triangle EBN has vertices E(-3, -3), B(-1, 1) and N(7, -3).

(a) Prove that triangle EBN is right angled.

(b) The **median** from E to BN meets the **median** from B to EN at point K.

Find the coordinates of K.

4. Triangle TVP has vertices T(1, 8), V(4, 2) and P(-2, 2).

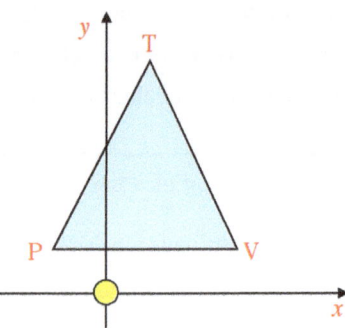

(a) Show that triangle TVP is isosceles.

(b) The **altitudes** PA and VB intersect at W, where A and B lie on TV and PT respectively.

Find the coordinates of W.

(c) Hence show that W lies one quarter way up the altitude CT, from C.

5. A, B and C are the points (5, 3), (-8, 7) and (1, -5) respectively.

(a) Find the equation of the **altitude** of triangle ABC from A to BC.

(b) The line through C parallel to the *y*-axis meets this altitude at H and the line through A parallel to the *x*-axis meets BC at L.

Show that LH is the **perpendicular bisector** of the line AC.

6. A triangle has vertices P(6, 3), Q(-4, 1) and R(4, -7).

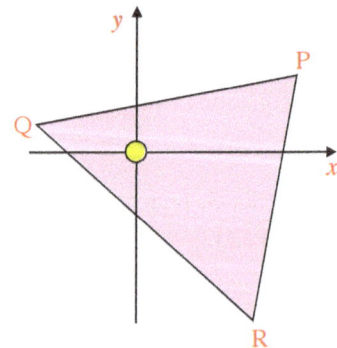

(a) Find the equations of the **medians** PL and QM.

(b) Find the coordinates of J, the point of intersection of PL and QM.

(c) Find the equation of RJ, and show that RJ produced bisects PQ.

Hint - before attempting these questions, you should consider making a sketch first.

7. The vertices of triangle ABC are A(-3, 11), B(11, 4) and C(1, -9).

   Find the point of intersection of the median BM and the altitude CP.

8. (a) Find the equation of the line through the origin and perpendicular to the line with equation $y - 4x = 34$.

   (b) Find the point of intersection of these two lines and hence find the shortest distance from O to the given line.

9. R is the point (2, 8), S(-1, 2) and T(5, 6).

   Show that the midpoint, M of RT lies on the line through the midpoint N of ST, which is parallel to the line RS.

10. EFGH is a square with E the point (-1, 2) and G(7, 6). Find the point of intersection of the diagonals and find also the coordinates of the points F and H.

11. OPQR is a parallelogram where O is the origin and Q is the point (8, 6).

   The equation of OP is $y = 4x$ and the equation of OR is $y = -\frac{1}{3}x$.

   (a) Find the equations of the two sides PQ and QR.

   (b) Use these answers to determine the coordinates of the two vertices P and R.

12. A, B and C have coordinates (-3, 2), (-2, 9) and (7, -3) respectively .

   (a) Find the equation of the altitude from A to BC.

   (b) Determine the coordinates of the point where the altitude meets the line BC and hence calculate the area of triangle ABC.

13. Triangle LMN has its three sides given by the equations $y - 2x - 7 = 0$, $2y + x + 1 = 0$ and $3x - y - 11 = 0$.

   Determine the coordinates of the vertices of triangle LMN.

14. Triangle RST has vertices at R(1, 3), S(-1, -5) and T (7, -1).

   (a) Find the equation of the median of triangle RST from point T.

contd……..

14. (b) Find the equation of the perpendicular bisector of side TR.

   (c) Determine the coordinates of the point of intersection of these two lines.

15. T(-3, 6), U(5, 7) and V(5, -6) are three vertices of a parallelogram TUVW, with diagonal TV.

   (a) Find the equation of the altitude from U to TV in triangle TUV.

   (b) Find the coordinates of where this altitude meets diagonal TV.

   (c) Determine the area of the parallelogram.

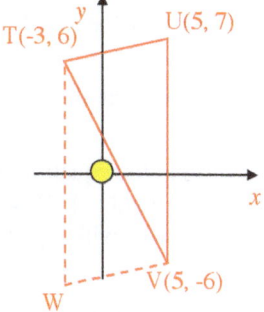

16. P is the point (1, 5).

   The two lines $2y - 3x + 6 = 0$ and $y - 2x + 5 = 0$ intersect at the point Q.

   Determine the gradient of PQ and show that PQ is perpendicular to only one of these lines.

17. (a) In the figure shown opposite, prove that triangle ABC is right angled at B.

   (b) Hence, calculate the blue area in the diagram.

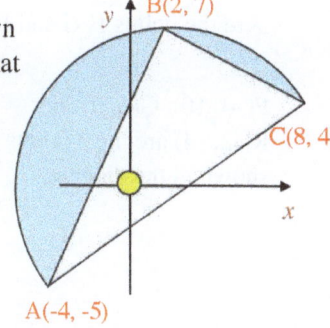

18. The line KL makes an angle of 21·8° with the x axis. K has coordinates (-6, 0).

   Find the equation of the line through L, perpendicular to KL.

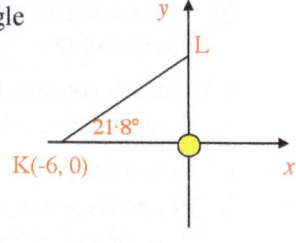

19. F, G and H have coordinates (-6, -1), (1, 8) and (9, 4) respectively.

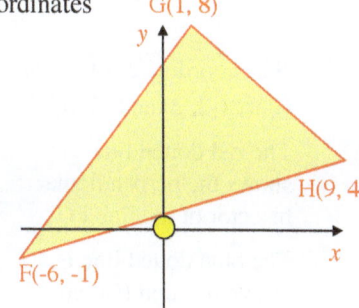

   Calculate the area of triangle FGH.

Exam Practice Exercise (H2)

1. $P(-5, 3)$, $Q(5, 7)$ and $R(0, 9)$ are the vertices of a triangle.

   Find the equation of the median through R.　(3)

2. S and T are the points $(-2, 5)$ and $(4, p)$.

   ST is perpendicular to the line with equation $5y + 3x - 7 = 0$.

   Determine the value of p.　(3)

3. Find the equation of the line passing through the point $(-4, 2)$, which is parallel to the line with equation $3x + 4y - 2 = 0$.　(3)

4. A and B are the points $(-d, 1)$ and $(1, d^2)$.

   AB is parallel to the line $2y - 6x + 3 = 0$.

   Determine the value(s) of d.　(3)

5. F and G are points on the line $y - \sqrt{3}x + 1 = 0$.

   H is a point, such that the line HG makes an angle of 60° with the positive direction of the x-axis.

   Are the points F, G and H collinear ?　(3)

6. $P(-4, 10)$, $Q(6, 0)$ and $R(-2, -4)$ are the 3 points shown in the diagram.

   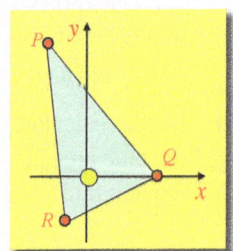

   (a) Find the equation of the perpendicular bisector of QR.　(4)

   (b) Find the equation of the median of the triangle through the vertex R.　(3)

   (c) Determine the coordinates of the point of intersection of the perpendicular bisector and the median.　(3)

7. The coordinates of F and G are $(-2, 2)$ and $(5, 0)$.

   The red dotted line shows the perpendicular bisector of the line FG.

   The blue dotted line is drawn through F at an angle of 45° to the x-axis.

   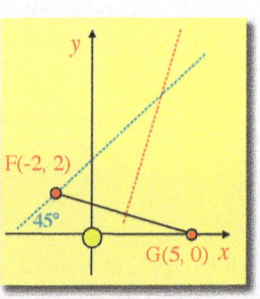

7. (a) Find the equation of the perpendicular bisector of FG.　(4)

   (b) Find the equation of the blue dotted line through F.　(2)

   (c) Find the coordinates of the point of intersection of the 2 dotted lines.　(3)

8. PQRS is a quadrilateral with vertices $P(-3, -1)$, $Q(-7, 7)$, $R(0, 8)$ and $S(8, 2)$.

   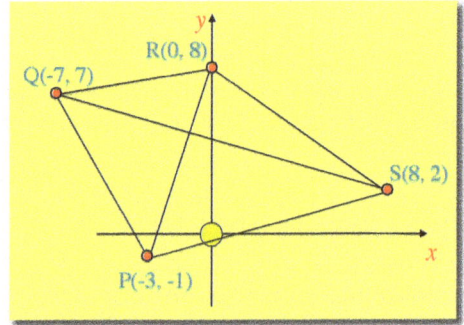

   (a) Find the equation of diagonal QS.　(3)

   (b) The equation of diagonal PR is
   $$y = 3x + 8.$$
   Find the coordinates of point T, where the two diagonals meet.　(3)

   (c) (i) Find the equation of the perpendicular bisector of PQ.

   (ii) Show that this line passes through T.　(5)

9. ABCD is a parallelogram.

   AB is parallel to the x-axis.

   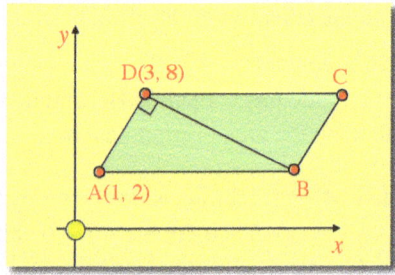

   A and D have coordinates $(1, 2)$ and $(3, 8)$.

   BD is perpendicular to side AD.

   (a) Show that the equation of BD is
   $$3y + x = 27.$$　(4)

   (b) Hence find the coordinates of the points B and C.　(3)

   (continued)

Chapter H3 - Functions and Graphs - Revision

1. Consider the function $f(x) = 3x - 4$, and the set of x-values $\{-1, 0, 1, 2, 3\}$.

   (a) Find $f(-1) = \boxed{3 \times (-1) - 4 \;=\; ...}$

   (b) Draw up and complete the table :-

x	-1	0	1	2	3
$f(x)$	-7	...	...	...	...

   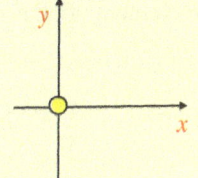

   (c) Plot the values as points on a Cartesian diagram to show the graph of $f(x) = 3x - 4$.

2. Consider this time the function $f(x) = 4x - 5$.

   (a) Calculate $f(2)$.

   (b) Calculate $f(10)$.

   (c) If $f(x) = 4x - 5$, write down an expression for $f(p)$ in terms p.

   (d) If $f(p) = 43$, form an equation in terms of p and solve it to find the value of p.

3. Consider the function $f(x) = x^2 + 1$ and the set of values $\{-3 \le x \le 3\}$.

   (a) Find $f(3) = \boxed{3^2 + 1 \;=\; 9 + 1 \;=\; ....}$

   (b) Similarly, find $f(2), f(1), f(0), f(-1), f(-2)$ and $f(-3)$.

   (c) Draw a coordinate diagram and plot the corresponding 7 points $(-3, 10)$, ..., ...

   (d) Join the points with a smooth curve to show the graph representing the quadratic function :-
   $$f(x) = x^2 + 1.$$

4. Consider the quadratic function :-
   $$f(x) = 4x - x^2 \qquad \{-1 \le x \le 5\}.$$

   (a) Find $f(-1) = \boxed{4 \times (-1) - (-1)^2 = -4 - 1 = ...}$

   (b) Similarly, find $f(0), f(1), ... f(5)$.

   (c) Plot these 7 points on a coordinate diagram and join with a smooth curve to represent the function.

   (d) What are the two **roots** of the function ?

   (e) State the equation of the **line of symmetry**.

   (f) What are the coordinates of the **maximum turning point** ?

5. A function is defined by $f(x) = x + 8$.

   Write an expression for $f(a^2)$ and determine the values of a, given that $f(a^2) = 57$.

6. A function is defined by $f(x) = 2\sqrt{x} - 6$.

   (a) Find the value of $f(25)$.

   (b) Calculate the value of h, given that
   $$f(h) = 12.$$

7. Without drawing the curves, describe what kind of turning point, (**maximum or minimum**), will be produced for the following quadratic functions :-

   (a) $f(x) = x^2 + 3x - 4$ (b) $f(x) = -x^2 + 7x$

   (c) $f(x) = 20 - 4x^2$ (d) $f(x) = x^2 - 8$

   (e) $f(x) = 10x - x^2$ (f) $f(x) = 3x^2 - 12x$.

8. (a) Draw the graph of the parabola corresponding to the quadratic function
   $$f(x) = 9 - x^2 \qquad \{-4 \le x \le 4\}.$$

   (b) What are the two **roots** of the function ?

   (c) Write down the equation of the **line of symmetry**.

   (d) Write down the coordinates of its **maximum turning point**.

9. Consider the function $f(x) = x(x + 2)$ and the set of values $\{-4 \le x \le 2\}$.

   (a) Find $f(-4), f(-3), ..., f(2)$.

   (b) Draw a Cartesian diagram and plot the corresponding 7 points $(-4, 8)$, $(-3, ...)$, ...

   (c) Join the points up to show yet again a smooth quadratic curve.

   (d) State the equation of the **line of symmetry**.

   (e) What are the coordinates of the **minimum turning point** ?

Sets and Set Notation

A **set**, is a group of items - numbers, letters, objects.

The items in the set are referred to as the **elements** of the set, and are enclosed in curly brackets :- {   }.

The symbol $\in$ means "is a member of" **or** " is an element of" the set. For example, $3 \in \{0, 1, 2, 3, 4\}$.

The symbol $\notin$ means "is **not** a member of" **or** " is **not** an element of" the set. For example, $5 \notin \{0, 1, 2, 3, 4\}$.

{ } means the **empty** set. i.e. the set with no elements (or members).

A **subset** ($\subset$) is simply a part of a set. e.g. $\{1, 2, 3\}$ $\subset$ $\{0, 1, 2, 3, 4, 5\}$. (*Note :- not part of the Higher Course*)

Standard Sets

the set of **Natural Numbers,** $N = \{1, 2, 3, 4, 5, 6, ...\}$ - the set you "naturally" count items with.

the set of **Whole Numbers,** $W = \{0, 1, 2, 3, 4, 5, ...\}$ - the set of Natural Numbers along with zero.

the set of **Integers,** $Z = (\{...-3, -2, -1, 0, 1, 2, 3, ...\}$ - the set of positive & negative whole numbers and 0.

the set of **Rational Numbers,** $Q = \{$all those numbers that can be written in the form $\frac{a}{b}$, where a and b are integers$\}$.

the set of **Real Numbers,** $R = \{$all rational and irrational numbers, including numbers like $\pi, \sqrt{2},$ sin 20°, etc$\}$.

Diagram showing relationships between Sets

$N \subset W \subset Z \subset Q \subset R$

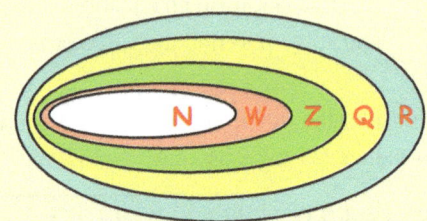

The Natural Numbers form a subset of the Whole Numbers, that form a subset of the Integers, that form a subset of the Rational Numbers, that form a subset of the Real Numbers.

Example :- The set of numbers defined by $P = \{x : -3 < x \le 3,\ x \in Z\}$ is simply the set $\{-2, -1, 0, 1, 2, 3\}$.
It reads as "*the set of values greater than -3 and less than or equal to 3, and they must be Integers*".

Definition :- A **function** is a relationship between elements of two sets, called the **domain** and the **range**.

If a function f is applied to a set of values A, and a new set of values B is generated,

we say that :-

> the function f "maps" the set A onto the set B.
> the set A is called the **domain**.
> the set B is called the **range** or **image set**.

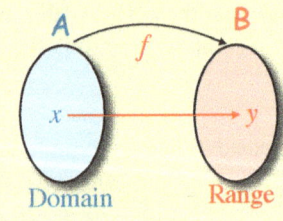

Domain   Range

Example :- The function that takes the set of numbers $\{-2, -1, 0, 1, 2\}$ and **squares** each number is given by :-

$f : x \rightarrow x^2$, with domain $\{-2, -1, 0, 1, 2\}$ but is usually shown using brackets as $f(x) = x^2$.

Since $f(-2) = (-2)^2 = 4$, $f(-1) = (-1)^2 = 1$, $f(0) = (0)^2 = 0$, $f(1) = (1)^2, = 1$, $f(2) = (2)^2 = 4$.

=> the **domain** here is $\{-2, -1, 0, 1, 2\}$ and the **range** is $\{0, 1, 4\}$.

=> we can now draw the graph of the function by plotting the 5 points $(-2, 4), (-1, 1), (0, 0), (1, 1), (2, 4)$.

=> Note - only the red dots • show the mapping.

=> * the dotted curve shows $f(x) = x^2, \{x : -2 \le x \le 2, x \in R\}$.

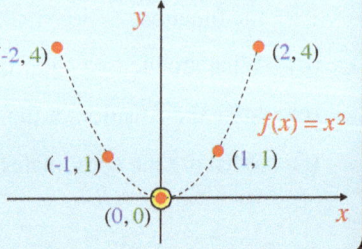

1. Consider the **quadratic** function $f(x) = 2x^2$, and the set of values $\{x : -2 \leq x \leq 2, x \in Z\}$.

   (a) A table :-

x	-2	-1	0	1	2
$f(x)$	8	...	...	...	...

   (b) Draw a coordinate diagram and plot the corresponding five points $(-2, 8), (-1, 2), ...$

   (c) Join the five points up with a smooth curve.

2. Consider the function $f(x) = x(x - 3)$ and the set of values $\{-1 \leq x \leq 4\}$.

   (a) Find $f(-1) = (-1) \times ((-1) - 3) = (-1) \times (-4)$.

   (b) Find $f(0), f(1), f(2), f(3)$ and $f(4)$.

   (c) Draw a coordinate diagram and plot the corresponding six points $(-1, 4), (0, 0), ...$

   (d) Join the 6 points up to form a smooth curve.

   > **Note the U-shape you obtain from a quadratic function - this is always the case - a parabola**.

3. (a) List all the integers between -5 and 3 inclusive.

   (b) List all the whole numbers less than 6.

4. Which of these statements is/are true ?

   (a) $5 \in W$

   (b) $-3 \in N$

   (c) $0.5 \notin R$

   (d) $-\frac{2}{5} \in Q$

   (e) $\sqrt{-1} \in R$

   (f) R is a subset of Z

   (g) the solution to $\{x : x^2 = 16, x \in R\}$ is $\{4\}$

   (h) the solution to $\{x : 2x - 1 < 3, x \in N\}$ is $\{1, 2\}$.

5. List the sets defined by the following :-

   (a) $A = \{x : x \leq 8, x \in W\}$

   (b) $P = \{x : -2 < x < 4, x \in Z\}$

   (c) $G = \{y : y \leq 15, y \text{ even}, y \in N\}$

   (d) $T = \{v : v^2 = 25, v \in R\}$

   (e) $F = \{t : t^2 + 8t + 12 = 0, t \in Q\}$

   (f) $C = \{x : 2x^2 - x = 0, x \in Z\}$

   (g) $M = \{n : n^2 + 1 = 0, n \in R\}$

   (h) $S = \{x : sinx° = 1, 0 \leq x \leq 360\}$.

6. $f(x) = 10 - x^2, x \in \{-3, -2, -1, 0, 1, 2, 3\}$.

   (a) What is the range of $f(x)$?

   (b) Draw a graph showing these 7 image points.

   (c) Now on your diagram, join the points up with a smooth curve to show the function :-
   $$f(x) = 10 - x^2, \{x : -3 \leq x \leq 3, x \in R\}.$$

7. $g(x) = x^2 - 2x, x \in \{-2, -1, 0, 1, 2, 3, 4\}$.

   (a) What is the range of $f(x)$?

   (b) Draw a graph showing all the image points.

   (c) On your diagram, show the function :-
   $f(x) = x^2 - 2x, \{x : -2 \leq x \leq 4, x \in R\}$.

8. $h(x) = x^3 + 1, \{x : -2 \leq x \leq 2, x \in R\}$.

   (a) Find $h(-2), h(-1), h(0), h(1)$ and $h(2)$.

   (b) Plot these five points and draw a smooth graph through them to show the function $h(x) = x^3 + 1$.

   (c) What kind of graph is this ?

   (d) Describe the range using set notation :-
   $\Rightarrow \{y : ... \leq y \leq ...., y \in R\}$.

9. Function $f(x) = x^2 - 3x - 4, \{x : -2 \leq x \leq 5, x \in R\}$.

   (a) Find $f(-2), f(-1), f(0), f(1), f(2), f(3), f(4), f(5)$.

   (b) By plotting these points, sketch the graph of $f(x)$.

   (c) What is the solution to $f(x) = 0$? (These are the **zeros** of the function. i.e. where $y = f(x) = 0$).

10. $f(x) = \sqrt{16 - x^2}$, with domain $\{x : -4 \leq x \leq 4, x \in R\}$.

    (a) Find $f(-4), f(-3), f(-2), ... f(3)$ and $f(4)$.

    (b) State the coordinates of the points and plot them on a Cartesian diagram.

    (c) Join the points up with a smooth curve and describe the shape of curve you have drawn.

11. $f(x) = sinx°$ has domain $\{x : 0 \leq x \leq 360, x \in R\}$.

    (a) Find $f(0), f(30), f(60), f(90), ... f(330), f(360)$.

    (b) Plot the points on a coordinate diagram.

    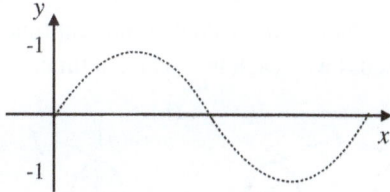

    (c) Describe the range using set notation.
    Range $= \{y : ... \leq y \leq ....., y \in ...\}$

Graphs of Functions

Not every relationship between two sets of values represents a function.

If the relationship $f(x)$ is such that each and every element of the domain maps onto **exactly one** element in the range, then the relationship is defined as a **function**.

We can see this better if we look at the relationship using an **arrow diagram**.

Examples :- All of these represent functions, since one and only one arrow leaves each element in set A.

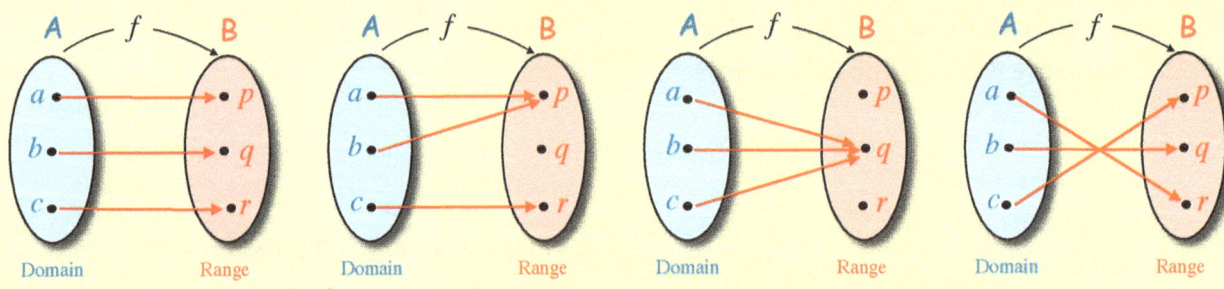

Examples :- Each of the following does **NOT** represent a function. - Can you see why each is **not** a function ?

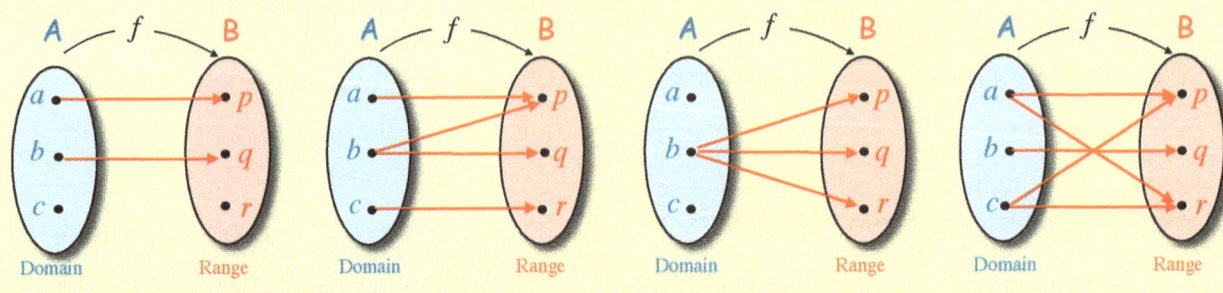

Recognising a Function from its Graph

As we saw above, since every value of the domain (x) must map onto exactly one point in the range (y), then we can check if a graph represents a function. Consider a series of vertical lines on the graph and check that every line cuts the graph at a unique point.

Example 1 :- By drawing a series of red vertical lines, we can see this **IS** a function since no line cuts the graph more than once.

Example 2 :- By drawing a series of red vertical lines, we can see this is **NOT** a function since some lines cut the graph more than once.

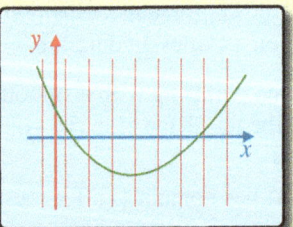

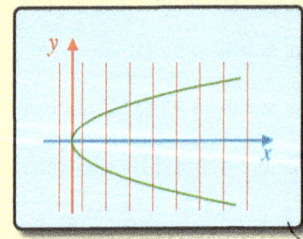

Exercise H3·2 – (for class discussion)

1. Decide which of these could represent functions, and discuss why each is **or** is not a function :-

(a)

(b)

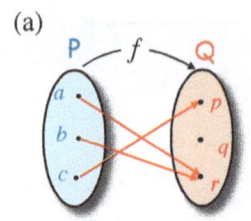

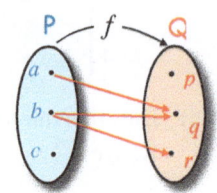

(c)

(d)

(e)

(f)

Composition of Functions

In the past, you have been asked to do something like this :-

"Think of a number (x), double it, then add on 3. What do you get ?"

This simple sentence, combines two separate functions, the first being $f(x) = 2x$, and the second being $g(x) = x + 3$.

We can look at this "combination" or "composition" of the two functions by studying the associated arrow diagram.

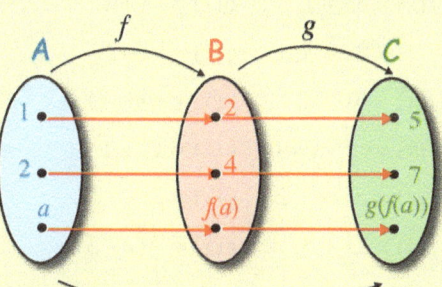

Can you see we have formed a new function $h(x)$ by combining the two function, performing f first, followed by g ?

This "combination" of two functions is called a "**composition**".

f takes any element a from **A** and produces the point $f(a)$ in **B**, then g takes $f(a)$ in **B** and produces a third point $g(f(x))$ in **C**.

We write this new function as :- $\boxed{h(x) = g(f(x))}$ (reads as g of f of x).

Example 1 :-

Two functions are defined by :-

$f(x) = 2x + 3$ and $g(x) = x^2 - 1$.

Find $h(x) = g(f(x))$ and $k(x) = f(g(x))$.

(a) $g(f(x))$ means $g[2x + 3]$

   (*note :- g squares each element then subtracts 1*)

=> $g[2x + 3] = (2x + 3)^2 - 1 = (4x^2 + 12x + 9) - 1$

=> $g(f(x)) = $ **$4x^2 + 12x + 8$**.

(b) $f(g(x))$ means $f[x^2 - 1]$

   (*note :- f doubles each element then adds 3*)

=> $f[x^2 - 1] = 2(x^2 - 1) + 3 = 2x^2 - 2 + 3$

=> $g(f(x)) = $ **$2x^2 + 1$**.

(*note :- g(f(x)) is not the same as f(g(x))*)

Example 2 :-

Two functions are defined by :-

$f(x) = 90 - x$ and $g(x) = sin2x°$.

Find $h(x) = g(f(x))$ and hence find $h(75)$.

(a) $g(f(x)) = g[90 - x]$

   (*note :- g doubles each element then finds its sine*).

=> $g[90 - x] = sin(2(90 - x))° = sin(180 - 2x)°$.

=> $h(x) = g(f(x)) = $ **$sin(180 - 2x)°$**

(b) $h(75) = sin(180 - 2 \times 75)° = sin30° = $ **$0\cdot5$**.

Example 3 :-

Here are two functions along with suitable domains :-

$f(x) = \dfrac{1}{x - 2} \{x \in R, x \neq 2\}$, $g(x) = \sqrt{x - 4}, \{x \in R, x \geq 4\}$.

Discuss in class why there are restrictions in both domains.

Exercise H3·3

1. Two functions are defined by $f(x) = 4x - 3$ and $g(x) = 1 - x$, both functions having domain $x \in R$.

    (a) Find $h(x) = g(f(x))$ and $k(x) = f(g(x))$.

    (b) Is it true that $g(f(x)) = f(g(x))$ for all values of x ?

    (c) Find $g(f(-1))$ and $f(g(-1))$.

2. In this question, $f(x) = x^2$ and $g(x) = x + 2, x \in R$. Find, in its simplest form :-

    (a) $g(f(x))$ (b) $f(g(x))$ (c) $g(g(x))$ (d) $f(f(x))$.

3. Here, $f(x) = x + 1$ and $g(x) = x^3, x \in \{1, 2, 3, 4\}$.

    (a) Find $h(x) = f(g(x))$ and state the range of $h(x)$.

    (b) Find $g(f(1)), g(f(2)), g(f(3)))$ and $g(f(4))$.

    (c) Find $k(x) = g(f(x))$, and expand the brackets.
         (Remember :- $(x + 1)^3 = (x + 1)[(x + 1)(x + 1)]$.)

4. $f(x) = x - 3, \{x \in R\}$ and $g(x) = \dfrac{1}{2x}, \{x \in R, x \neq 0\}$.

    (a) Find $h(x) = f(g(x))$ and $k(x) = g(f(x))$. *note

    (b) Find the value of $f(g(2)) - g(f(2))$.

    (c) State suitable domains for both $h(x)$ and $k(x)$.

5. These functions are on the set of Real Numbers.
    Find a formula each time for $f(g(x))$:-

    (a) $f(x) = 2x - 5,$ $g(x) = x^2$

    (b) $f(x) = x + 1,$ $g(x) = x^2 + x - 1$

    (c) $f(x) = x^2,$ $g(x) = 3x^2 + 1$

    (d) $f(x) = 3x - 1,$ $g(x) = x^2 + 1$

    (e) $f(x) = 2x - 5,$ $g(x) = x^2 - 2$

    (f) $f(x) = 6x - 1,$ $g(x) = \sin x$

    (g) $f(x) = \dfrac{1}{3x}$ $x \neq 0,$ $g(x) = x^3 + 1$

    (h) $f(x) = \cos x + 2,$ $g(x) = 2x^2 - 3$

    (i) $f(x) = 2x + 5,$ $g(x) = \tfrac{1}{2}(x - 5).$

6. $f(x) = x^2 + 2$ and $g(x) = 2x - 4.$

    (a) Find both $f(g(x))$ and $g(f(x)).$

    (b) Generally, $f(g(x)) \neq g(f(x)),$ but for specific
         values of $a,$ then $f(g(a)) = g(f(a)).$

         Find the value(s) of $a,$ (*to 2 decimal places*).

In question 5(i), you found $f(g(x)) = x.$ i.e. $h(x) = x.$

This function, $h(x) = x$ (or $y = x$) is called the :

     Identity Function   and is denoted by $I(x).$

It is called this because it maps each number identically
back onto itself.

7. For each pair of functions, check that $f(g(x)) = x.$
    (i.e., that the composition of f and g gives $h(x) = x$).

    (a) $f(x) = 3x,$ $g(x) = \tfrac{1}{3} x.$

    (b) $f(x) = x + 4$ $g(x) = x - 4$

    (c) $f(x) = x^2 + 1$ $g(x) = \sqrt{x - 1},$ $\{x \geq 1\}$

    (d) $f(x) = \dfrac{1}{x - 2},$ $\{x \neq 2\},$ $g(x) = \dfrac{1}{x} + 2,$ $\{x \neq 0\}.$

8. $f(x) = \dfrac{1}{x^2 - 4},$ $\{x \neq \pm 2\}$ and $g(x) = x + 2.$

    Find a formula for $h(x) = f(g(x)),$ and state a
    suitable domain for $h(x).$

9. Given that $f(x) = \dfrac{3}{x},$ $\{x \neq 0\},$ find $f(f(x)).$

Inverse of a Function

Earlier in the chapter, we defined a **function** as a relationship between two sets of values such that
each and every element of the domain maps onto **exactly one** element in the range.

The two diagrams on the right both show functions
from set **A** to set **B**, but there is a difference.

If we reversed the arrows in *figure 1*, we have created
a "**reverse**" function from **B** to **A**.

In *figure 2*, that is **not** the case, since there would be
two arrows leaving point p and none from point $q.$

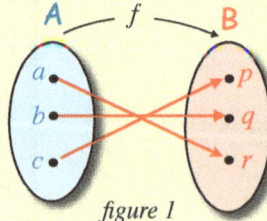
figure 1

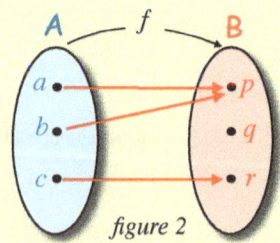
figure 2

If a function is such that for each point in set **A**, there is exactly one point in set **B**, and for each point in set **B**,
there is exactly one point in set **A**, we say there is a **one-to-one correspondence** between the sets.

For a one-to-one correspondence, it is possible to undo (or reverse) the function $f(x).$
This is called the **inverse function** and is denoted by :-

     The   **inverse function**   corresponding to $f(x)$ is :- $f^{-1}(x).$ (reads as "f to the negative one of x).

Example 1 :-
a	The reverse of "doubling" is "halving"	=> $f(x) = 2x$	=> $f^{-1}(x) = \tfrac{1}{2}x.$
b	The reverse of "adding 3" is "subtracting 3"	=> $f(x) = x + 3$	=> $f^{-1}(x) = x - 3.$
c	The reverse of "squaring" is "square rooting"	=> $f(x) = x^2$	=> $f^{-1}(x) = \sqrt{x}.$

The inverses of the above 3 functions were fairly obvious, but most functions are composite and have several steps.

Example 2 :- You might think that the inverse of the function :- $f(x) = 2x - 1$ is $f^{-1}(x) = \tfrac{1}{2}x + 1,$ but it is **NOT**.

     Think of how to undo the following :-   "put on your socks, then put on your shoes"

     Can you see the reverse of this is **NOT**   "take off your socks then take off your shoes" ?

Finding the Inverse of a Function Algebraically

There is a simple algorithm (rule) for finding the inverse of a composite function $f(x)$, and it consists of 4 steps.

Step 1 :- Re-write the function, but this time replace the term $f(x)$ with the letter y.

Step 2 :- Rearrange the formula using algebraic manipulation to make x the subject . (i.e. obtain x by itself).

Step 3 :- Interchange the letters x and y. (i.e. swap x for y and y for x).

Step 4 :- This is your inverse function, so simply replace x with $f^{-1}(x)$.

Example 1   Find the inverse of :- $f(x) = 2x - 1$.

Step 1 :- replacing $f(x)$ by y $y = 2x - 1$

Step 2 :- make x the subject
$$y = 2x - 1$$
$$2x - 1 = y$$
$$2x = y + 1$$
$$x = \tfrac{1}{2}(y + 1)$$

Step 3 :- Interchange x and y $y = \tfrac{1}{2}(x + 1)$

Step 4 :- Write as a function $f^{-1}(x) = \tfrac{1}{2}(x + 1)$.

Example 2   Find the inverse of :- $f(x) = x^2 + 3 . x \in R$.

Step 1 :- replacing $f(x)$ $y = x^2 + 3$

Step 2 :- rearranging
$$y = x^2 + 3$$
$$x^2 + 3 = y$$
$$x^2 = y - 3$$
$$x = \sqrt{(y-3)}, \quad y \geq 3$$

Step 3 :- interchange $y = \sqrt{(x-3)}, \quad x \geq 3$

Step 4 :- write as a function $f^{-1}(x) = \sqrt{(x-3)}, x \geq 3$.

Exercise H3·4

1. Use the "4 steps" to find $f^{-1}(x)$, given $f(x) = 5 - 3x$.

   Copy and **complete** :-

   Step 1 :- substitute y for $f(x)$ $y = 5 - \ldots$

   Step 2 :- make x the subject
   $$y = 5 - \ldots$$
   $$3x = 5 - \ldots$$
   $$x = \underset{\ldots}{\perp}(5 - \ldots)$$

   Step 3 :- interchange x and y $y = \underset{\ldots}{\perp}(\ldots - \ldots)$

   Step 4 :- inverse function is $f^{-1}(x) = \ldots\ldots$

2. For each function here, find the inverse function $f^{-1}(x)$.

   (a) $f(x) = 4x - 2$

   (b) $f(x) = 4 - 2x$

   (c) $f(x) = \tfrac{1}{3}x + 1$

   (d) $f(x) = 3(x - 2)$

   (e) $f(x) = \tfrac{3}{4}(4x + 5)$

   (f) $f(x) = x^3$

   (g) $f(x) = \dfrac{x + 1}{3}$

   (h) $f(x) = x^3 - 3$

   (i) $f(x) = \sqrt{x - 5},\ \{x:\ x \geq 5\}$.

3. (a) Show that the inverse of $f(x) = 3x + 1$ is given by $f^{-1}(x) = \tfrac{1}{3}(x - 1)$.

   (b) Find $h(x) = f(f^{-1}(x))$.

   (c) What special name do we have for $h(x)$?

Can you see that for any function $f(x)$, then $f^{-1}(f(x))$ will always produce the Identity Function $I(x) = x$, since when you apply $f(x)$ to any value a, then undo it by applying $f^{-1}(x)$ to this new value $f(a)$, it must take you back to the original value a, for all values of a ?

4. (a) Find $f^{-1}(x)$, given that $f(x) = 7 - 2x$.

   (b) Show that $f^{-1}(f(x)) = x$ (the identity function).

5. (a) $f(x) = 3 - x$.
   Find $f^{-1}(x)$ and show that $f(x) = f^{-1}(x)$.

   (b) $f(x) = \dfrac{12}{x}, x \neq 0$.
   Find $f^{-1}(x)$ and show again that $f(x) = f^{-1}(x)$.

6. For each function, find $f^{-1}(x)$ and in each case state a **suitable domain** for $f^{-1}(x)$.

   (a) $f(x) = \sqrt{4 - x}$

   (b) $f(x) = \sqrt{x + 5}$

   (c) $f(x) = x^2 + 2$

   (d) $f(x) = \dfrac{1}{x - 2}$ $\{x \neq 2\}$

   (e) $f(x) = \dfrac{1}{2x - 1}$ $\{x \neq \tfrac{1}{2}\}$ (f) $f(x) = \dfrac{6}{4 - x}$ $\{x \neq 4\}$.

7. Given $f(x) = x^2, (x : -3 < x < 3, x \in R\}$, explain why an inverse function does **NOT** exist.

8. Find the inverse, stating a suitable domain for $f^{-1}(x)$:-

   (a) $f(x) = \dfrac{x}{x + 1}, \{x \neq -1\}$ (b) $f(x) = \dfrac{x + 2}{x - 2}$ $\{x \neq 2\}$.

Exam Practice Exercise (H3)

1. A function, g, is defined by $g(x) = x^3 + 3$, where $x \in R$.

   Determine an expression for $g^{-1}(x)$. **(2)**

2. Functions f and g are defined on R, the set of real numbers and it is known that the inverse functions f^{-1} and g^{-1} both exist.

   (a) Given that $f(x) = 2x - 5$, find $f^{-1}(x)$. **(2)**

   (b) $g(3) = 2$. Find $g^{-1}(2)$. **(1)**

3. The functions f and g are defined on R, the set of real numbers.

   $$f(x) = 2x^2 - 3x + 1 \text{ and } g(x) = 4 - x.$$

   Find $h(x) = f(g(x))$. **(2)**

4. A function g is defined on R, the set of real numbers, by $g(x) = 8 - 3x$.

   (a) Determine an expression for $g^{-1}(x)$. **(2)**

   (b) Find an expression for $g(g^{-1}(x))$. **(2)**

5. Functions f and g are defined on suitable domains by $f(x) = 9 + x$ and $g(x) = (2 + x)(1 - x) + 1$.

   (a) Find an expression for $f(g(x))$. **(1)**

   (b) A function h is given by $h(x) = \dfrac{1}{f(g(x))}$.

   What values of x cannot be in the domain of h? **(2)**

6. Functions f and g are defined on suitable domains by $f(x) = x(x - 2) - p$ and $g(x) = x + 2$.

   (a) Find an expression for $f(g(x))$. **(1)**

   (b) Hence, find the value of p such that the equation $f(g(x)) = 0$ has roots, 2 and -4. **(2)**

7. Functions f and g are defined on the set of real numbers by $f(x) = x^2 + 2$ and $g(x) = x - 3$.

   (a) Find expressions for:

   (i) $f(g(x))$.

   (ii) $g(f(x))$. **(2)**

   (b) Show that $f(g(x)) + g(f(x)) = 0$ has no real roots. **(3)**

8. Functions f, g and h are defined on the set of real numbers by :-

   - $f(x) = x^2 + 2$
   - $g(x) = 2x$
   - $h(x) = 3x + 1$.

   (a) Find $g(f(x))$. **(2)**

   (b) Solve for x :- $g(f(x)) - \frac{1}{3} f(h(x)) = 0$. **(3)**

9. A function f is given by $f(x) = \sqrt{16 - 2x}$.

   What is a suitable domain for f? **(2)**

10. Functions f and g, defined on suitable domains, are given by $f(x) = x^2 + 1$ and $g(x) = 1 - 2x$.

    (a) Find $g(f(x))$ and $g(g(x))$. **(4)**

    (b) Solve for x :- $g(f(x)) - g(g(x)) = 0$. **(3)**

11. Functions f and g are given by $f(x) = 2(x + 1)$ and $g(x) = 2x - 1$, x being a real number.

    (a) Find expressions for :-

    (i) $g(f(x))$

    (ii) $g(g(x))$. **(3)**

    (b) Determine the value(s) of x for which :-

    $$g(f(x)) \times g(g(x)) = 16.$$ **(2)**

12. Functions $f(x) = 3x - 1$ and $g(x) = x^2 + 7$ are defined on the set of real numbers.

    (a) Find $h(x)$, where $h(x) = g(f(x))$. **(1)**

    (b) Solve the equation $h(x) - 11 = 0$ **(2)**

13. Function $f(x) = 2 - x$ and $g(x) = \dfrac{4}{x}$, $x \neq 0$.

    (a) Find $p(x)$, where $p(x) = f(g(x))$. **(1)**

    (b) If $q(x) = \dfrac{2}{3 - x}$, $x \neq 3$, find $p(q(x))$, in its simplest form. **(2)**

Home Exercise 1 (Chapters 1-3)

1. Determine the coordinates of the point of intersection of the line $y = 3x + 2$ and the parabola $y = 2x^2 - 4x + 5$.

2. Prove that the line $y = 2x - 11$ is a tangent to the circle $x^2 + y^2 - 6x - 10y + 14 = 0$, and determine the point of contact.

3. Find the equation of the line through A(-2, 7) and B(7, 1) and express it in the form $Ax + By + C = 0$, where A, B and C are integers.

4. Find the equation of the line perpendicular to the line with equation $2x - 3y + 7 = 0$, passing through the point P(-1, 5).

5. Show that the three points A(-5, 7), B(-2, 5) and C(7, -1) are collinear.

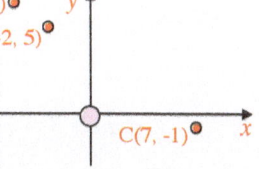

6. For the three points D(-1, 3), E(3, 6) and F(9, -2), prove that triangle DEF is right angled at E.

7. T(-1, -2), U(8, 1) and V(-2, 4) are the coordinates of triangle TUV.

   Find the equation of the altitude from V to side TU.

8. The vertices of triangle PQR are P(-1, -2), Q(7, 2) and R(3, 10).

   (a) Find the equation of the perpendicular bisector of the side PQ.

   (b) Find the equation of the median from P to side QR.

   (c) Find the coordinates of point T where these two lines meet.

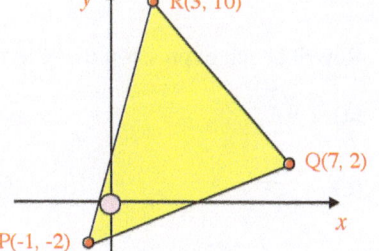

9. State a suitable domain for the function $f(x) = \dfrac{1}{\sqrt{x-2}}$.

10. Two functions are defined on suitable domains by $f(x) = 3x^2 - 2$ and $g(x) = x + 1$.
    (a) Find $f(g(x))$ and $g(f(x))$.
    (b) Solve for x :- $f(g(x)) - g(f(x)) = 0$.

11. Find $f^{-1}(x)$ for the function $f(x) = \dfrac{2x+1}{x-1}$ $\{x : x \neq 1, x \in R\}$ and state a suitable domain for $f^{-1}(x)$.

To succeed in this chapter on calculus, it is essential that you can express a function in the correct **index** form.

If you're unsure of how to express $\dfrac{3}{\sqrt{x}}$ as $3x^{-\frac{1}{2}}$, then you should complete this revision exercise.

Laws if Indices (should be known)

Law 1	**Law 2**	**Law 3**	**Law 4**	**Law 5**	**Law 6**
$a^m \times a^n = a^{m+n}$	$\dfrac{a^m}{a^n} = a^{m-n}$	$(a^m)^n = a^{mn}$	$a^0 = 1$	$a^{-m} = \dfrac{1}{a^m}$	$a^{\frac{m}{n}} = \sqrt[n]{a^m}$

Example 1 :- $3^{-2} = \dfrac{1}{3^2} = \dfrac{1}{9}$ and $8^{\frac{2}{3}} = \sqrt[3]{8^2} = 4$.

Example 2 :- $x + \dfrac{1}{x^7} - \sqrt[4]{x^3}$ expressed in the form ax^n.... $= x + x^{-7} - x^{\frac{3}{4}}$.

and $\dfrac{x-2}{x} = \dfrac{x}{x} - \dfrac{2}{x} = 1 - 2x^{-1}$.

Example 3 :- $\dfrac{1}{\sqrt{3}}$ with a rationalised denominator $= \dfrac{1}{\sqrt{3}} \times \dfrac{\sqrt{3}}{\sqrt{3}} = \dfrac{\sqrt{3}}{3}$.

1. Evaluate :-

    (a) 2^{-4} (b) 7^{-2} (c) 5^{-3} (d) 10^{-5}

    (e) $16^{\frac{1}{2}}$ (f) $27^{\frac{1}{3}}$ (g) $32^{\frac{1}{5}}$ (h) $256^{\frac{1}{4}}$

    (i) $8^{\frac{2}{3}}$ (j) $16^{\frac{3}{4}}$ (k) $25^{-\frac{1}{2}}$ (l) $27^{-\frac{1}{3}}$

    (m) $81^{-\frac{3}{4}}$ (n) $27^{-\frac{5}{3}}$ (o) $32^{-\frac{3}{5}}$ (p) $1000^{-\frac{2}{3}}$.

2. Rewrite each expression using terms in the form ax^n :-

    (a) $\sqrt[3]{x}$ (b) $\sqrt[4]{x^3}$ (c) $\dfrac{7}{x}$ (d) $\dfrac{5}{x^3}$

    (e) $\dfrac{4}{5x^2}$ (f) $\dfrac{-1}{2x^5}$ (g) $\dfrac{1}{\sqrt{x}}$ (h) $\dfrac{-2}{\sqrt[3]{x}}$

    (i) $\dfrac{1}{x^2} + \sqrt{x}$ (j) $x^3(1 + \sqrt{x})$ (k) $\sqrt{x}(10 - 5x)$ (l) $\left(x + \dfrac{1}{x}\right)^2$

    (m) $\left(x^4 + \dfrac{1}{x^3}\right)^2$ (n) $\left(\sqrt{x} + \dfrac{1}{\sqrt{x}}\right)^2$ (o) $\left(2x^2 - \dfrac{1}{x}\right)^2$ (p) $\dfrac{x+7}{x}$

    (q) $\dfrac{x^2 + \sqrt{x} - 1}{x}$ (r) $\dfrac{x-2}{\sqrt{x}}$ (s) $\dfrac{3 - 4x}{x^2}$ (t) $\dfrac{x+5}{3\sqrt{x}}$

    (u) $\dfrac{(1-x)^2}{6x}$ (v) $\dfrac{(1-x)(1-2x)}{x}$ (w) $\dfrac{x^2 + 5x}{x\sqrt{x}}$ (x) $\dfrac{4x^2 - x}{x^2\sqrt{x}}$.

3. Rationalise the denominator of each fraction, then express in the form ax^n :-

    (a) $\dfrac{1}{\sqrt{6}}$ (b) $\dfrac{2}{5\sqrt{3}}$ (c) $\dfrac{4}{\sqrt{8}}$ (d) $\dfrac{2}{1 - \sqrt{3}}$.

Introduction

Many people say that they never use the Mathematics they learn at school, but the topic we are about to introduce in this chapter, (**Calculus**) is probably one of the most important of all mathematic topics, and is used by mathematicians, scientists, statisticians, inventors, engineers, … the list goes on.

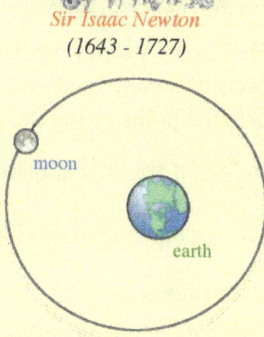

Sir Isaac Newton
(1643 - 1727)

- Scientists use calculus in the calculation of speed and acceleration
- Chemists use calculus to determine chemical reaction speeds
- We would never have been able to put a rocket into space without calculus
- Astronomers use calculus to determine the position and velocity of stars and planets
- A piece of music can be analysed as a series of resonances determinable by calculus
- Maximisation and minimisation problems are easily solved using calculus
- The study of how heat travels along an object or through the air involves calculus

- The list is endless….

So - what is calculus ?

Isaac Newton

Isaac Newton was a very famous scientist/mathematician/astronomer who lived in the 17th and early 18th centuries.

He is reputed to have invented calculus while studying the movement of the moon about the earth and the planets in the solar system around the sun.

To determine the position of a planet, it was important to be able to know its velocity (speed) at any instant in time, but this was almost impossible to do as the orbit of a planet is not a circle, but an ellipse, and the sun is not at the centre, but at a position slightly displaced from the centre, called the focus.

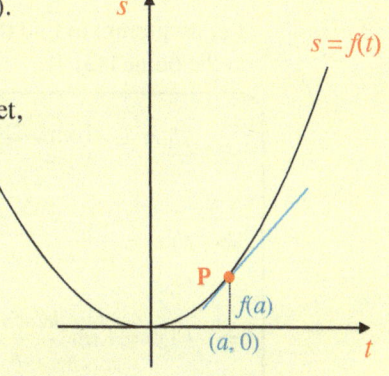

(figure 1)

Because of this, it was known that the planet was changing its speed and direction constantly as it travelled along its path in space.

Normally, to calculate speed, you divide the distance travelled by the time taken, but if the speed or velocity is always changing, that calculation can't be carried out.

> **Calculus was invented to solve this problem.**

To illustrate how calculus works, we are going to look initially at the simpler curve shown $s = f(t)$, where t is time and s distance (or displacement).

Some comets in the sky follow parabolic curves and some elliptical ones.

Newton knew that if for some reason, the sun instantly disappeared, the planet, no longer under the sun's gravitational pull, would leave its elliptical path at a tangent to the curve. (*See figure 1*).

Let us see if we can calculate the **rate of change** of the **function** $s = f(t)$, at the point **P** on the diagram with t coordinate a.

i.e. the **instantaneous speed** (or velocity) at **P**.

Can you see that the coordinates of **P** are **P**$(a, f(a))$, since when $x = a$, the y-coordinate of P will be $f(a)$?

Our task is to find a measure, (m) of the slope of the curve at this point.

On the next page we will begin by finding an estimate for this.

$s = f(t)$

P

$f(a)$

$(a, 0)$

t

The slope of the **blue** line indicates the rate of change of the curve with respect to time. (i.e. its velocity)

Let us begin by choosing a new point, **Q**, a short distance h to the right of **P** on the parabola.

This means the t-coordinate of **Q** is $(a + h)$, the s-coordinate of **Q** is $f(a + h)$, and the coordinates of **Q** are given by $Q((a + h), f(a + h))$.

Since we know the coordinates of $P(a, f(a))$ and $Q((a + h), f(a + h))$, we can determine the gradient of the green line joining **P** to **Q**. i.e. m_{PQ}.

$$\Rightarrow \qquad m_{PQ} = \frac{y_Q - y_P}{x_Q - x_P} = \frac{f(a + h) - f(a)}{(a + h) - a} = \boxed{\frac{f(a + h) - f(a)}{h}}$$

As you can see, the slope of PQ is not the same as that of the blue line at P.

However, you can see that since h was an arbitrary value, if we now make h become smaller and smaller, then the point **Q** moves closer and closer to our original point **P**, and the gradient m_{PQ} gradually gets closer to the slope at P(m).

In fact, if we let h approach a value of **zero**, the two gradients will become identical.

We say the **rate of change** of the curve at P is given by the :- $\underset{h \longrightarrow 0}{\text{Limit}} \dfrac{f(a + h) - f(a)}{h}$.

This reads as :-

"The rate of change of the curve (the speed) at point P is the limit, as h approaches 0, of the function $\dfrac{f(t + h) - f(t)}{h}$ ".

This **rate of change** can also be seen as a measure of the **gradient of the tangent** to the curve at point P and for any equation $y = f(t)$, we define this rate of change by the term $f'(t)$. It reads as "f **dash** t".

$$\boxed{f'(x) = \underset{h \to 0}{\text{Lim}} \frac{f(t + h) - f(t)}{h}}$$

New Terminology

Let us consider a general equation in terms of x and y, where $y = f(x)$, instead of the time-distance variables s and t.

Now, the new function, "derived" from the function $f(x)$ is called the "**derivative of $f(x)$**" and is referred to as $f'(x)$.

$\Rightarrow$ $\boxed{\begin{array}{l} f'(x) \text{ is simply a new function, derived from the old function } f(x) \text{ whose sole purpose is to} \\ \text{enable you to calculate the } \textbf{rate of change} \text{ of the function } f(x) \text{ at any point on the curve.} \\ \text{(We shall see later it can also help us calculate gradient of the tangent to the curve).} \end{array}}$

This might not seem very important, but you will find, as you develop your Calculus skills, that it **IS** very important.

Our formula for calculating the rate of change is now given by :- $\boxed{f'(x) = \underset{h \to 0}{\text{Lim}} \dfrac{f(x + h) - f(x)}{h}}$

Example :- Let us attempt to find the rate of change of the curve $f(x) = x^2$, at the point T(3, 9).

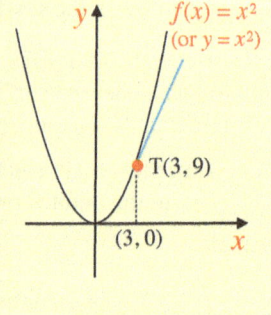

$$f'(x) = \underset{h \to 0}{\text{Lim}} \frac{f(x + h) - f(x)}{h} = \underset{h \to 0}{\text{Lim}} \frac{(x + h)^2 - (x)^2}{h}$$

$$\Rightarrow f'(x) = \underset{h \to 0}{\text{Lim}} \frac{x^2 + 2xh + h^2 - x^2}{h} = \underset{h \to 0}{\text{Lim}} \frac{2xh + h^2}{h} \quad \text{(the } x^2 \text{ disappear).}$$

$$\Rightarrow f'(x) = \underset{h \to 0}{\text{Lim}} \frac{h(2x + h)}{h} = \underset{h \to 0}{\text{Lim}} (2x + h) \quad \text{(the } h\text{'s cancel).}$$

now replace h by 0. $\Rightarrow$ $f'(x) = 2x.$ this is the derived function that will enable us to find the rate of change of the curve $y = f(x)$ at any point.

$\Rightarrow$ at T, with x-coordinate 3, the rate of change is $f'(3) = 2 \times 3 = $ **6.**

Exercise H4·1 - Practical

In this exercise, you are going to discover how to find the derivative (or derived function) of various known functions.

1. Find $f'(x)$, the derivative of the function $f(x) = x^3$, given that :- $(x + h)^3 = x^3 + 3x^2h + 3xh^2 + h^3$.

   Copy and **complete** :-

   Always start with $f'(x) = \underset{h \to 0}{\text{Lim}} \dfrac{f(x + h) - f(x)}{h}$

   $\Rightarrow f'(x) = \underset{h \to 0}{\text{Lim}} \dfrac{(x + h)^3 - x^3}{h}$

   $\Rightarrow f'(x) = \underset{h \to 0}{\text{Lim}} \dfrac{x^3 + 3x^2h + 3xh^2 + h^3 - x^3}{h}$

   $\Rightarrow f'(x) = \underset{h \to 0}{\text{Lim}} \dfrac{3x^2h + 3xh^2 + h^3}{h}$　　(the x^3 disappears)

   $\Rightarrow f'(x) = \underset{h \to 0}{\text{Lim}} \dfrac{h(3x^2 + 3xh + h^2)}{h}$　　(h - a common factor) (the h's cancel)

   $\Rightarrow f'(x) = \underset{h \to 0}{\text{Lim}} \; 3x^2 + 3xh + h^2$　　now, replace h by 0.

   $\Rightarrow f'(x) = \;.....$

2. Find $f'(x)$, the derivative of the function $f(x) = x^4$, given that :- $(x + h)^4 = x^4 + 4x^3h + 6x^2h^2 + 4xh^3 + h^4$.

   $\Rightarrow f'(x) = \underset{h \to 0}{\text{Lim}} \dfrac{(x + h)^4 - x^4}{h}$

   $\Rightarrow f'(x) = \underset{h \to 0}{\text{Lim}} \dfrac{x^4 + 4x^3h + 6x^2h^2 + 4xh^3 + h^4 - x^4}{h}$

   $\Rightarrow f'(x) = \underset{h \to 0}{\text{Lim}} \dfrac{4x^3h + 6x^2h^2 + 4xh^3 + h^4}{h}$　　(the x^4 disappears)

   $\Rightarrow f'(x) = \underset{h \to 0}{\text{Lim}} \dfrac{h(4x^3 + ... + ... + ...)}{h}$　　(h is a common factor) (the h's cancel)

   $\Rightarrow f'(x) = \underset{h \to 0}{\text{Lim}} \; 4x^3 + ... + ... + ...$　　now, replace h by 0.

   $\Rightarrow f'(x) = \;.....$

3. Find $f'(x)$, the derivative of the function $f(x) = x$. (x^1).

   $\Rightarrow f'(x) = \underset{h \to 0}{\text{Lim}} \dfrac{(x + h) - x}{h}$

   $\Rightarrow f'(x) = \underset{h \to 0}{\text{Lim}} \dfrac{h}{h}$　　(the x's disappears)

   $\Rightarrow f'(x) = \underset{h \to 0}{\text{Lim}} \dfrac{h}{h}$　　(h - a common factor) and they cancel now replace h by 0.

   $\Rightarrow f'(x) = \;.....$

4. Find $f'(x)$, the derivative of the function $f(x) = x^2 + x$.

Summarising

This table shows the derived functions we have found so far, :-

Original function $f(x)$	$f(x) = 1$	$f(x) = x$	$f(x) = x^2$	$f(x) = x^3$	$f(x) = x^4$	$f(x) = x^5$	$f(x) = x^6$
Derived function $f'(x)$	$f'(x) = ...$	$f'(x) = 1$	$f'(x) = 2x$	$f'(x) = 3x^2$	$f'(x) = 4x^3$	$f'(x) = ...$	$f'(x) = ...$

Observe the pattern for the functions $f(x) = x$, $f(x) = x^2$, $f(x) = x^3$, $f(x) = x^4$, etc .

Continuing the pattern leads to :-　　$f(x) = x^5 \Rightarrow f'(x) = 5x^4$; $f(x) = x^6 \Rightarrow f'(x) = 6x^5$.

What about $f(x) = 1$, which can be thought of as $f(x) = 1x^0$?　　$\Rightarrow$　If $f(x) = 1x^0$, then $f'(x) = 0 \times 1x^{-1} = 0$.

Finding the Derived Function :-

If $f(x) = x^n$, where n is a constant, then $\Rightarrow f'(x) = nx^{(n-1)}$ **Example** : $f(x) = x^{10} \Rightarrow f'(x) = 10x^9$.

If $f(x) = ax^n$, where a is a number, then $\Rightarrow f'(x) = anx^{(n-1)}$ **Example** : $f(x) = 5x^7 \Rightarrow f'(x) = 35x^6$.

If $f(x) = ax^n \pm bx^m$, then $\Rightarrow f'(x) = anx^{(n-1)} + bmx^{(m-1)}$ **Example** : $f(x) = 3x^6 + 4x^2 \Rightarrow f'(x) = 18x^5 + 8x$.

Note :- We haven't actually proven this work for all powers of x. If you do 6th Year Maths, you will meet the proofs then.

The Derivative of a Function - Differentiation

$f(x) = c$, where c is a constant, then

$$\Rightarrow f'(x) = \lim_{h \to 0} \frac{(x+h) - x}{h}$$

$$\Rightarrow f'(x) = \lim_{h \to 0} \frac{c - c}{h} = 0$$

The derivative of a constant function is zero.

Using what we have discovered earlier :-

Example 1 :-

Find the derivative of the function $f(x) = 10$.

$$f(x) = 10, \quad \Rightarrow \quad f'(x) = 0.$$

Example 2 :-

(a) Given $f(x) = x^3 - 8x + 5$, find $f'(x)$.

(b) Find the rate of change of the curve at $x = 2$

(a) $f(x) = x^3 - 8x + 5$

$$\Rightarrow f'(x) = 3x^2 - 8.$$

(b) $f'(2) = 3 \times 2^2 - 8 = 4.$

Example 3 :- Given $f(x) = (x^2 - 6)^2$, find $f'(x)$.

$$f(x) = (x^2 - 6)^2 = x^4 - 12x^2 + 36$$

$$f'(x) = 4x^3 - 24x.$$

*Note :- if asked to find the rate of change at $x = 3$, find $f'(3)$.

$$f'(3) = 4 \times 3^3 - 72 = 36.$$

Finding the **rate of change** of a function at a point on the curve with $x = a$, is the same as finding $f'(a)$.

Exercise H4·2

Find the derivative $f'(x)$ of each function :-

1. $f(x) = x^5$

2. $f(x) = x^9$

3. $f(x) = 5x^4$

4. $f(x) = \frac{1}{3}x^3$

5. $f(x) = \frac{2}{5}x^5$

6. $f(x) = -2x^6$

7. $f(x) = ax^2$

8. $f(x) = 10x$

9. $f(x) = 7$

10. $f(x) = 1$

11. $f(x) = x^2 + 5x + 5$

12. $f(x) = x^3 - 6x^2 + 1$

13. $f(x) = \frac{1}{3}x^3 + \frac{1}{4}x^2 + 3$

14. $f(x) = 5x^4 - x^2 + 11$

15. $f(x) = 7 - 3x^5 + 2x^7$

16. $f(x) = ax^3 - bx^2 + c$

17. $f(x) = (x - 1)^2$

18. $f(x) = (x + 2)^2$

19. $f(x) = (4x + 3)^2$

20. $f(x) = (x + 2)(3x - 1)$

21. $f(x) = (4x + 1)(4x - 1)$

22. $f(x) = (3 - x)(5 - x)$

23. $f(x) = (x^2 + 3)^2$

24. $f(x) = (x^3 - 2)^2$

25. $f(x) = (x^4 + 1)^2$

26. $f(x) = (x - 1)^3$

27. $f(x) = (x + 1)(x - 4)(2x - 5)$

28. $f(x) = (x + 3)^3$

29. Given $f(x) = 5 + x - x^2$, find the value of :-

(a) $f'(0)$ (b) $f'(\frac{1}{2})$ (c) $f'(1)$ (d) $f'(-5)$.

30. (a) Given a function $f(x) = (x^3 - 1)^2$, find a formula for the derived function $f'(x)$.

(b) Find the rate of change of f at $x = 1$ and $x = -2$.

31. If $f(x) = 7 - 8x - 2x^2$, find x for which :-

(a) $f'(x) = 4$ (b) $f'(x) = -10$ (c) $f'(x) > 0$.

32. Given $f(x) = \frac{1}{3}x^3 - x^2 - 8x$, find x for which :-

(a) $f'(x) = 0$ (b) $f'(x) = -9$ (c) $f'(x) < 0$.

33. For each function, find $f'(x)$ and sketch the graphs of both $f(x)$ and $f'(x)$.

(a) $f(x) = x$ (b) $f(x) = x^2$ (c) $f(x) = x^3$.

The Derivative of ax^n, where n is a Negative or a Rational Number

Similar rules apply.

If $f(x) = x^n$, where n is a negative integer, then $\Rightarrow f'(x) = nx^{(n-1)}$.

If $f(x) = ax^n$, where a is a rational number, then $\Rightarrow f'(x) = anx^{(n-1)}$.

Example 1 :- Given $f(x) = \frac{1}{4x^2}$, find $f'(x)$.

$f(x) = \frac{1}{4x^2} = \frac{1}{4} \times \frac{1}{x^2} = \frac{1}{4}x^{-2}$

$f'(x) = -\frac{2}{4}x^{-3}$

$= -\dfrac{1}{2x^3}$

Example 2 :- If $f(x) = \left(3x + \frac{1}{3x}\right)^2$, find $f'(x)$.

$f(x) = 9x^2 + 2 + \frac{1}{9x^2} = 9x^2 + 2 + \frac{1}{9}x^{-2}$

$f'(x) = 18x - \frac{2}{9}x^{-3}$

$= \boxed{18x - \dfrac{2}{9x^3}}$

Example 3 :- Given $f(x) = \frac{x+1}{\sqrt{x}}$, find $f'(x)$.

$f(x) = \frac{x+1}{\sqrt{x}} = \frac{x}{x^{\frac{1}{2}}} + \frac{1}{x^{\frac{1}{2}}} = x^{\frac{1}{2}} + x^{-\frac{1}{2}}$

$f'(x) = \frac{1}{2}x^{-\frac{1}{2}} - \frac{1}{2}x^{-\frac{3}{2}}$

$= \dfrac{1}{2x^{\frac{1}{2}}} - \dfrac{1}{2x^{\frac{3}{2}}}$ or $\boxed{\dfrac{1}{2\sqrt{x}} - \dfrac{1}{2\sqrt{x^3}}}$

Exercise H4·3

Express all **answers** with **positive indices**.

1. Find $f'(x)$ for each function :-

   (a) $f(x) = x^{\frac{5}{3}}$ (b) $f(x) = x^{\frac{3}{2}}$ (c) $f(x) = x^{\frac{7}{4}}$

   (d) $f(x) = x^{\frac{1}{2}}$ (e) $f(x) = x^{\frac{1}{4}}$ (f) $f(x) = x^{-1}$

   (g) $f(x) = x^{-3}$ (h) $f(x) = x^{-6}$ (i) $f(x) = 2x^{-2}$

   (j) $f(x) = -10x^{-5}$ (k) $f(x) = \frac{1}{2}x^{-6}$

   (l) $f(x) = -\frac{1}{4}x^{-2}$ (m) $f(x) = -\frac{5}{3}x^{-6}$.

2. Express each function in the form ax^n, and then find its derivative :-

   (a) $f(x) = \sqrt{x}$ (b) $f(x) = \sqrt[3]{x}$ (c) $f(x) = \sqrt[5]{x^2}$

   (d) $f(x) = \frac{1}{x^2}$ (e) $f(x) = \frac{1}{x}$ (f) $f(x) = \frac{1}{x^5}$

   (g) $f(x) = \frac{4}{x}$ (h) $f(x) = \frac{1}{\sqrt{x}}$ (i) $f(x) = \frac{-3}{\sqrt{x}}$

   (j) $f(x) = \frac{5}{x^4}$ (k) $f(x) = \frac{1}{2x^{\frac{1}{2}}}$ (l) $f(x) = \frac{2}{3x^3}$

   (m) $f(x) = \frac{4}{5x^5}$ (n) $f(x) = \frac{-1}{3x^6}$ (o) $f(x) = \frac{1}{8\sqrt{x}}$.

3. Express each of the following as a sum of terms in the form ax^n, and find its derivative :-

   (a) $f(x) = \frac{1}{x} + x$ (b) $f(x) = \frac{1}{\sqrt{x}} + \sqrt{x}$

   (c) $f(x) = 3x - \frac{3}{x}$ (d) $f(x) = 2x^2 - \frac{1}{3x^2}$

   (e) $f(x) = x^3 + 3 - \frac{1}{x^2}$ (f) $f(x) = \frac{7}{x} + \frac{x}{7}$

   (g) $f(x) = 3x^4 + \frac{1}{4x^3}$ (h) $f(x) = x^2(\sqrt{x} + 1)$

   (i) $f(x) = \sqrt{x}(3 - \sqrt{x})$ (j) $f(x) = \left(x - \frac{1}{x}\right)^2$

   (k) $f(x) = \left(x^3 + \frac{1}{x^2}\right)^2$ (l) $f(x) = \left(4x - \frac{4}{x}\right)^2$

   (m) $f(x) = \left(\sqrt{x} + \frac{1}{\sqrt{x}}\right)^2$ (n) $f(x) = \left(x - \frac{1}{x}\right)\left(x + \frac{1}{x}\right)$

   (o) $f(x) = \frac{x - 3}{x}$ (p) $f(x) = \frac{x^2 + 3x + 2}{x}$

   (q) $f(x) = \frac{4x^3 - x^2 + 3}{x}$ (r) $f(x) = \frac{x - 4}{x^{\frac{1}{2}}}$

   (s) $f(x) = \frac{5 + 8x}{x^2}$ (t) $f(x) = \frac{x + 3}{2x^{\frac{1}{3}}}$.

Leibniz Notation

Gottfried Leibniz* was a German mathematician who discovered/invented the notion of Differential Calculus about the same time as Isaac Newton, but he used a different notation.

Instead of writing the derivative as $f'(x)$, we can use the Leibniz Notation.

Leibniz notation helps to highlight that we are dealing with a rate of change in y over a rate in change of x by using the term Δx (reads as "delta" x) instead of the symbol h.

In Leibniz notation Δx denotes a small change in x and Δy denotes a small change in y.

For any function $y = f(x)$, the gradient of the chord between P(x, y) and

Q($x + \Delta x$, $y + \Delta y$) is $m = \dfrac{y + \Delta y - y}{x + \Delta x - x} = \dfrac{\Delta y}{\Delta x}$.

The **rate of change** of the curve at (x, y) is $\lim\limits_{\Delta x \to 0} \dfrac{\Delta y}{\Delta x}$.

This is normally written as $\dfrac{dy}{dx}$. (it reads as dy by dx).

$$\boxed{\dfrac{dy}{dx} = f'(x)}$$

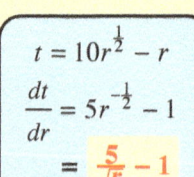

Gottfried Wilhem Leibniz
(1646 - 1716)

Example 1 :- Find the derivative of :-
$$y = 2x^4 + 4x^3 - 7x + 2,$$
with respect to x.

$$y = 2x^4 + 4x^3 - 7x + 2$$
$$\dfrac{dy}{dx} = 8x^3 + 12x^2 - 7$$

Example 2 :- Differentiate $t = 10r^{\frac{1}{2}} - r$ with respect to r.

$$t = 10r^{\frac{1}{2}} - r$$
$$\dfrac{dt}{dr} = 5r^{-\frac{1}{2}} - 1$$
$$= \dfrac{5}{\sqrt{r}} - 1$$

Example 3 :- Calculate the gradient of the tangent

to the curve $y = \dfrac{(x+1)(x+3)}{x^2}$ at $x = 4$.

$$y = \dfrac{x^2 + 4x + 3}{x^2} = \dfrac{x^2}{x^2} + \dfrac{4x}{x^2} + \dfrac{3}{x^2}$$
$$y = 1 + 4x^{-1} + 3x^{-2}$$
$$\dfrac{dy}{dx} = -4x^{-2} - 6x^{-3} = \dfrac{-4}{x^2} - \dfrac{6}{x^3}$$
At $x = 4$, $\dfrac{dy}{dx} = -\dfrac{4}{16} - \dfrac{6}{64}$
$$= -\dfrac{11}{32}$$

*The **calculus controversy** (often referred to with the German term *Prioritätsstreit*, meaning "priority dispute") was an argument between 17th-century mathematicians Isaac Newton and Gottfried Leibniz over who had first invented the mathematical study of rates of change, calculus. It is a question that had been the cause of a major intellectual controversy, one that began simmering in 1699 and broke out in full force in 1711.

Exercise H4·4

Find the derivative of each of the following with respect to the relevant variable, giving answers with positive indices when required :-

1. (a) $y = 8x^4 - 5x^2 + 3x - 2$ (b) $y = 4x^{\frac{3}{4}} - 10x^{\frac{1}{5}}$

    (c) $y = g + \dfrac{4}{g^2}$ (d) $y = \dfrac{2}{x} + \dfrac{5}{x^3}$

    (e) $v = u^2(u^3 - u)$ (f) $y = (x + \dfrac{10}{x})^2$

    (g) $w = \dfrac{(v-1)(v+3)}{2v^2}$ (h) $s = \dfrac{(4h-2)^2}{\sqrt{h}}$.

2. Given the function $y = 2x^4$, find the value of :-

    (a) $\dfrac{dy}{dx}$ at $x = 2$.

    (b) the derivative of y at $x = -1$.

3. (a) If $v = (u-1)(u^2 + 4)$, find $\dfrac{dv}{du}$ at $u = \frac{1}{2}$.

    (b) $y = \dfrac{x-4}{x^2}$. Find $\dfrac{dy}{dx}$ at $x = 2$.

4. Find the gradient of the tangent to each curve :-

    (a) $y = 5x^2 + 1$, at $x = -2$.

    (b) $y = 2x + \dfrac{1}{2x}$, at $x = \frac{1}{2}$.

    (c) $y = \dfrac{2}{\sqrt{x}}(1 + 2x)$, at $x = 4$.

5. Find the two values of x for which the value of the derivative to the curve $y = x^3 - 2x$ is 1.

6. Given that $s = \dfrac{2t^4 + 6t^2 - 2}{\sqrt{t}}$,

    calculate the value of $\dfrac{ds}{dt}$ at $t = 4$.

Practical uses for Calculus - Speed

Newton developed Calculus to help calculate the speed and direction of the movement of the planets around the sun. He discovered that the tangent to the curve could provide him with a means of calculating the **instantaneous** speed.

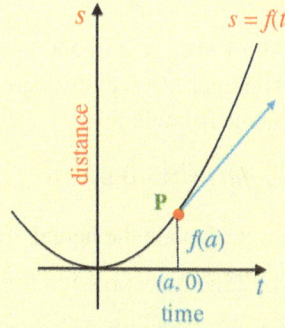

The curve shows the path of an object. The horizontal axis measures time (t) and the vertical axis the corresponding distance (s) travelled. The slope of the graph at P gives us the **rate of change** of distance with respect to time or in other words, the **speed**.

> If the distance-time graph is represented by $s = f(t)$, then $\dfrac{ds}{dt}$ allows us to calculate the speed at any point (a).

Example :- An object is moving along a parabolic path and its distance is given by the formula
$s = 5 + 30t - 3t^2$, where t is the time in seconds and s is the distance travelled in metres.

(a) Calculate the speed of the object after 2 seconds.

(b) At what time is the object stationary ?

> (a) Speed $= \dfrac{ds}{dt} = 30 - 6t$. At $t = 2$ seconds, speed $= 30 - 6 \times 2 =$ **18 m/s**.
>
> (b) For the object to be stationary, its speed must be 0. Solve $\dfrac{ds}{dt} = 30 - 6t = 0 \Rightarrow t =$ **5 secs**.

Acceleration

For this moving object, the horizontal axis measures time (t) but the vertical axis the corresponding speed (v).

The **rate of change** of speed with respect to time now gives us the **acceleration**.

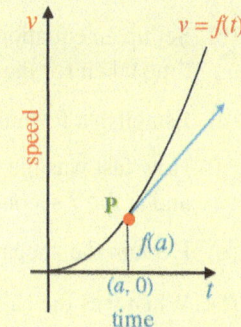

> If the speed-time graph is represented by $v = f(t)$, then $\dfrac{dv}{dt}$ represents the acceleration at any point (a).

Example :- A plane is flying with its velocity given by the formula :- $v = \frac{1}{3}t^3 + 2t^2 - 5t + \frac{2}{3}$, where $t \geq 0$.
where t is the time in seconds and v is the speed measured in metres per second.

(a) Calculate the **speed** of the plane after 10 seconds.

(b) Calculate the plane's **acceleration** after 2 seconds.

(c) At what time is the plane flying at a constant velocity ?

> (a) Velocity $= \frac{1}{3}$ of $10^3 + 2 \times 10^2 - 5 \times 10 + \frac{2}{3} =$ **484 m/s**
>
> (b) Acceleration $= \dfrac{dv}{dt} = t^2 + 4t - 5$. After $t = 2$ seconds, $acc^n = 2^2 + 4 \times 2 - 5 =$ **7 m/s**.
>
> (c) Constant speed means acceleration is **zero**.
> Set $\dfrac{dv}{dt} = t^2 + 4t - 5 = 0$ and solve $\Rightarrow (t + 5)(t - 1) = 0 \Rightarrow t = -5$ or 1,
> but since we do not have a negative time, then constant speed occurs after **1 second**.

Exercise H4·5

1. As a firework is lit and takes off, its height $h(t)$ metres is given by the formula :-

    $$h(t) = t^3, \quad 0 \le t \le 6.$$

    (a) Calculate the height after 1, 2 and 3 seconds.

    (b) Find an expression for its speed $v(t)$.

    (c) Calculate the firework's speed after 5 seconds.

2. When a ball it thrown up in the air, it follows a parabolic path as shown.

    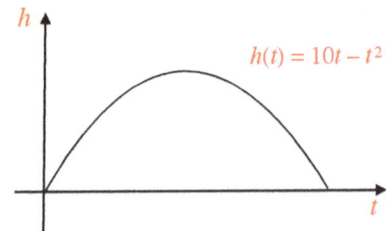

    h is the height in metres and t the time in seconds.

    (a) Use the formula for h to calculate the height after 2 seconds and after 8 seconds.

    (b) Set up an equation and use it to calculate the time taken for the ball to land again.

    (c) Establish a formula for the ball's speed $v(t)$.

    (d) How fast was the ball travelling at the 3 second and at the 7 second point on its journey ?

    (e) Explain the "negative" value.

    (f) When was the ball at its maximum height ?

3. When a marble is released and rolls along this slope, its drop in height d metres from the starting point is defined by the formula :-

    $$d(t) = 3t^2 - 18t, \quad 0 \le t \le 6, \; t \text{ in seconds.}$$

    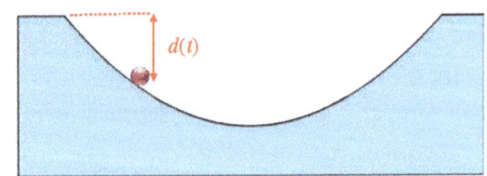

    (a) Find an expression for its speed, $v(t)$.

    (b) What is its speed after 2 and after 4 seconds ?

    (c) Explain your answers to part (b).

4. As a wheel turns, it drives a piston along a metal sleeve. The distance s cm of the piston from its starting point is defined by $s(t) = 6t - \frac{1}{2}t^2, \quad 0 \le t \le 12, \; t$ in seconds.

    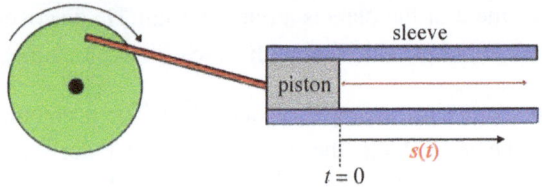

    (a) How far was the front of the piston from its starting point after 4 seconds ?

    (b) Find a formula for the piston's speed $v(t)$.

    (c) What was its speed after 4 seconds ?

5. The height in feet above ground of the car on a roller-coaster ride is defined by the formula :-

    $$h(d) = \tfrac{1}{200} d(d - 60)^2, \quad \{d : 0 \le d \le 90\},$$

    where d measures the horizontal distance, in feet.

    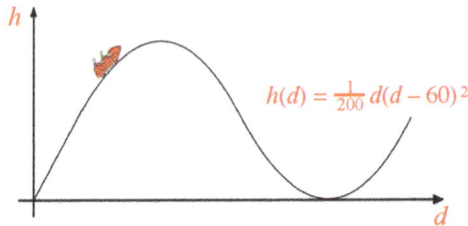

    (a) Calculate the height of the car when $d = 10$.

    (b) Find the two values for d when the car was at ground level.

    (c) Find the rate of change of the height with respect to the horizontal distance when $d = 10$.

    (d) Find d when the car was at the top of the ride.

6. When a stone is dropped into a pond, the ripples form circles radiating from the point of impact.

    The circumference, c metres, of the outer circle, at time t seconds, is given by $c(t) = 2\pi\sqrt{t}$.

    Calculate the rate of change of the circumference after 9 seconds.

7. The volume V (cm³) of air in a balloon as it is being inflated, is given by the formula $V(t) = 3t^3 + \frac{1}{3}t^2$, where t is the time in seconds.

    Calculate the rate of change of volume (how quickly it is expanding) in m³ per second, after 6 seconds.

8. The resistance R ohms in an electrical circuit is given by $R(i) = \dfrac{240}{i}$, where i is the current in amps.

    Calculate the rate of change in the resistance when the current is 10 amps.

The Equation of a Tangent to a Curve

Since a tangent is a straight line, its equation can be found using :- $y - b = m(x - a)$.
To find the equation of the tangent at any point on a curve we need two things :-
We need its gradient m, and the coordinates (a, b) at the point of contact with the curve.

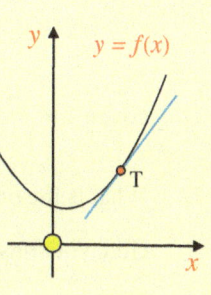

The derivative $f'(x)$ (or $\frac{dy}{dx}$) of a function $y = f(x)$ allows us to find the rate of change
of a curve at a point (T) on the curve, as shown by the blue line in the diagram.

This blue line is a tangent, and hence differentiation gives us the gradient of the tangent $\boxed{m_T}$.

Example 1 :- Find the equation of the tangent to the
curve with equation $y = 4x^2 + 2x - 1$,
at the point where $x = -1$.

> $y = 4x^2 + 2x - 1$
>
> $\frac{dy}{dx} = 8x + 2 \Rightarrow$ at $x = -1$, $\frac{dy}{dx} = -6$
>
> This means that the gradient, m, is -6.
> At $x = -1$, the value of y is $4 + (-2) - 1 = 1$.
>
> This means that the point (a, b) where
> the tangent meets the curve is (-1, 1).
>
> Therefore the equation of the tangent is
>
> $y - 1 = -6(x + 1)$ or $y = -6x - 5$.

Example 2 :- Find the points of contact on the curve
$f(x) = x^3 - 4x$ for tangents with gradient 8.

> $f(x) = x^3 - 4x$
>
> $f'(x) = 3x^2 - 4$
>
> (since gradient $m = 8$),
>
> $\Rightarrow \quad 3x^2 - 4 = 8$
>
> $\Rightarrow \quad x^2 = 4 \Rightarrow \quad x = \pm 2$
>
> At $x = -2$, the value of $y = f(-2)$ is 0.
> At $x = 2$, the value of $y = f(2)$ is also 0.
> Therefore the points of contact are
>
> (-2, 0) and (2, 0).

Exercise H4·6

1. Find the equation of the tangent to each curve at
   the given point :-

   (a) $y = x^2$, at (1, 1) (b) $y = 3x^3$, at (-1, -3)

   (c) $y = \sqrt{x}$, at (9, 3) (d) $y = \frac{1}{x}$, at $(2, \frac{1}{2})$.

2. Find the equation of the tangent to each of the
   following curves :-

   (a) $y = x^3$, at $x = 2$ (b) $y = x^3 - 4x$, at $x = 1$

   (c) $y = 2 - x^2$, at $x = 0$ (d) $y = 3x^4$, at $x = -1$

   (e) $y = 6\sqrt{x}$, at $x = 4$ (f) $y = \sqrt[3]{x}$, at $x = 8$

   (g) $y = \frac{3}{x^2}$, at $x = -1$ (h) $y = x - \frac{1}{x}$, at $x = \frac{1}{2}$

   (i) $y = x^3 - x + 2$, at $x = 2$

   (j) $y = (2x - 4)(x - 1)$, at $x = 3$.

3. Find the equation of the tangent to the curve
   $y = \frac{1}{4}x^2$ at the point given by $x = 4$.
   Show that if the tangent cuts the axes at A and B
   the midpoint of AB is (1, -2).

4. Find the equations of the tangent to the curve
   $y = 3x^2$ at the points given by $x = 1$ and $x = -1$.
   Find the point of intersection of these tangents.

5. Find the equation of the tangents to the parabola
   $y = x^2 + 2$ at the points P and Q with x-coordinates
   -1 and 2 respectively, and show that the tangents
   intersect at a point on the x-axis.

6. The tangent to the parabola $y = (x - 2)^2$ at the
   point (4, 4) cuts the x-axis at D and the y-axis at E.
   Find the length of the line DE, leaving your answer
   in surd form.

7. Find the points on the curve $y = x^2(x - 6)$ at which
   the gradient of the tangent is 15, and also find the
   equations of the tangents at these points.

8. On the curve $y = x^2 + 2x - 4$, the tangent at point
   R is parallel to the line $4x + 2y - 3 = 0$.
   Find the coordinates of R.

9. Find the equation of the tangent to the curve with
   equation $y = x^2 - \frac{1}{x}$ at the point where the curve
   crosses the x-axis.

10. The line with equation $y - x = 2$ is a tangent to
    the curve with equation $y = m\sqrt{x} + c$ at the point
    (9, 11). Calculate the values of m and c.

11. Find the points on the curve $y = \sqrt[3]{x}$ at which
    the tangents are perpendicular to the line with
    equation $y + 12x = 1$.

Exam Practice Exercise (H4)

1. Given $y = \dfrac{24}{\sqrt{x}}$, $x > 0$, find $\dfrac{dy}{dx}$. **(2)**

2. What is the derivative of $y = \dfrac{3}{4x^4}$, $x \neq 0$?

   Give your answer with a positive index. **(3)**

3. If $w = t\sqrt{t} - \dfrac{1}{t^4}$, $t \neq 0$, find $\dfrac{dw}{dt}$. **(4)**

4. Calculate the rate of change of
   $d(t) = \dfrac{1}{4t}$, at $t = 4$. **(4)**

5. If $y = 14x^3 + 10\sqrt{x}$, $x > 0$, find $\dfrac{dy}{dx}$. **(3)**

6. What is the rate of change of $x^2(\sqrt{x} - 2)$ at $x = 4$? **(4)**

7. Differentiate u with respect to t :-

   (a) $u = \dfrac{t^2 - 3t - 4}{t}$, **(4)**

   (b) $u = \dfrac{t + 4}{2t^{\frac{1}{3}}}$. **(4)**

8. The volume V (cm³) of air in a small balloon as it is being inflated, is given by the formula $V(t) = 2t^3 + \frac{1}{4}t^2$.

   Calculate the rate of change of the volume after 10 seconds.

   (i.e. how quickly it is growing in m³ per sec). **(4)**

9. A function $u(v)$ is defined on a suitable domain by $u(v) = \sqrt{v}(5v - \dfrac{4}{v\sqrt{v}})$. Find $u'(v)$. **(3)**

10. If $d(t) = 4t^2 - 10t + 6$, what is the rate of change of d with respect to t at $t = 3$? **(3)**

11. A tangent to the curve $y = 6x^3 - x$ is drawn through the point (-1, -5).

    What is its gradient ? **(3)**

12. A curve has equation $f(x) = 7x^3 - 11x$.

    What is the gradient of the tangent at the point (-1, 4) ? **(3)**

13. Find the equation of the tangent to the curve $y = 2x^3 + 5$ at the point with x-coordinate -3. **(3)**

14. A curve has equation $y = 2x^4 - 4x^3 + 2$.

    Find the equation of the tangent to this curve at the point where $x = 1$. **(3)**

15. The diagram shows a sketch of $y = \dfrac{12}{\sqrt{x}}$, $x > 0$.

    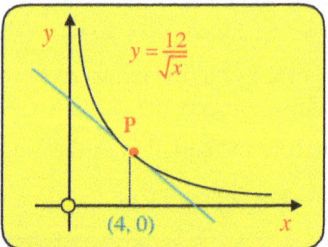

    Find the equation of the tangent at P. **(5)**

16. (a) Show that there is only one tangent to the curve $f(x) = 4 + 9x - x^2$ which makes an angle of 45° with the positive direction of the x-axis. **(3)**

    (b) Find its equation. **(2)**

17. The parabola with equation $f(x) = x^2 - 4x + 1$ has a tangent at the point T(6, 13).

    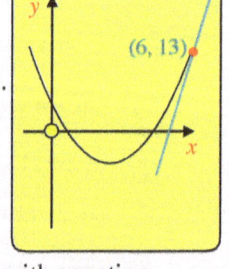

    (a) Find the equation of this tangent. **(3)**

    (b) Show that the tangent found in (a) is also a tangent to the parabola with equation $y = -x^2 - 51$ and find the coordinates of the point of contact C. **(3)**

18. The line with equation $y = x + 8$ is a tangent to the curve with equation $y = p\sqrt{x} + q$ at the point (4, 12).

    Find the values of p and q. **(5)**

Chapter H5 Transformation of Graphs - Revision

Standard Graphs

You should be able to recognise many graphs from their basic shapes and be able to sketch some of them from their functional definition.

This introductory exercise may be used for discussion.

1. Here is a list of functions and a set of graphs.

    The object of the exercise is to match up the functions to their most likely corresponding graphs.

    (a) $f(x) = x$

    (b) $y = 3x$

    (c) $y = -\frac{1}{2}x$

    (d) $f(x) = x^2$

    (e) $f(x) = x^3$

    (f) $y = \dfrac{1}{x}$

    (g) $y = \sin x°$

    (h) $f(x) = \cos x°$

    (i) $f(x) = -x^2$

    (j) $y = \tan x°$

    (k) $y = x^2 - 1$

    (l) $f(x) = \sqrt{x}$

    (m) $f(x) = 2^x$

    (n) $y = -x^3$

    (o) $y = 2x - 3$

    (p) $f(x) = -\sin x°$.

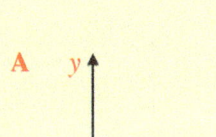
A

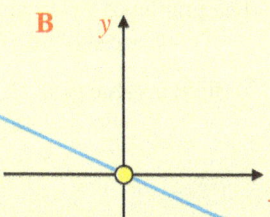
B

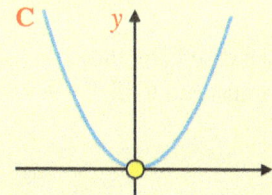
C

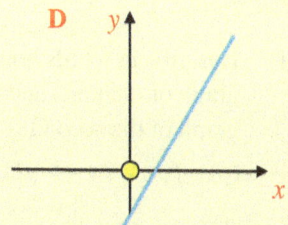
D

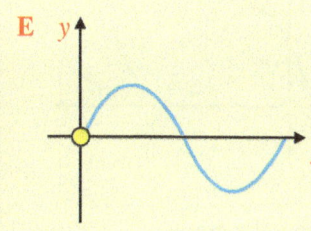
E

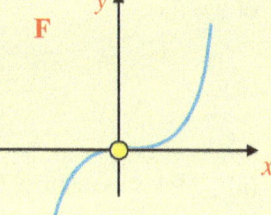
F

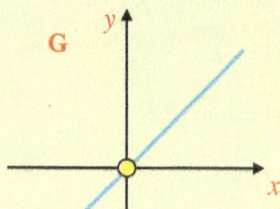
G

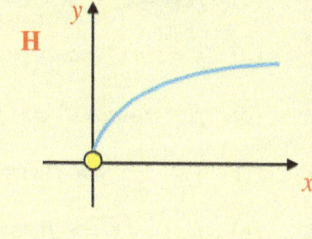
H

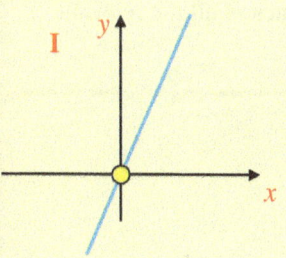
I

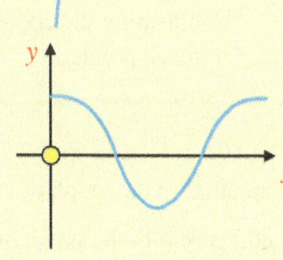
J

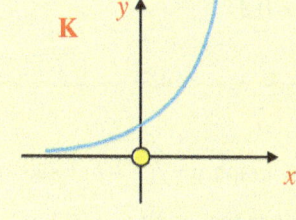
K

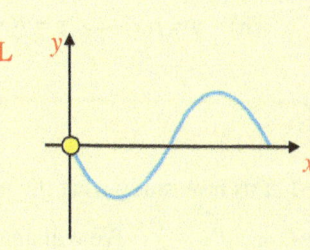
L

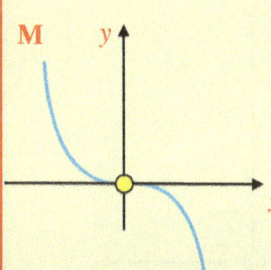
M

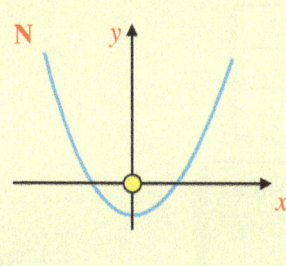
N

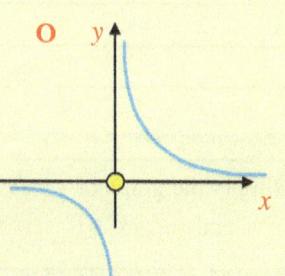
O

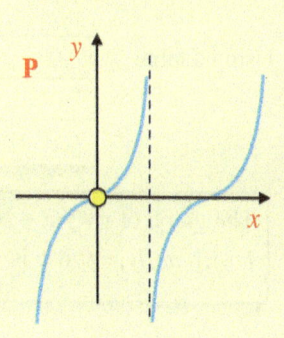
P

The graph of $y = f(x) + c$

Let us study what the new graph $y = f(x) + c$ looks like compared to the graph of $y = f(x)$.

Example :-   We will use the well known graph $y = x^2$ and compare it to the graph of $y = x^2 + 3$.

Using a table :-

x	-3	-2	-1	0	1	2	3
x^2	9	4	1	0	1	4	9
$x^2 + 3$	12	7	4	3	4	7	12

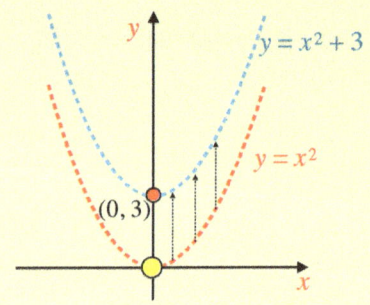

The graph of $y = f(x) + c$ is simply the graph of $y = f(x)$ translated *vertically*, **up** if c is **positive** and **down** if c is **negative**.

Exercise H5·1

1. Describe in words how in each case here, the graph of the first function is translated to the graph of the second :-

    (a) $f(x) = 2x \implies f(x) = 2x - 1$

    (b) $y = x^3 \implies y = x^3 + 2$

    (c) $f(x) = x^2 + 2x - 1 \implies f(x) = x^2 + 2x + 5$

    (d) $y = \sin x° \implies y = \sin x° - 2$

    (e) $f(x) = -\cos x° \implies f(x) = 1 - \cos x°$

    (f) $y = \dfrac{1}{x} \implies f(x) = 3 + \dfrac{1}{x}$

    (g) $f(x) = \sqrt{x} \implies f(x) = \sqrt{x} + 5$

    (h) $y = f(x) \implies y = f(x) - 0·8$.

2. The graphs of $y = x^3$ and $y = x^3 + k$ are shown.

    Write the value of k.

    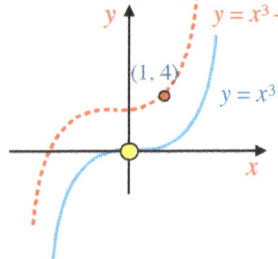

3. Shown is the graph of $y = f(x)$.

    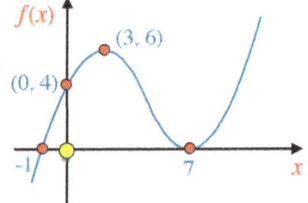

    (a) Make a sketch of $f(x)$.

    (b) On your diagram, show the graph of $y = f(x) + 2$, indicating the coordinates of all the relevant image points.

The graph of $y = f(x + b)$

Let us now study what the new graph $y = f(x + b)$ looks like compared to the graph of $y = f(x)$.

Example :-   We will again use the graph $y = f(x) = x^2$ and compare it to the graph of $y = f(x + 2) = (x + 2)^2$.

Using a table :-

x	-3	-2	-1	0	1	2
x^2	9	4	1	0	1	4
$(x + 2)^2$	1	0	1	4	9	16

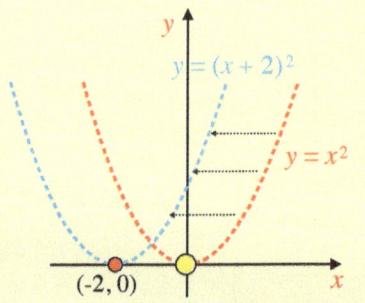

The graph of $y = f(x + b)$ is simply the graph of $y = f(x)$ translated *horizontally*, **left** if b is **positive** and **right** if b is **negative**.

Exercise H5·2

1. Describe in words how in each case here, the graph of the first function is translated to the graph of the second.

    (a) $f(x) = x^2 \implies f(x) = (x-1)^2$

    (b) $y = x^3 \implies y = (x+3)^3$

    (c) $f(x) = x^2 + 5x \implies (x+4)^2 + 5(x+4)$

    (d) $y = \sin x° \implies y = \sin(x-45)°$

    (e) $f(x) = \cos x° \implies f(x) = \cos(x+180)°$

    (f) $y = \dfrac{2}{x} \implies f(x) = \dfrac{2}{x-3}$

    (g) $f(x) = \sqrt{x+1} \implies f(x) = \sqrt{x-1}$

    (h) $y = f(x) - p \implies y = f(x) + p, \ \{p > 0\}$.

2. Shown is the graph of $f(x) = x^2 - 2x, \ -1 < x < 3$.

    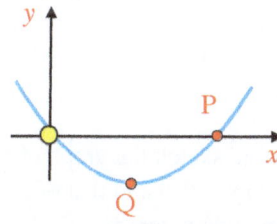

    (a) State the coordinates of points P and Q, the minimum turning point.

    (b) Copy the diagram and show the graph of $y = f(x-2)$, indicating clearly the coordinates of the images of points P and Q.

    (c) Copy the diagram again and show the graph of $y = f(x+3)$, indicating clearly the coordinates of the images of points P and Q.

3. Shown is the graph of $f(x) = 4 - x^2, \ -3 < x < 3$.

    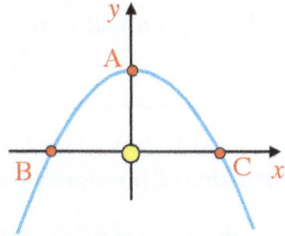

    (a) State the coordinates of points A, B and C, where A is the maximum turning point.

    (b) Copy the diagram and show the graph of $y = f(x+2)$, stating the coordinates of the images of points A, B and C.

    (c) Describe the position of $y = f(x+2) + 3$ compared to that of $y = f(x)$.

4. Describe in words how the graphs of functions $y = f(x)$ and $y = f(x+b) + c$ are related.

    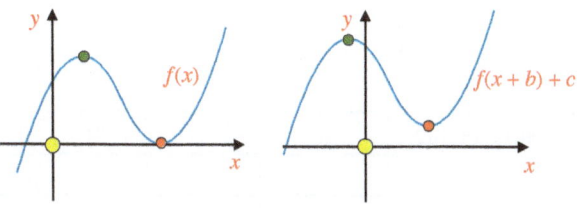

    Begin by writing "The graph of $y = f(x+b) + c$ is transformed by …….".

5. The graph of $y = x^2$ and the graph of $y = (x-3)^2 + 1$ are shown on these diagrams :-

    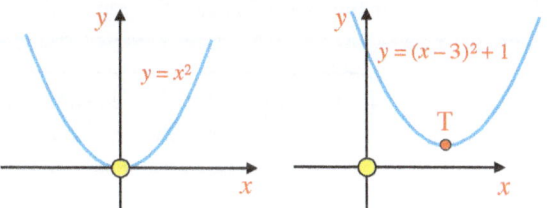

    State the coordinates of point T.

6. (a) Use the graph of $y = x^2$, to help sketch the the graph of $y = (x+2)^2 - 4$, showing the coordinates of the minimum turning point.

    (b) Sketch the graph of $y = (x-1)^2 + 6$.

7. Shown is a sketch of $f(x) = x^3$.

    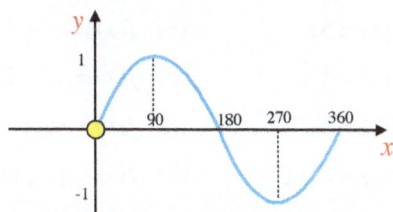

    Sketch the graph of the function $f(x) = (x-2)^3 - 3$, showing the coordinates of the image of the point $(0, 0)$.

8. Shown is the graph of $y = \sin x°, \ 0 \le x \le 360$.

    (a) Make a neat sketch of $y = \sin x°$ and on your diagram sketch the graph of $y = \sin(x-40)°$, indicating where it crosses the x-axis.

    (b) Now sketch of the graph of $y = \sin(x-40)° + 1$, indicating the coordinates of the maximum and the minimum turning points.

    (c) Sketch the graph of $y = \cos x°$ and show on the same diagram the graph of $y = \cos(x+30)° - 1$, indicating clearly where it cuts the axes, and the turning points.

The Graph of $y = -f(x)$ and the Graph of $y = f(-x)$

Let us now study what the new graphs $y = -f(x)$ and $y = f(-x)$ look like compared to the graph of $y = f(x)$.

Example :- Use the graph $f(x) = x^2 - x$ to compare it to the graphs of $g(x) = -(x^2 - x)$ and $h(x) = (-x)^2 - (-x)$.

Using a table :-

x	-2	-1	0	1	2
$x^2 - x$	6	2	0	0	2
$-(x^2 - x)$	-6	-2	0	0	-2
$(-x)^2 - (-x)$	2	0	0	2	6

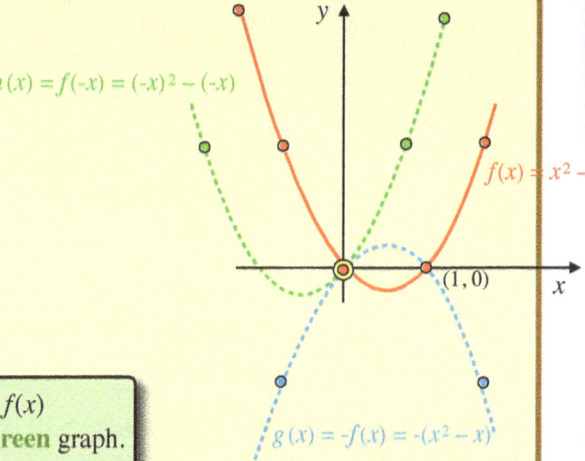

The graph of $y = -f(x)$ is simply the graph of $y = f(x)$ **reflected** over the *x*-axis, as can be seen by the **blue** graph.

The graph of $y = f(-x)$ is simply the graph of $y = f(x)$ **reflected** over the *y*-axis, as can be seen by the **green** graph.

Exercise H5·3

(*Remember* - to sketch the graph of $y = -f(x)$, simply reflect the graph of $y = f(x)$ over the *x*-axis).

1. Sketch the graph of $y = f(x) = 3x$ and $y = -f(x) = -3x$ on the same diagram. You should not need a table.

2. Draw the lines $f(x) = 2x - 1$ and $g(x) = -2x + 1$ on the same diagram and say, from studying the graphs why it must be true that $g(x) = -f(x)$.

3. For each function, sketch the graph of both the original function $y = f(x)$ and that of $y = -f(x)$ on the same diagram.

   (a) $f(x) = 5x$ (b) $f(x) = x^2 + 1$

   (c) $f(x) = \frac{1}{2}x$ (d) $f(x) = x^3 - 1$

   (e) $f(x) = 3x - 2$ (f) $f(x) = sin\,x°$

   (g) $f(x) = cos\,x°$ (h) $f(x) = \sqrt{x}, \{x \geq 0\}$.

(*Remember* - to sketch the graph of $y = f(-x)$, simply reflect the graph of $y = f(x)$ over the *y*-axis).

4. Sketch the graph of $y = f(x) = 2x$ and $y = f(-x) = -2x$ on the same diagram. No table.

5. Draw the lines $f(x) = 3x - 2$ and $h(x) = -3x - 2$ on the same diagram and say, from studying the graphs why it must be true that $h(x) = -f(x)$.

   Check by replacing *x* with *-x* in the function $y = f(x)$.

6. Sketch the graph of $y = f(x) = x^2$ and $y = f(-x) = (-x)^2$ on the same diagram. (You should not need a table).

7. For each function, sketch the graph of both the original function $y = f(x)$ and that of the function $y = f(-x)$ on the same diagram.

   (a) $f(x) = -3x$ (b) $f(x) = x^2 + 3$

   (c) $f(x) = \frac{1}{4}x$ (d) $f(x) = x^3 + 2$

   (e) $f(x) = x - 3$ (f) $f(x) = sin\,x°$

   (g) $f(x) = cos\,x°$ (h) $f(x) = \frac{1}{x}, \{0 < x \leq 4\}$.

Extension - *Even* and *Odd* Functions -

A function is said to be **even** if for all *x*, $f(x) = f(-x)$. Even functions are **symmetrical** about the *y*-axis.

A function is said to be **odd** if for all *x*, $f(x) = -f(-x)$. Odd functions have **half-turn symmetry** about the **origin**.

8. By replacing *x* with *-x* in $f(x) = x^2 - 2$, show that $f(x) = f(-x)$. What kind of function is $y = f(x)$?

9. By replacing *x* with *-x* in $f(x) = 2x^3$, show that $f(x) = -f(-x)$. What kind of function is $y = f(x)$?

10. Is the function $f(x) = 3x^4$, even or odd ?

11. Is the function $f(x) = cos\,x°$ even or odd ?

12. Look at all the functions in Questions 3 and 7, and decide which of them are even functions, which are odd functions and which are neither even nor odd.

The Graph of $y = kf(x)$, where k can be a Positive or Negative Number

Let us now study what the new graph $y = kf(x)$ looks like compared to the graph of $y = f(x)$.

Example 1 :- Use the graph $f(x) = 3x^2$ to compare it to the graphs of $f(x) = x^2$. (here $k = 3$)

Using a table :-

x	-3	-2	-1	0	1	2
x^2	9	4	1	0	1	4
$3x^2$	27	12	3	0	3	12

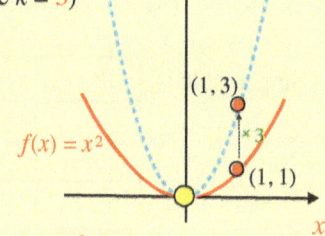

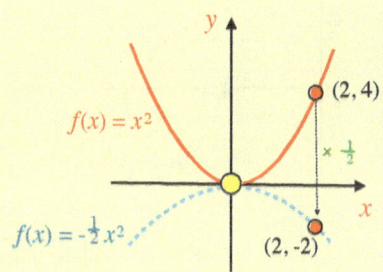

Example 2 :- Use the graph $f(x) = -\frac{1}{2}x^2$ to compare it to the graphs of $f(x) = x^2$. (here $k = -\frac{1}{2}$)

Using a table :-

x	-2	-1	0	1	2
x^2	4	1	0	1	4
$-\frac{1}{2}x^2$	-2	$-\frac{1}{2}$	0	$-\frac{1}{2}$	-2

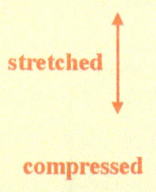

stretched

compressed

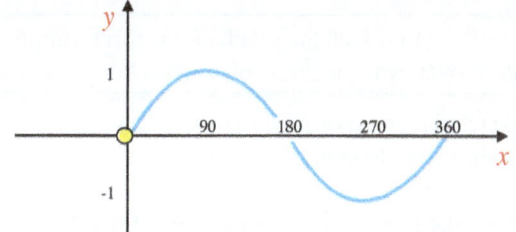

The graph of $y = kf(x)$ is simply the graph of $y = f(x)$ **stretched** (or **compressed**) **vertically** from the x-axis by a factor of k.

If $k > 1$, it is stretched.   If $k < 1$, it is compressed.

If k is **negative**, the graph is reflected in the x-axis.

Exercise H5·4

(*Remember* - to sketch the graph of $y = kf(x)$, simply stretch or compress the graph of $y = f(x)$ vertically).

1. Sketch the graph of $y = f(x) = x^2$ and $y = 2f(x) = 2x^2$ on the same diagram.

   Check that the 2nd graph is a 2 × stretch of the 1st.

2. Draw the lines $f(x) = 2x + 1$ and $g(x) = 3f(x) = 6x + 3$ on the same diagram and check the $g(x)$ is a 3 × stretch of the graph of $f(x)$.

3. For each of the following, sketch the graph of both the original function $y = f(x)$ and the function $y = 2f(x)$ on the same diagram.

   (a) $f(x) = 2x$ (b) $f(x) = x^2 + 1$

   (c) $f(x) = \frac{1}{2}x$ (d) $f(x) = \sqrt{x}$, $\{x \geq 0\}$.

4. For each of the following, sketch the graph of both the original function $y = f(x)$ and the function $y = \frac{1}{2}f(x)$ on the same diagram.

   (a) $f(x) = 4x + 2$ (b) $f(x) = x^2 + 2$

   (c) $f(x) = x$ (d) $f(x) = \sqrt{x}$, $\{x \geq 0\}$.

5. Shown is the graph of $f(x) = sinx°$, $\{0 \leq x \leq 360\}$.

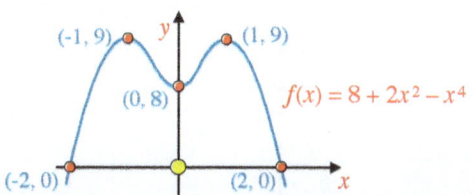

   (a) Make a neat sketch of the sine graph and show (dotted) what the graph of $y = 2f(x)$ looks like.

   i.e. sketch the graph of $y = 2sinx°$.

   (b) Sketch the sine graph again and show what the graph of $y = -3f(x) = -3sin x°$ looks like.

6. Shown is the graph of $f(x) = 8 + 2x^2 - x^4$.

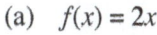
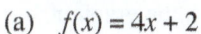

   (a) Sketch the graph of $y = 3f(x)$, showing the coordinates of all the corresponding new points.

   (b) Repeat (a) for the graph of $y = -\frac{1}{2}f(x)$.

The Graph of y = f(kx), where k can be a Positive or Negative Number

Let us now study what the new graph $y = f(kx)$ looks like compared to the graph of $y = f(x)$.

Example :- Use the graphs $g(x) = \sin 2x°$ and $h(x) = \sin\frac{1}{2}x°$, and compare them to the graph of $f(x) = \sin x°$.

Using a table :-

x	0	45	90	135	180	225	270	315	360
$\sin x°$	0	0·71	1	0·71	0	-0·71	-1	-0·71	0
$\sin 2x°$	0	1	0	-1	0	1	0	-1	0
$\sin\frac{1}{2}x°$	0	0·38	0·71	0·92	1	0·92	0·71	0·38	0

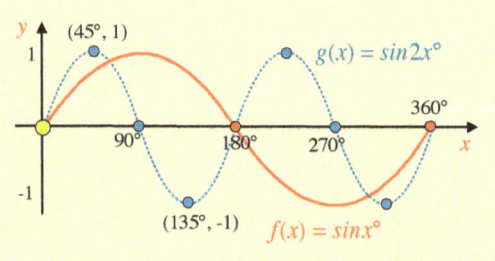

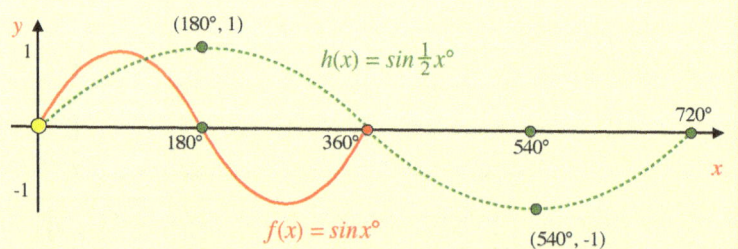

The graph of $y = f(kx)$ is simply the graph of $y = f(x)$
stretched (or **compressed**) **horizontally** by a factor of **k** from the y-axis.

If $k > 1$, it is compressed.   If $k < 1$, it is stretched.

Exercise H5·5

(***Remember*** - to sketch the graph of $y = f(kx)$, simply stretch or compress the graph of $y = f(x)$ horizontally).

1. Sketch the graph of $f(x) = x^2$ and $f(2x) = (2x)^2 = 4x^2$ on the same diagram.

2. Draw the lines $f(x) = x$ and $g(x) = f(3x) = 3x$ on the same diagram and check the $g(x)$ is a 3 × compression of the graph of $f(x)$.

3. Draw the cubic $f(x) = x^3$ and $g(x) = f(\frac{1}{2}x) = \frac{1}{8}x^3$ on the same diagram and check that $g(x)$ is a "2 times" stretch of the graph of $f(x)$.

4. Shown is the graph of a cubic $y = f(x)$, $\{-3 \le x \le 12\}$.

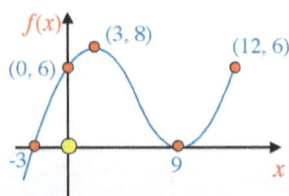

Make a neat sketch of the function $y = f(3x)$, showing clearly the coordinates of the five image points.

5. Shown is the graph of $y = f(x)$, $-5 \le x \le 8$.

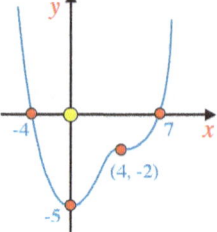

Make a sketch of the function $y = f(\frac{1}{2}x)$, showing clearly the coordinates of the 4 image points.

6. Shown is the graph of $f(x) = 2\cos x°$, $\{-90 \le x \le 450\}$.

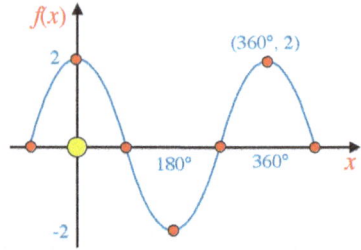

(a) Make a sketch of the graph of the function.

(b) On a new diagram, sketch the graph of $y = f(3x)$, showing the coordinates of the seven image points.

The Graph of $y = f^{-1}(x)$, the Inverse of the function $y = f(x)$

In Chapter 3, we saw how to algebraically find the inverse function $f^{-1}(x)$, corresponding to the function $f(x)$.

The table shows various functions, along with their inverses.

$f(x) =$	$2x$	$x + 1$	x^2	x^3	$1 - x$	$\dfrac{1}{x}$
$f^{-1}(x) =$	$\frac{1}{2}x$	$x - 1$	$\sqrt{x}$	$\sqrt[3]{x}$	$1 - x$	$\dfrac{1}{x}$

Each diagram illustrates the graph of $f(x)$ in **blue** and the graph of $f^{-1}(x)$ in **red**.

In each, we have shown the dotted line $y = x$, the Identity Function (see page 24).

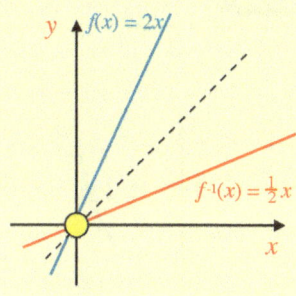
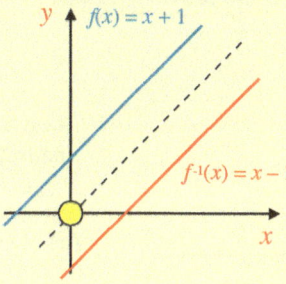
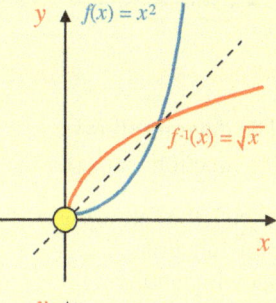

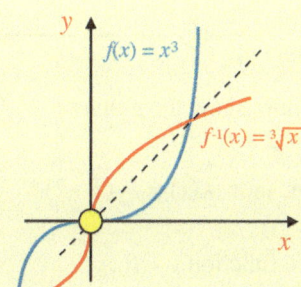
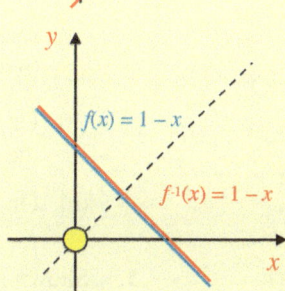
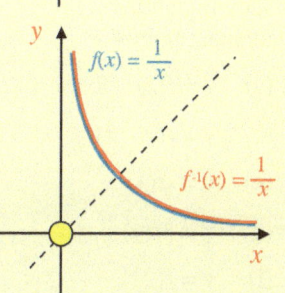

> The graph of the inverse of a function $f(x)$ may be obtained by **reflecting** the graph of $f(x)$ over the line $y = x$.

Note that the last two functions, $f(x) = 1 - x$ and $f(x) = \dfrac{1}{x}$, are their own inverses.

Exercise H5·6

> (*Remember* - to sketch the graph of $y = f^{-1}(x)$, simply reflect the graph of $y = f(x)$ over the line $y = x$).

1. (a) Sketch the graph of the line $f(x) = 2x + 4$.

    (b) Use the method shown on page 25 to find the inverse function $f^{-1}(x)$.

    (c) Sketch both lines on a coordinate diagram. Check that your $f^{-1}(x)$ **is** the inverse of $f(x)$.

2. Sketch the graph of each function $f(x)$.

    On the same diagram, sketch the graph of the identity function $y = x$, as well as that of the inverse function $f^{-1}(x)$.

    (a) $f(x) = 3x$ (b) $f(x) = 4x - 2$ (c) $f(x) = x^3 + 2$.

3. Copy each diagram and sketch the inverse function.

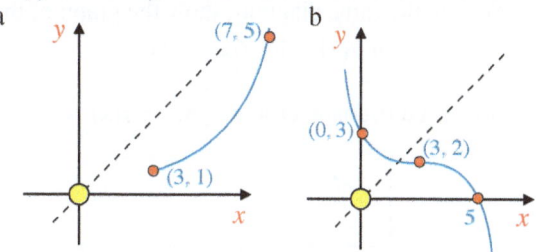

4. **Extension** - Shown is the exponential function $f(x) = 2^x$.

    Make a neat sketch of $f(x)$, and show its inverse on the same graph.

    *note - this new graph is an important function and has a special name :- it is called the **logarithmic function**.

    We will study it in a later Chapter.

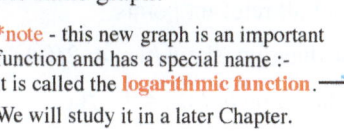

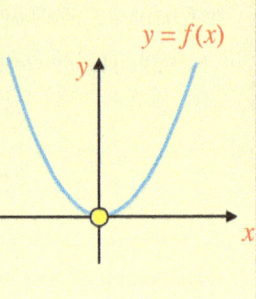
Exercise H5·7 - Mixed Exercise

1. The diagram shows the function $y = f(x)$.

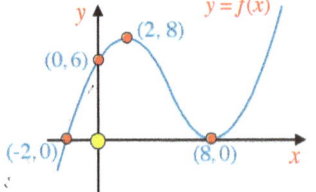

   Sketch the following new functions, showing all the relevant points :-

   (a) $y = f(x) - 2$ (b) $y = f(x) + 1$

   (c) $y = f(x - 2)$ (d) $y = f(x + 3)$

   (e) $y = -f(x)$ (f) $y = f(-x)$

   (g) $y = 3f(x)$ (h) $y = \frac{1}{2}f(x)$

   (l) $y = f(2x)$ (j) $y = f^{-1}(x)$.

2. The diagram shows the function $y = f(x)$.

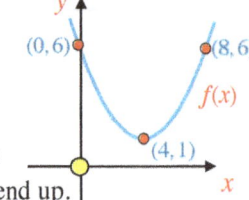

   (a) Draw the graph of the function $g(x) = -f(x)$, clearly showing where the three given points end up.

   (b) On the same diagram, show the graph of the function $h(x) = 1 - f(x)$. (*Hint :- -f(x) + 1*).

3. Shown is a trigonometric graph, $y = f(x)$:-

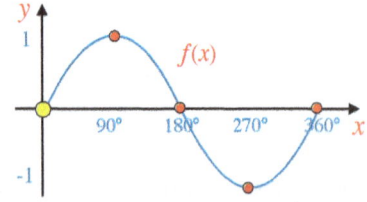

   (a) Sketch the graph of $g(x) = 2f(x)$, showing the coordinates of all relevant points.

   (b) On the same diagram, show $h(x) = -2f(x)$.

   (c) Also show the graph of $k(x) = 4 - f(x)$.

4. Shown is part of the quadratic function $f(x) = x^2 + 3$.

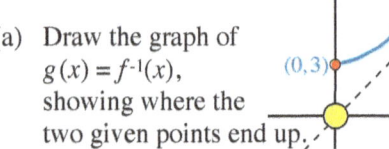

   (a) Draw the graph of $g(x) = f^{-1}(x)$, showing where the two given points end up.

   (b) On the same diagram, show the graph of the function $h(x) = 2 + f^{-1}(x)$.

   (c) On a new diagram, show $k(x) = f^{-1}(x - 2)$.

5. Shown is the graph of a function $y = f(x)$

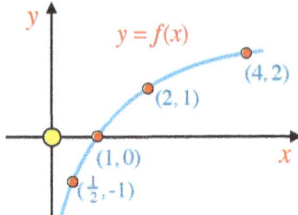

   On separate diagrams, show clearly, the graphs :-

   (a) $y = -f(x)$ (b) $y = f(x) + 1$

   (c) $y = 2f(x)$ (d) $y = f(x - 2)$

   (e) $y = f(2x)$ (f) $y = f^{-1}(x)$.

6. Sketch the graphs of the following composite functions, where $y = f(x)$ is the same graph as that shown in Question 5.

   (a) $y = 1 - f(x)$ (b) $y = 2f(x) - 1$

   (c) $y = f(x + 1) + 2$ (d) $y = f((2x) + 1$

   (e) $y = \frac{1}{2}f(2x)$ (f) $y = 1 + f^{-1}(x)$.

Exam Practice Exercise (H5)

1. The diagram below shows the graph of the function $y = f(x)$ where $x > 0$.

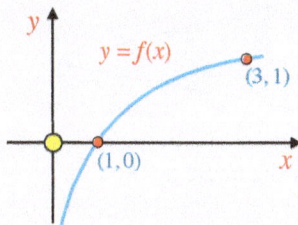

Sketch the inverse function $f^{-1}(x)$. **(2)**

2. The diagram shows part of the graph of $y = f(x)$.

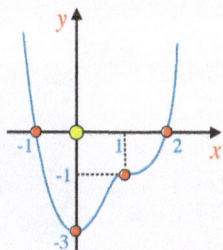

Sketch the function $y = 1 - 2f(x)$. **(3)**

3. Study the graph of $y = f(x)$, shown.

The graph has a vertical line of symmetry through the point $(4, 0)$.

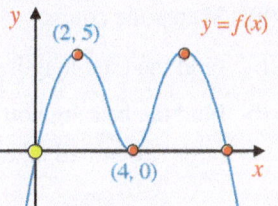

(a) Copy the diagram and on it sketch the graph of $y = f(2x)$. **(2)**

(b) On a separate diagram, show the graph of the function $y = 3 - f(2x)$, indicating all relevant coordinate points. **(3)**

4. The diagram shows the graph of $y = f(x)$, along with the graph of $g(x) = kf(x - a) + b$.

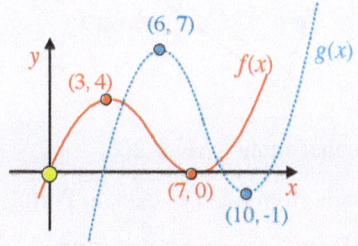

Write down the values of k, a and b. **(3)**

5. Sketch on the same diagram $f(x) = x^2$, and a a possible graph for

$$g(x) = kf(x - a) + b,$$

where $-1 < k < 0$, $a > 0$ and $b < 0$.

On your graph, indicate the position of the turning point of $g(x)$ in relation to k, a and b. **(3)**

6. The diagram shows part of the graph of the function $y = f(x)$, with $p > 5$.

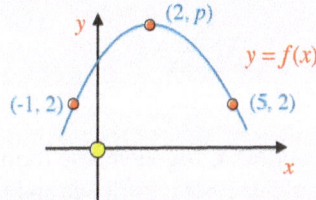

Sketch the diagram and on it show the graphs of the following, indicating the relevant coordinate points :-

(a) $y = f(x - 2)$ **(2)**

(b) $y = f(x - 2) - 3$. **(2)**

7. The graph of the function $f(x) = 2^x + 1$ is shown.

The graph passes through the point A$(2, a)$ and meets the x-axis at point B.

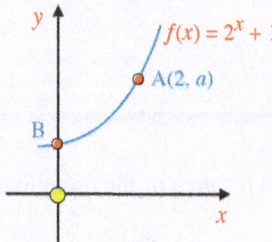

(a) What is the value of a ? **(1)**

(b) Copy the diagram and on it show the inverse function $y = f^{-1}(x)$. **(1)**

(c) Write down the coordinates of the images of points A and B. **(3)**

(d) The point C$(1, 3)$ also lies on the graph.

Find the coordinates of the image of C on the graph with equation

$$y = f(x - 1) + 2.$$ **(2)**

1. Solve for x :-

(a)

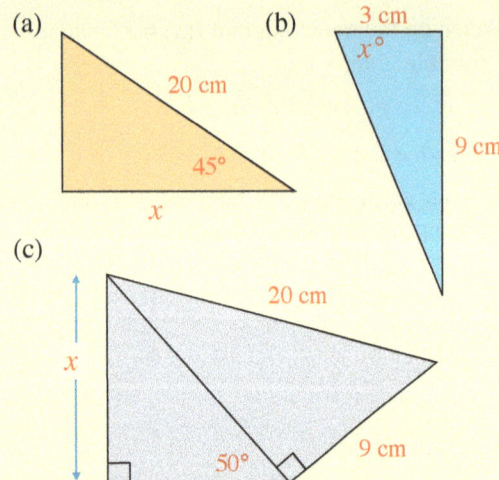

20 cm

45°

x

(b)

3 cm

$x°$

9 cm

(c)

20 cm

x

50°

9 cm

At Higher level, **ALL** trigonometric formula from **National 5** is prior knowledge and is **NOT** given in a formulae list.

(You **MUST** know the following).

Area of a triangle

$$A = \tfrac{1}{2}\, ab \sin C$$

Cosine Rule

$$a^2 = b^2 + c^2 - 2bc \cos A$$

$$\cos A = \frac{b^2 + c^2 - a^2}{2bc}$$

Sine Rule

$$\frac{a}{\sin A} = \frac{b}{\sin B} = \frac{c}{\sin C}$$

2. (a) Calculate the area of the triangle below :-

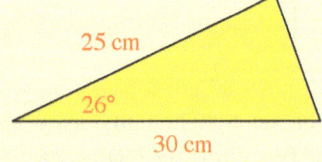

25 cm

26°

30 cm

(b) Calculate the size of the obtuse angle :-

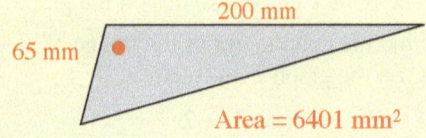

200 mm

65 mm

Area = 6401 mm²

3. (a) Find the length of the side marked x.

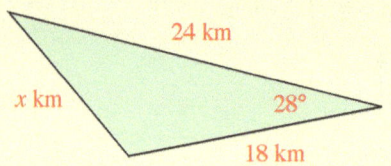

24 km

x km

28°

18 km

(b) Find the size of the angle marked $k°$.

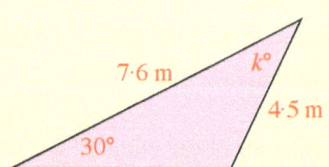

7·6 m

$k°$

4·5 m

30°

4. An orienteering course, from the Start, heads North West for 3 km to Control Point 1.

Control Point 2 is 7 km due South of Control Point 1.

After Control Point 2 the route then takes you directly back to the Start.

(a) Sketch the course.

(b) Find the total length of this course.

(c) Find the bearing you must take from Control Point 2 that will take you directly back to the Start.

5. A ship leaves Port **P** and travels 140 km on a bearing of 070° to Island **A**.

From **A** it sails on a bearing of 230° for 160 km to point **K**.

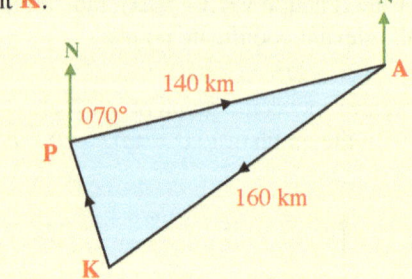

N

A

140 km

N

070°

P

160 km

K

(a) Prove that angle **PAK** is 20°.

The ship sails from point **K** back to Port **P**.

(b) How far will the ship travel from **K** to **P** **and** what bearing must it sail on ?

Radian Measure

So far in Mathematics we have measured the size of an angle in degrees.

There is a second way of measuring an angle, called its **radian** measure.

Imagine you take a piece of string, the same length as the radius (r) of a circle, and wrap it round the circumference, creating the pink sector as shown.

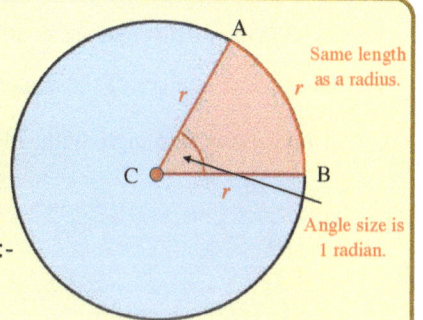

The angle, between the two radii, is called **1 radian**, and is defined as follows :-

> A **radian** is the angle subtended by an arc which is the same length as the radius (r) of the circle .

The sector looks like a little like an equilateral triangle, but is "flattened", so **1 radian is slightly less than 60°** ?

Radian measure = the ratio $\dfrac{\text{arc length}}{\text{radius}}$ =>   A whole revolution, 360° = $\dfrac{\text{circumference}}{\text{radius}} = \dfrac{2\pi r}{r} = 2\pi$.

This means that 2π radians are equivalent to 360°

=> **1 radian** = $360 \div 2\pi = 360 \div 6 \cdot 28318\ldots$

=> **1 radian = 57·3°** (*approximately*)

note :-
radians	degrees
2π ⟷	360
π ⟷	180*

(*this is the handiest fact to help you convert*).

Example 1 :-   Convert 60° to radians.

> Since $180° = \pi$ radians
> => $1° = \dfrac{\pi}{180}$ radians
> => $60° = 60 \times \dfrac{\pi}{180} = \dfrac{\pi}{3}$ (radians)

Example 2 :-   Convert $\dfrac{2\pi}{5}$ radians to degrees.

> Since π radians = 180°
> => $\dfrac{2\pi}{5}$ radians = $\dfrac{2}{5} \times 180 = \boxed{72°}$

Exercise H6·1

1.   Convert 45° to radian measure.

   Copy and **complete** :-

   > $180° = \pi$ radians
   > => $1° = \dfrac{\pi}{180}$ radians
   > => $45° = 45 \times \dfrac{\pi}{180} = \ldots$ **radians**.

2.   Convert each of the following to radians :-

   (a) 90°   (b) 270°   (c) 30°

   (d) 120°   (e) 210°   (f) 300°

   (g) 135°   (h) 225°   (i) 315°

   (j) 20°   (k) 147°   (l) 1·5°.

3.   Convert to degrees :-

   (a) $\dfrac{\pi}{8}$ (b) $\dfrac{3\pi}{8}$ (c) $\dfrac{11\pi}{12}$

   (d) $\dfrac{6\pi}{5}$ (e) $\dfrac{3\pi}{10}$ (f) $\dfrac{7\pi}{12}$

   (g) $\dfrac{2\pi}{15}$ (h) $\dfrac{9\pi}{4}$ (i) $\dfrac{11\pi}{2}$.

4.   (a) Sketch the graph of $y = \sin x$, converting all degrees to radians.

   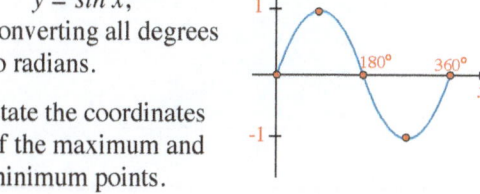

   (b) State the coordinates of the maximum and minimum points.

5.   Repeat Question 4 for $y = \cos x$ and $y = \tan x$.

   (When asked to find the sin, tan or cos of an angle in radian measure, you may or may not wish to consider changing the angle back to degrees first).

6.   **Copy** and **complete** :-

   $\sin \dfrac{5\pi}{6} = \sin (\ldots)° = \ldots\ldots$

7.   Find :-

   (a) $\sin \dfrac{\pi}{2}$ (b) $\cos \dfrac{\pi}{4}$ (c) $\sin \dfrac{\pi}{6}$

   (d) $\tan \dfrac{\pi}{3}$ (e) $\cos \dfrac{2\pi}{3}$ (f) $\cos \dfrac{3\pi}{2}$

   (g) $\sin \dfrac{7\pi}{12}$ (h) $\tan \dfrac{5\pi}{8}$ (i) $\cos 3\pi$.

Special Angles

There are many angles that are commonly used in trigonometric ratios, such as 0°, 30°, 45°, 60°, 90°, 120°, etc.

To find the *exact* values of these, possibly in surd form, we will study two special triangles :-

1. An *equilateral* triangle with side 2 units.

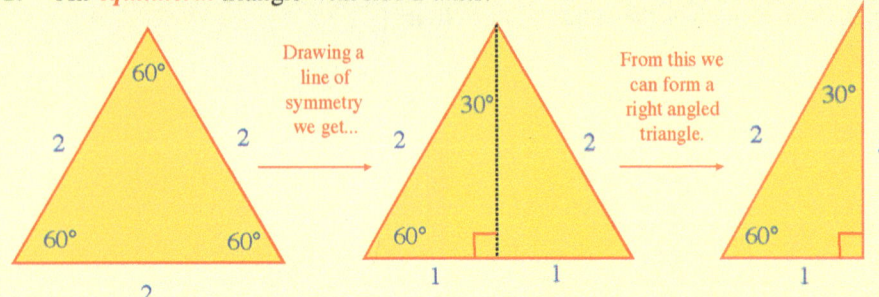 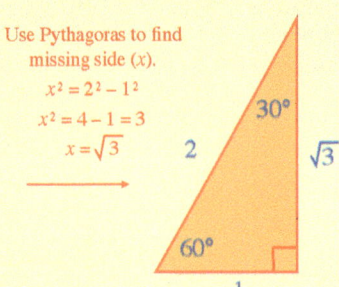

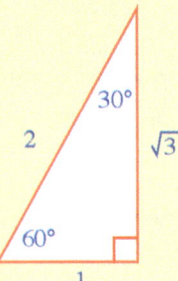

From this triangle we can use our trig ratios, along with (**SOHCAHTOA**), to obtain the following exact values :-

$$sin\,60° = \frac{\sqrt{3}}{2} \qquad cos\,60° = \frac{1}{2} \qquad tan\,60° = \sqrt{3}$$

$$sin\,30° = \frac{1}{2} \qquad cos\,30° = \frac{\sqrt{3}}{2} \qquad tan\,30° = \frac{1}{\sqrt{3}}$$

It is important you memorise these results,

(or at least, picture the triangle in your head and derive them).

2. A *right angled isosceles* triangle with two sides 1 unit.

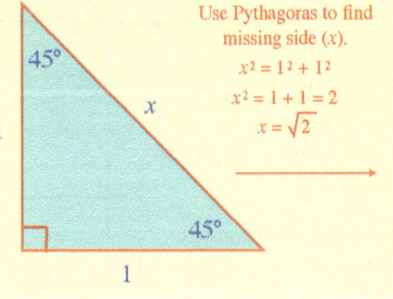 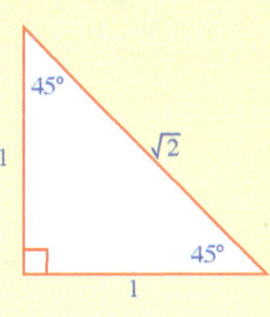

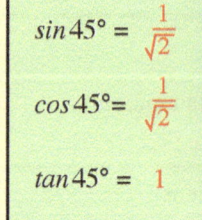

$$sin\,45° = \frac{1}{\sqrt{2}}$$

$$cos\,45° = \frac{1}{\sqrt{2}}$$

$$tan\,45° = 1$$

Memorise these results,

(or again, picture the triangle and work them out).

Exercise H6·2

1. Cover up the teaching panel above.

    Try to recreate the equilateral and isosceles triangles and reproduce the above results.

2. Construct a table of values to help you, either from memory or by picturing the triangles shown above.

angle	0°	30°	45°	60°	90°
sin	0	$\frac{1}{2}$	$\frac{1}{\sqrt{2}}$	$\frac{\sqrt{3}}{2}$	1
cos					
tan					

3. For each of the following, find the **exact** values :-

    (a) $sin\,60°$ (b) $cos\,60°$ (c) $tan\,30°$

    (d) $cos\,30°$ (e) $sin\,45°$ (f) $tan\,60°$

    (g) $tan\,45°$ (h) $sin\,30°$ (i) $cos\,45°$

    (j) $cos\,90°$ (k) $sin\,90°$ (l) $tan\,90°$

    (m) $sin\,\pi$ (n) $cos\,2\pi$ (o) $tan\,\pi$

    (p) $cos\,\frac{3\pi}{2}$ (q) $sin\,\frac{7\pi}{2}$ (r) $tan\,\frac{17\pi}{2}$.

Exact Values

Remember that all *sin*, *cos* and *tan* ratios may be extended from acute angles to **all** sizes $(0 \le \theta \le 2\pi)$, by using :-

$$\sin\theta = \frac{y}{r} \qquad \cos\theta = \frac{x}{r} \qquad \tan\theta = \frac{y}{x}$$

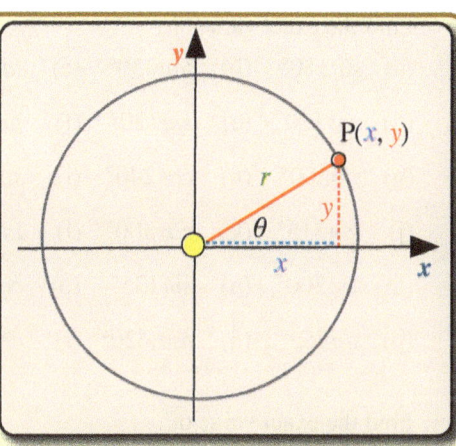

Every angle may be expressed in terms of their **related** (*acute*) angle.

Note :-

All angles **must** be expressed in relation to their position relative to the *x*-axis.

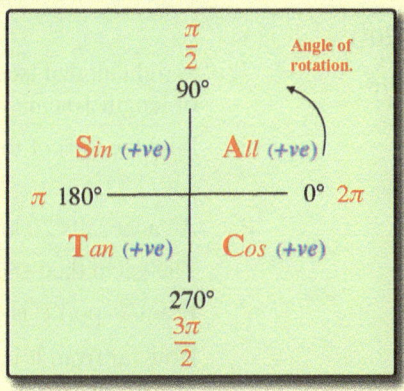

Example 1 :-

Find the exact value for sin 210°.

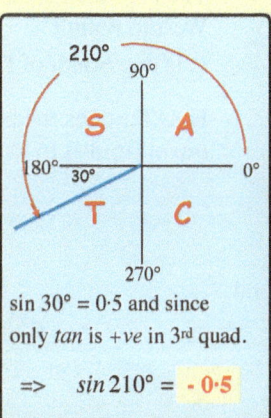

sin 30° = 0·5 and since only *tan* is +ve in 3rd quad.

=> $sin\,210° = $ **- 0·5**

Example 2 :-

Find an exact value for tan 120°.

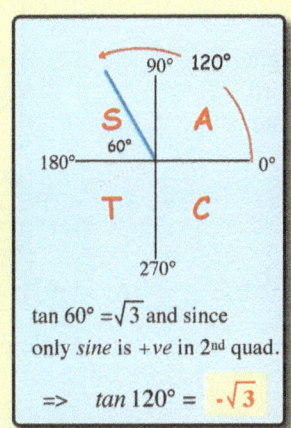

tan 60° = $\sqrt{3}$ and since only *sine* is +ve in 2nd quad.

=> $tan\,120° = $ **$-\sqrt{3}$**

Example 3 :-

Find an exact value for cos (-45°).

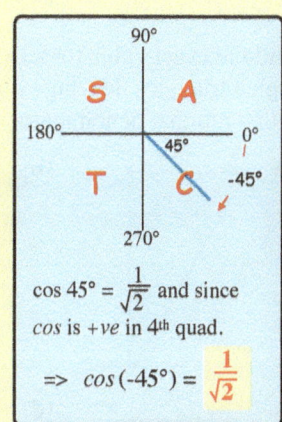

cos 45° = $\frac{1}{\sqrt{2}}$ and since *cos* is +ve in 4th quad.

=> $cos\,(-45°) = $ **$\frac{1}{\sqrt{2}}$**

Exercise H6·3

1. Use the diagrams below to help you find the exact value for each :-

(a) $cos\,150°$

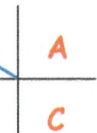

(b) $tan\,300°$

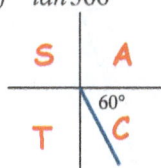

(e) $cos\,300°$

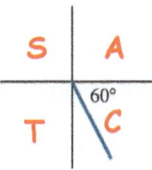

(f) $tan\,315°$

(c) $sin\,240°$

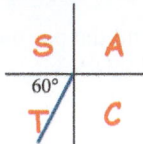

(d) $tan\,240°$

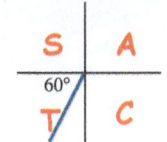

(g) $cos\,225°$

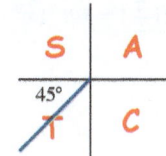

(h) $tan\,(-60°)$.

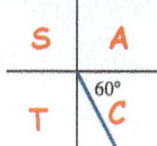

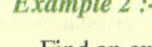

2. Find the exact value of :-

   (a) $sin\,150°$ (b) $tan\,330°$ (c) $tan(-30°)$

   (d) $cos\,120°$ (e) $sin\,120°$ (f) $tan\,120°$

   (g) $sin\,300°$ (h) $cos\,240°$ (i) $sin\,225°$

   (j) $tan\,315°$ (k) $cos\,300°$ (l) $tan\,240°$

   (m) $tan\,300°$ (n) $sin\,135°$ (o) $cos(-720°)$

   (p) $sin\,765°$ (q) $tan\,420°$ (r) $cos\,3600°$.

3. Find the exact value of :-

   (a) $sin\frac{\pi}{6}$ (b) $sin\frac{7\pi}{6}$ (c) $cos\frac{7\pi}{6}$

   (d) $tan\frac{2\pi}{3}$ (e) $cos(-\frac{\pi}{4})$ (f) $sin\frac{4\pi}{3}$

   (g) $cos\frac{9\pi}{4}$ (h) $sin\frac{11\pi}{2}$ (i) $tan(-\frac{5\pi}{4})$

   (j) $tan\frac{7\pi}{3}$ (k) $tan\frac{21\pi}{2}$ (l) $sin(-\frac{8\pi}{3})$.

4. Find the exact value for x in each of these right angled triangles, leaving your answer as a surd with a rational denominator where appropriate :-

   (a)   (b)

   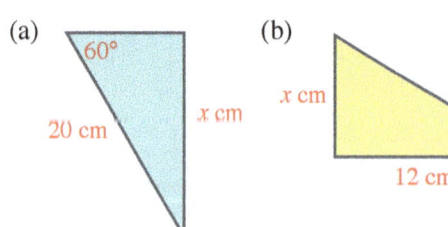

   (c)   (d)

   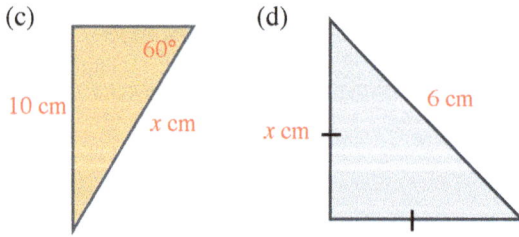

5. Find the exact value of :-

   (a) $sin\,30° \times cos\,60°$ (b) $tan\,30° sin\,60°$

   (c) $2sin\,45° cos\,30°$ (d) $4sin\,60° cos\,30°$

   (e) $sin^2 45°$ (f) $cos^2 30° + sin^2 30°$

   (g) $\sqrt{2}cos\,\pi\,tan(\frac{\pi}{3})$ (h) $cos^2(\frac{\pi}{4}) \div sin^2(\frac{2\pi}{3})$

   (i) $cos(\frac{\pi}{2})sin(-\frac{3\pi}{2})tan\,\pi$

   (j) $tan(\frac{\pi}{4})sin(\frac{\pi}{2})cos^2\pi \times cos(\frac{\pi}{6})tan(\frac{\pi}{6})$.

Note :-   *Formulae for the sine rule, cosine rule and area of a triangle are considered as prior knowledge and must be memorised.*
*They will **NOT** appear in the Higher formulae list.*

6. An equilateral triangle **PQR** has side length 3 cm.

   Find the exact value of the area of triangle **PQR**.

7. A right angled isosceles triangle has hypotenuse of length 10 cm.

   Find the area of this triangle.

8. A yacht sails 20 km from a port on a bearing of 045°.

   The yacht then sails due south to a point, **T**.

   From **T**, port **P** is on a bearing of 315°.

   How far from **P** is the yacht at point **T** ?

9. A boat at **B** is 30 km South East of port **P**.

   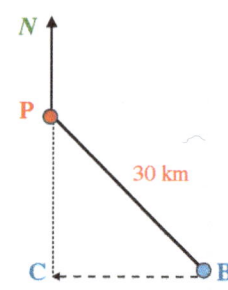

   The boat then sails due West to point **C**.

   C is due South of P.

   How far does the boat travel from **B** to **C** ?

10. **ABCD** is a quadrilateral.

    Angle **ABC** = 75°.

    Find the exact length of side x.

    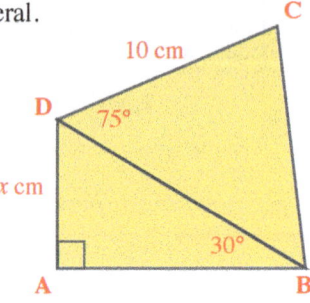

11. A *V*-kite **ABCD** is shown.

    • Angle **DAB** = 120°
    • Length **AB** = **AD** = 40 cm
    • Diagonal length **AC** = 5 cm.

    (a) Find the area of **ABCD**.

    (b) Find the size of angle **CBA**.

    (c) Find the perimeter of this *V*-kite.

Trigonometric Graphs - Revision of Prior Work

Remember that the basic trigonometric graphs, from 0° to 360° look like this :-

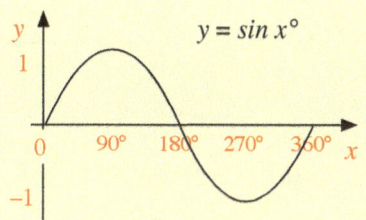

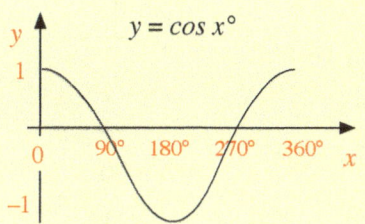

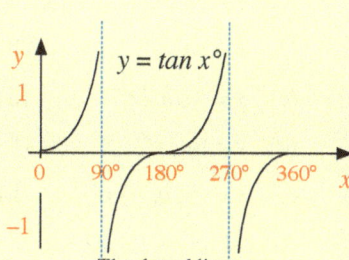

The dotted lines are called **Asymptotes**.

These are simply lines which the curve tends towards without actually crossing.

The waves continue in the same pattern infinitely in both directions on each graph.

(*Sine* of 18 000° would still be 0, and *cosine* of 360 000 000° would still be 1).

The **amplitude** of a wave is defined as :- *half the distance between the maximum turning point and minimum turning points.*	The **period** of a wave is defined as :- *the number of degrees required for one wave to complete its cycle.*	For $y = a\sin bx$ Amplitude = a. Period is $\dfrac{360}{b}$.

Also, remember from Chapter 5 that the graph of the function $f(x) + 3$ is simply the graph of $f(x)$ moved **up** 3 units.

Example 1 :-

The graph of $y = 4\sin 2x°$ is the *sine* wave with an amplitude of 4 and period of $(360 ÷ 2)°$.

=> 2 full sine waves between 0 and 360°, with a maximum of 4, and a minimum of -4.

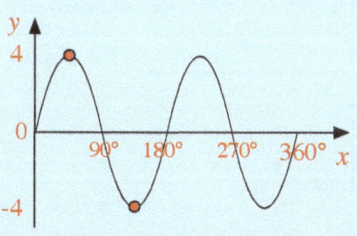

note The maximum turning point of the first wave has coordinates (45°, 4).

Example 2 :-

The graph of $f(x) = 5\cos 6x° + 3$ is the *cosine* wave with an amplitude of 5 and period of $(360 ÷ 6)°$.

=> Begin by drawing 6 *cos* waves between 0 and 360° (which would have a maximum of 5 and a minimum of -5), but which are then translated up by 3 units.

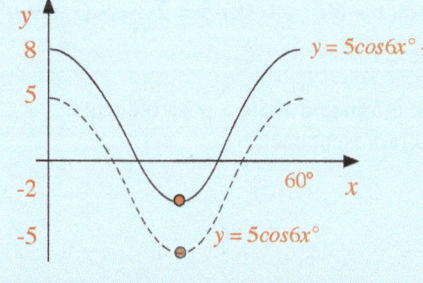

note The minimum turning point of the first wave has coordinates (30°, -2).

A **Phase Angle** is the angle through which a standard trig curve is translated left (or right) from its normal position.

Example 3 :-

The graph of $y = 9\sin(x - 40)°$ is the *sine* wave with an amplitude of 9 and *translated* to the **right** 40°.

The graph of $cos(x + 20)°$ would be the basic cosine graph, translated 20° to the **left**.

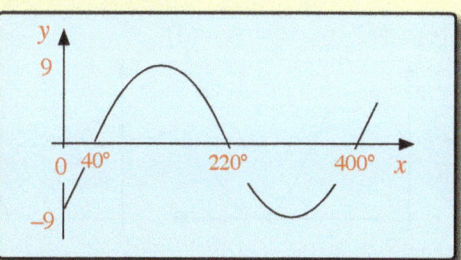

1. Sketch the trig. graph, $0 \le x \le 360°$, for each function, indicating where it cuts the axes :-

   (a) $y = \sin x°$ (b) $y = \cos 2x°$

   (c) $y = 4\sin 2x°$ (d) $y = -8\cos 3x°$

   (e) $y = \tan x°$ (f) $y = 2\tan x°$

   (g) $y = -5\sin \tfrac{1}{2}x°$ (h) $y = 0{\cdot}25\cos \tfrac{1}{3}x°$.

2. Sketch each trig. graph, for $0 \le x \le 360°$.

   (a) $y = 4\sin x° + 3$ (b) $y = 7\cos x° - 4$

   (c) $y = 1 - \cos 2x°$ (d) $y = 10\sin 3x° - 7$

   (e) $y = 2{\cdot}8\cos 2x° + 3$ (f) $y = \sqrt{2}\sin 2x° - \sqrt{2}$.

3. Sketch each graph with the given limits :-

   (a) $y = 3\sin 2x° + 5$ $0 \le x \le 180°$

   (b) $y = 15\cos 3x - 10$ $0 \le x \le \pi$

   (c) $y = \tan 2x + 3$ $0 \le x \le \pi$

   (d) $y = 4\cos 1{\cdot}5x - 6$ $0 \le x \le 2\pi$

   (e) $y = 2 - 0{\cdot}5\sin 2x°$ $-90° \le x \le 90°$

   (f) $y = 0{\cdot}25\cos 2x + 1$ $-\pi \le x \le \pi$

   (g) $y = 3\cos 6x - 2$ $-\pi \le x \le 0$

       Use a domain of $0 \le x \le 360$ for (h) to (k)

   (h) $y = \sin(x - 30)°$ (i) $y = \cos(x + 45)° + 1$

   (j) $y = 3\sin(x - 60)° - 1$ (k) $y = 2 - \cos(x + 90)°$.

4. Identify the graph and write a possible trig. equation to represent each :-

   (a)   (b)

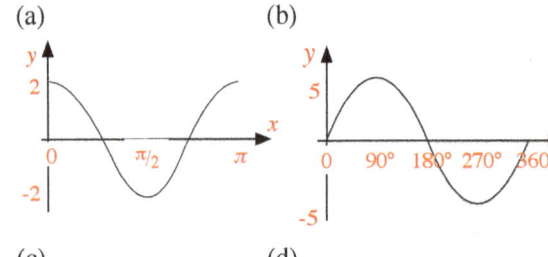

   (c)   (d)

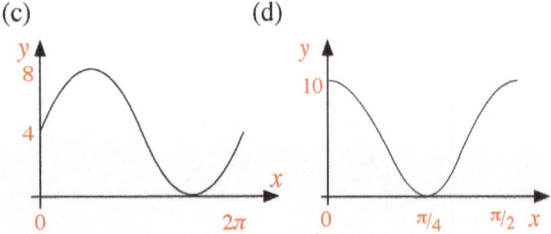

4.   (e)   (f)

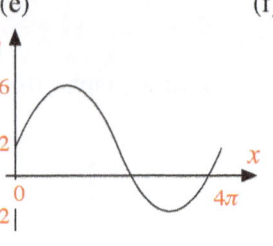 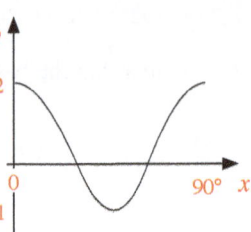

  (g)   (h)

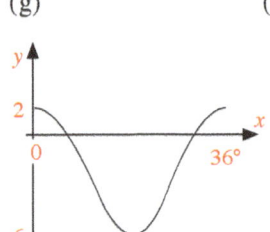 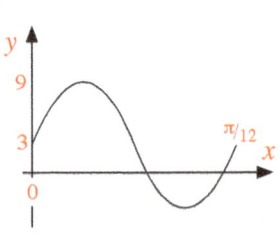

5. List the coordinates of the minimum turning point for each graph in Question 4.

6. State possible trig. equations to represent these :-

   (a)

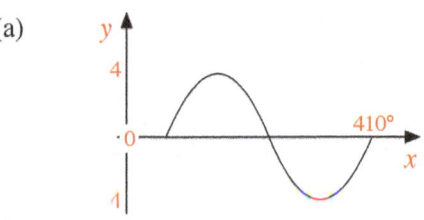

   (b)

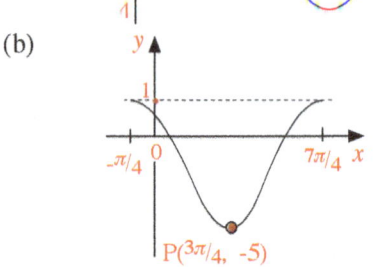

7. A *cosine* graph has a period of $45°$.

   It has a maximum value of 7 and a minimum value of -3.

   (a) State a trig. equation representing this wave.

   (b) Sketch the graph between $0°$ and $90°$.

8. Two trig. functions are defined as :-

       $f(x) = a\sin x°$ and $g(x) = a\cos(x + b)°$.

   Given that $f(x) = g(x)$, state a value for b.

Solving (basic) Trigonometric Equations

Remember - when solving trigonometric equations where $0 \le x \le 360$, there is often more than one answer.

Use trig graphs, (or remembering the $\boxed{All - Sin - Tan - Cos}$ rule will help).

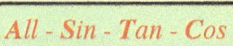

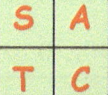

Example 1 :-

Solve $2\sin x° = 1$ $0 \le x < 360$.   *note :- Since the limits are in degrees, the answer must also be given in degrees.*

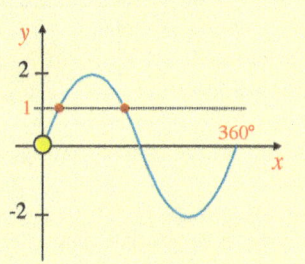

From the graph, we can see that when $y = 1$, we have two answers

Also, since *sine* is +ve the answers are in quadrants 1 & 2.

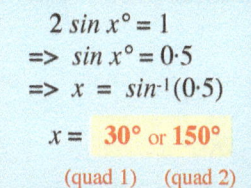

$2\sin x° = 1$
$\Rightarrow \sin x° = 0\cdot5$
$\Rightarrow x = \sin^{-1}(0\cdot5)$

$x = $ **30°** or **150°**
   (quad 1)   (quad 2)

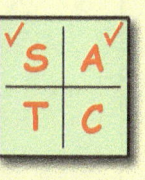

Example 2 :-

Solve $\sqrt{2}\cos x = -1$ $0 \le x < 2\pi$.   *note :- Since the limits are in radians, so answer must be given in radians.*

You may find it easier to work in degrees then convert to radians at the end

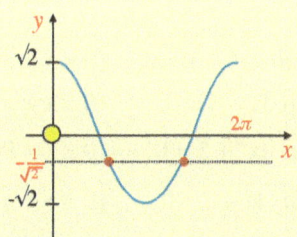

From the graph, we can see that when $y = -\frac{1}{\sqrt{2}}$, we have two answers

Also, since *cosine* is -ve the answers are in in quadrants 2 & 3.

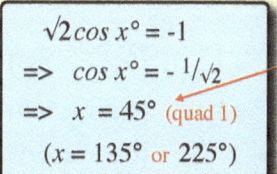

$\sqrt{2}\cos x° = -1$
$\Rightarrow \cos x° = -\frac{1}{\sqrt{2}}$
$\Rightarrow x = 45°$ (quad 1)
$(x = 135°$ or $225°)$
  (quad 2)   (quad 3)

$\Rightarrow x = \frac{3\pi}{4}$ or $\frac{5\pi}{4}$

Begin by ignoring the negative sign.

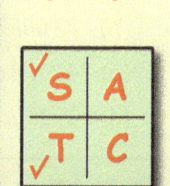

Exercise H6·5

1. Solve each equation for $0 \le x \le 360$:-

  (a) $2\cos x° = 1$ (b) $2\sin x° = \sqrt{3}$

  (c) $\sqrt{3}\tan x° = 1$ (d) $5\tan x° = 5\sqrt{3}$

  (e) $\sqrt{2}\sin x° = -1$ (f) $4\cos x° = -2\sqrt{3}$

  (g) $6\cos^2 x° = 3$ (h) $\sqrt{5}\tan^2 x° - \sqrt{5} = 0$.

2. Solve :-

  (a) $10\sin x + 5 = 0$, $0 \le x \le 2\pi$

  (b) $2\cos x + \sqrt{3} = 2\sqrt{3}$, $0 \le x \le 4\pi$

  (c) $8\sin^2 x - 4 = 0$, $0 \le x \le 2\pi$.

3. Solve for x, giving answers in terms of π :-

  (a) $2\cos x - 1 = 0$, $0 \le x \le \pi$

  (b) $2\sin x + \sqrt{3} = 0$, $0 \le x \le 2\pi$

  (c) $\sqrt{3}\tan x + 1 = 0$, $-\pi \le x \le 0$

  (d) $\sqrt{3} + \sqrt{12}\cos x = 0$, $0 \le x \le 4\pi$.

4. Solve for x, giving answers to 2 decimal places :-

  (a) $5\cos x = 3$, $0 \le x \le 2\pi$

  (b) $2\cdot5\tan x = 4$, $0 \le x \le 2\pi$

  (c) $7\cos x = -3$, $0 \le x \le \pi$

  (d) $\tan x = -\sqrt{2}$, $0 \le x \le \pi$.

5. Solve for x for $0 \le x \le 360$:-

  (a) $9\sin x° - 2 = 3\sin x° + 4$

  (b) $5\cos x° + 1 = 3\cos x° + 2$

  (c) $5\sqrt{3}\cos x° + 1 = \sqrt{3}\cos x° + 7$

  (d) $3\sqrt{2}\sin x° - 1 = 3 - \sqrt{2}\sin x°$.

6. Solve for x, $0 \le x < 360$.

  (a) $4\sin x° - 5 = 0$ (b) $\sqrt{2}\cos x° + \sqrt{3} = 0$.

7. Explain why there are no solutions to the equations in Question 6.

8. Solve for x :- $2\sin 2x° = 1$, $0 \le x < 360$.

Solving Multiple Angle Trigonometric Equations

When solving a trigonometric equation with a **multiple angle** (ie $2x$, $3x$, ...) we need to consider a larger domain.

Example :-

Solve :- $2\sin 2x° = 1$, $0 \le x < 360$.

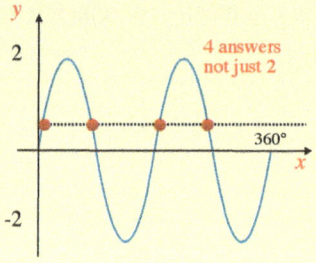

4 answers not just 2

> $\Rightarrow$ $2\sin 2x° = 1$ $\Rightarrow$ $\sin 2x° = \frac{1}{2}$
>
> Since sine is $+ve$, answers are in quadrants 1 and 2
>
> $\Rightarrow$ $2x = 30°, 150°,$ but $\ldots\ldots\ldots$
>
> *important*
>
> Since $0 \le x < 360$, the domain for for $2x$ is $0 \le 2x < 720$. (see graph)
>
> $\Rightarrow 2x = 30°, 150°, 390°, 510°\ldots$ (add $360°$ to each answer)
>
> $\Rightarrow$ $x =$ $15°, 75°, 195°, 255°$.

note :-

If the angle is $3x$ use domain $0 \le x \le 1080°$

If the angle is $5x$ use domain $0 \le x \le 1800°$ etc ....

Exercise H6·6

1. Solve for x :-

   (a) $\sqrt{2}\cos 2x° = 1$, $\{0 \le x < 360\}$

   (b) $\sqrt{3}\tan 2x° = 1$, $\{0 \le x < 360\}$

   (c) $4\cos 3x = -2$, $\{0 \le x < 2\pi\}$ *(radians)*

   (d) $2\sqrt{2}\sin 4x = \sqrt{6}$, $\{0 \le x < \pi\}$.

2. Solve for x :-

   (a) $\sqrt{2}\sin 2x° + 1 = 0$, $\{0 \le x < 360\}$

   (b) $8\cos 3x - 4 = 0$, $\{0 \le x < \pi\}$

   (c) $6\cos 4x° + 5 = 0$, $\{0 \le x < 90\}$

   (d) $9\tan^2 4x - 3 = 0$, $\{0 \le x < \frac{\pi}{2}\}$.

Solving Compound Angle Equations

A Compound Angle Equation gives rise to a trig. graph with a phase angle.

Example 1 :-

Solve for x :- $2\sin(x - 30)° = 1$, $0 \le x < 360$.

> $\Rightarrow$ $2\sin(x - 30)° = 1$
>
> $\Rightarrow$ $\sin(x - 30)° = \frac{1}{2}$
>
> $\Rightarrow$ $(x - 30) = 30°$ or $150°$
> $\qquad$ sine is $+ve \Rightarrow$ Quad 1 & 2
>
> $\Rightarrow$ $x =$ $60°, 180°$.

*Remember this is a **phase angle**.
It is the graph of $y = 2\sin x$ that
has been moved $30°$ to the right.*

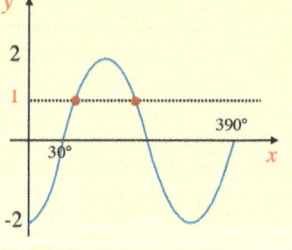

Exercise H6·7

1. Solve for x :-

   (a) $2\sin(x - 60)° = 1$ $0 \le x \le 360$

   (b) $\sqrt{3}\tan(x - \frac{\pi}{3}) = 1$ $0 \le x \le 2\pi$

   (c) $\sqrt{10}\sin(x + 25)° = \sqrt{5}$ $0 \le x \le 180$

   (d) $2\cos(x + \frac{\pi}{8}) = \sqrt{3}$ $\pi \le x \le 2\pi$

   (e) $\sqrt{2}\cos(x + \frac{\pi}{2}) + 1 = 0$ $0 \le x \le 2\pi$.

2. Solve for x :-

   (a) $2\sin(2x - 30)° = 1$ $0 \le x \le 360$

   (b) $3\cos(2x - 45)° = 1$ $0 \le x \le 360$.

3. The questions here are more difficult and include both re-arranging and factorising. Solve for x :-

   (a) $2\sin(x - 45)° - 1 = 0$ $0 \le x \le 360$

   (b) $2\sin(2x - \frac{\pi}{3}) - \sqrt{3} = 0$ $0 \le x \le 2\pi$

   (c) $\sqrt{3}\tan(3x - 45)° + 1 = 0$ $0 \le x \le 180$

   (d) $\cos x°(\cos x° + 1) = 0$ $0 \le x \le 360$

   (e) $\sin^2 x - \sin x = 0$ $0 \le x \le 2\pi$

   (f) $\sin^2 x - 1 = 0$ $0 \le x \le 2\pi$

   (g) $4\cos^2 x° - 1 = 0$ $0 \le x \le 360$

   (h) $2\sin^2 x° - \sin x° - 1 = 0$ $0 \le x \le 360$.

Exercise H6·8 (Contextualised)

1. A ferris wheel is constructed and the height of a capsule above ground can be calculated using the trigonometric equation

$$h(t) = 11 - 10\cos 18t°$$

where h is the height (in metres) and t is the time it takes to revolve (in seconds).

The wheel completes a revolution every 20 seconds.

(a) Sketch this function for one revolution of the wheel.

(b) At what height above the ground is the capsule at its lowest ?

(c) What is the maximum height of the capsule ?

(d) From $t = 0$, after how many seconds will it take to reach its maximum height ?

(e) I enter a capsule at the lowest point.

After how many seconds will the capsule be 12 metres above the ground ?

2. A child bounced up and down on a large trampoline.

Their height and time were recorded and plotted on a graph as shown, where H is height, (in feet) and T is time, (in seconds).

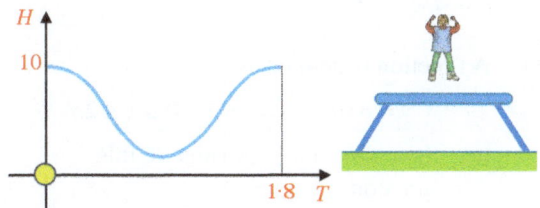

At $t = 0$ seconds the child's feet were at their maximum height of 10 feet above ground.

They returned to this position after 1·8 seconds. When stationary the child's feet were two feet from the ground.

(a) At what height was the trampoline set at above the ground ?

(b) Write a possible equation to represent this graph.

(c) How high was the child above ground after exactly 1 second ?

3. A cylindrical hot water tank has a minimum operating safety depth of $d = 30$ cm. If the water level falls below this, the heating element will be in danger of overheating.

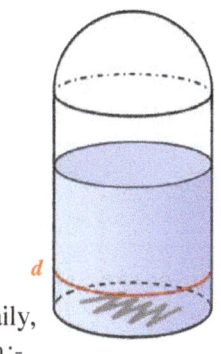

The water depth rises and falls daily, and is represented by the function :-

$$d(t) = 40\sin 15t° + 60, \quad 0 < t < 24,$$

where t is time (measured in hours from midnight), and d the depth in centimetres.

(a) Make a sketch of this function.

(b) State the maximum and minimum depths of the water and the times at which they occur each day.

(c) Between what times does the depth dip below the minimum operating safety depth ?

(d) To the nearest minute, for how long is the water level at or below the danger line ?

4. Water tide levels in a harbour are recorded over a 12 hour period and the results are represented by this sine graph.

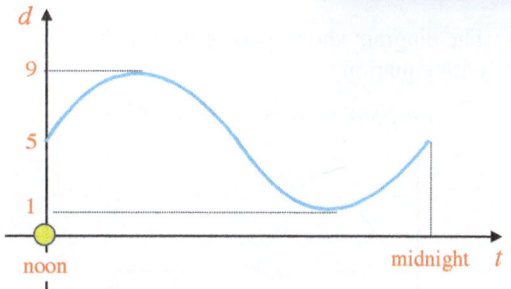

The water level at noon on the first day is 5 metres.

The maximum depth was recorded at 9 metres and the shallowest was 1 metre.

This sine wave was defined as $d = a\sin bt° + c$.

(a) State the values of $a, b,$ and c.

A boat is known to have a draught of 2 metres.
(Draught is a ship's depth below the waterline).

(b) At what time, to the nearest minute, will this boat moored in the harbour, run aground ?

1. The diagram shows part of the graph

$$y = a\cos bx + c.$$

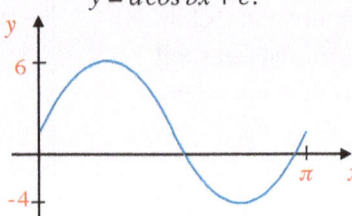

State the values of a, b and c. **(2)**

2. (a) Find the exact value of

$$1 - 2\cos^2 30°.$$ **(2)**

(b) Find the exact value of

$$1 - 2\sin^2 135°.$$ **(2)**

3. (a) Sketch the graph of $y = -3\sin x$, for $0 \le x < 2\pi$.

The graph of $y = -3\sin x$ and the graph of $y = 3\cos x$ will intersect at two points.

The first intersection point will occur within the range $\frac{\pi}{2} < x < \pi$.

(b) Within which range of values will the second point of intersection occur? **(2)**

4. Solve $\tan\left(\frac{x}{2}\right) = -1$, for $0 \le x < 2\pi$. **(2)**

5. The diagram shows part of the graph with equation :-

$$y = p\sin(x - q) + r, \quad 0 \le x \le 2\pi.$$

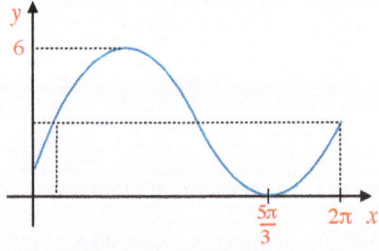

State the values of p, q and r. **(3)**

6. State the coordinates of the minimum T.P. of :-

$$y = 3 + 2\cos\left(x - \frac{\pi}{4}\right), \quad 0 \le x < 2\pi.$$ **(2)**

7. Solve for x :-

(a) $4\sin^2 x° - 3 = 0$, $\quad 0 \le x \le 360$ **(2)**

(b) $4\cos(2x - 30)° = 1$, $\quad 0 \le x \le 360$ **(3)**

(c) $\sqrt{2}\sin^2 x - \sin x = 0$, $\quad 0 \le x \le 2\pi$. **(3)**

8. The diagram below shows part of the graph of

$$y = p\cos qx° + r.$$

(a) Find the values of p, q and r. **(3)**

(b) Determine the x-coordinate of point P, where this graph intersects the x-axis. **(3)**

9. (a) Sketch the graph of :-

$$y = 5\cos(x - \frac{\pi}{6}) + 4, \quad 0 \le x \le 2\pi.$$ **(3)**

(b) Find the coordinates of the point where this graph cuts :-

(i) the y-axis **(3)**

(ii) the x-axis. **(2)**

10. Two equations are defined by

$$f(x) = a\cos(x - k)°, \text{ and}$$
$$g(x) = a\sin x°.$$

(a) State the values of k, such that $f(k) = g(k)$. **(2)**

(b) For this value of k, solve the equation $f(x) = 0$ for $-360 < x < 360$. **(2)**

11. A function is defined as :-

$$y = 6\sin(x + \frac{\pi}{6}) + 3, \quad 0 \le x \le 2\pi.$$

(a) State the minimum value of this function. **(1)**

(b) Find the coordinates of the minimum turning point of the function. **(3)**

(c) Find the coordinates of the point where the graph of the function intercepts the x-axis, between $x = \pi$ and $x = 2\pi$. **(2)**

12. Given $\sin(x + k)° = \cos x°$, state the value of k. **(1)**

13. Solve for x :-

$$\cos(3x - 60)° = 0·866, \quad 0 \le x \le 180.$$ **(3)**

Home Exercise 2 (Chapters 1–6)

1. The three points A$(8, p + 4)$, B$(4, 5)$ and C$(2p - 8, 2)$ are collinear.

    Find the value(s) of p.

2. The point W(-2, 5) lies on the parabola $y = ax^2 + b$.

    A tangent to the parabola is drawn through W. The equation of this tangent is $y = 4x + 13$.

    Determine the values of a and b.

3. A function $f(x)$ is defined by $f(x) = \dfrac{4x^3 - 6x + 2}{\sqrt{x}}$, $x \neq 0$.

    Calculate the gradient of the tangent to the curve $f(x)$ at the point where $x = 1$.

4. The diagram shows a line through M$(1, -6\sqrt{3})$ and N$(3, -4\sqrt{3})$.

    A second line KL makes an angle of 150° with the x-axis, as shown.

    Show that the line KL is perpendicular to the line MN.

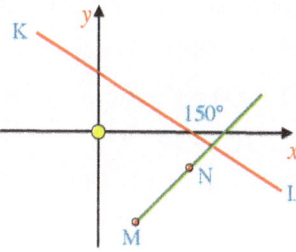

5. $f(x) = 3 - x$ and g$(x) = \dfrac{3}{x}$, $x \neq 0$.

    (a) Find $p(x)$ where $p(x) = f(g(x))$.

    (b) Find the inverse function, $p^{-1}(x)$, and state a suitable domain for $p^{-1}(x)$.

6. The diagram shows part of the graph of $y = f(x)$.

    (a) Copy the diagram and on it sketch the graph of $y = f(2x)$.

    (b) On a separate diagram, sketch the graph of $y = 1 - f(2x)$.

    (In each case, show the coordinates of the four image points).

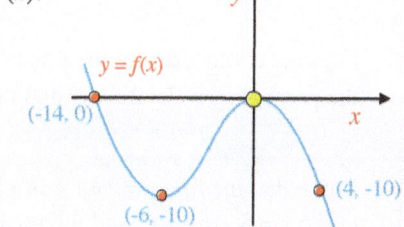

7. This diagram shows part of the graph of the curve $y = 5x^2 - x^3$ and the straight line $y = 4x$.

    The line intersects the curve at three points.

    (a) Find the coordinates of the points A and B.

    (b) The red dotted line is a tangent to the curve at B.

    Establish the equation of this line.

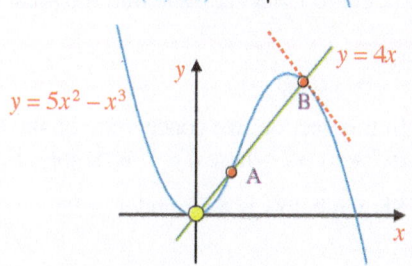

8. Find the coordinates of the point on the curve given by $y = 3x^2 + 7x + 2$,

    where the tangent to it makes an angle of 45° with the positive direction of the x-axis.

9. Solve the following trig. equations, showing all your working :-

    (a) $2\sin(x - 20)° + \sqrt{3} = 0$, $0 \leq x \leq 360$.

    (b) $2\cos^2 x - \cos x = 0$, $0 \leq x \leq 2\pi$.

10. The sketch represents part of the graph of $y = a\sin(x + b)° + c$.

    It crosses the y-axis at $(0, q)$ and has turning points at $(60°, -2)$ and $(p, 4)$.

    (a) Determine the values of a, b, c and p.

    (b) Calculate the value of q.

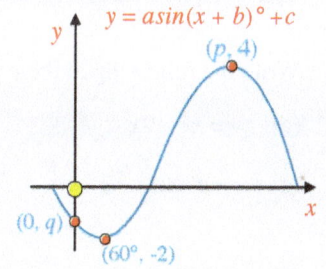

Chapter H7 - Quadratic Theory - Revision

1. Solve each quadratic equation by factorising :-

   (a) $x^2 + 7x = 0$ (b) $4x^2 - 12x = 0$

   (c) $1 - 64x^2 = 0$ (d) $x^2 + 11x + 30 = 0$

   (e) $42 - x - x^2 = 0$ (f) $5x^2 + 23x - 10 = 0$

   (g) $5x^2 - 20x + 15 = 0$ (h) $4x^2 - 20x + 9 = 0$

   (i) $x(x + 2) = 35$ (j) $3x(3x - 2) = 8$.

2. Sketch each function, write down its **roots** and state the equation of its **axis of symmetry** :-

   (a) $f(x) = x^2 - 6x$ (b) $y = x^2 - 2x - 3$

   (c) $f(x) = 16 - x^2$ (d) $y = x^2 + 2x - 8$

   (e) $y = 4x^2 - 12x + 8$ (f) $f(x) = 42 + x - x^2$.

3. Find the coordinates of the points of intersection of the parabola $y = x^2 - 2x - 5$ and the line $y + 4x = 10$.

4. Find the coordinates of the points of intersection of the parabola $y = 7 - 2x - x^2$ and the line $y - 3x = 1$.

5. Prove that the line $y = 2x + 6$ is a tangent to the curve $y = 5 - x^2$, and find the point of contact.

6. Is the line $y = 4x - 2$ a tangent to the parabola with equation $y = 2x^2 - 8$?   Explain.

In Questions 1 and 2, factorisation was used to help solve quadratic equations.

Remember :- factorisation does not always work !

Attempt to factorise the equation $4x^2 + 7x + 4 = 0$!

Such quadratic equations are solved using the

Quadratic Formula.

For $ax^2 + bx + c = 0$, use $x = \dfrac{-b \pm \sqrt{b^2 - 4ac}}{2a}$

7. Rewrite each equation in the form $ax^2 + bx + c = 0$ where necessary. Write the values of a, b and c. Use the quadratic formula to solve :-

   (a) $x^2 + 5x + 3 = 0$ (b) $x^2 - 10x - 2 = 0$

   (c) $2x^2 + 3x = 4$ (d) $4x^2 = 5(3x + 5)$.

8. Prove that the line with equation $y - 4x = -7$ does **not** intersect the parabola $y = x^2$.

9. Make a sketch of each function, indicating the roots, the turning point and the y-intercept :-

   (a) $f(x) = x^2 - 8x + 15$ (b) $f(x) = 3 - 2x - x^2$.

Revision of Completing the Square

In this section, we concentrate on the method used to "*complete the square*" of the quadratic expression, $ax^2 + bx + c$ where $a = 1$. Examples involving coefficients of x^2 other than 1, will appear in a later exercise.

Shown below is a reminder of how to "*complete the square*" :-

Example 1 :- $y = x^2 - 6x + 10$
$= (x^2 - 6x + 9 - 9) + 10$
$= (x - 3)^2 - 9 + 10$
$= (x - 3)^2 + 1$

The co-efficient of x-*term* (-6) is halved, then squared and finally *added* and *subtracted* inside a bracket.

Example 2 :- $y = x^2 + 12x + 30$
$= (x^2 + 12x + 36 - 36) + 30$
$= (x + 6)^2 - 36 + 30$
$= (x + 6)^2 - 6$

The co-efficient of the x-term (12) is halved, then squared and *added* and *subtracted* inside the bracket.

10. Write the following in the form $y = (x + a)^2 + b$:-

    (a) $y = x^2 - 2x$ (b) $y = x^2 - 2x - 3$ (c) $y = x^2 + 4x + 1$ (d) $t = s^2 - 6s + 3$

    (e) $s = t^2 - 3t - 2$ (f) $y = x^2 + 10x - 24$ (g) $y = x^2 + 5x - 6$ (h) $y = x^2 + 30x + 25$.

Solving Quadratic Inequalities

When we solve a quadratic equation like $x^2 - 2x - 3 = 0$, the first step is to factorise $x^2 - 2x - 3$, leading to $(x - 3)(x + 1) = 0$, giving the solutions $x = 3$ or $x = -1$.

You might therefore think that when solving the quadratic inequality $x^2 - 2x - 3 > 0$ you would arrive at the solution $x > 3$ or $x > -1$ (*a bit of a contradiction*).

Also, if we look at $x > -1$ and substitute a value (like 0) for x into the inequality, we get $-3 > 0$, which is false !

> The ideal way to solve a quadratic inequality is to **sketch of the graph the corresponding function**.

Example 1 :- Find the values of x for which $x^2 - 2x - 3 > 0$.

Start with the quadratic equation $x^2 - 2x - 3 = 0$
$$(x - 3)(x + 1) = 0$$
$$x = 3 \text{ or } x = -1.$$

Now sketch the parabola $y = x^2 - 2x - 3$.

From the graph, the part of the curve which is *above* the x-axis shows when $x^2 - 2x - 3 > 0$.

So, $x < -1$ or $x > 3$.

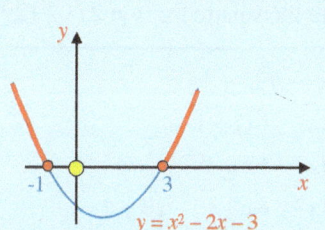

Example 2 :- Solve the quadratic inequality $6 - 5x - x^2 \le 0$.

Start with the quadratic equation $6 - 5x - x^2 = 0$
$$(6 + x)(1 - x) = 0$$
$$x = -6 \text{ or } x = 1.$$

Now sketch the parabola $y = 6 - 5x - x^2$.

From the graph, the part of the curve which is *below* the x-axis shows when $6 - 5x - x^2 \le 0$.

i.e. $x \le -6$ or $x \ge 1$.

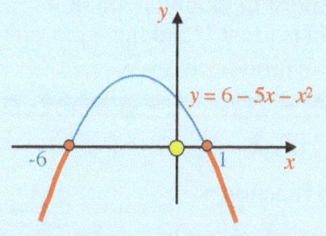

Note :- for $6 - 5x - x^2 > 0$, the part of the curve *above* the x-axis would provide the solution $-6 < x < 1$.

Exercise H7·1

1. Use the graph of the quadratic equation to find the values of x for each inequality :-

    (a) solve $x^2 + 2x - 8 > 0$ (b) solve $12 + x - x^2 > 0$.

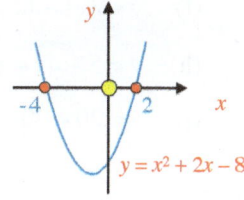   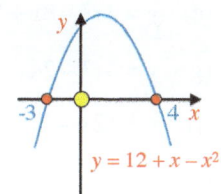

2. Solve for x :- (*Make a sketch each time*).

    (a) $x^2 + 5x + 4 > 0$ (b) $x^2 - 12x + 20 < 0$
    (c) $x^2 + 2x - 15 \ge 0$ (d) $x^2 - 3x - 18 \le 0$
    (e) $42 - x - x^2 > 0$ (f) $24 + 10x - x^2 < 0$
    (g) $14 + 5x - x^2 \le 0$ (h) $20 - x - x^2 \ge 0$
    (i) $2x^2 + 14x > 0$ (j) $9x^2 - 6x - 8 < 0$
    (k) $6x^2 - 7x - 3 \le 0$ (l) $3 - 2x - x^2 \ge 0$
    (m) $2x^2 > 7x - 5$ (n) $4x^2 - 8x < 5$.

Completing the Square in $ax^2 + bx + c = 0$, for any value for a.

By completing the square in a quadratic function it is possible to find the turning point of the parabola. This is particularly useful for parabolas which have no roots. (i.e. do **not** cut the x-axis).

To complete the square -

Step 1 :- Take out a as a common factor so that the coefficient of x^2 becomes $+ve$ 1.

Step 2 :- Halve the "new" coefficient of x and square it.

Step 3 :- Add and subtract the answer inside the bracket.

Step 4 :- Write in completed square form.

Note :- If the coefficient of x^2 is $+ve$, the parabola has a minimum turning point.
If the coefficient of x^2 is $-ve$, the parabola has a maximum turning point.

Example 1 :-

Complete the square for $y = 2x^2 - 12x + 1$.

$y = 2x^2 - 12x + 1$
$\quad = 2(x^2 - 6x) + 1$
$\quad = 2(x^2 - 6x + 9 - 9) + 1$
$\quad = 2(x^2 - 6x + 9) - 18 + 1$
$\quad = \mathbf{2(x - 3)^2 - 17}.$ *note* -17 and NOT -8.

Since it is a "completed square", the lowest value that $2(x - 3)^2$ can be is zero.

Hence, the **minimum** (since x^2 is $+ve$) value of y is -17, when $x = 3$.

The minimum turning point of the parabola is (3, -17) and the **equation of its axis of symmetry** is $x = 3$.

Example 2 :-

Complete the square for $y = 3 + 8x - x^2$ to find its turning point and find the equation of its axis of symmetry.

$y = 3 + 8x - x^2 = -x^2 + 8x + 3$
$\quad = -(x^2 - 8x) + 3$
$\quad = -(x^2 - 8x + 16 - 16) + 3$
$\quad = -(x^2 - 8x + 16) + 16 + 3$
$\quad = \mathbf{-(x - 4)^2 + 19}.$ *note* 19 and NOT -13.

Hence the **maximum** (since x^2 is $-ve$) value of y is 19, when $x = 4$.

The **maximum** T.P. of the parabola is (4, 19) and the **equation of its axis of symmetry** is $x = 4$.

The **y-intercept** where $x = 0$ is 3.

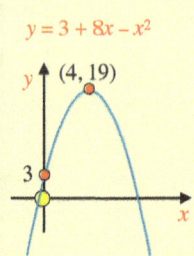
$y = 3 + 8x - x^2$

Exercise H7·2

1. For each function :-

    (i) State whether it has a minimum or maximum turning point.

    (ii) State the coordinates of the turning point.

    (iii) Write the equation of its axis of symmetry.

    (iv) Find the y-intercept.

    (a) $y = (x - 3)^2 + 4$
    (b) $y = (x - 2)^2 - 5$
    (c) $y = (x + 1)^2 - 1$
    (d) $y = (x + 6)^2$
    (e) $y = -(x + 1)^2 + 1$
    (f) $y = 8 - (x - 2)^2$
    (g) $y = -1 - (x - 4)^2$
    (h) $y = -(x - 5)^2$
    (i) $y = 2(x - 3)^2 + 2$
    (j) $y = 4(x - 1)^2 - 1$
    (k) $y = 8(x + 1)^2 - 6$
    (l) $y = -2(x + 3)^2 + 1$
    (m) $y = -5(x + 1)^2 + 4$
    (n) $y = 8 - 9(x - 2)^2$.

2. Express each function in the form $p(x + q)^2 + r$ and :-

    (i) State whether it has a minimum or maximum turning point.

    (ii) State the coordinates of the turning point.

    (iii) Write the equation of its axis of symmetry.

    (iv) Find the y-intercept.

    (v) Sketch the parabola.

    (a) $y = x^2 + 2x - 4$
    (b) $y = x^2 - 2x - 3$
    (c) $y = x^2 - 4x + 9$
    (d) $y = x^2 + 3x + 4$
    (e) $y = 2x^2 - 8x + 2$
    (f) $y = 3x^2 - 12x - 5$
    (g) $y = 4x^2 - 24x - 1$
    (h) $y = 5 + 4x - x^2$
    (i) $y = 12x - 2x^2$
    (j) $y = 20 - 40x - 5x^2$
    (k) $y = -18 - 12x - 3x^2$
    (l) $y = 5 - 3x - x^2$.

Parabolic Functions of the form $y = \pm(x - a)^2 + b$ and $y = kx^2$

You have already seen that :-

- Any quadratic function of the form $y = (x - a)^2 + b$ will have a minimum at (a, b).
- Any quadratic function of the form $y = b - (x - a)^2$ will have a maximum at (a, b).

Conversely :-

- Any quadratic function which has a minimum at (a, b) will have equation $y = (x - a)^2 + b$.
- Any quadratic function which has a maximum at (a, b) will have equation $y = b - (x - a)^2$.

Parabolas of the form $y = kx^2$

- All have a minimum (or maximum) turning point at $(0, 0)$.
- A second point on the parabola is required to obtain the value of k.

Example 1 :-

Find the equation of this parabola, which is of the form $y = (x - a)^2 + b$.

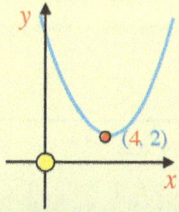

Minimum T.P. at $(4, 2)$
At (a, b) $a = 4$, $b = 2$
$y = (x - a)^2 + b$
$y = (x - 4)^2 + 2$.

Example 2 :-

Write the equation for this parabola.

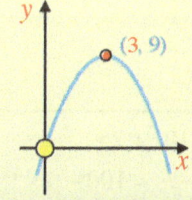

Maximum T.P. at $(3, 9)$
At (a, b) $a = 3$, $b = 9$
$y = b - (x - a)^2$
$y = 9 - (x - 3)^2$.

Example 3 :-

The parabola $y = kx^2$ passes through the point $(2, 20)$.

What is its equation ?

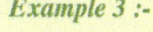
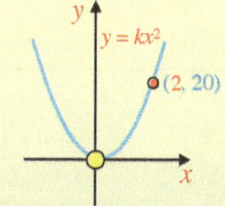

$y = kx^2$
$20 = k \times 2^2$
$k = 5 \Rightarrow y = 5x^2$.

Exercise H7·3

1. Determine the equation of each parabola and write the equation of its axis of symmetry :-
   (In parts (a) to (g), all the curves are of the form $y = \pm(x - a)^2 + b$. In parts (h) to (j), they are of the form $y = kx^2$.)

(a)
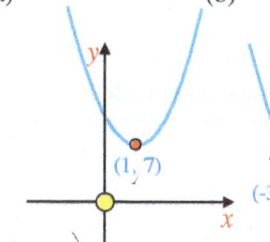

(b)

(c)
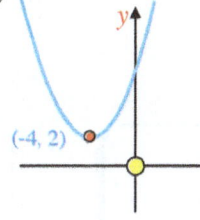

(d)
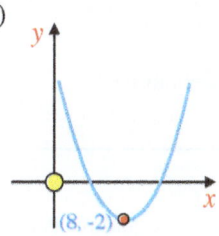

(e)
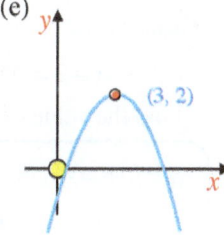

(f)
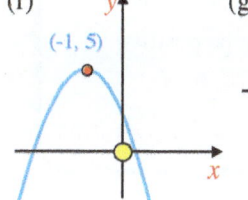

(g)
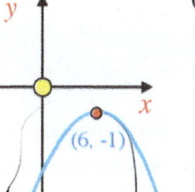

(h)
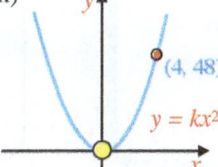

(i)
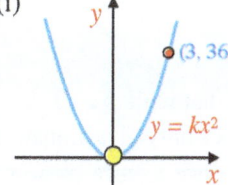

(j)
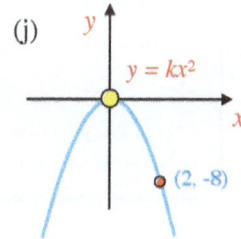

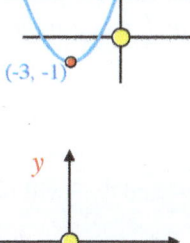

The Discriminant - Revision

Looking back at the quadratic formula, $x = \dfrac{-b \pm \sqrt{b^2 - 4ac}}{2a}$, consider the $b^2 - 4ac$ part in the numerator.

This expression is referred to as the **discriminant**.

There are **3 possibilities** for the roots of a quadratic function :-

- If the $b^2 - 4ac$ part is **positive**, you **can** find it and the $\pm\sqrt{b^2 - 4ac}$ will provide **2** answers.

- If the $b^2 - 4ac$ part is **zero**, then the $\pm\sqrt{b^2 - 4ac} = 0$, which means you only get **1** answer.

- If the $b^2 - 4ac$ part is **negative**, you **cannot** find the square root of a negative number => **0** answers.

Solutions obtained from solving a quadratic equation are referred to as the *roots* of the equation.

The **discriminant** very quickly tells us **how many roots** there are, and this in turn tells us how many times the **quadratic graph** (*the parabola*) cuts the *x*-axis. This helps us quickly see what the **parabola** looks like.

If $b^2 - 4ac > 0$, the quadratic has **two real roots** and the parabola cuts the *x*-axis at **two points**.	If $b^2 - 4ac = 0$, the quadratic has **two qual roots** and the parabola meets the *x*-axis at only **one point**.	If $b^2 - 4ac < 0$, the quadratic has **NO real roots**. The parabola does **not** cross the *x*-axis.

Example 1 :-

$y = x^2 + 5x + 4$
=> $b^2 - 4ac = 25 - 4 \times 1 \times 4 = 9$
=> Since $b^2 - 4ac > 0$
=> There are **2 real roots**.

Example 2 :-

$y = x^2 + 10x + 25$
=> $b^2 - 4ac = 100 - 4 \times 1 \times 25 = 0$
=> Since $b^2 - 4ac = 0$
=> There is only **1 real root**.

Example 3 :-

$y = -x^2 - 2x - 4$
=> $b^2 - 4ac = 4 - 4 \times \text{-}1 \times \text{-}4 = -12$
=> Since $b^2 - 4ac < 0$
=> There are **0 real roots**.

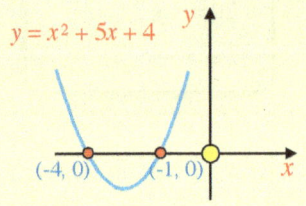

$y = x^2 + 5x + 4$
(-4, 0) (-1, 0)

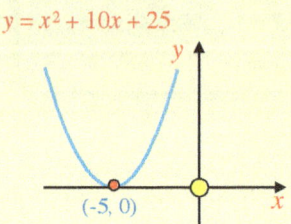

$y = x^2 + 10x + 25$
(-5, 0)

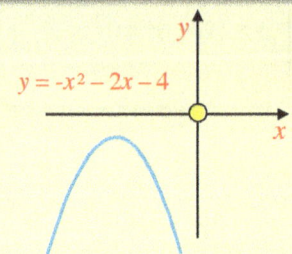

$y = -x^2 - 2x - 4$

Example 4 :-

$px^2 + 4x - 2 = 0$ has equal roots.
Find the value of p.

$a = p, b = 4, c = \text{-}2$.
$b^2 - 4ac = 0$ for two equal roots (*or only 1 root*)
=> $16 - 4 \times p \times \text{-}2 = 0$
=> $16 + 8p = 0$
=> $p = \text{-}2$.
(*It is easy to check that with $p = -2$
$-2x^2 + 4x - 2 = 0$ does only give 1 answer, $(x = 1)$)

Example 5 :-

Show that the roots of $mx^2 + nx - m = 0$
are always real if m and n are real.

$a = m, b = n, c = \text{-}m$.
=> $b^2 - 4ac = n^2 - 4 \times m \times \text{-}m$
$= n^2 + 4m^2$
but since m and n are both real
n^2 and $4m^2$ will both be positive
=> $b^2 - 4ac$ **will be** ≥ 0
=> we have **one or two real roots**.

Exercise H7·4

1. Find the discriminant for each equation and use it to determine the nature of the roots, (0, 1 or 2) :-

   (a) $x^2 + 5x + 1 = 0$

   (b) $x^2 + x + 4 = 0$

   (c) $x^2 - 4x + 4 = 0$

   (d) $x^2 + 10x + 25 = 0$

   (e) $2x^2 + 5x + 3 = 0$

   (f) $2x^2 - x + 1 = 0$

   (g) $4x^2 + 9x + 6 = 0$

   (h) $5x^2 + 11x + 7 = 0$

   (i) $9x^2 + 6x + 1 = 0$

   (j) $10x^2 - 5x - 1 = 0$

   (k) $2x^2 = 6 - 3x$

   (l) $5x - 7 = x^2$.

2. $x^2 + bx + 36 = 0$ has two equal roots.

   Find two values for b.

3. $mx^2 + 8x + 2 = 0$ has two real roots.

   Set up an inequality in m and solve for m.

4. $qx^2 + 10x + q = 0$ has only one root.

   Find the value of q for $q > 0$.

5. $x^2 + 6x + d^2 = 0$ has no real roots.

   Find the range of values for d.

6. Find h, given that $x^2 + 2hx + 4 = 0$ has real roots.

7. Find the value of v, if $x^2 + (1 + v)x + 16 = 0$ has two equal roots.

8. Show that the equation $(1 + 2m)x^2 - 2mx - 2m = 0$ has real roots for all values of $m \geq 0$.

9. Find the value of k for which the equation $x^2 + 4(k - 1)x = -4$ has two real roots.

10. $nx^2 + 2x + n = 0$ has two real distinct roots.

    Find the range of values for n.

11. (a) Find the value of t for which the equation $tx^2 + 2(1 - t)x - 4 = 0$ has only one root.

    (b) Find this root.

12. Use the discriminant and completing the square to prove that the equation $x^2 + 2qx + (q - 1) = 0$ has two real roots for all q.

13. Find the condition for $(ax + b)^2 = 4x$ to have equal roots.

14. Find n so that the roots of $nx^2 + 3x = n - 5$ are real and unequal.

15. Find the smallest positive integer value of p such that the graph of

    $y = px^2 - 8x + p$

    does **not** cut or touch the x-axis.

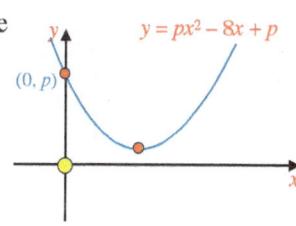

16. Find the condition for $x^2 + (x + c)^2 = 8$ to have no real roots.

17. Find r so that the equation $rx^2 + (r + 8)x + 9 = 0$ will have real and distinct roots.

18. $3px^2 + 4px + 4 = 0$ has only one root.

    Set up an equation in p and solve for p.

19. Show that if g is a real number, then the roots of $(x - 2)(x - 3) = g^2$ are real.

20. Show that the roots of $p(x + 1)(x + 4) = x$ are real only if $p \leq \frac{1}{9}$ or $p \geq 1$.

21. (a) Find u, given that $(3u - 2)x^2 + (u + 1)x + 1 = 0$ has only one root.

    (b) If u lies between these two values, how many distinct roots will there be ?

22. Find the value of t, if the equation $x^2 + (tx - 5)^2 = 16$ has equal roots.

23. Prove that $x^2 - (m + 3)x + (2m + 3) = 0$ has no real roots for $-1 < m < 3$.

24. Given that $\dfrac{x^2 + 4x + 10}{2x + 5} = c$, form a quadratic equation in x, and hence show that when c lies between -3 and 2, the function has no real roots.

Finding the Tangent to a Curve using the Discriminant

To detect whether a straight line cuts, just touches or does not intersect a parabola, the equation of the line has to be substituted into the equation of the parabola and the corresponding new quadratic equation solved.

From the resulting quadratic equation, the discriminant can be used to determine the number of points of intersection.

Case 1   *The line meets the curve at two points*

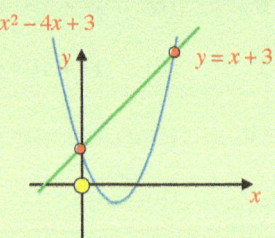

Curve $y = x^2 - 4x + 3$, Line $y = x + 3$.
$$x^2 - 4x + 3 = x + 3$$
$$x^2 - 5x = 0$$
Discriminant is $b^2 - 4ac = 25 - 4 \times 1 \times 0$
$$= 25, (> 0), \text{ so two real unequal roots.}$$
$$\Rightarrow \text{ 2 points of intersection.}$$

Case 2   *The line meets the curve at only one point*

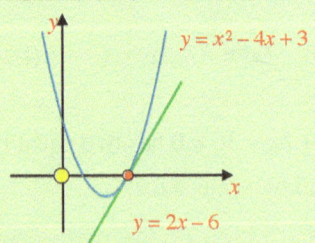

Curve $y = x^2 - 4x + 3$, Line $y = 2x - 6$.
$$x^2 - 4x + 3 = 2x - 6$$
$$x^2 - 6x + 9 = 0$$
Discriminant is $b^2 - 4ac = 36 - 4 \times 1 \times 9 = 0$
$$\Rightarrow \text{ so two equal roots } \Rightarrow \text{ 1 point of intersection.}$$

Case 3   *The line does NOT meet the curve*

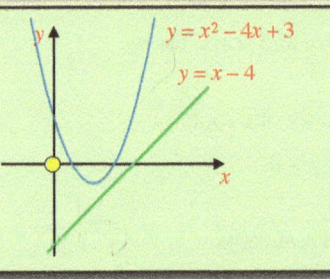

Curve $y = x^2 - 4x + 3$, Line $y = x - 4$.
$$x^2 - 4x + 3 = x - 4$$
$$x^2 - 5x + 7 = 0$$
Discriminant is $b^2 - 4ac = 25 - 4 \times 1 \times 7 = -3 \ (< 0)$
$$\Rightarrow \text{ no roots } \Rightarrow \text{ no point of intersection.}$$

When the equation of the straight line is substituted into the equation of the parabola the following outcomes are arrived at when the discriminant of the resulting quadratic equation is evaluated :-

- if $b^2 - 4ac > 0$, the line and the curve intersect at **2 points**
- if $b^2 - 4ac = 0$, the line and the curve intersect at **1 point**
- if $b^2 - 4ac < 0$, the line and the curve do **NOT** intersect.

Example 1 :-

Prove that $y = 4x - 4$ is a tangent to the parabola $y = x^2$ and find the point of intersection.

Set :- $x^2 = 4x - 4$
$\Rightarrow$ $x^2 - 4x + 4 = 0$
$\quad a = 1, b = -4, c = 4$

$b^2 - 4ac = 16 - 16 = 0$

Line and curve meet at one point.
Hence, the line is a tangent.
$x^2 - 4x + 4 = 0$,
$(x - 2)^2 = 0, \Rightarrow x = 2$.
Point of intersection is **(2, 4)**.

Example 2 :-

Find the equation of the tangent to the parabola $y = 2x^2 + 5$ with gradient 4.

The line with gradient 4 will take the form $y = 4x + p$.
Intersection $2x^2 + 5 = 4x + p$
$\quad 2x^2 - 4x + (5 - p) = 0$
For tangency $b^2 - 4ac = 0$
$\quad a = 2, b = -4, c = (5 - p)$.
$\quad 16 - 8(5 - p) = 0$
$\quad\quad 8p = 24 \Rightarrow p = 3$.
Equation of tangent is $y = 4x + 3$.

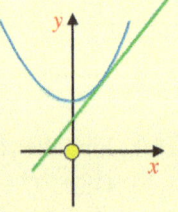

We could also have solved this question using calculus.

Example 3 :- Find the equations of the tangent(s) from the point $(0, -1)$ to the parabola $y = x^2 + 3$.

The line with gradient m passing through $(0, -1)$ will take the form $y = mx - 1$.

Intersection occurs when $\quad x^2 + 3 = mx - 1$

$\Rightarrow \quad x^2 - mx + 4 = 0 \qquad a = 1, b = -m, c = 4$

For tangency, we need $\quad b^2 - 4ac = 0$

$\Rightarrow \quad m^2 - 16 = 0$

$m = \pm 4$

The equations of the two tangents are :- $\boxed{y = 4x - 1}$ and $\boxed{y = -4x - 1}$. (*see diagram*)

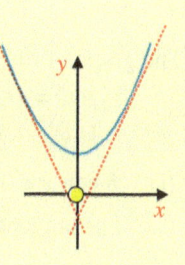

Exercise H7·5

1. For each pair of equations, prove that the line is a tangent to the curve and find the point of contact.

   (a) $y = x^2$ and $y = 2x - 1$

   (b) $y = x^2 - x$ and $y = x - 1$

   (c) $y = x^2 + 1$ and $y = -2x$

   (d) $y = x^2 - 4$ and $y = 4x - 8$

   (e) $y = 5x^2 + 5$ and $y = 10x$

   (f) $y = 2x^2$ and $y = 28x - 98$

   (g) $y = 4x^2 + 1$ and $y = 4x$

2. For each curve, find the equation of the tangent to to it with the given gradient :-

   (a) $y = x^2$, gradient 4   (b) $y = 2x^2$, gradient -8

   (c) $y = x^2 + 1$,   gradient 4

   (d) $y = 5x^2 - 1$,   gradient $-\sqrt{20}$

   (e) $y = x - x^2$,   gradient -3

   (f) $y = x^2 - x + 2$, gradient 1.

3. Find the equation of the tangent to the curve from the given point in each of these :-

   (a) $y = x^2$ $(0, -9)$ (b) $y = 2x^2$ $(0, -2)$

   (c) $y = x^2 + 16$ $(0, 0)$ (d) $y = -5x^2$ $(0, 5)$.

4. (a) Find k such that the line $y = x + k$ is a tangent to the curve $y = x^2 - 11x$.

   (b) Find the coordinates of the point of contact.

5. Prove that if the line $y = x + b$ is a tangent to the ellipse $x^2 + 9y^2 = 9$, then $b = \pm\sqrt{10}$.

1. Find the value of n for which the equation $x^2 - 4x + (n - 6) = 0$ has equal roots. **(3)**

2. Solve $8 - 2x - x^2 < 0$. **(2)**

3. Find the range of values for q such that $x^2 - 2x + 8 - q = 0$ has no real roots. **(3)**

4. $3x^2 + 12x + 15$ is expressed in the form $a(x + b)^2 + c$. What is the value of c ? **(3)**

5. Prove that the roots of the equation $2x^2 - mx - 2 = 0$ are real for all values of m. **(3)**

6. (a) Express $2x^2 + 6x - 3$ in the form $a(x + b)^2 + c$. **(3)**

   (b) Write the coordinates of the turning point for the parabola $f(x) = 2x^2 + 6x - 3$. **(1)**

7. Find the value of k such that the equation $kx^2 + kx + 9 = 0$, $k \neq 0$, has equal roots. **(4)**

8. The roots of the equation $(x + q)(x - 1) + 4 = 0$ are equal. Find values for q. **(4)**

9. (a) $f(x) = 2x + 1$ and $g(x) = x^2 - p$, where p is a constant.

   (i) Find $g(f(x))$ (ii) Find $f(g(x))$ **(4)**

   (b) (i) Show that $g(f(x)) - f(g(x)) = 0$ simplifies to give $2x^2 + 4x + p = 0$ **(2)**

   (ii) Determine the nature of the roots of this equation when $p = -1$. **(2)**

   (iii) Find the value of p for which $2x^2 + 4x + p = 0$ has equal roots. **(2)**

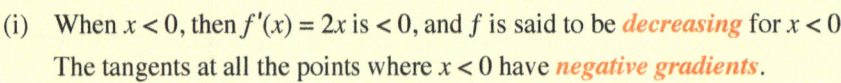

Increasing and Decreasing Functions

The graph of the parabola $f(x) = x^2 - 4$ is shown.

$f(x) = x^2 - 4$ has its derivative $f'(x) = 2x$.
(Remember - this tells us about the slope of the curve).

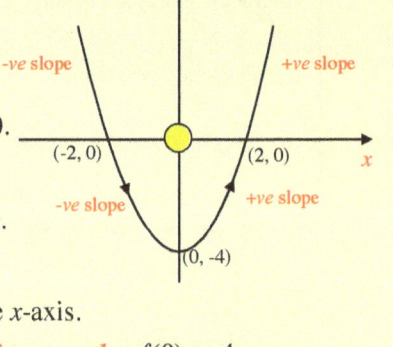

(i) When $x < 0$, then $f'(x) = 2x$ is < 0, and f is said to be *decreasing* for $x < 0$.
The tangents at all the points where $x < 0$ have *negative gradients*.

(ii) When $x > 0$, then $f'(x) = 2x$ is > 0, and f is said to be *increasing* for $x > 0$.
The tangents at all the points where $x > 0$ have *positive gradients*.

(iii) When $x = 0$, then $f'(x) = 2x = 0$, and the tangent at $(0, -4)$ is parallel to the x-axis.
At $x = 0$, f is *neither increasing nor decreasing* and is said to have a *stationary value* $f(0) = -4$.

> To find the values for which a function f is *decreasing* or *increasing*, simply
> find $f'(x)$ and determine the values of x for which $f'(x) < 0$ or $f'(x) > 0$

Example :- Find the intervals for which the function $f(x) = 4 + 2x^2 - \frac{1}{3}x^3$
is (a) decreasing and (b) increasing.

> Can you see that the derivative of a cubic
> function has to be a quadratic function ?

$f(x) = 4 + 2x^2 - \frac{1}{3}x^3$

$f'(x) = 4x - x^2 = x(4 - x)$

Set $f'(x) = 0$ and solve :- $x(4 - x) = 0$
$\Rightarrow x = 0$ or $x = 4$. (see graph)

$f(x)$ is decreasing when $f'(x) < 0$, $\Rightarrow x < 0$ or $x > 4$
(*From the graph, this is where $f'(x)$ lies below the x-axis*).

$f(x)$ is increasing when $f'(x) > 0$, $\Rightarrow 0 < x < 4$.
(*From the graph, this is where $f'(x)$ lies above the x-axis*).

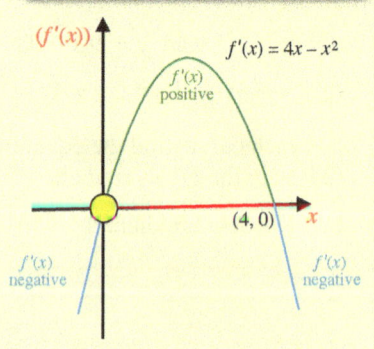

Exercise H8·1

1. For each function, find the intervals over which it is increasing and those over which it is decreasing :-

(a) $f(x) = x^2$
(b) $f(x) = x^2 - 4x$

(c) $f(x) = x^2 - 10x + 12$
(d) $f(x) = x - x^2$

(e) $f(x) = x^2 + 10x - 10$
(f) $f(x) = 2 - 4x + x^2$

(g) $f(x) = x^3$
(h) $f(x) = x^3 - 12x^2 + 4$

(i) $f(x) = 6x - 2x^3$
(j) $y = x^3 - \frac{9}{2}x^2 + 6x$

(k) $y = \frac{1}{3}x^3 - x^2 - 3x + 2$
(l) $y = x(x - 3)^2$

(m) $y = 3 + x - x^2 - x^3$
(n) $y = x^3 - x$.

2. Show that the function $y = \frac{x^3}{6}$ is never decreasing.

3. Show that the function $y = \frac{1}{3}x^3 - x^2 + x + 3$ is never decreasing.

4. Show that the function $y = \frac{x^2 + 2x - 3}{x}$ is increasing for all values of x, (except for $x = 0$).

5. Show that the function $y = \frac{2}{3}x^3 - 12x^2 + 72x + 10$ is never decreasing.

6. The height of a golf ball, as it travels from a point P on the green, to the pin, can be described by the function

$$h(m) = 2 - 9m - 3m^2 - \frac{1}{3}m^3,$$

where m is the number of metres along the horizontal and h is the height of the ball as it moves to the pin.

Does the green slope up or down from P ? Explain.

Stationary Points

Stationary points, (*i.e. points on the graph where it is no longer increasing or decreasing*), occur when $f'(x) = 0$.

The nature of a stationary point depends on the gradient of the slope on either side of the point.

There are four types of stationary point :-

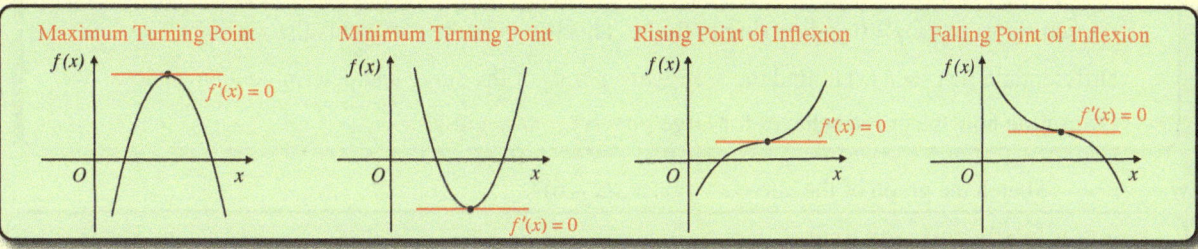

Maximum Turning Point   Minimum Turning Point   Rising Point of Inflexion   Falling Point of Inflexion

(A point of inflection is where the curve "flexes" from bending one way to bending the other way).

Determining Stationary Points and their Nature

To find each stationary point on $f(x)$, and its nature (maximum, minimum or point of inflexion), we :-

- find the derived function $f'(x)$.

- set $f'(x) = 0$ and solve it to find the x-coordinate of the turning points.

- substitute these x-values into the original function $f(x)$ to find the corresponding y-values.

- use a **table of signs**, as shown below, to determine the **nature** of the turning point.

Example :-   Find the stationary points on the curve $f(x) = x^3(x - 4)$ and determine the nature of each.

$f(x) = x^3(x - 4) = x^4 - 4x^3$

$f'(x) = 4x^3 - 12x^2 = 4x^2(x - 3)$

For stationary values of f, set $f'(x) = 0$, and solve

Hence $4x^2(x - 3) = 0$

$4x^2 = 0$ or $x - 3 = 0$

$x = 0$ or $x = 3$.

To find *stationary values*, find $f(0)$ and $f(3)$

$f(0) = 0$ and $f(3) = -27$

The turning points are at **(0, 0)** and **(3, -27)**.

The **nature of each stationary point** is found by drawing up a tables of signs.

(Your may need your teacher to explain this technique).

x	0^-	0	0^+
$f'(x)$	$-$	0	$-$
gradient	-ve	0	-ve
shape of graph	↘	→	↘

Falling point of inflection at (0, 0).

x	3^-	3	3^+
$f'(x)$	$-$	0	$+$
gradient	-ve	0	+ve
shape of graph	↘	→	↗

Minimum T.P. at (3, -27).

Exercise H8·2

1. Determine the turning point and the nature of the turning point for the function $f(x) = x^2$.

2. For the following, find the turning points and state the nature of each :-

    (a) $f(x) = x^2 - 3x$ (b) $f(x) = 10 - x^2$

    (c) $f(x) = 4 - 2x^2$ (d) $f(x) = (x + 3)(2 - x)$

    (e) $f(x) = (9 - x)^2$ (f) $f(x) = x^3$

    (g) $f(x) = 4 - x - 3x^2$ (h) $f(x) = 4 - x^3$.

3. For each function, find the turning points and state their nature :-

    (a) $y = x^3 - 6x$ (b) $y = x^3 - \frac{9}{2}x^2 + 6x$

    (c) $y = x(x - 3)^2$ (d) $y = x + \frac{1}{x}$

    (e) $y = \frac{1}{4}x^4 - 2x^2$ (f) $y = 6 + 3x^2 - 2x^3$

    (g) $y = x^3 - 12x^2 + 2$ (h) $y = x(4x^2 + 15x + 12)$.

    (i) $y = x(x + 3)^2$ (j) $y = 2x + \frac{1}{x^2}$

    (k) $y = x^3(8 - x)$ (l) $y = x - 2\sqrt{x}$.

Curve Sketching

To sketch the graph of a function $f(x)$, you must find 4 things :-

- Find the points where the curve cuts both axes - (the *x-intercept* and the *y-intercept*), by :-
  - setting $x = 0$ and finding y. This tells us where the curve cuts the y-axis.
  - setting y (or $f(x)$) $= 0$ and solving to find x. This is where the curve cuts the x-axis.
- Differentiate $f(x) \rightarrow f'(x)$ to find the *stationary points* of the curve and determine their *nature*.
- Determine how the curve behaves for large *positive and negative x*.

Example :-   Sketch the graph of the curve :- $f(x) = x(x - 6)^2$.

Points of intersection with axes

Substitute $x = 0$ into $f(x)$ => $y = 0(0 - 6)^2 = 0$. The y-intercept is at **(0, 0)**.

Now replace y (= $f(x)$) $= 0$ => $0 = x(x - 6)^2$ => $x = 0$ or 6. The x-intercepts are at **(0, 0)** and **(6, 0)**.

Stationary Points

$$f(x) = x(x - 6)^2 = x(x^2 - 12x + 36) = x^3 - 12x^2 + 36x$$

=> $f'(x) = 3x^2 - 24x + 36 = 3(x^2 - 8x + 12)$

=> The stationary values of $f(x)$ occur when $f'(x) = 0$.

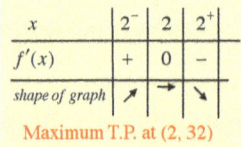

Hence, set $x^2 - 8x + 12 = 0$

$(x - 2)(x - 6) = 0$

$x - 2 = 0$ or $x - 6 = 0$

$x = 2$ or $x = 6$.

To find the coordinates of the turning points, find $f(2)$ and $f(6)$

$$f(2) = 2 \times (2 - 6)^2 = 32 \text{ and } f(6) = 6 \times (6 - 6)^2 = 0$$

The turning points are **(2, 32)** and **(6, 0)**.

     See table of signs :-

The shape of the curve for large x-values

Finally, check what happens as $x \rightarrow +\infty$ and $-\infty$

As $x \rightarrow +\infty$ (*large positive x value*), then $f(x) \rightarrow +\infty$

As $x \rightarrow -\infty$ (*large negative x value*), then $f(x) \rightarrow -\infty$.
(Suggestion :- substitute $x = \pm10, \pm100, \pm1000$ etc to see what happens).

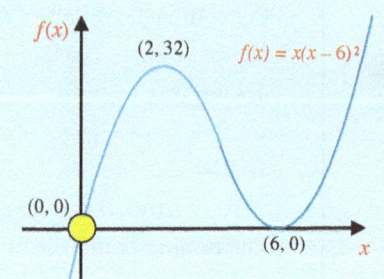

Now mark in all relevant points and join with a smooth curve.

Exercise H8·3

1. Sketch the following curves, by :-

   - finding where the curve crosses both axes.
   - differentiating the function to find the stationary points and their nature.
   - examining how the curve behaves for large positive and negative x.

   (a) $f(x) = x^2 - 4$ (b) $f(x) = 6x - x^2$

   (c) $f(x) = x^2 + 4x - 5$ (d) $f(x) = x^3 - 3x^2$

   (e) $f(x) = x^2(3 - x)$ (f) $f(x) = (x + 2)^2(x - 1)$.

2. Sketch each curve, showing all the important points and indicating clearly the shape of each graph :-

   (a) $y = x^4$ (b) $y = x(x - 1)^2$

   (c) $y = x^3 - 3x$ (d) $y = 1 - x^3$

   (e) $y = x(3 - x^2)$ (f) $y = 6x^2 - x^3$

   (g) $y = 4x^3 - x^4$ (h) $y = 2x^2 - x^4$

   (i) $y = 2(x - 1)^3$ (j) $y = x^4 - 2x^2 - 8$.

   (k) $y = (x - 1)^2(x + 1)$ (l) $y = 3x^5 - 5x^3$

   (m) $y = 2x^2(x - 3)$ (n) $y = x^3 + 6x^2 + 9x$.

Maximum and Minimum Values of a Function in a Closed Interval

For each graph the maximum and minimum values within a *closed interval* are given.

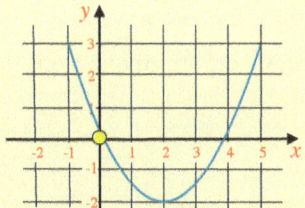

In the interval $0 \leq x \leq 5$
minimum value is -2
maximum value is 3.

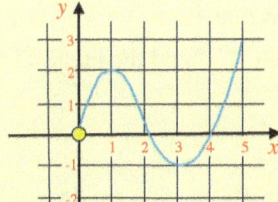

In the interval $0 \leq x \leq 5$
minimum value is -1
maximum value is 3.

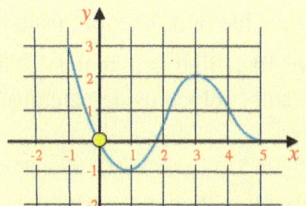

In the interval $-1 \leq x \leq 5$
minimum value is -1
maximum value is 3.

To find the **maximum** and **minimum** values of a function $f(x)$ (i.e. the y-values) in the closed interval, $a \leq x \leq b$,

- Find the values of the function (the y-values) at the **two end points** => Find $f(a)$ and $f(b)$.

- Find the values of $f(x)$ at all the stationary points, **but only for those within the closed interval.**

Now choose the highest and the lowest of these values.

Example :- Find the maximum and minimum value for $f(x) = x^3 - 12x$ in the closed interval $-1 \leq x \leq 3$.

- At the two end points, we find $f(-1) = $ **11** , and $f(3) = $ **-9** .

- Now we consider the stationary points on $f(x) = x^3 - 12x$

  => $f'(x) = 3x^2 - 12 = 3(x^2 - 4)$

  => For stationary values, set $f'(x) = 0$ and solve.

  => Hence $x^2 - 4 = 0$ => $x = 2$ or -2.

Since -2 does **not** lie in the interval, we simply **ignore** it.

Find the value of the function at $x = 2$ => $f(2) = $ **-16** .

Hence, by considering only those values of $f(x)$ at the end points, **and** at the single stationary point in the interval, we find the :-

  maximum value is   **11**

  minimum value is   **-16**

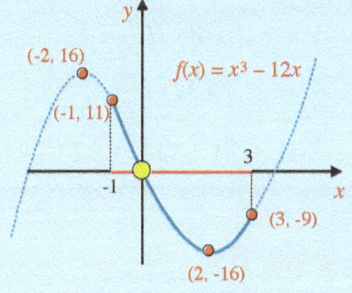

* Some textbooks use "square" brackets to denote a closed interval and round brackets for an open interval.
For example, $-1 \leq x \leq 3$ becomes **[-1, 3]**, $0 < x < 4$ becomes **(0, 4)**, $-5 \leq x < 5$ becomes **[-5, 5)**.

Exercise H8·4

Find the maximum and minimum values of each function in the given closed interval and illustrate with a sketch :-

1. $f(x) = -x^2$, $-3 \leq x \leq 3$

2. $f(x) = x^2 - 9$, $-5 \leq x \leq 5$

3. $f(x) = 2x - x^2$, $-1 \leq x \leq \frac{1}{2}$

4. $f(x) = 5 - 2x^2 - x^3$, $-1 \leq x \leq 3$

5. $f(x) = -2x^2$, $-2 \leq x \leq 3$

6. $f(x) = x(5 - x)$, $1 \leq x \leq 2$

7. $f(x) = x^3(6 - x)$, $-1 \leq x \leq 2$

8. $f(x) = x^4 - 4x^2$, $-\frac{1}{2} \leq x \leq 1\frac{1}{2}$.

Optimization - Problems involving Maxima and Minima

One of the main uses of Differential Calculus is in solving problems that require you to find the maximum or minimum value of a function, usually in a closed interval.

Questions like "find the greatest", "find the smallest", "find the highest", "find the fastest" etc are all questions that can be ideally solved using calculus.

Example :-

This cuboid, with an open top, measures x cm by $2x$ cm, is h cm deep and has an outer surface area (SA) of 24 cm².

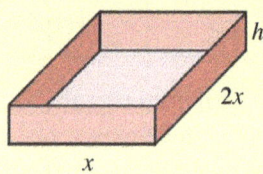

(a) Prove that the volume V cm³, of the cuboid is given by $V(x) = \frac{2}{3}x(12 - x^2)$.

(b) Find the value of x for which the volume is a maximum and calculate that volume.

(a) $Vol = L \times B \times H = x \times 2x \times h = 2x^2h$
   (*We now need to find an expression for h in terms of x*).

   We know that SA = area of base + area of 4 sides

   => SA $= 2x^2 + 2hx + hx + 2hx + hx$

   => SA $= 2x^2 + 6hx$

   => $2x^2 + 6hx = 24$ *

   We now need to make the letter h the subject in *.

   => $2x^2 + 6hx = 24$

   => $6hx = 24 - 2x^2$

   => $h = \dfrac{24 - 2x^2}{6x} = \dfrac{4}{x} - \dfrac{x}{3}$

   => $Vol = L \times B \times H$

   => $V(x) = x \times 2x \times \left(\dfrac{4}{x} - \dfrac{x}{3}\right)$

   => $V(x) = 8x - \frac{2}{3}x^3 = \boxed{\frac{2}{3}x(12 - x^2)}$

(b) We now have $V(x) = 8x - \frac{2}{3}x^3$

   => $V'(x) = 8 - 2x^2$

   => For stationary values, set $V'(x) = 0$.

   => $V'(x) = 2(2 - x)(2 + x) = 0$ => $\boxed{x = 2}$ (or -2).

   => -2 is impossible, so $V(2) = 16 - \frac{16}{3} = 10\frac{2}{3}$.

   i.e. the maximum volume is $\boxed{10\frac{2}{3}\,cm^3}$.

   We prove it is a **maximum**, by using a table of signs.

x	2^-	2	2^+
$V'(x)$	$+$	0	$-$
Shape of graph	↗	→	↘

   Maximum T.P. at $(2, 10\frac{2}{3})$

Exercise H8·5

1. The perimeter of a rectangular field is 140 metres.

q metres

p metres

(a) If its length is p metres and its breadth q metres, write an equation connecting p and q.

(b) Write a formula for the area A m² of the field and express A, purely in terms of p.

(c) Calculate the dimensions of the field which would give the largest area and state what that area would be.

2. The sum S of two numbers x and y is 60, and their product is P.

   i.e. $S = x + y = 60$ and $P = xy$.

   Find the greatest value of the product.

3. The height, h metres above ground, of a shell fired from a cannon after t seconds, is given by :-

   $$h(t) = 560t - 4t^2.$$

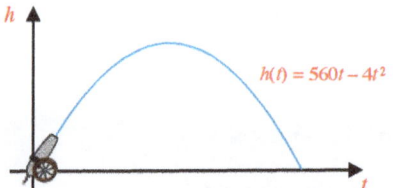

   $h(t) = 560t - 4t^2$

   Find the maximum height reached by the shell.

4. Square ABCD has sides 6 centimetres and triangle APQ is drawn on top of it as shown.

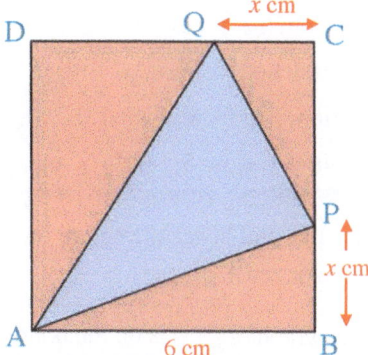

(a) Show that the area of triangle APQ is given by :-

$$A(x) = 18 - 3x + \tfrac{1}{2}x^2.$$

(b) Find the value of x that **minimises** the area of the triangle and calculate the area of the triangle when x takes this value.

5. Squares of side x cm are cut from a plastic square of side 9 cm.

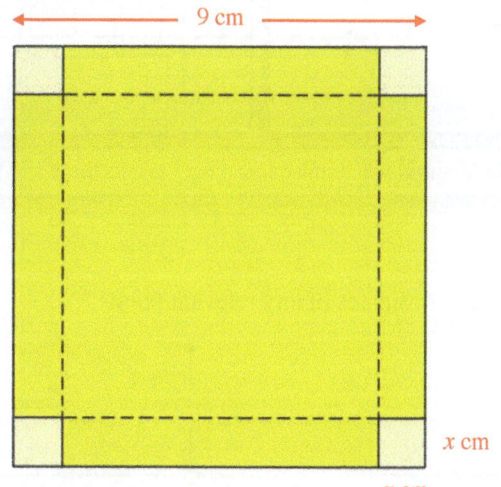

The flaps are then bent up and glued to form a shallow tray.

(a) Show that the volume V cm³ of the box is :-

$$V(x) = 81x - 36x^2 + 4x^3.$$

(b) Find the value of x which maximises the volume, and calculate that volume.

6. A store manager finds that the cost (£C) of storing stock depends on the amount of storage space (x cubic metres) there is.

(continued …)

6. The cost is given by the formula :-

$$C(x) = \frac{400}{x} + 4x + 500, \text{ where } x > 0.$$

(a) Calculate the amount of storage space needed for the store manager to minimise costs.

(b) Determine the actual cost incurred.

7. A rectangular box with no lid is made from 200 cm² of cardboard. Its base measures $2x$ cm by $3x$ cm.

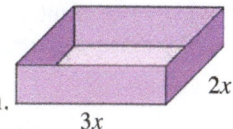

(a) Show that the height h of the box is given by

$$h = \frac{20}{x} - \frac{3x}{5}.$$

(b) Now show that its volume V cm³ is given by :-

$$V(x) = 120x - \tfrac{18}{5}x^3.$$

(b) Prove that the maximum volume occurs when $x = \tfrac{10}{3}$ and find this maximum volume.

8. The cost £C millions of laying an oil pipeline and operating it over a period of time is given by :-

$$C(r) = 16r + \frac{27}{r^2}.$$

where r is the radius of the pipe in metres.

Calculate the least cost of laying and operating the pipe and the corresponding radius of the pipe.

9. A vegetable gardener wants to rope off an allotment into eight individual rectangular plots measuring p metres by q metres with 4 strips of rope.

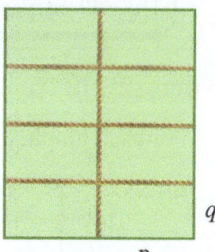

(a) Express the total length of rope in terms of p and q.

(b) Given that the total length of rope is 480 metres, show that the total area A m² of the eight plots is given by :-

$$A(p) = 960p - 12p^2.$$

(c) Find the values of p and q which give the maximum area and state this maximum area.

10. When a ship travels at a speed of v miles per hour, it uses $(1 + 0{\cdot}0005v^3)$ tonnes of fuel per hour.

(a) Prove that the total number of tonnes of fuel, T it uses on a 5000 mile journey at that speed is :-

$$T(v) = \frac{5000}{v} + 2{\cdot}5v^2. \quad (\textit{Hint} : \text{time} = \frac{\text{dist}}{\text{speed}}).$$

(b) Find the speed that gives the greatest fuel economy (i.e. the minimum amount of fuel used) and the amount of fuel used at that speed.

The Graph of the Derived Function

It is possible to sketch the graph of the function $f'(x)$, from the graph of the original function $f(x)$.

- The graph of a **quadratic** function like $y = x^2 - 3x$ will be a **linear** function, (i.e. $y = 2x - 3$).
- The graph of a **cubic** function like $y = x^3 + 4x^2 - 1$ will be a **quadratic** function, (i.e. $y = 3x^2 + 8x$).
- The graph of a **quartic** function like $y = 2x^4 - 5x^2$ will be a **cubic** function, (i.e. $y = 8x^3 - 10x$).
- The graph of a **quintic** function like $y = x^5 + 4x^3$ will be a **quartic** function, (i.e. $y = 5x^4 + 12x^2$), etc.

Remember :- $f'(x)$ indicates what the slope of the tangent to the curve looks like and hence the nature of curve itself, (i.e. whether the gradient $f'(x)$ is negative, positive or zero).

Examples :- Here, the original curve $y = f(x)$ is shown on top (**blue**) and the graph of $f'(x)$ is on the bottom. (**red**).

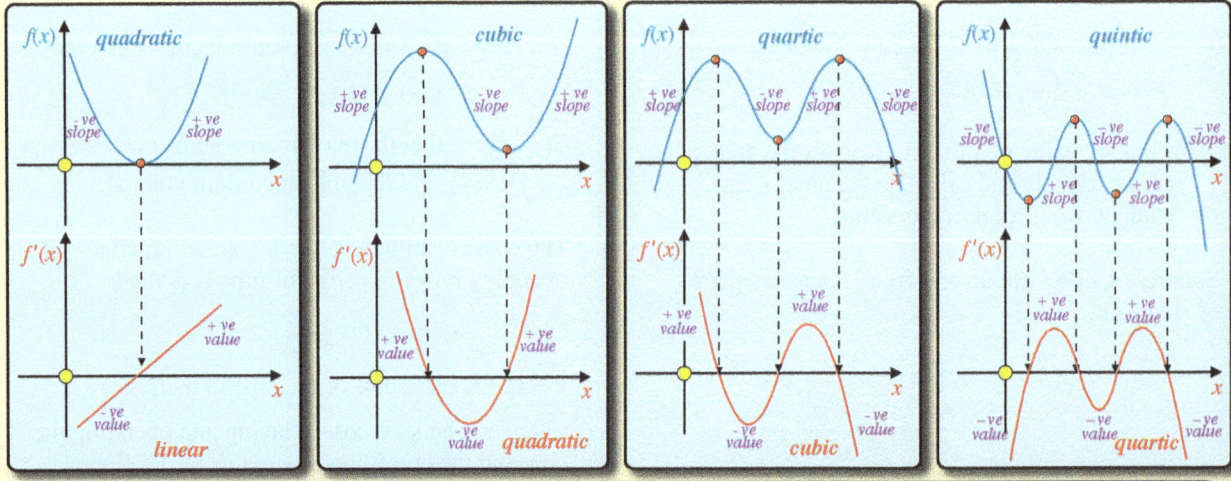

The stationary points (•) on $f(x)$ become the zeros in $f'(x)$. (i.e. the point(s) where the curve $y = f'(x)$ cuts the x-axis).

Exercise H8·6

1. For each graph, draw the graph of the derived function. Show the coordinates of any relevant points.

(a)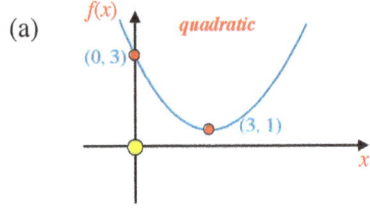

(b)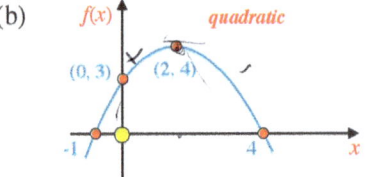

(c)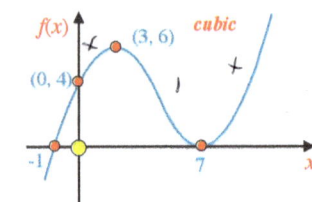

(d)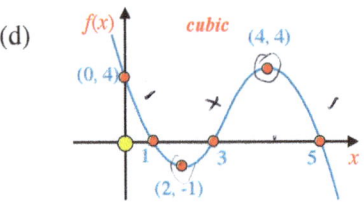

(e)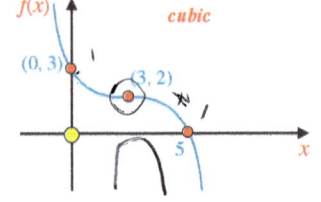

(f)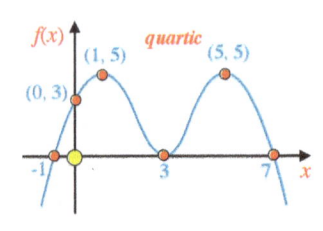

(g)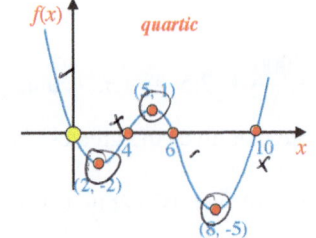

(h)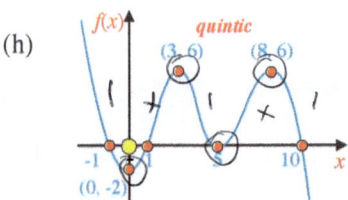

(i)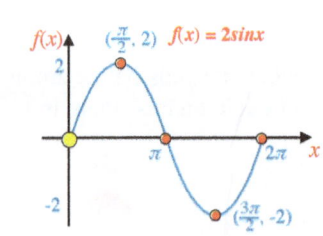

1. Show that the curve with equation :-
$$y = x^4 + 18x^2 + 1$$
has only one stationary point.

   Find its x-coordinate and determine the nature of the point. **(5)**

2. A function f is defined on the interval $0 \le x \le 2$ by
$f(x) = x^3 - \frac{1}{2}x^2 - 2x + 1$.

   Determine the maximum and minimum values of f in that closed interval. **(6)**

3. (a) Find the x-coordinate of the stationary point on the curve with equation $y = 12x - 4\sqrt{x^3}$ **(3)**

   (b) Hence, determine the greatest and least values of y in the interval $1 \le x \le 9$. **(3)**

4. (a) Given that $f(x) = x^3 + 12x^2 + 48x - 25$, find $f'(x)$. **(3)**

   (b) Hence, or otherwise, explain why the curve with equation $y = f(x)$ is strictly increasing for all values of x. **(3)**

5. (a) Find the x-coordinates of the stationary points on the graph with equation :-
$$f(x) = \tfrac{2}{3}x^3 + 2x^2 - 16x.$$ **(5)**

   (b) Hence, determine the range of values of x for which the function f is strictly decreasing. **(4)**

6. A curve has equation $y = 6x^2 - 2x^3$.

   (a) Find the coordinates of the stationary points on this curve and determine their nature. **(7)**

   (b) State the coordinates of the points where the curve meets the coordinate axes and and sketch the curve. **(5)**

7. The diagram shows the graph of a function $y = h(x)$.

   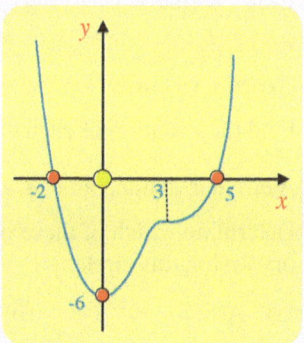

   Sketch the graph of $y = h'(x)$ **(4)**

8. A function f is defined on the set of real numbers by
$$f(x) = x^4 - 2x^2.$$

   (a) Find where the graph of $f(x)$ cuts both axes. **(3)**

   (b) On separate diagrams, sketch the graph of :-

   (i) $y = f(x)$ (ii) $y = f'(x)$. **(12)**

9. A landscape gardener sets out an area of land to test various types of grass seed. They plan to fence off 12 rectangular plots, each plot measuring a metres by b metres. He owns 720 square metres of land.

   (a) Show that the total length of fencing, F metres, needed is given by :-
$$F(a) = 16a + \frac{900}{a}.$$ **(4)**

   (b) Find the value of a that minimises the length of fencing required. **(5)**

10. ScotFun Theme Park has model cars which are used to transport visitors moving between the attractions. The daily cost £C of running a car is determined by the formula :-
$$C = \frac{400}{v} + 25v + 50,$$
v being the speed in km/hr of the car.

    Calculate the speed at which a car should travel to make the cost per day a minimum and find this cost. **(6)**

11. Ikera Store has designed an occasional coffee table, rectangular in shape, with a glass top of length x cm, breadth y cm and a perimeter of 360 cm.

    (a) Find an expression, in terms of x, for the area of the glass. **(3)**

    (b) Find the value of x which will give a maximum area. **(4)**

    (c) Calculate the maximum area of the glass top. **(1)**

Equation of a Circle

A circle is defined as the set of all points P(x, y) that are equidistant from a fixed point (*the centre*).

P(x, y) is a general point on the circumference of a circle, centre O(0, 0) and with radius r.

From Pythagoras' Theorem, the equation of the circle can be defined as :-

$$x^2 + y^2 = r^2.$$

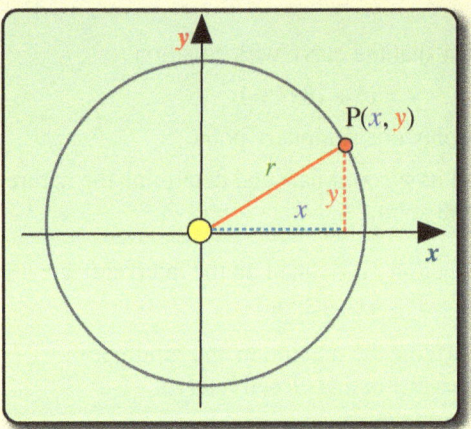

Example 1 :-   Write the equation of a circle with centre (0, 0) and radius 5 cm.

$$x^2 + y^2 = 5^2$$
$$=> \quad x^2 + y^2 = 25.$$

Example 2 :-   Write the equation of a circle with centre (0, 0) and radius $2\sqrt{3}$ cm.

$$x^2 + y^2 = (2\sqrt{3})^2$$
$$=> \quad x^2 + y^2 = 12.$$

Example 3 :-   Write the equation of the circle with centre (0, 0) passing through P(6, -8).

length of OP $= \sqrt{(6-0)^2 + (-8-0)^2} = 10$
$$x^2 + y^2 = (10)^2$$
$$=> \quad x^2 + y^2 = 100.$$

Note :-   To check if a point P lies inside, on or outside a circle, centre (0, 0) with radius r, use the distance formula to calculate the length of OP and compare OP to the radius.

Exercise H9·1

1. State the equation of each circle with centre (0, 0) and radius length :-

  (a)   3 units   (b)   10 units   (c)   4 units

  (d) $\sqrt{2}$ units   (e) $5\sqrt{2}$ units   (f) $\sqrt{13}$ units

  (g)   1·5 units   (h)   7·6 units   (i) $\frac{1}{2}$ unit.

2. For each circle below, state the radius :-

  (a) $x^2 + y^2 = 64$ (b) $x^2 + y^2 = 49$

  (c) $x^2 + y^2 = 1$ (d) $x^2 + y^2 = 144$.

3. Find the radius of each circle below, leaving your answer as a surd in its simplest form :-

  (a) $x^2 + y^2 = 10$ (b) $x^2 + y^2 = 50$

  (c) $x^2 + y^2 = 120$ (d) $x^2 + y^2 = 2000$.

4. Write the equation of the circle with centre the origin and passing through the point :-

  (a)   A(3, 4)   (b)   B(5, 12)   (c)   C(2, 5)

  (d)   D(7, 11)   (e)   E(1, 2)   (f)   F($\sqrt{2}, \sqrt{3}$).

5. A circle fits exactly into a square, which is drawn on a Cartesian diagram, with its centre the origin.

  The square measures 12 by 12 units.

  Find the equation of the circle.

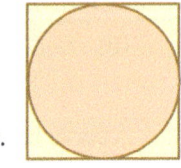

6. Three concentric circles, have their centres at the origin.

  The circles have diameters :-

  Blue - 8 cm

  Red - 10 cm

  Green - 15 cm.

  Find the equation of each circle.

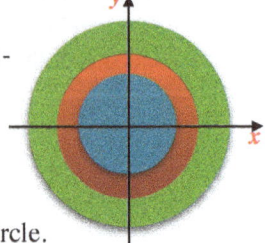

7. A circle is defined as $x^2 + y^2 = 100$.

  Determine which of these points lie **on, inside** or **outside** this circle :-

  (a)   A(6, 8)   (b)   B(6, 4)

  (c)   C(10, 0)   (d)   D(9, 5)

  (e)   E($\sqrt{10}, -\sqrt{10}$)   (f)   F($2\sqrt{2}, -\sqrt{80}$).

8. A circle and a point **on** its circumference are given in each of the following.

    Find **two** values for each missing variable :-

    (a) $x^2 + y^2 = 25$ $(a, 3)$

    (b) $x^2 + y^2 = 100$ $(8, b)$

    (c) $x^2 + y^2 = 50$ $(7, c)$

    (d) $x^2 + y^2 = 1$ $(d, (d + 1))$

    (e) $x^2 + y^2 = 2\sqrt{5}$ (g, g).

9. Explain why you would usually expect **two** values in Question 8, but not always.

10. The end points of the diameter of a circle, with centre the origin, have coordinates A(6, 8) and B(-6, -8).

    Find the equation of this circle.
    (A sketch might help).

11. A radar screen has its centre (0, 0). The screen is circular and it covers a radius of 50 km.

    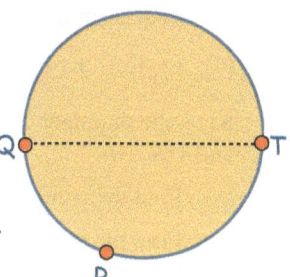

    Three aircraft, relative to the radar centre, have their coordinates P(20, 30), Q(30, -40) and R(-40, 40).

    Which of these aircraft are within the radar zone ?

12. A circle, with the origin as its centre, has a horizontal diameter QT where T(10, 0) is as shown.

    (a) Find the equation of this circle.

    A point R(-1, k) lies on the circumference of this circle.

    (b) Show that $k = -3\sqrt{11}$.

The Equation of a Circle with Centre (a, b) and Radius r

The equation of a circle with centre $C(a, b)$ and radius r is

$$(x - a)^2 + (y - b)^2 = r^2$$

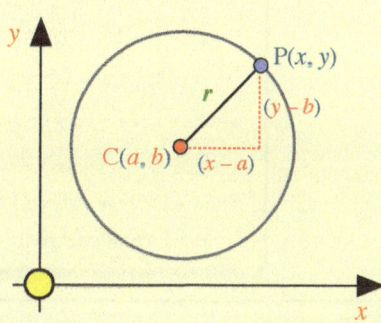

Proof

From Pythagoras' Theorem,

$(x - a)^2 + (y - b)^2 = CP^2$

$\Rightarrow (x - a)^2 + (y - b)^2 = r^2$

Example 1 :-   Find the equation of the circle with centre $(3, 4)$ and radius 2.

$(x - a)^2 + (y - b)^2 = r^2$

$(x - 3)^2 + (y - 4)^2 = 2^2$

$(x - 3)^2 + (y - 4)^2 = 4$

Example 2 :-   Find the equation of the circle with centre $(-1, 6)$ and radius $3\sqrt{2}$.

$(x - a)^2 + (y - b)^2 = r^2$

$(x - (-1))^2 + (y - 6)^2 = (3\sqrt{2})^2$

$(x + 1)^2 + (y - 6)^2 = 18$.

Exercise H9·2

1. State the equation of each circle :-

    (a) centre $(2, 5)$ (b) centre $(6, 3)$
         $r = 5$ $r = 7$

    (c) centre $(-1, 4)$ (d) centre $(-3, -2)$
         $r = 1$ $r = 10$

    (e) centre $(0, -7)$ (f) centre $(-8, -2)$
         $r = \sqrt{2}$ $r = 3\sqrt{5}$

    (g) centre $(k, -2k)$ (h) centre $(-31, 12)$
         $r = \sqrt{t}$ $r = 2^{\frac{3}{2}}$.

2. State the centre and radius of each circle :-

    (a) $(x - 4)^2 + (y - 1)^2 = 4$

    (b) $(x - 11)^2 + (y - 10)^2 = 9$

    (c) $(x + 2)^2 + (y - 3)^2 = 10$

    (d) $x^2 + (y + 2)^2 = 2$

    (e) $(x - k)^2 + (y - z)^2 = w$

    (f) $(x - \sqrt{5})^2 + (y + \sqrt{2})^2 = 1$

    (g) $(x - 2)^2 = 4 - (y + 3)^2$.

3. (a) Use the distance formula to find the radius of the circle shown.

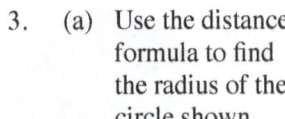

P(8, 8)

C(5, 4)

(b) State the equation of this circle.

(c) Determine the coordinates of point Q, where PQ is a diameter.

4. Find the equation of each circle below, given the centre C and a point on the circumference :-

(a) C(4, 1), T(9, 13)   (b) C(5, 0), R(11, 8)

(c) C(-1, 3), K(4, 4)   (d) C(-3, -5), H(-1, 6).

5. ST is the diameter of a circle where S(3, 2) and T(9, 10).

(a) Find the centre of this circle.

(b) Find the equation of this circle.

6. A circle has centre (-3, -5). The x-axis is a tangent to the circle.

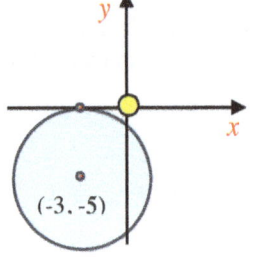

(-3, -5)

(a) Find the equation of the circle.

(b) Find the coordinates of the two points where the circle cuts the y-axis.

7. The equation of a circle is given as

$$(x + 7)^2 + (y - 6)^2 = 10.$$

Expand the brackets and simplify fully, and rearrange your equation into the form :-

$$x^2 + y^2 + ax + by + c = 0, \quad \text{(for some } a, b \text{ and } c\text{)}.$$

This form of the circle is called the :-
General Equation of the Circle,
and will be discussed in the next section.

The General Equation of a Circle

Expanding the equation of a circle :-

$$(x + g)^2 + (y + f)^2 = r^2,$$

$$\Rightarrow \ x^2 + 2gx + g^2 + y^2 + 2fy + f^2 - r^2 = 0$$

gives the general equation of a circle

$$\boxed{x^2 + y^2 + 2gx + 2fy + c = 0}$$

where $c = g^2 + f^2 - r^2$

Proof

$$x^2 + y^2 + 2gx + 2fy + c = 0$$

$$\Rightarrow x^2 + 2gx + y^2 + 2fy = -c \quad \text{(add } g^2 + f^2 \text{ to both sides)}$$

$$\Rightarrow x^2 + 2gx + g^2 + y^2 + 2fy + f^2 = -c + g^2 + f^2 \quad \text{(completed square form)}$$

$$\Rightarrow (x + g)^2 + (y + f)^2 = g^2 + f^2 - c$$

$$\Rightarrow (x - (-g))^2 + (y - (-f))^2 = g^2 + f^2 - c$$

Equation of circle with centre $(-g, -f)$ and $r = \sqrt{g^2 + f^2 - c}$.

This means that any equation, of the form :- $x^2 + y^2 + 2gx + 2fy + c = 0$ represents a circle with :-

centre at $(-g, -f)$ and **radius $= \sqrt{g^2 + f^2 - c}$.** (as long as $g^2 + f^2 - c > 0$) => i.e. $g^2 + f^2 - c$ must be $+ve$).

$x^2 + y^2 + 2gx + 2fy + c = 0$ is the expanded version of the equation of a circle.

You must be able to pick out the centre and radius when you meet this form of the circle, and be able to convert between both forms of the circle's equation.

Example 1 :- The equation of a circle is given as
$$x^2 + y^2 + 8x + 4y + 10 = 0.$$
Find its centre and its radius.

$x^2 + y^2 + 8x + 4y + 10 = 0$ centre is $(-g, -f)$

$2g = 8 \quad \Rightarrow \quad g = 4 \ (\text{so } -g = -4)$

$2f = 4 \quad \Rightarrow \quad f = 2 \ (\text{so } -f = -2)$

$c = 10$

$r = \sqrt{g^2 + f^2 - c} = \sqrt{4^2 + 2^2 - 10} = \sqrt{10}$

Centre $(-4, -2)$ radius $= \sqrt{10}$.

Example 2 :- A circle, centre C(2, -3) passes through point P(-1, 4). Find its General Equation.

Centre $(2, -3) \Rightarrow -g = 2, -f = -3, \Rightarrow g = -2, f = 3$.

$\Rightarrow \quad x^2 + y^2 + 2gx + 2fy + c = 0$

$\Rightarrow \quad x^2 + y^2 - 4x + 6y + c = 0$

but $(-1, 4)$ lies on the circumference, so

$\Rightarrow$ substitute $x = -1$ and $y = 4$ into the equation :-

$\Rightarrow 1 + 16 + 4 + 24 + c = 0 \quad \Rightarrow \quad c = -45$

$\Rightarrow \quad x^2 + y^2 - 4x + 6y - 45 = 0.$

note :- The easiest way to find the centre is to half both the x and y coefficients then change the sign of both.

Exercise H9·3

1. The equation of a circle is defined by :-

    $$x^2 + y^2 + 12x + 2y + 20 = 0.$$

    Find the centre and radius of this circle.

    Copy and **complete** :-

    > *From General Equation :-*
    >
    > $$x^2 + y^2 + 2gx + 2fy + c = 0.$$
    >
    > centre is $(-g, -f)$
    >
    > $2g = 12 \implies g = \dots \implies -g = \dots$
    >
    > $2f = \dots \implies f = \dots \implies -f = \dots$
    >
    > $c = 20$
    >
    > $r = \sqrt{g^2 + f^2 - c} \quad = \qquad = \dots$
    >
    > **Centre** (..., ...)   **Radius** = ...

2. Find the centre and radius of each circle :-

    (a) $x^2 + y^2 + 10x + 2y + 3 = 0$

    (b) $x^2 + y^2 + 16x + 20y + 2 = 0$

    (c) $x^2 + y^2 - 12x + 4y + 7 = 0$

    (d) $x^2 + y^2 - 2x - 6y - 11 = 0$

    (e) $x^2 + y^2 - x + 3y - 9 = 0.$

3. Find the General Equation of each circle :-

    (a)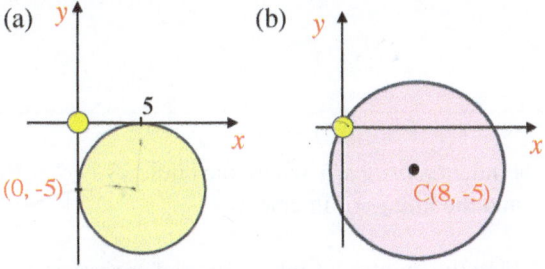

    (b)

4. A circle is defined by $x^2 + y^2 - 4x + 2y + c = 0$.

    Given that T(6, -8) lies on the circumference of the circle, find the value of c.

5. A circle has centre C(3, -7) and the point (4, 5) lies on its circumference.

    Find the equation of the circle.

6. The coordinates of the end points of a diameter of a circle are A(3, 6) and B(-3, 0).

    Find the equation of the circle.

7. (a) Explain why $x^2 + y^2 - 4x + 8y + 29 = 0$, though it looks like one, is **not** actually the equation of a circle.

    (b) If the +29 was changed to a -29, would the equation then represent a circle ?

8. The equation of the larger of two concentric circles is $x^2 + y^2 + 12x + 2y + 20 = 0$.

    The smaller circle has half the diameter of the larger circle.

    Find the equation of the smaller circle.

    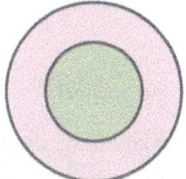

9. A smaller circle sits inside a larger circle with centre C(-2, -1).

    The circumference of the smaller circle passes through the centre of the larger circle and just touches the larger circle at the point T(4, 3).

    Find the equation of the smaller circle.

    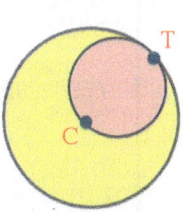

10. Two large circles and a smaller circle just touch as shown.

    All three centres are collinear.

    The equations of the two larger circles are :-

    $$x^2 + y^2 + 4x + 12y + 22 = 0 \quad \text{and}$$
    $$(x - 8)^2 + (y - 4)^2 = 18.$$

    Find the equation of the smaller circle.

    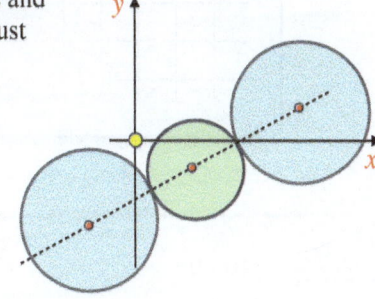

11. Diameter ST of a circle has end point S(3, 1). The equation of the circle is :-

    $$x^2 + y^2 - 4x + 6y - \sqrt{7} = 0.$$

    Find the coordinates of T.

12. These two circles intersect at a single point.

    $$x^2 + y^2 + 12x + 2y + 12 = 0$$
    $$(x - 2)^2 + (y + 7)^2 = 25.$$

    Find the coordinates of this point.

The Intersection of a Straight Line and a Circle

There are three ways a straight line and a circle can be drawn, relative to each other. They may :-

(i) have no points of intersection

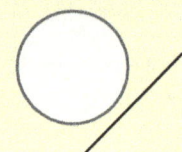

(ii) have two points of intersection

We have seen this in Chapter 1.

(iii) have one point of intersection. (i.e. tangency occurs)

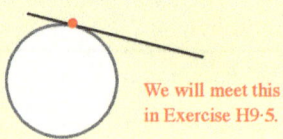

We will meet this in Exercise H9·5.

Example 1 :-

Sketch the circle $x^2 + y^2 = 4$ and the line $y = \frac{1}{2}x - 3$, to show graphically there are no points of intersection.

Circle , Centre $(0, 0)$
$\qquad r = 2$

Line $\quad m = \frac{1}{2}$

$\qquad$ *y-int* $(0, -3)$

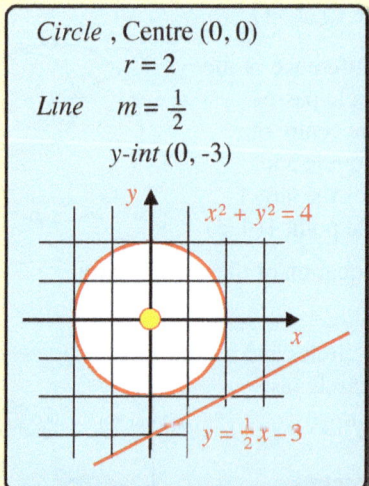

$x^2 + y^2 = 4$

$y = \frac{1}{2}x - 3$

Example 2 :-

Find where the circle $x^2 + y^2 = 125$ meets the line $y = 2x$.

Substitute $2x$ for y in the equation of the circle.

$$x^2 + (2x)^2 = 125$$

$\Rightarrow \qquad x^2 + 4x^2 = 125$

$\Rightarrow \qquad x^2 = 25 \Rightarrow x = \pm 5$

Replace $x = +5$ in $y = 2x \Rightarrow y = 2 \times 5 = 10$.

Replace $x = -5$ in $y = 2x \Rightarrow y = 2 \times -5 = -10$.

$\Rightarrow$ They intersect at **(5, 10)** and **(-5, -10)**.

Exercise H9·4

1. The equation of a circle is defined as :-
$$x^2 + y^2 = 9.$$
Make a sketch to show that the line $y = x + 5$ does **not** intersect this circle.

2. Sketch the circle $x^2 + y^2 = 16$.

Show *graphically* that both of these lines have **no** points of intersection with the above circle :-

(a) $y = \frac{1}{2}x - 6$ $\qquad$ (b) $y = 5$

3. (a) Sketch the circle $(x - 4)^2 + (y - 1)^2 = 1$ and show that the line $x = -4$ does not intersect this circle.

(b) Show that $y = -5$ does not intersect the circle $x^2 + y^2 + 12x + 2y + 20 = 0$.

4. Find, *algebraically* where the circle $x^2 + y^2 = 36$ and the line $y = x$ intersect.

5. Find the point(s) of intersection of each circle with the given line :-

(a) $x^2 + y^2 = 80$, $\qquad\qquad$ $y = 2x$

(b) $x^2 + y^2 = 25$, $\qquad\qquad$ $y = x - 1$

(c) $(x - 7)^2 + (y - 3)^2 = 16$, $\qquad$ $y = x$

(d) $x^2 + (y - 4)^2 = 40$, $\qquad\quad$ $y = 3x + 4$

(e) $x^2 + y^2 + 8x + 2y - 1 = 0$, $\quad$ $y = -x - 5$

(f) $x^2 + y^2 + 12x + 16y + 2 = 0$, $\;$ $y = x - 2$

(g) $x^2 + y^2 - 12x + 6y + 29 = 0$, $\;$ $x = 2y + 8$.

6. A circle has centre $(4, 3)$ and radius 5.

Find where the line $y = x$ intersects this circle.

7. For the circle found in Question 6, find where it intercepts both axes.

8. A circle has diameter with end points at P(-1, -7) and Q(-9, 1).

    (a) Find the centre of the circle.

    (b) Find the radius of the circle.

    (c) State the equation of the circle.

    (d) Find where this circle intersects the x-axis, to 1 decimal place.

9. The diameter of a circle has end points at A(-2, 0) and B(4, 6).

    (a) Find the equation of this circle.

    (b) Find the equation of diameter CD, which is perpendicular to AB. (Hint - use $m_1m_2 = -1$)

    (c) Find the end points of diameter CD.

10. The circle $x^2 + y^2 = 16$, has two vertical and two horizontal tangents.

    State the equation of all 4 lines. *(A sketch will help)*.

Tangents to a Circle

A tangent to a circle has only one point of contact with the circle.

Example :-   Show that the line $y = x - 10$ is a tangent to the circle $x^2 + y^2 + 4x + 8y - 12 = 0$.

Substitute $y = x - 10$ into the equation of the circle.

$\Rightarrow$ $x^2 + (x - 10)^2 + 4x + 8(x - 10) - 12 = 0$

$\Rightarrow$ $x^2 + (x^2 - 20x + 100) + 4x + (8x - 80) - 12 = 0$

$\Rightarrow$ $2x^2 - 8x + 8 = 0$

$\Rightarrow$ $2(x^2 - 4x + 4) = 0$

At this point we can choose two different methods.

Method 1	*Method 2*
by factorisation	use the discriminant
$\Rightarrow$ $x^2 - 4x + 4 = 0$	$\Rightarrow$ $b^2 - 4ac$
$(x - 2)(x - 2) = 0$	$= (-4)^2 - 4(1)(4) = 0$
$\Rightarrow$ **$x = 2$ or $x = 2$**	$\Rightarrow$ **since $b^2 - 4ac = 0$**
$\Rightarrow$ **since only 1 solution**	$\Rightarrow$ **there is only 1 solution**
$\Rightarrow$ **line must be a tangent**	$\Rightarrow$ **the line must be a tangent**.

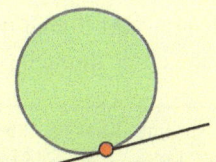

The point where the tangent meets the circle could also be found as follows :-

Using Method 1

$\Rightarrow$ substitute $x = 2$ into either equation.

$\Rightarrow$ $y = 2 - 10 = -8$

$\Rightarrow$ **Tangent at (2, -8).**

Exercise H9·5

1. The equation of a circle is defined by :-
    $$x^2 + y^2 - 6x - 4y + 8 = 0.$$

    (a) Show that the line $y = 2x + 1$ is a tangent to the circle.

    (b) Find the point where this tangent intersects the circle.

2. For the line, $y = 2x - 1$ and the circle
    $$x^2 + y^2 - 4x - 6y + 13 = 0,$$

    (a) use the substitution and *Method 1*, to show that the line is a tangent to the circle.

    (b) find the coordinates of the point P, where the tangent meets the circle.

3. Find the point of intersection for each circle and line.

    (a) $x^2 + y^2 - 6x - 4y - 4 = 0$, $y = 4x + 7$

    (b) $x^2 + y^2 = 2$, $y = x + 2$

    (c) $(x - 2)^2 + (y + 1)^2 = 5$, $y + 2x - 8 = 0$

    (d) $x^2 + y^2 = 13$, $2y = 3x - 13$. (hard)

4. A line is a tangent to the circle in Question 3(d), when $x = 3$.

    (a) Find the y-coordinate of the tangential point.

    (b) State the gradient of the radius joining the circle centre and this point.

    (c) State the gradient of the tangent.

The Equation of the Tangent to a Circle

We have already seen how to find the equation of a tangent to a curve using calculus.

However, we do not yet know how to apply differentiation to the equation of a circle like $x^2 + y^2 - 4x - 8y + 2 = 0$.

Remember :- $m_{tangent} \times m_{radius} = $ **-1**   (*the tangent is perpendicular to the radius at the point of contact*).

We can now find the **equation of the tangent to a circle**, since the radius and a tangent are **perpendicular**.

Example :-

(a) Show that the point P(5, 1) lies on the circumference of the circle with equation :-

$x^2 + y^2 - 4x - 8y + 2 = 0$.

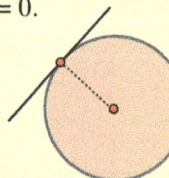

(b) Find the equation of the tangent to the circle through point P.

note :- to find the tangent to a circle does **NOT** require differentiation, but to find the tangent to any other curve generally **DOES**.

(a) Check that (5, 1) satisfies the equation of the circle.

$x^2 + y^2 - 4x - 8y + 2 = 5^2 + 1^2 - 4 \times 5 - 8 \times 1 + 2 = $ **0**

Hence, the point (5, 1) does lie **on** the circle.

(b) Since $-g = -2$ and $-f = -4$, then the centre is at C(2, 4).

$$\Rightarrow m_{(radius)} = m_{CP} = \frac{4-1}{2-5} = \frac{3}{-3} = -1.$$

$$\Rightarrow m_{(tangent)} = 1, \; since \; m_{(tangent)} \times m_{(radius)} = -1.$$

$\Rightarrow$ The equation of the tangent with $m = 1$ through (5, 1) is

$$y - b = m(x - a)$$
$$y - 1 = 1(x - 5)$$
$$y = x - 4.$$

---

5. A circle is defined by :-

$x^2 + y^2 - 2x - 10y + 1 = 0$.

(a) Show that the point P(5, 8) lies on the circumference of this circle.

(b) State the coordinates of the centre of the circle and find the equation of the tangent to the circle through P.

6. A circle has equation :-

$x^2 + y^2 - 4x - 6y - 12 = 0$.

(a) Show that the point Q(5, -1) lies on the circumference of this circle.

(b) Find the equation of the tangent to the circle through the point Q.

7. A circle has equation :-

$x^2 + y^2 + 2x + 2y - 66 = 0$.

(a) Show that the point S(7, 1) lies on the circumference of this circle.

(b) Find the equation of the tangent to the circle at the point S.

8. A circle has equation

$(x - 2)^2 + (y - 4)^2 = 25$.

Find the equation of the tangent to the circle through T(6, 7).

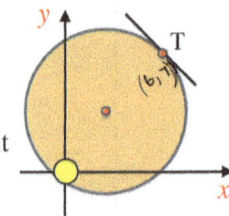

9. (a) Find the equation of the tangent to the circle $x^2 + y^2 + 2x - 4y - 12 = 0$, through P(3, 1).

(b) Find the equation of the line which passes through the centre of the circle and is parallel to this tangent.

10. A circle has centre (3, 2) and a radius of 5.

(a) Find the equations of the tangents to this circle through the points A(0, 6) and B(-1, -1), both of which lie on the circle.

(b) Find the coordinates of the point of intersection of the two tangents.

11. Two circles are given as :-

$x^2 + y^2 - 8x - 14y + 40 = 0$
$(x + 8)^2 + (y + 2)^2 = 100$.

These circles are known to touch at just one point.

(a) Find the point P where the two circles touch.

(b) Find the equation of the tangent through P.

1. The equation of a circle is defined by :-

   $$x^2 + y^2 = 29.$$

   Determine whether each of these points lie **inside**, **outside** or **on** the circumference of this circle :-

   (a) (-2, 5)   (b) ($\sqrt{29}$, -1)

   (c) (5, -3)   (d) (-1, -$\sqrt{28}$).

2. For each of the following, find the equation of the circle both in the form $(x - a)^2 + (y - b)^2 = r^2$, **and** in the form $x^2 + y^2 + 2gx + 2fy + c = 0$.

   (a) centre (3, -2), radius 6 units.

   (b) diameter 20 units, centre ($\sqrt{3}$, 7)

   (c) P(3, 1) lies on circumference, centre (-1, -4).

3. Two circles are defined by :-

   $$x^2 + y^2 + 4x - 6y + 2 = 0$$
   $$(x - 4)^2 + (y + 1)^2 = 5.$$

   (a) Find the centre and radius of each circle.

   (b) Calculate the distance between the centres.

   (c) Find the equation of the line that passes through these centres.

   (d) Find the equation of the perpendicular bisector of this line segment.

4. The line $y = x$ intersects the circle $x^2 + (y + 1)^2 = 25$. Find the coordinates of the points of intersection.

5. Find the equation of the tangent through the point S(2, 1), which lies on the circle :-

   $$x^2 + y^2 - 6x - 4y + 11 = 0.$$

6. Show that the line $x - 3y - 10 = 0$ is a tangent to the circle :-

   $$x^2 + y^2 = 10.$$

7. A circle is defined by $x^2 + y^2 - 8x - 16y + c = 0$.

   Given that (4, -6) lies on the circumference of this circle, determine the value of c.

8. A circle with equation $(x - 2)^2 + (y + 1)^2 = 100$ has a chord AB with equation $2y = x + 6$.

   Find the coordinates of the midpoint of AB.

9. A circle with equation $x^2 + y^2 + 10x - 2y - 38 = 0$, has a tangent at point Q(3, t), on the circle.

   (a) Determine the value of t.

   (b) Find the equation of this tangent.

10. The line $y = 2x + 1$ intercepts the circle

    $$x^2 + y^2 - 6x - 4y + 8 = 0.$$

    (a) Is this line a tangent to this circle ?

    (b) Find the coordinates of the point(s) of intersection.

11. A circle has a diameter QT, parallel to the x-axis, with T(6, 4) as shown.

    A point R lies on the circumference of this circle such that QR is 10 units in length and TR is 24 units long.

    Determine the equation of this circle.

12. A line passes through points P(8, 4) and Q(-4, 13). This line is a tangent to the circle

    $$x^2 + y^2 - 2x - 6y - 15 = 0.$$

    Find the equation of the line from the centre of the circle to the point where the line PQ meets the circle.

13. The straight line $y = 2x + c$ is a tangent to the circle

    $$x^2 + y^2 - 4y - 16 = 0.$$

    Calculate possible values for c.

14. Find the gradient of the tangent to the circle

    $$x^2 + y^2 = 9$$

    from the point P(0, 5), which lies outside the circle.
    (*Hint :- begin with the line through* (0, 5) *as* $y = mx + 5$).

15. (a) Show that the tangent to the circle
        $$x^2 + y^2 - 4x - 6 = 0,$$

        through the point (1, -3) on the circle is also a tangent to to the circle

        $$x^2 + y^2 - 8y - 24 = 0.$$

    (b) Find the length of the common tangent between the two tangential points.

Exam Practice Exercise (H9)

1. The equation $x^2 + y^2 - 8x + c = 0$ defines a circle, with a radius r.

   Set up an inequality and solve it to find the restriction on the value of c. **(3)**

2. A circle has centre C(3, 1) and a radius 5.

   (a) State the equation of this circle. **(2)**

   (b) Find the gradient of the line passing through the centre and point T(-1, -2) on the circle. **(2)**

   (c) Find the equation of the tangent to this circle through T. **(3)**

3. Two circles are defined by :-

   C1 : $x^2 + y^2 + 2x - 6y + 1 = 0$

   C2 : $(x - 5)^2 + (y + 1)^2 = 4$.

   (a) Find the centre and radius of each circle. **(3)**

   (b) Show that these circles do **not** intersect. **(3)**

   (c) Find the shortest distance between the circles. Leave your answer in surd form. **(3)**

4. A straight line passes through the point (-4, 0) and it makes an angle of 135° with the positive direction of the x-axis.

   (a) Show this line meets the y-axis at (0, -4). **(2)**

   These two points form the diameter of a circle.

   (b) Find the equation of the circle in the form
   $$x^2 + y^2 + ax + by + c = 0.$$ **(5)**

5. The line $y = 3 - 2x$ intersects the circle :-
   $$(x - 8)^2 + (y + 3)^2 = 25$$
   at points A and B.

   (a) Find the coordinates of A and B. **(3)**

   (b) Find the equation of the perpendicular bisector of AB. **(3)**

   (c) Show that this perpendicular bisector does indeed pass through the centre of the circle. **(2)**

   (d) CD is a diameter of the circle, where C lies on the x-axis.

   Find possible coordinates for C and D. **(3)**

6. Two *identical* circles have centres at :-

   C_1(-2, -5) and C_2(4, 3).

   The circles have a single point of contact at T.

   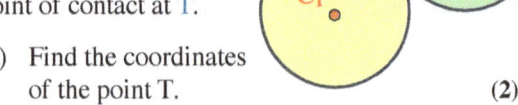

   (a) Find the coordinates of the point T. **(2)**

   (b) Find the equation of the tangent at T. **(3)**

   A third circle has its centre at T and just touches each of the other 2 circles at a single point.

   (c) Find the equation of this 3rd circle. **(3)**

7. The equation of a circle is defined as :-
   $$x^2 + y^2 + 6x - 4y - 3 = 0.$$

   (a) Show that P(1, 2) lies on the circumference of this circle. **(2)**

   The line $y - x - 1 = 0$ also passes through P.

   (b) Find the coordinates of the second point where this line intersects the circle. **(4)**

8. Find the point(s) of intersection of the circle
   $$(x - 5)^2 + (y + 10)^2 = 20$$
   and the line $x - \frac{1}{2}y - 5 = 0$. **(5)**

9. A circle is defined as follows :-
   $$(x + 3)^2 + (y - 8)^2 = k.$$

   Find all the values for k such that k is a whole number and the point Q(1, 3) lies outside this circle. **(4)**

10. A circle has a chord at A(7, 0) and B(9, 4).

    (a) Find the perpendicular bisector of AB. **(4)**

    (b) Given that the circle's centre is at (4, k), find the value of k. **(2)**

    (c) Find the equation of this circle. **(3)**

11. Find the coordinates of the point of intersection of the circle $(x - 10)^2 + y^2 = 160$ and the line $y = 2x$. **(4)**

Home Exercise 3 (Chapters 1-9)

1. A(-2, 4), B(-2, -2) and C(6, 2) are the vertices of a triangle ABC.

   Find the equation of AD, the altitude from A to BC.

2. On a suitable set of real numbers, functions f and g are defined by :-

   $$f(x) = \frac{1}{x+4} \quad \text{and} \quad g(x) = \frac{1}{x} - 4 \ .$$

   Find $f(g(2))$.

3. Differentiate with respect to x :-

   (a) $f(x) = 4x^3 + 5x - 11$ (b) $f(x) = 8x^2 + \frac{5}{x}$ (c) $f(x) = 8\sqrt{x}(x - 1)$.

4. The diagram shows part of the graph of $y = f(x)$.

   (a) Copy the diagram and on it sketch the graph of $y = f(x + 2)$.

   (b) On a separate diagram, sketch the graph of $y = 1 - f(x)$.

      (In each case show where each of the 4 points indicated end up).

   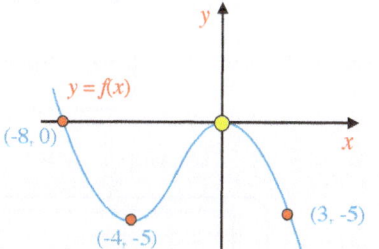

5. Solve for x :-   (a) $12\cos^2 x° - 5\cos x° - 2 = 0$ $\{0 \le x \le 360\}$.

                           (b) $2\sin^2 x - 1 = 0$ $\{-\pi < x < \pi\}$.

6. A parabola intercepts the x and y-axes at (-6, 0), (2, 0) and (0, 24).

   Find the equation of this parabola in the form $y = ax^2 + bx + c$.

7. A ball is thrown vertically upwards.

   The height (h) metres of the ball after t seconds is given by the formula $h(t) = 49t - 7t^2$.

   (a) Find the rate of change of height with respect to time, after one second.

   (b) Find the speed of the ball after 3·5 seconds. Explain your answer.

8. (a) Show that the line $y = -x + 2$ is a tangent to the circle $x^2 + y^2 + 10x + 2y - 6 = 0$.

   (b) Find the coordinates of the point where the tangent meets the circle.

9. A function is defined by :- $f(x) = (x - 4)^2 + 3$.

   (a) Sketch the graph of the function, showing the turning point and where it cuts the y-axis.

   (b) Sketch the graph of the derived function, $f'(x)$.

The General Term of a Sequence

A **sequence** is a **pattern** of numbers, defined by "**a given rule**".

A formula :- n_{th} **term = 3 × n + 1,**   or more mathematically :- $u_n = 3n + 1.$

This rule should allow you to determine any **term** of the sequence quite clearly.

There are two ways of defining patterns or sequences of numbers.

The first is to give a **general formula EXPLICITLY** which defines the nth term of the sequence in terms of n itself.

Example 1 :-   A sequence is defined by :- $u_n = 3n + 1$

To find the first term, you simply substitute **1** in place of n.

> => $u_1 = 3 \times 1 + 1 = 4$
>
> => $u_2 = 3 \times 2 + 1 = 7$
>
> => $u_3 = 3 \times 3 + 1 = 10$ etc.
>
> => the sequence is easily seen now as   4, 7, 10, 13, 16, ...

Example 2 :-   Develop a **formula** for the general term of the sequence :- 10, 16, 22, 28, 34, ...

Term	u_1	u_2	u_3	u_4	u_5
Value	10	16	22	28	34

6   6   6   6

You learned earlier in maths that if a "linear" sequence goes up in "**6**'s" you try the **6** times table first.

You also discovered how to use a "correction" factor (**4**).

=> $u_n = 6n + 4.$

Exercise H10·1

1. Write down the first **4 terms** for each of these sequences :-

    (a) $u_n = 4n$

    (b) $u_n = 5n - 1$

    (c) $u_n = n(n + 1)$

    (d) $u_n = n^2 + 1$

    (e) $u_n = 2^n$

    (f) $u_n = \dfrac{2}{n}$

    (g) $u_n = \dfrac{n(n - 1)}{2}$

    (h) $u_n = 10 - n$

    (i) $u_n = n(n + 1)(n + 2)$

    (j) $u_n = n^3 - 1$

    (k) $u_n = \dfrac{1}{n(n + 1)}$

    (l) $u_n = cos(180n)°.$

2. Look at the sequence $u_n = \dfrac{n}{n + 1}.$

    (a) Find $u_1, u_2, u_3, \dots u_{10}.$

    (b) Can you see that as n gets larger, u_n appears to **tend towards a particular value** ?

    What will u_n tend to, as $n \longrightarrow$ **infinity** ?

3. For the sequence $u_n = \dfrac{n(n - 1)}{2} + \dfrac{n(n + 1)}{2}$,

    (a) Find $u_1, u_2, u_3, \dots$ etc.

    (b) What do you notice about your answers ?

4. Look at the following sequences of numbers.

    In each case, try to find a **general formula** for the term u_n, in terms of n.

    (a) $3, 6, 9, 12, \dots$

    (b) $7, 12, 17, 22, \dots$

    (c) $20, 23, 26, 29, \dots$

    (d) $70, 67, 64, 61, \dots$

    (e) $1, 11, 21, 31, \dots$

    (f) $80, 68, 56, 44, \dots$

    (g) $6·7, 7·1, 7·5, 7·9, \dots$

    (h) $1, 4, 9, 16, 25, \dots$

    (i) $1, 8, 27, 64, \dots$

    (j) $2, 4, 8, 16, 32, \dots$

    (k) $1, 3, 9, 27, 81, \dots$

    (l) $2, 6, 12, 20, 30, \dots$

    (m) $\frac{1}{2}, \frac{1}{3}, \frac{1}{4}, \frac{1}{5}, \dots$

    (n) $\frac{1}{2}, \frac{2}{3}, \frac{3}{4}, \frac{4}{5}, \dots$

Recurrence Relations

As we stated earlier, there are two ways of defining patterns or **sequences** of numbers :-

A. An **Explicit Formulae** (*as in exercise 1*), is one in which u_n is given (**explicitly**) in terms of n.

This means it is easy to find the actual value of any term (for example u_{50}), without having to calculate $u_1, u_2, u_3, u_4, \ldots u_{49}$ first, because you have a (simple) formula, or rule, for calculating each term independently of any other term.

B. An **Implicit Formulae** (known as a **Recurrence Relation**).

This time, each term is determined (or **implied**) from the **previous** term.

When a **recurrence relation** is given, the connection between any term, u_n, and the previous term, u_{n-1}, (or u_{n+1}, and u_n), is given, along with the value of the **initial** term, usually u_0 or u_1.

Here are three examples of recurrence relations :-

(a) $u_n = 5u_{n-1}$, given that $u_0 = 2$.

(b) $u_n = u_{n-1} - 3$, given that $u_1 = 100$.

(c) $u_{n+1} = 0 \cdot 8u_n + 20$, given $u_0 = 200$.   These are all **recurrence relations**.

Example :-   Find the first **4 terms** of the recurrence relation, $u_n = \mathbf{0 \cdot 8 u_{n-1} + 20}$, with $u_0 = 200$.

$u_0 = 200$	=> $u_1 = 0 \cdot 8 \times u_0 + 20$	=> $u_1 = 0 \cdot 8 \times 200 + 20$	=> $u_1 = 180$
$u_1 = 180$	=> $u_2 = 0 \cdot 8 \times u_1 + 20$	=> $u_2 = 0 \cdot 8 \times 180 + 20$	=> $u_2 = 164$
$u_2 = 164$	=> $u_3 = 0 \cdot 8 \times u_2 + 20$	=> $u_3 = 0 \cdot 8 \times 164 + 20$	=> $u_3 = 151 \cdot 2$

We end up with the sequence :-   200, 180, 164, 151·2, ... (note the terms decrease)

Exercise H10·2

1. Use the recurrence relation and your calculator to find $u_1, u_2, u_3,$ and u_4 each time here :-

    (a) $u_n = u_{n-1} + 3$ $(u_0 = 5)$

    (b) $u_n = u_{n-1} + 5$ $(u_0 = 8)$

    (c) $u_n = u_{n-1} + 7$ $(u_0 = 12)$

    (d) $u_n = u_{n-1} - 2$ $(u_0 = 50)$

    (e) $u_n = u_{n-1} - 10$ $(u_0 = 80)$.

2. Consider the sequence given by $u_n = 5n + 3$.

    (a) Replace n by 1 to find u_1.

    (b) Replace n by 2 to find u_2.

    (c) Replace n by 3, then 4, to find, u_3 and u_4.

3. Use the same technique to find the first **4 terms** of the sequences defined by :-

    (a) $u_n = 3n + 5$ (b) $u_n = 80 - 10n$

    (c) $u_n = 50 - 2n$ (d) $u_n = 7n + 12$.

4. Look at your 5 answers to question 1 and your 7 answers to questions 2 and 3.

    Match up pairs of formulae where possible.

5. Use the recurrence relation and your calculator to find u_1, u_2, u_3, u_4 and u_5 each time here :-

    (a) $u_n = 3u_{n-1}$ $(u_0 = 2)$

    (b) $u_n = 0 \cdot 75u_{n-1}$ $(u_0 = 100)$

    (c) $u_n = 4u_{n-1}$ $(u_0 = 5)$

    (d) $u_n = 0 \cdot 8u_{n-1}$ $(u_0 = 3)$.

6. In question 5, two of the sequences appeared to get closer and closer to **zero**, whilst 2 of them appeared to get **bigger** and **bigger**.

    Which two appeared to approach a limit of 0 ? Try to explain the difference between these two sequences and the other two.

Developing an Explicit Formula from a Recurrence Relation (an Implicit one)

Though many patterns in real life are expressed as recurrence relations, it is always more useful to have the pattern described **explicitly**. We are going to show, over the next 2 examples, how to convert an **implicit** formula (a **recurrence relation**) into an **explicit** one.

Example 1 :- Develop an explicit formula for u_n, (in terms of n), for the recurrence relation :-
$u_n = 2u_{n-1}$, (with $u_0 = 3$), and use this to find u_{20}.

Follow carefully

$u_0 = 3$

$\Rightarrow \quad u_1 = 2u_0 \quad = \quad 2 \times 3 \quad\quad\quad\quad\quad\quad = \quad 3 \times 2^1$

$\Rightarrow \quad u_2 = 2u_1 \quad = \quad 2 \times (2 \times 3) \quad\quad\quad\quad = \quad 3 \times 2^2$

$\Rightarrow \quad u_3 = 2u_2 \quad = \quad 2 \times (2 \times 2 \times 3) \quad\quad\quad = \quad 3 \times 2^3$

$\Rightarrow \quad u_4 = 2u_3 \quad = \quad 2 \times (2 \times 2 \times 2 \times 3) \quad = \quad 3 \times 2^4$

$\Rightarrow \quad .... \quad = \quad .... \quad = \quad 3 \times .....$

$\Rightarrow \quad u_{10} = 2u_9 \quad = \quad 2 \times 2 \times .... \times (3) \quad = \quad 3 \times 2^{10}$

or in general $\Rightarrow \quad \boxed{u_n = 3 \times 2^n} \quad \Rightarrow \quad u_{20} = 3 \times 2^{20} = \boxed{3\,145\,728}.$

Exercise H10·3

1. Develop **explicit** formulae to represent each of these recurrence relations in the same way as above :-

(a) $u_n = 3u_{n-1}, \quad u_0 = 5.$ (b) $u_{n+1} = 2u_n, \quad u_0 = 510.$ (c) $u_n = 5u_{n-1}, \quad u_0 = 4.$

2. Develop an **explicit** formula for the recurrence relation $u_n = 4u_{n-1}, \; u_0 = 2$, and use it to find u_{10}.

Example 2 :- Develop an explicit formula for u_n, given that $u_n = u_{n-1} + 3, \quad u_0 = 5.$

Follow carefully

$u_0 = 5$ (leave as $5 + 3$)

$\Rightarrow \quad u_1 = u_0 + 3 \quad = \quad 5 + 3 \quad\quad\quad\quad\quad = \quad 5 + \mathbf{1} \times 3$

$\Rightarrow \quad u_2 = u_1 + 3 \quad = \quad (5 + 3) + 3 \quad\quad\quad = \quad 5 + \mathbf{2} \times 3$

$\Rightarrow \quad u_3 = u_2 + 3 \quad = \quad ((5 + 3) + 3) + 3 \quad = \quad 5 + \mathbf{3} \times 3$

$\Rightarrow \quad u_4 = u_3 + ... \quad = \quad (((5 + 3) + 3) + 3) + ... = \quad 5 + ... \times 3$

$\Rightarrow \quad u_{10} = u_9 + 3 \quad = \quad (5 + 3) + ... \quad\quad = \quad 5 + \mathbf{10} \times 3$

or in general $\Rightarrow \quad u_n = 5 + n \times 3 \Rightarrow \boxed{u_n = 5 + 3n}$

3. Develop **explicit** formulae to represent each of these recurrence relations in the same way as above :-

(a) $u_n = u_{n-1} + 4, \quad u_0 = 2$ (b) $u_{n+1} = u_n + 7, \quad u_1 = 5$ (c) $u_n = u_{n-1} - 2, \quad u_0 = 40.$

4. Develop an **explicit** formula for the recurrence relation $u_n = u_{n-1} + 6, \; u_0 = 2$, and use it to find u_{50}.

5. A car depreciates by 12% (0·12 *of its value that year*), by the end of each year.

Its value, V_n, at the end of each year is given by :-

$$V_n = 0·88\, V_{n-1}, \quad V_0 = 9000.$$

(a) Explain where the 0·88 comes from.

(b) What does the 9000 represent ?

(c) Why V_0 instead of V_1 ?

(d) Find an (**explicit**) formula for V_n, in terms of n.

(e) How much is the car worth after 4 years ?

(f) After how many years will the car have lost at least 60% of its original value ?

6. A large bulldozer, costing £28 000, loses 15% of its value each year.

(a) Set up the recurrence relation to show its value, after each year, n, of the form :-

$$V_n = \ldots \times V_{n-1}, \quad V_0 = \ldots$$

(b) Find an explicit formula for V_n and use it to determine the value of the bulldozer after 5 years.

7. A teenager, aged 14, inherits £5000.

It is placed in the bank, where the average **annual interest** rate is 8%, until their 21st birthday.

(a) Explain why the recurrence relation is given by :-

$$A_n, = 1·08\, A_{n-1}, \quad A_0 = 5000,$$

where n is the number of years the money is gaining interest, and A_n is the amount in the bank.

(b) Find an explicit formula for A_n and use it to find how much the teenager's £5000 will be worth when they reach the age of 21.

8. A certain population of bacteria **increases** at the rate of 13% per minute in a test tube.

(a) Set up the recurrence relation to find P_n, the population after n minutes, of the form :-

$$P_n = 1·\ldots P_{n-1},$$

where n represents the time in minutes.

(b) If the starting population (P_0), is 240, what will the population be after 3 minutes ?

(c) How long will it take for the population of bacteria to double ?

9. At the end of 1976, the population of India was 611 million.

The net rate of **increase** in the population (*births and deaths etc. taken into account*), was 2% per year.

(a) Set up a recurrence relation which shows how the population, P_n, is growing.

(b) Determine what the population was at the end of 1986.

10. In a marathon line dance competition, it was noted that 9% of the couples dropped out every hour.

There were 250 couples who entered the competition.

(a) Set up a recurrence relation to show how many couples, C_n, remained on the dance floor at the end of each hour period.

(b) How long did it take for there to be less than half the couples remaining on the dance floor ?

11. A Scottish artist became very well known in the 1980s and since then, his paintings increased in value by 50% every 5 years.

This piece of art was sold in 1985 for £120.

(a) What was it worth in 1990 ?

(b) Set up a recurrence relation to show its value V_n in relation to V_{n-1}, its value 5 years previously, where V_0 was its initial value.

(c) Find an explicit formula for V_n in terms of n.

(d) If you had bought the painting in 1985, what would it have been worth in 2015 ?

12. A jug of orange juice is left on a table and it begins to evaporate.

It loses 5% of its volume every hour.

(a) Assuming the jug holds 2 litres of juice to begin with, set up a recurrence relation to show how its volume V_n is dropping each hour.

(b) Find an explicit formula for V_n in terms of n.

(c) After how many hours will the jug have lost at least half of its volume ?

Linear Recurrence Relations

So far, we have looked at the following two types of recurrence relations :-

Multiplying.   => $u_n = a u_{n-1}$, $(u_0 = \dots\dots)$ for some value a.

Adding.   => $u_n = u_{n-1} + b$ $(u_0 = \dots\dots)$ for some value b.

What happens when we **combine** these two ideas ?

Multiplying and Adding.   => $u_n = a u_{n-1} + b$ $(u_0 = \dots\dots)$ for some fixed values of a and b.

This is a **Linear Recurrence Relation** of the form :-

$$u_n = a u_{n-1} + b, \ u_0 = \dots\dots$$ (it is called **linear** after :- $y = mx + c$).

Note :-   It is much more difficult to find a general (**explicit**) formula for u_n this time, and you will generally **not be required** to do this in the course of this chapter.

Example 1 :-   Consider the linear recurrence relation $u_n = 2 u_{n-1} + 3$, $u_0 = 5$.

$u_0 = 5$ => $u_1 = 2 \times u_0 + 3$ =   13
    => $u_2 = 2 \times u_1 + 3$ =   29
    => $u_3 = 2 \times u_2 + 3$ =   61
    => $u_4 = 2 \times u_3 + 3$ =   125 etc.

this produces the sequence, 5, 13, 29, 61, 125, ...

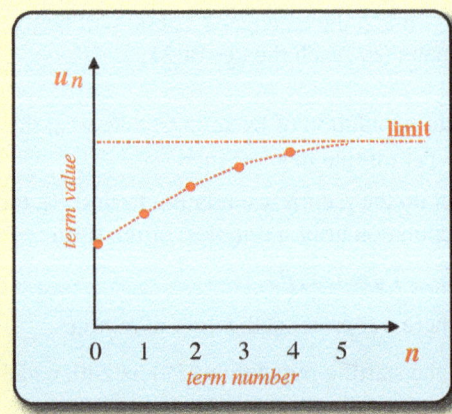

The graph of this sequence looks like this   —>

Note how, as the term number grows, the value gets bigger and bigger, quicker and quicker.

*(This is called **exponential growth**).*

=> We say the terms are **DIVERGENT** –   they do **not** appear to approach any fixed Limit.

Example 2 :-   This time, consider the linear recurrence relation $u_n = 0 \cdot 5 u_{n-1} + 3$, $u_0 = 2$.

$u_0 = 2$ => $u_1 = 0 \cdot 5 \times u_0 + 3$ =   4
    => $u_2 = 0 \cdot 5 \times u_1 + 3$ =   5
    => $u_3 = 0 \cdot 5 \times u_2 + 3$ =   5·5
    => $u_4 = 0 \cdot 5 \times u_3 + 3$ =   5·75 etc.

this produces the sequence, 2, 4, 5, 5·5, 5·75, ...

The graph of this sequence looks like this   —>

Note how as the term number grows, the value gets bigger but by a smaller and smaller amount each time.

*(We say that u_n tends towards a **LIMIT** this time).*

=> We say the terms are **CONVERGENT** – they **do** appear to **converge** to a specific Limit.

Exercise H10·4

1. For each of the following, use your calculator to find u_1, u_2, u_3 and u_4.

   State, also, if you think they appear to be approaching a **limit** or not. (i.e. are **convergent**).

   If they do, try to estimate what the limit will be.

   (a) $u_n = 1·1u_{n-1} + 2$, $\quad u_0 = 5$

   (b) $u_n = 0·7u_{n-1} + 10$, $\quad u_1 = 50$

   (c) $u_n = 1·5u_{n-1} - 3$, $\quad u_0 = 8$

   (d) $u_{n+1} = 0·55u_n + 20$, $\quad u_1 = 10$

   (e) $u_n = 1·6u_{n-1} + 12$, $\quad u_0 = 3$

   (f) $u_{n+1} = 0·2u_n + 8$, $\quad u_1 = 12$.

2. Three of the above recurrence relations converge to a limit as $n \longrightarrow \infty$. (*i.e. as n tends to infinity*).

   (a) Which three ?

   (b) Can you spot the difference between these three and the other three which might explain why this happens ?

3. Bradshaw Stores offer its customers a Credit Account and charges 3% per month on the 28th of the month on any balance outstanding.

   A customer buys a coat at the beginning of January priced £90, and pays back £10 per month on the last day of each month.

   (a) Explain, in words, why the recurrence relation representing this is :-

   $$B_n = 1·03B_{n-1} - 10, \quad B_0 = 90,$$

   where B_n is the balance due at the end of each month (n).

   (b) Use your calculator to determine in which month the customer will make their final payment to clear the balance.

   (c) How much will her £90 coat really have cost her in total ?

4. The pressure inside a boiler is 2000 Newtons, and is **rising** by 5% by the end of each hour.

   At the end of each hour a safety valve opens and reduces the pressure by 55 Newtons.

4. (a) Set up a recurrence relation indicating what the pressure (P_n), at the end of each hour will be.

   (b) **2200 Newtons** is the maximum safe pressure the boiler can withstand.

   Use your calculator to determine when the pressure in the boiler will exceed this limit.

5. 150 ml of a drug is injected into a patient just after an operation. It is known that the body rejects 30% of the drug over a 1 hour period.

   Every hour, an injection of 25 ml is given to the patient to compensate for this.

   (a) Set up a recurrence relation to show how much of the drug (D_n), is in the patient at the end of each hour period.

   (b) When will the drug drop below the 80 ml level, which is the minimum safety level needed by the patient ?

6. A hot air balloonist, at a height of 3000 feet, finds the balloon is dropping by 20% every minute.

   At the end of each minute period, the balloonist fires the burner for 10 seconds which is long enough for the balloon to rise by 50 feet.

   (a) Set up a recurrence relation which shows the height (H_n) feet, after n minutes.

   (b) When might the balloon land on the plateau of a 1600 foot tall mountain ?

7. A privet hedge grows by about 15% each year during the summer.

   The gardener prunes 40 cm off its height during the autumn to keep it healthy.

   If it was 300 cm tall on January 1st, 2000, set up a recurrence relation to show its height (H_n) at the end of each year and determine its height by the end of 2005.

8. A teenager receives a £50 birthday gift from an aunt every year, starting on their 16th.

   They always pay this into the same bank account, where the interest rate is 7·5% each year.

   Set up a recurrence relation to show its value, (V_n), each year, and calculate its value on their 21st birthday.

Finding the Limit (L) in a Linear Recurrence Relation

In the previous exercise, in Question 1, you found that the three recurrence relations given by :-

$$u_n = 0{\cdot}7u_{n-1} + 10, \qquad u_0 = 50$$

$$u_{n+1} = 0{\cdot}55u_n + 20, \quad u_1 = 10$$

$$u_{n+1} = 0{\cdot}2u_n + 8, \qquad u_1 = 12$$

They all appeared to approach a **limit** (L) as $n \longrightarrow \infty$.

> Every linear recurrence relation $u_n = au_{n-1} + b$, will tend to a limit (L) as long as **$-1 < a < 1$**.

If $a \geq 1$ (or $a \leq -1$), the recurrence relation will **NOT** approach a fixed limit.

Let us look at the recurrence relation :- $u_n = 0{\cdot}7\,u_{n-1} + 10, \; u_0 = 50$.

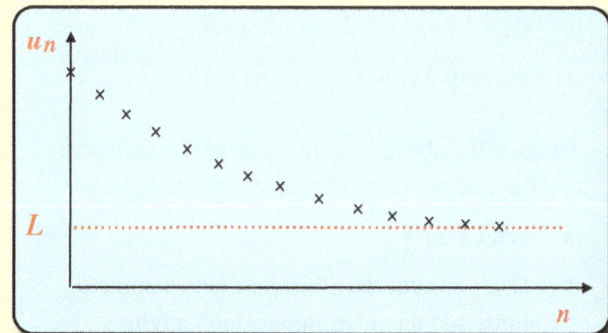

u_0	=	50	u_1 = 45	
u_2	=	41·5	u_3 = 39·05	
u_4	=	37·335	u_5 = 36·134...	
u_6	=	35·294...	u_7 = 34·70......	

There are three reasons you could offer as to why you believe that a recurrence relation is producing terms which appear to be approaching a limit, (i.e. is **convergent**).

- Though the terms are getting smaller, the actual amount they are decreasing by each time is getting smaller also and is tending to zero.

- The **graph** indicates that u_n is tending to a limit (L) as $n \longrightarrow \infty$.

- The multiplication factor $a = \mathbf{0{\cdot}7}$, (in the $u_n = 0{\cdot}7u_{n-1} + 10$), lies between -1 and 1 and this automatically produces a recurrence relation with a limit.

Finding the Limit (L) :-

Once you have established that a limit exists it is *straightforward* to find the limit (L).

Notice that if the sequence tends to a limit, L, then eventually after a while,

> $$u_n = u_{n+1} = u_{n+2} = u_{n+3} = u_{n+4} = u_{n+5} = \text{(etc.)} \Rightarrow L, \text{ as } n \text{ gets bigger.}$$

(i.e. all the terms, (*after a while*), will eventually be **the same** as each other and will have the value L).

To find L, simply :- | replace both u_n and u_{n+1} in the relation by the letter L and solve the equation.

Example :-   In the recurrence relation $u_n = 0{\cdot}7\,u_{n-1} + 10, \; u_0 = 50$, above, replace u_n and u_{n+1} by L.

> $\Rightarrow \qquad L = 0{\cdot}7L + 10$ Limit exists since $-1 < m < 1$.
>
> $\Rightarrow \qquad 1L - 0{\cdot}7L = 10 \qquad \Rightarrow \quad 0{\cdot}3L = 10$
>
> $\Rightarrow \qquad L = 10 \div 0{\cdot}3 \qquad \Rightarrow \quad \boxed{L = 33{\cdot}33..}$

this can be seen to be in agreement with the table and the graph above.

If the recurrence relation is $u_n = au_{n-1} + b$, $\Rightarrow \qquad L = aL + b$
(and if $-1 < a < 1$). $\Rightarrow \qquad L - aL = b$

$\Rightarrow \qquad L(1 - a) = b \qquad \Rightarrow \qquad \boxed{L = \dfrac{b}{1-a}}$

1. For each of these recurrence relations :-

    (i) Find the first four terms.

    (ii) Decide if u_n tends to a limit L as $n \longrightarrow \infty$.

    (iii) In the case(s) in which it does tend to a limit, find the limit L.

    (a) $u_n = 0·6u_{n-1} + 20$, $(u_0 = 60)$

    (b) $u_n = 0·88u_{n-1} + 5$, $(u_0 = 30)$

    (c) $u_n = 1·62u_{n-1} - 15$, $(u_1 = 25)$

    (d) $u_{n+1} = \frac{3}{4}u_n + 4$, $(u_0 = 20)$

    (e) $u_n = \frac{4}{3}u_{n-1} + 10$, $(u_1 = 30)$

    (f) $u_{n+1} = \frac{1}{10}u_{n-1} + 20$, $(u_1 = 50)$.

2. The Christmas tree in Dundee Square has 260 light bulbs, 15% of which fail each year.

    Dundee Council replace 30 failed bulbs each year.

    Set up a recurrence relation and use it to decide if this will guarantee that at least 65% of the bulbs will always be lit.

3. A car radiator holds 10 litres of water when full, but it leaks.

    Each month 12% of the water is lost and the owner adds 1 litre of water to top up the radiator.

    If the water level ever drops below 7 litres, the engine could be seriously damaged by overheating.

    Set up a recurrence relation and use it to check if the engine is ever in any danger.

4. At the beginning of a drought, a farmer has 10 000 pumpkins in their fields.

    The farmer estimates as follows :-

    - each month 20% of the pumpkins will be lost due to lack of water.

    - 800 new pumpkins will be planted at the end of each month.

    (a) How many pumpkins will be left after 1 month, 2 months and 3 months ?

    (b) What will the long-term position be if the drought continues indefinitely ?

5. A leak in a hot water tank means water is lost at the rate of 18% per hour.

    As a safety device, a valve opens at the end of each hour, allowing 30 litres of water to pour into the tank.

    The tank initially holds 180 litres.

    If the volume of the tank ever drops below 140 litres, the heating element will become exposed and it could be damaged.

    Will this eventually happen ?

6. A rottweiler weighs in at 76 kg and the vet decides to put it on a diet. The vet reckons that if the owner sticks to the diet the dog can shed 4% of its body-weight by the end of each month.

    However, as a special treat, at the end of each month the owner lets the dog have several treats and it puts on an average of 2·5 kg.

    The vet insists the dog has to get to 60 kg or less.

    Will the dog reach this goal at this rate ?

7. The gardens in Princes Street in Edinburgh are cleared once a week for litter, which results in 80% of the litter being removed.

    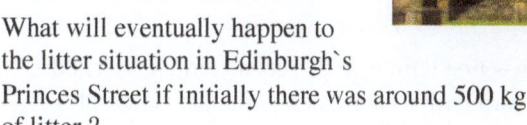

    Each week, visitors to Edinburgh are believed to drop around 100 kg of litter in Princes Street alone.

    What will eventually happen to the litter situation in Edinburgh`s Princes Street if initially there was around 500 kg of litter ?

8. The town of Drumnadobie has a population of 360.

    Every year, it is discovered that because of a lack of jobs, 15% of the population leave the town for the big city.

    To overcome this, Drumnadobie Council set about creating 40 new jobs in the town every year to encourage newcomers to join their community.

    (a) Set up a recurrence relation (P_n), to show the population at the end of each year, after the new lot of 40 jobs has been filled.

    (b) Calculate the population at the end of years 1, 2, 3, 4 and 5.

    (c) Calculate what the population of Drumnadobie will eventually become, if the pattern continues.

Determining a Recurrence Relation, given some of its Terms

Example :-

Given that 5, 13 and 29 are the first three terms of the linear recurrence relation $u_n = au_{n-1} + b$, determine the values of a and b and find the next two terms.

The information given is that $u_1 = 5$, $u_2 = 13$ and $u_3 = 29$.

We can use **simultaneous equation** techniques to find m and c.

From $u_n = au_{n-1} + b$, => $u_2 = au_1 + b$ => $13 = 5a + b$.

and => $u_3 = au_2 + b$ => $29 = 13a + b$.

we now have $\quad 5a + b = 13 \qquad$ **(1)**

and $\quad 13a + b = 29 \qquad$ **(2)**

(2) – (1) => $8a = 16 \qquad$ **(3)**

(3) ÷ 8 => $a = 2$

substitute $a = 2$ in **(1)** => $b = 3$.

=> recurrence relation is given by :- $\quad u_n = 2u_{n-1} + 3, \quad u_1 = 5$

$u_4 = au_3 + b$ => $u_4 = 2 \times 29 + 3 \quad = \quad$ 61

$u_5 = au_4 + b$ => $u_5 = 2 \times 61 + 3 \quad = \quad$ 125

Exercise H10·6

1. Given that the linear recurrence relation :-

    $$u_n = au_{n-1} + b$$

    has first term $u_1 = 2$, second term $u_2 = 4$ and third term $u_3 = 10$, determine the values of a and b and find the next two terms.

2. Given that the linear recurrence relation :-

    $$u_{n+1} = au_n + b$$

    has $u_3 = 28$, $u_4 = 30$ and $u_5 = 31$, determine the values of a and b and hence find the first two terms.

3. The linear recurrence relation, $u_n = au_{n-1} + b$ has $u_1 = 80$, $u_2 = 70$ and $u_3 = 62$.

    Determine the values of a and b and find the limit L to which the sequence of terms tends.

4. The linear recurrence relation, $u_n = au_{n-1} + b$ has $u_1 = 200$, $u_2 = 100$ and $u_3 = 90$.

    Determine the values of a and b and find the limit L to which the sequence of terms tends.

5. The linear recurrence relation, $u_{n+1} = au_n + b$ has $u_1 = 2$, $u_2 = 0$ and $u_3 = 4$.
    Determine the values of a and b and find the next four terms in the sequence.

6. The linear recurrence relation, $u_n = au_{n-1} + b$ has $u_0 = 3$, $u_1 = 12$ and $u_2 = 48$.

    (a) Determine the next two terms of the sequence.

    (b) Find an **explicit** formula for u_n and use it, along with a calculator to find u_{10}.

7. The linear recurrence relation, $u_{n+1} = 0·4u_n + b$ has limit $L = 20$. Determine the value of b.

8. The linear recurrence relation, $u_n = \frac{3}{5}u_{n-1} + b$ has limit $L = 30$. Determine the value of b.

9. The linear recurrence relation, $u_n = au_{n-1} + 14$ has limit $L = 20$. Determine the value of a.

10. The linear recurrence relation, $u_{n+1} = au_n + 10$ has limit $L = 25$. Determine the value of a.

Exam Practice Exercise (H10)

1. A sequence is generated by the recurrence relation
$$u_n = au_{n-1} + 4, \text{ where } a \text{ is a constant.}$$

   (a) Given that $u_1 = 18$ and $u_2 = 10$, find a. **(2)**

   (b) (i) Explain carefully why the sequence approaches a limit as $n \to \infty$. **(1)**

      (ii) Calculate this limit. **(2)**

2. A sequence is generated by the recurrence relation
$$u_n = pu_{n-1} - 8, \ u_0 = 4, \text{ where } p \text{ a real number.}$$

   (a) Show that $u_2 = 4p^2 - 8p - 8$. **(2)**

   (b) Determine the range of values for p for which $u_2 \geq u_0$. **(4)**

3. A sequence is defined by the recurrence relation
$$u_n = (a+1)u_{n-1} + 2.$$

   (a) Write down the condition on a for this sequence to have a limit. **(2)**

   (b) If the sequence tends to a limit of 10, as $n \to \infty$, determine the value of a. **(3)**

4. A sequence is defined by the recurrence relation
$$u_n = -\tfrac{1}{2}u_{n-1} - 8, \ u_4 = 16.$$

   (a) Find the value of u_5. **(1)**

   (b) Explain carefully why the sequence approaches a limit as $n \to \infty$. **(1)**

   (c) Calculate what this limit is. **(2)**

5. Two recurrence relations are defined by
$$u_n = \tfrac{2}{3}u_{n-1} + 8, \ u_0 = 150, \text{ and}$$
$$v_n = \tfrac{3}{4}v_{n-1} + 6, \ v_0 = -20.$$

   (a) Explain carefully why each sequence approaches a limit as $n \to \infty$. **(2)**

   (b) Prove that $\underset{n \to \infty}{Limit}(v_n - u_n) = 0$. **(3)**

6. A sequence is defined by the recurrence relation
$$u_{n+1} = (2a-5)u_n + 1, \ u_1 = 4.$$

   For what values of a does the sequence have a limit as $n \to \infty$? **(2)**

7. A sequence is generated by the recurrence relation
$$u_n = (sin^2 x)u_{n-1} + cos^2 x, \text{ with } u_0 = 1.$$

   (a) Explain why, as long as $0 < x < \pi/2$, the sequences formed always tend to a limit as $n \to \infty$. **(2)**

   (b) Prove that the limit is always 1. **(4)**

8. A linear recurrence relation, of the form
$$u_n = Au_{n-1} + B, \text{ with } u_1 = 8,$$
   generates the sequence $8, 16, 28, 46, \ldots$.
   A second sequence is defined by
$$u_n = -\tfrac{2}{3}u_{n-1} + 5, \text{ with } u_1 = 10.$$

   (a) Determine the values of A and B. **(3)**

   (b) One of these two sequences has a limit.

      (i) Calculate this limit.

      (ii) Explain clearly why the other sequence does not go towards a limit as $n \to \infty$. **(3)**

9. A sequence is generated by the recurrence relation
$$u_n = mu_{n-1} + (1 - m^2), \text{ with } u_0 = 1.$$

   (a) State the range of values for m if the sequence tends to a limit as $n \to \infty$. **(1)**

   (b) If m is restricted to this range of values, find the value of the limit in terms of m and show that the limit always lies between 0 and 2. **(4)**

10. Sequence A is defined by $u_{n+1} = pu_n + 6$, with $u_0 = 1$.

   Sequence B is defined by $v_{n+1} = qv_n - 6$, with $v_0 = 1$.

   It is stated that sequence A has a limit of 18 and sequence B has a limit of 12 as $n \to \infty$.

   (a) Determine the values of p and q. **(4)**

   (b) Explain why part of the statement, regarding the limits produced by sequences A and B, must be wrong. **(2)**

Introduction to Integration

The mathematics that we shall develop in this chapter was known to the famous Greek mathematician Archimedes of Syracuse, (287 - 212 BC) though it was not until the 17th century that it was thoroughly explored by Newton and Leibniz.

Calculus can be split into two basic parts. In an earlier chapter it was seen that the part which deals with rate of change requires the notion of a limit, and this was developed with the notation and ideas of differentiation.

In this chapter, we introduce the other part of Calculus called Integration, which initially can be thought of as anti-differentiation, the reverse (or inverse) process to differentiation.

- The derivative of $f(x) = x^4$ is $f'(x) = 4x^3$ so the **anti-derivative** of $f'(x) = 4x^3$ is $f(x) = x^4$.
- The derivative of $f(x) = x^{-5}$ is $f'(x) = -5x^{-6}$ so the **anti-derivative** of $f'(x) = -5x^{-6}$ is $f(x) = x^{-5}$.
- The derivative of $f(x) = x^{\frac{1}{2}}$ is $f'(x) = \frac{1}{2}x^{\frac{1}{2}}$ so the **anti-derivative** of $f'(x) = \frac{1}{2}x^{\frac{1}{2}}$ is $f(x) = x^{\frac{1}{2}}$.

Note that the derivative of $f(x) = x^3$, $f(x) = x^3 + 1$, $f(x) = x^3 - 102$ etc. is $f'(x) = 3x^2$.

This is because, any constant, added to the variable, when differentiated becomes zero.

Therefore, the anti-derivative of $3x^2$ has to take into account the fact that there could have been a constant present.

$$\text{If } f'(x) = nx^{n-1} \implies f(x) = x^n + C.$$

This technique of "working back" from differentiation is called **integration**.

We have a new symbol to represent the process, called the "**integral**" symbol -   *This is referred to as the "integration" symbol*

The Integral is written $\int x^n dx$, and it reads as the **Integral of x^n with respect to x.**

The 3 basic rules for integrating expressions are :-

$$\int x^n dx = \frac{x^{n+1}}{n+1} + C \quad \text{\small\color{orange}Add 1 to the power, then divide by the new power.}$$

$$\int ax^n dx = a\int x^n dx = \frac{ax^{n+1}}{n+1} + C$$

$$\int (f(x) + g(x))dx = \int f(x)dx + \int g(x)dx.$$

Example 1 :-

Find $\int x^5 dx$.

$$\int x^5 dx$$
$$= \frac{x^{5+1}}{5+1} + C$$
$$= \tfrac{1}{6}x^6 + C$$

Example 2 :-

Find $\int t^{-3} dt$.

$$\int t^{-3} dt$$
$$= \frac{t^{-3+1}}{-3+1} + C$$
$$= \frac{-1}{2t^2} + C$$

Example 3 :-

Find $\int 9x^3 dx$.

$$\int 9x^3 dx.$$
$$= 9\int x^3 dx$$
$$= 9\frac{x^{3+1}}{3+1} + C$$
$$= \tfrac{9}{4}x^4 + C$$

Example 4 :-

Find $\int 4t^{-\frac{3}{2}} dt$.

$$\int 4t^{-\frac{3}{2}} dt$$
$$= 4\int t^{-\frac{3}{2}} dt$$
$$= 4\frac{t^{-\frac{1}{2}}}{-\frac{1}{2}} + C$$
$$= -8t^{-\frac{1}{2}} + C$$

Example 5 :-

Find $\int 7 - 10v\, dv$.

$$\int 7 - 10v\, dv$$
$$= 7v - \frac{10v^2}{2} + C$$
$$= 7v - 5v^2 + C$$

Example 6 :-

Find $\int \sqrt{x} + \frac{1}{\sqrt{x}} dx$.

$$\int \sqrt{x} + \frac{1}{\sqrt{x}} dx$$
$$= \int x^{\frac{1}{2}} + x^{-\frac{1}{2}} dx$$
$$= \frac{x^{\frac{3}{2}}}{\frac{3}{2}} + \frac{x^{\frac{1}{2}}}{\frac{1}{2}} + C$$
$$= \tfrac{2}{3}x^{\frac{3}{2}} + 2x^{\frac{1}{2}} + C$$

As with differentiation, all terms must be in the form ax^n.

Exercise H11·1

1. Integrate the following with respect to x :-

   (a) x (b) x^2 (c) x^3

   (d) x^6 (e) x^{10} (f) $4x$

   (g) $5x^2$ (h) $7x^3$ (i) $-8x^2$

   (j) 12 (or $12x^0$)   (k) x^{-2} (l) x^{-4}

   (m) x^{-7} (n) $\dfrac{1}{x^4}$ (o) $\dfrac{-8}{x^3}$

   (p) $x^{\frac{1}{2}}$ (q) $x^{\frac{5}{2}}$ (r) $x^{-\frac{1}{2}}$

   (s) $x^{-\frac{7}{2}}$ (t) $\dfrac{4}{\sqrt{x}}$ (u) $\dfrac{1}{\sqrt[3]{x}}$.

2. Find the following integrals :-

   (a) $\int x^5\,dx$ (b) $\int (3x-2)\,dx$

   (c) $\int (5-x)\,dx$ (d) $\int (x^2-2)\,dx$

   (e) $\int (2-5x^3)\,dx$ (f) $\int (2x^2+5x-4)\,dx$

   (g) $\int (8x^2-7)\,dx$ (h) $\int (15x^4-3x^2)\,dx$

   (i) $\int (x-3)(x+3)\,dx$ (j) $\int (x-4)^2\,dx$

   (k) $\int (1-6x)^2\,dx$ (l) $\int x(x+2)(x-1)\,dx$.

3. Rearrange the following and integrate, giving answers with positive indices :-

   (a) $\int \dfrac{dx}{x^2}$ (b) $\int \dfrac{3}{x^8}\,dx$

   (c) $\int \sqrt[4]{x}\,dx$ (d) $\int 2\sqrt[3]{x^2}\,dx$

   (e) $\int \dfrac{-5}{\sqrt[3]{x^5}}\,dx$ (f) $\int 2x\left(3x+\dfrac{1}{x}\right)dx$

   (g) $\int x^{-1}(4x-x^2)\,dx$ (h) $\int \left(x-\dfrac{2}{x}\right)^2 dx$

   (i) $\int \dfrac{x^3-x}{x}\,dx$ (j) $\int \dfrac{5-x^4}{x^3}\,dx$

   (k) $\int \dfrac{(1+x^2)}{x^2}\,dx$ (l) $\int \dfrac{x^6-1}{x^2}\,dx$

   (m) $\int \left(3x-\dfrac{1}{x^3}\right)^2 dx$ (n) $\int x^{\frac{1}{2}}(8x^{\frac{1}{2}}-2)\,dx$

3. (o) $\int \dfrac{1}{\sqrt{x}}(\sqrt{x}-1)^2\,dx$ (p) $\int \left(4x+\dfrac{6}{x^3}\right)^2 dx$

   (q) $\int \dfrac{x(7x-5)}{\sqrt{x}}\,dx$ (r) $\int x\left(\sqrt{x}-\dfrac{1}{\sqrt{x}}\right)^2 dx$

Example 7 :-

Given that $f'(x) = 2x + 3$ and $f(3) = 20$, find the function $f(x)$.

$$f'(x) = 2x + 3$$
$$\Rightarrow f(x) = \int (2x+3)\,dx$$
$$= \dfrac{2x^2}{2} + 3x + C = x^2 + 3x + C$$

but since $f(3) = 20$

$$\Rightarrow f(3) = 9 + 9 + C = 18 + C = 20$$
$$\Rightarrow C = 2.$$

Hence $f(x) = x^2 + 3x + 2$.

---

4. Find $f(x)$ in each case, given that :-

   (a) $f'(x) = 6x$ and $f(1) = 7$

   (b) $f'(x) = 4x - 2$ and $f(3) = 10$

   (c) $f'(x) = 1 - 10x$ and $f(2) = 21$

   (d) $f'(x) = 9x^2$ and $f(1) = 7$

   (e) $f'(x) = 20x^4$ and $f(-1) = 5$

   (f) $f'(x) = x - \dfrac{2}{x^2}$ and $f(2) = 4$

   (g) $f'(x) = \dfrac{1}{\sqrt{x}} + 1$ and $f(16) = 20$

   (h) $f'(x) = 6(x^2 - 1)$ and $f(1) = -4$

   (i) $f'(x) = 3\left(x^2 - \dfrac{1}{x^2}\right)$ and $f(2) = 10$

   (j) $f'(x) = 1 - \sqrt[4]{x}$ and $f(1) = \frac{1}{5}$.

5. Find :-

   (a) $\int \dfrac{t^5 + 3t^2}{t}\,dt$ (b) $\int (4 + v\sqrt{v})^2\,dv$

   (c) $\int s^{\frac{1}{3}}(2s^{\frac{1}{2}} + s)\,ds$ (d) $\int \dfrac{h - 6h^2}{\sqrt{h}}\,dh$

   (e) $\int \dfrac{2 + \sqrt{z}}{z^2}\,dz$ (f) $\int \dfrac{3 + 15p}{p\sqrt{p}}\,dp$

Applications of Integration

For the curve $y = f(x)$, we used differentiation to determine the gradient of the tangent at any point on the curve.

Example :- If $f'(x) = x$ provides a formula for the gradient, then working backwards would allow us to find $f(x)$.

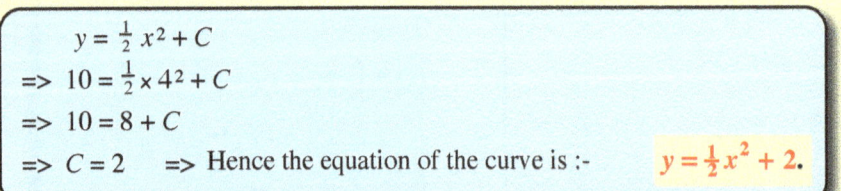

$$\frac{dy}{dx} = x \Rightarrow y = \int x\,dx \Rightarrow y = \tfrac{1}{2}x^2 + C.$$

C is called the constant of integration

Unfortunately, this gives rise to the equation of numerous parabolas, (some of which are shown in the sketch), but there is insufficient information to define the function **exactly**.

However, if, in addition, we are told that the parabola was to pass through the point, say (4, 10), then we could define the function exactly by substitution :-

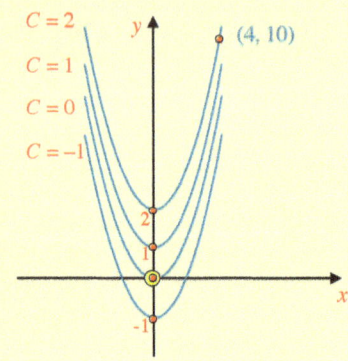

$$y = \tfrac{1}{2}x^2 + C$$
$$\Rightarrow 10 = \tfrac{1}{2} \times 4^2 + C$$
$$\Rightarrow 10 = 8 + C$$
$$\Rightarrow C = 2 \quad \Rightarrow \text{Hence the equation of the curve is :-} \quad y = \tfrac{1}{2}x^2 + 2.$$

Exercise H11·2

1. Find the equations of the curves which satisfy the following conditions at each point (x, y) :-

   (a) $\dfrac{dy}{dx} = 3x$, and the curve passes through the point (2, 7).

   (b) $\dfrac{dy}{dx} = 6x$, and the curve passes through the point (2, 16).

   (c) $\dfrac{dy}{dx} = 4x - 3$, and the curve passes through the point (1, 4).

   (d) $\dfrac{dy}{dx} = 3x^2 - 6x$, and the curve passes through the point (-1, 2).

   (e) $\dfrac{dy}{dx} = 9x^2 - 8x - 3$, and the curve passes through the point (2, 10).

   (f) $\dfrac{dy}{dx} = 3x(2x - 1)$, and the curve passes through the point (1, 1).

2. For a given function $y = f(x)$, $f'(x) = 6x^2 - 8x$, and $f(x) = 7$ when $x = -1$. Find $f(x)$ when $x = 2$.

3. The function $y = f(x)$ with $f'(x) = 12x^2 - 12x + 3$ passes through the point (1, 4).

   Show that it also passes through the point (-1, -10).

4. The curve with derivative $\dfrac{dy}{dx} = 8 - 2x$ has a maximum turning value of 0.

   Find the equation of the curve.

5. The gradient of the tangent to the curve at each point (x, y) is given by $\dfrac{dy}{dx} = 6x - 3x^2$.
   If this curve passes through the point (-2, 9), find its equation.

6. A function is such that its derivative is $\dfrac{dy}{dx} = 1 - \dfrac{5}{x^2}$.
   The curve passes through the point (5, 4).

   Find its equation.

7. The velocity-time graph of a body moving with velocity v at time t is a line with equation $v = 7 - 2t$.
   Given that $v = \dfrac{ds}{dt}$ and $s = 0$ when $t = 0$, this means that the displacement s at time t is $s = \int 7 - 2t\,dt$.
   Find a formula for the displacement s in terms of t.

8. The velocity v m/sec. of a body starting from rest is given by $v = \int (t^2 + 3t)\,dt$, where t seconds is the time from rest.

   Find a formula for v in terms of t, and use it to find the velocity of the body after 6 seconds.

9. The gradient of the tangent to a curve at each point (x, y) is given by $\dfrac{dy}{dx} = 3x^2 - 8x + 5$.
   If the curve passes through the point (3, 4) show that it also passes through (-1, -12).

10. The gradient of the tangent to a curve at each point (x, y) is given by $\dfrac{dy}{dx} = 1 - 4x$.

    If the maximum value of y is $8^1/_8$ find the equation of the curve.

Using Integration to find Areas

We've seen that Integration can be thought of as the reverse of Differentiation, but in fact, Integration, as we will see in the next part of this chapter, is a tremendous tool that enables us to calculate the area below, or between the curves of more complicated functions.

If we wish to find the (blue) area under the curve $y = f(x)$, between $x = a$ and $x = b$, up until now, we have had no way of doing that.

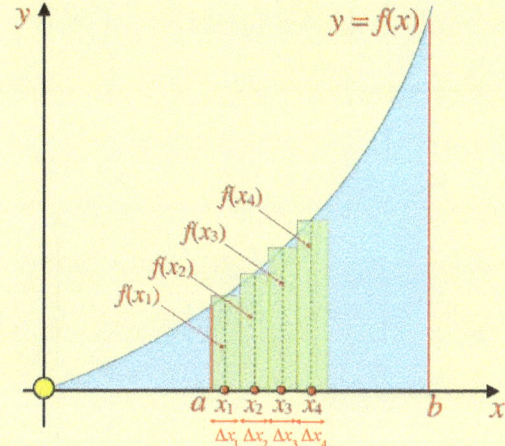

Let us study how, using integration, we CAN find the area.

We begin by estimating the area by creating small (green) rectangles as shown on the diagram opposite.

We will make each rectangle Δx wide and for each value of x, namely x_1, x_2, x_3, etc, the corresponding height of each rectangle will be $f(x_1)$, $f(x_2)$, $f(x_3)$ etc.

(Δx just means a "smallish" value for x).

The total green (approximate) area can be found from adding all the green rectangles.

(Approximate) Area = $f(x_1) \times \Delta x_1 + f(x_2) \times \Delta x_2 + f(x_3) \times \Delta x_3 + f(x_4) \times \Delta x_4 + \ldots\ldots + f(x_n) \times \Delta x_n$.

> This can be shortened, using mathematical language to (Approximate) **Area** $= \sum_{i=1}^{i=n} f(x_i) \times \Delta x_i$, where the Greek symbol $\sum$ (sigma) means the "sum of all the $f(x_i) \times \Delta x_i$ terms".

Just as we did in Differential Calculus, we can make our approximate area get closer and closer to the actual area, by making the rectangles become "thinner" and "thinner". To do this we take the "limit as each $\Delta x \longrightarrow 0$".

Can you see now that as Δx gets very very close to 0, we end up with the actual area under the curve ?

We finally end up with a formula for finding the exact area :- $\boxed{\textbf{AREA} = \int_{x=a}^{x=b} f(x)\,dx.}$

This reads as :- "The area under the curve $y = f(x)$ between $x = a$ and $x = b$ is the integral of $f(x)\,dx$ from a to b".

Example :- Find the area, under the curve $f(x) = x^2 + 1$, from $x = 1$ to $x = 3$.

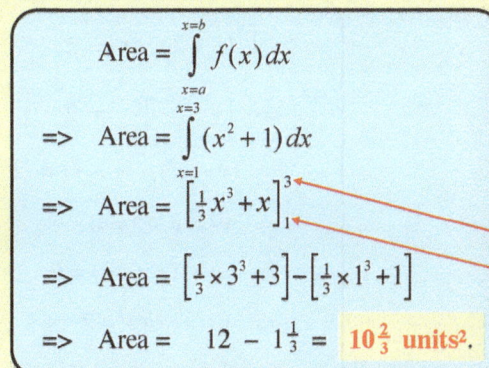

$$\text{Area} = \int_{x=a}^{x=b} f(x)\,dx$$

$$\Rightarrow \quad \text{Area} = \int_{x=1}^{x=3} (x^2 + 1)\,dx$$

$$\Rightarrow \quad \text{Area} = \left[\tfrac{1}{3}x^3 + x\right]_1^3$$

$$\Rightarrow \quad \text{Area} = \left[\tfrac{1}{3} \times 3^3 + 3\right] - \left[\tfrac{1}{3} \times 1^3 + 1\right]$$

$$\Rightarrow \quad \text{Area} = \quad 12 - 1\tfrac{1}{3} = \boxed{10\tfrac{2}{3} \text{ units}^2.}$$

> The rule here is to :-
> - replace the x with the upper limit (the 3).
> - replace the x with the lower limit (the 1).
> - Subtract the 2nd value from the 1st value.

Notice that here, the C disappears.

Exercise H11·3

1. Write each shaded area as an integral :-

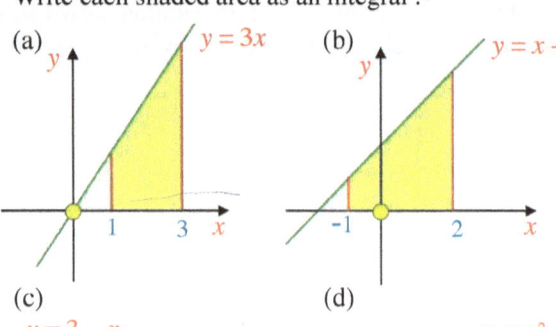

(a) $y = 3x$

(b) $y = x + 2$

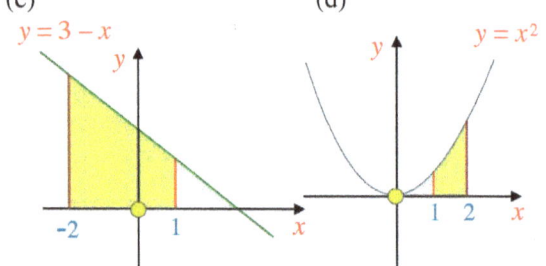

(c) $y = 3 - x$

(d) $y = x^2$

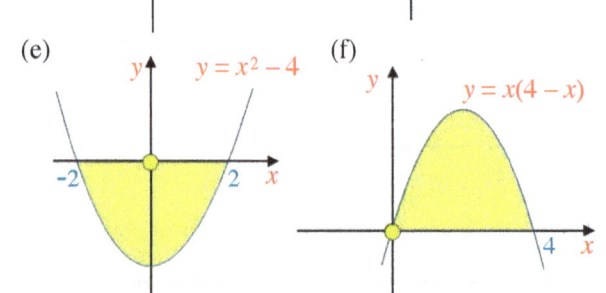

(e) $y = x^2 - 4$

(f) $y = x(4 - x)$

1. (g) $y = 3x^2$ (h) $y = x^3$

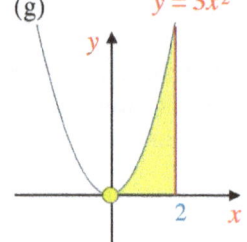 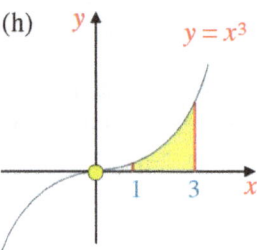

(i) $y = \sin 2x$ (j) $y = 12/x^2$

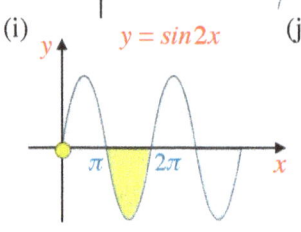 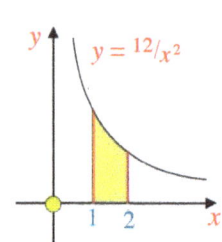

2. Sketch the area represented by the following definite integrals :-

(a) $\int_0^3 x\,dx$

(b) $\int_1^4 (x + 4)\,dx$

(c) $\int_1^6 (2x + 1)\,dx$

(d) $\int_0^2 x^2\,dx$

(e) $\int_{-1}^2 x^2 - 1\,dx$

(f) $\int_1^5 x^3\,dx$

(g) $\int_0^{\frac{\pi}{2}} \sin x\,dx$

(h) $\int_{\frac{\pi}{2}}^{\pi} \cos x\,dx$.

Definite Integrals

We saw on page 99 how to integrate a function $f(x)$ between a set of limits to find the area under the curve.

This technique is referred to as finding the **Definite Integral** of a function. Unlike basic integration that provides us with a set of functions, (remember the constant C ?), this process produces a **definite** answer.

For Definite Integrals :-   If $F(x)$ is the **anti-derivative** of $f(x)$, then ... $\int_a^b f(x)\,dx = F(a) - F(b)$ $(a \le x \le b)$

Example 1 :-

Evaluate the definite integral $\int_1^4 (x^2 + 4x)\,dx$.

$$\int_1^4 (x^2 + 4x)\,dx$$

$$= \left[\frac{x^3}{3} + 2x^2\right]_1^4$$

$$= \left(\frac{4^3}{3} + 32\right) - \left(\frac{1^3}{3} + 2\right)$$

$$= 53\tfrac{1}{3} - 2\tfrac{1}{3}$$

$$= \boxed{51}$$

Example 2 :-   Find the positive value of v for which $\int_1^v (1 - 2x)\,dx = -2$.

$$\int_1^v (1 - 2x)\,dx = -2$$

$$\Rightarrow \left[x - x^2\right]_1^v = -2$$

$$\Rightarrow (v - v^2) - (1 - 1) = -2$$

$$\Rightarrow v^2 - v - 2 = 0$$

$$\Rightarrow (v + 1)(v - 2) = 0$$

$$\Rightarrow v = -1 \text{ or } v = 2$$

Positive value $v = 2$

Exercise H11·4

1. **Copy** and **complete** :-

$$\int_0^1 6x\,dx$$

$$= \left[3x^2\right]_0^1$$

$$= \left(3 \times \ldots^2\right) - \left(3 \times \ldots^2\right)$$

$$= \ldots$$

2. **Copy** and **complete** :-

$$\int_1^4 (x^2 + 4x)\,dx$$

$$= \left[\tfrac{1}{3}x^3 + 2x^2\right]_1^4$$

$$= \left(\tfrac{1}{3}4^3 + 2 \times 4^2\right) - \left(\tfrac{1}{3}\ldots\ldots\right)$$

$$= \ldots - \ldots$$

$$= \ldots$$

3. Evaluate each definite integral :-

(a) $\displaystyle\int_0^4 (5 - x)\,dx$ (b) $\displaystyle\int_{-1}^1 x^6\,dx$

(c) $\displaystyle\int_0^1 (4x + 5)\,dx$ (d) $\displaystyle\int_1^2 x^3\,dx$

(e) $\displaystyle\int_1^2 (9x^2 + 2)\,dx$ (f) $\displaystyle\int_1^4 \frac{dx}{x^2}$

(g) $\displaystyle\int_2^5 (x^2 + 2x)\,dx$ (h) $\displaystyle\int_1^3 x^{-3}\,dx$

(i) $\displaystyle\int_0^4 x^{\frac{1}{2}}\,dx$ (j) $\displaystyle\int_1^2 4x^{-2} - x^{-4}\,dx$

(k) $\displaystyle\int_1^2 x^{-5}\,dx$ (l) $\displaystyle\int_1^8 3\sqrt[3]{x}\,dx$

(m) $\displaystyle\int_1^3 \frac{6}{x^2}\,dx$ (n) $\displaystyle\int_0^2 (6x^2 + 2x - 1)\,dx$

(o) $\displaystyle\int_0^1 \frac{8}{\sqrt[4]{x}}\,dx$ (p) $\displaystyle\int_1^2 \left(x^2 - \frac{1}{x^2}\right)dx$

(q) $\displaystyle\int_{-1}^1 \left(x - \frac{4}{x^2}\right)dx$ (r) $\displaystyle\int_1^2 \left(8x^2 - \frac{6}{x^2}\right)dx$

(s) $\displaystyle\int_1^{100} \left(\frac{x^2 - \sqrt{x}}{x}\right)dx$ (t) $\displaystyle\int_1^4 \left(\frac{\sqrt{x} + 1}{x^2}\right)dx$

(u) $\displaystyle\int_0^p x(x^2 - 1)\,dx$ (v) $\displaystyle\int_0^a (\sqrt{x} + 1)^2\,dx.$

4. Find :-

(a) $\displaystyle\int_{-4}^{-1} u^{-2}\,du$ (b) $\displaystyle\int_{-2}^{-1} p^{-6}\,dp$

(c) $\displaystyle\int_0^1 (t^3 - 1)\,dt$ (d) $\displaystyle\int_{-4}^{-1} w\,dw$

(e) $\displaystyle\int_1^4 (3z^{\frac{1}{2}} - 5z^{-2})\,dz$ (f) $\displaystyle\int_1^{25} (1 - 2s^{-\frac{1}{2}})\,ds$

(g) $\displaystyle\int_{-4}^1 \left(\frac{1 - h^3}{h^2}\right)dh$ (h) $\displaystyle\int_0^2 (2t - 3)(1 + 2t)\,dt$

(i) $\displaystyle\int_0^1 (\sqrt{p} - 1)^2\,dp$ (j) $\displaystyle\int_1^{25} \left(\frac{\theta^2 - \sqrt{\theta}}{\theta}\right)d\theta$

(k) $\displaystyle\int_0^{\frac{2\pi}{3}} w\,dw$ (l) $\displaystyle\int_{-\frac{\pi}{2}}^{\pi} 1\,d\theta.$

5. Find the positive value of a, given that:-

(a) $\displaystyle\int_0^a x^3\,dx = 4$ (b) $\displaystyle\int_0^a x^2\,dx = 9$

(c) $\displaystyle\int_1^a (6x - 4)\,dx = 5$ (d) $\displaystyle\int_0^a 4x^{-\frac{1}{3}}\,dx = 24$

(e) $\displaystyle\int_a^{2a} (1 - 2x)\,dx = -24$ (f) $\displaystyle\int_{-a}^{2a} (4x - 2)\,dx = 12.$

6. Find z in each case given that :-

(a) $\displaystyle\int_0^z 2x^{\frac{1}{2}}\,dx = 36$ (b) $\displaystyle\int_0^{3z} x(1 - x)\,dx = 0$

(c) $\displaystyle\int_{-1}^z \frac{dx}{x^2} = \frac{4}{3}$ (d) $\displaystyle\int_{-1}^z (2x - 1)\,dx = 10$

(e) $\displaystyle\int_0^z (4x^3 - 6x^2 + 2x)\,dx = 0$

(f) $\displaystyle\int_1^z \left(\frac{2x^3 - 1}{x^2}\right)dx = 2\tfrac{1}{2}.$

7. Verify each of these :-

(a) $\displaystyle\int_3^5 (5x + 2)\,dx = \int_3^5 5x\,dx + \int_3^5 2\,dx$

(b) $\displaystyle\int_0^2 \pi x^2\,dx = \int_0^1 \pi x^2\,dx + \int_1^2 \pi x^2\,dx$

(c) $\displaystyle\int_0^4 (4x^2 - 1)\,dx = -\int_4^0 (4x^2 - 1)\,dx.$

Areas Above and Below the x-axis

The diagram shows the graph of the function defined by $y = x(x-2)(x-4)$.
A_1 and A_2 represent the areas cut off above and below the x-axis.

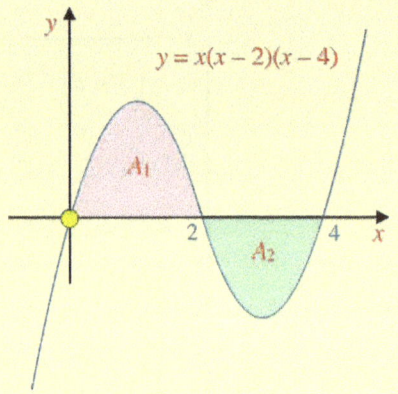

$$A_1 = \int_0^2 x(x-2)(x-4)\,dx \qquad A_2 = \int_2^4 x(x-2)(x-4)\,dx$$

$$= \int_0^2 x^3 - 6x^2 + 8x\,dx \qquad = \int_2^4 x^3 - 6x^2 + 8x\,dx$$

$$= \left[\tfrac{1}{4}x^4 - 2x^3 + 4x^2\right]_0^2 \qquad = \left[\tfrac{1}{4}x^4 - 2x^3 + 4x^2\right]_2^4$$

$$= \boxed{4} \qquad\qquad = \boxed{-4}$$

Any region formed between the x-axis and a part of the graph below the x-axis will be **negative**, as seen here.

Thus $\int_2^4 x(x-2)(x-4)\,dx$ represents the **magnitude** of A_2, but with a negative sign.

> The area between the curve and the x-axis (above the axis) is 4 units².
>
> The area between the curve and the x-axis (below the axis) is 4 units².
>
> The total area bounded by the x-axis is **8 units²**.

When integration is used to calculate area :-

- *Areas **above** the x-axis are positive*.
- *Areas **below** the x-axis are negative*.

When calculating the area between a curve and the x-axis :-

- **Make a sketch**
- **Calculate the area above and below the x-axis separately**
- **Ignore any negative sign and add.**

Example 1 :-

Calculate the total shaded area.

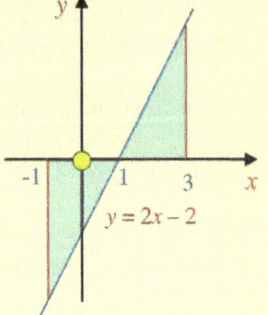

Example 2 :-

Calculate the total shaded area.

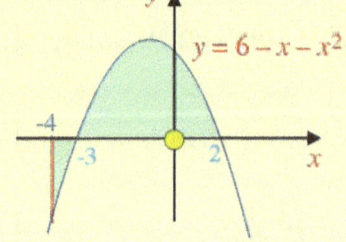

> The graph of $y = 6 - x - x^2$ cuts the x-axis when $y = 6 - x - x^2 = 0$. i.e. $x = -3$ or $x = 2$. (*factorise*)

Area below x axis $= \int_{-1}^{1} (2x - 2)\,dx$

$$= \left[x^2 - 2x\right]_{-1}^{1}$$

$$= (1 - 2) - (1 + 2)$$

$$= \boxed{-4}$$

Area above x axis $= \int_{1}^{3} (2x - 2)\,dx$

$$= \left[x^2 - 2x\right]_{1}^{3}$$

$$= (9 - 6) - (1 - 2)$$

$$= \boxed{4}$$

Total Area $= 4 + 4 = $ **8 units²**

Area below x axis $= \int_{-4}^{-3} (6 - x - x^2)\,dx$

$$= \left[6x - \tfrac{1}{2}x^2 - \tfrac{1}{3}x^3\right]_{-4}^{-3}$$

$$= (-13\tfrac{1}{2}) - (-10\tfrac{2}{3})$$

$$= \boxed{-2\tfrac{5}{6}}$$

Area above x axis $= \int_{-3}^{2} (6 - x - x^2)\,dx$

$$= \left[6x - \tfrac{1}{2}x^2 - \tfrac{1}{3}x^3\right]_{-3}^{2}$$

$$= (7\tfrac{1}{3}) - (-13\tfrac{1}{2})$$

$$= \boxed{20\tfrac{5}{6}}$$

Total Area $= $ **$23\tfrac{2}{3}$ units²**

Exercise H11·5

1. Calculate the shaded areas shown below by integration, and check each answer by using an appropriate geometrical formula :-

(a)
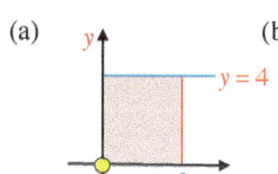

(b)
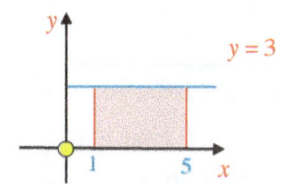

(c)
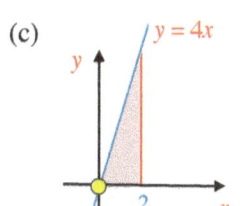

(d)
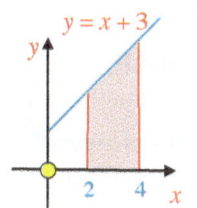

2. Use integration to calculate each shaded area :-

(a)
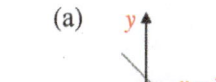

(b)
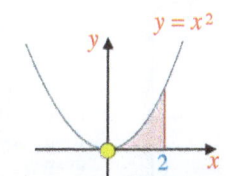

(c)
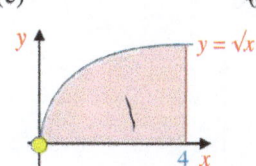

(d)
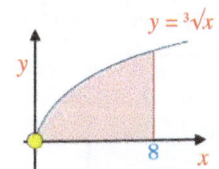

(e)

(f)
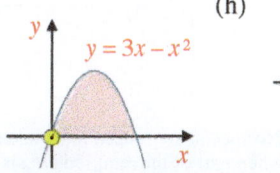

(g)
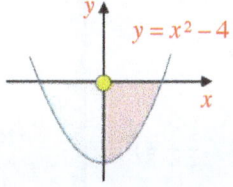

(h)

3. Calculate the area bounded by each of these curves and the x-axis :-

(a) $y = 4 - x^2$ (b) $y = x^2 - 5x$ (c) $y = x^2(2 - x)$.

4. Sketch the curve $y = (x - 3)^2$, and calculate the area enclosed by the curve, the x-axis and the y-axis.

5. The rectangle formed by the coordinate axes and the lines $x = 2$ and $y = 7$ is divided in two parts by the parabola $y = x^2$.

Calculate the area of each part.

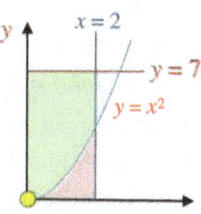

6. Find the points of intersection of the curve $y = x^3 - 9x$ with the x-axis and calculate the area enclosed by the curve and the x-axis.

7. Repeat Question 6 for the curve $y = x(4 - x^2)$.

8. In the sketch shown, the curve $y = x^2 - 5x + 4$ cuts the x-axis at P and Q and the y-axis at R.

Find the coordinates of P, Q and R, and calculate the total shaded area.

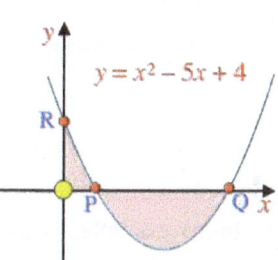

9. The parabola $y = (x - 1)(7 - x)$ cuts the x-axis at A and B and the y-axis at C.

Find the coordinates of A, B and C, and calculate the total area enclosed by the parabola and both axes.

10. Calculate the total shaded area in the sketch below.

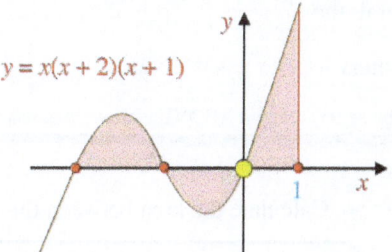

$y = x(x + 2)(x + 1)$

11. A parabola has an equation $y = (x + 3)(x - 2)$.

Prove that the area bounded by the x-axis and this parabola is divided by the y-axis into two parts in the ratio 81 : 44.

12. (a) Shown is the curve $y = \dfrac{1}{x^2}$.

Calculate the area enclosed by the curve and the x-axis from $x = -4$ and $x = -1$.

(b) Find the real number z such that the line $x = z$ splits this area in half.

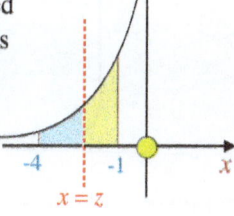

The Area Between Two Curves

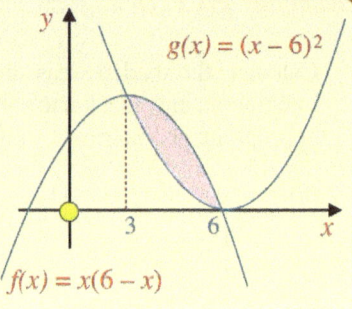

The diagram highlights the area between the curve $f(x) = x(6 - x)$ and the curve $g(x) = (x - 6)^2$.

(*It is useful if you are able to sketch these curves*).

To find the points of intersection and hence the interval of integration, set $f(x) = g(x)$, and solve.

In this case put $(x - 6)^2 = x(6 - x)$ and solve.

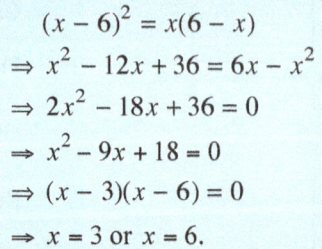

$$(x - 6)^2 = x(6 - x)$$
$$\Rightarrow x^2 - 12x + 36 = 6x - x^2$$
$$\Rightarrow 2x^2 - 18x + 36 = 0$$
$$\Rightarrow x^2 - 9x + 18 = 0$$
$$\Rightarrow (x - 3)(x - 6) = 0$$
$$\Rightarrow x = 3 \text{ or } x = 6.$$

These are the limits of integration

(which you should now insert into your sketch if you haven't done so already).

The area between the curves could be thought of as the difference of these two areas :-

i.e. $\int_3^6 f(x)\,dx - \int_3^6 g(x)\,dx$, usually written in the form $\int_3^6 f(x) - g(x)\,dx$.

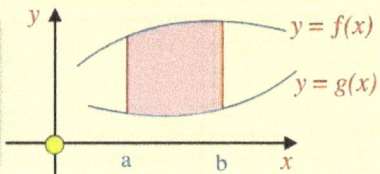

minus

In our example, we use :-

$$\int_3^6 (6x - x^2) - (x^2 - 12x + 36)\,dx$$
$$= \int_3^6 (18x - 2x^2 - 36)\,dx$$
$$= \left[9x^2 - \tfrac{2}{3}x^3 - 36x\right]_3^6$$
$$= (324 - 144 - 216) - (81 - 18 - 108)$$
$$= \boxed{9 \text{ units}^2}$$

*If you omit the sketch you might subtract the curves the wrong way round and hence obtain a negative answer !

In general, the **area enclosed between two curves** $y = f(x)$ and $y = g(x)$ in the interval $a \le x \le b$ is given by :- $\int_a^b f(x) - g(x)\,dx$

as long as $f(x)$ remains ABOVE $g(x)$ over the whole interval, $a \le x \le b$

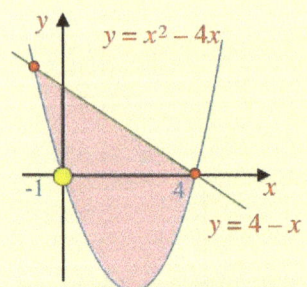

Example :- Calculate the area between the line $y = 4 - x$ and the curve $y = x^2 - 4x$.

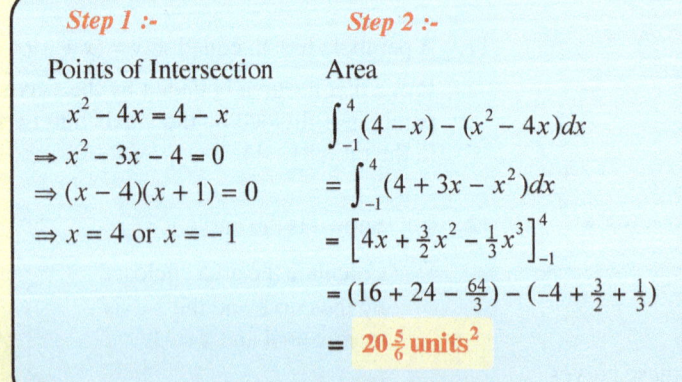

Step 1 :-

Points of Intersection
$$x^2 - 4x = 4 - x$$
$$\Rightarrow x^2 - 3x - 4 = 0$$
$$\Rightarrow (x - 4)(x + 1) = 0$$
$$\Rightarrow x = 4 \text{ or } x = -1$$

Step 2 :-

Area
$$\int_{-1}^4 (4 - x) - (x^2 - 4x)\,dx$$
$$= \int_{-1}^4 (4 + 3x - x^2)\,dx$$
$$= \left[4x + \tfrac{3}{2}x^2 - \tfrac{1}{3}x^3\right]_{-1}^4$$
$$= (16 + 24 - \tfrac{64}{3}) - (-4 + \tfrac{3}{2} + \tfrac{1}{3})$$
$$= \boxed{20\tfrac{5}{6} \text{ units}^2}$$

*No special steps need to be taken when part of the required area is above and part is below the x-axis, as long as $f(x)$ remains ABOVE $g(x)$ over the whole interval.

Exercise H11·6

1. Calculate the shaded area in each sketch :-

   (a)

   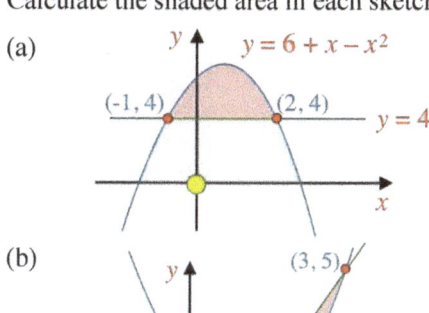

   (b)

   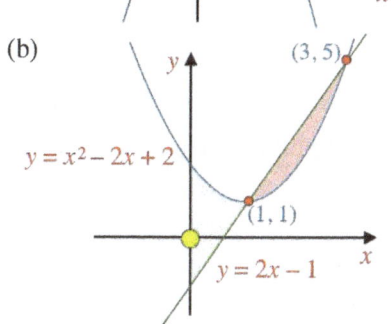

2. Calculate the areas enclosed by each pair of curves :-
   A sketch is recommended here :-

   (a) $y = x$, $y = 2x$ from $x = 0$ to $x = 4$

   (b) $y = x$ and $y = x^2$

   (c) $y = x^2$ and $y = 3x$

   (d) $y = x^3$ and $y = x$

   (e) $y = x^2$ and $y = x^3$

   (f) $y = x$ and $y = \sqrt{x}$

   (g) $y = x^2 + 2x$ and $y = -2x$

   (h) $y = x(x - 2)$ and $y = x(6 - x)$

   (i) $y = 10 - x^2$ and $y = x^2 + 4x + 4$

   (j) $y = x$ and $y = x^2 - 5x$

   (k) $y = 6 - \frac{3}{2}x^2$ and $y = 4 - x^2$

   (l) $y = 2 - x$ and $y = x^2 - 7x + 10$

   (m) $y = 6x - 3 - x^2$ and $y = x - 3$

   (n) $y = 24 + 2x - x^2$ and $y = x^2 + 8x + 16$

   (o) $y = x^4 - 4x^2$ and $y = 4 - x^2$.

3. The parabola with equation
   $$y = 3 + 2x - x^2$$
   meets the x-axis at P and Q
   where P is to the left of Q,
   and meets the y-axis at point R.

   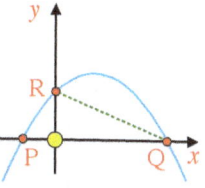

   (a) Find the coordinates of P, Q and R.

   (b) Calculate the finite area between the line
       QR and the parabola.

4. The roughcasting which surrounds the glass doors
   on the entrance to the Tunnel Restaurant has to be
   renewed.

   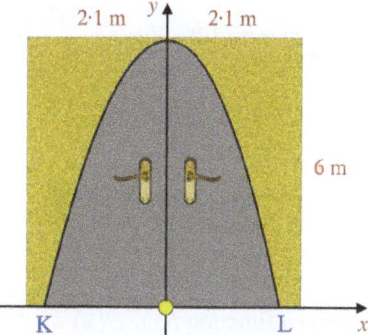

   Coordinate axes are chosen as shown in the
   diagram, with the scale of 1 unit equal to one metre.

   The glass door surrounds are in the shape of a
   parabola with equation $y = 6 - \frac{3}{2}x^2$.

   (a) Find the coordinates of the points K and L.

   (b) Calculate the cost of renewing the roughcasting
       at a cost of £50 per square metre.

5. The diagram shows a sketch of part of the graph
   of $f(x) = 9 - (x - 2)^2$.

   The graph cuts the y-axis at A
   and has a maximum
   turning point at B.

   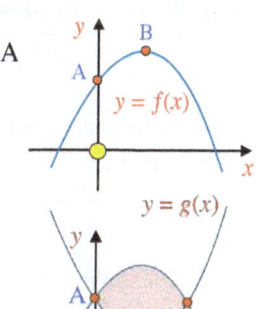

   (a) State the coordinates
       of A and B.

   (b) The second diagram
       shows the graphs of
       $y = f(x)$ and $y = g(x)$
       where
       $$g(x) = x^2 - 4x + 5.$$

   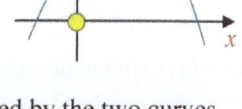

   Calculate the area enclosed by the two curves.

   (c) $f(x)$ can be written in the form $a + b \times g(x)$,
       where a and b are constants.
       Find the values of a and b.

1.   Integrate with respect to x :-

   (a) $x(x-3)(x+2)$ (b) $x^{\frac{1}{3}}(x^{\frac{2}{3}} - x^{-\frac{1}{3}})$

   (c) $\dfrac{1}{x^3} - \dfrac{1}{3x^4}$ (d) $\dfrac{\sqrt{x} + \dfrac{1}{\sqrt{x}}}{x}$.

2.   Find the following :-

   (a) $\int (2\sqrt{x} + 1)^2 dx$ (b) $\int \left(6x^2 + \dfrac{2}{x^3}\right) dx$

   (c) $\int \left(\dfrac{1}{4x^2} - \dfrac{4}{x^3}\right) dx$ (d) $\int \dfrac{3x^2 - 4x + 5}{\sqrt{x}} dx$.

3.   Evaluate each definite integral :-

   (a) $\displaystyle\int_{-1}^{0} (6 - 12x) dx$ (b) $\displaystyle\int_{1}^{8} \left(\sqrt[3]{x} + \dfrac{1}{\sqrt[3]{x}}\right) dx$.

4.   For a given function $f(x)$, $f'(x) = x^2 - \dfrac{1}{x^2}$,
   and $f(x) = -2\frac{1}{3}$ when $x = 1$.
   Find $f(x)$ when $x = 3$.

5.   The gradient of the tangent to a curve at any point
   $P(x, y)$ is found using $\dfrac{dy}{dx} = 4x - \dfrac{4}{x^2}$.

   If the curve passes through the point $(2, 9)$
   find its equation.

6.   If $\displaystyle\int_{-2}^{a} (x^3 - 4x) dx = 0$, find the value of a.

7.   Show by shading in a sketch the area enclosed by
   the curve $y = 4 - x^2$ and the line $y = 3x$.

8.   Calculate the area enclosed by the curve
   $y = x(x - 2)(x + 1)$ and the x-axis.

9.   (a)   Calculate the area enclosed by the x-axis, the
   parabola $y = x^2$, and the line with equation
   $x = 4$.

   (b)   Find the ratio in which the line $x = 2$ divides
   this area.

10.   The curve $y = x^3 - 9x$ meets a line at the points
   P(-2, 10) and Q(4, 28).

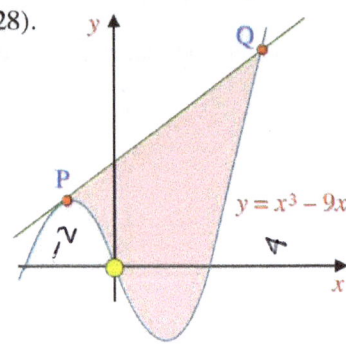

   (a)   Find the equation of the line joining P and Q.

   (b)   Calculate the finite area between this line and
   the curve.

11.   Calculate the finite area
   bounded by the parabola
   $y = -\frac{1}{4}x^2$, $-6 \le x \le 6$
   and the lines $y = -1$ and
   $y = -9$.

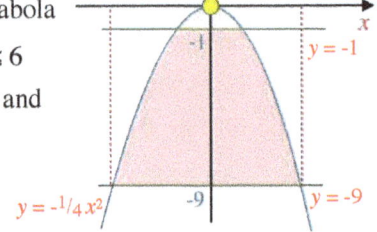

12.   (a)   Calculate the finite area between the curve
   $y = 4x - x^2$ and the x-axis.

   (b)   The parabola $y = x^2$ divides this area in two
   parts. What is the ratio of these areas ?

13.   The origin, and the points A and B are vertices
   of the shape below that is shaded.
   The edges lie on curves with equations :-

   $y = x(x + 7)$, $y = 2x - \frac{1}{2}x^2$ and $y = \dfrac{8}{x^2}$.

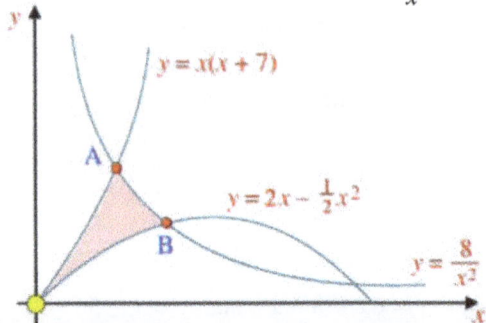

   (a)   A and B have coordinates $(a, 8)$ and $(b, 2)$.
   Find the values of a and b.

   (b)   Calculate the shaded area.

Exam Practice Exercise (H11)

1. Integrate :-

   (a) $\int x(5x-6)\,dx$ (b) $\int \dfrac{1}{4x^5}\,dx$.   **(3)(3)**

2. Integrate, answering with positive indices :-

   (a) $\int\left(8x^{\frac{1}{2}}+x^{-4}\right)dx$ (b) $\int \dfrac{6x^3-1}{x^2}\,dx$.   **(4)(4)**

3. The function $y = f(x)$ is such that $\dfrac{dy}{dx} = 6x-12x^2$.

   The curve passes through the point $(-1,0)$.

   Express y in terms of x.   **(4)**

4. For a function g, defined on a suitable domain,

   it is known that $g'(x) = \dfrac{2x-1}{\sqrt{x}}$, and $g(9)=28$.

   Find an expression for $g(x)$.   **(4)**

5. The rate of change of the temperature $T°C$ of
   stock in a jug is given by :-

   $$\frac{dT}{dt} = \tfrac{1}{16}t - k, \ \ 0 \le t \le 45,$$

   where t is the time in minutes after the stock has
   been poured, and k is a constant.

   The temperature of the stock is 90°C when first
   poured, but after 8 minutes its temperature falls
   to 76°C.

   Express T in terms of t.   **(6)**

6. Find the coordinates of the points where the curve
   $y = 14 - x^2$ meets the curve $y = 2x^2 + 2$
   and calculate the area between the curves.   **(6)**

7. The diagram below shows the curve
   $y = x^3 - 2x^2 - 6x + 4$ and the line $y = 2x + 4$.

   The curve and the line intersect at the points
   $(-2,0)$, $(0,4)$ and $(4,12)$.

   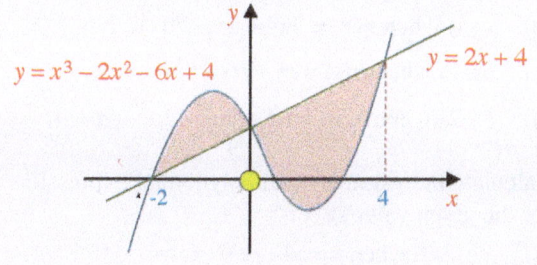

   Calculate the total shaded area.   **(10)**

8. The diagram shows two curves with equations
   $y = x^2$ and $y = \sqrt{x}$.

   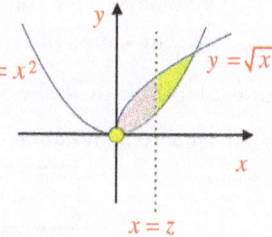

   The area
   completely
   enclosed between
   the two curves
   is split in half by the
   line with equation $x = z$.

   (a) Write these two equal areas as two separate
       integrals involving z.   **(3)**

   (b) Evaluate the integrals and show that z is
       given by the equation $2z^3 - 4z^{\frac{3}{2}} + 1 = 0$.   **(4)**

9. The parabola shown has equation $y = 18 - 2x^2$.

   The shaded area lies between the lines
   $y = 10$ and $y = 16$.

   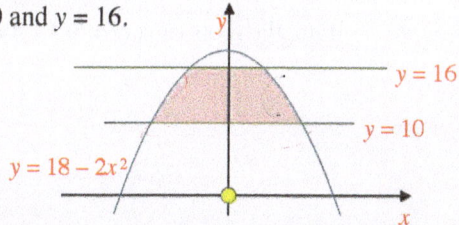

   Calculate the shaded area.   **(8)**

10. Land lying between a pathway and a stream is to be
    landscaped. This land is represented by the shaded
    area in the diagram below.

    The pathway is represented by the line $y = 2x$ and
    the stream by the parabola $y = 8x - x^2$.

    One square unit in the
    diagram represents
    10 m² of land.

    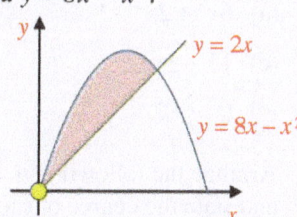

    (a) Calculate the area which is to be landscaped. **(5)**

    (b) A fence is to be erected parallel to the
        pathway and is a tangent to the stream.

        The land represented by the shaded area below
        is to be made into a children's play park.

        Calculate the area
        of the proposed
        play park.

         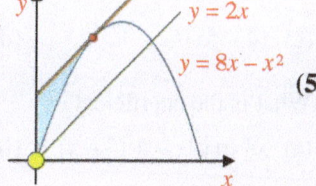

        (5)

What is a Polynomial ?

A polynomial is of the form $ax^n + bx^{n-1} + cx^{n-2} + dx^{n-3} + \ldots \beta x + \alpha$ where $a, b, c, d, e, f, \beta, \alpha$ etc. are constants.

$a, b, c, \ldots$ are called the *coefficients* of the polynomial. (i.e. the numbers in front of the powers of x).

For example :- in $4x^5 + 3x^4 - 8x^3 - 2x^2$, the coefficient of the x^5 term is 4 and the coefficient of the x^3 term is -8.

Often, functional notation is used, e.g. $f(x) = 5 - 4x^2 + 6x^5$.

> The **degree** of a polynomial is the **highest power** that appears in the expression.

Example :- $h(x) = 7x^3 - 6x^2 + x + 1$ has **degree 3**.

Note that $h(x)$ has descending powers, where as $f(x)$ above has ascending powers.

An expression such as $(x + 1)(x^2 + 2x - 1)$ is also a polynomial as it can be expressed in the form $x^3 + 3x^2 + x - 1$.

> A **root** of a polynomial function $f(x)$ is the **value of x** for which $f(x) = 0.$

Example :-　Find the roots of $f(x) = 6x^2 - 54$.

$$6x^2 - 54 = 0$$
$$\Rightarrow \quad 6(x^2 - 9) = 0$$
$$\Rightarrow \quad 6(x + 3)(x - 3) = 0$$
$$\Rightarrow \quad x + 3 = 0 \text{ or } x - 3 = 0$$
$$\Rightarrow \quad x = \text{-3 or } x = 3.$$

Hence the roots of $f(x) = 6x^2 - 54$ are **3 and -3.**

Exercise H12·1

1. State the degree of each polynomial expression :-

   (a) $6x^5 + 2x^4 - 1$　　　(b) $x^3 - 7x^2 - x$

   (c) $15 + 3x^7$　　　(d) $3 - x$

   (e) $(x - 4)^3$　　　(f) $x^2(2x + 1)^2$.

2. Arrange the following in **ascending** powers of x, and state the degree of each expression :-

   (a) $x^3 - 2 + x^4 - x^2$　　　(b) $3x^2 + 2x + 7 + x^3$

   (c) $x(x - 1)(x + 1)$　　　(d) $(2x - 5)^2$.

3. Arrange each expression in **descending** powers of x, and state the degree :-

   (a) $-x^2 + 3x^4 + x - 1$　　　(b) $4 + 5x^2 - 3x^8 + 7x$

   (c) $(4 - 5x)^2$　　　(d) $x^2(9 - x)^2$.

4. What is the coefficient of :-

   (a) x^2 in $(2x - 4)(3 - x)$　　(b) x in $(x - 5)(1 - 4x)$

   (c) x^3 in $(3x + 1)(5 - 2x^3)$　(d) x^4 in $(x^3 + 1)(x^4 - x)$?

5. Factorise each polynomial :-

   (a) $18x - 24$　　　(b) $16x^2 - 40x$

   (c) $49x^2 - 16$　　　(d) $5x^3 + 3x^2 - 2x$.

6. Find the roots of each polynomial function :-

   (a) $f(x) = x^2 - 81$　　(b) $g(x) = 9x^3 - 36x$

   (c) $h(t) = t^2 - 9t + 14$　(d) $k(a) = 3a^2 + 5a - 2$.

7. Calculate the value of :-

   (a) $f(1)$ when $f(x) = x^3 - 7x - 3$

   (b) $g(5)$ when $g(x) = 2x^2 + 5x - 70$

   (c) $h(-1)$ when $h(t) = t^4 - 2t^2 - 1$

   (d) $h(-2)$ when $h(a) = a^4 + 3a^3 - 2a^2 - a + 4$.

8. Calculate the value of each polynomial expression for the given value of x :-

   (a) $x - 3x^3$, when $x = -1$

   (b) $4x^2 - 16x^4$, when $x = 0{\cdot}5$

   (c) $(x - 1)^2(x + 1)$, when $x = -4$.

Evaluating Polynomials Using the Nested Form

Let $f(x) = ax^3 + bx^2 + cx + d$, and say we wish to find the value of $f(h)$, where h is any real number.
A substitution method requires the calculation $f(h) = ah^3 + bh^2 + ch + d$.

$ah^3 + bh^2 + ch + d$ can be expressed in **nested form** as follows :-
$$ah^3 + bh^2 + ch + d$$
$$= (ah^2 + bh + c)h + d$$
$$= [(ah + b)h + c]h + d$$

If we reverse the process, we can form $ah^3 + bh^2 + ch + d$ in this way :-

- *multiply* a by h and *add* b .... $ah + b$

- *multiply* $ah + b$ by h and *add* c .... $ah^2 + bh + c$

- *multiply* $ah^2 + bh + c$ by h and *add* d .... $ah^2 + bh + ch + d$

Artificial

This method is not often used in practice, but it leads to an easier method, called **synthetic division**, which is set down in tabular form as shown below, using the rule :-   "**add vertically and multiply diagonally**"

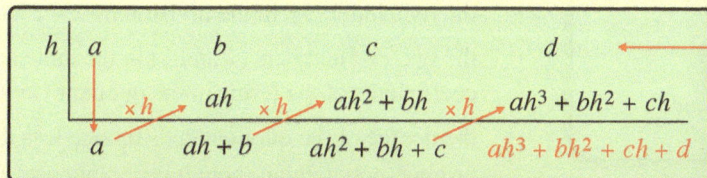

The coefficients of the polynomial in descending order

The nested form can be used to evaluate polynomials (*i.e. find the value of a polynomial, given the value of x*).

Example :-   Calculate $f(2)$ for $f(x) = 3x^5 + 2x^4 - x^3 - 4x - 1$.

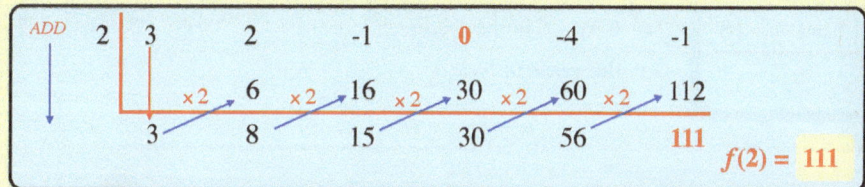

Note :- If there is a missing term in the polynomial, a "0" must be inserted in the appropriate place in the table.

In this case the x^2 is missing so a 0 is placed as the x^2 coefficient.

Exercise H12·2

1.   Use synthetic division to find $f(3)$ when
    $f(x) = 2x^3 + x^2 - 5x + 6$.
    Copy and **complete** :-

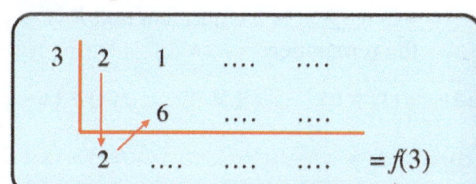

2.   In the same way, evaluate using synthetic division :-

   (a) $f(2)$ when $f(x) = 3x^3 + 4x^2 - 6x - 1$

   (b) $f(-1)$ when $f(x) = 6x^4 - 4x^2 + 1$

   (c) $f(4)$ when $f(x) = 2x^3 + 2x - 10$

   (d) $f(-3)$ when $f(x) = x^4 - 5x^3 + 2x + 9$

   (e) $f(5)$ when $f(x) = -2x^3 + 3x^2 - 12$.

3.   Calculate the value of each polynomial function for the given value of x :-

   (a) $f(x) = x^3 - 2x^2 + 3x + 1$ for $x = 2$

   (b) $f(p) = p^4 - p^2 - 7p - 20$ for $p = -4$

   (c) $f(t) = 2t^3 + 3t^2 + 15$ for $t = -2$

   (d) $f(m) = 2m^4 - m + 1$ for $m = 5$

   (e) $f(r) = r^6 + 2x^3 - 3$ for $r = -2$

   (f) $g(x) = x^4 - x^2 + x - 2$ for $x = -3$

   (g) $g(t) = 3t^6 + 2t^5 - 4t^4 + 5t^3 - 2t^2 + 1$ for $t = 1$

   (h) $g(p) = 2p^8 - 3p^5 + p^2 - 2$ for $p = -1$

   (i) $h(x) = 2x^4 - 3x^3 - 4x^2 + 12$ for $x = \frac{1}{2}$

   (j) $h(a) = 125a^3 - 25a^2 + 5a$ for $a = -\frac{1}{5}$.

Division of Polynomials - Division by $x - a$

In our "normal" numerical division calculations we either have one number dividing into another number exactly or what is more likely, there will be a remainder, as follows :- $45 \div 6 = 7$ remainder 3.

$$\begin{array}{r} 7\ r\ 3 \\ 6\,\overline{)\,4\,5} \end{array}$$

6 is the *divisor*, 7 is the *quotient*, and 3 is the *remainder*.

In algebraic division, we meet division examples such as :-

Example 1 :- $(2x^2 + 3x - 6) \div (x - 2)$

$$\begin{array}{r} 2x + 7 \quad r\ 8 \\ x - 2\,\overline{)\,2x^2 + 3x - 6} \\ \underline{2x^2 - 4x} \\ 7x - 6 \\ \underline{7x - 14} \\ 8 \end{array}$$

So $2x^2 + 3x - 6 = (x - 2)(2x + 7) + 8$

$x - 2$ is the *divisor*

$2x + 7$ is the *quotient*

8 is the *remainder*

(*note also that* $f(2) = 2 \times 2^2 + 6 - 6 = 8$).

We could use the *nested form*, (*synthetic division*), as in the previous exercise, for this kind of division, as follows :-

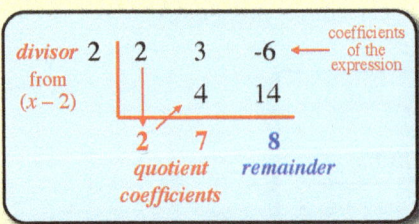

coefficients of the expression

We can see that :-

- the remainder (**8**), in the division by $x - 2$ has the **same** as $f(\mathbf{2})$.

- the two **red** numbers (**2** and **7**) in the table are the **same** as the coefficients of the terms in the quotient ($2x + 7$).

- the degree of the quotient ends up one less than the degree of the original polynomial: here it is x^1 compared with the original x^2.

Example 2 :-

Use synthetic division (nested form) to find the quotient and remainder for $(x^3 + 6x^2 + 3x - 15) \div (x + 3)$.

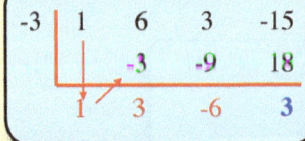

The divisor is
$x + 3$
(i.e. $x - (-3)$)

$(x + 3)$ is the *divisor*

$1x^2 + 3x - 6$ is the *quotient*

3 is the *remainder*.

*Note $x^3 + 6x^2 + 3x - 15$ can be expressed in the form $(x + 3)Q(x) + R$, where $Q(x)$ is the quotient and R is the remainder.

i.e. $x^3 + 6x^2 + 3x - 15 = (x + 3)(x^2 + 3x - 6) + 3$.

Exercise H12·3

1. Use synthetic division to find the quotient and remainder when :-

    (a) $2x^2 + 3x + 6$ is divided by $x - 1$

    (b) $8x^2 - 4x + 11$ is divided by $x + 5$

    (c) $x^3 + 2x^2 - 3x + 9$ is divided by $x - 2$

    (d) $2x^3 + 3x^2 - 5x + 12$ is divided by $x + 1$

    (e) $x^3 + 2x^2 - 3x + 4$ is divided by $x - 5$

    (f) $7x^4 - 2x^3 + 8x^2 - x + 20$ is divided by $x + 1$

    (g) $x^3 - 9x + 8$ is divided by $x + 5$

    (h) $x^4 - x^2 + 3$ is divided by $x + 1$

    (i) $10x^6 - 20x^5 - 20x - 60$ is divided by $x + 1$.

2. For each of the following :-

    (i)   Use synthetic division to find the quotient and remainder.

    (ii) Express $f(x)$ in the form $f(x) = (x - h)Q(x) + R$, where $Q(x)$ is the quotient and R is the remainder.

    (a) $f(x) = 6x^2 - 3x + 9.$ $f(x) \div (x - 2)$

    (b) $f(x) = x^3 - 6x + 7.$ $f(x) \div (x + 2)$

    (c) $f(x) = 4x^3 - 5x^2 - 1.$ $f(x) \div (x - 3)$

    (d) $f(x) = 5x^3 + 3x^2 - x + 9.$ $f(x) \div (x - 2)$

    (e) $f(x) = x^4 - x^2 + x - 2.$ $f(x) \div (x - 4)$.

3. What is special about the answer to :-
    $$(x^3 + 2x^2 - 5x - 6) \div (x + 3) ?$$

Instead of dividing by $x - 3$, $x + 5$ etc. you may be asked to divide a polynomial by $ax - b$ as in $2x - 1$, $4x + 5$ etc.

Example :-   Divide $(2x^3 + x^2 + 5x - 5)$ by $(2x - 1)$.

Since $2x - 1$ is the divisor, we evaluate the polynomial for the corresponding root $x = \frac{1}{2}$.
(i.e. set $2x - 1 = 0$ and solve, giving $x = \frac{1}{2}$)

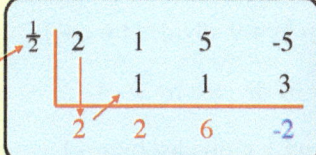

This means we can write $2x^3 + x^2 + 5x - 5$ as follows :-

$$2x^3 + x^2 + 5x - 5 = (x - \tfrac{1}{2})(2x^2 + 2x + 6) - 2$$

$$= 2 \times (x - \tfrac{1}{2}) \times \tfrac{1}{2} \times (2x^2 + 2x + 6) - 2$$

$$= (2x - 1)(x^2 + x + 3) - 2$$

$x^2 + x + 3$ is the *quotient*, -2 is the *remainder*

i.e. $2x^3 + x^2 + 5x - 5 = (2x - 1)(x^2 + x + 3) - 2$.

But we <u>don't</u> want $(x - \tfrac{1}{2})$ as the divisor. We want $(2x - 1)$ as the divisor,
⟹ We need to multiply $(x - \tfrac{1}{2})$ by 2.
To counteract this, we need to divide the quotient by 2 at the same time.

4.   Find the remainder on dividing :-

(a) $4x^2 + 8x - 2$ by $2x - 1$

(b) $9x^2 - 6x + 2$ by $3x - 1$

(c) $2x^3 + 5x^2 + 4x + 4$ by $2x - 3$

(d) $12x^2 - 8x - 10$ by $3x + 1$

(e) $4x^3 - 10x^2 + 8x$ by $2x - 1$

(f) $8x^3 + 2x - 6$ by $2x + 3$.

5.   Carry out the division, write your answer in the form $f(x) = (x - h)Q(x) + R$, and then write it in the form $(ax - b)Q(x) + R$:-

(a) $3x^3 + 8x^2 - 9x + 8 \div 3x - 1$

(b) $2x^3 + 7x^2 - 5x + 8 \div 2x + 1$

(c) $2x^3 - x^2 - 1 \div 2x + 3$

(d) $6x^2 - 11x + 6 \div 3x - 4$.

6. $12x^3 - 6x^2 - 18x + p$ is divisible by $2x + 3$. Calculate the value of p and the quotient.

The Remainder Theorem

Using the synthetic division method, we discovered that when we divided $f(x)$ by $(x - h)$, we got a remainder of $f(h)$.

If a polynomial $f(x)$ is divided by $(x - h)$, the remainder is $f(h)$.

Proof :-

Let $f(x) = (x - h)Q(x) + R$, where $Q(x)$ is the quotient and R is the remainder.

If $x = h$, $f(h) = (h - h)Q(h) + R$
$$= 0 \times Q(h) + R$$
$$= R.$$

This means that $f(x) = (x - h)Q(x) + f(h)$.

Example :-   Express $f(x) = (x^3 + 5x^2 - 5x + 1) \div (x - 2)$ in the form $f(x) = (x - 2)Q(x) + R$. Show that $R = f(h)$.

```
2 | 1    5    -5    1
  |      2    14    18
  --------------------
    1    7     9    19
```

$f(x) = (x - 2)(x^2 + 7x + 9) + 19$

$1x^2 + 7x + 9$ is the *quotient*,

19 is the *remainder*.

$f(2) = 2^3 + 5 \times 2^2 - 5 \times 2 + 1 = 19$

Exercise H12·4

Use Synthetic Division to express the answer to each division, either in the form $f(x) = (x - h)Q(x) + f(h)$ or $f(x) = (ax - b)Q(x) + f(h)$, depending on the divisor, and write the quotient and remainder each time :-

1. (a) $f(x) = x^3 + 27x^2 - 3x + 9$ divided by $x + 1$ (d) $f(x) = 4x^2 + 2x - 8$ divided by $2x - 1$

    (b) $f(x) = x^4 - 5x^2 - 36$ divided by $x - 4$ (e) $f(x) = 4x^2 - 8x - 8$ divided by $2x - 3$

    (c) $f(x) = x^7 - 2x^5 + x^3 + x$ divided by $x - 1$ (f) $f(x) = 6x^3 - 2x^2 - x + 11$ divided by $3x + 2$.

2. Find the value of a given that $x^3 - 5x^2 + ax - 2$ has a remainder 1 when divided by $x - 3$.
    (*Hint :- set up your synthetic division table, obtain the remainder, in terms of a, and set this equal to the 1 and solve for a*).

3. Find the value of b given that $2x^4 - bx^3 - 5$ has remainder 43 when divided by $x + 2$.

4. Find the value of c given that $cx^3 - 5x + 3$ has remainder 6 when divided by $x + 1$.

5. Find the value of d given that $6x^3 - 2dx + 2$ has remainder 10 when divided by $x - 2$.

The Factor Theorem

The Remainder Theorem can be used to factorise polynomials.

If $f(h) = 0$, then $x - h$ must be a factor of $f(x)$.
Also, if $x - h$ is a factor of $f(x)$, then $f(h) = 0$.

This is called the **Factor Theorem**.

Proof   For a function $f(x) = (x - h)Q(x) + f(h)$,   ← *the remainder*
If $f(h) = 0$, $f(x) = (x - h)Q(x)$
Therefore $x - h$ is a factor of $f(x)$.

and   If $x - h$ is a factor of $f(x)$, then $f(x) = (x - h)Q(x)$.

Example 1 :- Prove that $x - 1$ is a factor of $x^4 - 2x^3 + 4x^2 - 6x + 3$.

We require $f(1)$
to be zero (= 0)

1	1	-2	4	-6	3
		1	-1	3	-3
	1	-1	3	-3	0

$x^4 - 2x^3 + 4x^2 - 6x + 3 = (x - 1)(x^3 - x^2 + 3x - 3)$

$\Rightarrow$ $x - 1$ is a factor and 1 must be a root.

As the remainder is 0, $(x - 1)$ is a factor.

Example 2 :- Factorise fully :- $x^3 - 2x^2 - 11x + 12$.

To find the roots of this polynomial, consider all the factors of 12 :-

$\Rightarrow$ i.e. try $x = \pm1, \pm2, \pm3, \pm4, \pm6, \pm12$, until you find one that gives a remainder of 0 !

(This method of finding a linear factor by trial and improvement, making use of the fact that dividing by a factor gives a zero remainder leads to the notion called the *Factor Theorem*).

Here, $f(1) = 0$

1	1	-2	-11	12
		1	-1	-12
	1	-1	-12	0 √

$\Rightarrow$ $x - 1$ must be a factor

If 1, hadn't worked, you try -1, then 2, then -2 etc until you have exhausted all the factors of 12.

$x^3 - 2x^2 - 11x + 12 = (x - 1)(x^2 - x - 12)$

$= (x - 1)(x - 4)(x + 3)$

$x - 1$, $x - 4$ and $x + 3$ are factors

$\Rightarrow$ 1, 4 and -3 must be the roots.

On some occasions the quotient will not factorise - you may have to examine the discriminant to discover this.

Exercise H12·5

1. Show by means of the Factor Theorem that :-

   (a) $x - 1$ is a factor of $x^3 + x^2 - 5x + 3$

   (b) $x - 2$ is a factor of $x^3 + 3x^2 - 20$

   (c) $x - 4$ is a factor of $2x^4 - 9x^3 + 5x^2 - 3x - 4$

   (d) $x - 1$ is a factor of $x^3 + 3x^2 + x - 5$

   (e) $x + 2$ is a factor of $x^3 + 5x^2 + 9x + 6$

   (f) $x + 3$ is a factor of $x^4 - 7x^2 - 18$

   (g) $2x - 1$ is a factor of $2x^3 + x^2 + 5x - 3$

   (h) $2x - 5$ is a factor of $2x^3 + x^2 - 23x + 20$

   (i) $x - 1$ is a factor of $x^3 - (2p + 1)x^2 + (p^2 + 2p)x - p^2$.

2. Factorise fully :-

   (a) $x^3 - 7x + 6$

   (b) $x^3 - 8x^2 + 19x - 12$

   (c) $x^3 - 4x^2 - 31x + 70$

   (d) $2x^3 + 7x^2 + 2x - 3$

   (e) $2x^3 - 15x^2 + 22x + 15$

   (f) $4x^3 - 16x^2 - x + 4$

   (g) $x^4 + 2x^3 - 3x^2 - 4x + 4$

   (h) $x^4 - 5x^2 + 4$

   (i) $x^4 - 39x^2 + 70x$

   (j) $2x^5 - 2x^4 - 10x^3 + 10x^2 + 8x - 8.$

Finding the Unknown Coefficients of Polynomials

The Factor Theorem can also be used to determine unknown coefficients in polynomials.

Example 1 :-   If $x + 2$ is known to be a factor of $2x^3 + x^2 + mx - 8$, find the value of m.

> As $x + 2$ is a factor, this means $x = -2$ is a root, which means $f(-2) = 0$
>
> => We must evaluate $f(-2)$ using synthetic division and set the remainder = 0.
>
> | -2 | 2 | 1 | m | -8 |
> |------|---|---|-----|------|
> | | | -4 | 6 | $-2m - 12$ |
> | | 2 | -3 | $(m + 6)$ | $-2m - 20$ |
>
> Since the remainder is 0
> => we set $-2m - 20 = 0$
>
> $m = -10$

Example 2 :-   Find the values of a and b if $x - 2$ and $x - 1$ are factors of $x^4 - 4x^3 + ax^2 + bx - 4$.

> As $x - 2$ and $x - 1$ are factors, then $x = 2$ and $x = 1$ are roots, which means $f(2) = 0$ and $f(1) = 0$.
>
> => We must evaluate $f(2)$ and $f(1)$ using synthetic division and set both remainders = 0.
>
> | 2 | 1 | -4 | a | b | -4 |
> |---|---|------|-----|-----|------|
> | | | 2 | -4 | $2a - 8$ | $4a + 2b - 16$ |
> | | 1 | -2 | $(a - 4)$ | $(2a + b - 8)$ | $(4a + 2b - 20)$ |
>
> Hence, $4a + 2b - 20 = 0$
>
> | 1 | 1 | -4 | a | b | -4 |
> |---|---|------|-----|-----|------|
> | | | 1 | -3 | $a - 3$ | $a + b - 3$ |
> | | 1 | -3 | $(a - 3)$ | $(a + b - 3)$ | $(a + b - 7)$ |
>
> Hence, $a + b - 7 = 0$
>
> We now have to solve the simultaneous equations
>
> $4a + 2b = 20$
> $a + b = 7$
>
> which produces the answer => $a = 3,\ b = 4$

1. Find the value of m in each polynomial if :-

    (a) $x + 3$ is a factor of $x^3 - mx + 6$ (x^2 coefficient is 0)

    (b) $x - 3$ is a factor of $x^3 + mx^2 - x + 3$

    (c) $x - 2$ is a factor of $mx^4 - 10x^2 + 8$

    (d) $2x + 1$ is a factor of $4x^3 + 12x^2 + mx - 3$

    (e) $3x - 1$ is a factor of $6x^3 - 17x^2 + mx + 3$.

2. Find the values of a and b in :-

    (a) $x + 1$ and $x - 1$ are factors of $x^3 - ax^2 + bx + 2$

    (b) $x - 1$ and $x + 2$ are factors of $x^3 + ax^2 - bx + 4$

    (c) $x - 3$ and $x + 4$ are factors of $x^3 + ax^2 + bx + 24$

2. (d) $x - 2$ and $x + 3$ are factors of $2x^3 + x^2 + ax + b$

    (e) $x + 2$ and $x - 3$ are factors of $x^4 + ax^2 - 4x + b$

    (f) $x - 3$ and $x + 5$ are factors of
         $$x^4 + ax^3 - 29x^2 + bx + 180$$

    (g) $2x + 1$ and $3x - 1$ are factors of
         $$36x^4 + 36x^3 + 5x^2 + ax + b.$$

3. If $x + 1$ is a factor of $x^3 + qx^2 - x - 2$ find q and find the other factors when q has this value.

4. Show that $3x + 1$ is a factor of $27x^3 + 1$.

    Show that $27x^3 + 1$ has no other factors of the form $ax + b$, where a and b are real numbers.

Polynomial Equations

In chapter **8**, we were restricted in the number of curves we could sketch, as we were not able to factorise polynomials of degree greater than 2 (i.e. quadratics) to find the intersection with the x-axis. This exercise will resolve that !

Example :- Find the roots of $x^3 - 5x^2 + 2x + 8 = 0$.

Consider the roots $\pm 1, \pm 2, \pm 4, \pm 8$, by trial & improvement until you find one that gives a 0 remainder !

Eventually we find, $f(2) = 0$

$$\begin{array}{r|rrr} 2 & 1 & -5 & 2 & 8 \\ & & 2 & -6 & 8 \\ \hline & 1 & -3 & -4 & 0 \end{array}$$

This means that $(x - 2)$ is a factor as is $(1x^2 - 3x - 4)$.

*This would mean that the curve would meet the x-axis at $(-1, 0), (2, 0)$ and $(4, 0)$, and the y-axis at $(0, 8)$, and this now allows us to sketch the cubic function. (see below).

=> $x^3 - 5x^2 + 2x + 8 = (x - 2)(x^2 - 3x - 4)$
              $= (x - 2)(x - 4)(x + 1)$

=> **$(x - 2)$, $(x - 4)$ and $(x + 1)$ are factors.**
    and 2, 4 and -1 must be roots.

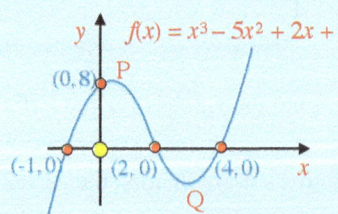

We could find the coordinates of P and Q using calculus.

1. Show that 1 is a root of $x^3 - 8x^2 - x + 8 = 0$ and find the other roots.

2. Show that 2 is a root of $x^3 - 6x^2 + 3x + 10 = 0$ and find the other roots.

3. Show that $\frac{1}{2}$ is a root of $2x^3 + x^2 - 13x + 6 = 0$ and find the other roots.

4. Show that $-\frac{1}{2}$ is a root of $4x^3 - 24x^2 + 27x + 20 = 0$ and find the other roots.

5. Find the roots of :-
    (a) $x^3 + 4x^2 + x - 6 = 0$
    (b) $x^3 - 4x^2 - 3x + 18 = 0$
    (c) $x^3 - 12x^2 + 27x + 40 = 0$
    (d) $x^4 - 8x^3 + 7x^2 + 36x - 36 = 0$.

6. Determine the coordinates of the points where each curve and the line intersects :-
    (a) $y = x^3 + 3x^2 - 5x - 6$ and $y = x + 2$
    (b) $y = x^3 + 4x^2 - 5x - 11$ and $y = 2x - 1$
    (c) $y = x^4 + 10x^3 + 23x^2 - 11x - 23$ and $y = 1 - x$.

7. Find the roots of :-

   (a) $2x^3 + 7x^2 - 5x - 4 = 0$

   (b) $3x^3 - 17x^2 - 8x + 12 = 0$

   (c) $6x^3 - 23x^2 - 6x + 8 = 0$

   (d) $5x^3 - 22x^2 - 52x + 24 = 0$.

8. The curve $f(x) = 3x^3 - 12x^2 - 21x + 30$ cuts the x-axis at three points.

   Find the coordinates of these points.

9. 4 is a root of $x^3 - 37x + p = 0$.

   Find the value of p and find the other roots.

10. Show that the equation $x^3 + 2x^2 - 2x + 3 = 0$ has only one real root.

11. Find the value of b if $x - 4$ is a factor of $2x^3 - 5x^2 + bx - 28$.

    Hence prove that $2x^3 - 5x^2 + bx - 28 = 0$ has only one solution.

Determining the Equation of a Function from its Graph

The equation of a function can be determined from its graph, as follows :-

Since this graph cuts the x-axis at p, q and r, (i.e. it has roots $x = p$, $x = q$ and $x = r$), then it must have factors $(x - p)$, $(x - q)$ and $(x - r)$.

This means, the function must be a cubic of the form :-

$$f(x) = k(x - p)(x - q)(x - r).$$

*The constant k has to be introduced into the equation - otherwise every equation of this type would have an x^3 coefficient of 1, which is not always the case.

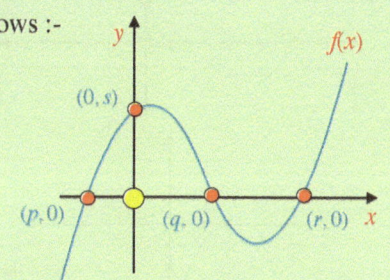

The graph crosses the y-axis at $(0, s)$.

Example :- For the graph shown, find the equation of the corresponding function.

The graph has zeros at -2, 3 and 8. (*i.e. its roots*)

Its factors are therefore $(x + 2)$, $(x - 3)$ and $(x - 8)$.

Its equation is $f(x) = k(x + 2)(x - 3)(x - 8)$

$\qquad = k(x + 2)(x^2 - 11x + 24)$

$\qquad = k(x^3 - 9x^2 + 2x + 48)$.   (*we need to find the value of k*).

Since $f(0) = 4 \Rightarrow k(0 + 2)(0 - 3)(0 - 8) = 4 \Rightarrow 48k = 4$, $\Rightarrow k = {}^1/_{12}$.

Hence $f(x) = \frac{1}{12}(x^3 - 9x^2 + 2x + 48)$ i.e. $f(x) = \frac{1}{12}x^3 - \frac{3}{4}x^2 + \frac{1}{6}x + 4$.

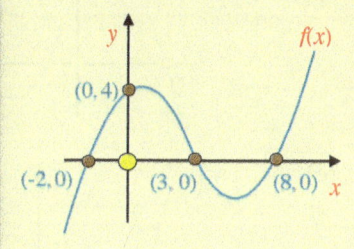

Exercise H12·8

Copy and **complete** :-

1.
   Zeros at -2, and 6.

   Factors are $(x + 2)$ and $(x - \ldots)$.

   Its equation is :-

   $f(x) = k(x + \ldots)(x - \ldots)$

   $f(x) = k(x^2 - \ldots x - \ldots)$

   (*we need to find the value of k*).

   Since $f(0) = -6$

   $\Rightarrow k(0 + 2)(0 - 6) = -6$

   $\Rightarrow -12k = -6$, $\Rightarrow k = {}^1/\ldots$

   $\Rightarrow f(x) = {}^1/\ldots(x^2 - \ldots x - \ldots)$

   $\Rightarrow f(x) = \ldots$

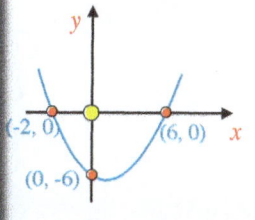

2. Use the graphs shown to determine the equation of the corresponding quadratic functions :-

   (a)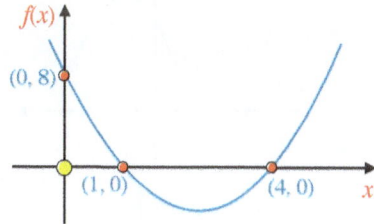

   (b)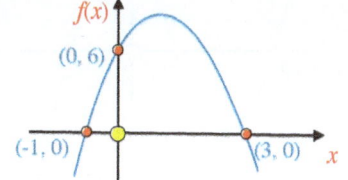

3. For each graph, determine the equation of the corresponding function :-

(a)
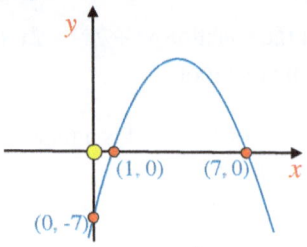

(b)
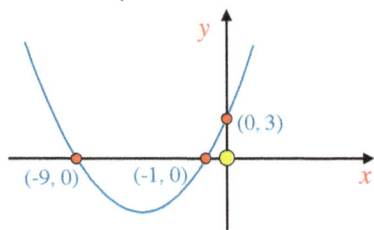

(c)
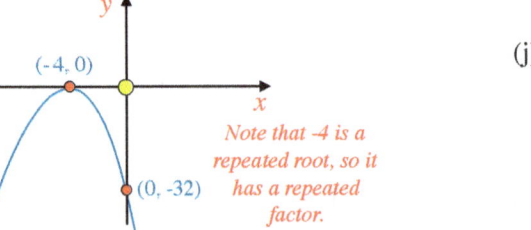

Note that -4 is a repeated root, so it has a repeated factor.

(d)
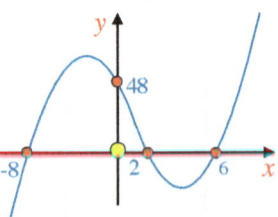

(e)
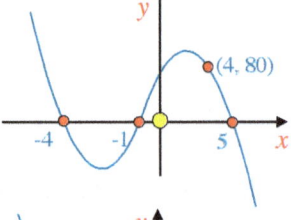

(f)
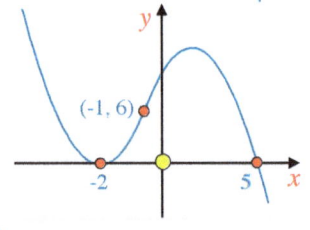

(g)
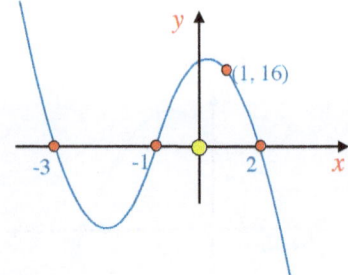

3. (h)
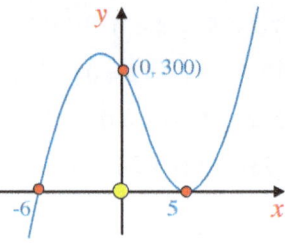

(i)
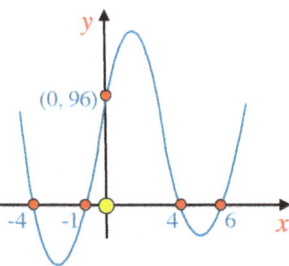

(j)
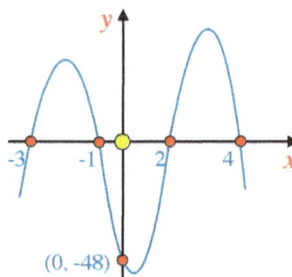

(k)
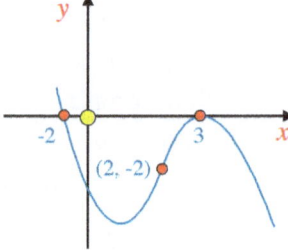

(l)
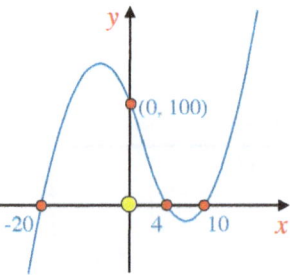

(m)
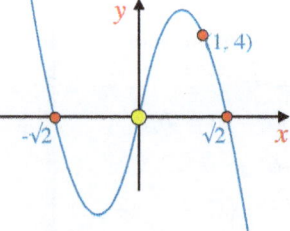

Sketching the Graphs of Polynomials

As shown earlier, we were restricted in the number of graphs we could sketch due the factorisation of polynomials with degrees of 3 and above. Now, by using synthetic division, we can factorise polynomials, find their roots where they exist and make improved sketches of curves.

Example :-   Sketch the graph of the curve :- $f(x) = x^3 - 4x^2 - 3x + 18$.

Step 1 :- Points of intersection with axes

(a) Substitute $x = 0$ into $y = f(x)$ => $f(0) = 0 - 0 - 0 + 18 = 18$ => cuts the y-axis at **(0, 18)**.

(b) Now replace $y (= f(x)) = 0$ => $0 = x^3 - 4x^2 - 3x + 18$

=> By trial &
improvement.
we find, $f(-2) = 0$

$$
\begin{array}{r|rrrr}
-2 & 1 & -4 & -3 & 18 \\
   &   & -2 & 12 & -18 \\
\hline
   & 1 & -6 & 9 & 0
\end{array}
$$

This means $x^3 - 4x^2 - 3x + 18$ has a factor of $(x + 2)$

=> $(x + 2)(x^2 - 6x + 9) = 0$

=> $(x + 2)(x - 3)(x - 3) = 0$

=> $x = -2$ or $x = 3$ **twice**

=> cuts x axis at **(-2, 0)** and **(3, 0)**

Step 2 :- Use Calculus to find the Stationary Points :-

$$f'(x) = 3x^2 - 8x - 3 = (3x + 1)(x - 3)$$

The stationary values of y occur when $f'(x) = 0$.

Hence, set $3x^2 - 8x - 3 = 0$

=> $(3x + 1)(x - 3) = 0$

=> $x = -^1/_3$ or $x = 3$.

To find the coordinates of the turning points, find $f(-^1/_3)$ and $f(3)$

=> $f(-^1/_3) = 18^{14}/_{27}$ and $f(3) = 0$

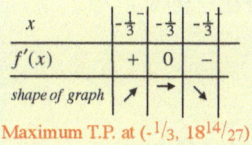

x	$-\frac{1}{3}^-$	$-\frac{1}{3}$	$-\frac{1}{3}^+$
$f'(x)$	+	0	−
shape of graph	↗	→	↘

Maximum T.P. at $(-^1/_3, 18^{14}/_{27})$

x	3^-	3	3^+
$f'(x)$	−	0	+
shape of graph	↘	→	↗

Minimum T.P. at (3, 0)

The turning points are **$(-^1/_3, 18^{14}/_{27})$** and **(3, 0)**.

See table of signs :-

Step 3 :- The shape of the curve for large x-values

Finally, check what happens as $x \rightarrow +\infty$ and $-\infty$

As $x \rightarrow +\infty$ (*large positive x value*), then $f(x) \rightarrow +\infty$

As $x \rightarrow -\infty$ (*large negative x value*), then $f(x) \rightarrow -\infty$.

Step 4 :- Join all points up with a smooth curve.

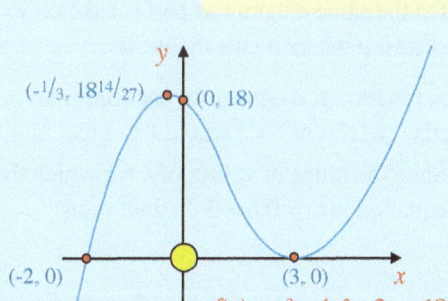

Exercise H12·9

Sketch each curve, illustrating the intersection with axes, the turning points and their nature, and how they behave for large and small values of x :-

1. $f(x) = x^3 + x^2 - x - 1$

2. $f(x) = x^3 - 3x + 2$

3. $f(x) = x^3 - x^2 - 5x - 3$

4. $f(x) = x^3 + 6x^2 + 9x$

5. $y = 4 - 9x + 6x^2 - x^3$

6. $y = 16 + 12x - x^3$

7. $y = -4x^3 + x^2 + 4x - 1$

8. $y = -4 + 5x^2 - x^4$.

Exercise H12·10   Mixed Exercise

1. Factorise fully :-

   (a) $2x^3 - 5x^2 - 4x + 3$ (b) $x - x^4$

   (c) $x^6 - x^4$ (d) $9x^2 - 4y^2$.

2. A function f is defined by $f(x) = x^3 - 3x^2 - 6x + 8$.

   (a) Factorise $f(x)$ fully.

   (b) A function h is such that $h(x) = \dfrac{1}{f(x)}$.

   For what values of x is the function h not defined ?

3. $(x - 3)$ is a factor of $3x^3 - 4x^2 + ax + 6$.

   Find the value of a and factorise the expression fully for this value of a.

4. A function f is defined on R by the formula :-

   $$f(x) = 4x^3 - 6x^2.$$

   (a) Find the stationary points of the function $y = f(x)$ and determine their nature.

   (b) Find the roots of $f(x)$.

   (c) Sketch the graph of f.

   (d) A function h is defined by the formula $h(x) = 4x^3 - 6x^2 + 2$.

   On the same diagram as part (c) sketch $y = h(x)$ showing where it cuts the y-axis.

   (e) A function p is defined by the formula $p(x) = 4x^3 - 6x^2 + k$ where k is a real number.

   State the range of values of k for which the equation $p(x) = 0$ has 3 distinct roots.

5. $(x + 2)$ is a factor of $3x^3 + px^2 - 17x + 6$.

   Find the value of p.

6. Prove that the polynomial with equation $f(x) = x^3 - 2x^2 + 2x - 1$ has only one real root.

7. When $x^2 + 3x - 2$ and $x^3 - 4x^2 + 5x + k$ are divided by $x + 1$, you end up with the same remainder.

   Find the value of k.

8. The diagram below shows the sketch of a function $y = f(x)$.

   The line $y = -8$ is a tangent to the curve at $x = 4$.

   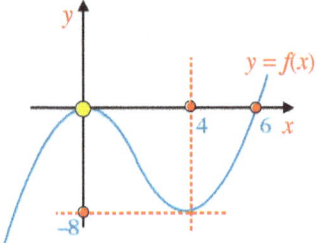

   Find the equation of the curve.

9. When $f(x) = 2x^4 - x^3 + px^2 + qx - 10$ is divided by $(x - 2)$ the remainder is 56.

   $(x - 1)$ is a factor of $f(x)$.

   Calculate the values of p and q.

10. The diagram below shows a sketch of the curve $y = -x^3 - x^2 + 16x + 16$.

    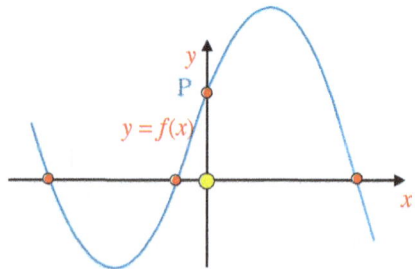

    (a) Write the coordinates of point P.

    (b) Find the coordinates of the points of intersection of the curve with the x-axis.

    (c) Find the x-coordinate of each of the turning points and justify the nature of each point.

11. A curve has equation $f(x) = x^3 + 2x^2 - 4x - 8$.

    (a) Show that $(x - 2)$ is a factor of $f(x)$ and completely factorise $f(x)$.

    (b) Find the coordinates of the points of intersection with both axes.

    (c) Find the stationary points of the curve and determine their nature.

    (d) Sketch the curve.

    (e) Calculate the finite area enclosed between the curve and the x-axis.

Exam Practice Exercise (H12)

1. $(x + 3)$ is a factor of $x^3 - x^2 + px + 24$.
   Find the value of p. (3)

2. (a) Show that $(x + 1)$ is a factor of $x^3 - 8x^2 + 5x + 14$.
   (b) Factorise $x^3 - 8x^2 + 5x + 14$ fully.
   (c) Solve $x^3 - 8x^2 + 5x + 14 = 0$. (6)

3. If $(x + 1)$ and $(x - 2)$ are factors of $3x^3 + ax^2 - 4x + b$ find the values of a and b. (4)

4. For the polynomial $2x^3 - 11x^2 + ax + b$,
   $(x + 1)$ is a factor, and when it is divided by $(x + 2)$ there is a remainder of -55.
   (a) Calculate the values of a and b. (4)
   (b) Hence factorise the polynomial completely. (3)

5. The diagram below shows the sketch of a cubic function $y = f(x)$ with the coordinates of the points of intersection with both axes shown.

   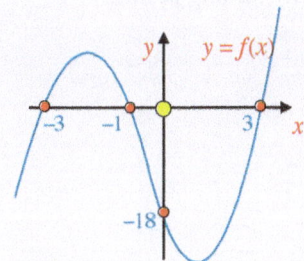

   Find the equation of the curve. (5)

6. (a) Given that $(x - 1)$ is a factor of $x^3 + 4x^2 + 3x - 8$, factorise it fully. (4)
   (b) Show that $y = 3x^4 + 16x^3 + 18x^2 - 96x + 2$ has only one stationary point. (3)
   (c) Find its x-coordinate and determine the nature of this turning point. (3)

7. The curve $y = 2x^3 + x^2 - 13x + q$ intersects the x-axis at the point $(-3, 0)$.
   (a) Find the value of q and hence write the coordinates of the point where the curve meets the y-axis. (3)
   (b) The curve meets the x-axis at another 2 points. Determine their coordinates. (3)

8. (a) Show that the tangent to the curve $y = x^3 - x^2 - 4x + 2$ at the point where $x = -1$ has equation $y = x + 5$. (4)
   (b) Find the coordinates of the point where this tangent meets the curve again. (3)

9. The curve with equation $y = 8 - x^3 - x^4$ cuts the x-axis at $(a, 0)$ and $(b, 0)$, where $a < 0$ and $b > 0$.
   (a) Find the value of a. (4)
   (b) Find the integer m such that $m \le b \le m + 1$. (2)

10. Find the coordinates of the points where the curve $y = x^3 - 2x^2 - 3x + 10$ meets the line with equation $y = 2x + 4$. (6)

11. A function g is defined by the formula :-
    $$g(x) = -2x^3 + 7x^2 - 9.$$
    (a) Show that $(x - 3)$ is a factor of $g(x)$ and factorise $g(x)$ fully. (4)
    (b) Find the coordinates of the points where the curve $y = g(x)$ crosses both axes. (2)
    (c) Find the greatest and least values of g in the interval $-0{\cdot}5 \le x \le 2$. (4)

12. Functions f, g and h are defined on the set of real numbers by :-
    $f(x) = x^3 + 1$, $g(x) = 3x - 7$ and $h(x) = 4x - 3$.
    (a) Find $g(f(x))$. (2)
    (b) Prove that :-
    $g(f(x)) + xh(x) = 3x^3 + 4x^2 - 3x - 4$. (1)
    (c) Factorise $3x^3 + 4x^2 - 3x - 4$ fully. (5)
    (d) Hence solve $g(f(x)) + xh(x) = 0$. (1)

13. The diagram shows the sketch of part of the graph of $y = x^3 - 4x^2 + x + 6$.

    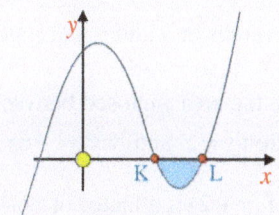

    (a) Find the coordinates of K and L. (4)
    (b) Calculate the shaded area. (5)

Home Exercise 4 (Chapters 1-12)

1. Points A(-4, -1), B(5, -1) and C(-1, 5) are vertices of ΔABC.

   (a) Find the equations of the median AD and of the altitude CE.

   (b) Determine the coordinates of the point of intersection of AD and CE.

2. Given $f(x) = \dfrac{x-1}{x}$, where $x \neq 0$, find $f^{-1}(x)$ and state a suitable domain for $f^{-1}(x)$.

3. (a) Find the equation of the tangent to the curve $f(x) = x^3 - 3x - 1$ at the point where $x = 2$.

   (b) Find the equation of the tangent to the curve $f(x) = x^2 - 6x - 3$ at its minimum turning point.

   (c) Find the coordinates of the point P, where these two tangents meet.

4. The graph $y = a^x + b$ is shown in the diagram.

   (a) Replace x by 0 and y by 4 to find the value of b, and then find the value of a.

   (b) Sketch the inverse of this function showing all relevant points.

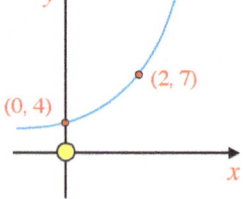

5. (a) Solve the equation $2\cos x° + \sqrt{3} = 0$ for $-180 < x < 180$, and hence list the coordinates of where the curve $y = 2\cos x° + \sqrt{3}$ meets the x axis.

   (b) Sketch the graph $y = 2\cos x° + \sqrt{3}$, for $-180 \leq x \leq 180$, indicating any turning points.

6. Find k, given that $x^2 + (k-3)x + 1 = 0$ has no real roots.

7. The line $y = x$ and the parabola $y = 10x - x^2$ intersect at two points.

   From each point of intersection, a tangent to the parabola is drawn.

   Find the coordinates of the point where the tangents meet.

8. Two points A(4, 4) and B(-4, 0) are the end points of the diameter of a circle, centre C.

   (a) Determine the equation of this circle.

   (b) A second circle lies inside the first circle.

   The centre of the first circle, C and the point D(2k, 0) are end points of a diameter of this second circle.

   Find the equation of this second circle in terms of x, y and k.

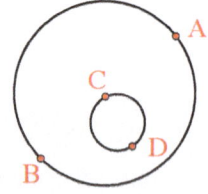

9. A sequence is defined as $u_{n+1} = au_n + b$ and its first three terms are 60, 40 and 30.

   Find the values of a and b and state the limit of this sequence as n tends to infinity.

10. Calculate the area enclosed between the graphs of the function $y = x$ and $y = x^2 - 6x + 10$.

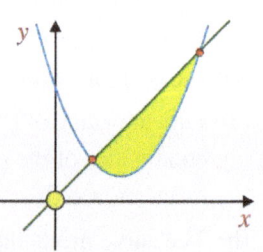

11. Find p, if $(x + 2)$ is a factor of $x^3 - px - 6$, and hence find all the roots of the equation $x^3 - px - 6 = 0$, with this value of p.

Chapter H13 - Revision of Trigonometry

1. Convert each angle to radian measure :-

   (a) 180°   (b) 45°   (c) 30°

   (d) 360°   (e) 270°   (f) 60°

   (g) 12°   (h) 8°   (i) 320°.

2. Convert each angle to degrees :-

   (a) 2π (b) $\pi/2$ (c) $\pi/6$

   (d) 3π (e) 8π (f) $\pi/8$

   (g) $\pi/4$ (h) $3\pi/2$ (i) $5\pi/3$.

3. Find the exact value of :-

   (a) $sin\,270°$ (b) $cos\,\pi$ (c) $sin\,\pi/6$

   (d) $tan\,\pi/2$ (e) $cos\,4\pi$ (f) $tan\,\pi/6$

   (g) $sin\,315°$ (h) $cos\,3\pi/4$ (i) $tan\,(-7\pi/3)$.

4. Find the exact value of :-

   (a) $cos\,45°\,sin\,45°$ (b) $tan\,60°\,sin\,315°$

   (c) $sin\,120°\,cos\,240°$ (d) $tan\,315°\,cos\,(-60°)$

   (e) $sin\,\pi\,cos\,2\pi$ (f) $tan\,\pi/6\,sin\,\pi/3$

   (g) $sin\,5\pi/4\,cos\,5\pi/3\,tan\,5\pi/6$.

5. Find the exact value of x, in each triangle :-

   (a)   (b)

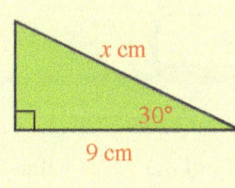

6. A helicopter leaves its pad and flies due south for 16 km.

It then flies on a bearing of 045° until it is due east of the helipad.

   (a) Make a sketch of this journey.

   (b) How far is the helicopter from the pad at this point ?

7. Sketch each of the following trigonometric graphs for $0 \le x \le 360$.

   (a) $y = 3\,sin\,x°$ (b) $y = cos\,x° + 2$

   (c) $y = 4\,cos\,2x°$ (d) $y = 5\,sin\,3x° + 2$

   (e) $y = tan\,2x°$ (f) $y = 6 - 2\,sin\,3x°$.

8. Identify the equation of each trig graph :-

   (a)   (b)

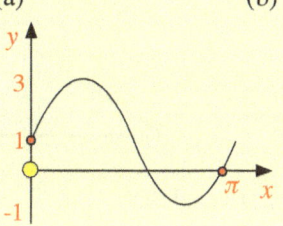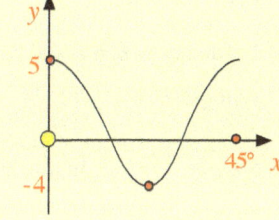

   (c)   (d)

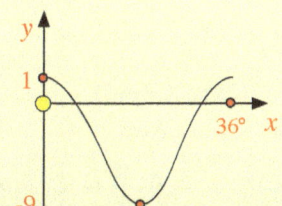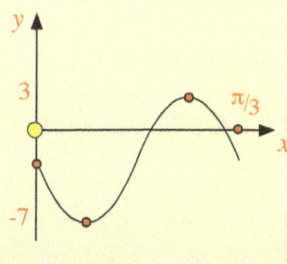

9. State the **period** and **amplitude** of $y = 6 - 5\cdot3\,sin\,4x$.

10. Solve each of these trigonometric equations :-

   (a) $2\,cos\,x° - \sqrt{3} = 0$ $0 \le x < 360$

   (b) $4\sqrt{3}\,tan\,x + 4 = 0$ $\pi \le x < 2\pi$

   (c) $4 - 5\,cos\,x = 1$ $0 \le x < \pi$

   (d) $\sqrt{3}\,cos\,(x - 45)° = 1$ $0 < x < 360$

   (e) $1 - cos\,0\cdot5x° = 0$ $0 \le x < 180$

   (f) $tan^2\,x° = 1/3$ $0 \le x < 360$

   (g) $2\,sin\,2x = 1$ $0 < x < \pi/4$

   (h) $2\,sin\,(2x - 30)° = 1$ $0 < x < 360$

   (i) $\sqrt{3}\,cos\,(3x - 45) + 1 = 0$ $0 < x < \pi$

   (j) $(sin\,x°)(sin\,x° + 1) = 0$ $0 < x \le 360$

   (k) $cos^2\,x - cos\,x = 0$ $-2\pi < x \le 2\pi$.

11. The line $y = -3$ and the curve $y = 2\,cos\,x - 3$ intersect at three points between 0 and 3π.

   Determine the coordinates of these three points.

The Compound Angle $sin(\alpha + \beta)$

When given a compound angle of the form $sin(\alpha + \beta)$, we can expand this to make difficult problems easier to solve. We can show that $sin(\alpha + \beta)$ does **NOT** equal to $sin\,\alpha + sin\,\beta$, by means of a simple example :-

Check for $\alpha = 30°$ and $\beta = 60°$ => $sin\,30° + sin\,60° = 0.5 + 0.866 = \mathbf{1\cdot366} \neq sin\,(30 + 60)° = \mathbf{1}.$

We are about to prove the following :- $sin\,(\alpha + \beta) = sin\,\alpha cos\,\beta + cos\,\alpha sin\,\beta$

Proof :-

Let **CD** = **h** (*height*)

Let angle ACB = $\alpha + \beta$

Using **SOH CAH TOA**

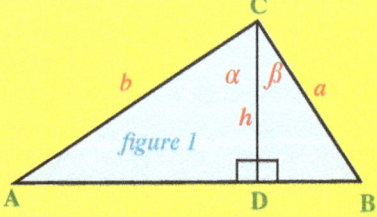

figure 1

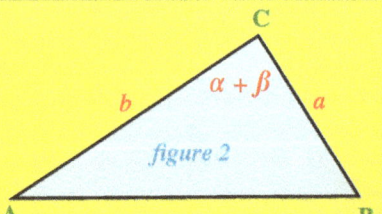

figure 2

From figure 1 :-   In triangles ADC and BDC :-

$$sin\,\alpha = \frac{AD}{b} \qquad cos\,\alpha = \frac{h}{b} \qquad sin\,\beta = \frac{BD}{a} \qquad cos\,\beta = \frac{h}{a}$$

=> $AD = b\,sin\,\alpha$ => $h = b\,cos\,\alpha$ => $BD = a\,sin\,\beta$ => $h = a\,cos\,\beta$

Area ACD = $\frac{1}{2}(AD)\,h = \frac{1}{2}(b\,sin\,\alpha)(a\,cos\,\beta)$ **Area BCD** = $\frac{1}{2}(BD)\,h = \frac{1}{2}(a\,sin\,\beta)(b\,cos\,\alpha)$

$\qquad\qquad = \frac{1}{2}\,ab\,sin\,\alpha cos\,\beta$ $\qquad\qquad = \frac{1}{2}\,ab\,cos\,\alpha sin\,\beta$

=> **Area ABC** = **Area ACD** + **Area BCD** = $\frac{1}{2}\,ab\,sin\,\alpha cos\,\beta + \frac{1}{2}\,ab\,cos\,\alpha sin\,\beta = \frac{1}{2}\,ab(sin\,\alpha cos\,\beta + cos\,\alpha sin\,\beta)$

From figure 2 :-   In triangle ACB :-

Area ABC = $\frac{1}{2}\,ab\,sin\,C = \frac{1}{2}\,ab\,sin\,(\alpha + \beta)$

$\qquad\qquad => \frac{1}{2}\,ab\,sin\,(\alpha + \beta) = \frac{1}{2}\,ab(sin\,\alpha cos\,\beta + cos\,\alpha sin\,\beta)$

(*divide each side by* $\frac{1}{2}ab$)   => $sin\,(\alpha + \beta) = sin\,\alpha cos\,\beta + cos\,\alpha sin\,\beta$

$sin\,(\alpha + \beta) = sin\,\alpha cos\,\beta + cos\,\alpha sin\,\beta$

Example 1 :-

Expand the compound angle $sin(x + 60)°$ and simplify

$$sin(x + 60)° = sin\,x°\,cos\,60° + cos\,x°\,sin\,60°$$
$$= sin\,x°(\tfrac{1}{2}) + cos\,x°(\tfrac{\sqrt{3}}{2})$$
$$= \frac{1}{2}(sin\,x° + \sqrt{3}cos\,x°)$$

Example 2 :-

Find the **exact** value of $sin\,105°$.

$$sin(60 + 45)° = sin\,60°\,cos\,45° + cos\,60°\,sin\,45°$$
$$= (\tfrac{\sqrt{3}}{2})(\tfrac{1}{\sqrt{2}}) + (\tfrac{1}{2})(\tfrac{1}{\sqrt{2}})$$
$$= \frac{\sqrt{3}}{2\sqrt{2}} + \frac{1}{2\sqrt{2}}$$
$$= \frac{\sqrt{3} + 1}{2\sqrt{2}}$$

Example 3 :-

This diagram shows that $sin\,\alpha = \frac{3}{5}$.

(a) Use Pythagoras' Theorem
     to find the length of **AB**.

(b) State the value of $cos\,\alpha$.

(c) State the value of $tan\,\alpha$.

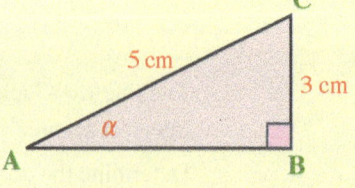

5 cm

3 cm

(a) **AB** = $\sqrt{5^2 - 3^2}$ = **4**

(b) $cos\,\alpha = \frac{adj}{hyp} = \frac{4}{5}$

(c) $tan\,\alpha = \frac{opp}{adj} = \frac{3}{4}$

Exercise 13·1

1. Expand each compound angle and simplify where possible and then simplify :-

    (a) $sin(x + 30)°$
    (b) $sin(x + 120)°$
    (c) $sin(x + 45)°$
    (d) $sin(x + 90)°$
    (e) $sin(x + \pi/3)$
    (f) $sin(x + 2\pi)$.

2. Write as a compound angle :-

    (a) $sin P cos K + cos P sin K$
    (b) $sin Y cos T + cos Y sin T$
    (c) $sin 45° cos 15° + cos 45° sin 15°$
    (d) $sin \pi/4 cos \pi/2 + cos \pi/4 sin \pi/2$.

3. By expressing $75°$ as $45° + 30°$, find the exact value of $sin 75°$.

4. This diagram shows that $sin A = \frac{4}{5}$.

    (a) Calculate the length of the 3rd side AB.

    (b) Now state the value of $cos A$.

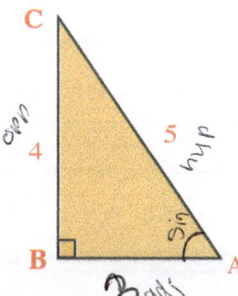

5. This diagram shows that $sin P = \frac{12}{13}$.

    Find the exact value of $cos P$.

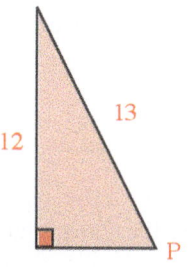

6. (a) Given that $sin T = \frac{8}{17}$, find $cos T$.

    (b) Given $sin \phi = \frac{3}{4}$, find $cos \phi$ and $tan \phi$.

7. Two right angled triangles are as shown.

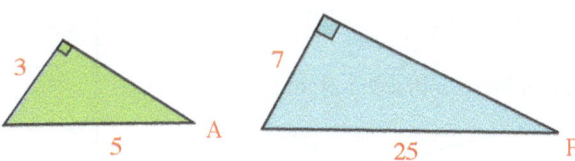

    (a) Find $sin A$, $cos A$, $sin P$ and $cos P$.

    (b) Show that $sin(A + P) = \frac{4}{5}$.

8. Given $sin B = \frac{1}{\sqrt{2}}$ and $sin C = \frac{2}{\sqrt{5}}$,

    (a) Draw two triangles to represent this information, filling in possible dimensions.

    (b) Show that $sin(B + C) = 0.3\sqrt{10}$.

Expanding $sin(\alpha - \beta)$

We can determine a similar formula for $sin(\alpha - \beta)$ by using the expansion of $sin(\alpha + \beta)$.

We simply replace β by $-\beta$ in the formula.

We need to remember that :-

$sin(-x) = -sin x$ and $cos(-x) = cos x$.

(This can be seen by looking at the graph of $y = sin x$ and the graph of $y = cos x$).

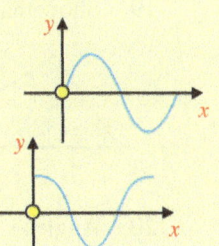

Proof

$sin(\alpha - \beta) = sin(\alpha + (-\beta))$

$= sin \alpha cos(-\beta) + cos \alpha sin(-\beta)$

$= sin \alpha cos \beta - cos \alpha sin \beta$

$sin(\alpha - \beta) = sin \alpha cos \beta - cos \alpha sin \beta$

---

9. Expand each compound angle and simplify where possible :-

    (a) $sin(x - 45)°$
    (b) $sin(3t - 5k)°$
    (c) $sin(2Q - 30)°$
    (d) $sin(x - 60)°$
    (e) $sin(x - \pi/2)$
    (f) $sin(x - \pi)$
    (g) $sin(\pi/3 - \phi)$
    (h) $sin(x - 2\pi)$.

10. Find the exact value of :-

    (a) $sin 15°$
    (b) $sin 75°$.
    (hint use $45° - 30°$).

11. Write as a single trig. expression and simplify :-

    (a) $sin C cos H - cos C sin H$
    (b) $sin 2T cos G - cos 2T sin G$
    (c) $sin 45° cos 15° - cos 45° sin 15°$
    (d) $sin \pi/2 cos \pi/4 - cos \pi/2 sin \pi/4$
    (e) $sin \pi/3 cos \pi/4 - cos \pi/3 sin \pi/4$
    (f) $sin \pi/2 cos \pi/3 + cos \pi/2 sin \pi/3$.

12. Shown are two right angled triangles.

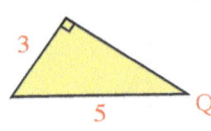 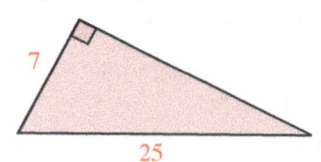

Use the above triangles to show that the value of $sin(Q - W) = \frac{44}{125}$.

13. x and y are two acute angles, such that :-

$$sin x = \tfrac{1}{\sqrt{2}} \text{ and } sin y = \tfrac{2}{\sqrt{5}},$$

Find the exact value of $sin(x - y)$.

14. Given $sin V = \tfrac{1}{2}$ and $cos K = \tfrac{1}{3}$, find the exact value of $sin(V - K)$.

Expanding $cos(\alpha + \beta)$ and $cos(\alpha - \beta)$

We will now use the 2 formulae for $sin(\alpha + \beta)$ and $sin(\alpha - \beta)$ to find similar formulae for $cos(\alpha + \beta)$ and $cos(\alpha - \beta)$.

It can be seen that in a right angle triangle :-

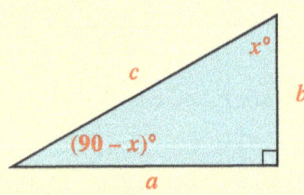

$$cos x° = \frac{b}{c} = sin(90 - x)°$$

(*i.e. cos* of any angle = *sine* of its complement).

Proof

$$cos x = sin(\tfrac{\pi}{2} - x)$$
$$\Rightarrow cos(\alpha + \beta) = sin(\tfrac{\pi}{2} - (\alpha + \beta))$$
$$= sin((\tfrac{\pi}{2} - \alpha) - \beta)$$
expand $\Rightarrow$
$$= sin(\tfrac{\pi}{2} - \alpha) cos\beta - cos(\tfrac{\pi}{2} - \alpha) sin\beta$$
$$= cos\alpha cos\beta - sin\alpha sin\beta$$

$$cos(\alpha + \beta) = cos\alpha cos\beta - sin\alpha sin\beta$$

Similarly $cos(\alpha - \beta)$ can be expanded, by writing it as $cos(\alpha + (-\beta))$, to

give $\quad cos(\alpha - \beta) = cos\alpha cos\beta + sin\alpha sin\beta$

Note the change of sign.
"–" becomes "+" and "+" becomes "–".

---

15. Expand each compound angle and simplify where necessary :-

   (a) $cos(x + y)$ (b) $cos(t - k)°$

   (c) $cos(2P - Q)$ (d) $cos(x + 60)°$

   (e) $cos(x - 45)°$ (f) $cos(x + 30)°$

   (g) $cos(x - \tfrac{\pi}{3})$ (h) $cos(x + \pi)$.

16. Write as a single trig. expression and simplify :-

   (a) $cos C cos H - sin C sin H$

   (b) $cos 2W cos T + sin 2W sin T$

   (c) $cos 45° cos 15° - sin 45° sin 15°$

   (d) $cos 45° cos 15° + sin 45° sin 15°$

   (e) $cos \tfrac{\pi}{2} cos \tfrac{\pi}{3} - sin \tfrac{\pi}{2} sin \tfrac{\pi}{3}$.

17. Prove that :-

   (a) $cos(90° - P) = sin P$

   (b) $sin(180° - T) = sin T$

   (c) $cos(180° - B) = -cos B$

   (d) $cos(-x) = cos x$ *(hint use cos(0° - x))*

   (e) $sin(-y) = -sin y$.

18. Given that $cos A = \tfrac{12}{13}$, find $tan A$.

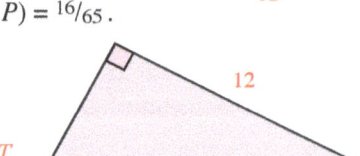

19. Show that $cos(T + P) = \tfrac{16}{65}$.

20. Angles x and y are such that :-

$$cos x = \tfrac{1}{\sqrt{2}} \text{ and } cos y = \tfrac{1}{\sqrt{3}},$$

Find the exact value of $cos(x - y)$.

21. Given $sin D = \tfrac{2}{3}$ and $cos E = \tfrac{1}{3}$, find the exact value of $cos(D - E)$.

22. Two right angled triangles are as shown.

   (a) Show that $cos(x + y) = \tfrac{\sqrt{5}}{5}$.

   (b) Find $cos(y - x)$.

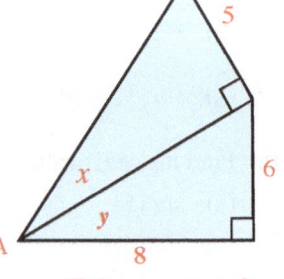

Trigonometric Identities

An "Identity" is a statement that is always true for **all** values of any variables involved. (e.g. $(a + b)^2 = a^2 + 2ab + b^2$).

We already know two **trig identities**.

$$\boxed{sin^2\theta + cos^2\theta = 1}$$

$$\boxed{\frac{sin\,\theta}{cos\,\theta} = tan\,\theta}$$

This can also lead to
$sin^2\theta = 1 - cos^2\theta$ and
$cos^2\theta = 1 - sin^2\theta$.

We can now use the trigonometric expansions developed earlier in this chapter to discover others.

Remember that an identity involving a variable (x) is a rule that can be proven to be true *for all* values of x.

To prove an identity, you generally :-

- Begin with the left hand side (**L.H.S.**) (or occasionally the (**R.H.S.**))

- Rearrange it using various techniques, and eventually

- Show that it is **identical to** the other side. (**L.H.S.**) or (**R.H.S.**).

Example 1 :-

Prove that

$(sin\,x - cos\,x)(sin\,x - cos\,x) = 1 - 2\,sin\,x\,cos\,x.$

L.H.S. $= (sin\,x - cos\,x)(sin\,x - cos\,x)$

$= sin^2x - sin\,x\,cos\,x - sin\,x\,cos\,x + cos^2x.$

$= (sin^2x + cos^2x) - 2\,sin\,x\,cos\,x$

$= 1 - 2\,sin\,x\,cos\,x$ *Remember* $sin^2x + cos^2x = 1$

$= $ **R.H.S.**   hence - proven !

Example 2 :-

Prove that $\dfrac{sin(x - y)}{cos\,x\,cos\,y} = tan\,x - tan\,y.$

L.H.S. $= \dfrac{sin(x - y)}{cos\,x\,cos\,y}$

$= \dfrac{sin\,x\,cos\,y - cos\,x\,sin\,y}{cos\,x\,cos\,y}$

$= \dfrac{sin\,x\,cos\,y}{cos\,x\,cos\,y} - \dfrac{cos\,x\,sin\,y}{cos\,x\,cos\,y}$

$= \dfrac{sin\,x}{cos\,x} - \dfrac{sin\,y}{cos\,y}$

$= tan\,x - tan\,y$ $=$ **R.H.S.** *as required*.

Exercise 13·2

1. Prove each identity :-

(a) $(sin\,x + cos\,x)(sin\,x - cos\,x) = 1 - 2\,cos^2x$

(b) $\dfrac{cos\,x\,tan\,x}{sin\,x} = 1$

(c) $sin(180 + x)° = \text{-}sin\,x°$

(d) $cos(A - B) - cos(A + B) = 2\,sin\,A\,sin\,B$

(e) $sin(p + q)\,sin(p - q) = sin^2p - sin^2q$

(f) $\dfrac{1 - sin^2 x}{sin^2 x} = \dfrac{1}{tan^2 x}$

(g) $\dfrac{cos(90 - x)°}{sin\,x°} = 1$.

2. Prove each of the following :-

(a) $\dfrac{sin\,x}{cos\,x} + \dfrac{cos\,x}{sin\,x} = \dfrac{1}{cos\,x\,sin\,x}$

(b) $(2\,cos\,x + 3\,sin\,x)^2 + (3\,cos\,x - 2\,sin\,x)^2 = 13$

(c) $(sin\,x + cos\,x)^2 - (sin\,x - cos\,x)^2 = 4\,sin\,x\,cos\,x$

(d) $\left(\dfrac{1 - cos^2 x}{cos^2 x}\right)\left(\dfrac{1 - sin^2 x}{sin^2 x}\right) = 1$

(e) $cos^4y - sin^4y = cos^2y - sin^2y.$

3. Use $2x = (x + x)$ to find an expansion for $sin\,2x$.

The Double Angle Formulae involving 2α

The "**Addition Formulae**" can also be used to expand expressions like $\sin 2\alpha$ and $\cos 2\alpha$.

$$\sin 2\alpha = 2\sin\alpha\cos\alpha$$

$$\cos 2\alpha = \cos^2\alpha - \sin^2\alpha$$

$$\cos 2\alpha = 2\cos^2\alpha - 1$$
$$= 1 - 2\sin^2\alpha$$

Proof
$$\begin{aligned}\sin 2\alpha &= \sin(\alpha + \alpha) \\ &= \sin\alpha\cos\alpha + \cos\alpha\sin\alpha \\ &= 2\sin\alpha\cos\alpha\end{aligned}$$

Proof
$$\begin{aligned}\cos 2\alpha &= \cos(\alpha + \alpha) \\ &= \cos\alpha\cos\alpha - \sin\alpha\sin\alpha \\ &= \cos^2\alpha - \sin^2\alpha\end{aligned}$$

By using the result of the 2nd *proof*
$$\begin{aligned}\cos 2\alpha &= \cos^2\alpha - \sin^2\alpha \\ &= \cos^2\alpha - (1 - \cos^2\alpha) \\ &= 2\cos^2\alpha - 1\end{aligned}$$

Try to prove the second one yourself.

Example :-

Given that α is an acute angle and $\sin\alpha = {}^3/_5$, find :-

(a) $\sin 2\alpha$ (b) $\cos 2\alpha$.

The first thing to do is sketch a right angled triangle :-

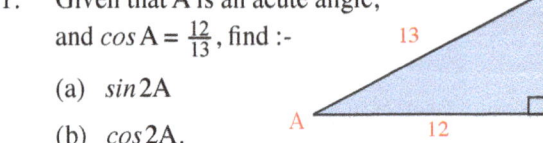

(a) $\begin{aligned}\sin 2\alpha &= 2\sin\alpha\cos\alpha \\ &= 2 \times \tfrac{3}{5} \times \tfrac{4}{5} \\ &= \boxed{\tfrac{24}{25}}\end{aligned}$

(b) $\begin{aligned}\cos 2\alpha &= \cos^2\alpha - \sin^2\alpha \\ &= (\tfrac{4}{5})^2 - (\tfrac{3}{5})^2 \\ &= \tfrac{16}{25} - \tfrac{9}{25} \\ &= \boxed{\tfrac{7}{25}}\end{aligned}$

Then use Pythagoras' Theorem to calculate the missing side which turns out to be **4.**

Exercise 13·3

1. Given that A is an acute angle, and $\cos A = \frac{12}{13}$, find :-

    (a) $\sin 2A$

    (b) $\cos 2A$.

2. Q is an acute angle and $\sin Q = \frac{8}{17}$, find :-

    (a) $\sin 2Q$ (b) $\cos 2Q$.

3. (a) From the diagram below show that $\sin 2\alpha = \frac{24}{25}$.

    (b) Prove that $\cos\beta = -\frac{7}{25}$.

4. Find the exact value of each expression :-

    (a) $2\sin 15°\cos 15°$ (b) $2\cos^2 15° - 1$

    (c) $1 - 2\sin^2(\pi/3)$ (d) $\cos^2(\pi/6) - \sin^2(\pi/6)$.

5. (a) By expressing 4α as $2 \times 2\alpha$ show that :-
    $$\sin 4\alpha = 4\sin\alpha\cos^3\alpha - 4\sin^3\alpha\cos\alpha.$$

    (b) Find $\cos 4Q$ in terms of $\cos Q$.

    (c) Prove that $\cos 3P = 4\cos^3 P - 3\cos P$.

6. Given that ϕ is an acute angle and $\sin\phi = \frac{4}{5}$, find $\sin 2\phi$, $\cos 2\phi$ and $\tan 2\phi$.

7. Given both A and B are acute angles with $\sin A = \frac{4}{5}$ and $\cos B = \frac{5}{13}$, find the value of :-

    (a) $\sin(2A - B)$ (b) $\cos(A + 2B)$.

Solving Trigonometric Equations involving the Double Angle Formulae

We can solve trig equations involving $2x$, by expanding the expression and factorising where possible.

Example 1 :-

Solve :- $\sin 2x° + \sin x° = 0$, where $0 < x < 360$.

$$\sin 2x° + \sin x° = 0$$
$$\Rightarrow\ 2\sin x°\cos x° + \sin x° = 0$$
$$\Rightarrow\ \sin x°(2\cos x° + 1) = 0$$
$$\Rightarrow\ \sin x° = 0\ \Rightarrow\ x = 0, \textbf{180}, 360$$
$$\textbf{or}\ \ 2\cos x° + 1 = 0$$
$$\Rightarrow\ \cos x° = -\tfrac{1}{2}\ \Rightarrow\ x = \textbf{120}, \textbf{240}$$

$$\boxed{x = 120,\ 180,\ 240.}$$

Note :- the limits do **not** include 0° or 360° so we ignore these two values.

Example 2 :-

Solve :- $\cos 2x - \cos x = 0$, where $0 \le x \le 2\pi$.

$$\cos 2x + \cos x = 0$$
$$\Rightarrow\ 2\cos^2 x - 1 + \cos x = 0$$
$$\Rightarrow\ 2\cos^2 x + \cos x - 1 = 0$$
$$\Rightarrow\ (2\cos x - 1)(\cos x + 1) = 0$$
$$\Rightarrow\ 2\cos x - 1 = 0\ \ \textbf{or}\ \ \cos x + 1 = 0$$
$$\Rightarrow\ \cos x = \tfrac{1}{2}\ \ \textbf{or}\ \ \cos x = -1$$
$$\Rightarrow\ x = \pi/3,\ ^{5\pi}/3\ \ \textbf{or}\ \ x = \pi.$$

$$\boxed{x = \pi/3,\ \pi,\ ^{5\pi}/3.}$$

Note :- this time the limits **do** include 0 and 2π.

Exercise 13·4

1. Solve :- $\sin 2x° - 2\sin x° = 0$, where $0 < x \le 360$.

   Copy and **complete** :-

   $$\sin 2x° - 2\sin x° = 0$$
   $$\Rightarrow\ 2\sin x°\cos x° - 2\sin x° = 0$$
   $$\Rightarrow\ 2\sin x°(\cos x° - ...) = 0$$
   $$\Rightarrow\ \sin x° = 0 \Rightarrow x = \underline{0}, 180, 360$$
   $$\textbf{or}\ \ \cos x° = ...\ \Rightarrow x = ...$$
   $$\therefore\ \ x = ...$$

2. Solve for $0 \le x < 360°$:-

   (a) $\cos 2x° - \sin x° = 0$

   (b) $\cos 2x° + \sin x° = 0$

   (c) $\sin 2x° + \cos x° = 0$

   (d) $\cos 2x° - \sin x° - 1 = 0$.

3. Solve, where $0 \le x < 180$:-

   (a) $\cos 2x° - 4\sin x° + 5 = 0$

   (b) $\cos 2x° - 3\cos x° = -1$

   (c) $1 - \cos x° - 2\cos 2x° = 0$.

4. Solve, where $0 \le x < 2\pi$:-

   (a) $\sin 2x = \sin x$

   (b) $\sqrt{2}\sin 2x = 2\sin x$

   (c) $\cos 2x = 7\sin x + 4$.

5. (a) Make a sketch of $y = \sin x$, where $0 \le x < 2\pi$.

   (b) Show $y = \cos 2x$ on the same diagram.

   (c) Determine where these two graphs intersect.

   (d) State what your answers would be if the limits were :-

   (i) $0 \le x < 4\pi$ \quad (ii) $4\pi \le x < 6\pi$.

6. Solve $sin\,4\alpha = 2\,sin\,2\alpha$ for $\{0 < \alpha \le 2\pi\}$.

   (Hint :- use the fact that $4a = 2 \times (2a)$).

7. Shown are parts of the graphs of :-

   $y = cos\,2x°$ and

   $y = -sin\,x°$.

   Find the coordinates of the points where the graphs intersect, given $0 < x < 360$.

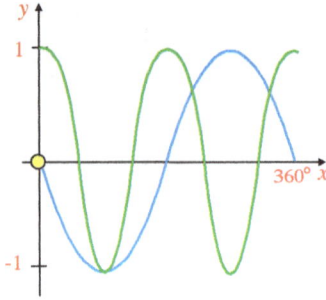

8. For each diagram :-
   (i) state a possible equation of each trig. graph
   (ii) find where each pair of graphs intersect in the domain indicated by the diagrams.

   (a)   (b)

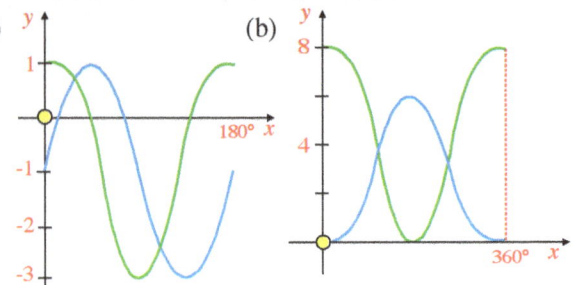

Further Trigonometric Identities

We will now look at rearranging the two "double angle" formulae to create a further two new identities :-

$$cos\,2\alpha = 2\,cos^2\alpha - 1 \quad - \quad 1$$
$$\text{and} \quad cos\,2\alpha = 1 - 2\,sin^2\alpha \quad - \quad 2$$

$$sin\,2\alpha = 2\,sin\,\alpha\,cos\,\alpha$$
$$cos\,2\alpha = cos^2\alpha - sin^2\alpha$$
$$= 2\,cos^2\alpha - 1$$
$$= 1 - 2\,sin^2\alpha$$

From **1**, $cos\,2\alpha = 2\,cos^2\alpha - 1$

$\Rightarrow \quad 2\,cos^2\alpha - 1 = cos\,2\alpha$

$\Rightarrow \quad 2\,cos^2\alpha = 1 + cos\,2\alpha$

$\Rightarrow \quad cos^2\alpha = \frac{1}{2}(1 + cos\,2\alpha)$

From **2**, $cos\,2\alpha = 1 - 2\,sin^2\alpha$

$\Rightarrow \quad 1 - 2\,sin^2\alpha = cos\,2\alpha$

$\Rightarrow \quad 2\,sin^2\alpha = 1 - cos\,2\alpha$

$\Rightarrow \quad sin^2\alpha = \frac{1}{2}(1 - cos\,2\alpha)$

Two New Identities :-

$$cos^2\alpha = \tfrac{1}{2}(1 + cos\,2\alpha)$$
$$sin^2\alpha = \tfrac{1}{2}(1 - cos\,2\alpha)$$

Example

Express $cos^2\alpha - 2\,sin^2\alpha$ in terms of $cos\,2\alpha$.

$$cos^2\alpha - 2\,sin^2\alpha$$
$$= \tfrac{1}{2}(1 + cos\,2\alpha) - 2(\tfrac{1}{2}(1 - cos\,2\alpha))$$
$$= \tfrac{1}{2} + \tfrac{1}{2}\,cos\,2\alpha - 1 + cos\,2\alpha$$
$$= \tfrac{3}{2}\,cos\,2\alpha - \tfrac{1}{2}$$

Exercise 13·5

1. Using $cos^2\alpha = \frac{1}{2}(1 + cos\,2\alpha)$

   and $\quad sin^2\alpha = \frac{1}{2}(1 - cos\,2\alpha)$,

   prove that $cos^2\alpha + sin^2\alpha = 1$.

2. Express each of the following in terms of $cos\,2x$:-

   (a) $2\,cos^2x$ (b) $4\,sin^2x$

   (c) $(cos^2x)^2$ (d) sin^4x.

3. (a) Prove $cos^4x - sin^4x = cos\,2x$.

   (b) Prove that $(sin\,\frac{1}{2}y - cos\,\frac{1}{2}y)^2 = 1 - sin\,y$.

4. Prove each of the following :-

   (a) $\dfrac{1 - cos\,2x}{sin\,2x} = tan\,x$ (b) $\dfrac{2\,tan\,y}{1 + tan^2\,y} = sin\,2y$

   (c) $\left(\dfrac{1 - cos\,2w}{1 + cos\,2w}\right) = -tan^2\,w$

   (d) $tan(P + Q) = \dfrac{tan\,P + tan\,Q}{1 - tan\,P\,tan\,Q}$.

5. Solve :-

   $cos\,2x° + 2\,cos^2x° = 4\,sin\,x° + 3$, when $0 \le x \le 360$.

Exercise 13·6   Mixed Exercise

1. Write *True* or *False* for each statement:-

    (a) $cos(-x) = sin x$

    (b) $-cos x = sin x$

    (c) $cos(180 - B)° = -cos B°$

    (d) $sin(90 - k)° = -sin k°$

    (e) π radians is equivalent to 360°

    (f) $cos(a + b) = cos a \cos b + sin a \sin b$

    (g) $\dfrac{1}{tan\, y} = \dfrac{cos\, y}{sin\, y}$

    (h) $tan\, {}^{\pi}\!/6 = \sqrt{3}$

    (i) $y = 3\,cos\,2x - 2$ has a minimum value of -5.

2. Expand fully and simplify where possible :-

    (a) $sin(x + 60)°$ (b) $cos(x - y)°$

    (c) $sin(x - {}^{\pi}\!/4)$ (d) $cos(2x + 4\pi)$.

3. Simplify fully :-

    (a) $sin\,45° \cos 15° + cos\,45° \sin 15°$

    (b) $sin\, {}^{\pi}\!/3 \, cos \, {}^{\pi}\!/6 + cos\, {}^{\pi}\!/3 \, sin\, {}^{\pi}\!/6$.

4. Find the exact value of :-

    (a) $sin\,75°$ (b) $cos\,105°$.

5. Find the exact value of :-

    (a) $2\,sin\,15° \cos 15°$ (b) $1 - 2\,sin^2 15°$

    (c) $2\,cos^2({}^{\pi}\!/6) - 1$ (d) $cos^2({}^{\pi}\!/4) - sin^2({}^{\pi}\!/4)$.

6. Given that $sin\,A = {}^1\!/2$, find :-

    (a) $cos\,A$

    (b) $tan\,A$.

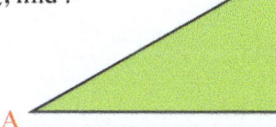

7. Find $tan\,2\alpha$, given α is an acute angle and $sin\,\alpha = {}^4\!/5$.

8. Given both P and Q are acute angles with $sin\,P = {}^3\!/5$. and $cos\,Q = {}^5\!/13$, find the value of :-

    (a) $sin(2P - Q)$ (b) $cos(2P + Q)$.

9. (a) Sketch on the same diagram :-

        $y = sin\,x$ and $y = cos\,x$, where $\pi \le x \le 2\pi$.

    (b) Find, algebraically, the points of intersection of these two curves between the stated limits.

10. Solve :-

    (a) $sin\,2x° - cos\,x° = 0$ for $0 \le x \le 360$

    (b) $cos\,2y - 2\,sin\,y - 1 = 0$ for $0 < x < 2\pi$

    (c) $cos\,2x° - 7\,sin\,x° - 4 = 0$ for $0 \le x \le 180$

    (d) $\frac{1}{2}(1 + cos\,2x) - 1 = 0$ for $0 \le x \le {}^{\pi}\!/2$

    (e) $2\,cos\,2x° + 3\,sin\,x° - 1 = 0$ for $0 \le x \le 360$.

11. (a) State a possible equation for each of the trig. graphs shown in the diagram below.

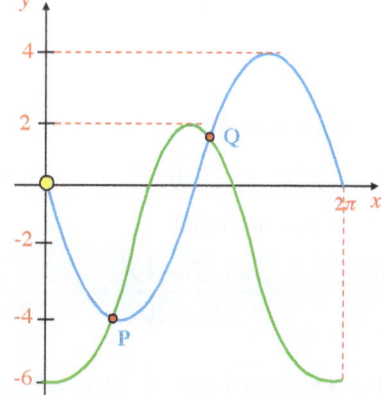

    (b) Find the coordinates of the points of intersection of these two graphs.

12. (a) Sketch on the same diagram the graphs of $y = sin\,2x°$ and $y = cos\,x°$, for $0 \le x \le 360$.

    (b) Find any point(s) of intersection with domain $0 \le x \le 90$.

13. Prove :-

    (a) $sin(180 - (x + y)) = sin(x + y)$

    (b) $cos(x - y) - cos(x + y) = 2\,sin\,x\,sin\,y$

    (c) $2\,cos(x + \pi)\,cos(x - \pi) = cos\,2x + 1$

    (d) $tan\,x\,sin\,2x = 1 - cos\,2x$

    (e) $tan(x - y) = \dfrac{tan\,x - tan\,y}{1 + tan\,x\,tan\,y}$.

1. The right angled triangle below has dimensions as shown.

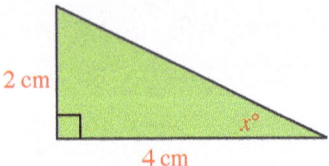

Find the exact values of :-

(a) $sin x$ **(2)**

(b) $sin 2x$ **(3)**

2. Given that $sin x = 0.6$, find the **exact** value of $sin 2x$. **(4)**

3. (a) Find in its simplest form $sin(270 - k)°$. **(2)**

(b) Find in its simplest form $cos(k + 180)°$. **(2)**

(c) Hence show that

$$\frac{sin(270-k)°}{cos(k+180)°} = 1$$ **(2)**

4. State a suitable range of values for p, if $p - 3\cos 2x > 0$. **(2)**

5. Sketch the graph of $y = 3\cos 2x - 2$ for $0 < x < \pi$. **(3)**

6. The diagram shows part of the graph of the function

$$y = a\, sin\, bx + c.$$

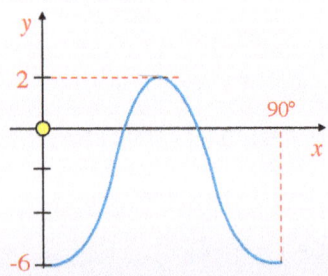

State the values of a, b and c. **(3)**

7. Solve the equation

$$cos x - 2\cos 2x - 2 = 0,$$

for $0 < x < \pi$. **(5)**

8. (a) Write a possible equation for each of the two trig functions shown below, with domain $-360 \le x \le 0$. **(2)**

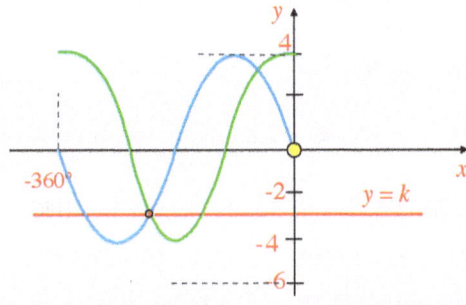

(b) The line $y = k$ (*in red*) passes through the point of intersection of these two graphs.

Find the value of k. **(4)**

9. (a) Use the fact that $\pi/12 = \pi/3 - \pi/4$ to find the exact value of $sin(\pi/12)$. **(3)**

(b) Hence or otherwise find the exact value of $sin(\pi/12) + sin(\pi/4)$. **(1)**

10. Show that :-

$$\frac{sin 2x}{tan x} - 1 = cos 2x.$$ **(3)**

11. Solve $cos 2x° = sin^2 x°$, given $0 < x < 180$. **(5)**

12. Using $sin^2 y = \frac{1}{2}(1 - cos 2y)$, express $sin^4 y$ in the form $a + b\cos 2y + c\cos^2 2y$, stating the values of a, b and c. **(4)**

13. Prove that :-

$$\left(\frac{1 - tan^2 x}{1 + tan^2 x}\right) = cos 2x.$$ **(4)**

A Review of Vector Work

There are two types of measurable quantities in this world :-   **SCALARS**   and   **VECTORS**.

> A **scalar** quantity is one that only requires **size** (or **magnitude**) to define it fully, and does **not** require a sense of "**direction**" to be assigned to it.
>
> *Examples :-*   time, length, area, speed, etc.

> A **vector** quantity is one that requires, not just **magnitude** (or **size**) to define it, but needs an indication of its **direction**.
>
> *Examples :-*   displacement, velocity, force, etc.
>
> A vector can be thought of as a **journey** or **displacement** from point A to point B.

We can represent a vector by a **directed line segment**, and use the end point capital letters (A and B) or a small underline letter to represent the vector.

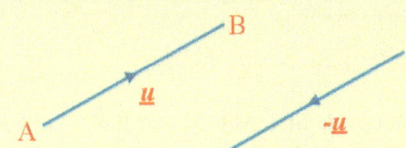

The vector shown opposite is represented by $\overrightarrow{AB}$ = **_u_**

Note :- If $\overrightarrow{AB}$ = **_u_**, then $\overrightarrow{BA}$ = **-_u_**, => $\overrightarrow{BA}$ = $-\overrightarrow{AB}$.

> **Note** :- throughout this chapter we will represent a vector as a small bold, underlined single letter. e.g. **_p_**, **_a_**, **_v_**, etc so that the vectors stand out clearly on the page. Other books and exam papers may omit the "underlining".

We can think of vectors as "journeys" and can add vectors to create equivalent vectors as follows :-

$$\overrightarrow{AB} + \overrightarrow{BC} = \overrightarrow{AC} = \textbf{\textit{u}} + \textbf{\textit{v}}.$$

Note the "add nose to tail" arrangement.

To subtract vectors like **_u_** – **_v_**, we simply add **_u_** + **-_v_**,

or $\overrightarrow{PQ} - \overrightarrow{RQ} = \overrightarrow{PQ} + \overrightarrow{QR} = \overrightarrow{PR}$ (*note the change of order*).

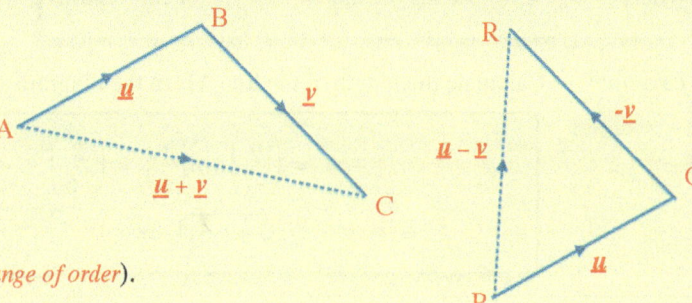

We can multiply a vector **_u_** by a scalar **_k_** to produce the vector **_ku_**.

This vector **_ku_** will be parallel to **_u_**, but will be **_k_** times as long.

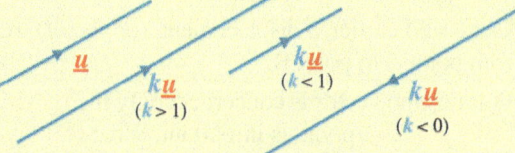

We can represent a vector in two dimensions using a grid system. In this figure :-

$$\overrightarrow{AB} = \textbf{\textit{n}} = \begin{pmatrix} 6 \\ 4 \end{pmatrix}, \quad \overrightarrow{RT} = \textbf{\textit{s}} = \begin{pmatrix} 4 \\ -5 \end{pmatrix}, \quad \overrightarrow{PQ} = \textbf{\textit{r}} = \begin{pmatrix} -9 \\ -2 \end{pmatrix}.$$

These 2 numbers are referred to as the **components** of the vector.

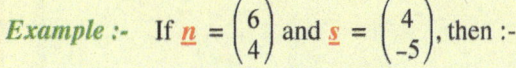

We can add and subtract vectors and multiply vectors by a scalar, as before, using these columnar representations of them as follows :-

Example :-   If $\textbf{\textit{n}} = \begin{pmatrix} 6 \\ 4 \end{pmatrix}$ and $\textbf{\textit{s}} = \begin{pmatrix} 4 \\ -5 \end{pmatrix}$, then :-

$$\textbf{\textit{n}} + \textbf{\textit{s}} = \begin{pmatrix} 6 \\ 4 \end{pmatrix} + \begin{pmatrix} 4 \\ -5 \end{pmatrix} = \begin{pmatrix} 10 \\ -1 \end{pmatrix}$$ $$\textbf{\textit{n}} - \textbf{\textit{s}} = \begin{pmatrix} 6 \\ 4 \end{pmatrix} - \begin{pmatrix} 4 \\ -5 \end{pmatrix} = \begin{pmatrix} 2 \\ 9 \end{pmatrix}$$ $$3\textbf{\textit{s}} = 3 \times \begin{pmatrix} 4 \\ -5 \end{pmatrix} = \begin{pmatrix} 12 \\ -15 \end{pmatrix}$$ $$-\tfrac{1}{2}\textbf{\textit{n}} = -\tfrac{1}{2} \begin{pmatrix} 6 \\ 4 \end{pmatrix} = \begin{pmatrix} -3 \\ -2 \end{pmatrix}.$$

Position Vector

We can show vectors in a coordinate diagram. In this diagram,

$$\overrightarrow{OP} = \underline{p} = \begin{pmatrix} 2 \\ 5 \end{pmatrix}, \quad \overrightarrow{OQ} = \underline{q} = \begin{pmatrix} 8 \\ 2 \end{pmatrix}, \quad \overrightarrow{OR} = \underline{r} = \begin{pmatrix} 4 \\ -3 \end{pmatrix}.$$

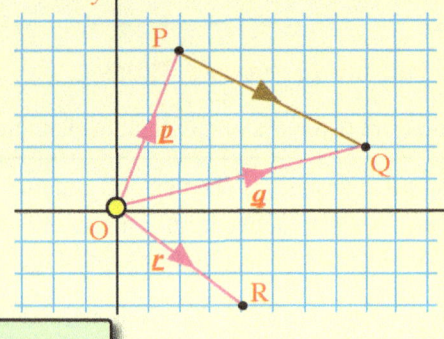

If A has coordinates A(6, -3) its **position vector** is $\overrightarrow{OA} = \underline{a} = \begin{pmatrix} 6 \\ -3 \end{pmatrix}$.

IMPORTANT :- If we are given two points P(2, 6) and Q(8, 2), then we can find the vector joining them $\overrightarrow{PQ}$, as follows :-

$$\overrightarrow{PQ} = \overrightarrow{OQ} - \overrightarrow{OP} = \begin{pmatrix} 8 \\ 2 \end{pmatrix} - \begin{pmatrix} 2 \\ 5 \end{pmatrix} = \begin{pmatrix} 6 \\ -3 \end{pmatrix} \quad \text{or} \quad \overrightarrow{PQ} = \underline{q} - \underline{p}.$$

Magnitude of a Vector

Given two points, A(1, 5) and B(9, -1), we could find the magnitude or length of AB by using Pythagoras' Theorem, or the distance formula.

A second way is to use vectors, as follows :-

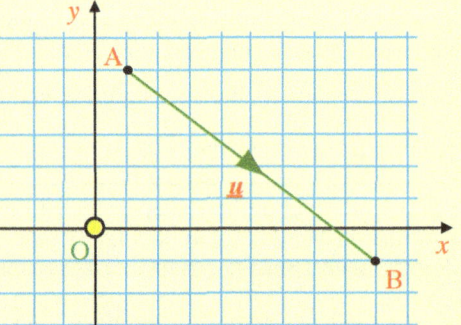

If vector $\overrightarrow{AB} = \underline{u} = \begin{pmatrix} x \\ y \end{pmatrix}$, then $|\overrightarrow{AB}| = |\underline{u}| = \sqrt{x^2 + y^2}$,
where $|\overrightarrow{AB}| = |\underline{u}|$ stands for the **magnitude** of the vector.

Example :- Calculate the length of the line AB in the diagram shown.

$$\overrightarrow{AB} = \underline{u} = \underline{b} - \underline{a} = \begin{pmatrix} 9 \\ -1 \end{pmatrix} - \begin{pmatrix} 1 \\ 5 \end{pmatrix} = \begin{pmatrix} 8 \\ -6 \end{pmatrix}$$

$$\Rightarrow |\overrightarrow{AB}| = |\underline{u}| = \sqrt{8^2 + (-6)^2} = 10$$

$|\overrightarrow{AB}|$ is referred to as the **magnitude** or the **modulus** of the vector $\overrightarrow{AB}$.

Alternative Vector Journeys

As we said earlier, a displacement, (or vector), represents a journey from point A to point B.

As far as the vector is concerned, only the **finishing** point, **in relation to the starting** point, is important. What **route** you take is **irrelevant**.

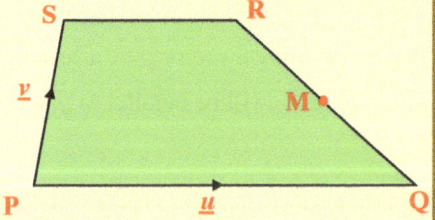

Example :- SPQR is a **trapezium** with side PQ equal to **2 ×** side SR in length.

Vector $\overrightarrow{PQ} = \underline{u}$ and vector $\overrightarrow{PS} = \underline{v}$.

Find, in terms of $\underline{u}$ and $\underline{v}$, the following vectors :-

(a) $\overrightarrow{SR}$ (b) $\overrightarrow{PR}$ (c) $\overrightarrow{SQ}$ (d) $\overrightarrow{RQ}$ (e) $\overrightarrow{PM}$, (*where M is the mid-point of RQ*).

(a) $\overrightarrow{SR}$	(b) $\overrightarrow{PR}$	(c) $\overrightarrow{SQ}$	(d) $\overrightarrow{RQ}$	(e) $\overrightarrow{PM}$
$= \frac{1}{2}\overrightarrow{PQ}$	$= \overrightarrow{PS} + \overrightarrow{SR}$	$= \overrightarrow{SP} + \overrightarrow{PQ}$	$= \overrightarrow{RS} + \overrightarrow{SQ}$	$= \overrightarrow{PS} + \overrightarrow{SR} + \overrightarrow{RM}$
$= \frac{1}{2}\underline{u}$	$= \underline{v} + \frac{1}{2}\underline{u}$	$= -\underline{v} + \underline{u}$	$= -\frac{1}{2}\underline{u} + \underline{u} - \underline{v}$	$= \underline{v} + \frac{1}{2}\underline{u} + \frac{1}{2}(\frac{1}{2}\underline{u} - \underline{v})$
		$= \underline{u} - \underline{v}$	$= \frac{1}{2}\underline{u} - \underline{v}$	$= \frac{3}{4}\underline{u} + \frac{1}{2}\underline{v}$

Exercise H14·1

1. Sketch this vector $\underline{w}$. On the same diagram,

   (a) sketch the vector $2\underline{w}$.

   (b) Show the vector $4\underline{w}$.

   (c) Show the vector $-\underline{w}$.

   (d) Show the vector $-3\underline{w}$.

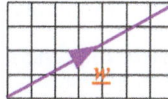

2. Sketch these two vectors $\underline{u}$ and $\underline{v}$.

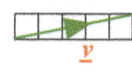

   (a) Now sketch the vector $2\underline{v}$.

   (b) Sketch the vector showing $\underline{u} + \underline{v}$ and mark $\underline{u} + \underline{v}$ on your diagram.

   (c) Sketch the vector $2\underline{u} + \underline{v}$.

   (d) Sketch the vector $-(\underline{u} + \underline{v})$.

3. Sketch the vectors $\underline{a}$ and $\underline{b}$.

   (a) Sketch the vector $\underline{a} + \underline{b}$.

   (b) Now sketch and label vector $\underline{a} - \underline{b}$.

   (c) Sketch the vector $\underline{b} - \underline{a}$. (*Draw $\underline{b}$ first*).

   (d) Show the vector $3\underline{b} - 2\underline{a}$.

   (e) Show the vector vector $\underline{b} + -\underline{b}$.

   When you add a vector to its negative, you end up where you started. (*They cancel each other*).

   > This is referred to as the **zero vector**.
   > $\underline{b} + -\underline{b}$ is the same as $\underline{b} - \underline{b} = \underline{0}$. (*Note how it is written*).

4. (a) Draw a Cartesian diagram and plot the 2 points P(3, 2) and Q(5, 7).

   (b) Write the components of the position vectors $\underline{p}$ and $\underline{q}$. (i.e. $\begin{pmatrix} 3 \\ ? \end{pmatrix}$ and $\begin{pmatrix} ? \\ ? \end{pmatrix}$).

   (c) Find vector $\overrightarrow{PQ}$, using $\overrightarrow{PQ} = \underline{q} - \underline{p}$.

   (d) Write down the vector $\overrightarrow{QP}$.

5. For each of the following pairs of points, find the components of the vector joining the first point to the second :-

   (a) A(3, 1), B(8, 4) (i.e. find vector $\overrightarrow{AB}$).

   (b) C(0, 6), D(5, 3)

   (c) E(1, -4), F(7, -2)

   (d) G(m, p), H(s, t).

6. The coordinates of 6 points are H(-1, -1), I(3, 2), J(1, -4), K(5, -1), L(-6, 0) and M(-2, 3).

   (a) Find the vector $\overrightarrow{HI}$. i.e. ($\underline{i} - \underline{h}$).

   (b) Find the vectors $\overrightarrow{JK}$ and $\overrightarrow{LM}$.

   (c) What does this tell you about the three lines, HI, JK and LM ?

7. P(-2, -3), Q(1, 3), R(6, 5) and S(3, -1).

   (a) Without plotting the points, find the components of the vectors $\overrightarrow{PQ}$ and $\overrightarrow{RS}$.

   (b) What can you say about lines PQ and RS ?

   (c) What type of quadrilateral does this fact tell you PQRS must be ?

8. Calculate the magnitude of the vector joining M(5, 3) and N(9, 6).

   Copy and **complete** :-

   $$\overrightarrow{MN} = \underline{n} - \underline{m} = \begin{pmatrix} 9 \\ 6 \end{pmatrix} - \begin{pmatrix} \dots \\ \dots \end{pmatrix} = \begin{pmatrix} \dots \\ \dots \end{pmatrix}.$$
   $$|\overrightarrow{MN}| = \sqrt{\dots^2 + \dots^2} = \dots$$

9. In a similar way, calculate the **magnitude**, of the vector joining each pair of points :-

   (a) E(8, 5), F(11, 9)   (b) Q(-2, 3), R(10, -2)

   (c) S(4, -1), T(12, 5)   (d) U(-4, -5), V(5, 7).

10. A(-1, -4), B(1, 0) and C(-5, -2) are 3 points.

    (a) Use the above method to calculate the lengths of the 3 sides of triangle ABC.

    (b) Use your answer to part (a) to explain clearly what kind of triangle ABC is.

11. Given C(4, 5), K(10, 13), L(12, -1) and M(-4, 11), show that K, L and M could be points which lie on the circumference of a circle having its centre at point C.

12. A force is applied to a large box in order to slide it from point R to point S.

This force is represented by the vector $\overrightarrow{RS}$.

A second force is then applied to move the box from point S to a new point T.

This force is represented by the vector $\overrightarrow{ST}$.

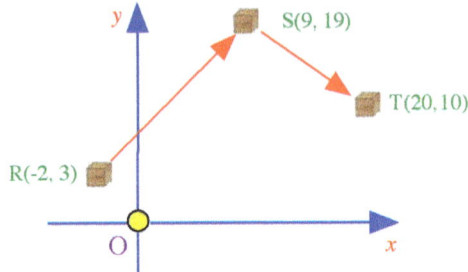

(a) Find the components of forces $\overrightarrow{RS}$ and $\overrightarrow{ST}$.

(b) Find the component of the **resultant** force (*i.e. the single force*), which if applied, would have moved the box directly from point R to point T.

13. The coordinate diagram shows the position of two ships, the **J**eronimo and the **P**eacock, in relation to **O**rly harbour, (1 *unit* = 10 *km*).

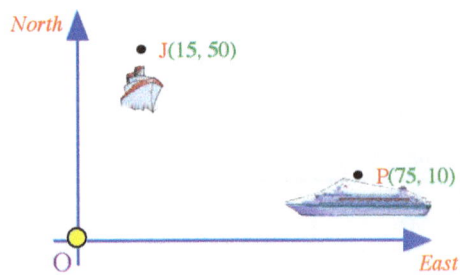

(a) Describe, using components, the vector journey that the Jeronimo would have to travel to end up to meet up with the Peacock.

(b) Use this to determine the distance Jeronimo had sailed, (*the magnitude*).

14. Three ropes are tied to a box and the ropes are pulled in various directions as shown below.

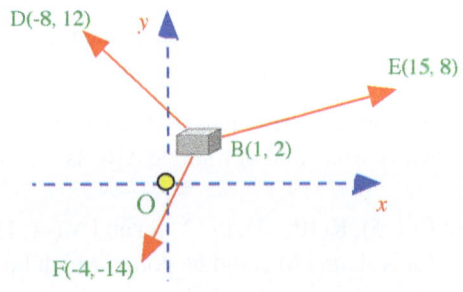

The coordinates of the box are (1, 2)

14. The vectors $\overrightarrow{BD}$, $\overrightarrow{BE}$ and $\overrightarrow{BF}$ represent the **strength** and **direction** of the forces being applied to the box.

(a) Determine the component values of the three forces, $\overrightarrow{BD}$, $\overrightarrow{BE}$ and $\overrightarrow{BF}$.

(b) Find the **magnitude** of each force.

(c) Add the 3 forces together, $\overrightarrow{BD} + \overrightarrow{BE} + \overrightarrow{BF}$.

(d) Explain how far, and in which direction, the box actually moves.

15. Shown is parallelogram ABCD, with vector $\overrightarrow{AB} = \underline{p}$ and vector $\overrightarrow{AD} = \underline{q}$.

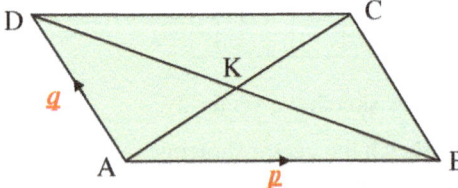

Find the following vectors in terms of $\underline{p}$ and $\underline{q}$:-

(a) $\overrightarrow{BC}$ (b) $\overrightarrow{DC}$ (c) $\overrightarrow{AC}$

(d) $\overrightarrow{BD}$ (e) $\overrightarrow{AK}$ (f) $\overrightarrow{DK}$.

16. Trapezium EFGH has EF parallel to HG and EF = 2 × HG in length. $\overrightarrow{HG} = \underline{u}$ and $\overrightarrow{GF} = \underline{v}$.

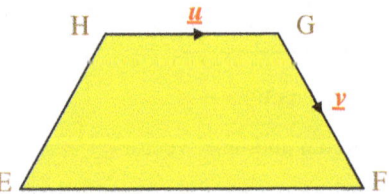

(a) Find these vectors in terms of $\underline{u}$ and $\underline{v}$:-

(i) $\overrightarrow{EF}$ (ii) $\overrightarrow{HF}$

(iii) $\overrightarrow{EG}$ (iv) $\overrightarrow{EH}$.

In fact, $\underline{u} = \begin{pmatrix} 4 \\ 0 \end{pmatrix}$ and $\underline{v} = \begin{pmatrix} 2 \\ -4 \end{pmatrix}$.

(b) Find the components of $\overrightarrow{EF}$, $\overrightarrow{HF}$ and $\overrightarrow{HE}$.

(c) Find $|\overrightarrow{GF}|$, $|\overrightarrow{HF}|$ and $|\overrightarrow{GE}|$.

17. PQRSTU is a regular hexagon with centre M.

$\overrightarrow{PQ} = \underline{a}$ and $\overrightarrow{UT} = \underline{b}$.

Express each vector in terms of $\underline{a}$ and $\underline{b}$:-

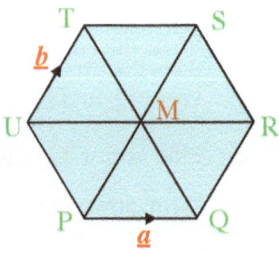

(a) $\overrightarrow{TS}$ (b) $\overrightarrow{QR}$

(c) $\overrightarrow{UR}$ (d) $\overrightarrow{PU}$

(e) $\overrightarrow{QT}$ (f) $\overrightarrow{PT}$.

Vectors in 3 Dimensions (Revision)

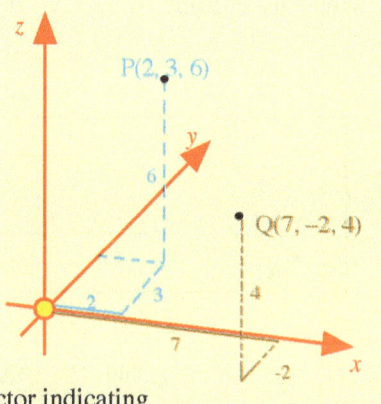

We also saw, in **National 5**, how to represent a point in 3 dimensions using 3 coordinates instead of just 2.

The x and y-axes are lain in a **horizontal** plain and the z axis is **vertical** in relation to the other two axes.

Can you see that the 2 points are **P(2, 3, 6)** and **Q(7, –2, 4)**?

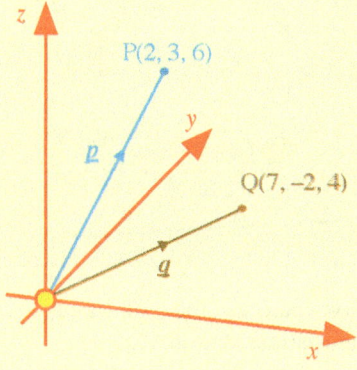

The **blue** arrow shows a 3-dimensional vector indicating the position of the point **P(2, 3, 6)**, from the origin.

The **brown** arrow shows a 3-dimensional vector giving the position of the point **Q(7, –2, 4)**, from the origin.

These two **position vectors** can be represented by :-

$$\Rightarrow \overrightarrow{OP} = \underline{p} = \begin{pmatrix} 2 \\ 3 \\ 6 \end{pmatrix} \text{ and } \overrightarrow{OQ} = \underline{q} = \begin{pmatrix} 7 \\ -2 \\ 4 \end{pmatrix}.$$

⟵ the x component
⟵ the y component
⟵ the z component

We can find the vector joining two points P and Q :-

$$\overrightarrow{PQ} = \underline{q} - \underline{p} = \begin{pmatrix} 7 \\ -2 \\ 4 \end{pmatrix} - \begin{pmatrix} 2 \\ 3 \\ 6 \end{pmatrix} = \begin{pmatrix} 5 \\ -5 \\ -2 \end{pmatrix}$$

Also, the **magnitude** can be found using **Pythagoras' Theorem**, (*applied in 3 dimensions*).

$$|\overrightarrow{OP}| = \sqrt{2^2 + 3^2 + 6^2} = \sqrt{4 + 9 + 36} = \sqrt{49} = 7.$$

$$|\overrightarrow{PQ}| = |\underline{q} - \underline{p}| = \sqrt{5^2 + (-5)^2 + (-2)^2} = \sqrt{25 + 25 + 4} = \sqrt{54} = 7.35.$$

Exercise H14·2

1. Given that $\underline{v} = \begin{pmatrix} 5 \\ 2 \\ -1 \end{pmatrix}$ and $\underline{w} = \begin{pmatrix} 3 \\ -4 \\ -2 \end{pmatrix}$, find :-

   (a) $2\underline{v}$ (b) $3\underline{w}$ (c) $\underline{v} + \underline{w}$

   (d) $\underline{v} - \underline{w}$ (e) $3\underline{v} + 2\underline{w}$ (f) $-4(\underline{v} + \underline{w})$.

2. Given that $\underline{a} = \begin{pmatrix} 2 \\ -4 \\ 4 \end{pmatrix}$ and $\underline{b} = \begin{pmatrix} -4 \\ 5 \\ 10 \end{pmatrix}$, find :-

   (a) $\underline{a} + \underline{b}$ (b) $\underline{a} - \underline{b}$ (c) $-2\underline{a}$

   (d) $|\underline{a}|$ (e) $|\underline{b}|$ (f) $|\underline{a} + \underline{b}|$

   (g) Is it true that $|\underline{a}| + |\underline{b}| = |\underline{a} + \underline{b}|$?

3. Solve these **vector equations** for vector $\underline{x}$:-

   (a) $\underline{x} + \begin{pmatrix} 2 \\ 3 \\ 5 \end{pmatrix} = \begin{pmatrix} 8 \\ 3 \\ 2 \end{pmatrix}$ (b) $\underline{x} - \begin{pmatrix} 4 \\ -2 \\ 10 \end{pmatrix} = \begin{pmatrix} -4 \\ 2 \\ -10 \end{pmatrix}$

3. (c) $2\underline{x} = \begin{pmatrix} -12 \\ 8 \\ -2 \end{pmatrix}$ (d) $-3\underline{x} = \begin{pmatrix} -21 \\ 0 \\ 9 \end{pmatrix}$

   (e) $4\underline{x} - \begin{pmatrix} 3 \\ 6 \\ 10 \end{pmatrix} = \begin{pmatrix} -7 \\ 10 \\ -18 \end{pmatrix}$ (f) $6\underline{x} - \begin{pmatrix} 3 \\ -1 \\ 2 \end{pmatrix} = 4\underline{x} + \begin{pmatrix} 11 \\ 3 \\ -4 \end{pmatrix}$.

4. S(2, 6, 9), T(5, 0, 3) and U(7, 4, -5) are 3 points.

   (a) State the position vectors, $\underline{s}$, $\underline{t}$ and $\underline{u}$ of the 3 points S, T and U. (i.e. $\overrightarrow{OS}$ = etc.)

   (b) Using $\overrightarrow{ST} = \underline{t} - \underline{s}$, find vector $\overrightarrow{ST}$.

   (c) Similarly, find vectors $\overrightarrow{TS}$, $\overrightarrow{TU}$ and $\overrightarrow{US}$.

   (d) Find $\overrightarrow{ST} + \overrightarrow{TS}$ and explain your answer.

   (e) Now find $\overrightarrow{ST} + \overrightarrow{TU} + \overrightarrow{US}$.

   (f) Explain this answer.

5. Sketch the cuboid GHIJKLMN.

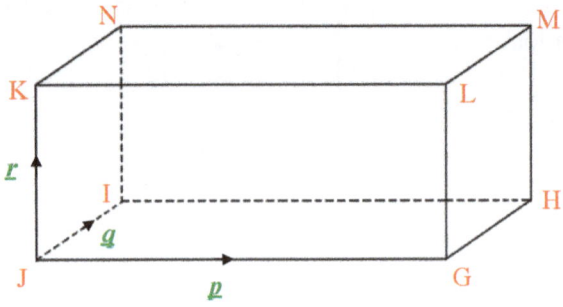

$\overrightarrow{JG} = \underline{p}$, $\overrightarrow{JI} = \underline{q}$ and $\overrightarrow{JK} = \underline{r}$.

Find, in terms of $\underline{p}$, $\underline{q}$ and $\underline{r}$, the vector :-

(a) $\overrightarrow{KL}$ (b) $\overrightarrow{GH}$ (c) $\overrightarrow{JL}$

(d) $\overrightarrow{JN}$ (e) $\overrightarrow{GM}$ (f) $\overrightarrow{JM}$.

On your sketch, show the point V, the mid-point of GH, the point W, the middle of face GHML and X at the very centre of the cuboid. Find :-

(g) $\overrightarrow{GV}$ (h) $\overrightarrow{JV}$ (i) $\overrightarrow{GW}$

(j) $\overrightarrow{JW}$ (k) $\overrightarrow{JX}$ (l) $\overrightarrow{NX}$.

6. In the above, $\underline{p} = \begin{pmatrix} 15 \\ 0 \\ 0 \end{pmatrix}$, $\underline{q} = \begin{pmatrix} 0 \\ 3 \\ 0 \end{pmatrix}$, and $\underline{r} = \begin{pmatrix} 0 \\ 0 \\ 5 \end{pmatrix}$.

Find the following :-

(a) $\overrightarrow{JN}$ (b) $\overrightarrow{JL}$ (c) $\overrightarrow{JM}$

(d) $|\overrightarrow{JN}|$ (e) $|\overrightarrow{JL}|$ (f) $|\overrightarrow{JX}|$.

7. Shown is a rectangular based pyramid with lengths 12 units and 5 units and with point T directly above the centre of rectangle CDEF.

CD is parallel to the x-axis.

The height of the pyramid is 15 units and the coordinates of point C are C(6, 4, 2).

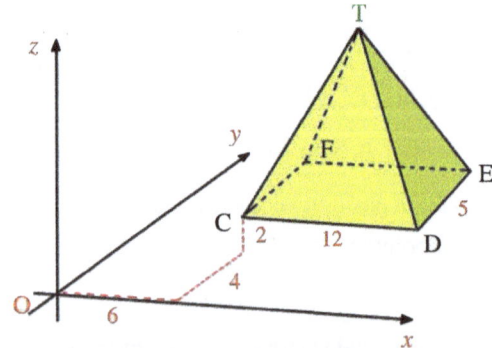

(a) Give the components of vector $\overrightarrow{OC}$.

(b) Find the position vectors of the other four points, D, E, F and T.

(c) Find vectors $\overrightarrow{CD}$, $\overrightarrow{DE}$ and $\overrightarrow{CT}$.

7. (d) Calculate the **magnitude** of the face diagonal vector $\overrightarrow{CE}$, (i.e. $|\overrightarrow{CE}|$).

(e) Calculate the **length** of CT.

8. From a weather station (O), the flight path of a weather balloon is being tracked.
(*Distances are in miles*).

A shows where the balloon is at 1330.

B shows where the balloon is at 1530.

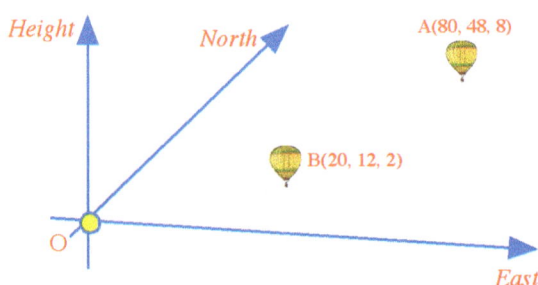

(a) Write the position vectors $\underline{a}$ and $\underline{b}$ of A and B in relation to the weather station.

(b) Calculate how far away the balloon is from the weather station at 1330 and 1530 (**magnitude**).
(*Give each answer to the nearest mile*).

(c) Determine the components of the journey from A to B. (i.e. $\overrightarrow{AB}$).

(d) By calculating $|\overrightarrow{AB}|$, find the speed of the balloon from A to B.

(e) Explain why, if the balloon keeps on its present flight path, it will land at the weather station.

9. A rubber, air filled car, advertising a car sale in a garage, is tethered from a wheel W to 3 points R, S and T on the ground.

$\begin{pmatrix} 0 \\ 0 \\ 240 \end{pmatrix}$

The coordinates of R, S, T and W are given in relation to another point O.

The coordinates are :-

R(16, 20, 0),   S(40, 10, 0),

T(34, 60, 0),   W(30, 30, 80).

The vectors $\overrightarrow{WR}$, $\overrightarrow{WS}$ and $\overrightarrow{WT}$ represent the forces acting on the ropes holding the balloon.

The upward arrow shows the vertical force acting on the balloon caused by the helium inside it.

(a) Find the vectors $\overrightarrow{WR}$, $\overrightarrow{WS}$ and $\overrightarrow{WT}$.

(b) By adding all 4 (force) vectors together, explain why the car remains in its fixed position.

Vectors in 3 Dimensions - Collinearity

We saw in Chapter 2 that it was possible to prove that three points A, B and C were collinear by considering the gradients of AB (m_{AB}) and BC (m_{BC}) and showing the gradients were the same, with a common point B.

We don't use gradients in 3 dimensions, but we can still prove that 3 points are collinear using a vector approach.

Example :-

Prove that the three points P(-1, 3, 5), Q(3, 1, 3) and R(5, 0, 2) are collinear.

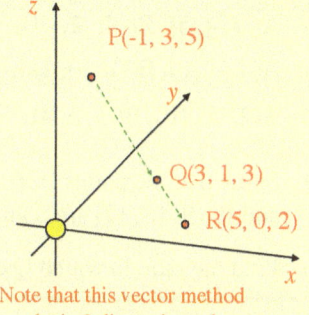

Find vectors $\overrightarrow{PQ}$ and $\overrightarrow{QR}$ first.

$$\Rightarrow \overrightarrow{PQ} = \underline{q} - \underline{p} = \begin{pmatrix} 3 \\ 1 \\ 3 \end{pmatrix} - \begin{pmatrix} -1 \\ 3 \\ 5 \end{pmatrix} = \begin{pmatrix} 4 \\ -2 \\ -2 \end{pmatrix} \quad \overrightarrow{QR} = \underline{r} - \underline{q} = \begin{pmatrix} 5 \\ 0 \\ 2 \end{pmatrix} - \begin{pmatrix} 3 \\ 1 \\ 5 \end{pmatrix} = \begin{pmatrix} 2 \\ -1 \\ -1 \end{pmatrix}$$

We can now see that since $\overrightarrow{PQ} = 2 \times \overrightarrow{QR}$, vectors must be **parallel**.

Also, they have a point (Q) in common => they must be **collinear**.

Note that this vector method works in 2 dimensions also.

Exercise H14·3

1. Plot the points A(3, 1), B(4, 3) and C(6, 7) on a Cartesian diagram.

   (a) Find the gradients m_{AB} and m_{BC}.

   (b) Prove using gradients, that A, B and C are collinear.

   (c) Find the vectors $\overrightarrow{AB}$ and $\overrightarrow{BC}$.

   (d) Prove using vectors, that A, B and C are collinear.

2. Which of the following sets of points are collinear :-

   (a) A(2, 3 5), B(8, 6, 2) and C(10, 7, 1)

   (b) F(-3, 2, -5), G(5, -2, -3) and H(9, -4, -2)

   (c) P(6, 0, -1), Q(2, 2, 0) and R(0, 3, ¹/₂) ?

3. The points D(-2, 8, -10), E(2, 4, -4) and F(4, 2, k) are known to be collinear.

   Determine the value of k.

4. P(1, -3, -2), Q(5, a, 7) and R(7, 1, b) are collinear.

   Determine the values of a and b.

5. Only three of the following points are collinear :-

   R(-4, -6, 2), S(-1, -2, 3), T(2, 3, 4) and U(5, 6, 5).

   Which three ?

6. A piece of string is stretched tightly between 2 points A(16, 20, 24) and B(28, 11, 21), relative to a set of 3 dimensional axes.

   Will the string pass through the point P(20, 17, 23) ?

The Section Formula

If 3 points are **collinear**, the **section formula** is a useful tool to enable us to find the coordinates of an in-between point, if we know the coordinates of the end points and the ratio into which the line has been divided.

The diagram shows three collinear points A, P and B with position vectors $\underline{a}$, $\underline{p}$ and $\underline{b}$.

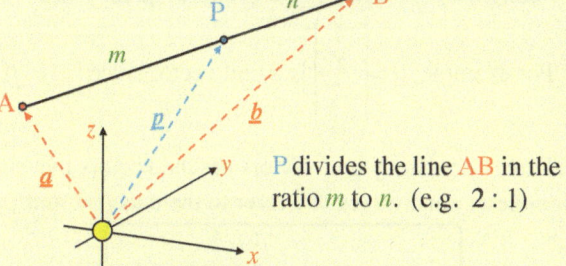

P divides the line AB in the ratio m to n. (e.g. 2 : 1)

$\dfrac{\overrightarrow{AP}}{\overrightarrow{PB}} = \dfrac{m}{n}$

$\Rightarrow n\overrightarrow{AP} = m\overrightarrow{PB}$

$\Rightarrow n(\underline{p} - \underline{a}) = m(\underline{b} - \underline{p})$

$\Rightarrow n\underline{p} - n\underline{a} = m\underline{b} - m\underline{p}$

$\Rightarrow m\underline{p} + n\underline{p} = n\underline{a} + m\underline{b}$

$\Rightarrow (m + n)\underline{p} = n\underline{a} + m\underline{b}$

$\Rightarrow \boxed{\underline{p} = \dfrac{1}{(m+n)}(n\underline{a} + m\underline{b})}$

This is called the **section formula**.

Example :- Two points A(-3, -1, 5) and B(3, 2, 8) are divided by a third point P in the ratio 2 : 1. Find P

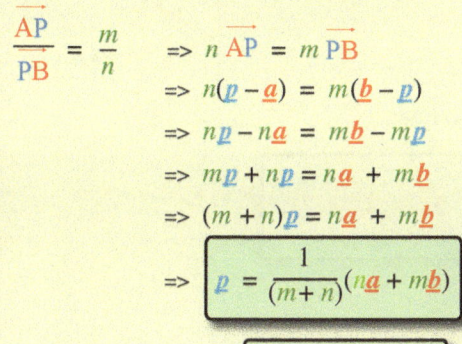

Here $m = 2$, $n = 1$, A(-3, -1, 5), B(3, 2, 8) and $m + n = 3$

$\Rightarrow$ A(-3, -1, 5)   B(3, 2, 8)

2   :   1

Notice how we multiply across the way.

$P\left(\dfrac{(2 \times 3 + 1 \times -3)}{3}, \dfrac{(2 \times 2 + 1 \times -1)}{3}, \dfrac{(2 \times 8 + 1 \times 5)}{3}\right) = $ **P(1, 1, 7)**

Exercise H14·4

1. Given that P divides AB in the given ratio, find the coordinates of point P each time :-

   (a) A(5, 3, 0), B(-5, 8, 5),   AP : PB = 1 : 4

   (b) A(-1, 4, 5), B(-4, -2, -4),   AP : PB = 1 : 2

   (c) A(4, -5, 0), B(-1, 10, 15),   AP : PB = 2 : 3

   (d) A(2, 7, -10), B(-5, 0, 4),   AP : PB = 5 : 2.

2. (a) Show that the points P(-6, -7, 2), Q(4, 3, 6) and R(19, 18, 12) are collinear.

   (b) Find the ratio in which Q divides PR.

M divides AB in the ratio 1 : 1. (i.e. M is the **mid-point** of the line AB. $A(x_1, y_1, z_1)$ and $B(x_2, y_2, z_2)$.

Show that a formula for the position vector $\underline{m}$, of M, the mid-point of the line AB is :-

$$\underline{m} = \tfrac{1}{2}((x_1 + x_2), (y_1 + y_2), (z_1 + z_2)).$$

This is called the **mid-point formula**.

To find the mid-point between two points, simply add the two x-coordinates, the two y-coordinates and the two z-coordinates, then halve your answers.

---

3. Use your formula to find the midpoint of the following lines :-

   (a) A(2, 5, -3), B(-4, 1, 5)   (b) S(8, 13), T(-2, 5)

   (c) E(-1, 5, -3), F(1, -5, 3)   (d) U(-3, 6), V(2, -1).

4. The three points P(-1, 3, -5), Q(5, -6, k) and R(9, -12, 0) are collinear.

   (a) Find the value of k.

   (b) Determine the ratio in which Q divides PR.

5. These 4 points, A(-2, 3, -4), B, C and D(8, 8, 11) are collinear.

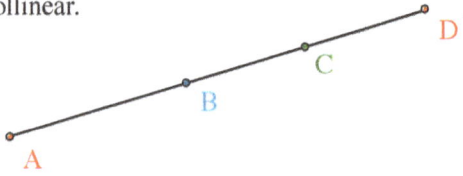

   B divides AD in the ratio 2 : 3.

   C is the mid-point of BD.

   Find the coordinates of C.

6. Triangle FGH is shown with L, M and N the mid-points of FG, GH and FH.

   The coordinates of the vertices of the triangle are F(-2, 5, 8), G(6, -1, 2) and H(10, 11, 0).

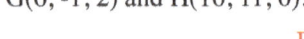

   (a) Find the coordinates of L, M and N.

   (b) T is the centroid of triangle FGH. It is known that T is a point of trisection of each of the 3 medians. (i.e. LT : TH = 1 : 2 etc.)

   Find the coordinates of T.

Unit Vectors

A unit vector $\underline{u}$, is one whose **magnitude** is **1**.

For example, $\underline{u} = \begin{pmatrix} \frac{1}{3} \\ \frac{2}{3} \\ -\frac{2}{3} \end{pmatrix}$ is a unit vector since $|\underline{u}| = \sqrt{(\frac{1}{3})^2 + (\frac{-2}{3})^2 + (\frac{2}{3})^2} = \sqrt{\frac{1}{9} + \frac{4}{9} + \frac{4}{9}} = \sqrt{\frac{9}{9}} = 1$

Three very handy unit vectors are the vectors that run parallel to the x, y and z axes. We refer to them as $\underline{i}$, $\underline{j}$, and $\underline{k}$, where :-

$$\underline{i} = \begin{pmatrix} 1 \\ 0 \\ 0 \end{pmatrix} \qquad \underline{j} = \begin{pmatrix} 0 \\ 1 \\ 0 \end{pmatrix} \qquad \underline{k} = \begin{pmatrix} 0 \\ 0 \\ 1 \end{pmatrix}.$$

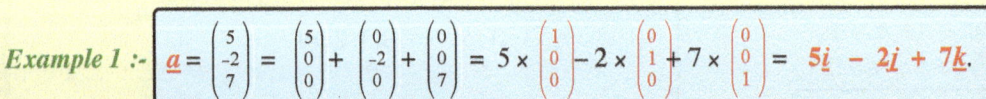

Every vector can be expressed in terms of the three vectors $\underline{i}$, $\underline{j}$, and $\underline{k}$, as follows :-

Example 1 :- $\underline{a} = \begin{pmatrix} 5 \\ -2 \\ 7 \end{pmatrix} = \begin{pmatrix} 5 \\ 0 \\ 0 \end{pmatrix} + \begin{pmatrix} 0 \\ -2 \\ 0 \end{pmatrix} + \begin{pmatrix} 0 \\ 0 \\ 7 \end{pmatrix} = 5 \times \begin{pmatrix} 1 \\ 0 \\ 0 \end{pmatrix} - 2 \times \begin{pmatrix} 0 \\ 1 \\ 0 \end{pmatrix} + 7 \times \begin{pmatrix} 0 \\ 0 \\ 1 \end{pmatrix} = 5\underline{i} - 2\underline{j} + 7\underline{k}.$

Example 2 :- $\underline{b} = 6\underline{i} - 2\underline{k} = 6\begin{pmatrix} 1 \\ 0 \\ 0 \end{pmatrix} + 0\begin{pmatrix} 0 \\ 1 \\ 0 \end{pmatrix} - 2\begin{pmatrix} 0 \\ 0 \\ 1 \end{pmatrix} = \begin{pmatrix} 6 \\ 0 \\ -2 \end{pmatrix}$

Exercise H14·5 Mixed Exercise

1. Express each vector in terms of $\underline{i}$, $\underline{j}$ and $\underline{k}$:-

   (a) $\begin{pmatrix} 3 \\ -1 \\ 4 \end{pmatrix}$ (b) $\begin{pmatrix} 6 \\ 8 \\ -1 \end{pmatrix}$ (c) $\begin{pmatrix} 8 \\ 0 \\ -1 \end{pmatrix}$

   (d) $\begin{pmatrix} 0 \\ 4 \\ 0 \end{pmatrix}$ (e) $\begin{pmatrix} \frac{1}{2} \\ 2 \\ -\frac{3}{4} \end{pmatrix}$ (f) $\begin{pmatrix} p \\ (p-1) \\ (p+2) \end{pmatrix}$.

2. Express as column vectors :-

   (a) $2\underline{i} + 3\underline{j} - 7\underline{k}$ (b) $5\underline{i} - 6\underline{j} + 3\underline{k}$

   (c) $\underline{i} + \underline{j} - 2\underline{k}$ (d) $4\underline{i} - \underline{k}$

   (e) $3\underline{j} + 3\underline{k}$ (f) $6\underline{i}$.

3. Express each vector in terms of $\underline{i}$, $\underline{j}$ and $\underline{k}$:-

   (a) Given A(-1, 3, 2), and B(4, -2, 1), find $\overrightarrow{AB}$.

   (b) Given M(4, 0, -1), and N(5, 3, -12), find $\overrightarrow{MN}$.

   (c) Given R(-3, -5, 4), and S(0, -5, 2), find $\overrightarrow{RS}$.

4. Calculate the magnitude of each vector, leaving your answer in surd form simplified as far as possible :-

   (a) $\underline{u} = 2\underline{i} + 2\underline{j} - 4\underline{k}$ (b) $\underline{v} = 3\underline{i} - 3\underline{j} + 3\underline{k}$

   (c) $\underline{w} = \sqrt{2}\underline{i} - 4\underline{k}$ (d) $\underline{s} = \sqrt{3}\underline{i} - \sqrt{5}\underline{j} + \sqrt{10}\underline{k}$.

5. Given that $\underline{x} = 3\underline{i} + a\underline{j} - 6\underline{k}$, and $|\underline{x}| = 9$, find a.

6. $\underline{p} = 2\underline{i} - 3\underline{j} + 5\underline{k}$ and $\underline{q} = \underline{i} - \underline{j} + 3\underline{k}$. Find :-

   (a) $\underline{p} + \underline{q}$ (b) $\underline{p} - \underline{q}$

   (c) $2\underline{q}$ (d) $3\underline{p} - 2\underline{q}$

   (e) $|\underline{p} + \underline{q}|$ (f) $|\underline{p}| \times |\underline{q}|$.

To find a **unit vector** parallel to a given vector, $\underline{a}$:-

Step 1 :- Find the magnitude $|\underline{a}|$ of $\underline{a}$.

Step 2 :- Divide each component of $\underline{a}$ by $|\underline{a}|$.

Example :- Find a unit vector $\underline{u}$, parallel to $\underline{a} = \begin{pmatrix} 4 \\ -4 \\ 2 \end{pmatrix}$.

$$|\underline{a}| = \sqrt{4^2 + (-4)^2 + 2^2} = \sqrt{36} = 6.$$

$$\Rightarrow \underline{u} = \frac{1}{6}\begin{pmatrix} 4 \\ -4 \\ 2 \end{pmatrix} = \begin{pmatrix} \frac{2}{3} \\ -\frac{2}{3} \\ \frac{1}{3} \end{pmatrix} \text{ (or } \begin{pmatrix} -\frac{2}{3} \\ \frac{2}{3} \\ -\frac{1}{3} \end{pmatrix})$$

---

7. (a) Find a unit vector parallel to :-

   (i) $\underline{b} = \underline{i} - 2\underline{j} + 2\underline{k}$ (ii) $\underline{d} = \sqrt{3}\underline{i} - \sqrt{5}\underline{j} + 2\sqrt{2}\underline{k}$.

   (b) Find a unit vector parallel to :-

   (i) $\underline{p} = 6\underline{i} - 8\underline{k}$ (ii) $\underline{q} = 2a\underline{i} - 4a\underline{j} + \sqrt{5}a\underline{k}$.

8. A, P and B are collinear. The position vectors of A and B are given by $\underline{a} = 3\underline{i} + \underline{j} - 4\underline{k}$ and $\underline{b} = -2\underline{i} - 9\underline{j} + \underline{k}$.

   Find the position vector $\underline{p}$ of P, given AP : PB = 3 : 2.

9. Points E, T and F are collinear.

   T divides EF in the ratio 4 : 1.

   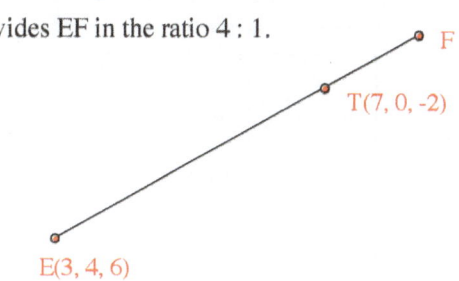

   Determine the coordinates of point F.

10. The diagram shows a cruiser (C), a radio ship (R) and a helicopter (H), with all units in kilometres.

    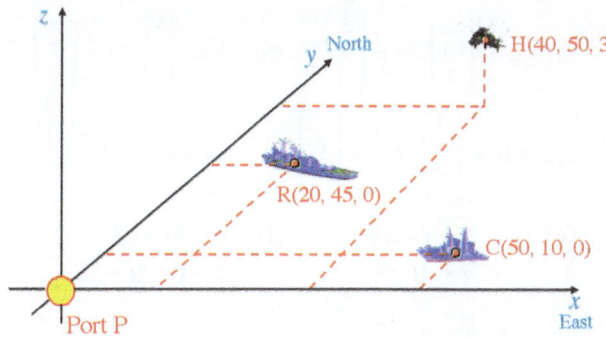

    (a) Determine the position of the helicopter in relation to each boat. (i.e. find $\overrightarrow{RH}$ and $\overrightarrow{CH}$.)

    (b) Which boat is closer to the helicopter ?

11. (a) Prove that the three points P(6, 8, 2), Q(4, 4, 6) and R(7, 5, 6) lie on the surface of a sphere with centre C(5, 6, 4).

    (b) Determine the coordinates of point S that lies diametrically opposite point R.

Scalar (or Dot) Product - Part 1

The **product** of 2 numbers or algebraic expressions is the answer you get by combining them using multiplication.

In this part of the chapter, we are going to introduce a new type of product, between 2 vectors, that will provide a excellent tool that allows us to calculate the size of an angle between two lines in 3-dimensions (or in 2-dimensions).

Let $\underline{a} = \begin{pmatrix} a_1 \\ a_2 \\ a_3 \end{pmatrix}$ and $\underline{b} = \begin{pmatrix} b_1 \\ b_2 \\ b_3 \end{pmatrix}$

Reads as $\underline{a}$ dot $\underline{b}$

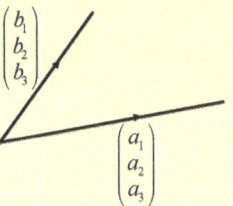

We define the **Scalar Product** of two vectors $\underline{a}$ and $\underline{b}$ as $\boxed{\underline{a} \cdot \underline{b}}$ where

$$\underline{a} \cdot \underline{b} = a_1 b_1 + a_2 b_2 + a_3 b_3.$$

*It is called **scalar** (or **dot** product)because it produces a scalar quantity from 2 vectors.*

Example 1 :- If $\underline{a} = \begin{pmatrix} 3 \\ -2 \\ 5 \end{pmatrix}$ and $\underline{b} = \begin{pmatrix} 2 \\ -3 \\ -1 \end{pmatrix}$

$\Rightarrow \underline{a} \cdot \underline{b} = a_1 b_1 + a_2 b_2 + a_3 b_3.$

$= 3 \times 2 + (-2) \times (-3) + 5 \times (-1)$

$= \boxed{7}$

Example 2 :- If $\underline{p} = 2\underline{i} + \underline{j} - 4\underline{k}$ and $\underline{q} = 3\underline{i} + 2\underline{k}$

$\Rightarrow \underline{p} \cdot \underline{q} = a_1 b_1 + a_2 b_2 + a_3 b_3.$

$= 2 \times 3 + 1 \times \underline{0} + (-4) \times 2$

$= \boxed{-2}$

We will find later how this version of the scalar product, along with a 2nd version enables us to calculate angles between lines in 3-dimensions.

Exercise H14·6

1. Calculate the **scalar product** of these two vectors :-

   (a) $\underline{a} = \begin{pmatrix} 2 \\ -4 \\ 3 \end{pmatrix}$, $\underline{b} = \begin{pmatrix} 5 \\ 3 \\ -1 \end{pmatrix}$ (b) $\underline{s} = \begin{pmatrix} 0 \cdot 5 \\ -1 \\ 0 \cdot 3 \end{pmatrix}$, $\underline{t} = \begin{pmatrix} -6 \\ 5 \\ 10 \end{pmatrix}$

   (c) $\overrightarrow{AB} = \begin{pmatrix} 3 \\ 5 \\ -4 \end{pmatrix}$, $\overrightarrow{AC} = \begin{pmatrix} -3 \\ 0 \\ -2 \end{pmatrix}$ (d) $\overrightarrow{AB} = \begin{pmatrix} 1 \\ 0 \\ 0 \end{pmatrix}$, $\overrightarrow{AC} = \begin{pmatrix} 0 \\ 0 \\ 1 \end{pmatrix}$

   (e) $\underline{u} = 3\underline{i} + \underline{j} - 5\underline{k}$ (f) $\underline{p} = 6\underline{i} + 2\underline{k}$
   $\underline{v} = 4\underline{i} + 3\underline{j} - \underline{k}$ $\underline{q} = \underline{i} + 3\underline{j} - 5\underline{k}.$

2. From the figure, find :-

   (a) $\overrightarrow{AP}$ and $\overrightarrow{AQ}$.

   (b) $\overrightarrow{AP} \cdot \overrightarrow{AQ}$.

   Q(0, 6, 7)

   P(4, -1, 5)

   A(1, 2, 3)

3. Find $\overrightarrow{RS} \cdot \overrightarrow{RT}$ and $\overrightarrow{MN} \cdot \overrightarrow{MP}$.

   $M(\frac{1}{4}, \frac{1}{3}, \frac{1}{2})$

   S(1, 3, 1)

   R(-2, -3, -4)

   T(-1, 0, 3) $N(\frac{3}{4}, \frac{2}{3}, 1)$

   $P(\frac{1}{2}, \frac{4}{3}, 0)$

4. The coordinates of three points are E(2, 1, -1), F(3, -1, 4) and G(0, -3, 5).

   Find :-

   (a) $\overrightarrow{EF} \cdot \overrightarrow{EG}$ (b) $\overrightarrow{FG} \cdot \overrightarrow{FE}$.

5. Shown is triangle XYZ.

   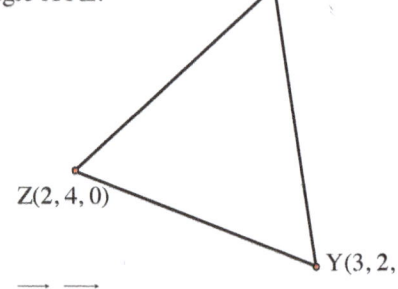

   X(1, 2, 3)

   Z(2, 4, 0)

   Y(3, 2, 1)

   (a) Show that $\overrightarrow{YZ} \cdot \overrightarrow{YX} = 0$.

   (b) Prove that $\overrightarrow{YX} \cdot \overrightarrow{YX} + \overrightarrow{ZX} \cdot \overrightarrow{ZY} + \overrightarrow{XZ} \cdot \overrightarrow{XY} = 14$.

6. $\underline{a} = \begin{pmatrix} x \\ 2 \\ 1 \end{pmatrix}$ and $\underline{b} = \begin{pmatrix} x \\ -1 \\ x \end{pmatrix}$. Find x, given that $\underline{a} \cdot \underline{b} = 0$.

7. Solve the following equations for x :-

   (a) $\begin{pmatrix} x \\ x \\ 2 \end{pmatrix} \cdot \begin{pmatrix} x \\ -2 \\ 1 \end{pmatrix} = 10$ (b) $\begin{pmatrix} x \\ x \\ -2 \end{pmatrix} \cdot \begin{pmatrix} x \\ -4 \\ x \end{pmatrix} + 9 = 0$

   (c) $\begin{pmatrix} x \\ x \\ x \end{pmatrix} \cdot \begin{pmatrix} x^2 \\ -3x \\ 2 \end{pmatrix} = 0$ (d) $\begin{pmatrix} \sin x \\ -2 \\ \sin x \end{pmatrix} \cdot \begin{pmatrix} \sin x \\ \sin x \\ 1 \end{pmatrix} = 0$.

   $0 \leq x < 2\pi.$

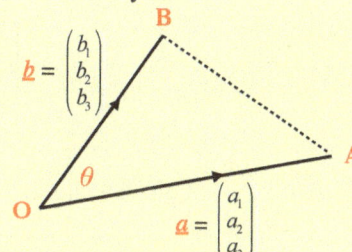

Scalar Product – Part 2

The component form of the **scalar product** in the previous section, on its own, has no intrinsic value, but as we shall see here, there is a second form of the product, which when combined with the first, is extremely useful.

If $\underline{a}$ and $\underline{b}$ are vectors and θ is the angle between them, then we can also define the **Scalar Product** of two vectors $\underline{a}$ and $\underline{b}$ as $\boxed{\underline{a}.\underline{b}}$ where

$$\underline{a}.\underline{b} = |\underline{a}||\underline{b}|\cos\theta$$

$\underline{b} = \begin{pmatrix} b_1 \\ b_2 \\ b_3 \end{pmatrix}$

$\underline{a} = \begin{pmatrix} a_1 \\ a_2 \\ a_3 \end{pmatrix}$

We can prove that $\underline{a}.\underline{b} = |\underline{a}||\underline{b}|\cos\theta = a_1b_1 + a_2b_2 + a_3b_3$ as follows :-

Proof :-

In triangle OAB, $\overrightarrow{AB} = \underline{b} - \underline{a}$

and $|\underline{a}|^2 = |\overrightarrow{OA}|^2 = a_1^2 + a_2^2 + a_3^2$ and $|\underline{b}|^2 = |\overrightarrow{OB}|^2 = b_1^2 + b_2^2 + b_3^2$

also, $|\overrightarrow{AB}|^2 = |\underline{b} - \underline{a}|^2 = (b_1 - a_1)^2 + (b_2 - a_2)^2 + (b_3 - a_3)^2$

We now use the cosine rule on triangle ABC as follows :-

$$|\overrightarrow{AB}|^2 = |\overrightarrow{OA}|^2 + |\overrightarrow{OB}|^2 - 2 \times |\overrightarrow{OA}||\overrightarrow{OB}|\cos\theta$$

$\Rightarrow (b_1 - a_1)^2 + (b_2 - a_2)^2 + (b_3 - a_3)^2 = (a_1^2 + a_2^2 + a_3^2) + (b_1^2 + b_2^2 + b_3^2) - 2 \times |\underline{a}||\underline{b}|\cos\theta$

$\Rightarrow b_1^2 - 2a_1b_1 + a_1^2 + b_2^2 - 2a_2b_2 + a_2^2 + b_3^2 - 2a_3b_3 + a_3^2 = a_1^2 + a_2^2 + a_3^2 + b_1^2 + b_2^2 + b_3^2 - 2 \times |\underline{a}||\underline{b}|\cos\theta$

$\Rightarrow 2|\underline{a}||\underline{b}|\cos\theta = 2a_1b_1 + 2a_2b_2 + 2a_3b_3 \Rightarrow \boxed{|\underline{a}||\underline{b}|\cos\theta = a_1b_1 + a_2b_2 + a_3b_3}$

Example 1 :-   If $|\underline{a}| = \sqrt{3}$, $|\underline{b}| = 4$ and $\theta = \pi/6$, find $\underline{a}.\underline{b}$.

$\underline{a}.\underline{b} = |\underline{a}||\underline{b}|\cos\theta = \sqrt{3} \times 4 \times \cos(\pi/6)$

$\Rightarrow \underline{a}.\underline{b} = \sqrt{3} \times 4 \times \dfrac{\sqrt{3}}{2}$

$\Rightarrow \underline{a}.\underline{b} = \boxed{6}$.

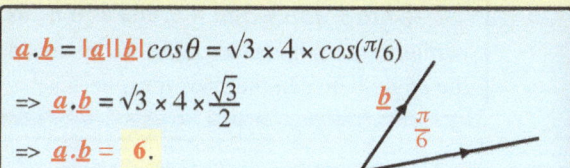

Example 2 :-   If $|\underline{p}| = 2$, $|\underline{q}| = 5$ and $\underline{p}.\underline{q} = 5\sqrt{2}$, find θ.

$\underline{p}.\underline{q} = |\underline{p}||\underline{q}|\cos\theta$

$\Rightarrow 5\sqrt{2} = 2 \times 5 \times \cos\theta$

$\Rightarrow \cos\theta = 5\sqrt{2} \div 10 = \sqrt{2}/2 = 1/\sqrt{2}$

$\Rightarrow \theta = \pi/4$ or **45°**.

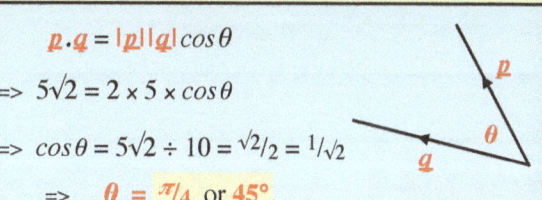

Exercise H14·7

1. Find the value of the scalar product in each case :-

(a) $|\underline{a}| = 2$, $|\underline{b}| = 3$. with angle $\dfrac{\pi}{3}$

(b) $|\underline{p}| = 2$, $|\underline{q}| = 2\sqrt{2}$. with angle $\dfrac{\pi}{4}$

(c) $|\underline{u}| = \sqrt{3}$, $|\underline{v}| = \sqrt{5}$. with angle $\dfrac{\pi}{6}$

(d) $|\underline{d}| = 4\cdot2$, $|\underline{e}| = 3\cdot9$.

(e) $|\underline{r}| = 12$, $|\underline{s}| = 10$. with angle $\dfrac{2\pi}{3}$

(f) $|\underline{x}| = \sqrt{12}$, $|\underline{y}| = 5\cdot5$. with angle 150°

2. (a) Use $\underline{a}.\underline{b} = a_1b_1 + a_2b_2 + a_3b_3$ to find the scalar product :-

$\underline{b} = \begin{pmatrix} -1 \\ 2 \\ 2 \end{pmatrix}$ $\underline{a} = \begin{pmatrix} 4 \\ 0 \\ 3 \end{pmatrix}$ with angle 82·34°

(b) Given that $|\underline{a}| = 3$ and $|\underline{b}| = 5$, show you obtain the same answer as in part (a) by using the 2nd form of the scalar product.

3. Use both forms of the scalar product to find $\underline{a}.\underline{a}$, and show that both answers are the same.

$\underline{a} = \begin{pmatrix} 6 \\ 8 \\ -1 \end{pmatrix}$

The Scalar Product and Angles

Neither form of the scalar product, on its own, is as powerful as when we combine them, as follows.

As we have shown, $\underline{a}.\underline{b} = |\underline{a}||\underline{b}|\cos\theta$. If we rearrange this, we obtain a formula for calculating θ.

$$\cos\theta = \frac{\underline{a}.\underline{b}}{|\underline{a}||\underline{b}|}$$ where $\underline{a}.\underline{b} = a_1b_1 + a_2b_2 + a_3b_3$.

Example 1 :- Calculate the size of angle θ here :-

$$\underline{b} = \begin{pmatrix} 4 \\ -4 \\ -2 \end{pmatrix} \qquad \underline{a} = \begin{pmatrix} 0 \\ -8 \\ 6 \end{pmatrix}$$

Step 1 :- Find $\underline{a}.\underline{b} = a_1b_1 + a_2b_2 + a_3b_3$
$$= 4 \times 0 + (-4) \times (-8) + (-2) \times 6$$
$$= 20$$

Step 2 :- Find $|\underline{a}| = \sqrt{4^2 + (-4)^2 + (-2)^2}$
$$= 6$$
and $|\underline{b}| = \sqrt{0^2 + (-8)^2 + (6)^2}$
$$= 10$$

Step 3 :- Now use $\cos\theta = \frac{\underline{a}.\underline{b}}{|\underline{a}||\underline{b}|} = \frac{20}{6 \times 10} = 0.333..$

$$=> \theta = 70.5° .$$

Example 2 :- Show that the following two vectors, $\underline{p}$ and $\underline{q}$, are perpendicular :-

$$\underline{p} = \underline{i} - 2\underline{j} + 2\underline{k}, \quad \underline{q} = 4\underline{i} + 3\underline{j} + \underline{k}.$$

$\underline{a}.\underline{b} = a_1b_1 + a_2b_2 + a_3b_3$
$$= 1 \times 4 + (-2) \times 3 + 2 \times 1 = 4 - 6 + 2 = \mathbf{0}$$
$|\underline{a}| = \sqrt{1^2 + (-2)^2 + 2^2} = 3$
$|\underline{b}| = \sqrt{4^2 + 3^2 + 1^2} = \sqrt{26}$

$$=> \cos\theta = \frac{\underline{a}.\underline{b}}{|\underline{a}||\underline{b}|} = \frac{0}{3 \times \sqrt{26}} = \mathbf{0}$$

but the angle with cosine is 0 *is* **90°**.

=> the two vectors **are perpendicular**.

Important :- To prove that 2 vectors are perpendicular, show that the scalar product $\underline{a}.\underline{b} = a_1b_1 + a_2b_2 + a_3b_3 = \mathbf{0}$, and as long as neither $\underline{a}$ nor $\underline{b}$ is the zero vector, this means the angle between the lines must be **90°**.

Exercise H14·8

1. Calculate the size of angle POR.

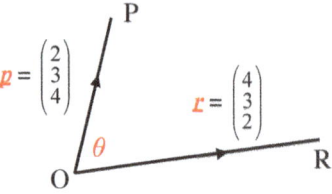

$$\underline{p} = \begin{pmatrix} 2 \\ 3 \\ 4 \end{pmatrix} \qquad \underline{r} = \begin{pmatrix} 4 \\ 3 \\ 2 \end{pmatrix}$$

2. Calculate the size of the angle between the vectors :-

   (a) $\underline{a} = \begin{pmatrix} 2 \\ -4 \\ 3 \end{pmatrix}, \; \underline{b} = \begin{pmatrix} 5 \\ 3 \\ 1 \end{pmatrix}$ (b) $\underline{p} = \begin{pmatrix} 2 \\ -4 \\ 3 \end{pmatrix}, \; \underline{q} = \begin{pmatrix} 5 \\ 3 \\ -1 \end{pmatrix}$

   (c) $\underline{u} = 3\underline{i} - 5\underline{j} + 10\underline{k}$ and $\underline{v} = 10\underline{i} - 3\underline{j} + 5\underline{k}$

   (d) $\overrightarrow{AB} = \begin{pmatrix} 3 \\ -4 \\ -12 \end{pmatrix}, \; \overrightarrow{AC} = \begin{pmatrix} -3 \\ 0 \\ -4 \end{pmatrix}$ (e) $\overrightarrow{PQ} = \begin{pmatrix} 1 \\ 0 \\ 0 \end{pmatrix}, \; \overrightarrow{PR} = \begin{pmatrix} 0 \\ 1 \\ 1 \end{pmatrix}$

3. Prove that the vectors $\overrightarrow{OF} = \begin{pmatrix} 3 \\ 5 \\ -4 \end{pmatrix}$ and $\overrightarrow{OG} = \begin{pmatrix} 1 \\ 5 \\ 7 \end{pmatrix}$ are perpendicular.

4. A(2, -1, 3), B(3, 1, 1) and C(6, 2, 3) are the three vertices of triangle ABC.
   Find $\overrightarrow{AB}$ and $\overrightarrow{AC}$, and show that angle BAC = 48·2°.

5. P(5, 4, -5), Q(7, 4, 1) and R(3, 0, -1) are the three vertices of triangle PQR.
   Calculate the size of angle PRQ. (Use $\overrightarrow{RP}$ and $\overrightarrow{RQ}$.)

6. P(1, -1, 4), Q(4, -3, 8) and R(5, 5, 4).
   (a) Use the distance formula to calculate the values of PQ², QR² and PR², then use the Converse of Pythagoras' Theorem to prove triangle PQR is right angled at P.
   (b) Find vectors $\overrightarrow{PQ}$ and $\overrightarrow{PR}$ and prove, using vectors, that triangle PQR is right angled at P.

7. Vectors, $\underline{u} = 2\underline{i} - 4\underline{j} + \underline{k}$ and $\underline{v} = a\underline{i} + 2\underline{j} - 2\underline{k}$ are perpendicular. Find the value of a.

8. Vector $\underline{d} = 2\underline{i} + a\underline{j} + b\underline{k}$ is perpendicular to both vectors $\underline{p} = 5\underline{i} - \underline{j} + 6\underline{k}$ and $\underline{q} = -3\underline{i} + 2\underline{j} + 2\underline{k}$.
   Set up simultaneous equations and solve for a and b.

9. $\underline{s} = 3\underline{i} + m\underline{j} + n\underline{k}$ is a vector that is perpendicular to both vectors $\underline{u} = 4\underline{i} + 8\underline{j} - \underline{k}$ and $\underline{v} = -2\underline{i} + 6\underline{j} + 3\underline{k}$.
   Find the values of m and n.

Properties of the Scalar Product

There are two properties of the scalar product we need to prove.

Property A - The scalar product is **commutative**.

What this means is $\quad \boxed{\underline{a}\cdot\underline{b} = \underline{b}\cdot\underline{a}}$

$$
\begin{aligned}
Proof:- \quad \underline{a}\cdot\underline{b} &= a_1b_1 + a_2b_2 + a_3b_3 \\
&= b_1a_1 + b_2a_2 + b_3a_3 \\
&= \underline{b}\cdot\underline{a}.
\end{aligned}
$$

Property B - The scalar product is **associative**.

What this means is $\quad \boxed{\underline{a}\cdot(\underline{b}+\underline{c}) = \underline{a}\cdot\underline{b} + \underline{a}\cdot\underline{c}}$

$$
\begin{aligned}
Proof:- \quad \underline{a}\cdot(\underline{b}+\underline{c}) &= a_1(b_1 + c_1) + a_2(b_2 + c_2) + a_3(b_3 + c_3) \\
&= a_1b_1 + a_1c_1 + a_2b_2 + a_2c_2 + a_3b_3 + a_3c_3 \\
&= (a_1b_1 + a_2b_2 + a_3b_3) + (a_1c_1 + a_2c_2 + a_3c_3) \\
&= \underline{a}\cdot\underline{b} + \underline{a}\cdot\underline{c}.
\end{aligned}
$$

Example 1 :- Calculate $\underline{p}\cdot(\underline{q}+\underline{r})$ given that
$|\underline{p}| = 2$, $|\underline{q}| = \sqrt{3}$, and $|\underline{r}| = 2\sqrt{2}$
and with the angles between them as shown

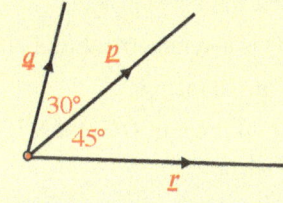

$$
\begin{aligned}
\underline{p}\cdot(\underline{q}+\underline{r}) &= \underline{p}\cdot\underline{q} + \underline{p}\cdot\underline{r} \\
&= |\underline{p}||\underline{q}|\cos 30° + |\underline{p}||\underline{r}|\cos 45° \\
&= 2 \times \sqrt{3} \times \frac{\sqrt{3}}{2} + 2 \times 2\sqrt{2} \times \frac{1}{\sqrt{2}} \\
&= 3 + 4 = \boxed{7.}
\end{aligned}
$$

Example 2 :- (a) If $|\underline{a}| = 3$, $|\underline{b}| = 3\sqrt{2}$, find $\underline{a}\cdot(\underline{a} + \underline{b})$

(b) What does that tell you about $\underline{a}$ and $(\underline{a} + \underline{b})$?

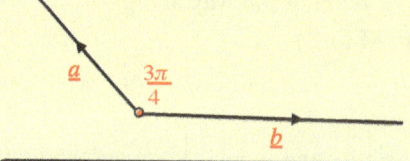

(a)
$$
\begin{aligned}
\underline{a}\cdot(\underline{a}+\underline{b}) &= \underline{a}\cdot\underline{a} + \underline{a}\cdot\underline{b} \\
&= |\underline{a}||\underline{a}|\cos 0° + |\underline{a}||\underline{b}|\cos 135° \\
&= 3 \times 3 \times 1 + 3 \times 3\sqrt{2} \times (-\tfrac{1}{\sqrt{2}}) \\
&= 9 - 9 = \boxed{0.}
\end{aligned}
$$

(b) $\quad \Rightarrow \quad \underline{a}$ must be **perpendicular** to $(\underline{a} + \underline{b})$.

Exercise H14·9

1. (a) Calculate $\underline{a}\cdot(\underline{b} + \underline{c})$,
   given that $|\underline{a}| = 8$,
   $|\underline{b}| = 10$ and $|\underline{c}| = 4\sqrt{3}$.

   (b) Show that :-
   $\underline{b}\cdot(\underline{a} + \underline{c}) = \underline{b}\cdot\underline{a} = 40$.

2. Given that $\underline{p} = \begin{pmatrix} 5 \\ 3 \\ -1 \end{pmatrix}$, $\underline{q} = \begin{pmatrix} 2 \\ 1 \\ -3 \end{pmatrix}$ and $\underline{r} = \begin{pmatrix} 1 \\ 4 \\ 3 \end{pmatrix}$, find :-

   (a) $\underline{p}\cdot(\underline{q} + \underline{r})$ (b) $\underline{q}\cdot(\underline{q} + \underline{r})$ (c) $\underline{r}\cdot(\underline{p} - \underline{q})$.

3. $\underline{s} = 2\underline{i} - 3\underline{j} + \underline{k}$, $\underline{u} = 4\underline{i} + 2\underline{j} - 5\underline{k}$ and $\underline{v} = 3\underline{i} + 4\underline{k}$.
   Find :-

   (a) $\underline{s}\cdot(\underline{u} + \underline{v})$ (b) $\underline{u}\cdot(\underline{u} + 2\underline{v})$ (c) $\underline{v}\cdot(\underline{v} - \underline{u})$.

4. (a) Given $|\underline{a}| = 5$, what is the value of $\underline{a}\cdot\underline{a}$?

   (b) If $|\underline{a} + \underline{b}| = 6$, what is $(\underline{a} + \underline{b})\cdot(\underline{a} + \underline{b})$?

5. If $\underline{p}\cdot\underline{q} = \underline{p}\cdot\underline{r}$, and neither $\underline{p}$, $\underline{q}$ nor $\underline{r}$ are zero vectors, which of the following statements is/are true ?

   (a) $\underline{p}\cdot(\underline{q} - \underline{r}) = 0$ (b) $\underline{q} = \underline{r}$

   (c) $\underline{p}$ is perpendicular to $(\underline{q} - \underline{r})$.

6. (a) $\underline{i}, \underline{j}$ and $\underline{k}$ are the standard unit vectors. What is :-

   (i) $\underline{i}\cdot\underline{i}$ (ii) $\underline{i}\cdot\underline{j}$ (iiii) $\underline{j}\cdot\underline{k}$?

   (b) Copy and complete this (scalar) multiplication table for $\underline{i}, \underline{j}$ and $\underline{k}$:-

·	$\underline{i}$	$\underline{j}$	$\underline{k}$
$\underline{i}$	1		
$\underline{j}$			
$\underline{k}$			

7. Triangle PQR is equilateral with all sides 2 units long.

   (a) Find $\underline{a}\cdot\underline{b}$.

   (b) Express $\overrightarrow{QR}$ in terms of $\underline{a}$ and $\underline{b}$.

   (c) Find $\overrightarrow{PQ}\cdot\overrightarrow{QR}$.

   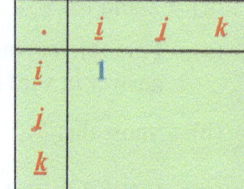

8. (a) Explain why $\underline{a}\cdot\underline{b} \leq |\underline{a}||\underline{b}|$.

   (b) If $\underline{a}\cdot\underline{b} = |\underline{a}||\underline{b}|$, what is true about $\underline{a}$ and $\underline{b}$?

9. In this figure, $|\underline{a}| = 6$, $|\underline{p}| = 3\sqrt{3}$, $|\underline{q}| = 3$ and $|\underline{r}| = 4$.

   Find $\underline{a}\cdot(\underline{p} + \underline{q} + \underline{r})$.

   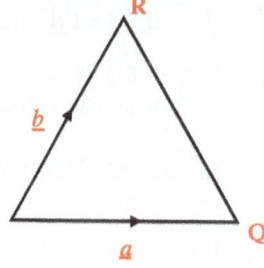

Exercise H14·10 Mixed Exercise

1. A(1, 3, -2), B(5, 4, 1) and C(-2, 6, 3) are three vertices of a parallelogram ABCD.

    Find the coordinates of the fourth vertex D.

2. Prove that P(-1, 3, 6), Q(7, -1, -6) and R(13, -4, -15) are collinear.

    Find also the ratio in which Q divides PR.

3. A(-3, 1, 5), B(5, -1, -1) and C(7, 3, -1) are three vertices of a triangle.

    M is the mid point of AB and G is the centroid of the triangle. (i.e. it is $^1/_3$ of the way along from M to C).

    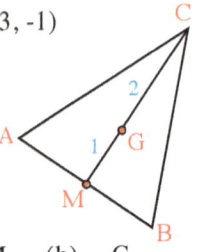

    Find the coordinates of   (a) M   (b) G.

4. If $\underline{u} = \begin{pmatrix} 3 \\ a \\ -1 \end{pmatrix}$ and $\underline{v} = \begin{pmatrix} 3 \\ -3 \\ 6 \end{pmatrix}$ are perpendicular, find a.

5. $\underline{m} = \begin{pmatrix} -1 \\ 2 \\ 2 \end{pmatrix}$ and $\underline{n} = \begin{pmatrix} 3 \\ 4 \\ 0 \end{pmatrix}$.

    Calculate the size of acute angle θ.

6. Given the 4 points, R(1, 3, 6), S(-1, 2, 7), T(4, 1, 5) and V(1, 6, 5), prove that RT is perpendicular to SV.

7. In the right angled triangle shown, $|\underline{a}| = 2$ and $|\underline{b}| = 4$.

    (a) Find $|\underline{c}|$, leaving your answer in surd form.

    (b) Show that $\underline{b} \cdot (\underline{a} + \underline{c}) = 16$.

    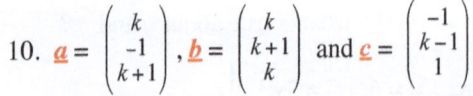

8. (a) Expand $(\underline{p} + \underline{q}) \cdot (\underline{p} - \underline{q})$.

    (b) If $|\underline{p}| = |\underline{q}|$, simplify your answer to part (a).

    (c) If neither $\underline{p} + \underline{q}$ nor $\underline{p} - \underline{q}$ is the zero vector, what can you say about $\underline{p} + \underline{q}$ and $\underline{p} - \underline{q}$?

9. In triangle LMN, $\overrightarrow{LM}$ represents $\underline{u}$ and $\overrightarrow{MN}$ represents $\underline{v}$.

    If $(\underline{u} + \underline{v}) \cdot (\underline{u} + \underline{v}) = \underline{u} \cdot \underline{u} + \underline{v} \cdot \underline{v}$, prove that triangle LMN is right angled at M.

10. $\underline{a} = \begin{pmatrix} k \\ -1 \\ k+1 \end{pmatrix}$, $\underline{b} = \begin{pmatrix} k \\ k+1 \\ k \end{pmatrix}$ and $\underline{c} = \begin{pmatrix} -1 \\ k-1 \\ 1 \end{pmatrix}$.

    (a) Find $\underline{a} \cdot (\underline{b} - \underline{c})$.

    (b) If $\underline{a}$ is perpendicular to $(\underline{b} - \underline{c})$, find the value(s) of k.

11. OPQRSTUV is a cube with sides 4 units.

    A is the centre of face PQTU and B is the centre of face VUTS.

    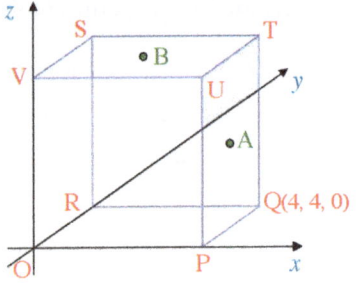

    (a) What are the coordinates of point U ?

    (b) Find $\underline{a}$ and $\underline{b}$, the position vectors of points A and B.

    (c) Calculate the size of angle AOB.

12. OABCPQ is a symmetrical roof structure.

    All units are in metres.

    M is the mid point of OC and N is the mid point of AB.

    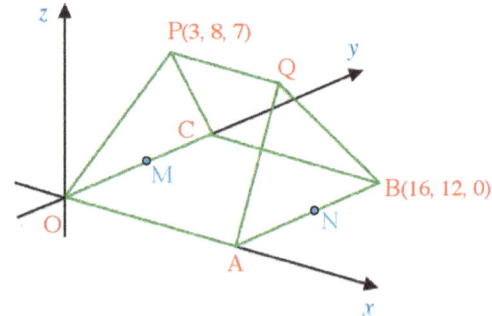

    (a) Write the coordinates of points M, N and Q.

    (b) Find vectors $\overrightarrow{QM}$ and $\overrightarrow{QN}$.

    (c) Hence, calculate the size of angle MQN.

13. The diagram shows a cone with its base circle on the x-y plane, and with height 12 units.

    In this plane, the equation of the circular base is :-
    $$x^2 + y^2 - 12x - 14y + 60 = 0.$$

    (a) Determine the coordinates of the centre C, of the circle and the coordinates of P.

    (b) E and F lie on the circle with E(12, 7, 0) and F(3, n, 0).

    Find the value of n.

    (c) Find the vectors $\overrightarrow{PE}$ and $\overrightarrow{PF}$.

    (d) Hence calculate the size of angle FPE.

Exam Practice Exercise (H14)

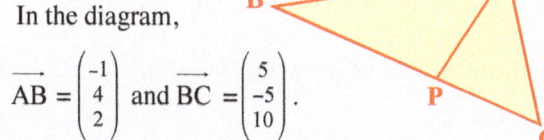

1. In the diagram,

$$\overrightarrow{AB} = \begin{pmatrix} -1 \\ 4 \\ 2 \end{pmatrix} \text{ and } \overrightarrow{BC} = \begin{pmatrix} 5 \\ -5 \\ 10 \end{pmatrix}.$$

(a) Find the vector $\overrightarrow{AC}$ in component form. **(2)**

Point P divides BC in the ratio 3 : 2.

(b) Show that $\overrightarrow{AP} = \begin{pmatrix} 2 \\ 1 \\ 8 \end{pmatrix}.$ **(2)**

(c) Find the size of angle BAP. **(5)**

2. $P(1, -3, 5)$ and $Q(-5, 0, -1)$.

g is such that the magnitude $\left| g\overrightarrow{PQ} \right| = 1$.

Find the value of g. **(3)**

3. (a) Show that $E(-2, 5, 3)$, $P(6, 1, 7)$ and $F(12, -2, 10)$ are collinear and find the ratio in which P divides EF. **(3)**

(b) G is a point on the z-axis and GP is perpendicular to EF.

Find the coordinates of G. **(5)**

4. Shown is an equilateral triangle.

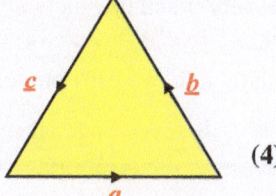

Prove that :-
$\underline{a}.(\underline{a} + \underline{b} + \underline{c}) = 0.$ **(4)**

5. PQR is an equilateral triangle and QRST is a square.

All sides are 2 units.

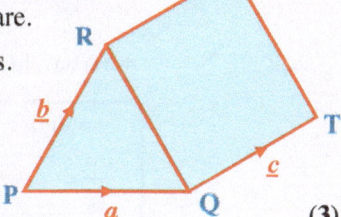

(a) Find $\underline{a}.\underline{c}$. **(3)**

(b) Show that $\underline{b}.(\underline{a} + \underline{c}) = 2 + 2\sqrt{3}$. **(5)**

6. $|\underline{p}| = 4, |\underline{q}| = 7$ and $|\underline{r}| = 11$.

$\underline{p}.\underline{q} = 6$ and the angle between $\underline{p}$ and $\underline{r}$ is 120°.

Find $\underline{p}.(\underline{p} + \underline{q} + \underline{r})$. **(3)**

7. Three identical plastic bricks are glued and stacked as shown.

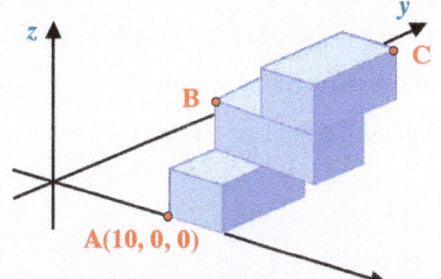

The dimensions of each brick are 6 cm by 12 cm by 4 cm high.

(a) Find the coordinates of points B and C. **(2)**

(b) Write the components of $\overrightarrow{CA}$ and $\overrightarrow{CB}$. **(2)**

(c) Calculate the size of angle ACB. **(5)**

8. The points K, L and M shown are collinear.

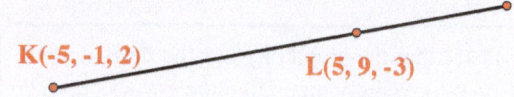

$K(-5, -1, 2)$ · · · · · · L(5, 9, -3) · · · · · · M

L is such that $2KL = 5LM$.

Determine the coordinates of M. **(4)**

9. Triangle RST lies on the x-y plane with $\overrightarrow{RT} = \underline{a}$, $\overrightarrow{RS} = \underline{b}$, and angle TRS = 120°.

$\underline{c}$ is a vector parallel to the z-axis.

$|\underline{a}| = |\underline{b}| = 3$ units and $|\underline{c}| = 2$ units.

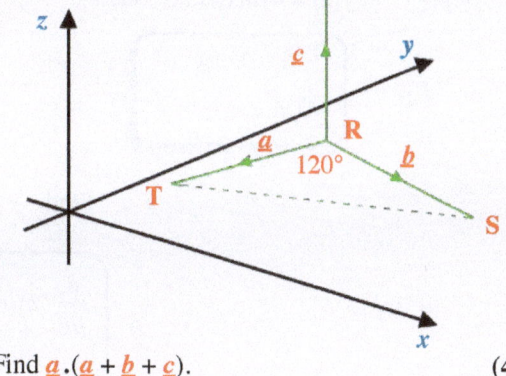

Find $\underline{a}.(\underline{a} + \underline{b} + \underline{c})$. **(4)**

Differentiation of Trigonometric Functions

To find the derivative of $f(x) = sinx$ and $f(x) = cosx$, where x is in radian measure, we use a graphical approach.

In Chapter 8, page 74, we looked at drawing the graph of the derivative, $f'(x)$ of a function $y = f(x)$.

Let us look at the slope of the tangent to the functions $f(x) = sinx$ and $f(x) = cosx$.

In this situation, we are going to use **radians** so we can draw the graph with the **same scale on both axes**.

The diagrams below show what is happening to the gradients (m) of the tangents to the curves.

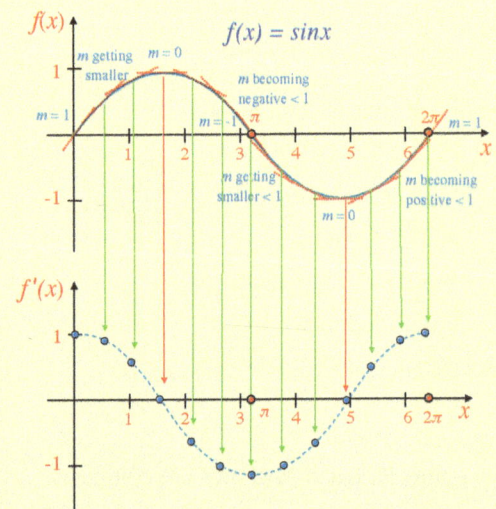
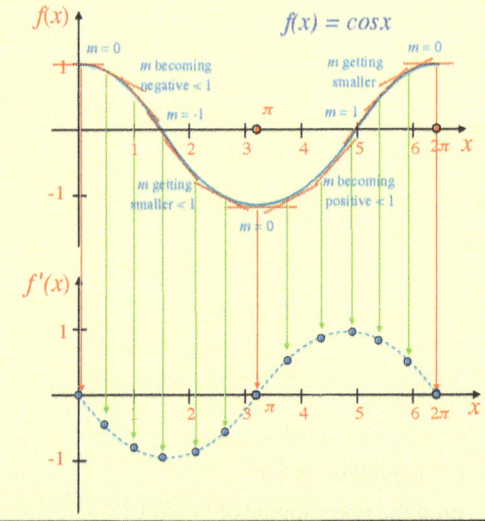

Can you see that the graph of $f'(x)$, the derivative of $f(x) = sinx$, looks very much like the **cosine** graph ? Though we can't prove it at this stage, this is true.

If $f(x) = sinx$, then $f'(x) = cosx$.

This time the graph of $f'(x)$, the derivative of $f(x) = cosx$, looks very much like the **sine** graph, but this time the sine graph is "**upside down**". i.e. it is the **negative sine** graph.

Again though, we can't prove it at this stage, this is true.

If $f(x) = cosx$, then $f'(x) = -sinx$.

In Leibniz Notation, $\dfrac{d}{dx}sin\,x = cos\,x$, and $\dfrac{d}{dx}cos\,x = -sin\,x$.

For these results to be true, x must be measured in radians. This was one of the main reasons for introducing radians.

Example 1 :- $f(x) = 4sinx$, find $f'(x)$.

$$f(x) = 4sinx$$
$$f'(x) = \textbf{4cosx}$$

Example 2 :- $y = 8cosx$, find $\dfrac{dy}{dx}$.

$$y = 8cosx$$
$$\dfrac{dy}{dx} = \textbf{-8sinx}$$

$\frac{1}{3}x \; \frac{-3x}{1}$

Example 3 :-   Find $\dfrac{d}{dx}(2sinx - 3cosx)$.

$$\dfrac{d}{dx}(2sinx - 3cosx) = 2cosx - 3(-sinx)$$
$$= \textbf{2cosx + 3sinx}$$

1. Find $f'(x)$ for each of the following :-

(a) $f(x) = 5cosx$ (b) $f(x) = -3sinx$

(c) $f(x) = 10cosx$ (d) $f(x) = 6sinx + cosx$

(e) $f(x) = 4sinx - 7cosx$ (f) $f(x) = 9cosx - sinx$

(g) $f(x) = 12sinx + x^4$ (h) $f(x) = 4cosx - 10x^5$

(i) $f(x) = 2cosx - 5sinx + 4\sqrt{x}$

(j) $f(x) = 8sinx - 3cosx + \sqrt[4]{x}$.

2. Find $\dfrac{dy}{dx}$ if :-

(a) $y = x + sinx$ (b) $y = x^3 - cosx$

(c) $y = -2sinx + \sqrt[3]{x^2}$ (d) $y = 2cosx - \dfrac{2}{x}$.

3. Evaluate :-

(a) $\dfrac{d}{dp}(11sinp)$ (b) $\dfrac{d}{dr}(-6cosr)$

(c) $\dfrac{d}{dt}(-2sint - 12cost)$

(d) $\dfrac{d}{d\theta}\left(8cos\theta + 10sin\theta + \dfrac{2}{\theta^2}\right)$.

4. Find the gradient of $f(x) = sinx + cosx$ at :-

(a) $x = 0$ (b) $x = \frac{\pi}{2}$

(c) $x = \frac{\pi}{4}$ (d) $x = \frac{3\pi}{4}$.

5. (a) Use differentiation to show that the maximum turning point on the graph of $y = 3sinx$ in the interval $0 < x < \pi$ is at $(\frac{\pi}{2}, 3)$.

(b) Use differentiation to show that the minimum turning point on the graph of $y = 2cosx$ in the interval $0 < x < 2\pi$ is at $(\pi, -2)$.

6. Find the **equation** of the tangent to the curve :-

(a) $y = 2sinx$ at the point where $x = \frac{\pi}{3}$.

(b) $y = 5cosx$ at the point where $x = \frac{5\pi}{3}$.

(c) $y = 3cosx + 4sinx$ at the point where $x = \frac{\pi}{2}$.

7. Show that the following functions are never decreasing :-

(a) $f(x) = x + sinx$

(b) $f(x) = x - cosx$.

8. For the curve with equation $f(x) = \sqrt{3}sinx + cosx$:-

(a) Find $f(0)$ and $f(2\pi)$.

(b) Calculate the roots of the function.

(c) Determine the stationary values of f and their nature.

(d) Sketch the curve.

Integration of Trigonometric Functions

As integration is the reverse process to differentiation, it follows that :-

$$\int cos\,x\,dx = sin\,x + C$$

$$\int sinx\,dx = -cosx + C$$

For these results to be true, x must be measured in radians.

Example 1 :- Find $\int 3sin\,x - cos\,x\,dx$.

$$\int 3sin\,x - cos\,x\,dx$$
$$= -3cos\,x - sin\,x + C$$

Example 2 :- Evaluate $\int_0^{\frac{\pi}{4}} \sqrt{2}\,cosx - 3sinx\,dx$.

$$\int_0^{\frac{\pi}{4}} \sqrt{2}\,cosx - 3sinx\,dx$$
$$= \left[\sqrt{2}\,sinx + 3cosx\right]_0^{\frac{\pi}{4}}$$
$$= \left(\sqrt{2}\,sin\frac{\pi}{4} + 3cos\frac{\pi}{4}\right) - \left(\sqrt{2}\,sin0 + 3cos0\right)$$
$$= \left(1 + \frac{3}{\sqrt{2}}\right) - \left(0 + 3\right)$$
$$= \frac{3}{\sqrt{2}} - 2$$

Exercise H15·2

1. Find :-

   (a) $\int 3\cos x\,dx$ (b) $\int 6\sin x\,dx$

   (c) $\int -2\sin x\,dx$ (d) $\int (5\cos x + 8\sin x)\,dx$

   (e) $\int (\cos x - 4\sin x)\,dx$ (f) $\int (9\sin x - 10\cos x)\,dx$

   (g) $\int (x^2 + 3\cos x)\,dx$ (h) $\int (\sqrt{x} - \cos x)\,dx$

   (i) $\int \left(4\sin x - 7\cos x - \dfrac{2}{x^2}\right)dx.$

2. Find :-

   (a) $\int (2\cos t - 8\sin t)\,dt$ (b) $\int (-4\sin\theta - 6\cos\theta)\,d\theta.$

3. Evaluate each definite integral :-

   (a) $\int_0^{\frac{\pi}{2}} 4\cos x\,dx$ (b) $\int_0^{\frac{\pi}{2}} 6\sin x\,dx$

   (c) $\int_0^{\frac{\pi}{6}} \cos x\,dx$ (d) $\int_{\frac{\pi}{4}}^{\pi} 5\cos x\,dx$

   (e) $\int_0^{\frac{\pi}{4}} (2\cos x - \sin x)\,dx$ (f) $\int_0^{\pi} (\sin x + \cos x)\,dx$

   (g) $\int_0^{\frac{\pi}{2}} (1 + \cos x)\,dx$ (h) $\int_0^{\frac{\pi}{3}} (1 + 4\sin x)\,dx$

   (i) $\int_{-\pi}^{\pi} (2x - \sin x)\,dx$ (j) $\int_0^{\frac{\pi}{3}} (2 + 6\cos x)\,dx$

   (k) $\int_0^{\frac{\pi}{6}} (9 - 2\cos x)\,dx$ (l) $\int_{-\pi}^{\pi} (x^2 + 2\sin x)\,dx$

   (m) $\int_{\frac{\pi}{2}}^{\pi} (x + 8\sin x)\,dx$ (n) $\int_{-\pi}^{\frac{\pi}{2}} (2\sin x - 6\cos x)\,dx.$

4. Evaluate $\int_0^{\frac{\pi}{2}} \cos x\,dx$ and show the area represented by this integral in a sketch.

5. Evaluate $\int_0^{\pi} \sin x\,dx$ and show the area represented by this integral in a sketch.

6. Shown is the curve representing $y = 2 + \sin x$.

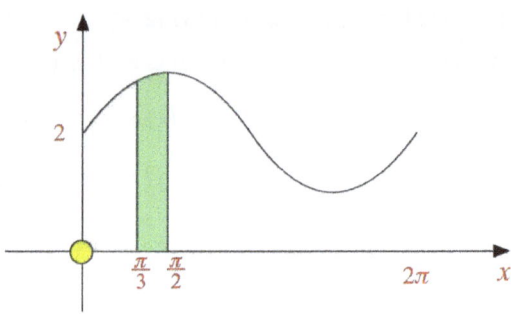

Calculate the shaded area.

7. (a) Prove that for $0 \le x \le \pi$, the curve $y = \sqrt{3}\sin x$ meets the curve $y = \cos x$ at the point with x-coordinate $\frac{\pi}{6}$.

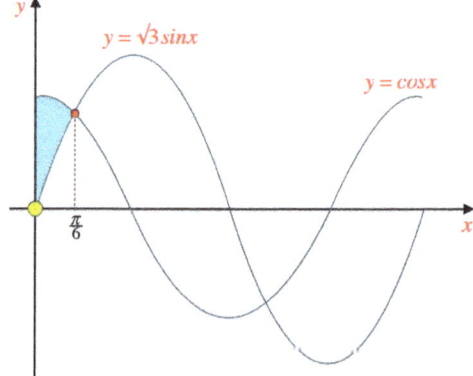

   (b) Calculate the shaded area shown above.

8. (a) Prove that for $0 \le x \le 2\pi$, the curve $y = \sqrt{3}\cos x$ meets the curve $y = \sin x$ at the points with x-coordinates $\frac{\pi}{3}$ and $\frac{4\pi}{3}$.

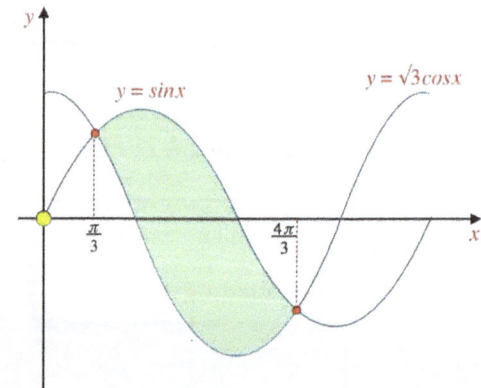

   (b) Calculate the shaded area shown above.

The Derivative of $(x + a)^n$ and The Derivative of $(ax + b)^n$

The derivative of expressions of the form $(x + a)^n$ or $(ax + b)^n$ can be found by expanding the brackets to expand the function and then differentiating each individual terms.

We will look at 2 examples using this method, but then ask .... what if the power (index) was very large, was a fraction or even a negative number ?

Example 1 :- Find $\dfrac{d}{dx}(x + 3)^3$.

$$\dfrac{d}{dx}(x + 3)^3$$
$$= \dfrac{d}{dx}(x + 3)(x + 3)^2$$
$$= \dfrac{d}{dx}(x + 3)(x^2 + 6x + 9)$$
$$= \dfrac{d}{dx}(x^3 + 9x^2 + 27x + 27)$$
$$= 3x^2 + 18x + 27$$
$$= 3(x^2 + 6x + 9)$$
$$= 3(x + 3)^2$$

You can see that going directly from line 1 to the last line ... the power appears to come to the front of the bracket and the power of the bracket decreases by 1.

$$\dfrac{d}{dx}(x + 3)^3 = 3(x + 3)^{3-1}$$

In general

$$\boxed{\dfrac{d}{dx}(x + a)^n = n(x + a)^{n-1}}$$

Example 2 :- Find $\dfrac{dy}{dx}$ if $y = (2x - 5)^3$.

$$y = (2x - 5)^3$$
$$= (2x - 5)(2x - 5)^2$$
$$= (2x - 5)(4x^2 - 20x + 25)$$
$$= 8x^3 - 60x^2 + 150x - 125$$
$$\dfrac{dy}{dx} = 24x^2 - 120x + 150$$
$$= 6(4x^2 - 20x + 25)$$
$$= 6(2x - 5)^2 \ \left(i.e.\ 3(2x - 5)^2 \times 2\right)$$

We can see that going directly from line 1 to the last line .... the power comes to the front of the bracket, the power of the bracket is reduced by 1 and the expression is then multiplied by the **coefficient of x**.

$$\dfrac{d}{dx}(2x - 5)^3 = 3(2x - 5)^{3-1} \times 2$$

In general

$$\boxed{\dfrac{d}{dx}(ax + b)^n = an(ax + b)^{n-1}}$$

This is called the **Chain Rule** for differentiation.

Example 3 :- Find $\dfrac{d}{dx}(x + 6)^5$.

$$\dfrac{d}{dx}(x + 6)^5$$
$$= 5(x + 6)^4$$

Example 4 :- Find $\dfrac{dy}{dx}$ if $y = \dfrac{1}{(x - 7)^4}$.

$$y = \dfrac{1}{(x - 7)^4}.$$
$$= (x - 7)^{-4}$$
$$\dfrac{dy}{dx} = -4(x - 7)^{-5}$$

Example 5 :- Differentiate $y = (4x + 9)^6$.

$$y = (4x + 9)^6.$$
$$\dfrac{dy}{dx} = 6(4x + 9)^5 \times 4$$
$$\dfrac{dy}{dx} = 24(4x + 9)^5$$

Example 6 :- If $f(x) = \dfrac{1}{\sqrt{6x - 8}}$, find $f'(x)$.

$$f(x) = \dfrac{1}{\sqrt{6x - 8}},$$
$$= (6x - 8)^{-\frac{1}{2}}$$
$$f'(x) = -\dfrac{1}{2}(6x - 8)^{-\frac{3}{2}} \times 6 \quad \text{← note}$$
$$f'(x) = \dfrac{-3}{\sqrt{(6x - 8)^3}}$$

Exercise H15·3

1. For each function below, find its derived function :-
   (i) by expanding the brackets and differentiating.
   (ii) using the rules applied in the worked examples.
   (a) $f(x) = (x - 4)^2$ (b) $g(t) = (t + 7)^2$
   (c) $h(m) = (2m - 1)^3$.

2. Differentiate :-
   (a) $f(x) = (x + 3)^5$
   (b) $f(x) = (x - 2)^4$
   (c) $f(x) = \sqrt{x - 8}$
   (d) $f(x) = \dfrac{1}{x + 7}$
   (e) $f(x) = \dfrac{1}{(x - 10)^2}$
   (f) $f(x) = \sqrt[5]{(x + 1)^2}$
   (g) $f(p) = (p - 2)^2 + \cos p$ (h) $f(t) = \sin t + \sqrt{t - 9}$
   (i) $f(r) = \dfrac{1}{\sqrt{r + 4}} - \cos r$ (j) $f(v) = (8 - v)^{-9}$.

3. Find :-
   (a) $\dfrac{d}{dx}(2x + 5)^5$
   (b) $\dfrac{d}{dx}(2 - 5x)^6$
   (c) $\dfrac{d}{dx}(7x - 2)^7$
   (d) $\dfrac{d}{dx}(\tfrac{1}{5}x - 3)^{-5}$
   (e) $\dfrac{d}{dx}(6 - 8x)^{\frac{3}{4}}$
   (f) $\dfrac{d}{dx}\left(\dfrac{2}{x - 5}\right)$
   (g) $\dfrac{d}{dt}(6 + \tfrac{1}{2}t)^{-\frac{1}{10}}$
   (h) $\dfrac{d}{dt}(2 - 5t)^{-\frac{1}{3}}$
   (i) $\dfrac{d}{dt} = \sqrt[4]{10 - 4t}\,dt$
   (j) $\dfrac{d}{d\theta}\sqrt{(12\theta + 2)}$
   (k) $\dfrac{d}{d\theta}\dfrac{1}{(4\theta - 1)^2}$
   (l) $\dfrac{d}{d\theta}\dfrac{1}{\sqrt[5]{(1 - 10\theta)^4}}$
   (m) $\dfrac{d}{dr}\dfrac{8}{(4r + 5)^2}$
   (n) $\dfrac{d}{dr}\dfrac{3}{\sqrt[3]{(3 - 8r)}}$.

The Chain Rule

The process you have been using in the last exercise is referred to as the **chain rule**. Let us explain how it works.

We will use the Leibniz notation to explain why $\dfrac{d}{dx}(ax + b)^n = a \times n(ax + b)^{n-1}$

> To differentiate $y = (ax + b)^n$, let us firstly replace $(ax + b)$ by a new letter v.
>
> => $y = (ax + b)^n$ becomes $y = v^n$, where $v = (ax + b)$.
>
> We can now find both $\dfrac{dy}{dv}$ and $\dfrac{dv}{dx}$.
>
> => $\dfrac{dy}{dv} = nv^{n-1}$ and $\dfrac{dv}{dx} = a$.
>
> Though it is outwith the scope of Higher Maths, it can be proved that :-
>
> $\dfrac{dy}{dx} = \dfrac{dy}{dv} \times \dfrac{dv}{dx}$ => $\dfrac{dy}{dx} = a \times nv^{n-1} = an(ax + b)^{n-1}$.

This is known as *the chain rule*, and can be used for any term, thought of as being in brackets.

> To differentiate a term in brackets, think of the brackets as v, find $\dfrac{dv}{dx}$, then multiply by the derivative of the brackets.

Example 1 :-
Differentiate $(3x^2 - 2)^4$

$y = (3x^2 - 2)^4$
Let $v = 3x^2 - 2$, then $y = v^4$
$\dfrac{dv}{dx} = 6x$ $\dfrac{dy}{dv} = 4v^3$
$\dfrac{dy}{dx} = \dfrac{dy}{dv} \times \dfrac{dv}{dx}$
$= 24x v^3$
$= 24x(3x^2 - 2)^3$

Example 2 :-
Differentiate $\sqrt{x^2 + 5x}$.

$y = \sqrt{x^2 + 5x} = (x^2 + 5x)^{\frac{1}{2}}$
Let $v = x^2 + 5x$, then $y = v^{\frac{1}{2}}$
$\dfrac{dv}{dx} = 2x + 5$ $\dfrac{dy}{dv} = \tfrac{1}{2}v^{-\frac{1}{2}}$
$\dfrac{dy}{dx} = \dfrac{dy}{dv} \times \dfrac{dv}{dx}$
$= \tfrac{1}{2}v^{-\frac{1}{2}} \times (2x + 5)$
$= \dfrac{(2x + 5)}{2\sqrt{x^2 + 5x}}$

Exercise H15·4

1. Use the chain rule to differentiate :-

   (a) $f(x) = (x + 1)^5$ (b) $f(x) = (2x - 4)^3$

   (c) $f(x) = (7 + x)^6$ (d) $f(x) = (3x - 5)^7$

   (e) $f(x) = (1 - x)^8$ (f) $f(x) = (4 - 3x)^3$

   (g) $f(x) = (2 - x)^9$ (h) $f(x) = (7 - 5x)^5$

   (i) $f(x) = (x^2 + 1)^4$ (j) $f(x) = (x^3 - 2)^3$

   (k) $f(x) = (x^4 + 10)^6$ (l) $f(x) = (1 - x^5)^3$

   (m) $f(x) = (2x + 4)^{\frac{1}{2}}$ (n) $f(x) = (3x - 6)^{\frac{1}{3}}$

   (o) $f(x) = (x - 1)^{-3}$ (p) $f(x) = (2 - 9x)^{-2}$

   (q) $f(x) = (x^2 + 6x)^3$ (r) $f(x) = (x^2 + x + 3)^2$

   (s) $f(x) = (x^3 - x)^8$ (t) $f(x) = (x^2 + 2x - 6)^{\frac{1}{2}}$

   (u) $f(x) = \sqrt{2x - 3}$ (v) $f(x) = \sqrt{1 - 8x}$

   (w) $f(x) = \sqrt[3]{x^3 + 6x}$ (x) $f(x) = \sqrt[4]{10 - x^2}$.

2. Find the derivative of :-

   (a) $f(x) = \dfrac{1}{x + 9}$ (b) $f(x) = \dfrac{10}{1 - x}$

   (c) $f(x) = \dfrac{1}{(2x + 5)^2}$ (d) $f(x) = \dfrac{6}{\sqrt{6x + 2}}$

   (e) $f(x) = (x^2 - 2)^2$ (f) $f(x) = \left(x - 1 + \dfrac{1}{x} \right)^2$.

3. Find the stationary value of the function f defined by $f(x) = 8x - (3x - 1)^{\frac{4}{3}}$, and determine its nature.

4. (a) Show that if $f(x) = (x - 2)^{\frac{3}{2}} - 3(x - 2)^{\frac{1}{2}}$,

   then $f'(x) = \dfrac{3(x - 3)}{2(x - 2)^{\frac{1}{2}}}$.

   (b) Find the stationary value of the function and determine its nature.

5. (a) Find $\dfrac{d}{dx} \left(\dfrac{3}{x - 5} \right)$.

   (b) Find the equation of the tangent to the graph of the function $y = \dfrac{3}{x - 5}$ at the point where $x = 4$.

6. Calculate the coordinates of the points on the graph of $f(x) = \dfrac{-9}{x + 2}$ where the tangent is at an angle of 45° with the positive direction of the x-axis.

Using the Chain Rule to Differentiate Trigonometric Functions

The chain rule can be used in the differentiation of trigonometric functions but, although the idea is similar, it can be expressed in simpler ways.

Example 1 :- Find $\dfrac{d}{dx} \sin 3x$.

In this case, think simply about differentiating sin(3x), then differentiating the "brackets" and finally, multiplying the two terms.

- Differentiate the "trig part"
  i.e. $\dfrac{d}{dx} \sin... \rightarrow \cos...$
- Differentiate the "3x part"
  i.e. $\dfrac{d}{dx} 3x \rightarrow 3$
- Now multiply.

  $\dfrac{d}{dx} \sin 3x = $ **$3\cos 3x$**

Example 2 :- Find $\dfrac{d}{dx} \cos^4 x$.

Think of it as $(\cos x)^4$, and differentiate the power (the $(...)^4$), then differentiate the $(\cos x)$ and finally, multiply the two terms.

- Deal with the "power part"
  i.e. $\dfrac{d}{dx}(....)^4 \rightarrow 4 \times (...)^3$
  $\Rightarrow \dfrac{d}{dx} \cos^4 = 4\cos^3 ..$
- Differentiate the "trig part"
  i.e. $\dfrac{d}{dx} \cos x = -\sin x$
- Now multiply.
  $\dfrac{d}{dx} \cos^4 x = 4\cos^3 x \times -\sin x$

  $= $ **$-4\cos^3 x \sin x$**

Example 3 :- Find $\dfrac{d}{dx} \sin^8 5x$.

Think of it as $(\sin 5x)^8$, and differentiate the power (the $(...)^8$), then differentiate the $(\sin 5x)$ in the same way as in example 1 and finally, multiply the three terms.

- Deal with the "power part"
  i.e. $\dfrac{d}{dx}(....)^8 \rightarrow 8 \times (...)^7$
  $\Rightarrow \dfrac{d}{dx} (\sin...)^8 = 8(\sin...)^7$
- Differentiate the "trig part"
  i.e. $\dfrac{d}{dx} \sin 5x \rightarrow 5\cos 5x$
- Now multiply.
  $\dfrac{d}{dx} \sin^8 5x = 8\sin^7 5x \times 5\cos 5x$

  $= $ **$40\sin^7 5x \cos 5x$**

Exercise H15·5

1. Use the chain rule to differentiate :-

   (a) $\sin 2x$ (b) $\sin(5x+1)$

   (c) $\sin(ax+b)$ (d) $\sin\frac{1}{4}x$

   (e) $\cos 2x$ (f) $\cos(6x-2)$

   (g) $\cos(mx+n)$ (h) $\cos\frac{1}{3}x$

   (i) $\sin^2 x$ (j) $\sin^5 x$

   (k) $\cos^2 x$ (l) $\cos^7 x$

   (m) $\sin(4x-8)$ (n) $\cos(9-10x)$

   (o) $2\cos 4x$ (p) $3\sin 6x$

   (q) $(1+\cos x)^2$ (r) $(1-\cos x)^2$

   (s) $\dfrac{4}{\sin x}$ (t) $(\cos^2 x+\sin^2 x)$.

2. Differentiate :-

   (a) $\frac{1}{4}(x+\sin x)^3$ (b) $(4-\cos x)^{\frac{1}{2}}$

   (c) $(5\sin x-2)^{-2}$ (d) $(\sin x)^{\frac{3}{4}}$

   (e) $(x-\sin x)^{\frac{1}{3}}$ (f) $(1-\cos x)(1+\cos x)$

   (g) $\sin^2 4x$ (h) $\cos^2 3x$

   (i) $\sin^3(4x^2)$ (j) $\cos^4(5x^3)$

   (k) $(x+\cos 2x)^2$ (l) $(\sin 5x-x^2)^{\frac{1}{2}}$.

3. Find the x-coordinates of the stationary points for :-

   (a) $f(x)=4\sin x+\cos 2x$ $0\le x\le 2\pi$,

   (b) $f(x)=\sin 2x+2\sin x$, $0\le x\le 2\pi$.

4. (a) Show that the function defined by
   $y=2x+4\cos\frac{1}{2}x$ is never decreasing.

   (b) Find the x-coordinate of the point of inflexion of the function, in the interval $0\le x\le 2\pi$.

Further Integration

Though we can use the chain rule to differentiate $(3x^2-2)^5$, we cannot easily integrate functions like $(3x^2-2)^5$.

We **can** integrate certain "**special**" functions - those where the term in the brackets, or in trig functions is a simple linear function like $2x-1, 3x+5, 6-\frac{1}{2}x$ etc. i.e. of the form **(ax + b)**.

Here are a final 3 **special** integrals for you to use :-

Since $\dfrac{d}{dx}(ax+b)^n = n(ax+b)^{n-1}$ Since $\dfrac{d}{dx}\cos(ax+b)=-a\sin(ax+b)$ Since $\dfrac{d}{dx}\sin(ax+b)=a\cos(ax+b)$

$$\int(ax+b)^n\,dx = \frac{(ax+b)^{n+1}}{(n+1)a} + C$$
$$n\ne -1$$

$$\int\sin(ax+b)\,dx = -\frac{1}{a}\cos(ax+b)+C$$

$$\int\cos(ax+b)\,dx = \frac{1}{a}\sin(ax+b)+C$$

Example 1 :-

Find $\int(5x+2)^3\,dx$

$$\int(5x+2)^3\,dx$$
$$= \frac{(5x+2)^4}{4\times 5}+C$$
$$= \frac{1}{20}(5x+2)^4+C$$

Example 2 :-

Find $\int\sin(8x+1)\,dx$

$$\int\sin(8x+1)\,dx$$
$$= -\frac{1}{8}\cos(8x+1)+C$$

Example 3 :-

Find $\int_1^2\dfrac{dx}{\sqrt{6x-3}}$

$$\int_1^2\frac{dx}{\sqrt{6x-3}}$$
$$= \int_1^2(6x-3)^{-\frac{1}{2}}dx$$
$$= \left[\frac{(6x-3)^{\frac{1}{2}}}{\frac{1}{2}\times 6}\right]_1^2$$
$$= \left(\frac{(12-3)^{\frac{1}{2}}}{3}\right) - \left(\frac{(6-3)^{\frac{1}{2}}}{3}\right)$$
$$= 1-\frac{\sqrt 3}{3}$$

Exercise H15·6

1. Integrate the following with respect to x :-

   (a) $(x + 2)^4$

   (b) $(2x + 5)^7$

   (c) $(px - q)^5$

   (d) $(1 - 8x)^3$

   (e) $(x + 6)^{-2}$

   (f) $(7x - 1)^{-4}$

   (g) $(4x - 9)^{\frac{1}{2}}$

   (h) $(1 - 4x)^{\frac{3}{2}}$

   (i) $\dfrac{1}{(x + 2)^2}$

   (j) $\dfrac{2}{(x + 4)^2}$

   (k) $(12 - x)^{-\frac{2}{3}}$

   (l) $\dfrac{1}{\sqrt{(2x + 9)}}$

   (m) $\dfrac{1}{\sqrt[3]{(x - 4)^2}}$

   (n) $\dfrac{4}{\sqrt{(8x + 12)}}$.

2. Evaluate each definite integral :-

   (a) $\displaystyle\int_0^1 (2x + 2)^3\, dx$

   (b) $\displaystyle\int_{-1}^1 (1 - x)^4\, dx$

   (c) $\displaystyle\int_0^4 \sqrt{(4 - x)}\, dx$

   (d) $\displaystyle\int_1^2 \frac{dx}{(x + 3)^2}$

   (e) $\displaystyle\int_2^3 \sqrt{(10 - 3x)}\, dx$

   (f) $\displaystyle\int_1^5 \frac{dx}{\sqrt{(2x - 1)}}$

   (g) $\displaystyle\int_{-1}^4 (3x + 4)^{\frac{3}{2}}\, dx$

   (h) $\displaystyle\int_2^{10} \frac{3}{\sqrt{(2x + 5)}}\, dx$.

3. Integrate with respect to x :-

   (a) $2\sin x$

   (b) $\cos 2x$

   (c) $\sin 3x$

   (d) $\cos(4x - 1)$

   (e) $-\cos 7x$

   (f) $\sin\frac{1}{2}x$

   (g) $\cos(2 - x)$

   (h) $x^2 - 4\cos 4x$

   (i) $\sin\left(\dfrac{4x + 2}{8}\right)$

   (j) $\frac{2}{3}\cos(3x - 6)$

   (k) $6x^3 - \sin(6x - 5)$

   (l) $8x^{\frac{3}{2}} + 8\sin\frac{1}{2}x$.

4. Evaluate each definite integral :-

   (a) $\displaystyle\int_0^{\frac{\pi}{3}} \cos 3x\, dx$

   (b) $\displaystyle\int_0^{\frac{\pi}{3}} \sin 4x\, dx$

   (c) $\displaystyle\int_{-\frac{\pi}{2}}^{\frac{\pi}{2}} \cos(x + \frac{\pi}{4})\, dx$

   (d) $\displaystyle\int_{-\frac{\pi}{4}}^{\frac{5\pi}{6}} \sin 6x\, dx$

4. (e) $\displaystyle\int_0^{\frac{\pi}{2}} \sin 2x - \cos 2x\, dx$

   (f) $\displaystyle\int_0^{\frac{\pi}{12}} \sin 4x - \cos 6x\, dx$

   (g) $\displaystyle\int_{-\frac{\pi}{6}}^{\frac{\pi}{6}} 2\cos 3x - 3\cos 2x\, dx$.

5. Evaluate $\displaystyle\int_0^{\frac{\pi}{2}} \sin 2x\, dx$ and illustrate in a sketch the area given by this integral.

6. Calculate the area between the x-axis and the curve $y = 3\sin 4x$ from $x = \pi$ to $x = \frac{5\pi}{4}$.

7. We cannot use this special integration method to find
   $$\int \sin^2 x\, dx.$$

   (a) Remember, from page 128 :-
   $$\sin^2 x = \tfrac{1}{2}(1 - \cos 2x)$$
   $$\Rightarrow \quad \int \sin^2 x\, dx = \int \tfrac{1}{2}(1 - \cos 2x)\, dx$$

   Use this to find $\int \sin^2 x\, dx$.

   (b) Similarly, find $\int \cos^2 x\, dx$.

8. Calculate the area enclosed by the x-axis and :-

   (a) $y = \sin 2x$, between $x = 0$ and $x = \frac{\pi}{2}$.

   (b) $y = \cos 4x$, between $x = 0$ and $x = \frac{\pi}{6}$.

9. Calculate the shaded area shown in the diagram below :-

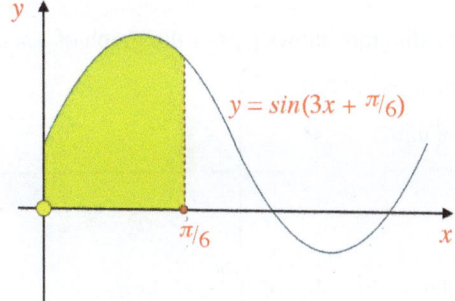

$y = \sin(3x + \pi/6)$

Exam Practice Exercise (H15)

1. Find :-

   (a) $\int (3x - 8)^5 dx$ (2)

   (b) $\int (4x - 1)^{\frac{1}{2}} dx$ (2)

   (c) $\int 6\cos(3x + 1) dx$ (2)

   (d) $\int (8x^3 - \cos 8x) dx$ (3)

   (e) $\int \dfrac{dx}{\sqrt{1 - 4x}}$. (4)

2. If $y = 3\cos^6 x$, find $\dfrac{dy}{dx}$. (3)

3. If $f(x) = 6\cos 3x$, find $f'(0)$. (3)

4. Find the derivative of $y = \sqrt{9 - 4x^4}$. (3)

5. If $y = \sin(x^2 - 7)$, find $\dfrac{dy}{dx}$. (2)

6. Given that $f(x) = \sin\sqrt{(6 - 3x^4)}$ for a suitable domain, find $f'(x)$. (3)

7. If $y = (x^2 + 9)^{\frac{1}{2}}$, find $\dfrac{dy}{dx}$. (2)

   Hence find $\int \dfrac{2x}{\sqrt{x^2 + 9}} dx$. (1)

8. $\int_2^p (4x + 1)^{-\frac{1}{2}} dx = 1$, find the value of p. (5)

9. $\int_0^b (7\sin 3x) dx = \dfrac{14}{3}, 0 < b < \pi$.

   Calculate the value of b. (5)

10. The diagram shows part of the graph of $y = a\sin bx$.

    The area shaded is $\dfrac{3}{8}$ unit^2.

    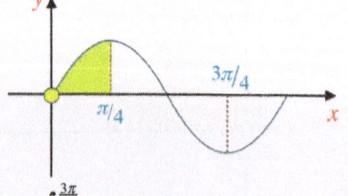

    What is the value of $\int_{\frac{\pi}{4}}^{\frac{3\pi}{4}} a\sin bx\, dx$? (2)

11. (a) A curve has equation $y = (2x - 4)^{\frac{1}{2}}$.

    Show that the equation of the tangent to this curve at the point where $x = 4$ is $y = \frac{1}{2}x$. (5)

    (b) Diagram 1 shows part of the curve and the tangent.

    The curve cuts the x-axis at point P.

    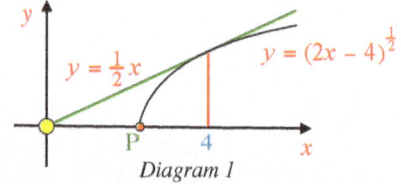

    Diagram 1

    Find the coordinates of P. (1)

    (c) Calculate the shaded area shown in diagram 2. (7)

    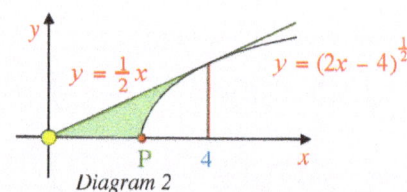

    Diagram 2

12. Acceleration is defined as the rate of change of velocity with respect to time.

    An object is travelling in a straight line.

    The velocity, v m/s, of the object, t seconds after the start of the motion, is given by

    $$v(t) = 10\cos(2t - \tfrac{\pi}{2}).$$

    (a) Find a formula for $a(t)$, the acceleration of the object, t seconds after the start of the motion. (3)

    (b) Determine whether the velocity of this object is increasing or decreasing when $t = 8$. (2)

13. (a) Find $\int_{\frac{\pi}{2}}^{\frac{3\pi}{2}} \sin 2x\, dx$. (4)

    (b) Draw a sketch and use it to explain your answer to part (a). (2)

1. Points P(0, 2), Q(3, 5) and R(10, 4) are the vertices of ΔPQR.

   Find the coordinates of the point of intersection of the median QS and the altitude PT.

2. Find the equation of the tangent to the curve $y = x^3 - 5x^2 + 3x - 1$ at the point where $x = -2$.

3. The sketch of the quartic function, $y = f(x)$ is shown.

   Sketch a possible graph for $y = f'(x)$, indicating all relevant points.

   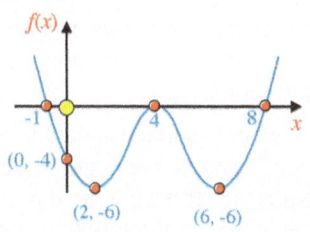

4. Show that a line segment joining the minimum turning point of the function $y = x^2 - 6x + 5$ to the maximum turning point of the function $y = 2x - x^2$ has length $\sqrt{29}$.

5. Sketch the graph of $y = \frac{1}{3}x^3 - x^2 - 3x + 4$ in the closed interval $\{x: -2 \le x \le 4, x \in R\}$, showing where the graph cuts the y-axis, and any relevant turning points.

6. Part of the graph of the cubic function $y = f(x)$ is shown.

   Find the equation of this function and express it in the form
   $$f(x) = ax^3 + bx^2 + cx + d.$$

   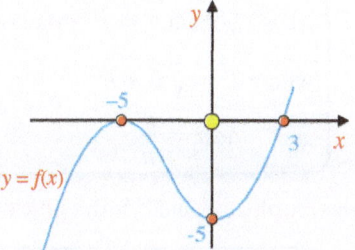

7. A sequence is defined by $u_n = 0{\cdot}6u_{n-1} + 2$, with $u_0 = 10$.

   (a) Find the value of u_3.

   (b) Determine the limit of this sequence, as n tends towards infinity.

8. A(-2, 1) and B(8, 11) are the end points of the diameter of a circle with centre C.

   A second circle is drawn such that P is the centre of the circle with diameter AC.

   Find the equation of this circle.

   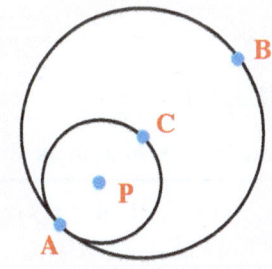

9. Solve the trig. equation $5\cos 2x° - 1 = 4\cos x°$, for $0 < x < 180$.

10. Three vectors, $\underline{p}, \underline{q}$ and $\underline{r}$ are given as $\underline{p} = 3\underline{i} + 4\underline{j} - \underline{k}$, $\underline{q} = \underline{i} - 3\underline{k}$ and $\underline{r} = 5\underline{j} + \underline{k}$.

    (a) Evaluate $\underline{p}.\underline{q} + \underline{q}.\underline{r}$.   (b) Find the size of the angle between vectors $\underline{p}$ and $\underline{q}$.

11. Differentiate :-   (a) $f(x) = \dfrac{3}{\sqrt{x^2 - 2x}}$ (b) $y = (1 - \sin^2 x)^{\frac{1}{3}}$.

12. Find :-   (a) $\int (3x+1)^4 \, dx$ (b) $\int_{\frac{\pi}{2}}^{\pi} 5\cos x - 4\sin 2x \, dx$.

Expressing $a\cos x + b\sin x$ in the form $k\cos(x - \alpha)$

When an expression involves a combination of sine and cosine functions, it is possible to express them as a **single trigonometric function**.

For example, look at the graphs of $y = \sin x$ and $y = \cos x$, showing all major points.

If we wish to add these functions to form $y = \sin x + \cos x$, we could do so by considering all the coloured points at $x = 0°, 45°, 90°, \dots 360°.$, and adding their y-values together to create a set of points for our new graph.

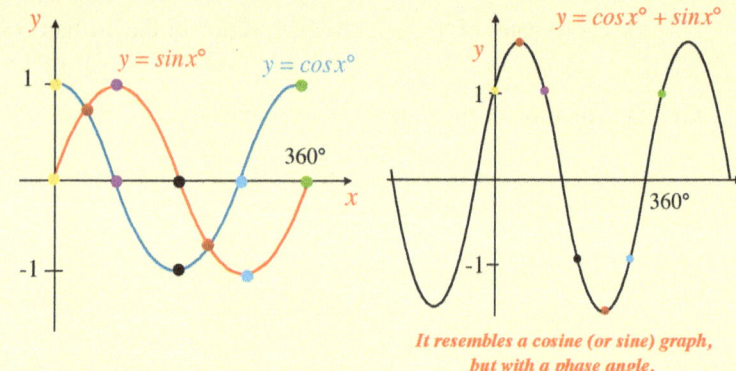

It resembles a cosine (or sine) graph, but with a phase angle.

Any trig expression of the form $a\cos x + b\sin x$ can be represented by the single trig expression :-
$$k\cos(x - \alpha).$$

i.e.
> $a\cos x + b\sin x = k\cos(x - \alpha),$
>
> where $k = \sqrt{a^2 + b^2}$
>
> and $\tan\alpha = \dfrac{b}{a}.$

k is the **amplitude** and α is the **phase angle**.

> $k\cos(x - \alpha),$ is called a **wave function**.

Proof :-

Let $a\cos x + b\sin x = k\cos(x - \alpha)$

$\qquad\qquad = k(\cos x\cos\alpha + \sin x\sin\alpha)$ *R.H.S. expanded*

$\qquad\qquad = k\cos x\cos\alpha + k\sin x\sin\alpha$ *(now rearrange)*

$\qquad\qquad = k\cos\alpha\cos x + k\sin\alpha\sin x$

We now equate the coefficients of this equation and this gives :-

$\qquad a = k\cos\alpha$ and $b = k\sin\alpha$

Note :- $\quad a^2 + b^2 = (k\cos\alpha)^2 + k\sin\alpha^2$

$\qquad\qquad\quad = k^2\cos^2\alpha + k^2\sin^2\alpha$

$\qquad\qquad\quad = k^2(\cos^2\alpha + \sin^2\alpha)$

$\qquad\qquad\quad = k^2$ this means $k = \sqrt{a^2 + b^2}.$

Also :- $\dfrac{b}{a} = \dfrac{k\sin\alpha}{k\cos\alpha} \quad \Rightarrow \quad \dfrac{b}{a} = \tan\alpha.$

Example 1 :-

Write $\cos x + \sin x$ in the form $k\cos(x - \alpha)$.

$\begin{aligned}
1\cos x° + 1\sin x° &= k\cos(x - \alpha)° \\
&= k(\cos x°\cos\alpha° + \sin x°\sin\alpha°) \\
&= k\cos x°\cos\alpha° + k\sin x°\sin\alpha°
\end{aligned}$

$\Rightarrow \underline{1}\cos x° + \underline{1\sin} x° = \underline{k\cos\alpha°}\cos x° + \underline{k\sin\alpha°}\sin x°$

now, by equating coefficients, we get :-

$\underline{k\cos\alpha°} = 1$ and $\underline{k\sin\alpha°} = 1$

α in the 1st quadrant

Hence $\dfrac{k\sin\alpha}{k\cos\alpha} = \dfrac{1}{1} \Rightarrow \tan\alpha° = 1$

$\alpha = 45$

and $\quad k = \sqrt{1^2 + 1^2} \quad \Rightarrow \quad k = \sqrt{2}$

$\Rightarrow \cos x° - \sin x° = \boxed{\sqrt{2}\cos(x - 45)°}.$

Example 2 :-

Write $3\cos x + 4\sin x$ in the form $k\cos(x - \alpha)$.

$\begin{aligned}
3\cos x° + 4\sin x° &= k\cos(x - \alpha)° \\
&= k(\cos x°\cos\alpha° + \sin x°\sin\alpha°) \\
&= k\cos x°\cos\alpha° + k\sin x°\sin\alpha°
\end{aligned}$

$\Rightarrow \underline{3}\cos x° + \underline{4\sin} x° = \underline{k\cos\alpha°}\cos x° + \underline{k\sin\alpha°}\sin x°$

by equating coefficients, we get

$\underline{k\cos\alpha°} = 3$ and $\underline{k\sin\alpha°} = 4$

α in the 1st quadrant

Hence $\dfrac{k\sin\alpha}{k\cos\alpha} = \dfrac{4}{3} \Rightarrow \tan\alpha° = {}^4/_3$

$\alpha = 53·1$

and $\quad k = \sqrt{4^2 + 3^2} \quad \Rightarrow \quad k = 5$

$\Rightarrow 3\cos x° - 4\sin x° = \boxed{5\cos(x - 53·1)°}.$

Exercise 16·1

1. Write $12\cos x° + 5\sin x°$ in the form $k\cos(x - \alpha)°$.

   Copy and **complete** :-

   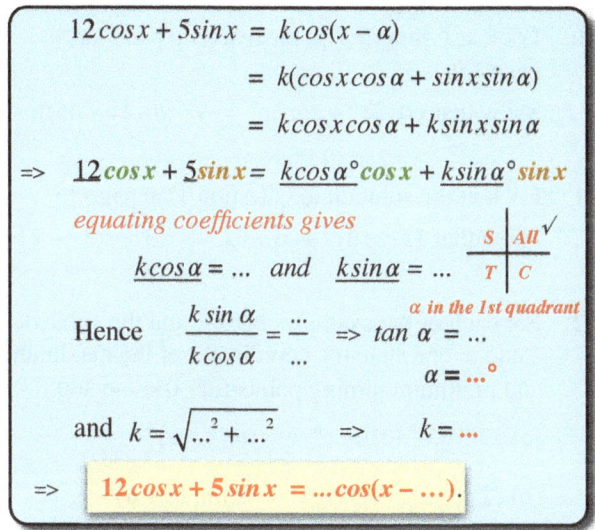

   $$12\cos x + 5\sin x = k\cos(x - \alpha)$$
   $$= k(\cos x\cos\alpha + \sin x\sin\alpha)$$
   $$= k\cos x\cos\alpha + k\sin x\sin\alpha$$
   $$\Rightarrow \quad \underline{12}\cos x + \underline{5}\sin x = \underline{k\cos\alpha°\cos x} + \underline{k\sin\alpha°\sin x}$$

   equating coefficients gives

   $$k\cos\alpha = \ldots \quad and \quad k\sin\alpha = \ldots$$

   $$Hence \quad \frac{k\sin\alpha}{k\cos\alpha} = \frac{\ldots}{\ldots} \Rightarrow \tan\alpha = \ldots$$

   $$\alpha \text{ in the 1st quadrant}$$
   $$\alpha = \ldots°$$

   $$and \quad k = \sqrt{\ldots^2 + \ldots^2} \quad \Rightarrow \quad k = \ldots$$

   $$\Rightarrow \quad \boxed{12\cos x + 5\sin x = \ldots\cos(x - \ldots).}$$

2. Write each expression in the form
   $k\cos(x - \alpha)°$ for $0 \le x \le 360$.

   (a) $8\cos x° + 6\sin x°$ (b) $4\cos x° + \sin x°$

   (c) $3\cos x° + 7\sin x°$ (d) $\sqrt{3}\cos x° + 2\sin x°$

   (e) $\cos x° + \sqrt{5}\sin x°$ (f) $1·2\cos x° + 5·3\sin x°$.

It is quite difficult to find the maximum or minimum turning points of a function like :-

$$f(x) = 12\cos x° + 5\sin x°,$$

but by changing it to $13\cos(x - 22·6)°$, as we did in Question 1, the problem becomes much easier.

Since $-1 \le \cos x \le 1$, the maximum and minimum values of $13\cos(x - 22·6)°$ must be **13** and **-13**.

Example :-

Find the coordinates of the turning points of :-

$$f(x) = 12\cos x° + 5\sin x°, \quad for \ 0 \le x \le 360.$$

Change to a wave function $\Rightarrow f(x) = 13\cos(x° - 22·6)°$.

Maximum occurs when	**Minimum** occurs when
$13\cos(x - 22·6)° = 13$	$13\cos(x - 22·6)° = -13$
$\Rightarrow \cos(x - 22·6)° = 1$	$\Rightarrow \cos(x - 22·6)° = -1$
$\Rightarrow \quad x - 22·6 = 0$	$\Rightarrow \quad x - 22·6 = 180$
$\Rightarrow \quad x = 22·6$	$\Rightarrow \quad x = 202·6$

$\Rightarrow$ Max T.P. **(22·6°, 13)**. $\Rightarrow$ Min T.P. **(202·6°, -13)**.

3. Use your answers to Question 2 to determine the coordinates of the maximum and minimum turning points for each trig function.

Expressing $a\cos x - b\sin x$ in the form $k\cos(x - \alpha)$

If this time we have the **difference**, instead of the **sum** of a sine and cosine function, it is still possible to find a single equivalent cosine (or sine) function to represent it.

Example :-

Write $3\cos x - 4\sin x$ in the form $k\cos(x - \alpha)$.

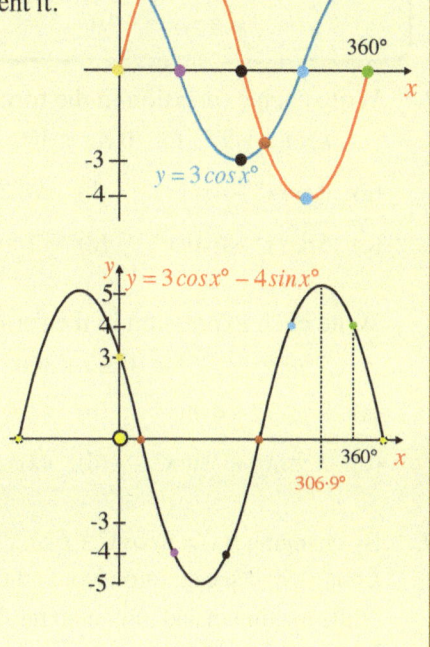

$$3\cos x° - 4\sin x° = k\cos(x - \alpha)°$$
$$= k(\cos x°\cos\alpha° + \sin x°\sin\alpha°)$$
$$= k\cos x°\cos\alpha° + k\sin x°\sin\alpha°$$
$$\Rightarrow \quad \underline{3}\cos x° \underline{-4}\sin x° = \underline{k\cos\alpha°\cos x°} + \underline{k\sin\alpha°\sin x°}$$

by equating coefficients, we get

$$\underline{k\cos\alpha°} = +3 \quad and \quad \underline{k\sin\alpha°} = -4$$

Note :- if $k > 0$, then $\cos\alpha$ is **+ve** and $\sin\alpha$ is **-ve**.

$\Rightarrow \alpha$ must be in the **4th quadrant**.

$$Hence, \quad \frac{k\sin\alpha°}{k\cos\alpha°} = \frac{-4}{3} \Rightarrow \tan\alpha° = -4/3 \quad (126·9° \text{ or } 306·9°)$$

$$\alpha = 306·9° \ (\text{not } 53·1°)$$

$$and \quad k = \sqrt{(-4)^2 + 3^2} \quad \Rightarrow \quad k = 5$$

$$\Rightarrow \quad 3\cos x° - 4\sin x° = \boxed{5\cos(x - 306·9)°.}$$

4. Write each of the following in the form
$k\cos(x - \alpha)°$ for $0 \le x \le 360$.

(a) $8\cos x° - 6\sin x°$ (b) $4\cos x° - \sin x°$

(c) $2\cos x° - 8\sin x°$ (d) $\sqrt{2}\cos x° - \sin x°$

(e) $\sqrt{2}\cos x° - \sqrt{5}\sin x°$ (f) $2·3\cos x° - 3·6\sin x°$.

5. By changing $f(x) = 8\cos x° + 6\sin x°$ to the form $k\cos(x + \alpha)°$, find the coordinates of the maximum and minimum turning points of $f(x)$, between $0°$ and $360°$.

> We can also express a combination of sine and cosine functions as a single sine function as follows :-
>
> $$a\cos x° + b\sin x° = k\sin(x \pm \alpha)°.$$

6. **Copy** and **complete** :-

Re-write $4\cos x° - 4\sin x°$ in the form $k\sin(x + \alpha)°$.

$4\cos x° - 4\sin x° = k\sin(x + \alpha)°$

$\qquad = k(\sin x° \cos\alpha° + \cos x° \sin\alpha°)$

$\qquad = k\sin x° \cos\alpha° + k\cos x° \sin\alpha°$

$\underline{4}\cos x° - \underline{4}\sin x° = \underline{k\cos\alpha°}\sin x° + \underline{k\sin\alpha°}\cos x°$

equating coefficients gives

$k\cos\alpha° = \text{-}4$ and $k\sin\alpha° = ...$

√ S	All
T	C

this time $\cos\alpha$ is -ve and $\sin\alpha$ is +ve,

α *in the 2nd quadrant*

$\Rightarrow \dfrac{k\sin\alpha}{k\cos\alpha} = \dfrac{...}{...} \qquad \Rightarrow \alpha = ...$

$\Rightarrow k = \sqrt{...^2 + ...^2} \qquad \Rightarrow k = ...$

$\Rightarrow 4\cos x° - 4\sin x° = \boxed{...\sin(x + ...)°}$

7. Write each expression in the form
$k\sin(x + \alpha)°$ for $0 \le x \le 360$.

(a) $3\cos x° - 4\sin x°$ (b) $\cos x° - 3\sin x°$

(c) $5\cos x° - 6\sin x°$ (d) $\sqrt{2}\cos x° - 4\sin x°$.

8. Write each expression in the form
$k\sin(x - \alpha)°$ for $0 \le x \le 360$.

(a) $8\cos x° + 6\sin x°$ (b) $4\cos x° + \sin x°$

(c) $3\cos x° + 7\sin x°$ (d) $\sqrt{2}\cos x° - 3\sin x°$.

9. By changing $f(x) = 8\cos x° + 6\sin x°$ to the form $k\sin(x - \alpha)°$ (see question 8a), find the coordinates of the maximum and minimum turning points of $f(x)$, between $0°$ and $360°$.

> The wave function can be used in problems involving **multiple angles**.
>
> The process is exactly the same.

10. Look at **Example 1** in the teaching panel on page 156.

Show that $\cos 2x° + \sin 2x° = \sqrt{2}\cos(2x - 45)°$.

11. Look at the solution to Question 1 on page 157.

Show that $12\cos 3x° + 5\sin 3x° = 13\cos(3x - 22·6)°$.

12. For each of the examples below, find the value of k and α and state the coordinates of the maximum and minimum turning points for $0 < x < 360$.

(a) $3\cos x° + 4\sin x° = k\sin(x - \alpha)°$

(b) $2\cos 2x° + 7\sin 2x° = k\sin(2x + \alpha)°$

(c) $\cos x° - \sqrt{2}\sin x° = k\sin(x - \alpha)°$

(d) $1·2\cos x° + 5·6\sin x° = k\cos(x + \alpha)°$.

.

13. An oscilloscope registers two sound waves
$d = 25\sin t°$ and $d = 75\cos t°$,

where d is the decibel level and t is the time in seconds.

(a) Find the combined resultant wave in the form
$d = 25\sin t° + 75\cos t° = k\sin(t - \alpha)°$.

(b) Find the maximum decibel level of the resultant wave and the first time, after $t = 0$, that this maximum occurs.

14. Two waves W_1 and W_2 are created in a water tank by dropping two bricks in the water simultaneously, and this causes a combined wave effect.

It is known that after the bricks are dropped in the water, the waves are defined by :-

$W_1 = 30\cos t°$ and $W_2 = 45\sin t°$.

(W is the wave height created in centimetres and t is the time in seconds).

(a) Find the combined resultant wave caused by $W_1 + W_2$, in the form $k\sin(t + \alpha)°$.

(b) Will the combined wave manage to flow over a 55 centimetre high wall ?

Solving Equations Involving the Wave Function

Equations in the form $a\cos x + b\sin x = c$ are much easier to solve if we rewrite them as wave functions.

Example :-

Solve $4\cos x° + 3\sin x° = \sqrt{2}$ for $0 \le x \le 360$. *In this format, solving the equation is difficult*

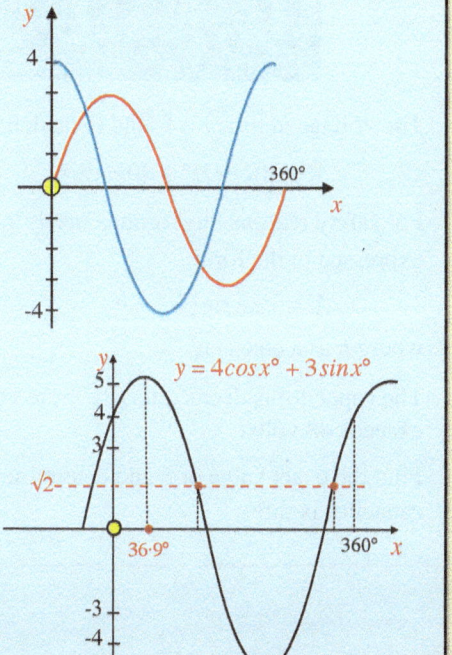

$$4\cos x° + 3\sin x° = k\cos(x - \alpha)°$$
$$= k(\cos x° \cos \alpha° + \sin x° \sin \alpha°)$$
$$= k\cos x° \cos \alpha° + k\sin x° \sin \alpha°$$

$\Rightarrow \underline{4}\cos x° + \underline{3}\sin x° = \underline{k\cos \alpha°}\cos x° c + \underline{k\sin \alpha°}\sin x°$

$\Rightarrow$ *equating coefficients gives* $k\cos \alpha° = 4$ and $k\sin \alpha° = 3$

$\Rightarrow \quad \dfrac{k\sin \alpha}{k\cos \alpha} = \dfrac{3}{4} \Rightarrow \tan \alpha = {}^3/_4 \Rightarrow \alpha = \mathbf{36 \cdot 9}$

Also $\quad k = \sqrt{4^2 + 3^2} \Rightarrow \mathbf{k = 5}$

$\Rightarrow \quad 4\cos x + 3\sin x = \mathbf{5\cos(x - 36 \cdot 9°)}.$

Therefore, $5\cos(x - 36 \cdot 9)° = \sqrt{2}$

$\Rightarrow \cos(x - 36 \cdot 9)° = {}^{\sqrt{2}}/_5 = 0 \cdot 283$

$\Rightarrow (x - 36 \cdot 9)° = 73 \cdot 6°$ or $286 \cdot 4°$

$\Rightarrow \quad x° = \boxed{\mathbf{110 \cdot 5°, \ 323 \cdot 3°}}.$

Exercise 16·2

1. Solve $12\cos x° + 5\sin x° = 13, \ 0 \le x \le 360$

   Copy and complete :-

   $$12\cos x° + 5\sin x° = k\cos(x - \alpha)°$$
   $$= k(\cos x° \cos \alpha° + \sin x° \sin \alpha)°$$
   $$= k\cos x° \cos \alpha° + k\sin xv \sin \alpha°$$

   $\Rightarrow 12\cos x° + 5\sin x° = k\cos x° \cos \alpha° + k\sin x° \sin \alpha°$

   equating both sides gives

   $k\cos \alpha° = \ldots$ and $k\sin \alpha° = \ldots$

   therefore $\dfrac{k\sin \alpha}{k\cos \alpha} = \dfrac{\ldots}{\ldots} \Rightarrow \tan \alpha = \ldots$

   $\alpha = \ldots$

   also $k = \sqrt{\ldots^2 + \ldots^2} \Rightarrow k = \ldots$

   $\therefore 12\cos x° + 5\sin x° = \boxed{\ldots\cos(x - \ldots)°}$

   Therefore $\ldots\cos(x - \ldots) = 13$

   .... and solve ....

2. Solve :-

   (a) $2\cos x° + 5\sin x° = 1$ $\qquad 0 \le x \le 360$

   (b) $\cos x° + \sqrt{3}\sin x° = 2$ $\qquad 0 \le x \le 360$

   (c) $6\cos x + 8\sin x = 5$ $\qquad 0 \le x \le 2\pi.$

   > If not specifically told to do so, you can choose any of the wave functions to work with.
   >
   > i.e. $k\cos(x \pm \alpha)$ or $k\sin(x \pm \alpha)$.
   >
   > The suggestion is that you pick a wave that makes the calculation easier. (*i.e. avoid double negatives etc.*)

3. Solve :-

   (a) $8\cos x° - 4\sin x° = 1$ $\qquad 0 \le x \le 360$

   (b) $6\cos x° - \sin x° = 2$ $\qquad 0 \le x \le 360$

   (c) $2\cos x + 2\sin x = {}^1/_2$ $\qquad 0 \le x \le \cancel{2\pi} \, 360$

   (d) $\cos 4x - \sin 4x = \sqrt{2}$ $\qquad 0 \le x \le {}^\pi/_2.$

4. A metal coil in a complex flux capacitor is rotated in a magnetic field and generates an alternating current.

The voltage at time t is found to be defined by

$$V = 30\cos 2t° + 40\sin 2t°.$$

For safety reasons this formula needs to be expressed in the form

$$V = V_{max}\sin(2t° + b),$$

where b as a constant.

The capacitor is deemed unsafe if the voltage exceeds 48 volts.

Find the exact value of b and determine if this capacitor is safe.

5. Two sound waves are recorded on an oscilloscope.

The two waves are defined as

$$y = 20\cos x° - 2 \text{ and}$$

$$y = 25\sin x° + 2 \text{ for } 0 < x < 180.$$

Sketch the resultant wave created by these waves and state the maximum decibel level.

6. A right angled triangle has an angle $x°$ and a hypotenuse of length h cm.

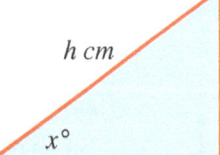

(a) Given that the perimeter of this triangle is 100 cm, show that

$$h = \frac{100}{\sin x + \cos x + 1}.$$

(b) Express $\sin x + \cos x$ in the form $k\sin(x + a)$ and find the minimum value of h.

Exam Practice Exercise (H16)

1. A function is defined by
$$f(x) = 3\cos x° + 4\sin x°.$$

   (a) Express this function in the form
   $$f(x) = k\cos(x - a)°$$
   where $k > 0$ and $0 < a < 360$ **(4)**

   (b) Hence, state the minimum value of
   $$3\cos x + 4\sin x.$$ **(1)**

2. (a) Express $f(x) = 9\cos x° + 40\sin x°$
   in the form $k\cos(x - a)°$. **(4)**

   (b) Hence sketch the graph of
   $f(x)$, over 1 complete cycle **(2)**

   (c) Sketch $f'(x)$ the derivative of $f(x)$. **(2)**

3. (a) Express $y = \cos x° - \sqrt{3}\sin x°$
   in the form $y = k\sin(x - a)°$. **(4)**

   (b) Find the coordinates of the points
   of contact where the line $y = -1$
   intersects the curve
   $$y = \cos x° - \sqrt{3}\sin x°.$$ **(3)**

4. (a) Express $y = 4\sin 2x° + 3\cos 2x°$
   in the form $y = k\cos(2x - t)°$. **(4)**

   (b) Hence solve
   $$4\sin 2x° + 3\cos 2x° = 5.$$ **(3)**

5. Solve $\sin t + \cos t = -1$ for $0 < t < 2\pi$. **(4)**

Revision of Surds and Indices (Reminder)

In **Chapter 4, on page 28**, you revised the work of surds and indices.

If you feel confident with working with both surds and indices, you may decide to skip **Exercise H17·1**.

If you would like some extra practice, here is a summary of what you should know, followed by a short exercise.

Rule 1
$$a^m \times a^n = a^{m+n}$$

Rule 2
$$\frac{a^m}{a^n} = a^{m-n}$$

Rule 3
$$(a^m)^n = a^{mn}$$

Rule 4
$$a^0 = 1$$

Rule 5
$$a^{-m} = \frac{1}{a^m}$$

Rule 6
$$a^{\frac{m}{n}} = \sqrt[n]{(a^m)}$$

Example 1 :- $\quad 3^{-2} = \frac{1}{3^2} = \frac{1}{9}$ and $8^{\frac{2}{3}} = \sqrt[3]{8^2} = 4$

Example 2 :- $\quad x + \frac{1}{x^7} - \sqrt[4]{x^3}$ expressed in the form $ax^n \dots = x + x^{-7} - x^{\frac{3}{4}}$

and $\dfrac{x-2}{x} = \dfrac{x}{x} - \dfrac{2}{x} = 1 - 2x^{-1}$

Example 3 :- $\quad \dfrac{1}{\sqrt{3}}$ with a rationalised denominator $= \dfrac{1}{\sqrt{3}} \times \dfrac{\sqrt{3}}{\sqrt{3}} = \dfrac{\sqrt{3}}{3}$

Example 4 :- $\quad (2x^{\frac{1}{2}} + x^{-\frac{1}{2}})(2x^{\frac{1}{2}} - x^{-\frac{1}{2}}) = 4x + 2 - 2 - x^{-1} = 4x - \dfrac{1}{x}$

Exercise H17·1

1. Simplify :-

   (a) $a^2 \times a^3$
   (b) $a^6 \div a^2$
   (c) $(a^3)^4$

   (d) $2p^2 \times 5p^4$
   (e) $(2x^2)^3$
   (f) $20n^{20} \div 10n^{10}$

   (g) $5t^3 \times 3t^{-2}$
   (h) $m^5 \div m^{-5}$
   (i) $3ab^2 \times 4a^2b^3$

   (j) $(10d^4 e^{-2})^3$
   (k) $8v^4 \div 2v^{-4}$
   (l) $6jh^2 \div 4j^{-1}h^{-2}$.

2. Evaluate without a calculator :-

   (a) 3^3
   (b) 2^{-3}
   (c) 5^{-1}

   (d) 27^0
   (e) $36^{\frac{1}{2}}$
   (f) $125^{\frac{1}{3}}$

   (g) $8^{\frac{2}{3}}$
   (h) $4^{\frac{3}{2}}$
   (i) $16^{-\frac{1}{2}}$

   (j) $27^{-\frac{2}{3}}$
   (k) $\dfrac{1}{16^{-\frac{3}{4}}}$
   (l) $(\sqrt{7})^2$

   (m) $\frac{1}{2} \times 16^{\frac{3}{2}}$
   (n) $\dfrac{4^{\frac{3}{2}}}{8^{-\frac{2}{3}}}$
   (o) $\dfrac{3 \times 1000^{\frac{5}{3}}}{4 \times 25^{\frac{3}{2}}}$.

3. Simplify :-

   (a) $2x^3(3x^2 + 5x^{-1})$
   (b) $x^{\frac{1}{2}}(x^{\frac{1}{2}} + x^{-\frac{1}{2}})$

   (c) $4x^2(5x - \dfrac{1}{x})$
   (d) $(x^{\frac{1}{2}} + x^{-\frac{1}{2}})^2$

   (e) $(x^{\frac{1}{2}} + x^{-\frac{1}{2}})(x^{\frac{1}{2}} - x^{-\frac{1}{2}})$
   (f) $x^{\frac{2}{3}}(3x^{\frac{1}{3}} - x^{-\frac{2}{3}})$

4. Rewrite as surds :-

   (a) $x^{\frac{2}{3}}$
   (b) $a^{\frac{3}{4}}$
   (c) $p^{\frac{5}{4}}$

   (d) $m^{-\frac{1}{4}}$
   (e) $\dfrac{1}{z^{-\frac{2}{5}}}$
   (f) $\dfrac{3}{b^{-\frac{2}{3}}}$.

5. Re-write as a power of x :-

   (a) $\sqrt[3]{x^4}$
   (b) $\sqrt[5]{x^2}$
   (c) $\sqrt[10]{x}$

   (d) $\dfrac{1}{\sqrt{x}}$
   (e) $\dfrac{2}{\sqrt[5]{x^2}}$
   (f) $-\dfrac{3}{\sqrt[4]{x^{\frac{1}{2}}}}$.

The Logarithm Function

In **Chapter 5, on page 45**, we looked at how to create the graph of the inverse of a function $f(x)$, where it existed.
To find the inverse, $f^{-1}(x)$, you reflected the graph of $y = f(x)$ over the line $y = x$, (*the Identity Function*).

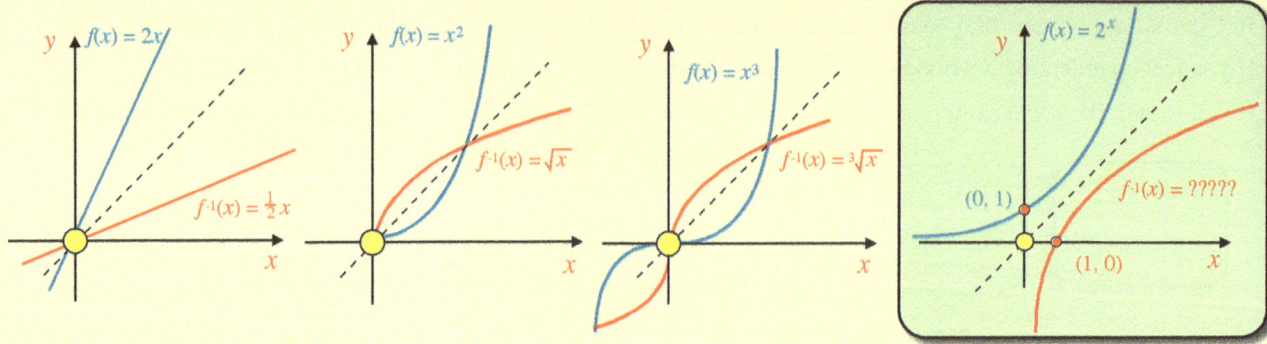

In this chapter, we are going to study the 4th function $f(x) = 2^x$, and its corresponding inverse function $f^{-1}(x)$.
Functions like $f(x) = 2^x$, $f(x) = 10^x$, $f(x) = (\frac{1}{2})^x$, or in general, $f(x) = a^x$, are called **exponential** or **power functions**.

We call the **inverse** of an exponential function a **logarithmic function**, and represent it as follows :-

$f(x) = log_2 x$, or in general $\boxed{f(x) = log_a x,}$ where the a is the base corresponding to the power of the related
exponential function.

Properties of the Log Function

1. Since every exponential function $f(x) = a^x$ passes through $(0, 1)$, (*because anything to the power 0 is 1*), then every corresponding logarithmic (log) function must pass through the point **$(1, 0)$**.

2. For each exponential function $f(x) = a^x$, a is called the "base" and x the "exponent". For the corresponding inverse function $f(x) = log_a x$, the a is called the base and it reads as "*log to the base a, of x*"

3. Since every "basic" exponential function tends towards 0, as $x \rightarrow -\infty$, then every basic log function will tend towards $-\infty$ as $x \rightarrow 0$.

4. Since every exponential function $f(x) = a^x$ increases quickly as $x \rightarrow \infty$, every corresponding log function will increase more **slowly** as $x \rightarrow \infty$.

5. When the base of the exponential function increases, i.e. 2^x to 3^x to 4^x etc, the function grows more quickly. Hence as the base of the log increases, $log_2 x$, $log_3 x$, $log_4 x$, etc, the log function increases **more slowly**.

Exercise H17·2

1. (a) Draw up a table of values for $y = 2^x$.

x	-3	-2	-1	0	1	2	3
2^x	$^1/_8$	...	....	1	2	4	...

(b) Draw a set of axes, plot these points and show the graph of $y = 2^x$.

(c) Draw up a second table, "reversing" the first :-

x	$^1/_8$	...	....	1	2	4	...
$log_2 x$	-3	-2	-1	0	1	2	3

1. (d) On the same set of axes, plot these points and show the graph of $y = log_2 x$.

2. Repeat Question 1 (a) to (d), but this time for $y = 3^x$.

x	-3	-2	-1	0	1	2	3
3^x	....	$^1/_9$	....	1	3	....	....

3. Repeat for $y = 10^x$ and $y = (^1/_2)^x$.

(i)

x	-3	-2	-1	0	1	2	3
10^x	....	$^1/_{100}$	....	1	....	....	1000

(ii)

x	-3	-2	-1	0	1	2	3
$(^1/_2)^x$	....	4	....	1	$^1/_2$	....	....

Evaluating the Logarithmic Function

It is fairly easy to handle exponential calculations like 2^4, 10^{-2}, $(-4)^3$, $(\frac{1}{3})^5$, etc, but what does $log_2 16$ actually mean ?

Let us look at the function $f(x) = 2^x$, with domain $\{-2, -1, 0, 1, 2\}$.

As we can see, the log function "**undoes**" the exponential function.

The easiest way to find $log_2 16$ is to ask the question :-

What power of 2 is needed to create the number 16 ? - answer is **4**.

In general, remember the connection between logs and exponentials.

Hence, if $log_a x = y$ <=> $a^y = x$.

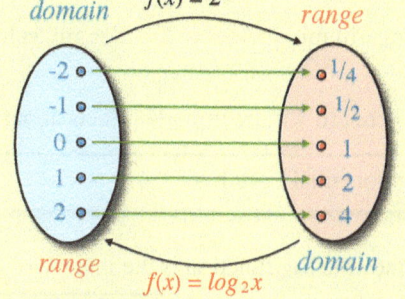

Example 1 :-

Find $log_2 8$

What power of 2 gives 8 ? (**3**)

=> $log_2 8 = $ **3** .

Example 2 :-

Find $log_3 81$

What power of 3 gives 81 ? (**4**)

=> $log_3 81 = $ **4** .

Example 3 :-

Find $log_{10} 1\,000\,000$

What power of 10 gives $1\,000\,000$? (**6**)

=> $log_{10} 1\,000\,000 = $ **6** .

Example 4 :-

Find $log_9 3$

What power of 9 gives 3 ? ($^1/_2$)
(i.e. $9^{\frac{1}{2}} = \sqrt{9} = 3$)

=> $log_9 3 = \frac{1}{2}$.

Example 5 :-

Find $log_4(\frac{1}{64})$

What power of 4 gives $^1/_{64}$? (**-3**)
(i.e. $4^{-3} = 1/4^3 = 1/64$)

=> $log_4(\frac{1}{64}) = $ **-3** .

Example 6 :-

Find $log_8 4$

What power of 8 gives 4 ? ($^2/_3$)
(i.e. $8^{\frac{2}{3}} = \sqrt[3]{8^2} = 4$)

=> $log_8 4 = \frac{2}{3}$.

Exercise H17·3

1. **Copy** and **complete** :-

   (a) $log_2 16 = $ .... since $2^{...} = 16$

   (b) $log_{10} 1000 = $ .... since $10^{...} = 1000$

   (c) $log_3 27 = $ .... since $3^{...} = 27$

   (d) $log_2 128 = $ .... since $2^{...} = 128$.

2. Find the the value of :-

   (a) $log_2 4$ (b) $log_3 9$ (c) $log_7 1$

   (d) $log_9 9$ (e) $log_4 64$ (f) $log_{10} 100\,000$

   (g) $log_5 125$ (h) $log_3 729$ (i) $log_6 216$.

3. **Copy** and **complete** :-

   (a) $log_4 2 = $ .... since $4^{...} = 2$

   (b) $log_8 2 = $ .... since $8^{...} = 2$

   (c) $log_{27} 9 = $ .... since $27^{...} = 9$

   (d) $log_{10} \sqrt{10} = $ .... since $10^{...} = \sqrt{10}$.

4. Find the value of :-

   (a) $log_{25} 5$ (b) $log_{100} 10$ (c) $log_8 4$

   (d) $log_9 9$ (e) $log_{16} 8$ (f) $log_9 27$.

5. **Copy** and **complete** :-

   (a) $log_2(^1/_8) = $ .... since $2^{...} = {}^1/_8$

   (b) $log_{10}(^1/_{100}) = $ .... since $10^{...} = {}^1/_{100}$

   (c) $log_5(^1/_{125}) = $ .... since $5^{...} = {}^1/_{125}$.

6. Find the the value of :-

   (a) $log_4(^1/_{16})$ (b) $log_3(^1/_{81})$ (c) $log_{10}(^1/_{10000})$

   (d) $log_5(^1/_{625})$ (e) $log_4(^1/_2)$ (f) $log_8(^1/_4)$.

7. (a) Calculate :- $log_2 4 - log_4 2$.

   (b) Calculate :- $2 \times log_5(^1/_{25}) - 1$.

8. Solve for x :-

   (a) $log_3 x = 3$ (b) $3log_2 x = 12$

   (c) $log_4(8x) = 3$ (d) $2log_5 x - 4 = 2$

   (e) $6 - log_{10} x = 1$ (f) $\sqrt{log_2 x} = 2$.

Properties of the Log Function

We have already met two important facts (**rules**) relating to the log function.

Logarithmic **Property 1 :-** for any value a, $\boxed{log_a a = 1,}$ since for exponentials, a to the power $1 = a$. $(a^1 = a)$

Logarithmic **Property 2 :-** for any value a, $\boxed{log_a 1 = 0,}$ since for exponentials, a to the power $0 = 1$. $(a^0 = 1)$

There are 3 more important facts about logs and to study them, we consider exponential facts first.

Exponential Fact 1 :- $a^x \times a^y = a^{(x+y)}$ **Exponential Fact 2 :-** $a^x \div a^y = a^{(x-y)}$ **Exponential Fact 3 :-** $(a^x)^y = a^{xy}$

Since the log function is the inverse of the exponential function, we can find 3 similar facts about logs :-

Log **Property 3 :-** $\boxed{log_a x + log_a y = log_a(xy)}$

Log **Property 4 :-** $\boxed{log_a x - log_a y = log_a(\frac{x}{y})}$

Log **Property 5 :-** $\boxed{log_a(x)^p = p \, log_a x}$

Proof of log Property 3 - $log_a x + log_a y = log_a(xy)$

Let $m = a^x$ and let $n = a^y$

$\Rightarrow m \times n = a^x \times a^y = a^{x+y}$

From $m = a^x$ we can write the log equivalent $x = log_a m$

From $n = a^y$ we can write the log equivalent $y = log_a n$

From $mn = a^{x+y}$ we can write the log equivalent $x + y = log_a(mn)$

$\Rightarrow x + y = log_a(mn)$ or $log_a m + log_a n = log_a(mn)$.

Example 1 :-

Find $log_{12} 2 + log_{12} 6$

$= log_{12}(2 \times 6) = log_{12}(12)$ *(prop 3)*

$= \boxed{1}$ *(prop 1)*

Example 2 :-

Find $log_6 48 - log_6 16 + log_6 12$

$= log_6((\frac{48}{16}) \times 12) = log_6(36)$ *(prop 3 and 4)*

$= \boxed{2}$ *(since $6^2 = 36$)*

Example 3 :-

Solve $log_6(x + 1) + log_6(x + 2) = 1$

$\Rightarrow log_6(x + 1)(x + 2) = 1$ *(prop 3)*

$\Rightarrow (x + 1)(x + 2) = 6^1$ *(change from logs to exponentials)*

$\Rightarrow x^2 + 3x - 4 = 0 \Rightarrow (x + 4)(x - 1) = 0 \Rightarrow x = 1$ or -4

but $x = -4 \Rightarrow log_6(-3)$ and $log_6(-2)$ *(which do not exist)*

$\Rightarrow x = \boxed{1}$

Example 4 :-

Find $2 log_5 8 - 3 log_5 4$

$= log_5 8^2 - log_5 4^3 = log_5 64 - log_5 64$ *(prop 5)*

$= log_5(\frac{64}{64})$ *(fact 4)* $= log_5(1) = \boxed{0}$ *(prop 2)*

Exercise H17·4

1. Simplify :-
   (a) $log_{12} 4 + log_{12} 3$ (b) $log_2 32 - log_2 8$
   (c) $log_6 12 - log_6(1/3)$ (d) $log_4 6 + log_4 8 - log_4 3$
   (e) $log_{10} 25 - log_{10}(1/4)$
   (f) $log 4 + log 6 + log(1/3) + log(1/8)$.

2. Show that :-
   (a) $log 2 + log(1/2) = 0$ (b) $log(1/3) = -log 3$.

3. Find :-
   (a) $log_6 60 + log_6(0·6)$ (b) $2 log_6 3 + 2 log_6 2$
   (c) $\frac{1}{2} log_4 16 - \frac{1}{3} log_4 8$ (d) $3 log x - log x^3$.

4. Show that :-
   (a) $log 4 + log(1/4) = 0$ (b) $log(1/5) = -log 5$.

5. Solve for x where x is positive :-
   (a) $log x + log 4 = log 12$
   (b) $log_9 15 - log_9 x = log_9 5$
   (c) $log x + log(x + 1) = log 30$
   (d) $log x^2 + log 3 = log 75$
   (e) $log_8(x + 1) + log_8(x - 1) = log_8 24$
   (f) $log_4(3x - 1) - log_4(x - 1) = 1$.

6. (a) Show that $log 32 = 5 \, log 2$.
   (b) Hence, simplify :-
   (i) $log 32 - log 8$ (ii) $\frac{log 32}{log 8}$.

7. (a) Prove Log **Property 4** in same way as shown above.
   (b) Prove Log **Property 5**.

Transformation of the Logarithmic Graph

In **Chapter 5,** we saw how to transform a graph.

To find the inverse, $f^{-1}(x)$, you reflected the graph of $y = f(x)$ over the line $y = x$, (*the Identity Function*).

- $f(x) + a$ translates the graph of $f(x)$ vertically up (or down if a is negative).
- $f(x + b)$ translates the graph of $f(x)$ horizontally left (or right if b is negative).
- $-f(x)$ reflects the graph over the x-axis.
- $f(-x)$ reflects the graph over the y-axis.
- $kf(x)$ stretches (or compresses if $k < 1$) the graph vertically from the x-axis.
- $f(kx)$ stretches (or compresses if $k > 1$) the graph horizontally from the y-axis.
- $f^{-1}(x)$, the inverse function, reflects the graph over the line $y = x$.

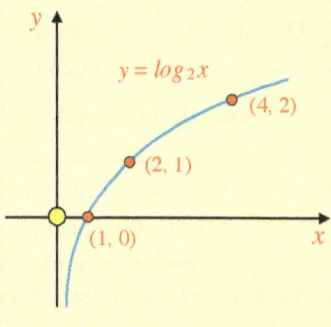

Examples :- Sketch the graphs of :-

  (a) $f(x) = \log_2 x + 2$,   (b) $f(x) = \log_2(x + 3)$,   (c) $f(x) = 2\log_2 x$,   (d) $f(x) = 1 - \log_2 x$.

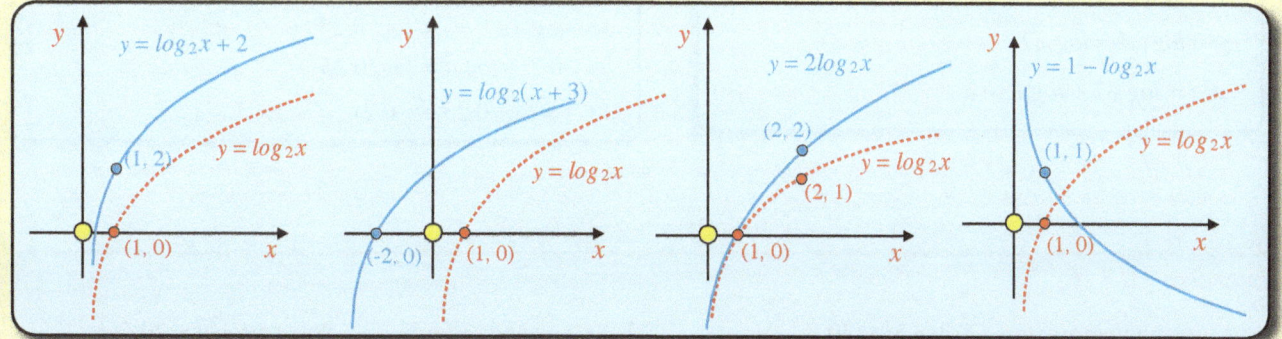

Exercise H17·5

1.   (a)   Sketch the graph of $y = \log_2 x$, showing the three points $(1, 0), (2, 1)$ and $(4, 2)$ on it.

    (b)   On the same diagram, show (dotted) the graph of $y = \log_2 x + 4$, indicating clearly the new image points corresponding to the three points.

2.   Repeat for the graph of $y = \log_2 x - 2$.

3.   (a)   Sketch the graph of $y = \log_3 x$, showing it passing through points $(1, 0), (3, 1)$ and $(9, 2)$.

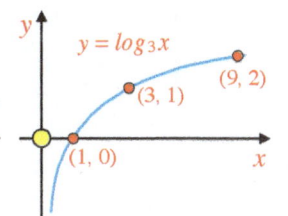

    (b)   On the same diagram, show the graph of $y = \log_3(x + 2)$, indicating clearly the new image points corresponding to the original three points.

4.   Repeat parts (a) and (b) above for $y = \log_3(x - 1)$.

5.   Sketch these graphs, listing clearly 3 points on each.

    (a) $y = \log_3 x + 3$ (b) $y = -\log_3 x$.

6.   Sketch the graphs of $y = \log_2 x$, $y = 2\log_2 x$ and $y = \log_2 2x$ on the same diagram.

     Show the images of points $(1, 0), (2, 1)$ and $(4, 2)$ (on $y = \log_2 x$), on the other two graphs.

7.   These are a combination of transformations. Sketch each graph, showing 3 points on each :-

    (a) $y = \log_2(x - 1) + 2$ (b) $y = 3\log_2(x + 4)$
    (c) $y = 3 - \log_2 x$ (d) $y = \log_2(x + 1) - 2$.

8.   Write the equation of the log function for each graph :-

    (a)   (b)

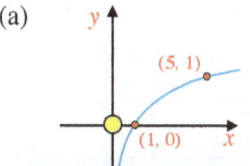 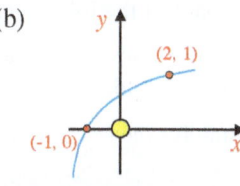

    (c)   (d)

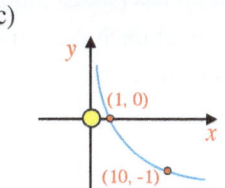 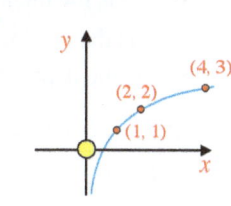

Using your Calculator for Logarithms

If you look at your calculator, you will find two logarithm buttons.

The "**log**" button refers to "base 10" (i.e. $log_{10}x$). Can you see the inverse is 10^x ?

The second one, "**ln**" is called the "**natural log**" or "**log to the base e**" button (i.e. $log_e x$), where e is a very special number in maths, which, like π, is irrational.

* e is called **the** "exponential number" with a value of :- $e = 2.71828.....$ e, like π, is an irrational number.

> (Check that $log_{10}10 = 1$, $log_{10}100 = log_{10}10^2 = 2log_{10}10 = 2$ etc...)
>
> (To find a better value for e, enter 1 in your calculator and press e^x button.)

We may use logs to help solve exponential problems.

Example 1 :- Solve $3^x = 7$.

> The simplest way to solve an exponential equation like this is to **take the log of both sides**.
>
> => $log_{10}3^x = log_{10}7$ (or find $log_e 3^x = log_e 7$).
>
> => $x\, log_{10}3 = log_{10}7$ (*using log Rule 5*)
>
> => $x = log_{10}7 \div log_{10}3$ = **1·7712...**   (*calculator*)

Example 1 :- Solve $200e^{-0.2t} = 50$.

> Divide by 200 then take the log_e (**ln**) of both sides.
>
> (*Can you see why we chose e ?*)
>
> => $e^{-0.2t} = 50 \div 200 = 0.25$
>
> => $log_e(e^{-0.2t}) = log_e 0.25$ (*we could use log_{10} instead*)
>
> => $-0.2t \times log_e e = log_e 0.25$ (*using log Rule 5*)
>
> => $t = log_e 0.25 \div (-0.2)$ = **6·931...**   (*since $log_e e = 1$*)

Though in Higher Maths we are not able to differentiate exponential functions like $f(x) = 2^x$, $f(x) = 10^x$ etc, the importance of the exponential number $e = 2.7182818284...$ is that, except for the basic function $f(x) = 0$, $f(x) = e^x$ is the only other function whose derivative is itself.
i.e Given $f(x) = e^x$, then $f'(x) = e^x$.

Exercise H17·6

1. **Copy** and **complete** :-   Solve $5^x = 30$.

   > Take the log of both sides.
   >
   > => $log_{10}5^x = log_{10}...$
   >
   > => $...log_{10}... = log_{10}...$
   >
   > => $x = log_{10}... \div log_{10}...$ = ...

3. **Copy** and **complete** :-   Solve $5.6e^{3d} = 20$.

   > => $e^{3d} = 20 \div 5.6 = ...$
   >
   > => $log_e(e^{..d}) = log_e ...$
   >
   > => $...d \times log_e e = log_e ...$
   >
   > => $d = log_e ... \div ...$ = ...

   We take log_e here because $log_e e = 1$.

2. Solve for x :-

   (a) $2^x = 17$ (b) $4^x = 100$ (c) $12^x = 7000$

   (d) $(0.5)^x = 0.1$ (e) $10^x = 5$ (f) $3^x = 59$.

4. Solve :-

   (a) $10e^{2x} = 3$ (b) $0.2e^{0.1t} = 1$ (c) $100e^{-0.3d} = 15$

Exponential Functions in Practical Use

Let us consider the following *Example :-*

As sunlight passes through a cloud, it loses some of its intensity, and that is dependant on the thickness (*depth*) of the cloud.

A formula for the intensity is $I(d) = I_0 e^{-0.03d}$, where :-

- $I(d)$ is the intensity after it has passed through the cloud.
- I_0 is the original intensity of the light as it enters the cloud.
- d is the depth of the cloud in metres.

Qu 1 :- If $I_0 = 80$ units what will the intensity be after the sunlight has passed through a cloud 30 metres deep ?

Qu 2 :- What depth of cloud would cause a reduction in intensity of a half ?

Qu 1 :- Simply substitute $d = 30$ in $I(d) = I_0 e^{-0.03d}$.

$\Rightarrow \quad I(30) = 80 \times e^{-0.03 \times 30} = 80 \times e^{-0.9} = $ **32·5 units.** (*calculator*)

Qu 2 :- (*Harder*) This time, set $I(d) = 40$ (*half of 80*) and solve for d.

$\Rightarrow \quad 80 \times e^{-0.03d} = 40$ (*we saw how to solve this type of equation on the previous page*)

$\Rightarrow \quad e^{-0.03d} = 40 \div 80 = 0.5$ (*now we take the* log *of both sides and here we use* log_e)

$\Rightarrow \quad log_e e^{-0.03d} = log_e 0.5$

$\Rightarrow \quad -0.03d \times log_e e = log_e 0.5$ (*using log Fact 5*)

$\Rightarrow \quad d = log_e 0.5 \div (-0.03) = $ **23·1 metres** (*since* $log_e e = 1$)

Exercise H17·7

1. 120 grams of a radioactive isotope of Plutonium give off radiation, and hence mass is being lost.

   The formula for the remaining mass, is given by $M(t) = 120 e^{-0.005t}$, where t is the time in years.

   (a) How much of the isotope will remain after a period of 50 years ?

   (b) After how many years will the mass be reduced by half ? (*the half-life*).

2. A scientist grows a culture of bacteria in her lab.

   The graph shows the number of bacteria, as they grow after 2, 3, 4, ... hours.

   The equation for the number of bacteria is $N(t) = N_0 e^{0.3t}$. (*t* measured in hours).

   (a) What is the value of N_0 ? (i.e. at $t = 0$ hours)

   (b) How many bacteria are there after 3 hours ?

   (c) How long will it take for the number of bacteria to grow to 10 times the original number ?

3. The population of elephants is known to be dropping in a nature reserve. The present population is 160.

   The equation for the population in t years time is predicted to be :-

   $$P(t) = P_0 e^{-0.03t}.$$

   (a) How many of the 160 elephants are expected to be left after 1 year ?

   (b) After how many years will 25% of the elephants have disappeared ?

4. Banks once offered good interest rates to savers, and you could expect your money, if you left it in the bank, to grow in value, exponentially.

   The value of your money could be calculated using $V(t) = V_0 e^{0.05t}$, where V_0 was your initial deposit and t was the number of years it remained in your account.

   Tom's grandmother deposited £500 in his account when he was born, at a fixed annual interest rate, and the value of his money grew slowly, but steadily.

   (a) If Tom withdrew the money on his 18th birthday, how much would he have received ?

   (b) Tom instead decided to wait until his savings had reached at least £2000.

   How old would he be when that occurred ?

5. Population growth/fall can be represented by the equation $W(t) = W_0 e^{kt}$, where W_0 is the population in 2018, t the number of years on from 2018, and k is the annual growth or fall rate.

   Country A, population 254 000 and Country B, population 371 000 (in 2018) are two small countries.

   Country A's population growth is $M(t) = M_0 e^{0.05t}$, and Country B's population decline is $R(t) = R_0 e^{-0.02t}$.

   (a) What will the populations of both countries be in 2020 ?

   (b) In which year will both populations be the same ?

6. The **drop** in atmospheric pressure, P at a height h km, is given by the formula $P(h) = P_0(1 - e^{-kh})$, where P_0 is the atmospheric pressure at sea level, which is 750 units.

   (a) At a height (h) of 1 km, the drop in pressure $P(h)$ is 104 units. Show that $k = 0.15$.

   (b) Calculate the drop in pressure, from the original 750 units at a height of 20 kilometres.

Using Logs to determine the connection between Two Variables

Introduction :- This table shows the cost of hiring a cement mixer for 1, 2, 3, ... days.

Days (d)	1	2	3	4	5	6
Cost (£C)	17	24	31	38	45	52

As you would expect, if we draw a graph showing the costs, it will be a straight line, and it is quite easy to show the line has a gradient of 7 and cuts the C-axis at $(0, 10)$.

This means, a formula connecting C to d is :- $C = 7d + 10$.

Let us now study a slightly more complex set of pairs of values.

Example :- In a scientific experiment, connecting the volume V (cm³) of a gas to its temperature t (°C), the following readings were recorded :-

temp ($t°C$)	10	20	30	40	50	60
Vol (V cm³)	6·3	17·9	33·0	50·6	71·0	93·0

Table 1.

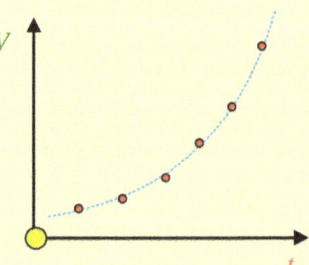

When the scientist drew a graph of this, he discovered it did not give a straight line.
Therefore, the equation joining the two quantities was definitely **NOT** of the form $V = mt + c$.

He **DID** think though the graph resembled some kind of **exponential** or **polynomial type** function, so he decided to draw up a new table containing $\log t$ and $\log V$ (either to base 10 or base e).

$\log_{10} t$	1·00	1·30	1·48	1·60	1·70	1·78
$\log_{10} V$	0·80	1·25	1·52	1·70	1·85	1·97

Table 2.

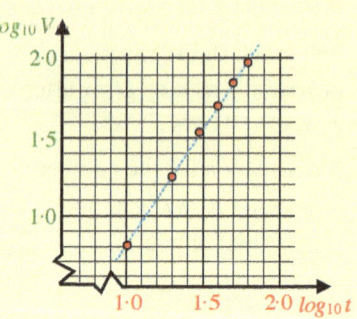

When the scientist drew the new graph of this, it **DID** produce a straight line.

This meant that the equation of the line became $\boxed{\log_{10} V = m \log_{10} t + c.}$

By choosing 2 well spaced points on the graph $(1·0, 0·8)$ and $(1·6, 1·7)$, and setting up two simultaneous equations, we can show that $m = 1·5$ and $c = -0·7$.

This means the equation connecting t and V was :- $\boxed{\log_{10} V = 1·5 \log_{10} t - 0·7.}$

$1·6m + c = 1·7$
$1·0m + c = 0·8$
Subtract
$\Rightarrow \quad 0·6m = 0·9$
$\Rightarrow \quad\quad m = 1·5$
and $\quad\quad c = -0·7$

This formula connecting t and V can be improved as follows :-

The first thing we have to do is express the $(-0·7)$ as $\log_{10}$ (of something), and to do this we use the *inverse* $\log_{10}$ button on the calculator, (better known as the 10^x button).

$\Rightarrow$ enter -0·7 in your calculator and press 10^x $\Rightarrow$ $-0·7 = \log_{10} 0·199526...$ or $\log_{10} 0·2$.

Finally, rewrite the equation as :-

$\quad\quad \log_{10} V = 1·5 \log_{10} t + \log_{10} 0·2$.

$\Rightarrow \quad \log_{10} V = \log_{10} t^{1·5} + \log_{10} 0·2$.   (*using Log Property 5*)

$\Rightarrow \quad \log_{10} V = \log_{10} (0·2 \times t^{1·5})$.   (*using Log Property 3*)

$\Rightarrow \quad\quad \boxed{V = 0·2 \times t^{1·5}.}$

This is the formula connecting t and V. You could check the points in **Table 1** satisfy this equation.

Exercise H17·8

1. Use the technique shown on the previous page to devise a formula connecting x and H of the form $H = kx^n$, from this table of values.

x	1	2	3	4	5
H	2	16	54	128	250

Step 1 :- Begin by drawing up a new table listing the values of $\log_{10} x$ and $\log_{10} H$.

Step 2 :- Draw the graph, choose two points on the graph and use simultaneous equation methods to find m and c.

Step 3 :- Rearrange your equation :-
$\log_{10} H = m \log_{10} x + c$ as shown in the example to obtain the formula $H = kx^n$.

2. In an experiment, the pressure P and the volume v of a gas were recorded as follows :-

v	20	40	60	80	100
P	13·7	19·9	24·5	28·3	31·6

Devise a formula connecting v and P of the form $P = kv^n$, from this table.

3. An engineer took readings of two variables, t and D and recorded them in this table :-

t	1	3	5	7	9
D	20	3·85	1·79	1·08	0·74

Devise a formula connecting t and D of the form $D = kt^n$, from this table.

Determining the connection between Two Variables from their Graphs - Type 1

If the graph, showing the connection between 2 variables looks like this, the chances are the formula is of the form $y = kx^n$.

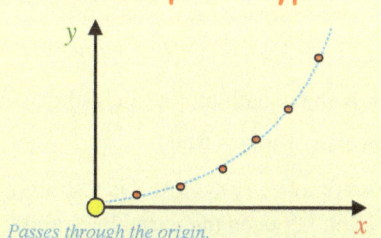

Passes through the origin.

If this is the case, we can express $y = kx^n$ in the form of a line by taking the log (*to any base*) of both sides, as follows :-

$$y = kx^n$$
$$\Rightarrow \quad \log y = \log kx^n$$
$$\Rightarrow \quad \log y = \log k + \log x^n$$
$$\Rightarrow \quad \log y = n \log x + \log k \quad (\textit{of the form } y = mx + c)$$

(which is the equation of a line if the axes are $\log x$ and $\log y$.)

The reverse of this is also true :-

If the graph of $\log y$ against $\log x$ is a straight line, then the connection between the variables x and y is $y = kx^n$.

Example :- Two variables y and x are connected by the formula $y = kx^n$.

When $\log y$ is plotted against $\log x$, we get the graph shown below, passing through the points $(0, 3)$ and $(8, 7)$.

Find the values of k and n.

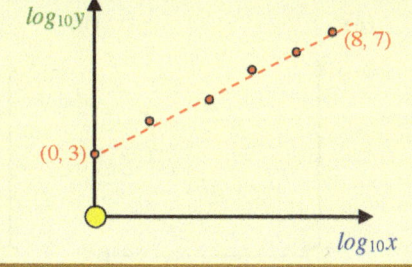

$$\Rightarrow \quad \log_{10} y = m \log_{10} x + c$$
$$\Rightarrow \quad \text{from the diagram, we have } c = 3$$
$$\Rightarrow \quad \text{and } m = \frac{7-3}{8-0} = \frac{1}{2}$$
$$\Rightarrow \quad \log_{10} y = \frac{1}{2} \log_{10} x + 3$$
$$\Rightarrow \quad \log_{10} y = \log_{10} x^{\frac{1}{2}} + \log_{10} 1000$$
$$\Rightarrow \quad \log_{10} y = \log_{10} (1000 x^{\frac{1}{2}}) \qquad \log_{10} 1000 = 3$$
$$\Rightarrow \quad \boxed{y = 1000 \, x^{\frac{1}{2}}}$$

Exercise H17·9

Each diagram in this exercise shows that when the logs of two variables are plotted against each other, a straight line graph is produced.

Determine the value of k and n each time.

1. (a) **Copy** and **complete** to find k and n, given $G = kp^n$.

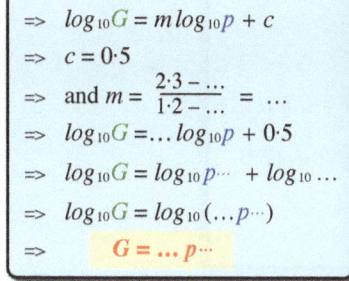

$$\Rightarrow \quad \log_{10} G = m \log_{10} p + c$$
$$\Rightarrow \quad c = 0.5$$
$$\Rightarrow \quad \text{and } m = \frac{2.3 - \ldots}{1.2 - \ldots} = \ldots$$
$$\Rightarrow \quad \log_{10} G = \ldots \log_{10} p + 0.5$$
$$\Rightarrow \quad \log_{10} G = \log_{10} p^{\ldots} + \log_{10} \ldots$$
$$\Rightarrow \quad \log_{10} G = \log_{10} (\ldots p^{\ldots})$$
$$\Rightarrow \quad \boxed{G = \ldots p^{\ldots}}$$

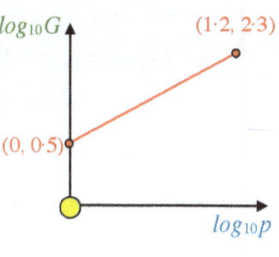

1. Repeat for parts (b) to (e) :-

(b)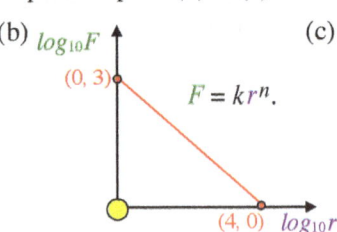

(c)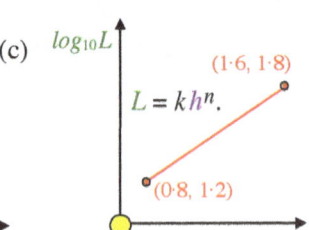

(d)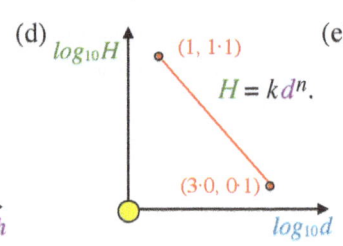

(e)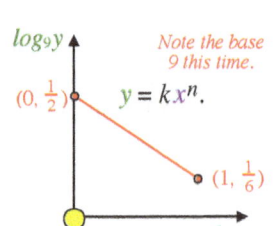

Determining the connection between Two Variables from their Graphs – Type 2

If the graph, showing the connection between 2 variables looks like this, the chances are the formula is of the form $y = ab^x$. (*exponential*)

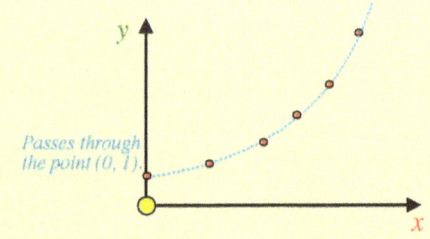

If this is the case, we can express $y = ab^x$ in the form of a line by taking the log (*to any base*) of both sides, as follows :-

$$y = ab^x$$
$$\Rightarrow \quad \log y = \log ab^x$$
$$\Rightarrow \quad \log y = \log a + \log b^x$$
$$\Rightarrow \quad \log y = (\log b)\,x + \log a \quad (\textit{of the form } y = mx + c)$$

(which is the equation of a line if the axes are x and $\log y$.)

The reverse of this is true :-

just x this time - not logx

If the graph of $\log y$ against x is a straight line, then the connection between the variables x and y is $y = ab^x$.

Example :- Two variables y and x are related by the formula :- $y = ab^x$.

When $\log_3 y$ is plotted against x, we get the graph shown below, passing through the points $(0, 2)$ and $(2, 0)$. Find the values of a and b.

$$\Rightarrow \quad \log_3 y = mx + c$$
$$\Rightarrow \quad \text{from the diagram, we have } c = 2$$
$$\Rightarrow \quad \text{and } m = \frac{2-0}{0-2} = -1$$
$$\Rightarrow \quad \log_3 y = -1x + 2$$

$\log_3 \frac{1}{3} = -1$
$\log_3 9 = 2$

$$\Rightarrow \quad \log_3 y = x(\log_3 \tfrac{1}{3}) + \log_3(9)$$
$$\Rightarrow \quad \log_3 y = \log_3(\tfrac{1}{3})^x + \log_3(9)$$
$$\Rightarrow \quad \log_3 y = \log_3(9 \times (\tfrac{1}{3})^x)$$
$$\Rightarrow \quad y = 9 \times (\tfrac{1}{3})^x$$

This time, express the -1 and 2 in terms of log₃.

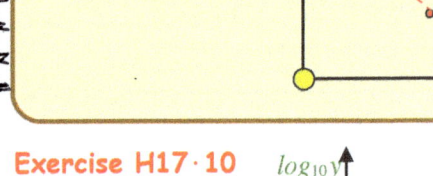

$(0, 2)$

$(2, 0)$ *not log x this time*

Exercise H17·10

1. **Copy** and **complete** to find the values of a and b, given :-
$$y = ab^x.$$

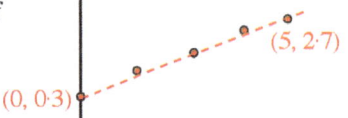

$(5, 2·7)$

$(0, 0·3)$

$$\Rightarrow \quad \log_{10} y = mx + c$$
$$\Rightarrow \quad \text{we can see that } c = 0·3$$
$$\Rightarrow \quad \text{and } m = \frac{2·7 - \ldots}{5 - \ldots} = \ldots$$
$$\Rightarrow \quad \log_{10} y = \ldots x + 0·3$$
$$\Rightarrow \quad \log_{10} y = x(\log_{10}(\ldots)) + \log_{10}(\ldots)$$
$$\Rightarrow \quad \log_{10} y = \log_{10}(\ldots)^x + \log_{10}(2·0)$$
$$\Rightarrow \quad \log_{10} y = \log_{10}(2·0) \times (\ldots)^x$$
$$\Rightarrow \quad y = 2 \times \ldots^x$$

This time, use the 10ˣ button to change the ... and the 0·3 to log₁₀.

2. Find a formula of the form $y = ab^x$.

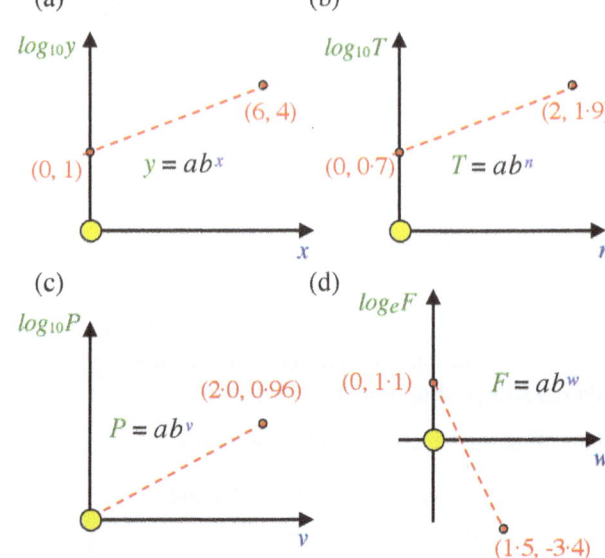

(a)

$(6, 4)$

$(0, 1)$ $y = ab^x$

(b)

$(2, 1·9)$

$(0, 0·7)$ $T = ab^n$

(c)

$(2·0, 0·96)$

$P = ab^v$

(d)

$(0, 1·1)$ $F = ab^w$

$(1·5, -3·4)$

Exam Practice Exercise (H17)

1. Solve the equation
   $$\log_6(7-x) - \log_6(2-x) = 2, \quad x < 2. \qquad \textbf{(4)}$$

2. The function g is of the form $g(x) = \log_b(x-a)$.

   The graph of $y = g(x)$ is shown below.

   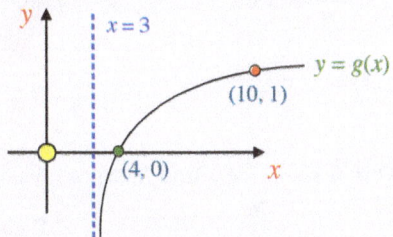

   (a) Write the values of a and b. **(2)**

   (b) State the domain of g. **(1)**

3. The curve with equation $y = \log_3(x-1) - 4$, where $x > 1$, cuts the x-axis at the point $B(b, 0)$.

   Find the value of b. **(3)**

4. As part of a thesis, a student is researching the growth of a breed of bacteria. The number of bacteria present is given by the formula
   $$B(t) = 300\,e^{0.105t},$$
   where t represents the number of hours since commencing her experiment.

   (a) What was the amount of bacteria present at the start of her research ? **(1)**

   (b) Calculate the time taken for the number of bacteria to treble. **(4)**

5. Solve the equation :-
   $$\log_5(3+2x) + \log_5(2-x) = 1, \text{ where } x \text{ is real. } \textbf{(4)}$$

6. Two variables, x and y, are connected by the equation $y = kx^n$.

   The graph of $\log_2 y$ against $\log_2 x$ is a straight line as shown.

   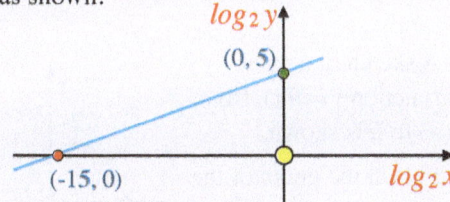

   Find the values of k and n. **(5)**

7. (a) Given that $\log_{16} x = R$, show that
   $$\log_4 x = 2R. \qquad \textbf{(3)}$$

   (b) Solve $\log_4 x + \log_{16} x = 6$. **(3)**

8. Two variables, x and y, are related by the equation $y = ka^x$.

   When $\log_4 y$ is plotted against x, a straight line passing through the points $(0, 2)$ and $(8, 6)$ is obtained, as shown in the diagram.

   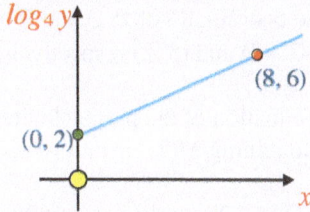

   Find the values of k and a. **(5)**

9. The diagram below shows the graph of the function $h(x) = \log_6 x$, where $x > 0$.

   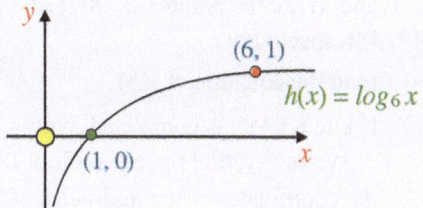

   The inverse function h^{-1}, exists.

   Draw a Cartesian diagram and on it sketch the graph of the inverse function. **(2)**

10. The concentration of the lawn weedkiller *Weedo* can be modelled by the equation
    $$C_t = C_0\,e^{-kt},$$
    where C_0 is the initial concentration; C_t is the concentration at time t, and t is the time in hours, after the application of weedkiller.

    (a) Once on a lawn, the half-life of the weedkiller is the time taken for its concentration to be reduced to one half of its initial strength.

    If the half-life of *Weedo* is 10 hours, find the value of k to 1 sig. fig. **(4)**

    (b) What is the percentage decrease in concentration of *Weedo*, two days after the initial application ? **(3)**

Equations of Lines

1. Find the equation of the straight line which passes through the point (-2, 6) and is :-

    (a) parallel to the line with equation $x = 3$.

    (b) perpendicular to the line with equation $y + 2x = 0$.

    (c) parallel to the line with equation $y - 3x = 4$.

2. Find the equation of the median PS of ΔPQR where the coordinates of P, Q and R are (-2, 3), (-3, -4) and (5, 2) respectively.

3. Find the equation of the perpendicular bisector of the line joining M(2, -1) and N(8, 3).

4. P(-3, 5), Q(-1, -2) and R(5, 1) are the vertices of ΔPQR.

    Find the equation of PS, the altitude from P to QR.

5. K, L and M are the points (-5, -8), (12, -1) and (13, 4) respectively.

    (a) Find the equation of KM.

    (b) If kite KLMN is completed, with KM the axis of symmetry, find the equation of LN and the coordinates of the mid-point of LN.

6. C has coordinates (4, 7), D(-2, 3) and E(1, 9).

    (a) Find the equation of the line through the mid-point of CD, parallel to DE.

    (b) Verify that this line passes through the mid-point of CE.

7. Points G(0, -10), H(10, 3) and I(-4, 10) are vertices of ΔGHI. Find :-

    (a) the equations of the altitude GP and of median HQ of this triangle.

    (b) the coordinates of the point of intersection of GP and HQ.

8. OPQR is a kite.

    Calculate the gradient of line OR, to 2 decimal places.

    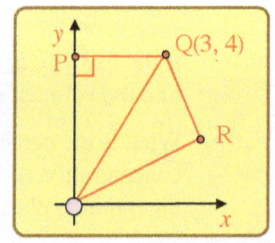

Differentiation

9. Differentiate with respect to x :-

    (a) $f(x) = 5x^2 - 3x - 17$ (b) $y = 6x^2 - \dfrac{3}{x}$

    (c) $y = \dfrac{9}{x^2} + x\sqrt{x}$ (d) $f(x) = 3\sqrt{x}(x-3)$

    (e) $f(x) = \dfrac{6x^2 - 8x - 5}{2x}$.

10. If $f(x) = \sqrt[4]{x} - \dfrac{1}{\sqrt[4]{x}}$, find $f'(x)$.

11. A ball is thrown upwards.

    The height H metres of the ball t seconds after it is thrown, is given by the formula :-

    $$H(s) = 36t - 6t^2$$

    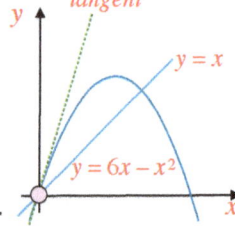

    (a) Find the rate of change of height, with respect to time, of the ball, just as it is thrown.

    (b) Find the speed of the ball after 3 seconds and explain your answer.

12. (a) Find the equation of the tangent to the curve with equation :-

    $$y = 5x^3 - 8x^2,$$

    where $x = 1$.

    (b) Find the x coordinate of each point on the curve

    $$y = 2x^3 - 3x^2 - 12x + 12,$$

    where the tangent is parallel to the x–axis.

13. (a) Find the gradient of the tangent to the parabola $y = 6x - x^2$ at (0, 0).

    (b) Hence calculate the size of the angle between the line $y = x$ and this tangent.

14. A sketch of a cubic function $y = f(x)$, from -3 to 5 is shown.

    Sketch the graph of the derived function $f'(x)$, over the same domain.

15. Find the maximum and minimum values of
$f(x) = 6x^2 - x^3$ in the closed interval $-2 \leq x \leq 2$.

16. Find the stationary values of the function defined
by $f(x) = 2 + 3x - x^3$.

Hence, or otherwise, sketch the graph of $y = f(x)$,
stating where the graph meets the axes.

(Note :- You will need to factorise $2 + 3x - x^3$).

17. (a) Given that $f(x) = \sqrt{x}(x - 3)$, $x > 0$, where only
the positive value of $\sqrt{x}$ is taken, find $f'(x)$.

(b) State the coordinates of the point on the
curve $y = f(x)$ where $x = 4$ and obtain the
the equation of the tangent to the curve at
this point.

(c) Show that $(1, -2)$ is a stationary point on the
curve and sketch the curve in the interval
$0 \leq x \leq 4$ showing where it cuts the x and y axes.

Graphs and Functions

18. On a suitable set of real numbers, functions f and g
are defined by :–
$$f(x) = \frac{1}{(x + 3)}, (x \neq 3) \text{ and } g(x) = \frac{1}{x} - 3, (x \neq 0).$$
Find $f(g(2))$.

19. The functions h and k are defined as :-
$$h(x) = x^2 \text{ and } k(x) = x + 1.$$
Find in its simplest form $h(k(p)) - k(h(p))$.

20. $g(x) = x^2 - 1$; $x \in R$, defines a function $g(x)$.

$$h(x) = \frac{x - 2}{x}, x \in R, x \neq 0, \text{ defines a function } h(x).$$

(a) Explain why g has no inverse function.

(b) Find the inverse function $h^{-1}(x)$, stating
the largest suitable domain.

21. The graph of $y = f(x)$ is shown below for $-1 \leq x \leq 3$.

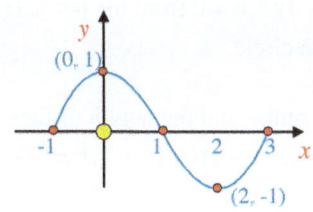

21. On separate diagrams, sketch the graphs of :-

(a) $y = f(x) + 1$ (b) $y = f(x + 1)$

(c) $y = -f(x)$ (d) $y = -f(x - 2)$

(e) $y = 2(f(x))$ (f) $y = 1 - f(x)$.

22. Part of the graph
$y = a^x + b$ is shown.

Find the values of
a and b.

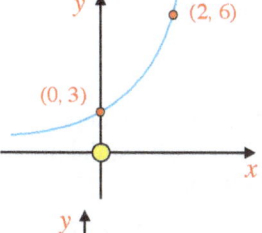

23. The sketch shows
part of a logarithmic
function.

Find the value of c.

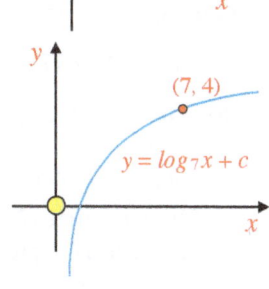

24. Let $p(x) = \sin x°$, $q(x) = x^2$ and $r(x) = 1 - 2x$ be
functions on the set of Real Numbers.

(a) Find a formula, in its simplest form, for the
function $s(x)$, such that $s(x) = r(q(p(x)))$.

Hence, or otherwise, find the image of the
number 30, under the function $s(x)$.

(b) State, for each of p, q and r, whether there
exists an inverse function on R. Where it
does exist, state its formula.

Completing the Square

25. Express each of these in the form $f(x) = a(x + p)^2 + q$.

(a) $f(x) = x^2 + 6x$ (b) $f(x) = x^2 + 10x + 1$

(c) $f(x) = 5 + 4x - 2x^2$ (d) $f(x) = 2x^2 + 6x + 1$

(e) $f(x) = 4 + 6x - 3x^2$ (f) $f(x) = 1 + x - x^2$.

26. In each of the above cases, find the maximum or
minimum turning value of the function, and
the corresponding value of x each time.

27. (a) Express $2 + 4x - x^2$ in the form $a - (x + b)^2$.

(b) Hence find the coordinates of the minimum
turning point on the curve
$$f(x) = \frac{12}{2 + 4x - x^2} \ .$$

Trigonometry

28. Sketch the graph of :-

    (a) $y = 2\sin 3x°$ $0 \leq x \leq 360$

    (b) $y = \cos(x - 30)° + 1$ $0 \leq x \leq 360$.

29. Solve the following for $0 \leq x \leq 2\pi$.

    (a) $\cos^2 x = \frac{1}{2}$ (b) $\sqrt{2}\sin^2 x - \sin x = 0$

    (c) $2\sin x + \sqrt{3} = 0$ (d) $2\sin(2x + {}^\pi/6) = 1$.

30. The minimum depth, d feet, of water in a marina, t hours after midnight, can be estimated by the function :-

    $$d(t) = 21 + 12\cos(15t)°, \text{ where } 0 \leq t \leq 24.$$

    (a) At midnight, a yacht, with a draft of 15 feet, is in the marina.(i.e. it needs a clear 15 ft depth of water to prevent being grounded).

    By what time (24 hour clock) must it leave the marina to prevent being left aground ?

    (b) What is the earliest time after that the yacht can return to the marina ?

Recurrence Relations

31. A sequence is defined by the recurrence relation :-

    $$V_n = 0{\cdot}8\,V_{n-1} + 3, \qquad V_1 = 4.$$

    (a) Calculate the value of V_2.

    (b) What is the smallest value of n for which $V_n > 11$?

    (c) Find the limit of this sequence as $n \longrightarrow$ infinity.

32. On the day of her 16th birthday, Amal is given a sum of money by her uncle to put into the Building Society until she is 21.

    The money she invests gains compound interest of 7% per annum, which is added to her savings on each of her following birthdays.

    The amount she has each year is hence given by :-

    $$A_n = 1{\cdot}07A_{n-1}$$

    By what percentage will Amal's investment have increased when she is allowed to withdraw her money on her 21st birthday ?

33. The first three terms of the linear recurrence relation $V_{n+1} = aV_n + b$ are 14, 12 and 10 respectively.

    Find the values of a and b.

34. Once a week, the greenkeeper at a golf club removes leaves from the pond at the 12th hole.

    They manage to remove 92% of the leaves each week.

    Each week, 20 kg of leaves build up in the pond.

    This is represented by $W_n = 0{\cdot}08W_{n-1} + 20$, where W_n is the weight of leaves present on day n.

    The greenkeeper knows the pond life will suffer if ever the amount of debris reaches 22kg.

    Is the pond life safe in the long run? (Explain clearly).

35. The adult population of Wellington is 20 000, all of whom are avid supporters of one or other of the two local teams, Rovers and United.

    In 2021, it was estimated that half supported Rovers whilst the other half supported United, but they tended to change their loyalty every so often.

    The Rovers' management estimate that they lose about 20% of their support to United each season.

    United estimate that they lose 3 000 supporters to Rovers each year.

    (a) If $R_n =$ represents the total Rovers' support in season n, show that
    $$R_{n+1} = 0{\cdot}8R_n + 3\,000, \quad R_0 = 10\,000.$$

    (b) What would the Rovers' support be in :-

    (i) 2022   (ii) 2023   (iii) 2024 ?

    (c) If this situation were to continue, how many fans would each team have in the long run ?

The Circle

36. Show that the equation of the tangent to the circle $x^2 + y^2 = 10$ from T(1, -3) is $x - 3y - 10 = 0$.

37. The point (4, -6) lies on the circumference of the circle $x^2 + y^2 - 8x - 16y + c = 0$.
    Find the value of c.

38. Find the equation of the tangent to the circle $x^2 + y^2 + 2x - 3y - 6 = 0$ from the point T(2, 1) that lies on the circle.

39. (a) Find the centre and the length of the radius of the circle $(x - 2)^2 + (y + 1)^2 = 100$.

cont'd...

39. (b) A chord AB of this circle is given by $2y = x + 6$.

   Find the coordinates of the points A and B and write down the coordinates of the mid point of the chord AB.

40. Find the coordinates of the centre, and the length of the radius of the circle :-

   $$x^2 + y^2 - 2p\cos\theta x - 2p\sin\theta y + p^2\cos^2\theta = 0,$$

   in terms of p and θ, and show that the circle just touches the x–axis.

41. (a) Show that the y-axis is a tangent to the circle $x^2 + y^2 - 2x - 10y + 25 = 0$.

   (b) Find the equation of the other tangent to the circle through the origin.

   (c) If $y = mx$ cuts this circle in two distinct points, find the range of values of m.

42. Find an expression, in terms of t, for the length of the radius of the circle :-

   $$x^2 + y^2 - 2(t-1)x - 2(t+1)y + 2 = 0.$$

Trigonometric Formulae

43. PQRST is a pyramid on a square base PQRS with each of its eight edges of length 2 units.

   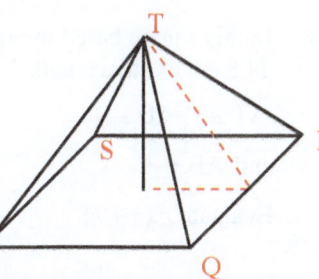

   Find the size of the angle between the planes QRT and PQRS.

44. Calculate the exact value of $sin(x - y)$ if x and y are acute angles, given that $tan x = \frac{3}{4}$ and $tan y = \frac{5}{12}$.

45. Solve the equation $3\cos 2x° - 2 = 13\cos x°$, for $0 \le x < 360$.

46. Solve for x :-

   $$\cos x°\cos 25° - \sin x°\sin 25° = 0\cdot5,$$

   given $0 \le x \le 360$.

47. If $\cos\theta = \frac{4}{5}, 0 \le \theta \le \frac{\pi}{2}$, find the exact value of :-

   (a) $\sin 2\theta$ (b) $\sin 4\theta$.

48. The diagram shows two right angled triangles ABC and BDE.

   AB is perpendicular to BE

   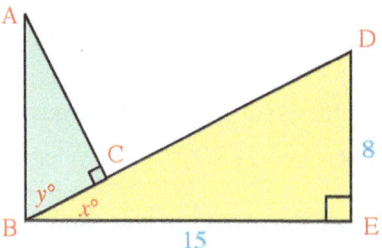

   (a) Find the exact values of $sin x°$ and $cos x°$.

   (b) Express y in terms of x.

   (c) Use this to show that $sin y° = \frac{15}{17}$.

Polynomials

49. A(1, 0) and B(-2, 0) are the two points at which the curve $y = x^4 + 2x^3 - 3x^2 - 4x + 4$ cuts the x–axis.

   By factorising $x^4 + 2x^3 - 3x^2 - 4x + 4$ fully, prove that there are no other points of intersection with this axis.

50. Find the quotient and remainder when polynomial $6x^3 + 7x^2 - x - 2$ is divided by $2x - 1$.

51. Find n if $(x + 3)$ is a factor of $3x^3 + 2x^2 + nx + 6$, and factorise the expression fully when n has this value.

52. A function is defined as $g(x) = x^3(3x + 2)$.

   (a) Find the stationary values of g and determine the nature of each.

   (b) Find where the graph of $g(x)$ cuts the x axis.

   (c) Sketch the graph of $g(x)$.

53. A function is defined by $p(x) = x^3 + k$ where k is a constant.

   When $p(x)$ is divided by $x - 3$, the remainder is 36.

   Find k and hence solve the equation $p(-2x) = -18$.

54. (a) Find the stationary points of the function given by $f(x) = x^2 - \frac{1}{3}x^3$ and determine their nature.

   (b) Find where the graph of $f(x)$ cuts both the x-axis and the y-axis.

   (c) Sketch the graph of $f(x)$.

55. Show that the equation of the tangent to the curve
$y = 5 - 2x^2 - x^3$ at $x = -2$ is $y + 4x + 3 = 0$.

Quadratic Theory

56. Find the values(s) of c for which the quadratic
equation $x^2 - 2x + 21 = 2c(3x - {}^{17}/_2)$ has equal roots.

57. Find the equation of the parabola shown.

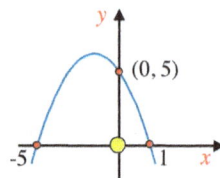

58. Find t, given that $x^2 + (t - 3)x = -1$ has no real roots.

59. x is a real number and $m = \dfrac{x^2 + 4x + 10}{2x + 5}$.

By rearranging, form a quadratic equation in x and
show that m cannot have a value between -3 and 2.

60. Given that $\dfrac{x}{p} + \dfrac{p + 2}{x + 1} = 2$, rearrange to show that

$x^2 + (1 - 2p)x + p^2 = 0$.

Hence determine the set of values for p for which
the equation has real roots.

61. Find the condition for the quadratic equation
$(mx + c)^2 = 4x$ to have equal roots.

62. (a) Show that the line $y = 3x - c$ meets the parabola
$y = 2x^2 + x - 4$ where $2x^2 - 2x + (c - 4) = 0$.

(b) Find the value of c for the line to be a tangent
to the parabola.

(c) Find the point of contact.

Integration

63. Find :-

(a) $\int (\sqrt[4]{x} - 3)dx$
(b) $\int \dfrac{6x^3 - 4x^2 + 2x}{x} \, dx$

(c) $\int_{-1}^{2} (x^2 - \dfrac{1}{x^3}) \, dx$
(d) $\int_{1}^{3} (\dfrac{1 + \sqrt{w}}{\sqrt{w}}) \, dw$.

64. Calculate the coloured areas :-

(a) 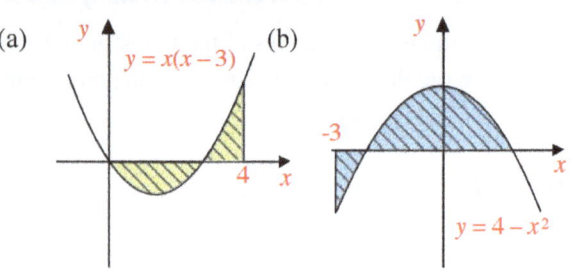 (b)

65. The gradient of a tangent to a curve is given by

$$\dfrac{dy}{dx} = 4 - \dfrac{1}{x^2}.$$

If the curve passes through the point $(1, 6)$, find its
equation.

66. Calculate the area enclosed
between the functions

$g(x) = x$ and $h(x) = x^2 - 3x + 3.$

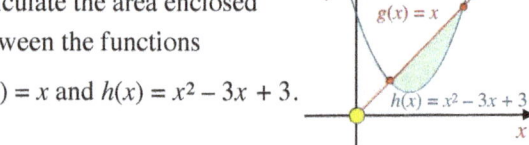

Vectors

67. K, L and M are the points $(4, 6, 3)$, $(3, 1, 1)$ and
$(5, 11, 5)$ respectively.

(a) Show that K, L and M are collinear.

(b) Find the coordinates of N such that $\overrightarrow{KN} = 3\overrightarrow{KL}$.

68. In this square based pyramid,
all 8 edges have length 2 units.

$\overrightarrow{AT} = \underline{p}$, $\overrightarrow{AD} = \underline{q}$

and $\overrightarrow{AB} = \underline{r}$.

Evaluate $\underline{p}.(\underline{q} + \underline{r})$.

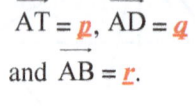

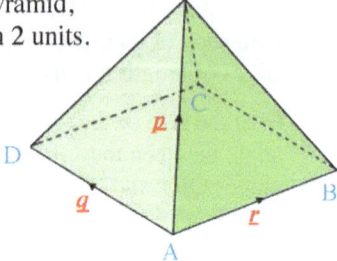

69. The vectors $\underline{a}, \underline{b}$ and $\underline{c}$ are defined as follows :-

$\underline{a} = 4\underline{i} - 2\underline{k}$; $\underline{b} = 2\underline{i} + 4\underline{j} + 2\underline{k}$; $\underline{c} = 2\underline{j} + 2\underline{k}.$

(a) Evaluate $\underline{a}.\underline{b} + \underline{a}.\underline{c}$.

(b) What does your answer tell you about the
vector $(\underline{b} + \underline{c})$?

70. Shown opposite is a right
angled isosceles triangle
whose sides represent the
vectors $\underline{r}, \underline{s}$ and $\underline{t}$.
The two equal sides have
length 4 units.
Find the value of $\underline{s}.(\underline{r} + \underline{s} + \underline{t})$.

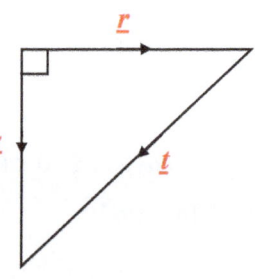

71. Calculate the size of the angle between the two vectors, $\underline{p} = \underline{i} + 2\underline{j} - 2\underline{k}$ and $\underline{q} = 2\underline{i} + \underline{j} + \underline{k}$.

72. OPQR is a parallelogram.

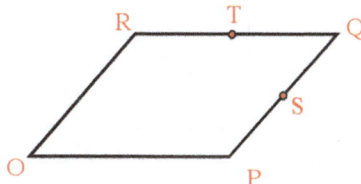

S is the mid point of PQ and T the midpoint of QR. Relative to the origin O, $\underline{p}, \underline{q}, \underline{r}, \underline{s}$ and $\underline{t}$ are the position vectors of P, Q, R, S and T respectively.

(a) Express $\underline{q}$ in terms of $\underline{p}$ and $\underline{r}$.

(b) Express $\underline{t}$ in terms of $\underline{q}$ and $\underline{r}$.

(c) Hence, show that $4(\underline{s} + \underline{t}) = 3(\underline{p} + \underline{q} + \underline{r})$.

73. Find the coordinates of M that divides K(2, 1, 3) and N(6, 5, 11) in the ratio 3 : 1.

74. P, Q and R are the points $(0, 5, 5), (4, 1, 1)$ and $(2\frac{1}{2}, 2\frac{1}{2}, 2\frac{1}{2})$ respectively.

(a) Prove that P, Q and R are collinear and find the ratio in which R divides PQ.

(b) If O is the origin, prove that OR bisects angle POQ.

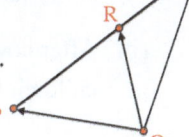

Further Calculus

75. If $f(x) = \sqrt{1 + x^2}$, find $f'(x)$.

76. Given that $f(x) = \cos^2 x$, find $f'(x)$ and hence solve the equation $f'(x) = -\frac{1}{2}$ $0 \le x < \pi$.

77. A curve has equation $f(x) = (x + 3)^{\frac{1}{2}}$.

Find the equation of the tangent at the point on the curve where $x = 6$.

78. If $f(t) = 2\sin 2t + \cos^3 t$, find $f'(t)$.

79. A function $f(x) = 1 + \cos(x + \pi/4)$, where $0 \le x \le 2\pi$.

(a) Find the value of x for which $f(x) = 0$.

(b) Find the values of x for which $f'(x) = 0$.

Hence obtain the stationary values of f in the given interval.

80. For $0 \le x \le 2\pi$, find the coordinates of the stationary points on the curve
$$y = \sin 2x + 2\sin x.$$

81. Find :-

(a) $\int (6x - 5)^5 dx$

(b) $\int_0^2 \sqrt{4x + 1} \, dx$

(c) $\int_0^2 \frac{1}{(3 + 2x)^2} dx$

(d) $\int (3\sin x + 2\sin 2x) \, dx$.

The Wave Function

82. (a) Express $4\sin x° - 8\cos x°$ in the form :-
$R\sin(x - \alpha)°$ where $R > 0$ and $0 \le \alpha < 360$.

(b) Find the maximum value of
$$f(x) = 4\sin x° - 8\cos x°,$$
and state the value of x at which this maximum occurs.

83. Express $\sqrt{3}\cos x° + \sin x°$ in the form $k\cos(x - \alpha)°$, and hence solve the equation :-
$$\sqrt{3}\cos x° + \sin x° = 1·6, \quad 0 \le x \le 360.$$

84. Show that $3\cos x° - 2\sin x°$ may be expressed as $\sqrt{13}\cos(x + 33·7)°$, and hence solve the equation :-
$$3\cos x° - 2\sin x° = 1, \quad 0 \le x < 360.$$

85. $E = 3\cos^2 x° + 2\sin x° \cos x° - 3\sin^2 x°$.

(a) Express E in the form $A\cos 2x° + B\sin 2x°$.

(b) Hence express E in the form $P\cos(2x - \alpha)°$.

(c) State the maximum and minimum values of E.

86. Find the maximum value of $20\cos 4x + 20\sin 4x$, where $0 \le x \le \pi$, and state both values of x at which this maximum occurs.

87. The expression $25\sin 10t° + 50\cos 10t°$ represents the displacement of a wave after t seconds.

This expression may be written in the form :-

$A\sin(10t + \alpha)°$ where $A > 0$ and $0 \le \alpha \le 360$.

(a) Find the values of A and α.

(b) What is the amplitude of the wave ?

(c) Use your values of A and α to sketch the graph of $y = A\sin(10t + \alpha)°$ against t for $0 \le t \le 36$, showing clearly the stationary points, and where the graph cuts the x-axis.

88. $3\log_x 4 - \log_x 8 - \log_x 2 = 1$. Find the value of x.

89. Given $x = \log_3 6 + \log_3 4$, find the value of x, correct to 2 decimal places.

90. Medical students, studying the growth of a strain of bacteria, notice that the number of bacteria present after t hours is given by the formula
$$B(t) = 40e^{1\cdot 5t}.$$

    (a) How many bacteria were present at the start of the experiment ?

    (b) How many hours will it take for the bacteria to double in number ?

91. The graph shows a relationship between two variables B and C.

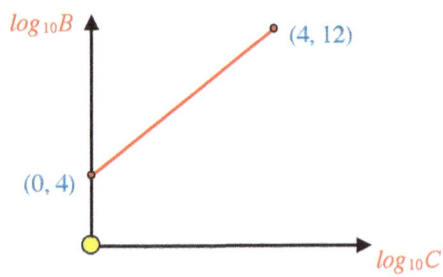

    Show there is a formula connecting B and C of the form $B = kC^n$ and find the values of k and n.

92. This graph shows the connection between two quantities P and t.

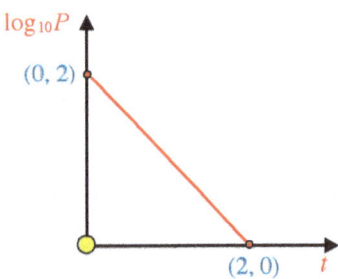

    Show there is a formula connecting P and t of the form $P = ab^t$ and find the values of a and b.

93. Shown is part of the graph of $Y = Pe^{0\cdot 3x}$.

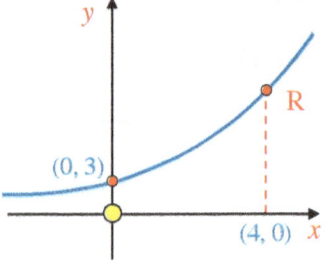

    (a) State the value of P.

    (b) Determine the coordinates of R.

94. A study was made in 2020 to look at the decline in the number of children attending football matches in Scotland.

    The formula representing the number of children, is given by :-
$$C(t) = 3000e^{-0\cdot 2t}, \text{ where}$$

    • t is the number of years after 2020.
    • $C(t)$ is the number of children attending matches in year t.

    (a) How many children were attending matches at the start of 2020 ?

    (b) After how many years will the number of children have fallen by half ?

The TeeJay Team
wish you

in your Higher Exam

Higher Maths Paper 1 (Non-Calculator)
(1 hour 30 minutes)

Total marks — 70

Attempt ALL questions.

You may NOT use a calculator.

Full credit will be given only to solutions which contain appropriate working.

State the units for your answer where appropriate.

Answers obtained by readings from scale drawings will not receive any credit.

Use **blue** or **black** ink.

FORMULAE LIST

Circle:

The equation $x^2 + y^2 + 2gx + 2fy + c = 0$ represents a circle centre $(-g, -f)$ and radius $r = \sqrt{g^2 + f^2 - c}$.

The equation $(x - a)^2 + (y - b)^2 = r^2$ represents a circle centre (a, b) and radius r.

Scalar Product: $\underline{a}.\underline{b} = |\underline{a}| \, |\underline{b}| \cos \theta$, where θ is the angle between **a** and **b**

or $\underline{a}.\underline{b} = a_1 b_1 + a_2 b_2 + a_3 b_3$, where and $\underline{a} = \begin{pmatrix} a_1 \\ a_2 \\ a_3 \end{pmatrix}$ and $\underline{b} = \begin{pmatrix} b_1 \\ b_2 \\ b_3 \end{pmatrix}$.

Trigonometric formulae:

$$sin(A \pm B) = sin\,A\,cos\,B \pm cos\,A\,sin\,B$$
$$cos(A \pm B) = cos\,A\,cos\,B \mp sin\,A\,sin\,B$$
$$sin\,2A = 2\,sin\,A\,cos\,A$$
$$cos\,2A = cos^2 A - sin^2 A = 2\,cos^2 A - 1 = 1 - 2\,sin^2 A$$

Table of standard derivatives:

$f(x)$	$f'(x)$
$sin\,ax$	$a\,cos\,ax$
$cos\,ax$	$-a\,sin\,ax$

Table of standard integrals:

$f(x)$	$\int f(x)dx$
$sin\,ax$	$-\dfrac{1}{a} cos\,ax + c$
$cos\,ax$	$\dfrac{1}{a} sin\,ax + c$

1. (a) If $\underline{a} = \begin{pmatrix} 3 \\ -3 \\ 3 \end{pmatrix}$ and $\underline{b} = \begin{pmatrix} -1 \\ 1 \\ 5 \end{pmatrix}$, write the components of $\underline{a} + \underline{b}$ and $\underline{a} - \underline{b}$. **(1)**

   (b) Hence show that $\underline{a} + \underline{b}$ and $\underline{a} - \underline{b}$ are perpendicular. **(2)**

   (c) Find the magnitude of $\underline{a} - \underline{b}$. **(2)**

2. A function h is defined on a suitable domain by $h(x) = \dfrac{4(\sqrt{x} - 2x)}{x\sqrt{x}}$.

   Find $h'(1)$. **(4)**

3. (a) Show that $x = \frac{1}{2}$ is a root of the equation $2x^3 + x^2 - 13x + 6 = 0$. **(1)**

   (b) Hence, find the other roots. **(3)**

4. Find the coordinates of the point on the curve $y = 4\sqrt{x} - 2$, at which the tangent has gradient $\frac{2}{3}$. **(4)**

5. Given that $log_b 18 - log_b 9 = \frac{1}{4}$, find the value of b. **(3)**

6. The diagram shows part of the graph of the function $y = a\sin bx + c$.

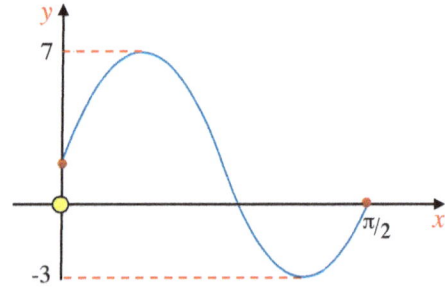

   What are the values of a, b and c ? **(3)**

7. A function f is defined on R, the set of real numbers, by $f(x) = 5 - 4x^2, \ \{x : x \geq 0\}$.

   (a) Determine an expression for the inverse function $f^{-1}(x)$. **(3)**

   (b) Given that $g(x) = 5 - x^2$, find $f^{-1}(g(x))$, and express it in its simplest form. **(3)**

8. If $\cos\alpha = \frac{\sqrt{5}}{3}$, $0 \leq \alpha < \frac{\pi}{2}$, find the exact value of :-　　　　　　　**MARKS**

   (a)　$\sin2\alpha$　　　　　　　　　　　　　　　　　　　　　　　　　　　　　(2)

   (b)　$\sin4\alpha$.　　　　　　　　　　　　　　　　　　　　　　　　　　　　(3)

9. P, Q and R are points such that PQ is perpendicular to the line with equation $x - \sqrt{3}y = 0$ and QR makes an angle of 120° with the positive direction of the x-axis.

   Prove that the points P, Q and R are collinear.　　　　　　　　　　　(3)

10. A right angled triangular lawn with dimensions x metres by $(x - 4)$ metres, is shown.

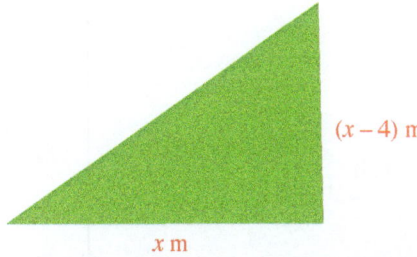

$(x - 4)$ m

x m

   If the area of the lawn has to be less than 30 square metres, determine the range of possible values for x.　(4)

11. The equation of the smaller circle is $(x - 1)^2 + (y - 3)^2 = 5$ and the larger circle has equation $(x - 11)^2 + (y - 8)^2 = 80$.

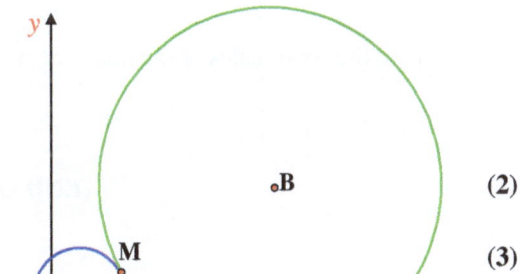

   (a)　Write the coordinates of the centre of each circle and calculate lengths of both radii, leaving the answers in surd form.　(2)

   (b)　Prove that the two circles touch at one point, M.　(3)

   (c)　Find the coordinates of the point of intersection.　(2)

   (d)　Find the equation of the common tangent to both circles at this point.　(3)

12. The curve $y = f(x)$ passes through the point $P(\frac{\pi}{3}, 1)$, and $f'(x) = -\sin 2x$.

   Find $f(x)$.　　　　　　　　　　　　　　　　　　　　　　　　　　　　(3)

13. For what range of values of q does the equation $x^2 + y^2 + 6x - 8y + q = 0$ represent a circle ? **(3)**

14. (a) Given that $\dfrac{a}{x} + \dfrac{x+2}{a+1} = 2$, show that :- $a^2 + a(1 - 2x) + x^2 = 0$. **(2)**

    (b) Hence, determine the set of values for x for which a is not real. **(4)**

15. The function $f(x) = 3^x + 4$ is defined on R, the set of real numbers.

The graph with equation $y = f(x)$ passes though the point
A$(1, a)$ and cuts the y-axis at C as shown.

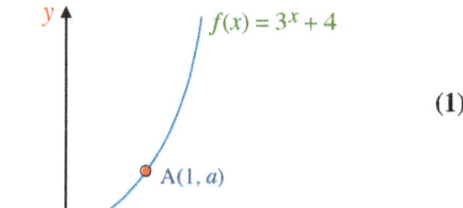

    (a) Determine the value of a. **(1)**

    (b) (i) Copy the diagram.

            On the same diagram, sketch the graph
            with equation $y = f^{-1}(x)$. **(1)**

        (ii) Write the coordinates of the images of A and C. **(3)**

    (c) B$(3, 31)$ also lies on the curve $y = f(x)$.

       A new function $g(x)$ is such that $g(x) = 6 - f(x + 2)$.

       Find the coordinates of the image of B on the graph of $g(x)$. **(2)**

[END OF QUESTION PAPER]

Higher Maths Paper 2 (Calculator)

(1 hour 45 minutes)

Total marks — 80

Attempt ALL questions.

You may use a calculator.

Full credit will be given only to solutions which contain appropriate working.

State the units for your answer where appropriate.

Answers obtained by readings from scale drawings will not receive any credit.

Use **blue** or **black** ink.

FORMULAE LIST

Circle:

The equation $x^2 + y^2 + 2gx + 2fy + c = 0$ represents a circle centre $(-g, -f)$ and radius $r = \sqrt{g^2 + f^2 - c}$.

The equation $(x - a)^2 + (y - b)^2 = r^2$ represents a circle centre (a, b) and radius r.

Scalar Product: $\quad \underline{a}.\underline{b} = |\underline{a}||\underline{b}|\cos\theta$, where θ is the angle between **a** and **b**

$\quad\quad$ or $\quad \underline{a}.\underline{b} = a_1b_1 + a_2b_2 + a_3b_3$, where and $\underline{a} = \begin{pmatrix} a_1 \\ a_2 \\ a_3 \end{pmatrix}$ and $\underline{b} = \begin{pmatrix} b_1 \\ b_2 \\ b_3 \end{pmatrix}$.

Trigonometric formulae:

$$sin(A \pm B) = sin\, A\, cos\, B \pm cos\, A sin\, B$$
$$cos(A \pm B) = cos\, A\, cos\, B \mp sin\, A sin\, B$$
$$sin\, 2A = 2sin\, A cos A$$
$$cos\, 2A = cos^2 A - sin^2 A = 2\, cos^2 A - 1 = 1 - 2\, sin^2 A$$

Table of standard derivatives:

$f(x)$	$f'(x)$
$sin\, ax$	$a\, cos\, ax$
$cos\, ax$	$-a\, sin\, ax$

Table of standard integrals:

$f(x)$	$\int f(x)dx$
$sin\, ax$	$-\dfrac{1}{a} cos\, ax + c$
$cos\, ax$	$\dfrac{1}{a} sin\, ax + c$

Attempt ALL Questions
Total Marks - 80

MARKS

1. A triangle PQR has vertices P(-5, 2), Q(11, 4) and R(6, -6).

   (a) Find the equation of the median RS. **(3)**

   (b) Find the equation of the altitude PT. **(3)**

   (c) Find the coordinates of the points of intersection of RS and PT. **(2)**

2. The diagram illustrates three functions f, g and h.

   The functions f and g are defined by

   $f(x) = 2x + 4$ and $g(x) = x^2 - 36$.

   A new function is $h(x) = g(f(x))$

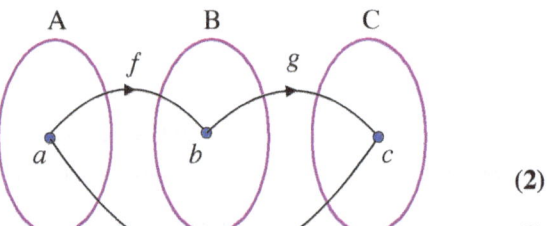

   (a) If $b = 8$, find the values of a and c. **(2)**

   (b) Find a formula for $h(x)$ in terms of x. **(3)**

   (c) Express $h(x)$ in the form $p(x + q)^2 + r$. **(3)**

   (d) Another function k is given by $k(x) = \dfrac{1}{h(x)}$.

   Define the largest suitable domain for $k(x)$. **(2)**

3. Concerned about their health, a vet puts two overweight dogs on a diet.

   If rottweiler Mick, who weighs 89 kg sticks to his diet, he will lose 2·5% of his body weight each month.

   As a treat at the end of the month, Mick's owner lets him have whatever he wants to eat, but he then puts on 2 kg each time.

   (a) Let U_n represent Mick's weight at the end of month n.

   Write a recurrence relation for his weight U_{n+1}, at the end of the following month. **(2)**

   (b) What will Mick's weight eventually settle at under this arrangement ? **(3)**

   (c) In his diet, mastiff Joe, is able to lose 4·5% of his body weight each month.

   How many kilograms can he afford to gain at the end of each month so that the long term effect on his weight will be the same as that of Mick's ? **(2)**

4. The diagram shows an isosceles triangle, with its base on the x-axis. A parabola with equation $y = 40 - \dfrac{x^2}{10}$ is drawn inside the triangle, the edges of which are tangents to the parabola, as shown.

Calculate the area (shaded) between the triangle and the parabola.

(5)

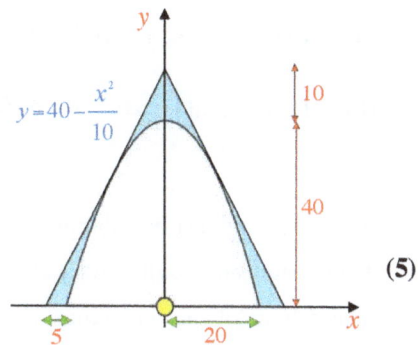

5. The circle with equation $x^2 + y^2 - 10x - 2y - 14 = 0$ and the line with equation $y = -2x + 1$ are shown in the diagram opposite.

The line intersects the circle at P and Q.

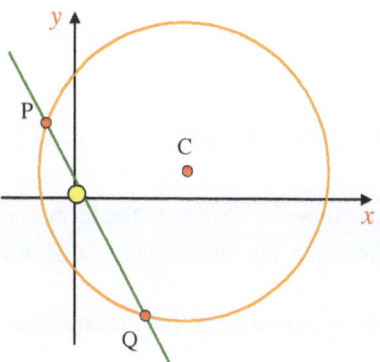

(a) Find the coordinates of P and Q. (4)

(b) Find the equation of the circle which has PQ as diameter. (3)

6. (a) U, V and W are the points $(1, 2, 3)$, $(2, 2, 2)$ and $(4, 3, 1)$ respectively.

Q is a point that divides UW in the ratio $1 : 2$.

(i) Find the coordinates of Q. (2)

(ii) Find $\overrightarrow{VU}$ and $\overrightarrow{VQ}$, and calculate the size of angle UVQ. (5)

(b) The sides of an equilateral triangle are 3 units long and represent the vectors $\underline{a}$, $\underline{b}$ and $\underline{c}$ as shown in the diagram.

Evaluate $\underline{a} \,.\, (\underline{a} + \underline{b} + \underline{c})$. (5)

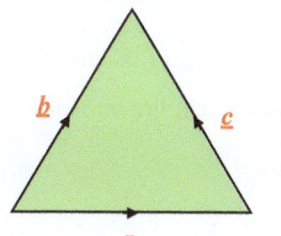

7. (a) Express $(cosx + sinx)^2$ in terms of $sin2x$. **(2)**

   (b) Hence, find $\int (cosx + sinx)^2 dx$. **(4)**

8. The chief engineer of a shipping company designs metal storage crates. Each crate is in the shape of a cuboid with a square floor base. The volume of each crate must be 216 m^3.

   (a) If the length of each edge of the base is m metres, show that the surface area of a crate is given by :- $A = 2m^2 + \dfrac{864}{m}$. **(4)**

   (b) The cost of manufacturing is directly proportional to the surface area of the crate. Calculate the dimensions of the crate that will ensure that the cost of the steel required to make it is kept to a minimum. **(6)**

9. (a) Show that $2cos(x + 30)° - sinx°$ can be expressed as $\sqrt{3}cosx° - 2sinx°$. **(3)**

   (b) Write $\sqrt{3}cosx° - 2sinx°$ in the form $kcos(x + \alpha)°$ where $k > 0$ and $0 < \alpha < 360$ and find the value of k and the value of α. **(4)**

   (c) Hence, or otherwise, solve the equation $2cos(x + 30)° = sinx° + 1, 0 \le x \le 360$. **(3)**

10. A radioactive object, made of *Bismol,* is giving off radiation and is losing some mass in the process. The mass, R grams, of the radioactive material remaining after a time t minutes is given by :-

$$R = R_0 e^{-kt}$$

where R_0 is the initial mass of the material and k is a constant.

In 4 minutes, 6 grams of the *Bismol* are reduced to 5 grams through decay.

   (a) Find the value of k. **(3)**

   (b) The half-life of the material is the length of time it takes for half of the matter to disappear. Find the half life of *Bismol.* **(2)**

[END OF QUESTION PAPER]

Answers to TeeJay Higher Book

1. a $3a^2 - ab - 10b^2$
   b $4x^2 - 28x + 49$
   c $x^3 - 9x^2 + 27x - 27$
   d $20x$
   e $3x^2 - 5x + 3$
   f $14t^2 - 32t + 1$
2. $2x^2 + 6x + 2$
3. a $5^{3}/_{4}$ b $5^{1}/_{6}$ c $^{13}/_{30}$ d $9^{3}/_{8}$
   e $11^{5}/_{12}$ f $^{1}/_{2}$ g $17^{1}/_{12}$ h $34^{4}/_{9}$
4. a $^{3}/_{5}$ b $^{7}/_{20}$ c $8^{1}/_{4}$ d $5^{1}/_{4}$
   e $1^{1}/_{4}$ f $^{5}/_{9}$ g $3^{1}/_{7}$ h 1
5. a $2x(4x + 3)$ b $abc(b - 2c)$
   c $(x + 7)(x - 4)$ d $(x - 4)^2$
   e $(x - 9)(x + 7)$ f $(x + 5y)(x - 3y)$
   g $3(x - 5)(x + 5)$ h $2p((x - 3)(x + 3)$
   i $(2x + 3)(x - 4)$ j $2(3x - 1)(x + 5)$
   k $(5a - 2b)(2a - 5b)$
   l $(5 + x)(4 - x)$
6. a $\dfrac{y-x}{xy}$ b $\dfrac{11}{3x}$
   c $\dfrac{3x-2}{x(x-1)}$ d $\dfrac{x-10}{x^2-4}$
   e $\dfrac{2-5x}{x^2}$ f $\dfrac{4(x+2)}{x(x-1)(x+3)}$
   g $\dfrac{5x+1}{(x+2)(x^2-1)}$ h $\dfrac{22-2x}{x(x-3)(x+5)}$
   i $\dfrac{2x-1}{x(x^2-1)}$
7. a $\dfrac{1}{x}$ b $\dfrac{x-2}{x}$
   c $\dfrac{1}{x}$ d $\dfrac{x+4}{x}$
   e $\dfrac{x+3}{x+4}$ f $\dfrac{x-6}{x+2}$
8. a $x = \dfrac{y-c}{m}$ b $b = a - \dfrac{C}{3}$
   c $h = \dfrac{3V}{\pi r^2}$ d $r = \sqrt{\dfrac{3V}{\pi h}}$
   e $x = \dfrac{r-n}{m-p}$ f $h = \dfrac{3g}{2T}$
   g $M = \frac{1}{2}(9q^2 + n)$ h $w = \frac{1}{3}(8b - 2a)$
9. a $x = 3, y = 4$ b $x = 1, y = -1$
   c $x = 4, y = 6$ d $x = 6, y = 2$
10. a $5\sqrt{2}$ b $10\sqrt{3}$
    c $26\sqrt{2}$ d $10\sqrt{2}$
    e $15\sqrt{2}$ f $10\sqrt{10}$
    g $2\sqrt{2}$ h 72
    i $60\sqrt{2}$ j $60 - 4\sqrt{3}$
    k 12 l $41 - \sqrt{7}$
    m $68 - 16\sqrt{15}$
11. a $20x^5$ b $5p^6$
    c $64m^6$ d $81r^8s^{12}$
    e $9x^2 + 6 + \dfrac{1}{x^2}$ f $6h^3 - 10$
    g $x - 2 + x^{-1}$ h $4m$
    i $2b^8$ j n^7
    k 2 l $t/5$
    m $12ab$ n $5p^4q$
12. a 6 b 4 c $^{1}/_{8}$ d $1^{1}/_{2}$
    e 10 f $^{1}/_{4}$ g $4^{1}/_{2}$ h 16
13. a $\sqrt{6}/2$ b $\sqrt{5}$ c $\sqrt{2}/2$ d $7\sqrt{6}/3$
14. a 9 b -45 c 12 d 6

14. e $8p^3 - 4p^2 + 1$ f 5 g 3 or -3
    h 6 or -1 i 2
15.

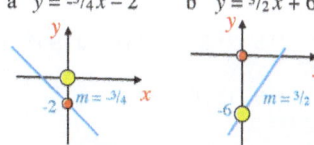

16. a $0, 7$ b $0, -3$ c $0, ^{1}/_{2}$ d $4, -4$
    e $5, -5$ f $^{5}/_{6}, -^{5}/_{6}$ g $-4, -3$ h $7, -3$
    i $5, -8$ j $3, -^{1}/_{2}$ k $-^{5}/_{2}, ^{2}/_{3}$ l $8, -2$
17. P$(-1, 0)$, Q$(4, 0)$, R$(0, -4)$, S$(0, -3)$,
    T$(0, 9)$, U$(-5, 0)$, V$(0, 10)$, W$(2, 0)$
18. a $y = (x - 2)^2 - 1$ b $y = (x + 5)^2 - 5$
    c $y = (x + ^{3}/_{2})^2 - ^{13}/_{4}$ d $y = (x - 3)^2 - 9$
    e $y = -(x - 2)^2 + 12$ f $y = -(x - 6)^2 + 36$
19. a -0.6 or -5.4 b 4.6 or 0.4
    c 7.1 or -0.1 d -0.7 or -2.8
    e 1.2 or -1.5 f 3.2 or -1.2
20. a (i) $a = 5, b = 2$, (ii) $x = 5$, (iii) $(0, 27)$
    b (i) $a = 1, b = 4$, (ii) $x = 1$, (iii) $(0, 3)$
    c (i) $a = -4, b = -3$, (ii) $x = -4$, (iii) $(0, 13)$
    d (i) $a = 6, b = 0$, (ii) $x = 6$, (iii) $(0, -36)$
21. a $y = 2x^2$ b $y = -^{1}/_{4}x^2$
22. a $24 \Rightarrow$ 2 unequal roots
    b $-16 \Rightarrow$ no roots
    c $44 \Rightarrow$ 2 unequal roots
    d $0 \Rightarrow$ 1 real root
23. $a = 6$ or -6
24. $b < 2$
25. $p = 5$ or -5
26. P$(1.78, 0)$

Answers to Chapter 1 - Page 4

Exercise H1·1 - Page 4

1. a $(1, -9), (3, -5)$ b $(2, 7), (-2, -5)$
   c $(-2, -8), (1, 4)$ d $(1, 9)$
   e $(5, 25), (-1, -5)$ f $(7, 35), (-2, 8)$
   g $(3, 0), (-1, -4)$ h $(3, 1), (-3, 1)$

Exercise H1·2 - Page 5

1. a $(0, -4), (4, 0)$ b $(3, 1), (-^{1}/_{3}, -2^{1}/_{3})$
   c $(1, 0), (3, 2)$ d $(-1, -1), (0, -^{1}/_{2})$
   e $(-1, -5), (5, 1)$ f $(3, 4), (-2, -6)$
   g $(4, 2)$ h $(4, 3), (4, -3), (-5, 0)$
2. $(1, -4)$ and $(-1, 2)$
3. substitute $y = 3x + 10$
   $\Rightarrow 10x^2 + 40x + 40 = 0$ or $x^2 + 4x + 4 = 0$
   $\Rightarrow (x + 2)^2 = 0 \Rightarrow x = -2, y = 4$ and since
   there is only 1 answer, it must be a tangent

Answers to Chapter 2 - Page 6

Exercise H2·1 - Page 7

1. 2
2. a $^{1}/_{3}$ b $^{1}/_{2}$ c 3 d $^{7}/_{3}$

3. undefined
4. $p = 10$
5. a $m_{QR} = -^{3}/_{2}$, $m_{PS} = -^{3}/_{2}$
   b $m_{PQ} = ^{1}/_{8}$, $m_{RS} = ^{1}/_{8}$
   c parallelogram
6. a $m = 4, (0, 1)$ b $m = 6, (0, -4)$
   c $m = -3, (0, 6)$ d $m = ^{1}/_{2}, (0, 5)$
   e $m = -^{1}/_{3}, (0, -7)$ f $m = -2, (0, 10)$
7. a $y = 2x + 1$ b $y = -3x + 5$
   c $y = -^{1}/_{2}x + 4$
8. a (i) $^{1}/_{3}$ (ii) $(0, 2)$ (iii) $y = ^{1}/_{3}x + 2$
   b (i) 2 (ii) $(0, 1)$ (iii) $y = 2x + 1$
   c (i) $^{2}/_{3}$ (ii) $(0, 2)$ (iii) $y = ^{2}/_{3}x + 2$
   d (i) -2 (ii) $(0, 6)$ (iii) $y = -2x + 6$
9. a -2 b 2 c $y = 2x - 2$
10. a B b C c E
    d D e A f F
11. a $y = -^{3}/_{4}x - 2$ b $y = ^{3}/_{2}x + 6$

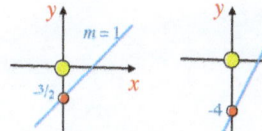

   c $y = x - ^{3}/_{2}$ d $y = 2x - 4$

   e $y = -^{1}/_{3}x + 1$ f $y = x - 3$

12.

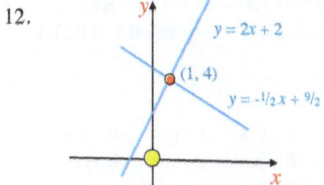

13. a $x = 3, y = 0$ b $x = 26, y = -10$
    c $x = 6, y = 9$ d $x = 0, y = 2$
14. $p = -1$
15. a $y = 5x - 3$ b $y = 2x - 4$
    c $y = 4x + 16$ d $y = x - 1$
    e $y = -2x + 18$ f $y = -4x - 3$
16. a $y = 5x - 15$ b $y = -x$
    c $y = 3x - 14$ d $y = -2x - 7$
    e $y = -^{2}/_{3}x - 4$
17. R$(8, 8)$
18. a $y = 2x + 4$ b $y = 2x + 1$
    c $y = x$ d $y = -x + 8$
    e $y = x + 3$ f $y = -^{1}/_{2}x - ^{3}/_{2}$
19. $y = ^{5}/_{3}x$ and $y = -2x$. They meet at $(0, 0)$
20. $t = 6$
21. a C$(1, 7)$ b $y = -x + 8$
22. a T$(15, 0)$, V$(7, 6)$ b $y = -^{3}/_{4}x + ^{45}/_{4}$

c 36·9° and 106·2°

23. a Pythagoras => P(5, √75) = P(5, 5√3)
   b y = -√3x + 10√3

Exercise H2·2 - Page 9

1. a $m_{AB} = -1/3$ and $m_{BC} = -1/3$
   b they are collinear c see diagram
2. $m_{UV} = -1/2$ and $m_{VW} = -1/2$
   UV and VW are parallel with point V in common so they must be collinear.
3. a $m_{FG} = 1$ and $m_{GH} = 1$
   FG and GH are parallel with point G in common so they must be collinear.
   b $m_{RS} = -1/2$ and $m_{ST} = -1/2$
   RS and ST are parallel with point S in common so they must be collinear.
   c $m_{DE} = 3/2$ and $m_{EF} = 3/2$
   DE and EF are parallel with point E in common so they must be collinear.
4. $p = -3$
5. $t = 0$

Exercise H2·3 - Page 10

1. 15·9°
2. a 68·2° b 21·8° c 26·6° d 8·1°
3. 153·4°
4. a 111·8° b 122·0°
5. $m = 2$
6. $m = 3$
7. $m = 0·25$
8. $m = -2$

Exercise H2·4 - Page 11

1. 8·25
2. a 5·66 b 8·94 c 6·08 d 8·54
3. JL = 8·60, KM = 9·43 => KM longer
4. a 5   b 5   c isosceles
5. PA = 5, PB = 5, PC = 5
   A, B and C lie on a circle centre P
6. RS = 10, ST = 5, RT = √125
   RS² + ST² = 100 + 25 = 125 = RT²
   By converse of Pythagoras, it is a R.A.T.

Exercise H2·5 - Page 12

1. a no   b yes   c no   d yes
   e no   f yes   g yes   h yes
2. a -2   b 1/3   c -1/7
   d 2/7   e 1   f -9/5
   g 2/11 h -3/7   i undefined
3. $y = -1/5x + 4$
4. $y = -3/2x$
5. a yes   b yes   c yes   d no
6. $y = -2/5x + 4$
7. $y = -5x$ b $y = -3/5x$
8. $y = 2x - 8$
9. $p = 2, q = 2$
10. a $x = 3$ b $y = 4$ c $x = -1$
11. a $y = -2$ b $x = 4$ c $y = 8$
12. a $y = 1/4x + 4$ b $y = -4x - 13$
    c $y = -2/3x - 7$ d $y = 3/2x + 6$
13. $k = 4/3$
14. $m_{PR} = 1/2$ and $m_{QS} = -2 => m_{PR} × m_{QS} = -1$
15. $m_1 = -p/q$ and $m_2 = q/p => m_1 × m_2 = -1$

16. $m_{RT} = -1/2$ (approx)

Exercise H2·6 - Page 13

1. $y = 1/2x$
2. $y = -2x + 1$
3. $y = 2x - 7$
4. a $y = 1/6x$ b $y = 7/3x - 13/3$
   c use 6y - x and 3y - 7x = -13 and simultaneous equations => (2, 1/3)
   d equation of 3rd median is $y = -5/9x + 13/9$ and (2, 1/3) lies on this line.
6. medians through A is $y = -1/5x + 14/5$
   medians through B is $y = 7x - 14$
   medians through C is $y = -2x + 7$
   medians 2 and 3 meet at (7/3, 7/3)
   the first median passes through this point.

Exercise H2·7 - Page 14

1. $y = -2x - 7$
2. $y = 8x + 7$
3. a $y = x$ b $y = -2/3x - 2$ c $y = -3/2x - 3$
   c Proof and (-6/5, -6/5)
4. a Altitude from E is $y = 2x - 6$
   Median through F is $y = -14/3x + 47/3$
   b they meet at the point (3¼, ½)

Exercise H2·8 - Page 15

1. $y = -3/2x + 17/2$
2. $y = x + 5$ and $y = 6x - 10$
3. a $y = -2x + 5$ b $y = 3x - 5$
   c (2, 1)   d $y = 1/7x + 5/7$
   => (2, 1) lies on this last line
4. a $y = 2x - 1$ b C lies on this line
   c It must be an isosceles triangle

Exercise H2·9 - Page 16

1. a $y = 2x - 9$ b $y = -3x + 26$
   c (7, 5)
2. a $y = -4x + 27$ b (5, 7)
   c $y = -1/7x + 46/7$
3. a $m_{EB} × m_{BN} = 2 × -1/2 = -1$ perpendicular
   b (1, -5/3)
4. a TV = √45 = TV => isosceles
   b W(1, 7/2)
   c CT = 6, CW = 3/2 = CW = 1/4 CT
5. a $y = 3/4x - 3/4$ H(1, 0), L(-5, 3)
   b perp bisector of AC is $y = -1/2x + 1/2$ and both H and L lie on this line.
6. a $y = x - 3$ and $y = -1/3x - 1/3$
   b J(2, -1)   c $y = -3x + 5$
   mid pt of PQ (1, 2) lies on this line
7. (7, 3)
8. a $y = -1/4x$ b (-8, 2), √68
9. M(3½, 7), line through N is $y = 2x$ and M lies on this line.
10. M(3, 4), F(5, 0), G(1, 8)
11. a PQ: $y = 4x - 26$, QR: $y = -1/3x + 26/3$
    b P(6, -2), Q(2, 8)
12. a $y = 3/4x + 17/4$
    b (1, 5),   Area = 37½ units²
13. (-3, 1), (3, -2) and (18, 43)
14. a $y = -1$ b $y = 3/2x - 5$ c (8/3, -1)
15. a $y = 2/3x + 11/3$
    b (-1, 3), Area = 104·8 units²

16. $m_{PQ} = -2/3$ and PQ is perpendicular to the line with equation $2y - 3x + 6 = 0$
17. a $m_{CB} = -1/2$ and $m_{AB} = 2 => 2 × -1/2 = -1$
    b A = (225/8 π - 45) units²
18. $y = -5/2x + 12/5$
19. A = 50 units²

Exam Practice Ch 2 - Page 18

1. $x = 0$
2. $p = 15$
3. $y = -3/4x - 1$
4. $d = 4$
5. yes, since $tan60° = √3$ and gradient of the line = √3, with G a common point
6. a $y = -2x + 2$
   b $y = 3x + 2$
   c (0, 2)
7. $y = 7/2x - 17/4$
   b $y = x + 4$
   c (33/10, 73/10)
8. a $y = -1/3x + 14/3$
   b T(-1, 5)
   c (i) $y = 1/2x + 11/2$
     (ii) $x = -1, => y = -1/2 × -1 + 11/2 = 5 = y$, so line passes through point (-1, 5)
9. a proof using (3, 8) and $m = -1/3$
   b B(21, 2) and C(23, 8)

Answers to Chapter 3 - Page 19

Revision Exercise - Page 19

1. a -7   b -4, -1, 2, 5
   c straight line through (0, -1) with $m = 3$
2. a -3   b 35   c $4p - 5$ d 12
3. a 10   b 5, 2, 1, 2, 5, 10
   c/d
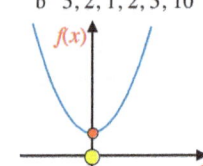
4. a -5   b/c 0, 3, 4, 3, 0, -5
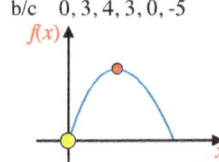
   d 0, 4   e $x = 2$ f (2, 4)
5. a $f(a²) = a² + 8$
     => $f(a²) = a² + 8 = 57 => a = ±7$
6. a 4   b 81
7. a min   b max   c max
   d min   e max   f min
8. a
   (0, 9)
   (-3, 0)   (3, 0)
   b 3, -3
   c $x = 0$
   d (0, 9)
9. a 8, 3, 0, -1, 0, 3, 8   b/c
   d $x = -1$
   e (-1, -1)
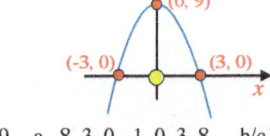
(-2, 0)
(-1, -1)

Exercise H3·1 - Page 21

1. a $8, 2, 0, 2, 8$
   b/c
   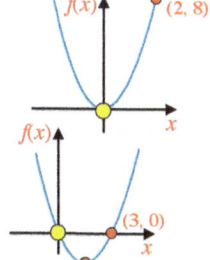

2. a 4
   b $0, -2, -2, 0, 4$
   c/d

3. a $-5, -4, -3, -2, -1, 0, 1, 2, 3$
   b $0, 1, 2, 3, 4, 5$
4. a true   b false   c false   d true
   e false   f false   g false   h false
5. a $\{0, 1, 2, 3, 4, 5, 6, 7, 8\}$
   b $\{-1, 0, 1, 2, 3\}$
   c $\{2, 4, 6, 8, 10, 12, 14\}$
   d $\{-5, 5\}$
   e $\{-6, -2\}$
   f $\{0\}$
   g $\{ \}$ - the empty set
   h $\{90\}$

6. a $\{1, 6, 9, 10\}$
   b/c graph

7. a $\{-1, 0, 3, 8\}$
   b/c graph

8. a $-7, 0, 1, 2, 9$
   b graph
   c a cubic
   d $\{y : -7 \le y \le 9, y \in R\}$

9. a $6, 0, -4, -6, -6, -4, 0, 6$
   b graph   c $-1, 4$

10. a $0, \sqrt{7}, \sqrt{12}, \sqrt{15}, 4, \sqrt{15}, \sqrt{12}, \sqrt{7}, 0$
    b $(-4, 0), (-3, \sqrt{7}), (-2, \sqrt{12}), (-1, \sqrt{15})$
      $(0, 4), (1, \sqrt{15}), (2, \sqrt{12}), (3, \sqrt{7}), (4, 0)$

    c graph
      a semicircle

11. a $0, 0·5, 0·87, 1, 0·87, 0·5, 0, -0·5, -0·87,$
      $-1, -0·87, -0·5, 0,$
    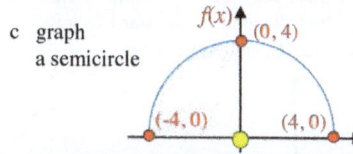
    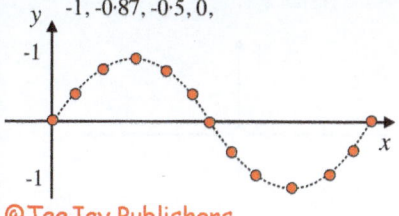

@TeeJay Publishers

---

b graph   c $\{y : -1 \le y \le 1, y \in R\}$

Exercise H3·2 - Page 22

1. a yes since 1 arrow leaves each and
      every element from the domain.
   b no since 2 arrows leave element b
      and no arrows leave element c.
   c yes
   d no since each x-value (domain) maps
      on to 2 y-values (range)
   e yes
   f no since each x-value (domain) maps
      on to 2 y-values (range)

Exercise H3·3 - Page 23

1. a $h(x) = 4 - 4x$ and $k(x) = 1 - 4x$
   b no   c 8 and 5
2. a $g(f(x)) = x^2 + 2$ b $f(g(x)) = (x + 2)^2$
   c $g(g(x)) = x + 4$ d $f(f(x)) = x^4$
3. a $h(x) = x^3 + 1$, range $= \{2, 9, 28, 65\}$
   b $8, 27, 64, 125$
   c $k(x) = (x + 1)^3 = x^3 + 3x^2 + 3x + 1$
4. a $h(x) = 1/2x - 3$, $k(x) = 1/(2x - 6)$
   b $-2\frac{1}{4} - (-\frac{1}{2}) = -2\frac{1}{4}$
   c $h(x) = \{ x \in R, x \ne 0\}$
      $k(x) = \{ x \in R, x \ne 3\}$
5. a $f(g(x)) = 2x^2 - 5$
   b $f(g(x)) = x^2 + x$
   c $f(g(x)) = (3x^2 + 1)^2$
   d $f(g(x)) = 3x^2 + 2$
   e $f(g(x)) = 2x^2 - 9$
   f $f(g(x)) = 6\sin x - 1$
   g $f(g(x)) = 1/(3x^3 + 3)$
   h $f(g(x)) = \cos(2x^2 - 3) + 5$
   i $f(g(x)) = x$.
6. a $f(g(x)) = (2x - 4)^2 + 2$
      $g(f(x)) = 2x^2$
   b if $f(g(a)) = g(f(a))$
      $\Rightarrow a = 1·35$ or $6·65$
7. They all give $f(g)x)) = x$
8. $h(x) = 1/(x^2 + 4x)$ $\{x : x \ne 0, -4\}$
9. $f(f(x)) = x$

Exercise H3·4 - Page 25

1. $f^{-1}(x) = 1/3 (5 - x)$
2. a $f^{-1}(x) = 1/4 (x + 2)$
   b $f^{-1}(x) = 2 - 1/2x$
   c $f^{-1}(x) = 3x - 3$
   d $f^{-1}(x) == 1/3 x + 2$
   e $f^{-1}(x) = 1/3 x - 5/4$
   f $f^{-1}(x) = {}^3\sqrt{x}$
   g $f^{-1}(x) = 3x - 1$
   h $f^{-1}(x) = {}^3\sqrt{(x + 3)}$
   i $f^{-1}(x) = x^2 + 5$
3. a proof b x c Identity function
4. a $f^{-1}(x) = 1/2(7 - x)$ b   proof
5. a $f^{-1}(x) = 3 - x$ and proof
   b $f^{-1}(x) = 12/x$ and proof
6. a $f^{-1}(x) = 4 - x^2$, $\{x : x \in R\}$
   b $f^{-1}(x) = (x - 5)^2$, $\{x : x \in R\}$
   c $f^{-1}(x) = \sqrt{(x - 2)}$, $\{x : \ge 2, x \in R\}$
   d $f^{-1}(x) = 1/x + 2$, $\{x : \ne 0, x \in R\}$
   e $f^{-1}(x) = 1/2x + 1/2$, $\{x : \ne 0, x \in R\}$
   f $f^{-1}(x) = 4 - 6/x$, $\{x : \ne 0, x \in R\}$

page 189

---

7. The inverse "relationship" would be
   $f^{-1}(x) = \pm\sqrt{x}$ which gives two answers each
   time so $f^{-1}(x) = \pm\sqrt{x}$ is not a function
   $\Rightarrow$ inverse does not exist.
8. a $f^{-1}(x) = x/(1 - x)$, $\{x : \ne 1, x \in R\}$
   b $f^{-1}(x) = (2x + 2)/(x - 1)$, $\{x : \ne 1, x \in R\}$

Exam Practice Ch 3 - Page 26

1. $g^{-1}(x) = {}^3\sqrt{x - 3}$, $\{x \ge 3, x \in R\}$
2. a $f^{-1}(x) = 1/2(x + 5)$
   b $g^{-1}(2) = 3$
3. $h(x) = f(4 - x) = 2x^2 - 13x + 21$
4. a $g^{-1}(x) = 1/3(8 - x)$
   b $g(g^{-1}(x)) = x$
5. a $f(g(x)) = (2 + x)(1 - x) + 10$
   b domain for $h(x)$ is $\{x : x \ne 3, -4, x \in R\}$
6. a $f(g(x)) = x^2 + 2x - p$
   b $p = 8$
7. a (i) $f(g(x)) = x^2 - 6x + 11$
      (ii) $g(f(x)) = x^2 - 1$
   b $f(g(x)) + g(f(x)) = 2x^2 - 6x + 10 = 0$
      since $b^2 - 4ac = 36 - 40 = -4$, no roots
8. a $g(f(x)) = 2x^2 + 4$
   b $x = 1$ or -3
9. Domain $= \{x : x \le 8, x \in R\}$
10. a $g(f(x)) = -2x^2 - 1$, $g(g(x)) = 4x - 1$
    b $x = 0$ or -2
11. a (i) $g(f(x)) = 4x + 3$, $g(g(x)) = 4x - 3$
      (ii) $x = 5/4$ or $-5/4$
12. a $h(x) = 9x^2 - 6x + 8$
    b $x = 1$ or $-1/3$
13. a $p(x) = 2 - 4/x$
    b $q(x) = 2x - 4$

Answers to Chapter 4 - Page 28

Revision Exercise - Page 28

1. a $1/16$ b $1/49$ c $1/125$ d $1/100000$
   e 4 f 3 g 2 h ±4
   i 4 j 8 k $1/5$ l $1/3$
   m $1/27$ n $1/243$ o $1/8$ p $1/100$.
2. a $x^{1/3}$ b $x^{3/4}$ c $7x^{-1}$ d $5x^{-3}$
   e $4/5x^{-2}$ f $-1/2x^{-5}$ g $x^{-1/2}$ h $-2x^{-1/3}$
   i $x^{-2} + x^{1/2}$ j $x^3 + x^{7/2}$
   k $10x^{1/2} - 5x^{3/2}$ l $x^2 + 2 + x^{-2}$
   m $x^8 + 2x + x^{-6}$ n $x + 2 + x^{-1}$
   o $4x^4 - 4x + x^{-2}$ p $1 + 7x^{-1}$
   q $x + x^{-1/2} - x^{-1}$ r $x^{1/2} - 2x^{-1/2}$
   s $3x^{-2} - 4x^{-1}$ t $1/3x^{1/2} + 5/3x^{-1/2}$
   u $1/6x^{-1} - 1/3 + 1/6x$
   v $x^{-1} - 3 + 2x$ w $x^{1/2} + 5x^{-1/2}$
   x $4x^{-1/2} - x^{-3/2}$.
3. a $\sqrt{6}/6$ b $2\sqrt{3}/15$ c $\sqrt{2}$ d $-1 - \sqrt{3}$.

Exercise H4·1 Page 31

1. $3x^2$ 2. $4x^3$ 3. 1.   4. $2x + 1$

Answers

Exercise H4·2 Page 32

1. $5x^4$
2. $9x^8$
3. $20x^3$
4. x^2
5. $2x^4$
6. $-12x^5$
7. $2ax$
8. 10
9. 0
10. 0
11. $2x + 5$
12. $3x^2 - 12x$
13. $x^2 + {}^1/_2 x$
14. $20x^3 - 2x$
15. $-15x^4 + 14x^6$
16. $3ax^2 - 2bx$
17. $2x - 2$
18. $2x + 4$
19. $32x + 24$
20. $6x + 5$
21. $32x$
22. $2x - 8$
23. $4x^3 + 12x$
24. $6x^5 - 12x^2$
25. $8x^7 + 8x^3$
26. $3x^2 - 6x + 3$
27. $6x^2 - 22x + 7$
28. $3x^2 + 18x + 27$
29. a 1 b 0 c -1 d 11
30. a $6x^5 - 6x^2$ b 0 and -216
31. a $x = -3$ b $x = {}^1/_2$ c $x < -2$
32. a $x = 4$ or $x = -2$
    b $x = 1$ c $-2 < x < 4$
33. a 1 $f'(x)$ b $2x$ $f'(x)$
    c $3x^2$.

Exercise H4·3 Page 33

1. a ${}^5/_3 x^{2/3}$ b ${}^3/_2 x^{1/2}$ c $7x^{3/4}$ d ${}^1/_2 x^{1/2}$
   e ${}^1/_4 x^{-3/4}$ f $-{}^1/_x{}^2$ g $-{}^3/_x{}^4$ h $-{}^6/_x{}^7$
   i $-{}^4/_x{}^3$ j ${}^{50}/_x{}^6$ k $-{}^3/_x{}^7$ l ${}^1/_{2x^3}$
   m ${}^{10}/_x{}^7$.

2. a ${}^1/_{2x^{1/2}}$ b ${}^1/_{3x^{2/3}}$ c ${}^2/_{5x^{3/5}}$ d $-{}^2/_x{}^3$
   e $-{}^1/_x{}^2$ f $-{}^5/_x{}^6$ g $-{}^4/_x{}^2$ h $-{}^1/_{2x^{3/2}}$
   i ${}^3/_{2x^{3/2}}$ j $-{}^{20}/_x{}^5$ k $-{}^1/_{4x^{3/2}}$ l $-{}^2/_x{}^4$
   m $-{}^4/_x{}^6$ n ${}^2/_x{}^7$ o $-{}^1/_{16}x^{3/2}$.

3. a $-{}^1/_x{}^2 + 1$ b $-{}^1/_{2x^{3/2}} + {}^1/_{2x^{1/2}}$
   c $3 + {}^3/_x{}^2$ d $4x + {}^2/_{3x^3}$
   e $3x^2 + {}^2/_x{}^3$ f $-{}^7/_x{}^2 + {}^1/_7$
   g $12x^3 - {}^3/_{4x^4}$ h ${}^5/_{2x^{3/2}} + 2x$
   i ${}^3/_{2x^{1/2}} - 1$ j $2x - {}^2/_x{}^3$
   k $6x^5 + 2 - {}^4/_x{}^5$ l $32x - {}^{32}/_x{}^3$
   m $1 - {}^1/_x{}^2$ n $2x + {}^2/_x{}^3$
   o ${}^3/_x{}^2$ p $1 - {}^2/_x{}^2$
   q $8x - 1 - {}^3/_x{}^2$ r ${}^1/_{2x^{1/2}} + {}^2/_{x^{3/2}}$
   s $-{}^{10}/_x{}^3 - {}^8/_x{}^2$ t ${}^1/_{3x^{1/3}} - {}^1/_{2x^{4/3}}$

Exercise H4·4 Page 34

1. a $32x^3 - 10x + 3$ b ${}^3/_{x^{1/4}} - {}^2/_{x^{4/5}}$
   c $1 - {}^8/_g{}^3$ d $-{}^2/_x{}^2 - {}^{15}/_x{}^4$

e $5u^4 - 3u^2$ f $2x - {}^{200}/_x{}^3$
g $-{}^1/_v{}^2 - {}^3/_v{}^3$
h $24h^{1/2} - {}^8/_h{}^{1/2} - {}^2/_h{}^{3/2}$.

2. a 64 b -8
3. a $3{}^3/_4$ b ${}^3/_4$
4. a -20 b 0 c ${}^7/_8$
5. $x = \pm 1$
6. $242{}^1/_8$

Exercise H4·5 Page 36

1. a 1 m, 8 m, 27 m b $v(t) = 3t^2$
   c 75 m/sec
2. a 16 m, 16 m
   b $h(t) = t(10 - t)$ 10 secs
   c $v(t) = 10 - 2t$ d 4 m/sec
   e ball falling f 5 secs
3. a $v(t) = 6t - 18$
   b 6 m/sec c rolling back down
4. a 16 cm b $v(t) = 6 - t$
   c 2 cm/sec
5. a 125 feet
   b $d = 0$ or $d = 60$
   c $7·5$ feet/feet
   d $d = 20$ feet
6. $\pi/_3$ meters/sec
7. 328 m³/sec
8. $-2·4$

Exercise H4·6 Page 37

1. a $y = 2x - 1$
   b $y = 9x + 6$
   c $y = {}^1/_6 x + {}^3/_2$
   d $y = -{}^1/_4 x + 1$
2. a $y = 12x - 16$ b $y = -x - 2$
   c $y = 2$ d $y = -12x - 9$
   e $y = {}^3/_2 x + 6$ f $y = {}^1/_{12} x + {}^4/_3$
   g $y = 6x + 9$ h $y = 5x - 4$
   i $y = 11x - 14$ j $y = 6x - 14$
3. $y = 2x - 4$, Proof.
4. $y = -6x - 3$ and $y = 6x - 3$ $(0, -3)$
5. $y = 4x - 2$, and $y = -2x + 1$ $({}^1/_2, 0)$ x-axis
6. $y = 4x - 12$, $\sqrt{153}$
7. $(5, -25)$ & $(-1, -7)$
   $y = 15x - 100$, $y = 15x + 8$
8. $R(2, 4)$
9. $y = 3x - 3$
10. $m = 6$, $c = -7$
11. $y = {}^1/_{12} x + {}^4/_3$, $(8, 2)$

Exam Practice Ch 4 Page 38

1. $-{}^{12}/_{\sqrt{x^3}}$.
2. $-{}^3/_x{}^5$.

3. ${}^3/_2 t^{1/2} + {}^1/_t{}^5$.
4. $-{}^1/_{64}$.
5. $42x^2 + {}^5/_{\sqrt{x}}$.
6. 4.
7. a $1 + {}^4/_t{}^2$ b ${}^1/_3 t^{-1/3} - {}^2/_3 t^{-4/3}$.
8. 605 m³/sec.
9. ${}^{15}/_2 v^{1/2} + {}^4/_v{}^2$.
10. 14.
11. 17.
12. 10.
13. $y = 54x + 113$.
14. $y = -4x + 4$.
15. $y = -{}^3/_4 x + 9$.
16. a one point of contact $(4, 24)$
    b $y = x + 20$.
17. a $y = 8x - 35$.
    b 1 pt. contact $(-4, -67)$
18. $p = 4$, $q = 4$.

Answers to Chapter 5 - Page 39

Revision Exercise - Page 39

1. a G b I c B d C
   e F f O g E h J
   i A j P k N l H
   m K n M o D p L

Exercise H5·1 - Page 40

1. a trans 1 down b trans 2 up
   c trans 6 up d trans 2 down
   e trans 1 up f trans 3 up
   g trans 5 up h trans $0·8$ down
2. $k = 3$
3.

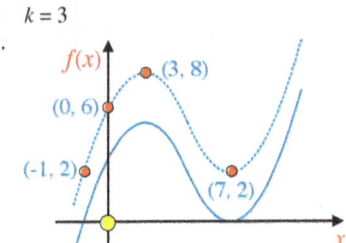

Exercise H5·2 - Page 41

1. a trans 1 right b trans 3 left
   c trans 4 left d trans $45°$ right
   e trans $180°$ left f trans 3 right
   g trans 2 right h trans $2p$ left
2. a $P(2, 0)$, $Q(1, -1)$
   b

3. a A(0, 4), B(-2, 0), C(2, 0)
   b
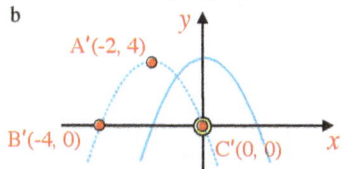

   c from $f(x)$, all points translate by 2 units
      left then 3 units up.

4. The graph of $y = f(x + b) + c$ is the same
    shape as that of $y = f(x)$, but it has been
    translated b units horizontally and by c
    units vertically, left if b is +ve, right if b is
    -ve, up if c is +v and down if c is negative.

5. T(3, 1)

6. a b
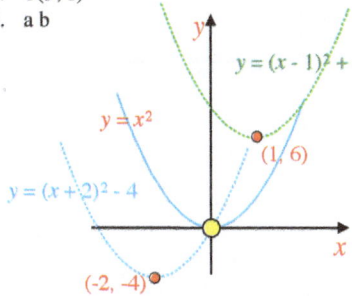

7.
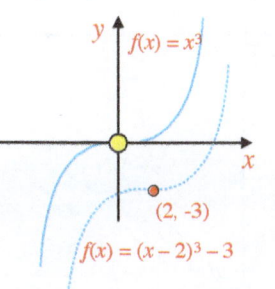

8. a
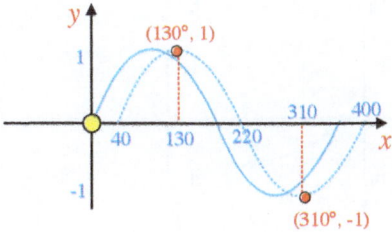

    b

c
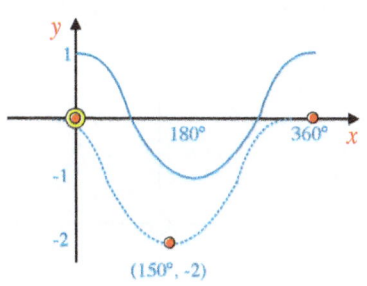

Exercise H5·3 - Page 42

1.
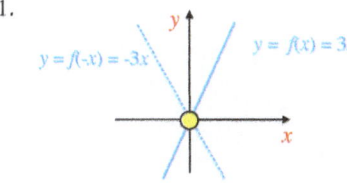

2.
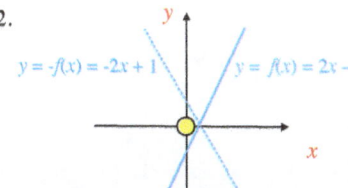

3. In each case, the graph of $y = -f(x)$ should
    be the same as that of $y = f(x)$, but
    reflected over the x-axis.

4.
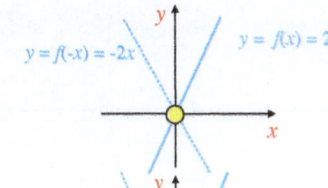

5.
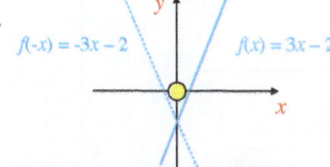

    must be $f(-x)$ since it is a reflection of
    $y = 3x - 2$ over the y-axis.

6.
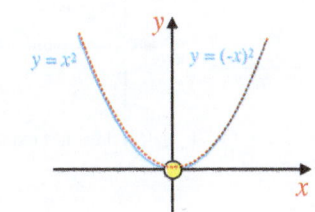

7. In each case, the graph of $y = f(-x)$ should
    be the same as that of $y = f(x)$, but reflected
    over the y-axis.

8. $f(-x) = (-x)^2 - 2 = x^2 - 2 = f(x)$ => even

9. $f(-x) = 2(-x)^3 = -2x^3 = -f(x)$ => odd

10. even

11. even

12. 3a odd   b even   c odd   d no
    e no   f odd   g even   h no
    7a odd   b even   c odd   d no
    e no   f odd   g even   h odd

Exercise H5·4 - Page 43

1.
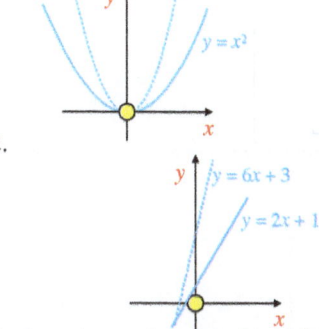

2.

3. In each case, the graph of $y = 2f(x)$ should
    be the same as that of $y = f(x)$, but
    stretched vertically by a factor of 2.

4. In each case, the graph of $y = 2f(x)$ should
    be the same as that of $y = f(x)$, but
    compressed vertically by a factor of $^1/_2$.

5. a
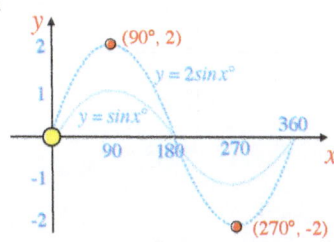

    b
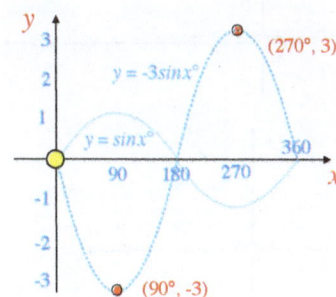

6. a
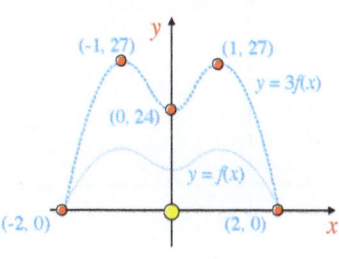

    b

Exercise H5·5 - Page 44

1.
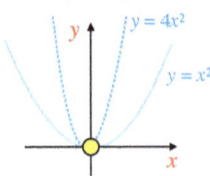

2.
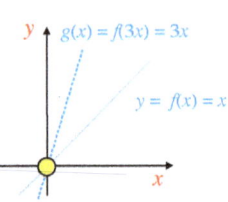

3.
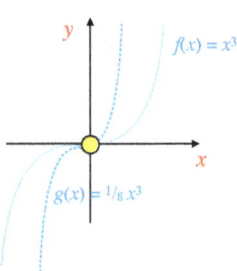

4.
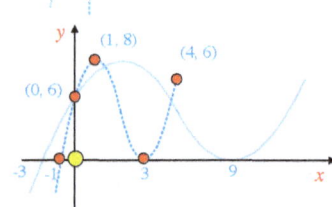

5.
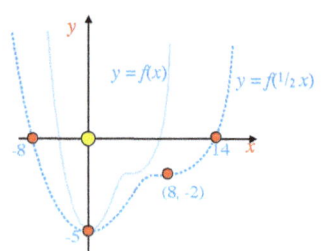

6
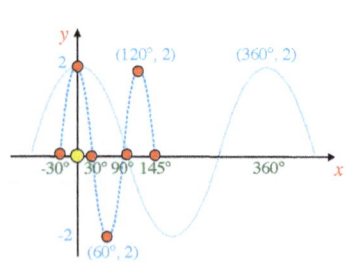

Exercise H5·6 - Page 45

1. a   see drawing
b $f^{-1}(x) = \frac{1}{2}x - 2$
c   see drawing

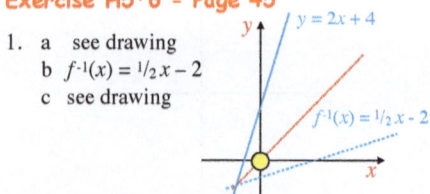

2. a   See sketch of $f(x)$ and $f^{-1}(x) = \frac{1}{3}x$

---

b   Sketch of $f(x)$ and $f^{-1}(x) = \frac{1}{4}x + \frac{1}{2}$
c   Sketch of $f(x)$ and $f^{-1}(x) = \sqrt[3]{(x-2)}$

3. a   b
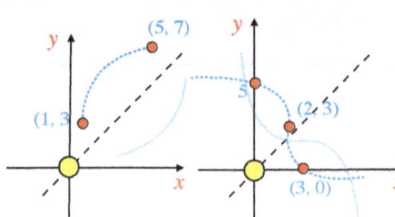

4.
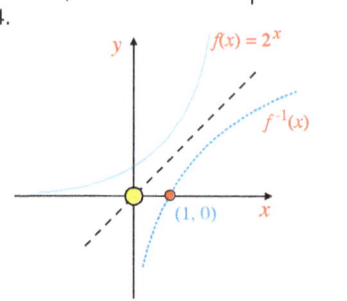

Exercise H5·7 - Page 46

1. a   b
c   d
e   f
g   h
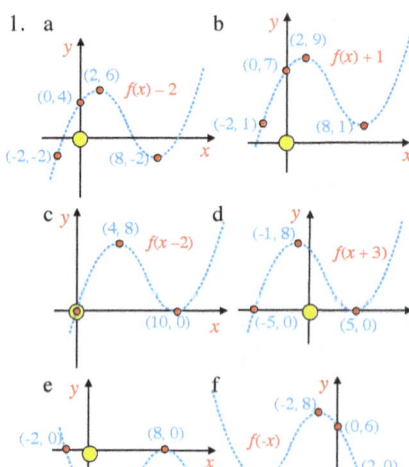

i   j $f^{-1}(x)$ does not exist
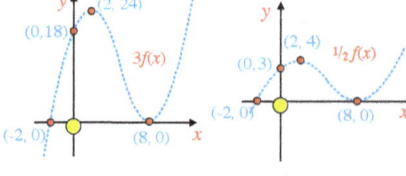

2.
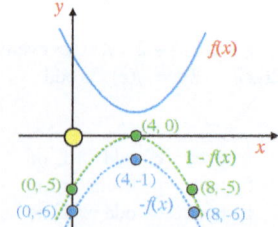

---

3. a/b
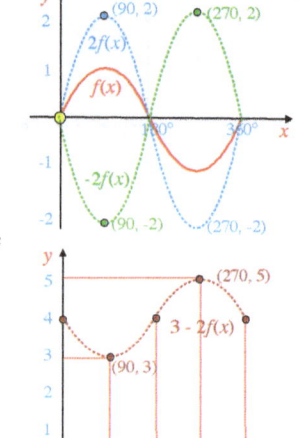
c

4. a/b
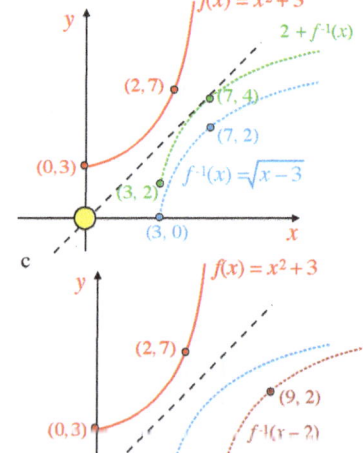
c

5. a   b
c   d
e   f
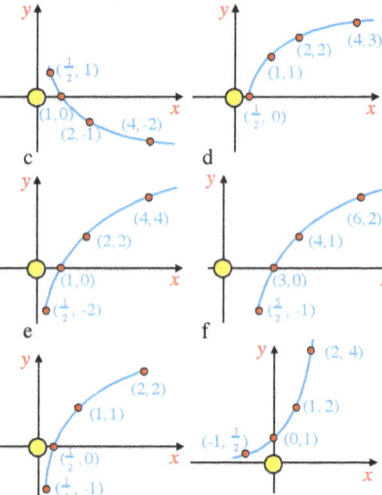

6. a   b

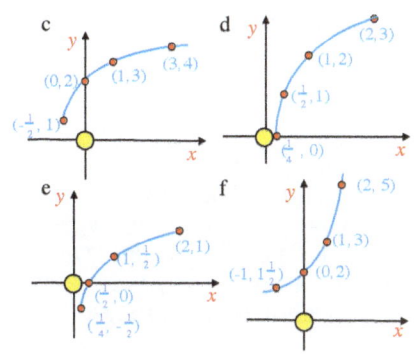

c

(0,2) (1,3) (3,4)
(-½,1)

d

(2,3)
(1,2)
(½,1)
(¼,0)

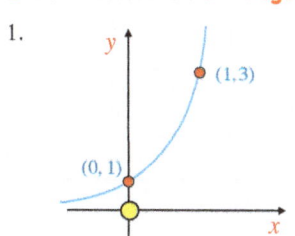

e

(1,½) (2,1)
(½,0)
(¼,-½)

f

(2,5)
(1,3)
(-1,1½) (0,2)

Exam Practice Ch 5 - Page 47

1.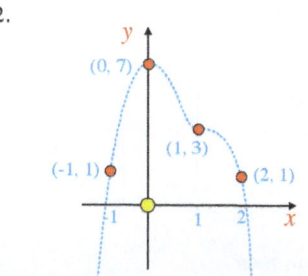

(1,3)
(0,1)

2.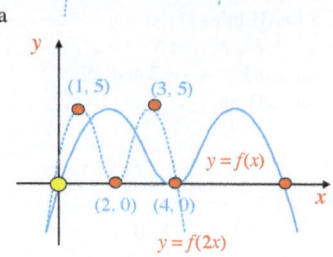

(0,7)
(1,3)
(-1,1) (2,1)

3. a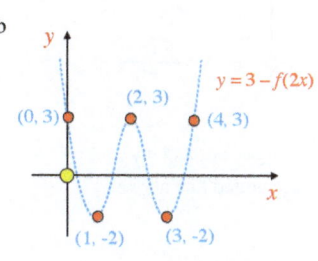

(1,5) (3,5)
$y = f(x)$
(2,0) (4,0)
$y = f(2x)$

b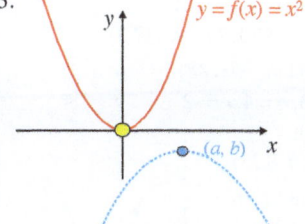

$y = 3 - f(2x)$
(0,3) (2,3) (4,3)
(1,-2) (3,-2)

4. $k = 2$, $a = 3$, $b = -1$

5.

$y = f(x) = x^2$
(a, b)

5. k between -1 and 0 means the graph is reflected over the x-axis and "compressed"

6.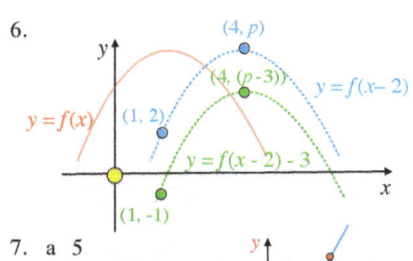

(4, p)
(4, (p-3))
$y = f(x-2)$
$y = f(x)$
(1, 2)
$y = f(x-2) - 3$
(1, -1)

7. a 5
   b see sketch
   c A'(2, 0), B'(5, 2)
   d C'(2, 5)

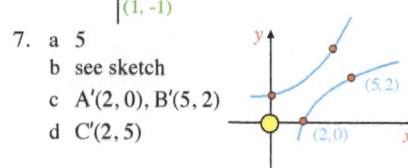

(5, 2)
(2, 0)

Answers to Chapter 6 - Page 48

Revision Exercise - Page 48

1. a 14·1 cm   b 71·6°
   c 13·6 cm
2. a 164·4 cm²   b 80°
3. a 11·7 km   b 27·6°
4. a 15·3 km   b 023·5°
5. a proof
   b 55·7 km   354°

Exercise H6·1 - Page 49

1. $\pi/4$
2. a $\pi/2$ b $3\pi/2$ c $\pi/6$
   d $2\pi/3$ e $7\pi/6$ f $5\pi/3$
   g $3\pi/4$ h $5\pi/4$ i $7\pi/4$
   j $\pi/9$ k 2·57   l 0·026
3. a 22·5°   b 67·5°   c 165°
   d 216°   e 54°   f 105°
   g 24°   h 405°   i 990°

4.

$y = \sin x$
$\pi/2$ π $3\pi/2$ 2π

5. a

$\pi/2$ π $3\pi/2$ 2π

b

$\pi/2$ π $3\pi/2$ 2π

6. $\sin 5\pi/6 = \sin 150° = 0·5$
7. a 1   b 0·707   c 0·5
   d 1·73   e -0·5   f 0
   g 0·966   h -2·414 i -1

Exercise H6·2 - Page 50

1. Practical
2.

	0°	30°	45°	60°	90°
$\sin x°$	0	1/2	1/√2	√3/2	1
$\cos x°$	1	√3/2	1/√2	1/2	0
$\tan x°$	0	1/√3	1	√3	undefined

3. a √3/2   b 1/2   c 1/√3
   d √3/2   e 1/√2   f √3
   g 1   h 1/2   i 1/√2
   j 0   k 1   l undefined
   m 0   n 1   o 0
   p 0   q -1   r undefined

Exercise H6·3 - Page 51

1. a -√3/2   b -√3   c -√3/2   d √3
   e 1/2   f -1   g -1/√2   h -√3
2. a 1/2   b -1/√3 c -1/√3
   d -1/2   e √3/2   f -√3
   g -√3/2   h -1/2   i -1/√2
   j -1   k 1/2   l √3
   m -√3   n 1/√2   0 1
   p 1/√2   q √3   r 1
3. a 1/2   b -1/2   c -√3/2
   d -√3   e 1/√2   f -√3/2
   g 1/√2   h -1   i -1
   j √3   k undefined l -√3/2
4. a 10√3 cm   b 4√3 cm
   c 20√3/3 cm   d 3√2 cm
5. a 1/4   b 1/2   c √6/2   d 3
   e 1/2   f 1   g -√6   h 2/3
   i 0   j 1/2
6. 9/4√3 cm²
7. 25 cm²
8. 20 km
9. 15√2 km
10. 5√6/2 cm
11. a 100√3 cm²   b 6·59°   c 155·5 cm

Exercise H6·4 - Page 54

1. a
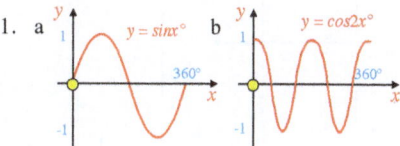
$y = \sin x°$ b $y = \cos 2x°$
360°   360°

c
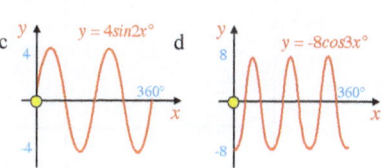
$y = 4\sin 2x°$ d $y = -8\cos 3x°$
360°   360°

e
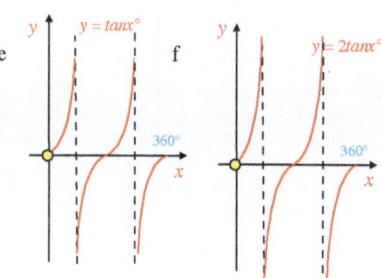
$y = \tan x°$ f $y = 2\tan x°$
360°   360°

1. g

$y = -5sin^{1}/_{2}x°$

(graph with 360°)

h

$y = 0.25cos^{1}/_{3}x°$

(graph with 360°, 0.25, -0.25)

j

$y = 3sin(x - 60)° - 1$

(graph)

k

$y = 2 - cos(x +90)°$

(graph, 360°)

2. a

$y = 4sinx° + 3$

(graph, 7, 3, 360°)

b

$y = 7cosx° - 4$

(graph, 3, -11, 360°)

c

$y = 1 - cos2x°$

(graph, 2, 360°)

d

$y = 10sin3x° - 7$

(graph, 3, -7, -17, 360°)

e

$y = 2.8cos2x° + 3$

(graph, 5.8, 0.2, 180°)

f

$y = \sqrt{2}sin2x° - \sqrt{2}$

(graph, 2√2, √2, 180°)

3. a

$y = 3sin2x° + 5$

(graph, 8, 5, 2, 180°)

b

$y = 15cos3x° - 10$

(graph, 5, -23, π)

c

$y = tan2x° + 3$

(graph, 3, π/2, π)

d

$y = 4cos1.5x° - 6$

(graph, -2, -10, 2π)

e

$y = 2 - 0.5sin2x°$

(graph, 2.5, 2, 1.5, -90°, 90°)

f

$y = 0.25cos2x° + 1$

(graph, 1.25, 1, 0.75, -π, π)

g

$y = 3cos6x° - 2$

(graph, 1, -2, -5, -π)

h

$y = sin(x - 30)°$

(graph, 1, -1, 30°, 210°, 360°)

i

$y = cos(x + 45)° + 1$

(graph, 2, 1, 135°, 360°)

4. a $y = 2cos2x$ b $y = 5sinx°$
  c $y = 4sinx + 4$ d $y = 5cos4x + 5$
  e $y = 4sin^{1}/_{2}x + 2$
  f $y = 1.5cos4x° + 0.5$
  g $y = 4cos10x° - 2$
  h $y = 6sin24x + 3$

5. a $(π/2, -2)$ b $(270°, -5)$
  c $(^{3π}/_{2}, 0)$ d $(π/4, 0)$
  e $(3π, -2)$ f $(45°, -1)$
  g $(18°, -6)$ h $(π/16, -3)$

6. a $y = 4sin(x - 50)°$
  b $y = 3cos(x + π/4) - 2$

7. a $y = 5cos8x° + 2$
  b

$y = 5cos8x° + 2$

(graph, 7, 2, -3, 45°, 90°)

8. b could be 270 or -90, or .....

Exercise H6·5 - Page 55

1. a 60, 300 b 60, 120
  c 30, 210 d 60, 240
  e 225, 315 f 150, 210
  g 45, 135, 225, 315
  h 45, 135, 225, 315
2. a $7π/6$ or $^{11π}/_{6}$
  b $π/6, ^{11π}/_{6}, ^{13π}/_{6}, ^{23π}/_{6}$
  c $π/4$ or $^{3π}/_{4}$ or $^{5π}/_{4}$ or $^{7π}/_{4}$
3. a $π/3$,
  b $^{4π}/_{3}, ^{5π}/_{3}$
  c $-^{π}/_{6}$
  d $^{2π}/_{3}, ^{4π}/_{3}, ^{8π}/_{3}, ^{10π}/_{3}$
4. a 0·93 or 5·36 b 1·01 or 4·15
  c 2·01 d 2·19
5. a 90 b 60, 300
  c 30, 330 d 45, 135
6. a no solution b no solution
7. sin and cos must lie between -1 and 1
8. 15, 75, (and 195, 225)

Exercise H6·6 - Page 56

1. a 22·5, 157·5, 202·5, 337·5
  b 15, 105, 195, 285
  c $^{2π}/_{9}, ^{4π}/_{9}, ^{8π}/_{9}, ^{10π}/_{9}, ^{14π}/_{9}, ^{16π}/_{9}$
  d $π/12, ^{π}/_{6}, ^{7π}/_{12}, ^{2π}/_{3}$
2. a 112·5, 157·5, 292·5, 337·5
  b $π/9, ^{5π}/_{9}, ^{7π}/_{9}$,
  c 36·6, 53·4, 81·6
  d $π/24, ^{5π}/_{24}, ^{7π}/_{24}, ^{11π}/_{24}$

Exercise H6·7 - Page 56

1. a 90, 210 b $π/2, ^{3π}/_{2}$,
  c 20, 110 d $π/24, ^{41π}/_{24}$
  e $π/4, ^{3π}/_{4}$
2. a 30, 90, 210, 270
  b 57·8, 167·3, 237·8, 347·3
3. a 75, 195 b $π/3, ^{π}/_{2}, ^{4π}/_{3}, ^{3π}/_{2}$
  c 65, 125, 185 d 90, 180, 270
  e 0, $^{π}/_{2}$, π, 2πf $^{π}/_{2}, ^{3π}/_{2}$
  g 60,120,240,300 h 90, 210, 330

Exercise H6·8 - Page 57

1. a graph
  b 1 metre
  c 21 metres
  d 10 seconds
  e 5·32 secs

$h = 11 - 10cos18t°$

(graph, h, 21, 11, 1, 10, 20, t)

2. a 6 feet
  b $H = 6 + 4cos200T°$
  c 2·24 metres

3. a graph
  b max = 100 cm
    at 6 am
    min = 20 cm
    at 6 pm

$d = 40sin15t° + 60$

(graph, d, 100, 60, 20, 12, 24, t)

  c 1514 to 2046
  d 5 hrs 31 mins
4. a $a = 4, b = 30, c = 5$
  b set $4sin30t° + 5 = 2$ and solve
    => 7.37pm

Exam Practice Ch 6 Page 58

1. $a = 5, b = 2, c = 1$
2. a $-^{1}/_{2}$ b 0
3. a

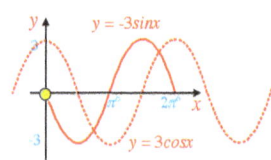

$y = -3sinx$

$y = 3cosx$

  b between $^{3π}/_{2}$ and $2π$
    (see dotted line above)
4. $^{3π}/_{2}$
5. $p = 3, q = ^{π}/_{6}, r = 3$
6. $(^{5π}/_{4}, 1)$
7. a {60, 120, 240, 300}
  b {52·8, 157·3, 232·8, 337·3}
  c {0, $^{π}/_{4}$, π, $^{3π}/_{4}$, 2π}
8. a $p = 3, q = 4, r = -2$ b 78°
9. a graph
  b (i) (0, 8·33)
    (ii) (3·02, 0)
      (4·3, 0)

(graph, y, 9, -1, 2π, x)

10. a $k = 90$
  b {-180, 0, 180}

11. a -3   b $(4\pi/3, -3)$ c $(5\pi/3, 0)$
12. $k = -90$, or 270, or 630, or ....
13. $x = 30, 130$ or 150

Answers to Chapter 7 Page 60

Revision Exercise Page 60

1. a $x = 0, x = 7$ b $x = 0, x = 3$
   c $x = \frac{1}{8}, x = -\frac{1}{8}$ d $x = -6, x = -5$
   e $x = 6, x = -7$ f $x = \frac{2}{5}, x = -5$
   g $x = 1, x = 3$ h $x = 4\frac{1}{2}, x = \frac{1}{2}$
   i $x = 5, x = -7$ j $x = \frac{4}{3}, x = -\frac{2}{3}$,
2. a $x = 0, x = 6$, $x = 3$
   b $x = 3, x = -1$, $x = 1$
   c $x = 4, x = -4$, $x = 0$
   d $x = -4, x = 2$, $x = -1$
   e $x = 1, x = 2$, $x = 1.5$
   f $x = -6, x = 7$, $x = 0.5$.
3. $(-5, 30)$ & $(3, -2)$.
4. $(1, 4)$ & $(-6, -17)$.
5. Proof $(-1, 4)$.
6. No - two points of contact.
7. a $x = -0.7, x = -4.3$
   b $x = 10.2, x = -0.2$
   c $x = 0.85, x = -2.4$
   d $x = 5, x = -1.25$.
8. $b^2 - 4ac < 0$ - No real roots.
9. a 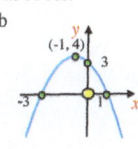   b

10. a $(x - 1)^2 - 1$ b $(x - 1)^2 - 4$
    c $(x + 2)^2 - 3$ d $(s - 3)^2 - 6$
    e $(t - \frac{3}{2})^2 - \frac{17}{4}$ f $(x + 5)^2 - 49$
    g $(x + \frac{5}{2})^2 - \frac{49}{4}$ h $(x + 15)^2 - 200$.

Exercise H7·1 Page 61

1. a $x < -4$ or $x > 2$ b $-3 < x < 4$.
2. a $x < -4$ or $x > -1$ b $2 < x < 10$
   c $x \le -5$ or $x \ge 3$ d $-3 \le x \le 6$
   e $-7 < x < 6$ f $x < -2$ or $x > 12$
   g $x \le -2$ or $x \ge 7$ h $-5 \le x \le 4$
   i $x < -7$ or $x > 0$ j $-\frac{2}{3} < x < \frac{4}{3}$
   k $-\frac{1}{3} \le x \le \frac{3}{2}$ l $-3 \le x \le 1$
   m $x < 1$ or $x > 2\frac{1}{2}$ n $-\frac{1}{2} < x < 5$.

Exercise H7·2 Page 62

1. a Min.T.P., $(3, 4)$, $x = 3$, $(0, 13)$
   b Min.T.P., $(2, -5)$, $x = 2$, $(0, -1)$
   c Min.T.P., $(-1, -1)$, $x = -1$, $(0, 0)$
   d Min.T.P., $(-6, 0)$, $x = -6$, $(0, 36)$
   e Max.T.P., $(-1, 1)$, $x = -1$, $(0, 0)$
   f Max.T.P., $(2, 8)$, $x = 2$, $(0, 4)$
   g Max.T.P., $(4, -1)$, $x = 4$, $(0, -17)$
   h Max.T.P., $(5, 0)$, $x = 5$, $(0, -25)$
   i Min.T.P., $(3, 2)$, $x = 3$, $(0, 20)$
   j Min.T.P., $(1, -1)$, $x = 1$, $(0, 3)$
   k Min.T.P., $(-1, -6)$, $x = -1$, $(0, 2)$

l Max.T.P., $(-3, 1)$, $x = -3$, $(0, -17)$
m Max.T.P., $(-1, 4)$, $x = -1$, $(0, -1)$
n Max.T.P., $(2, 8)$, $x = 2$, $(0, -28)$.
2. a Min.T.P., $(-1, -5)$,
      $x = -1$, $(0, -4)$
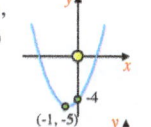

   b Min.T.P., $(1, -4)$,
      $x = 1$, $(0, -3)$
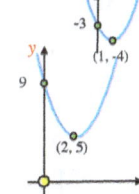

   c Min.T.P., $(2, 5)$,
      $x = 2$, $(0, 9)$
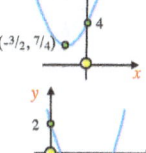

   d Min.T.P., $(-3/2, 7/4)$,
      $x = -3/2$, $(0, 4)$
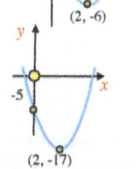

   e Min.T.P., $(2, -6)$,
      $x = 2$, $(0, 2)$
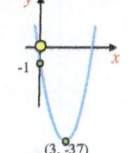

   f Min.T.P., $(2, -17)$,
      $x = 2$, $(0, -5)$
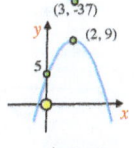

   g Min.T.P., $(3, -37)$,
      $x = 3$, $(0, -1)$
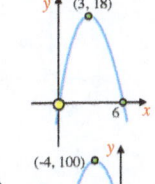

   h Max.T.P., $(2, 9)$,
      $x = 2$, $(0, 5)$
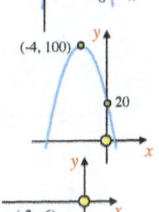

   i Max.T.P., $(3, 18)$,
      $x = 3$, $(0, 0)$
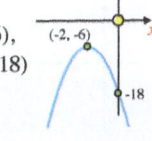

   j Max.T.P., $(-4, 100)$,
      $x = -4$, $(0, 20)$

   k Max.T.P., $(-2, -6)$,
      $x = -2$, $(0, -18)$
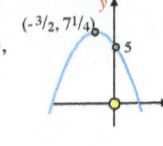

   l Max.T.P., $(-3/2, 7\frac{1}{4})$,
      $x = -3/2$, $(0, 5)$.

Exercise H7·3 Page 63

1. a $y = (x - 1)^2 + 7$ $x = 1$
   b $y = (x + 3)^2 - 1$ $x = -3$
   c $y (x + 4)^2 + 2$ $x = -4$
   d $y = (x - 8)^2 - 2$ $x = 8$
   e $y = 2 - (x - 3)^2$ $x = 3$
   f $y = 5 - (x + 1)^2$ $x = -1$
   g $y = -1 - (x - 6)^2$ $x = 6$
   h $y = 3x^2$ $x = 0$
   i $y = 4x^2$ $x = 0$
   j $y = -2x^2$ $x = 0$.

Exercise H7·4 Page 65

1. a 21   Real & Distinct
   b -15   Not Real
   c 0   Real & Equal
   d 0   Real & Equal
   e 1   Real & Distinct
   f -7   Not Real
   g -15   Not Real
   h -19   Not Real
   i 0   Real & Equal
   j 65   Real & Distinct
   k 57   Real & Distinct
   l -3   Not Real.
2. $b = \pm 12$.
3. $64 - 8m > 0$ $m < 8$.
4. $q = 5$.
5. $d < -3$ or $d > 3$.
6. $h \le -2$ or $h \ge 2$.
7. $v = 7$ or $v = -9$.
8. $20m^2 + 8m \ge 0$.
9. $k < 0$ or $k > 2$.
10. $-1 < n < 1$.
11. a $t = -1$ b $x = 2$.
12. $b^2 - 4ac > 0$ roots real.
13. $ab = 1$.
14. $n < 0.5$ or $n > 4.5$.
15. 5
16. $c < -4$ or $c > 4$.
17. $r < 4$ or $r > 16$.
18. $p = 0$ or $p = 3$.
19. $1 + (2g)^2 > 0$ roots real.
20. Proof
21. a $u = 1$ or $u = 9$ b Not real.
22. $t = \pm 3/4$.
23. Proof $b^2 - 4ac < 0$.
24. $x^2 + (4 - 2c) + 10 - 5c = 0$
    $b^2 - 4ac < 0$ No real roots.

Exercise H7·5 Page 67

1. a $(1, 1)$ b $(1, 0)$
   c $(-1, 2)$ d $(2, 0)$
   e $(1, 10)$ f $(7, 98)$
   g $(1/2, 2)$.
2. a $y = 4x - 4$ b $y = -8x - 8$
   c $y = 4x - 3$ d $y = -\sqrt{20}x - 2$
   e $y = -3x + 4$ f $y = x + 1$.
3. a $y = \pm 6x - 9$ b $y = \pm 4x - 2$
   c $y = \pm 8x$ d $y = \pm 10x + 5$.

4. a $k = -36$ b $(6, -30)$
5. Proof.

Exam Practice Ch 7 Page 67

1. $n = 10$.
2. $x < -4$ or $x > 2$.
3. $q < 7$.
4. $c = 3$.
5. $m^2 + 16 > 0$ Roots real.
6. a $2(x + {}^3/_2)^2 - 7{}^1/_2$.
    b $(-{}^3/_2, -{}^{15}/_2)$
7. $k = 0$ or $k = 36$.
8. $q = -5$ or $q = 3$.
9. a i $(2x + 1)^2 - p$ ii $2(x^2 - p) + 1$
    b i Proof   ii Real, Distinct Roots
       iii $p = 2$.

Answers to Chapter 8 Page 68

Exercise H8·1 Page 68

1. a $inc. x > 0,$ $dec. x < 0$
    b $inc. x > 2,$ $dec. x < 2$
    c $inc. x > 5,$ $dec. x < 5$
    d $inc. x < 0.5,$ $dec. x > 0.5$
    e $inc. x > -5,$ $dec. x < -5$
    f $inc. x > 2,$ $dec. x < 2$
    g $inc. x > 0,$ $dec. x < 0$
    h $inc. x < 0$ or $x > 8, dec. 0 < x < 8$
    i $inc. -1 < x < 1, dec. x < -1$ or $x > 1$
    j $inc. x < 1$ or $x > 2, dec. 1 < x < 2$
    k $inc. x < -1$ or $x > 3, dec. -1 < x < 3$
    l $inc. x < 1$ or $x > 3, dec. 1 < x < 3$
    m $inc. -1 < x < {}^1/_3,$
       $dec. x < -1$ or $x > {}^1/_3$
    n $inc. x < -{}^1/\sqrt{3}$ or $x > {}^1/\sqrt{3},$
       $dec. -{}^1/\sqrt{3} < x < {}^1/\sqrt{3}.$

2. ${}^1/_2 x^2 \geq 0$ never decreasing
3. $(x - 1)^2 \geq 0$ never decreasing
4. $1 + {}^3/x^2 > 0$ for all $x, x \neq 0$
5. $(x - 6)^2 \geq 0$ never decreasing
6. Downhill

Exercise H8·2 Page 69

1. $(0, 0)$ Min T.P.
2. a $(1{}^1/_2, -2{}^1/_4)$ Min T.P.
    b $(0, 10)$ Max T.P.
    c $(0, 4)$ Max T.P.
    d $(-{}^1/_2, 6{}^1/_4)$ Max T.P.
    e $(9, 0)$ Min T.P.
    f $(0, 0)$ Rising P.I.
    g $(-{}^1/_6, 4{}^1/_{12})$ Max T.P.
    h $(0, 4)$ Falling P.I.
3. a $(-\sqrt{2}, 4\sqrt{2})$ Max T.P.
       $(\sqrt{2}, -4\sqrt{2})$ Min T.P.
    b $(1, 2{}^1/_2)$ Max T.P.
       $(2, 2)$ Min T.P.
    c $(1, 4)$ Max T.P.
       $(3, 0)$ Min T.P.
    d $(-1, -2)$ Max T.P.
       $(1, 2)$ Min T.P.
    e $(-2, -4)$ Min T.P.

$(0, 0)$ Max T.P.
$(2, -4)$ Min T.P.
f $(0, 6)$ Min T.P.
   $(1, 7)$ Max T.P.
g $(0, 2)$ Max T.P.
   $(8, -254)$ Min T.P.
h $(-2, 4)$ Max T.P.
   $(-{}^1/_2, -{}^{11}/_4)$ Min T.P.
i $(-1, -4)$ Min T.P.
   $(-3, 0)$ Falling P.I.
j $(1, 3)$ Min T.P.
k $(0, 0)$ Rising P.I.
   $(6, 432)$ Max T.P.
l $(1, -1)$ Min T.P.

Exercise H8·3 Page 70

1. a 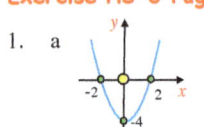   b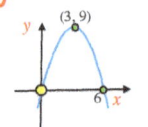

    c 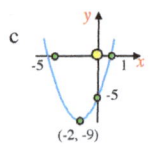   d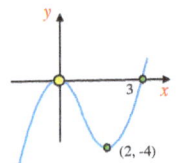

    e 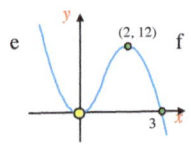   f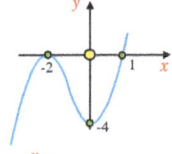

2. a 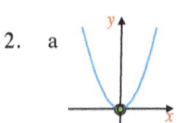   b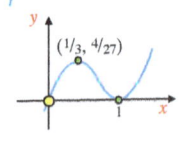

    c   d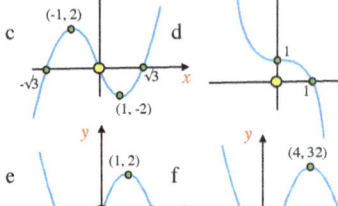

    e   f

    g   h

    i   j

    k   l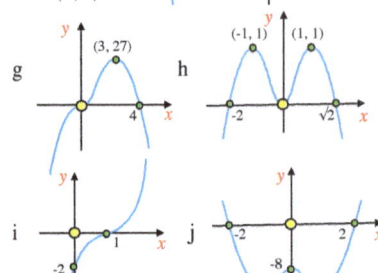
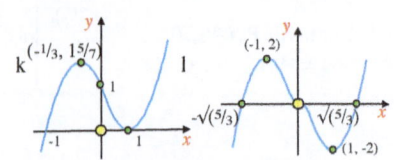

m 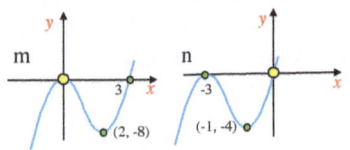   n

Exercise H8·4 Page 71

1. Max. Value 0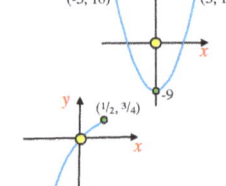
    Min. Value -9

2. Max. Value 16
    Min. Value -9

3. Max. Value ${}^3/_4$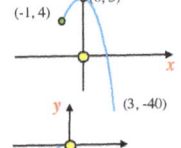
    Min. Value -3

4. Max. Value 5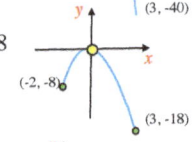
    Min. Value -40

5. Max. Value 0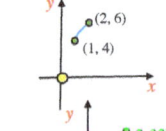
    Min. Value -18

6. Max. Value 6
    Min. Value 4

7. Max. Value 32
    Min. Value -7

8. Max. Value 9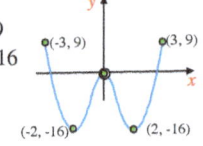
    Min. Value -16

Exercise H8·5 Page 72

1. a $p + q = 70$ b $A = 70p - p^2$
    c 35 m by 35 m 1225 m^2 .
2. a $x + y = 60$ $P = x(60 - x)$
    b 900.
3. 19600 metres.
4. a Proof   b $x = 3$ 13·5 cm^2 .
5. a Proof
    b $x = 1.5$ 54 cm^3 .
6. a 10 m^3 b £580.
7. a Proof
    b Proof and V$_{max}$ = 166$^2/_3$ cm^3
8. £36 million.
9. a $6p + 4q$
    b Proof
    c $p = 40, q = 60$ 19200 m^2 .
10. a Proof
    b 10 mph   750 tonnes.

1. a   b

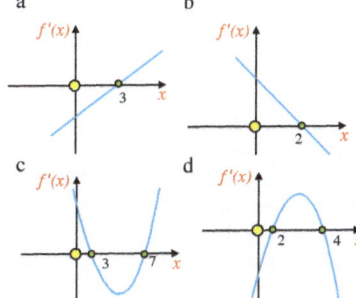

c   d

e   f

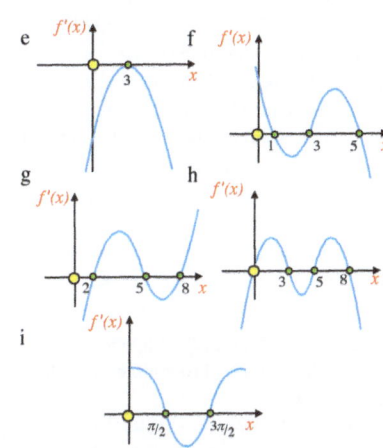

g   h

i

Exam Practice Ch 8 Page 75

1. Stationary point at $x = 0$.
   $(0, 1)$ Min. T.P.
2. Max. Value 3   Min. Value -0·5.
3. a $x = 4$
   b Max. Value 16   Min. Value 0.
4. a $3x^2 + 24x + 48$
   b $(x + 4)^2 \geq 0$ strictly increasing.
5. a $x = 2, x = -4$
   b $-4 < x < 2$.
6. a Min T.P. $(0, 0)$ Max. T.P. $(2, 8)$
   b $(0, 0)$ & $(3, 0)$.

7.

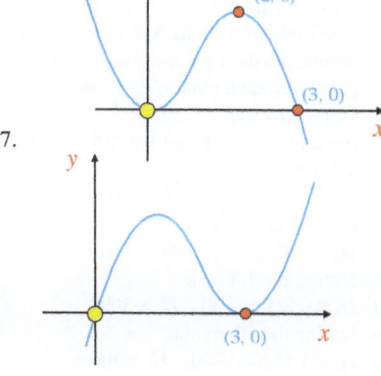

8. a $(0, 0), (\sqrt{6}, 0), (-\sqrt{6}, 0)$

b (i)

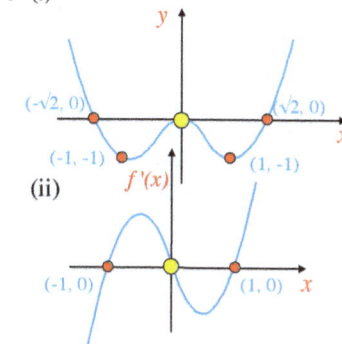

(ii)

9. Proof   b $a = 7·5$.
10. 4 km/hr, £250.
11. a $A = 180x - x^2$
    b $x = 90$
    c 8100 cm².

Answers to Chapter 9 Page 76

Exercise H9·1 Page 76

1. a $x^2 + y^2 = 9$
   b $x^2 + y^2 = 100$
   c $x^2 + y^2 = 16$
   d $x^2 + y^2 = 2$
   e $x^2 + y^2 = 50$
   f $x^2 + y^2 = 13$
   g $x^2 + y^2 = 2·25$
   h $x^2 + y^2 = 57·76$
   i $x^2 + y^2 = 1/4$
2. a $r = 8$ b $r = 7$
   c $r = 1$ d $r = 12$
3. a $r = \sqrt{10}$ b $r = 5\sqrt{2}$
   c $r = 2\sqrt{30}$ d $r = 20\sqrt{5}$
4. a $x^2 + y^2 = 25$ b $x^2 + y^2 = 169$
   c $x^2 + y^2 = 29$ d $x^2 + y^2 = 170$
   e $x^2 + y^2 = 5$ f $x^2 + y^2 = 5$
5. $x^2 + y^2 = 36$
6. Blue $x^2 + y^2 = 16$ Red $x^2 + y^2 = 25$
   Green $x^2 + y^2 = 56·25$
7. a on   b inside
   c on   d outside
   e inside   f inside
8. a $a = \pm4$ b $= \pm6$
   c $c = \pm1$ d $d = 0$ or $d = -1$
   e $e = \pm\sqrt{5}$
9. Vert/horiz lines would produce 2
   intercept values
   (unless line misses or is tangent to circle)
10. $x^2 + y^2 = 100$
11. P is inside zone   Q on radar perimeter
    R outside zone
12. a $x^2 + y^2 = 100$ b proof

Exercise H9·2 Page 77

1. a $(x - 2)^2 + (y - 5)^2 = 25$
   b $(x - 6)^2 + (y - 3)^2 = 49$
   c $(x + 1)^2 + (y - 4)^2 = 1$
   d $(x + 3)^2 + (y + 2)^2 = 100$

e $x^2 + (y + 7)^2 = 2$
f $(x + 8)^2 + (y + 2)^2 = 45$
g $(x - k)^2 + (y + 2k)^2 = t$
h $(x + 31)^2 + (y - 12)^2 = 8$
2. a $C(4, 1)$ $r = 2$
   b $C(11, 10)$ $r = 3$
   c $C(-2, 3)$ $r = \sqrt{10}$
   d $C(0, -2)$ $r = \sqrt{2}$
   e $C(k, z)$ $r = \sqrt{w}$
   f $C(\sqrt{5}, -\sqrt{2})$ $r = 1$
   g $C(2, -3)$ $r = 2$
3. a $r = 5$
   b $(x - 5)^2 + (y - 4)^2 = 25$
   c $Q(2, 0)$
4. a $(x - 4)^2 + (y - 1)^2 = 169$
   b $(x - 5)^2 + y^2 = 100$
   c $(x + 1)^2 + (y - 3)^2 = 26$
   d $(x + 3)^2 + (y + 5)^2 = 125$
5. a $C(6, 6)$
   b $(x - 6)^2 + (y - 6)^2 = 25$
6. a $(x + 3)^2 + (y + 5)^2 = 25$
   b $(0, -1)$ and $(0, -9)$
7. $x^2 + y^2 + 14x - 12y + 85 = 0$

Exercise H9·3 Page 79

1. $C(-6, -1)$ $r = \sqrt{17}$
2. a $C(-5, -1)$ $r = \sqrt{23}$
   b $C(-8, -10)$ $r = \sqrt{162}$
   c $C(6, -2)$ $r = \sqrt{33}$
   d $C(1, 3)$ $r = \sqrt{21}$
   e $C(1/2, -3/2)$ $r = 11\,1/2$
3. a $x^2 + y^2 - 10x + 10y + 25 = 0$
   b $x^2 + y^2 - 16x + 10y = 0$
4. $c = -60$
5. $x^2 + y^2 - 6x + 14y - 87 = 0$
6. $x^2 + y^2 - 6y - 9 = 0$
7. a $r = -\sqrt{9}$ not a real circle
   b yes
8. $(x + 6)^2 + (y + 1)^2 = 17/4$ **or**
   $x^2 + y^2 + 12x + 2y + 32\,3/4 = 0$
9. $x^2 + y^2 - 2x - 2y - 11 = 0$
10. $x^2 + y^2 - 6x + 2y + 2 = 0$
11. $(1, -7)$
12. $(-2, -4)$

Exercise H9·4 Page 80

1. 2. 3. see diagrams
4. $(3\sqrt{2}, 3\sqrt{2})$ and $(-3\sqrt{2}, -3\sqrt{2})$
5. a $(4, 8)$ and $(-4, -8)$
   b $(4, 3)$ and $(-3, -4)$
   c $(3, 3)$ and $(7, 7)$
   d $(2, 10)$ and $(-2, -2)$
   e $(-1, -4)$ and $(-7, 2)$
   f $(1, -1)$ and $(-13, -15)$
   g $(2, -3)$ and $(8\,2/5, 1/5)$
6. $(0, 0)$ and $(7, 7)$
7. $(0, 0), (0, 6)$ and $(8, 0)$
8. a $(-5, -3)$ b $\sqrt{32}$
   c $(x + 5)^2 + (y + 3)^2 = 32$
   d $(-0·2, 0)$ and $(-9·8, 0)$

9. a $x^2 + y^2 - 2x - 6y - 8 = 0$
   b CD: $y = -x + 4$
   c $(4, 0)$ and $(-2, 6)$
10. $x = 4$, $x = -4$, $y = 4$, $y = -4$

Exercise H9·5 Page 81

1. a Proof   b $(1, 3)$
2. a Proof   b $(2, 3)$
3. a $(-1, 3)$ b $(-1, 1)$
   c $(4, 0)$ d $(3, -2)$
4. a $y = 2$ tangent at $(3, 2)$
   b $m = ^2/_3$
   c $m = -^3/_2$,
5. a Proof
   b Centre $(1, 5)$ $y = -^4/_3 x + ^{44}/_3$
6. a Proof   b $y = ^3/_4 x - ^{19}/_4$
7. a Proof   b $y = -4x + 29$
8. $y = -^4/_3 x + 15$
9. a $y = 4x - 11$
   b $y = 4x + 6$
10. a A : $y = ^3/_4 x + 6$
    B : $y = -^4/_3 x - ^7/_3$
    b $(-4, 3)$
11. a $(0, 4)$
    b $y = -^4/_3 x + 4$

Exercise H9·6 Page 83

1. a on   b outside
   c outside   d on
2. a $(x - 3)^2 + (y + 2)^2 = 36$
     $x^2 + y^2 - 6x + 4y - 23 = 0$
   b $(x - \sqrt{3})^2 + (y - 7)^2 = 100$
     $x^2 + y^2 - 2\sqrt{3}x - 14y - 48 = 0$
   c $(x + 1)^2 + (y + 4)^2 = 41$
     $x^2 + y^2 + 2x + 8y - 24 = 0$
3. a $C_1(-2, 3)$ $r = \sqrt{11}$
     $C_2(4, -1)$ $r = \sqrt{5}$
   b $2\sqrt{13}$
   c $y = -^2/_3 x + ^5/_3$
   d $y = ^3/_2 x - ^1/_2$
4. $(3, 3)$ and $(-4, -4)$
5. $y = -x + 3$
6. Proof   tangent at $(1, -3)$
7. $c = -116$
8. $(0, 3)$
9. a $t = 1$
   b $x = 3$ (vertical line)
10. a yes   b $(1, 3)$
11. $(x + 7)^2 + (y - 4)^2 = 169$
12. $y = ^4/_3 x + ^5/_3$
13. $c = 12$ or -8
14. $m = ^4/_3$ or $-^4/_3$
15. a Proof and tangent is $y = -^1/_3(x + 8)$ and
      this can be shown to be a tangent to
      the 2nd circle at the point $(-2, -2)$.
    b $\sqrt{10}$

Exam Practice Ch 9 Page 84

1. $0 < c < 16$
2. a $(x - 3)^2 + (y - 1)^2 = 25$
   b $m_{CT} = ^3/_4$ c $y = -^4/_3 x - ^{10}/_3$
3. a $C_1(-1, 3)$ $r = 3$
     $C_2(5, -1)$ $r = 2$
   b Proof $(3 + 2 < 2\sqrt{13})$
   c $2\sqrt{13} - 5$
4. a $y = ^1/_2 x + 2$
   b $x^2 + y^2 + 4x + 4y = 0$
5. a A$(3, -3)$ B$(5, -7)$
   b $y = ^1/_2 x - 7$ c Proof
   d C$(4, 0)$, D$(12, -6)$ or C$(12, 0)$, D$(4, -6)$
6. a T$(1, -1)$ b $y = -^3/_4 x - ^1/_4$
   c $(x - 1)^2 + (y + 1)^2 = 100$
7. a Proof   b $(-3, -2)$
8. $(1, -8)$
9. $0 < k \le 6$
10. a $y = -^1/_2 x + 6$ b $k = 4$
    c $(x - 4)^2 + (y - 4)^2 = 25$
11. $(6, 12)$ and $(-2, -4)$

Answers to Chapter 10 Page 86

Exercise H10·1 - Page 86

1. a $4, 8, 12, 16$ b $4, 9, 14, 19$
   c $2, 6, 12, 20$ d $2, 5, 10, 17$
   e $2, 4, 8, 16$ f $2, 1, ^2/_3, ^1/_2$
   g $0, 1, 3, 6$ h $9, 8, 7, 6$
   i $6, 24, 60, 120$ j $0, 7, 26, 63$
   k $^1/_2, ^1/_6, ^1/_{12}, ^1/_{20}$ l $-1, 1, -1, 1$
2. a $^1/_2, ^2/_3, ^3/_4, ^4/_5, ... ^{10}/_{11}$
   b 1
3. a $1, 4, 9, 16, ... n^2$ - they are all squares
4. a $u_n = 3n$ b $u_n = 5n + 2$
   c $u_n = 3n + 17$ d $u_n = 73 - 3n$
   e $u_n = 10n - 9$ f $u_n = 92 - 12n$
   g $u_n = 0.4n + 6.3$ h $u_n = n^2$
   i $u_n = n^3$ j $u_n = 2^n$
   k $u_n = 3^{n-1}$ l $u_n = n(n + 1)$
   m $u_n = ^1/_{n+1}$ n $u_n = ^n/_{(n+1)}$

Exercise H10·2 - Page 87

1. a $8, 11, 14, 17$ b $13, 18, 23, 28$
   c $19, 26, 33, 40$ d $48, 46, 44, 42$
   e $70, 60, 50, 40$
2. a 8 b 13 c $18, 23$
3. a $8, 11, 14, 17$ b $70, 60, 50, 40$
   c $48, 46, 44, 42$ d $19, 26, 33, 40$
4. $u_n = u_{n-1} + 3$ matches $u_n = 3n + 5$
   $u_n = u_{n-1} + 7$ matches $u_n = 7n + 12$
   $u_n = u_{n-1} - 2$ matches $u_n = 50 - 2n$
   $u_n = u_{n-1} - 10$ matches $u_n = 80 - 10n$
5. a $6, 18, 54, 162, 486$
   b $75, 56.25, ..., 23.7304..$
   c $20, 80, 320, 1280, 5120$
   d $2.4, 1.92, 1.536, ..., 0.98304$
6. (b) and (d) appear to approach a limit,
   because the multiplication factor in both
   these cases (0.75 and 0.8) is < 1

Exercise H10·3 - Page 88

1. a $u_n = 5 \times 3^n$ b $u_n = 510 \times 2^n$
   c $u_n = 4 \times 5^n$
2. $u_n = 2 \times 4^{n-1}$ => $u_{10} = 524288$
3. a $u_n = 2 + 4n$ b $u_n = 5 + 7n$
   c $u_n = 40 - 2n$
4. $u_n = 2 + 6n$ => $u_{50} = 302$
5. a loses 12% means 88% (0.88) remains
   b starting value
   c V_1 will be the end of year 1 so
     V_0 will be the end of year 0 (the start)
   d $V_n = 9000 \times (0.88)^n$
   e $V_4 = £5397$ (approx)
   f after 8 years (£3237 approx)
6. a $V_n = 0.85 \times V_{n-1}$, $V_0 = 28000$
   b $V_n = 28000 \times (0.85)^n$ => $V_5 = £12424$
7. a If 8% is added on, the new value is
     108% (1.08) times the old value
   b $A_n = 5000 \times (1.08)^n$ => $A_7 = £8569$
8. a $P_n = 1.13 \times P_{n-1}$
   b 346 (approx)   c 6 minutes
9. a $P_n = 1.02 \times P_{n-1}$, $P_0 = 611$ (million)
   b $P_n = 611 \times (1.02)^n$ => $A_{10} = 745$ million
10. a $C_n = 0.91 \times C_{n-1}$, $C_0 = 250$
    b $C_n = 250 \times (0.91)^n$
      after 7 hours, 129 couples
      after 8 hours, 118 couples => 8 hours
11. a £180
    b $V_n = 1.5V_{n-5}$, $V_0 = 120$
    c $V_n = 120 \times (1.5)^{n-5}$ (where n is in
      multiples of 5)
    d $V_6 = 120 \times (1.5)^6$ => $V_6 = £1367$ (approx)
12. a $V_n = 0.95V_{n-1}$, $V_0 = 2000$ ml
    b $V_n = 2000 \times (0.95)^n$
    c After 14 hours, vol = 975 ml (approx)

Exercise H10·4 - Page 91

1. a $7.5, 10.25, 13.275, 16.6025, ...$ (no)
   b $45, 41.5, 39.05, 37.335, ...(33.3)$
   c $9, 10.5, 12.75, 16.125, ...$ (no)
   d $25.5, 34.025, 38.71375, ... (44.4)$
   e $16.8, 38.88, 74.208, 130.733, ...$ (no)
   f $10.4, 10.08, 10.016, 10.0032, ...$ (10)
2. a (b), (d) and (f)
   b these 3 have a multiplication factor < 1,
     the others do not
3. a The 1.03 refers to the 3% increase each
     month and the 10 is the amount she
     pays back each month. B_0 is cost of coat
   b 10 months and
   c the coat will have cost her £10 + £6.31
     = £106.31.
4. a $P_n = 1.05P_{n-1} - 55$, $P_0 = 2000$
   b During the 5th hour
5. a $D_n = 0.7D_{n-1} + 25$, $D_0 = 150$
   b During the 4th hour
6. a $H_n = 0.8H_{n-1} + 50$, $H_0 = 3000$
   b During the 4th minute
7. a $H_n = 1.15H_{n-1} - 40$, $H_0 = 300$
   b about 334 centimetres
8. a $V_n = 1.075V_{n-1} + 50$, $V_0 = 50$
   b About £362

Exercise H10·5 - Page 93

1. a $60, 56, 53·6, 52·16,$ Yes, 150
   b $30, 31·4, 32·6.., 33·7..,$ Yes, 41·67
   c $25, 25·5, 26·31, 27·62…$ No
   d $20, 19, 18·25, 17·6875, ..$ Yes, 16
   e $30, 50, 76·7, 112·2…,$ No
   f $50, 25, 22·5, 22·25, ..$ Yes 22·22..

2. $L_n = 0·85L_{n-1} + 30$, $L_0 = 260$
   Limit = 200 => but drops to 170, then rises back to 170 etc which is more than 65% (169)

3. $W_n = 0·88W_{n-1} + 1$, $L_0 = 10$
   Safe as limit = 8·33.., and does not drop below 7·33.. litres

4. $P_n = 0·8P_{n-1} + 800$, $P_0 = 10000$
   a 8800, 7840, 7072
   b Eventually, they will be left with about 4000 pumpkins (the limit)

5. $W_n = 0·82W_{n-1} + 30$, $W_0 = 180$
   Limit = 166·666. but the pressure will drop to 0·82 of this = 136·7, so it will become unsafe at some point

6. $W_n = 0·96W_{n-1} + 2·5$, $W_0 = 76$
   Limit = 62·5, but if the dog then loses 4%, its weight just tips the 60 kg mark, so yes, it could reach this goal

7. $L_n = 0·8L_{n-1} + 100$, $L_0 = 500$
   The limit is 500, so the litter will remain about the same as it started.

8. a $P_n = 0·85P_{n-1} + 40$, $L_0 = 360$
   b 346, 334, 323, 315
   b The limit is 267 in the long run

Exercise H10·6 - Page 94

1. $a = 3$, $b = -2$, $u_4 = 28$, $u_5 = 82$
2. $a = 1/2$, $b = 16$, $u_1 = 16$, $u_2 = 24$
3. $a = 0·8$, $b = 6$, $L = 30$
4. $a = 0·1$, $b = 80$, $L = 88·888…$
5. $u_4 = -4$, $u_5 = 12$, $u_6 = -20$, $u_7 = 44$
6. a $a = 4$, $b = 0$, $u_3 = 192$, $u_4 = 768$
   b $u_n = 3 \times 4^n$
7. $b = 12$
8. $b = 12$
9. $a = 3/10$
10. $a = 3/5$

Exam Practice Ch 10 - Page 95

1. a $a = 1/3$
   b since $-1 < 1/3 < 1$ it has a limit of 6
2. a proof   b $p \le -1·5$ or $p \ge 2$
3. a $-2 < a < 0$ b $a = -1/5$
4. a $u_5 = -16$
   b/c since $-1 < -1/2 < 1$ it has a limit $-16/3$
5. a since $-1 < 2/3 < 1$ it has a limit
   since $-1 < 3/4 < 1$ it has a limit
   b Proof
6. $2 < a < 3$
7. a for $0 < x < \pi/2$ => $0 < sin^2x < 1$
   b proof
8. a $A = 3/2$ and $B = 4$
   b (i) $L = 3$ (ii) $a = 3/2 > 1$ so no limit

---

9. a $-1 < a < 1$
   b Limit is $1 + m$ => lies between 0 and 2
10. a $p = 2/3, q = 3/2$
    b If $q = 3/2$ => no limit exists

Answers to Chapter 11 Page 96

Exercise H11·1 Page 97

1. a $1/2x^2 + C$ b $1/3x^3 + C$
   c $1/4x^4 + C$ d $1/7x^7 + C$
   e $1/11x^{11} + C$ f $2x^2 + C$
   g $5/3x^3 + C$ h $7/4x^4 + C$
   i $-8/3x^3 + C$ j $12x + C$
   k $-x^{-1} + C$ l $-1/3x^{-3} + C$
   m $-1/6x^{-6} + C$ n $-1/3x^{-3} + C$
   o $4x^{-2} + C$ p $2/3x^{3/2} + C$
   q $2/7x^{7/2} + C$ r $2x^{1/2} + C$
   s $-2/5x^{-5/2} + C$ t $8x^{1/2} + C$
   u $3/2x^{2/3} + C.$

2. a $1/6x^6 + C$
   b $3/2x^2 - 2x + C$
   c $5x - 1/2x^2 + C$
   d $1/3x^3 - 2x + C$
   e $2x - 5/4x^4 + C$
   f $2/3x^3 + 5/2x^2 - 4x + C$
   g $8/3x^3 - 7x + C$
   h $3x^5 - x^3 + C$
   i $1/3x^3 - 9x + C$
   j $1/3x^3 - 4x^2 + 16x + C$
   k $x - 6x^2 + 12x^3 + C$
   l $1/4x^4 + 1/3x^3 - x^2 + C.$

3. a $-1/x + C$
   b $-3/7x^7 + C$
   c $4/5x^{5/4} + C$
   d $6/5x^{5/3} + C$
   e $-15/2x^{-2/3} + C$
   f $2x^3 + 2x + C$
   g $4x - 1/2x^2 + C$
   h $1/3x^3 - 4x - 4/x + C$
   i $1/3x^3 - x + C$
   j $-5/2x^2 - 1/2x^2 + C$
   k $-1/x + x + C$
   l $2/13x^{13/2} - 2x^{1/2} + C$
   m $3x^3 + 6/x - 1/5x^5 + C$
   n $4x^2 - 4/3x^{3/2} + C$
   o $2/5x^{5/2} - x^2 + 2/3x^{3/2} + C$
   p $16/3x^3 - 48/x - 36/5x^5 + C$
   q $14/5x^{5/2} - 10/3x^{3/2} + C$
   r $1/3x^3 - x^2 + x + C.$

4. a $f(x) = 3x^2 + 4$
   b $f(x) = 2x^2 - 2x - 2$
   c $f(x) = -5x^2 + x + 39$

---

   d $f(x) = 3x^3 + 4$
   e $f(x) = 4x^5 + 9$
   f $f(x) = 1/2x^2 + 2/x + 1$
   g $f(x) = 2\sqrt{x} + x - 4$
   h $f(x) = 2x^3 - 6x$
   i $f(x) = x^3 + 3/x + 1/2$
   j $f(x) = x - 4/5x^{5/4}.$

5. a $1/5t^5 + 3/2t^2 + C$
   b $16v + 16/5v^{5/2} + 1/4v^4 + C$
   c $s^2 + 2/5s^{5/2} + C$
   d $2/3h^{3/2} - 12/5h^{5/2} + C$
   e $-2/z - 2/z_{1/2} + C$
   f $-6/p^{1/2} + 30p^{1/2} + C$

Exercise H11·2 Page 98

1. a $y = 3/2x^2 + 1$
   b $y = 3x^2 - 11$
   c $y = 2x^2 - 3x + 5$
   d $y = x^3 - 3x^2 + 6$
   e $y = 3x^3 - 4x^2 - 3x + 8$
   f $y = 2x^3 - 3/2x^2 - 1/2$
2. 13.
3. Proof
4. $y = -x^2 + 8x - 16.$
5. $y = -x^3 + 3x^2 - 11.$
6. $y = x + 5/x - 2.$
7. $s = 7t - t^2.$
8. $v = 1/3t^3 + 3/2t^2$ 126 m/sec.
9. Proof.
10. $y = -2x^2 + x + 8.$

Exercise H11·3 Page 100

1. a $\int_1^3 3x \, dx$ b $\int_{-1}^2 (x + 2) dx$
   c $\int_{-2}^1 (3 - x) dx$ d $\int_1^2 x^2 \, dx$
   e $\int_{-2}^2 (x^2 - 4) dx$ f $\int_0^4 x(4 - x) dx$
   g $\int_0^2 3x^2 \, dx$ h $\int_1^3 x^3 \, dx$
   i $\int_\pi^{2\pi} sin \, 2x \, dx$ j $\int_1^2 \frac{12}{x^2} dx,$

2. a   b

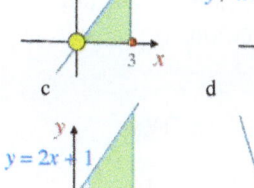

---

e   f

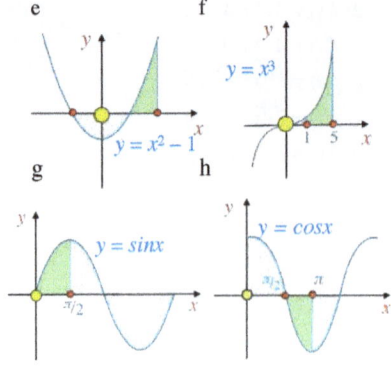

g   h

Exercise H11·4 Page 101

1. 3
2. 51
3. a 12   b $2/7$ c 7
    d $3^3/4$ e 23   f $3/4$
    g 60   h $4/9$ i $5^1/3$
    j $1^{17}/24$ k $15/64$ l $33^3/4$
    m 4   n 18   o $10^2/3$
    p $1^5/6$ q 8   r $15^2/3$
    s $4981^1/2$
    t $1^3/4$
    u $1/4p^4 – 1/2p^2$
    v $1/2a^2 + 4/3a^{3/2} + a$.
4. a $3/4$ b $-3/8$ c $-3/4$
    d $-7^1/2$ e $10^1/4$ f 8
    g $6^1/4$ h $-3^1/3$ i $1/6$
    j 304   k $2/9\pi^2$ l $3\pi/2$.
5. a 2   b 3   c 2
    d 8   e 3   f 2.
6. a 9   b 0, $1/2$ c 3
    d -3, 4   e 0, 1   f 2.
7. a/b/c   Proofs.

Exercise H11·5 Page 103

All answers to areas are in *squared units*.

1. a 12   b 12   c 8   d 12.
2. a $4^1/2$ b $2^2/3$
    c $17^1/3$ d 4
    e $5^1/3$ f 12
    g $4^1/2$ h $14\sqrt{7}/3$.
3. a $10^2/3$ b $20^5/6$ c $1^1/3$.
4. 9.
5. $2^2/3$ & $11^1/3$.
6. $x = -3, 0$ & 3, $40^1/2$.
7. $x = -2, 0$ & 2,   8.
8. P(1, 0), Q(4, 0), R(0, 4), $6^1/3$.
9. A(1, 0), B(7, 0), C(0, -7), $39^1/3$.
10. $2^3/4$.
11. Proof.
12. a $3/4$ b $1^3/5$.

Exercise H11·6 Page 105

All answers to areas are in *squared units*.

1. a $4^1/2$ b $1^1/3$.

2. a 8   b $1/6$
    c $4^1/2$ d $1/2$
    e $1/12$ f $1/6$
    g $10^2/3$ h $21^1/3$
    i $21^1/3$ j 36
    k $5^1/3$ l $1^1/3$
    m $20^5/6$ n $41^2/3$
    o $19^1/5$.
3. a P(-1, 0), Q(3, 0), R(0, 3)
    b $4^1/2$.
4. a K(-2, 0), L(2, 0),
    b £460.
5. a A(0, 5), B(2, 9),
    b $21^1/3$
    c $a = 10, b = -1$.

Exercise H11·7 Page 106

All answers to areas are in *squared units*.

1. a $1/4x^4 – 1/3x^3 – 3x^2 + C$
    b $1/2x^2 – x + C$
    c $-1/2x^{-2} + 1/9x^{-3} + C$
    d $2x^{1/2} – 2x^{-1/2} + C$.
2. a $2x^2 + 8/3x^{3/2} + x + C$
    b $2x^3 – x^{-2} + C$
    c $-1/4x^{-1} + 2x^{-2} + C$
    d $6/5x^{5/2} – 8/3x^{3/2} + 10x^{1/2} + C$.
3. a 12   b $15^3/4$.
4. $5^2/3$.
5. $y = 2x^2 + 4/x – 1$.
6. $a – 2$
7.

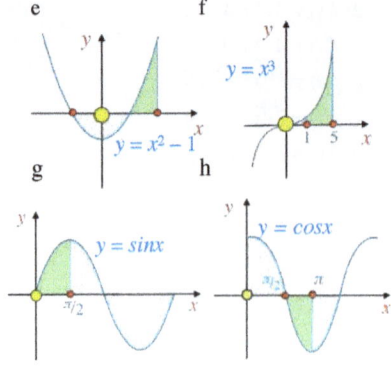

8. $3^1/12$.
9. a $21^1/3$ b 1 : 7.
10. a $y = 3x + 16$ b 108.
11. $69^1/3$.
12. a $10^2/3$ b 1 : 3.
13. a $a = 1, b = 2$,   b $5^1/6$.

Exam Practice Ch 11 – Page 107

1. a $5/3x^3 – 3x^2 + C$
    b $-1/16x^{-4} + C$.
2. a $16/3x^{3/2} – 1/3x^3 + C$
    b $3x^2 + 1/x + C$.
3. $y = -4x^3 + 3x^2 – 7$.
4. $g(x) = 4/3x^{3/2} – 2x^{1/2} – 2$.
5. $T = 1/32t^2 – 2t + 90$.
6. (-2, 10) & (2, 10), 32 sq. units.
7. $49^1/3$ sq. units.

8. a
    $$\int_0^z \left(x^{\frac{1}{2}} – x^2 \right) dx$$
    $$\int_z^1 \left(x^{\frac{1}{2}} – x^2 \right) dx$$
    b Proof.
9. $18^2/3$ sq. units.
10. a 360 m²   b 90 m².

Answers to Chapter 12 Page 108

Exercise H12·1 Page 108

1. a 5   b 3   c 7
    d 1   e 3   f 4.
2. a $2 – x^2 + x^3 + x^4$ 4
    b $7 + 2x + 3x^2 + x^3$ 3
    c $-x + x^3$ 3
    d $25 – 20x + 4x^2$ 2.
3. a $3x^4 – x^2 + x – 1$ 4
    b $-3x^8 + 5x^2 + 7x + 4$ 8
    c $25x^2 – 40x + 16$ 2
    d $x^4 – 18x^3 + 81x^2$ 4.
4. a -2   b 21   c -2   d 0.
5. a $6(3x – 4)$ b $8x(2x – 5)$
    c $(7x – 4)(7x + 4)$
    d $x(x + 1)(5x – 2)$.
6. a $x = ±9$
    b $x = -2, x = 0, x = 2$
    c $t = 2, t = 7$
    d $a = -2, a = 1/3$.
7. a 9   b 5   c -2   d -10.
8. a 2   b 0   c -75.

Exercise H12·2 Page 109

1. 54.
2. a 27   b 3   c 126
    d 219   e -187.
3. a 7   b 248   c 11   d 1246
    e 45   f 67   g 5   h 4
    i $10^3/4$ j -3.

Exercise H12·3 Page 110

1. a $2x + 5$ R11
    b $8x – 44$ R231
    c $x^2 + 4x + 5$ R19
    d $2x^2 + x – 6$ R18
    e $x^2 + 7x + 32$ R164
    f $7x^3 – 9x^2 + 17x – 18$ R38
    g $x^2 – 5x + 16$ R-72
    h $x^3 – x^2$ R3
    i $10x^5 – 30x^4 + 30x^3 – 30x^2 + 30x$
                     $– 50$ R $– 10$.

2. a $6x + 9$ R27
        $(x - 2)(6x + 9) + 27$
    b $x^2 - 2x - 2$ R11
        $(x + 2)(x^2 - 2x - 2) + 11$
    c $4x^2 + 7x + 21$ R62
        $(x - 3)(4x^2 + 7x + 21) + 62$
    d $5x^2 + 13x + 25$ R59
        $(x - 2)(5x^2 + 13x + 25) + 59$
    e $x^3 + 4x^2 + 15x + 61$ R242
        $(x - 4)(x^3 + 4x^2 + 15x + 61) + 242$

3. 0 remainder. $(x + 3)$ is a factor.

4. a 3   b 1   c 28
    d -6   e 2   f -36.

5. a $(3x - 1)(x^2 + 3x - 2) + 6$
        Quotient $(x^2 + 3x - 2)$ R6
    b $(2x + 1)(x^2 + 3x - 4) + 12$
        Quotient $(x^2 + 3x - 4)$ R12
    c $(2x + 3)(x^2 - 2x + 3) - 10$
        Quotient $(x^2 - 2x + 3)$ R -10
    d $(3x - 4)(2x - 1) + 2$
        Quotient $(2x - 1)$ R2.

6. $p = 27$.   Quotient $(6x^2 - 12x + 9)$.

Exercise H12·4 Page 112

1. a $(x + 1)(x^2 + 26x - 29) + 38$
        Quot. $(x^2 + 26x - 29)$ R38
    b $(x - 4)(x^3 + 4x^2 + 11x + 44) + 140$
        Quot. $(x^3 + 4x^2 + 11x + 44)$ R140
    c $(x - 1)(x^6 + x^5 - x^4 - x^3 + 1) + 1$
        Quot. $(x^6 + x^5 - x^4 - x^3 + 1)$ R1
    d $(2x - 1)(2x + 2) - 6$
        Quot. $(2x + 2)$ R -6
    e $(2x - 3)(2x - 1) - 11$
        Quot. $(2x - 1)$ R -11
    f $(3x + 2)(2x^2 - 2x + 1) + 9$
        Quot. $(2x^2 - 2x + 1)$ R9.

2. $a = 7$.
3. $b = 2$.
4. $c = 2$.
5. $d = 10$.

Exercise H12·5 Page 113

1. All proofs, showing 0 remainder.
2. a $(x - 1)(x - 2)(x + 3)$
    b $(x - 1)(x - 3)(x - 4)$
    c $(x - 2)(x - 7)(x + 5)$
    d $(x + 1)(x + 3)(2x - 1)$
    e $(x - 3)(x - 5)(2x + 1)$
    f $(x - 4)(2x + 1)(2x - 1)$
    g $(x - 1)(x + 1)(x - 2)(x + 2)$
    h $x(x - 2)(x + 7)(x - 5)$
    i $2(x - 1)(x - 1)(x + 1)(x - 2)(x + 2)$.

Exercise H12·6 Page 114

1. a $m = 7$ b $m = -3$
    c $m = 2$ d $m = -1$
    e $m = -4$.
2. a $a = 2$, $b = -1$
    b $a = -1$, $b = 4$
    c $a = -1$, $b = -14$
    d $a = -13$, $b = 6$
    e $a = -9$, $b = 12$
    f $a = 1$, $b = -9$
    g $a = -4$, $b = -1$.
3. $q = 2$. $(x - 1)(x + 2)$.
4. Proof, using discriminant.

Exercise H12·7 Page 114

1. Proof.   Other roots -1 and 8.
2. Proof.   Other roots -1 and 5.
3. Proof.   Other roots -3 and 2.
4. Proof.   Other roots $2^1/_2$ and 4.
5. a -2, -3, 1   b -2, 3
    c -1, 5, 8   d -2, 1, 3, 6.
6. a (-1, 1), (2, 4), (-4, -2)
    b $x = -1, x = 2, x = 5$
    c $x = -1, x = 1, x = -4, x = -6$.
7. a -4, -$^1/_2$, 1   b -1, $^2/_3$, 6
    c -$^2/_3$, $^1/_2$, 4   d -2, $^2/_5$, 6.
8. (-2, 0), (1, 0), (5, 0).
9. $p = 84$.   Other roots -7 and 3.
10. Proof, using discriminant. 1 root at -3
11. $b = -5$.   Proof, using discriminant.

Exercise H12·8 Page 115

1. $f(x) = {}^1/_2x^2 - 2x - 6$.
2. a $f(x) = 2x^2 - 10x + 8$
    b $f(x) = -2x^2 + 4x + 6$.
3. a $f(x) = -x^2 + 8x + 7$
    b $f(x) = {}^1/_3x^2 + {}^{10}/_3x + 3$
    c $f(x) = -2x^2 - 16x - 32$
    d $f(x) = {}^1/_2x^3 - 26x + 48$
    e $f(x) = -2x^3 + 42x + 40$
    f $f(x) = -x^3 + x^2 + 16x + 20$
    g $f(x) = -2x^3 - 4x^2 + 10x + 12$
    h $f(x) = 2x^3 - 8x^2 - 70x + 300$
    i $f(x) = x^4 - 5x^3 - 22x^2 + 80x + 96$
    j $f(x) = -2x^4 + 4x^3 + 26x^2 - 28x - 48$
    k $f(x) = -^1/_2x^3 + 2x^2 + ^3/_2x - 9$
    l $f(x) = {}^1/_8x^3 + ^3/_4x^2 - 30x + 100$
    m $f(x) = -4x^3 + 8x$.

Exercise H12·9 Page 117

1.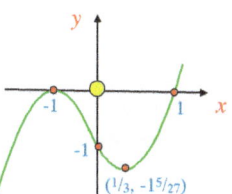

2.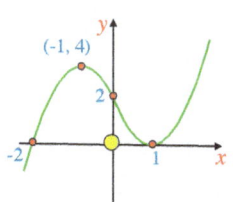

3.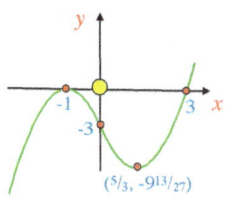

4.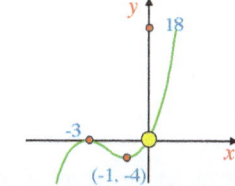

5.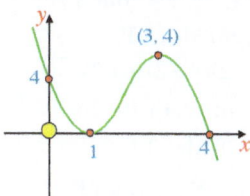

6.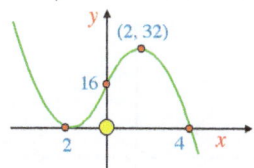

7.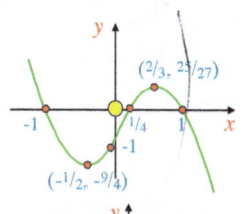

8.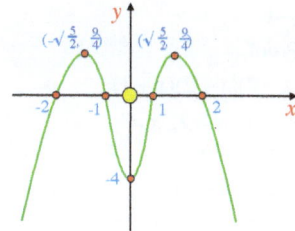

Exercise H12·10 Page 118

1. a $(x-3)(x+1)(2x-1)$
   b $x(x-1)(-x^2-x-1)$
   c $x^4(x-1)(x+1)$
   d $(3x-2y)(3x+2y)$
2. a $(x-1)(x+2)(x-4)$
   b $-2, 1, 4$.
3. $a = -17.$ $(x-3)(x+2)(3x-1)$.
4. a $(0,0)$ Max.T.P. $(1,-2)$ Min. T.P.
   b $0, {}^3/_2$
   c/d

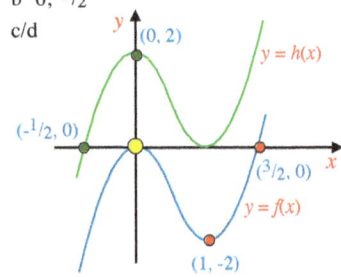

   e $0 < k < 2$.
5. $p = -4$.
6. Proof.
7. $k = 6$.
8. $y = {}^1/_4 x^2(x-6)$.
9. $p = 12,$ $q = -3$.
10. a $(0,16)$
    b $(-4,0)$ $(-1,0)$ $(4,0)$
    c $(-{}^8/_3, -{}^{400}/_{27})$ Min. T.P.
       $(2,36)$ Max.T.P.
11. a $(x-2)(x+2)(x+2)$
    b $(-2,0)$ $(2,0)$ $(0,-8)$
    c $(-2,0)$ Max.T.P.
       $({}^2/_3, -{}^{256}/_{27})$ Min.T.P.
    d

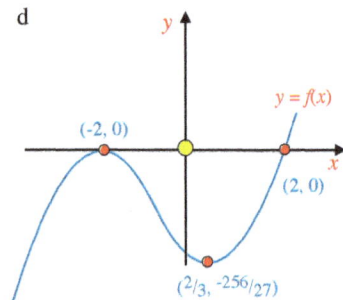

    e ${}^{64}/_3$ units^2

Exam Practice Ch 12 Page 119

1. $p = -4$.
2. a Proof
   b $(x-7)(x-2)(x+1)$
   c $x = -1, x = 2, x = 7$.
3. $a = -5, b = 4$.
4. a $a = 8, b = 21$
   b $(x-3)(x+1)(2x-7)$.

---

5. $f(x) = 2x^3 + 2x^2 - 18x - 18$.
6. a $(x-1)(x^2+5x+8)$
   b Proof
   c $(1,-57)$. Min. T.P.
7. a $q = 6, (0,6)$
   b $(2,0)$ $({}^1/_2, 0)$.
8. a Proof
   b $(3,8)$.
9. a $a = -2$
   b $m = 1$.
10. $(1,6)$ $(3,10)$ $(-2,0)$.
11. a Proof $(x-3)(x-1)(3-2x)$
    b $(3,0)$ $(-1,0)$ $(1{}^1/_2, 0)$ $(0,-9)$
    c Min. -9 Max. 3
12. a $3x^3 - 4$
    b Proof
    c $(x-1)(x+1)(3x+4)$
    d $x = 1, x = -1, x = -{}^4/_3$.
13. a $K(2,0)$ $L(3,0)$
    b ${}^7/_{12}$ units^2.

Answers to Chapter 13 Page 121

Revision Exercise Page 121

1. a πb ${}^\pi/_4$ c ${}^\pi/_6$ d 2π
   e ${}^{3\pi}/_2$ f ${}^\pi/_3$ g ${}^\pi/_{15}$ h ${}^{2\pi}/_{45}$
   i ${}^{16\pi}/_9$
2. a $360°$ b $90°$ c $30°$ d $540°$
   e $1440°$ f $22·5°$ g $45°$ h $270°$
   i $300°$
3. a -1 b -1 c ${}^1/_2$ d undefined
   e 1 f ${}^{\sqrt3}/_3$ g $-{}^{\sqrt2}/_2$ h $-{}^{\sqrt2}/_2$
   i $-\sqrt3$
4. a ${}^1/_2$ b $-{}^{\sqrt6}/_2$ c $-{}^{\sqrt3}/_4$ d $-{}^1/_2$
   e 0 f ${}^1/_2$ g ${}^{\sqrt6}/_{12}$
5. a ${}^{10\sqrt3}/_3$ b $6\sqrt3$
6. a

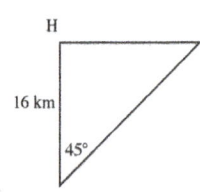

   H

   16 km

   45°

   b 16 km
7. a

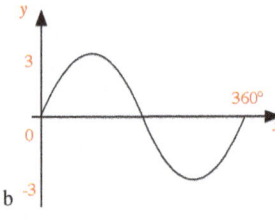

   b

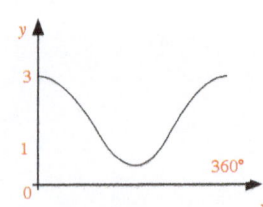

---

c

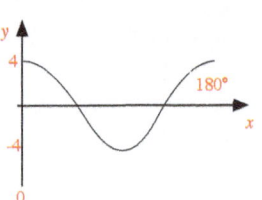

d

e

f

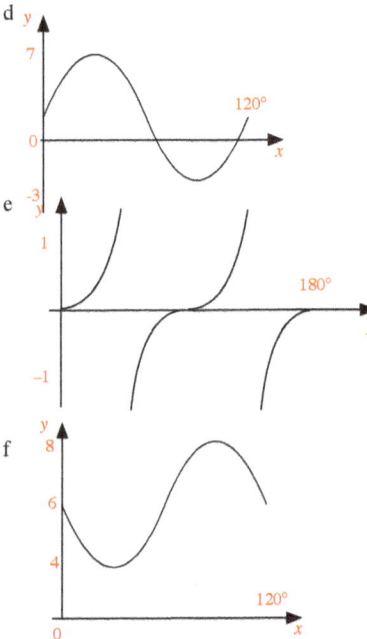

8. a $y = 2sin2x + 1$
   b $y = 4·5cos8x° + 0·5$
   c $y = 5cos10x° - 4$
   d $y = -5sin6x - 2$
9. period $= 90°$ $({}^\pi/_2)$ amplitude $5·3$
10. a $30°, 330°$ b ${}^{11\pi}/_6$
    c ${}^{53\pi}/_{180}$ d $99·7°, 350·3°$
    e $0°$
    f $30°, 150°, 210°, 330°$
    g ${}^\pi/_{12}$
    h $30°, 90°, 210, 270°$
    i ${}^{56·8\pi}/_{180}$ and ${}^{93·2\pi}/_{180}$
    j $180°, 270°, 360°$
    k $-2\pi, -{}^{3\pi}/_2, -{}^\pi/_2, 0, {}^\pi/_2, {}^{3\pi}/_2$
11. $({}^\pi/_2, 0)$ $({}^{3\pi}/_2, 0)$ $({}^{5\pi}/_2, 0)$

Exercise H13·1 Page 123

1. a ${}^1/_2(\sqrt3sin\,x + cos\,x)$
   b ${}^1/_2(-sin\,x + \sqrt3cos\,x)$
   c ${}^1/_{\sqrt2}(sin\,x + cos\,x)$
   d $cos\,x$
   e ${}^1/_2(sin\,x + \sqrt3cos\,x)$
   f $sin\,x$
2. a $sin(P+K)$ b $sin(Y+T)$
   c $sin(45+15)° = sin\,60° = {}^{\sqrt3}/_2$
   d $sin({}^\pi/_4 + {}^\pi/_3) = sin\,{}^{3\pi}/_4 = {}^{\sqrt2}/_2$
3. ${}^1/_4(\sqrt6 + \sqrt2)$
4. a 3 b ${}^3/_5$
5. ${}^5/_{13}$
6. a ${}^{15}/_{17}$ b ${}^{\sqrt7}/_4$ and ${}^3/_{\sqrt7}$
7. a $sin\,A = {}^3/_5,$ $cos\,A = {}^4/_5,$
      $sin\,P = {}^7/_{15},$ $cos\,P = {}^{24}/_{25}.$
   b Proof

8. a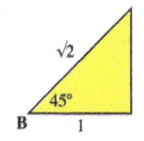

 b Proof

9. a $\frac{\sqrt2}{2}(\sin x - \cos x)$
 b $\sin 3t \cos 5k - \cos 3t \sin 5k$
 c $\frac12(\sqrt3 \sin 2Q - \cos 2Q)$
 d $\frac12(\sin x - \sqrt3 \cos x)$
 e $-\cos x$
 f $-\sin x$
 g $\frac12(\sqrt3 \cos \phi - \sin \phi)$
 h $\sin x$

10. a $\frac{(\sqrt6 - \sqrt2)}{4}$ b $\frac{(\sqrt6 + \sqrt2)}{4}$

11. a $\sin(C - H)$
 b $\sin(2T - G)$
 c $\sin(45 - 15)° = \sin 30° = \frac12$
 d $\sin(\pi/2 - \pi/4) = \sin(\pi/4) = \frac{1}{\sqrt2}$
 e $\sin(\pi/3 - \pi/4) = \sin(\pi/12) = \frac{(\sqrt6 - \sqrt2)}{4}$
 f $\frac12$

12. Proof

13. $-\frac{\sqrt{10}}{10}$

14. $\frac16 - \frac{\sqrt6}{3}$

15. a $\cos x \cos y - \sin x \sin y$
 b $\cos t \cos k + \sin t \sin k$
 c $\cos 2P \cos Q + \sin 2P \sin Q$
 d $\frac12(\cos x - \sqrt3 \sin x)$
 e $\frac{\sqrt2}{2}(\cos x + \sin x)$
 f $\frac12(\sqrt3 \cos x - \sin x)$
 g $\frac12(\cos x + \sqrt3 \sin x)$
 h $-\cos x$

16. a $\cos(C + H)$
 b $\cos(2W - T)$
 c $\cos(45 + 15)° = \cos 60° = \frac12$
 d $\cos(30°) = \frac{\sqrt3}{2}$
 e $\cos(\pi/2 + \pi/3) = \cos(5\pi/6) = -\frac{\sqrt3}{2}$

17. a - e proofs

18. $\frac{5}{12}$

19. Proof

20. $\frac{(\sqrt2 + 1)}{\sqrt6} = \frac{(2\sqrt3 - \sqrt6)}{6}$

21. $\frac19(\sqrt5 - 4\sqrt2)$

22. a Proof   b $\frac{11\sqrt5}{25}$

Exercise H13·2 Page 125

1. 2. Proofs
3. $\sin 2x = 2\sin x \cos x$

Exercise H13·3 Page 126

1. a $\frac{120}{169}$ b $\frac{119}{169}$
2. a $\frac{240}{289}$ b $\frac{161}{289}$
3. a Proof   b Proof
4. a $\frac12$ b $\frac{\sqrt3}{2}$
 c $-\frac12$ d $\frac12$
5. a Proof
 b $\cos 4Q = 8\cos^4 Q - 8\cos^2 Q + 1$
 c Proof
6. $\frac{24}{25}$, $-\frac{7}{25}$ and $-\frac{24}{7}$
7. a $\frac{204}{325}$ b $-\frac{837}{845}$

Exercise H13·4 Page 127

1. 180°, 360°
2. a 30°, 150°, 270°
 b 90°, 210°, 330°

 c 90°, 210°, 270°, 330°
 d 0°, 30°, 150°, 180°
3. a 90°   b 90°, 270°
 c 41·4°
4. a 0, $\pi/3$, π, $5\pi/3$ b 0, $\pi/4$, π, $7\pi/4$
 c $7\pi/6$, $11\pi/6$
5. ab

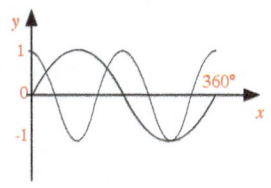

 c $\pi/6$, $5\pi/6$, $3\pi/2$
 d (i) $\pi/6$, $5\pi/6$, $3\pi/2$, $13\pi/6$, $17\pi/6$, $7\pi/2$
  (ii) $25\pi/6$, $29\pi/6$, $11\pi/2$
6. π, 2π
7. 90°, 210°, 330°
8. a (i) $y = 2\sin 2x - 1$
   $y = 2\cos 2x - 1$
  (ii) 22·5°, 112·5°
 b (i) $y = 4\cos x + 4$
   $y = -3\cos x + 3$
  (ii) 98·2°, 261·8°

Exercise H13·5 Page 128

1. Proof
2. a $\cos 2x - 1$ b $2 - 2\cos 2x$
 c $\frac14(1 + \cos 2x)^2$ d $\frac14(1 - \cos 2x)^2$
3. ab Proofs
4. a-d   Proofs
5. 0°, 180°, 270°, 360°

Exercise H13·6 Page 129

1. a F   b F   c T   d F
 e F   f F   g T   h F
 i T
2. a $\frac12(\sin x + \sqrt3 \cos x)$
 b $\cos x \cos y + \sin x \sin y$
 c $\frac{\sqrt2}{2}(\sin x - \cos x)$
 d $\cos 2x$
3. a $\frac{\sqrt3}{2}$ b 1
4. a $\frac{(\sqrt6 + \sqrt2)}{4}$ b $\frac{(\sqrt2 - \sqrt6)}{4}$
5. a $\frac12$ b $\frac{\sqrt3}{2}$ c $\frac12$ d 0
6. a $\frac{\sqrt3}{2}$ b $\frac{1}{\sqrt3}$
7. $-\frac{24}{7}$
8. a $\frac{36}{325}$ b $-\frac{253}{325}$
9. a

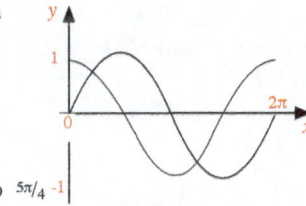

 b $5\pi/4$
10. a 30°, 90°, 150°, 270°
 b π, $3\pi/2$
 c no solution for $\{0 \le x \le 180\}$
 d 0°
 e 33·4°, 90°, 146·6°
11. a $y = -4\sin x$, $y = -4\cos x - 2$
 b $\pi/4$, $5\pi/4$

12. a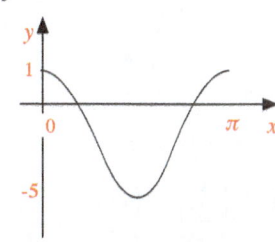

 b 30°

13. a-e   Proofs

Exam Practice Ch 13 Page 130

1. a $\frac{\sqrt5}{5}$ b $\frac45$
2. $\frac{24}{25}$
3. a $-\cos k$ b $-\cos k$
 c Proof
4. $p > 3$
5.

 y
 1
 0   π x
 -5

6. a = -4, b = 4, c = -2
7. $\pi/2$, $75·5\pi/180$
8. a $y = 4\cos x$, $y = -4\sin x$
 b $k = -2\sqrt2$ (-2·83)
9. a $\frac{(\sqrt3 - 1)}{2\sqrt2}$ b $\frac{(\sqrt3 + 1)}{2\sqrt2}$
10. Proof
11. 35·3°, 144·7°
12. a = $\frac14$, b = $\frac12$, c = $\frac14$
13. Proof

Answers to Chapter 14 Page 131

Exercise H14·1 Page 133

1. a $2\underline{w}$ is 14 right and 8 up
 b $4\underline{w}$ is 28 right and 16 up
 c $-\underline{w}$ is 7 left and 4 down
 d $-3\underline{w}$ is 21 left and 12 down
2. a $2\underline{v}$ is 10 right and 2 up
 b $\underline{u} + \underline{v}$ is 4 left and 5 down
 c $2\underline{u} + \underline{v}$ is 13 left and 11 down
 d $-(\underline{u} + \underline{v})$ is 4 right and 5 up
3. a $\underline{a} + \underline{b}$ is 9 right and 3 down
 b $\underline{a} - \underline{b}$ is 9 right and 9 up
 c $\underline{b} - \underline{a}$ is 9 left and 9 down
 d $3\underline{b} - 2\underline{a}$ is 18 left and 24 down
 e The zero vector
4. a see diagram   b $\underline{p} = \begin{pmatrix} 3 \\ 2 \end{pmatrix}$ $\underline{q} = \begin{pmatrix} 5 \\ 7 \end{pmatrix}$
 c $\begin{pmatrix} 2 \\ 5 \end{pmatrix}$ d $\begin{pmatrix} -2 \\ -5 \end{pmatrix}$
5. a $\begin{pmatrix} 5 \\ 3 \end{pmatrix}$ b $\begin{pmatrix} 5 \\ -3 \end{pmatrix}$ c $\begin{pmatrix} 6 \\ 2 \end{pmatrix}$ d $\begin{pmatrix} s - m \\ t - p \end{pmatrix}$
6. a $\begin{pmatrix} 4 \\ 3 \end{pmatrix}$ b $\begin{pmatrix} 4 \\ 3 \end{pmatrix}$ and $\begin{pmatrix} 4 \\ 3 \end{pmatrix}$ c parallel
7. a $\begin{pmatrix} 3 \\ 6 \end{pmatrix}$ and $\begin{pmatrix} -3 \\ -6 \end{pmatrix}$
 b same vector but opposite direction
 c at least a parallelogram
8. 5

9 a 5   b 13   c 10   d 15
10 a $\sqrt{20}$, $\sqrt{40}$ and $\sqrt{20}$ b a R.A.T.
11. CK =10, CL = 10 and CM = 10
12. a $\begin{pmatrix}11\\16\end{pmatrix}$ and $\begin{pmatrix}11\\-9\end{pmatrix}$ b $\begin{pmatrix}22\\7\end{pmatrix}$
13. a $\begin{pmatrix}60\\-40\end{pmatrix}$ b 720 km (approx)
14. a $\begin{pmatrix}-9\\10\end{pmatrix}$, $\begin{pmatrix}14\\6\end{pmatrix}$ and $\begin{pmatrix}-5\\-16\end{pmatrix}$
   b $\sqrt{181}$, $\sqrt{232}$ and $\sqrt{281}$ c $\begin{pmatrix}0\\0\end{pmatrix}$
   c The forces are perfectly balanced
      so the box stays where it is.
15. a $\underline{q}$ b $\underline{p}$
   c $\underline{p}+\underline{q}$ d $\underline{q}-\underline{p}$
   e $\frac{1}{2}(\underline{p}+\underline{q})$ f $\frac{1}{2}(\underline{p}-\underline{q})$
16. a (i) $2\underline{u}$ (ii) $\underline{u}+\underline{v}$
   (iii) $2\underline{u}-\underline{v}$ (iv) $\underline{u}-\underline{v}$
   b $\begin{pmatrix}8\\0\end{pmatrix}$, $\begin{pmatrix}6\\-4\end{pmatrix}$ and $\begin{pmatrix}-2\\-4\end{pmatrix}$
   c $\sqrt{20}$, $\sqrt{52}$ and $\sqrt{52}$
17. a $\underline{a}$ b $\underline{b}$
   c $2\underline{a}$ d $\underline{b}-\underline{a}$
   e $2\underline{b}-2\underline{a}$ f $2\underline{b}-\underline{a}$

Exercise H14·2 Page 135

1. a $\begin{pmatrix}10\\4\\-2\end{pmatrix}$ b $\begin{pmatrix}9\\-12\\-6\end{pmatrix}$ c $\begin{pmatrix}8\\-2\\-3\end{pmatrix}$
   d $\begin{pmatrix}2\\6\\1\end{pmatrix}$ e $\begin{pmatrix}21\\-2\\-7\end{pmatrix}$ f $\begin{pmatrix}-32\\8\\12\end{pmatrix}$
2. a $\begin{pmatrix}-2\\1\\14\end{pmatrix}$ b $\begin{pmatrix}6\\-9\\-6\end{pmatrix}$ c $\begin{pmatrix}-4\\8\\-8\end{pmatrix}$
   d 6   b $\sqrt{141}$ c $\sqrt{201}$
3. a $\underline{x}=\begin{pmatrix}6\\0\\-3\end{pmatrix}$ b $\underline{x}=\begin{pmatrix}0\\0\\0\end{pmatrix}$
   c $\underline{x}=\begin{pmatrix}-6\\4\\-1\end{pmatrix}$ d $\underline{x}=\begin{pmatrix}7\\0\\-3\end{pmatrix}$
   e $\underline{x}=\begin{pmatrix}-1\\4\\-2\end{pmatrix}$ f $\underline{x}=\begin{pmatrix}7\\1\\-1\end{pmatrix}$
4. a $\begin{pmatrix}2\\6\\9\end{pmatrix}$, $\begin{pmatrix}5\\0\\3\end{pmatrix}$ and $\begin{pmatrix}7\\4\\-5\end{pmatrix}$
   b $\begin{pmatrix}3\\-6\\-6\end{pmatrix}$ c $\begin{pmatrix}-3\\6\\6\end{pmatrix}$, $\begin{pmatrix}2\\4\\-8\end{pmatrix}$ and $\begin{pmatrix}-5\\2\\14\end{pmatrix}$
   d $\begin{pmatrix}0\\0\\0\end{pmatrix}$ journey returns to start point
   e/f $\begin{pmatrix}0\\0\\0\end{pmatrix}$ journey returns to start point
5. a $\underline{p}$ b $\underline{q}$
   c $\underline{p}+\underline{r}$ d $\underline{q}+\underline{r}$
   e $\underline{q}+\underline{r}$ f $\underline{p}+\underline{q}+\underline{r}$
   g $\frac{1}{2}\underline{q}$ h $\underline{p}+\frac{1}{2}\underline{q}$
   i $\frac{1}{2}(\underline{q}+\underline{r})$ j $\underline{p}+\frac{1}{2}(\underline{q}+\underline{r})$
   k $\frac{1}{2}(\underline{p}+\underline{q}+\underline{r})$ l $\frac{1}{2}(\underline{p}-\underline{q}-\underline{r})$
6. a $\begin{pmatrix}0\\3\\5\end{pmatrix}$ b $\begin{pmatrix}15\\0\\5\end{pmatrix}$ c $\begin{pmatrix}15\\3\\5\end{pmatrix}$
   d $\sqrt{34}$ e $\sqrt{250}$ f $\sqrt{259}/2$
7. a $\begin{pmatrix}6\\4\\2\end{pmatrix}$ b $\begin{pmatrix}18\\4\\2\end{pmatrix}$, $\begin{pmatrix}18\\9\\2\end{pmatrix}$, $\begin{pmatrix}6\\9\\2\end{pmatrix}$ and $\begin{pmatrix}12\\6·5\\17\end{pmatrix}$
   c $\begin{pmatrix}12\\0\\0\end{pmatrix}$, $\begin{pmatrix}0\\5\\0\end{pmatrix}$ and $\begin{pmatrix}6\\2·5\\15\end{pmatrix}$
   d 13   e 16·3 approx
8. a $\begin{pmatrix}80\\48\\8\end{pmatrix}$ and $\begin{pmatrix}20\\12\\2\end{pmatrix}$ b 94 and 23 miles
   c $\begin{pmatrix}-60\\-36\\-6\end{pmatrix}$ d 35 miles per hour

d We can show O, B and A are collinear
9. a $\begin{pmatrix}-14\\-10\\-80\end{pmatrix}$, $\begin{pmatrix}10\\-20\\-80\end{pmatrix}$ and $\begin{pmatrix}4\\30\\-80\end{pmatrix}$
   b the sum of all 4 vectors is $\begin{pmatrix}0\\0\\0\end{pmatrix}$

Exercise H14·3 Page 137

1. a $m_{AB} = 2$, $m_{BC} = 2$
   b parallel with B in common - collinear
   c $\begin{pmatrix}1\\2\end{pmatrix}$ and $\begin{pmatrix}2\\4\end{pmatrix}$
   d second vector is a multiple of the first
      with a point B in common - collinear
2. a yes   b yes   c yes
3. a $k = -1$ b ratio is 3 : 2
4. $a = -1/3$, $b = 23/2$
5. R, S and U are collinear
6. yes

Exercise H14·4 Page 138

1. a P(3, 4, 1)   b P(-2, 2, 2)
   c P(2, 1, 6)   d P(-3, 2, 0)
2. a proof   b 2 : 3
3. a (-1, 3, 1)   b (3, 9)
   c (0, 0, 0)   d $(-1/2, 2\,1/2)$
4. $k = -2$ and ratio = 3 : 2
5. B(2, 5, 2) and C(5, $6\,1/2$, $6\,1/2$)
6. a L(2, 2, 5), M(8, 5, 1) and N(4, 8, 4)
   b T($4\,2/3$, 5, $3\,2/3$)

Exercise H14·5 Page 139

1. a $3\underline{i} - \underline{j} + 4\underline{k}$ b $6\underline{i} + 8\underline{i} - \underline{k}$
   c $8\underline{i} - \underline{k}$ d $4\underline{i}$
   e $\frac{1}{2}\underline{i} + 2\underline{i} - \frac{3}{4}\underline{k}$
   f $p\underline{i} + (p - 1)\underline{i} + (p + 2)\underline{k}$
2. a $\begin{pmatrix}2\\3\\-7\end{pmatrix}$ b $\begin{pmatrix}5\\-6\\3\end{pmatrix}$ c $\begin{pmatrix}1\\1\\-2\end{pmatrix}$
   d $\begin{pmatrix}4\\0\\-1\end{pmatrix}$ e $\begin{pmatrix}0\\3\\3\end{pmatrix}$ f $\begin{pmatrix}0\\6\\0\end{pmatrix}$
3. a $5\underline{i} - 5\underline{i} - \underline{k}$ b $\underline{i} + 3\underline{i} - 11\underline{k}$
   c $3\underline{i} - 2\underline{k}$
4. a $2\sqrt{6}$ b $3\sqrt{3}$ c $3\sqrt{2}$ d $3\sqrt{2}$
5. 6 or -6
6. a $3\underline{i} - 4\underline{i} + 8\underline{k}$ b $\underline{i} - 2\underline{i} + 2\underline{k}$
   c $2\underline{i} - 2\underline{i} + 6\underline{k}$ d $4\underline{i} - 7\underline{i} + 9\underline{k}$
   e $\sqrt{89}$ f $\sqrt{418}$
7. a (i) $\frac{1}{3}\underline{i} - \frac{2}{3}\underline{j} + \frac{2}{3}\underline{k}$
   (ii) $\frac{\sqrt{3}}{4}\underline{i} - \frac{\sqrt{5}}{4}\underline{j} + \frac{\sqrt{2}}{2}\underline{k}$
   b (i) $\frac{3}{5}\underline{i} - \frac{4}{5}\underline{k}$
   (ii) $\frac{2}{5}\underline{i} - \frac{4}{5}\underline{j} + \frac{\sqrt{5}}{5}\underline{k}$
8. $\underline{p} = -5\underline{j} - \underline{k}$
9. F(8, -1, -4)
10. a $\begin{pmatrix}20\\5\\3\end{pmatrix}$ and $\begin{pmatrix}-10\\40\\3\end{pmatrix}$ b Radio ship
11. a PC = QC = RC = 3 units
   b S(3, 7, 2)

Exercise H14·6 Page 140

1. a -5   b -5   c -1
   d 0   e 20   f -4
2. a $\begin{pmatrix}-1\\4\\4\end{pmatrix}$ and $\begin{pmatrix}3\\-3\\2\end{pmatrix}$ b -7
3. 56 and $5/24$

4. a 36   b -6
5. a proof   b proof
6. $x = 1$ or -2
7. a 4, -2   b 3
   c 0, 1, 2   d $0, \pi/2, \pi, 2\pi$

Exercise H14·7 Page 141

1. a 3   b 4   c $3\sqrt{5}/2$
   d 0   e -60   f -16·5
2. a 2   b 2 (approx)
3. 101

Exercise H14·8 Page 142

1. 30·5°
2. a 88·2° b 99° c 44·9°
   d 53·1° e 90°
3. Scalar product is zero
4. $\begin{pmatrix}1\\2\\-2\end{pmatrix}$ and $\begin{pmatrix}4\\3\\0\end{pmatrix}$ and proof
5. 116·4°
6. a PQ² = 29, QR² = 81, PR² = 52
      since PQ² + PR² = QR², right angled
   b $\begin{pmatrix}3\\-2\\4\end{pmatrix}$ and $\begin{pmatrix}4\\6\\0\end{pmatrix}$ => scalar product = 0
7. $a = 5$
8. $10 - a + 6b = 0$, $-6 + 2a + 2b = 0$
   => $a = 4$, $b = -1$
9. $m = -1$, $n = 4$

Exercise H14·9 Page 143

1. a 88   b proof
2. a 30   b 11   c 17
3. a 7   b 29   c 33
4. a 25   b 36
5. a T   b F   c T
6. a 1   b 0   c 0

.	$\underline{i}$	$\underline{j}$	$\underline{k}$
$\underline{i}$	1	0	0
$\underline{j}$	0	1	0
$\underline{k}$	0	0	1

7. a 2   b $\underline{b}-\underline{a}$ c -2
8. a $\underline{a}.\underline{b} = |\underline{a}||\underline{b}|\cos\theta$ but $-1 \le \cos\theta \le 1$
      so $\underline{a}.\underline{b} \le |\underline{a}||\underline{b}|$ b $\underline{a}$ and $\underline{b}$ parallel
9. 36

Exercise H14·10 Page 144

1. D(-6, 5, 0)
2. Proof and 4 : 3
3. a M(1, 0, 2)   b (3, 1, 1)
4. $a = 1$
5. 70·5°
6. proof
7. a $c = 2\sqrt{3}$ b proof
8. a $\underline{p}.\underline{p} - \underline{q}.\underline{q}$ b 0
   c they are perpendicular
9. Proof
10. a $2k^2 + k - 3$ b $k = 1$ or $-3/2$
11. a U(4, 0, 4)   b $\begin{pmatrix}4\\2\\2\end{pmatrix}$ and $\begin{pmatrix}2\\2\\4\end{pmatrix}$
   c 33·6°
12. a M(0, 8, 0), N(16, 8, 0) and Q(13, 8, 7)
   b $\begin{pmatrix}-13\\0\\-7\end{pmatrix}$ and $\begin{pmatrix}3\\0\\-7\end{pmatrix}$ c 84·9°
13. a C(6, 7, 0) and P(6, 7, 12)

13. b $n = 3$

c $\begin{pmatrix} 6 \\ 0 \\ -12 \end{pmatrix}$ and $\begin{pmatrix} -3 \\ -4 \\ -12 \end{pmatrix}$ d 43·7°

Exam Practice Ch 14 Page 145

1. a $\begin{pmatrix} 4 \\ -1 \\ 12 \end{pmatrix}$ b proof c 61·8°

2. $g = {}^1/_9$

3. a proof and 4 : 3
   b G(0, 0, 18)

4. proof

5. a $2\sqrt{3}$ b proof

6. 0

7. a B(10, 6, 8) and C(22, 18, 12)
   b $\begin{pmatrix} -12 \\ -18 \\ -12 \end{pmatrix}$ and $\begin{pmatrix} -12 \\ -12 \\ -4 \end{pmatrix}$ c 18·9°

8. M(9, 13, -5)

9. $4^1/_2$

Answers to Chapter 15 Page 146

Exercise H15·1 Page 147

1. a $-5sinx$ b $-3cosx$
   c $-10sinx$ d $6cosx - sinx$
   e $4cosx + 7sinx$ f $-9sinx - cosx$
   g $12cosx + 4x^3$ h $-4sinx - 50x^4$
   i $-2sinx - 5cosx + 2x^{-1/2}$
   h $8cosx + 3sinx + {}^1/_4x^{-3/4}$.

2. a $1 + cosx$ b $3x^2 + sinx$
   c $-2cosx + {}^2/_3x^{-1/3}$
   d $-2sinx + {}^2/x^2$.

3. a $11cosp$ b $6sinr$
   c $-2cost + 12sint$
   d $-8sinx + 10cosx - {}^4/x^3$.

4. a 1   b -1
   c 0   d $-\sqrt{2}$.

5. a/b Proof.

6. a $y = x + \sqrt{3} - {}^\pi/_3$
   b $y - 3\sqrt{3} = -3(x - {}^\pi/_6))$
   c $y = -3x + 4 + {}^{3\pi}/_2$.

7. a $f'(x) = 1 + cosx \geq 0$ never decr.
   b $f'(x) = 1 + sinx \geq 0$ never decr.

8. a 1, 1
   b ${}^{5\pi}/_6$, ${}^{11\pi}/_6$.
   c -2 Min., 2 Max.

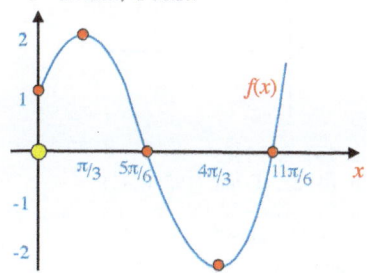

Exercise H15·2 Page 148

1. a $3sinx + C$ b $-6cosx + C$
   c $2cosx + C$ d $5sinx - 8cosx + C$
   e $sinx + 4cosx + C$
   f $-9cosx - 10sinx + C$
   g ${}^1/_3x^3 + 3sinx + C$
   h ${}^2/_3x^{3/2} - sinx + C$
   i $-4cosx - 7sinx + {}^2/x + C$.

2. a $2sint + 8cost + C$
   b $4cos\theta - 6sin\theta + C$

3. a 4   b 6
   c ${}^1/_2$ d -5
   e ${}^3/\sqrt{2} - 1$ f 2
   g ${}^\pi/_2 + 1$ h ${}^\pi/_3 + 2$
   i 0   j ${}^{2\pi}/_3 + 3\sqrt{3}$
   k ${}^{3\pi}/_2 - 1$ l ${}^2/_3\pi^3$
   m ${}^3/_8\pi^2 + 8$ n -8.

4. 1.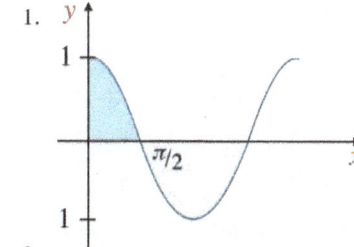

5. 2.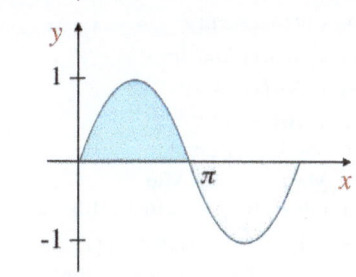

6. ${}^\pi/_3 + {}^1/_2$ sq. units.

7. a Proof   b $2 - \sqrt{3}$ sq. units.

8. a Proof   b 4 sq. units.

Exercise H15·3 Page 150

1. a $2x - 8$ b $2t + 14$
   c $24m^2 - 24m + 6$.

2. a $5(x + 3)^4$ b $4(x - 2)^3$
   c ${}^1/_2(x - 8)^{-1/2}$ d $-(x + 7)^{-2}$
   e $-2(x - 10)^{-3}$ f ${}^2/_5(x + 1)^{-3/5}$
   g $2(p - 2) - sinp$ h $cost + {}^1/_2(t - 9)^{-1/2}$
   i $-{}^1/_2(x + 4)^{-3/2} + sinx$
   j $-9(8 - v)^{-10}$.

3. a $10(2x + 5)^4$ b $-30(2 - 5x)^5$
   c $49(7x - 2)^6$ d $-{}^1/_5(x - 3)^{-6}$
   e $-6(6 - 8x)^{-1/4}$ f $-2(x - 5)^{-2}$
   g $-{}^1/_{20}(6 + {}^1/_2t)^{-11/10}$
   h $(2 - 5t)^{-6/5}$ i $-(10 - 4t)^{-3/4}$

j $6(12\theta + 2)^{-1/2}$
k $-8(4\theta - 1)^{-3}$ l $8(1 - 10\theta)^{-9/5}$
m $-64(4r + 5)^{-3}$ n $8(3 - 8r)^{-4/3}$.

Exercise H15·4 Page 151

1. a $5(x + 1)^4$ b $6(2x - 4)^2$
   c $6(7 + x)^5$ d $21(3x - 5)^6$
   e $-8(1 - x)^7$ f $-9(4 - 3x)^2$
   g $-9(2 - x)^8$ h $-25(7 - 5x)^4$
   i $8x(x^2 + 1)^3$ j $9x^2(x^3 - 2)^2$
   k $24x^3(x^4 + 10)^5$
   l $-15x^4(1 - x^5)^2$
   m $(2x + 4)^{-1/2}$ n $(3x - 6)^{-2/3}$
   o $-3(x - 1)^{-4}$ p $18(2 - 9x)^{-3}$
   q $(6x + 18)(x^2 + 6x)^2$
   r $(4x + 2)(x^2 + x + 3)$
   s $(24x^2 - 8)(x^3 - x)^7$
   t $(x + 1)(x^2 + 2x - 6)^{-1/2}$
   u $(2x - 3)^{-1/2}$ v $-4(1 - 8x)^{-1/2}$
   w $(x^2 + 2)(x^3 + 6x)^{-2/3}$
   x $-{}^1/_2x(10 - x^2)^{-3/4}$.

2. a $-(x - 9)^{-2}$ b $10(1 - x)^{-2}$
   c $-4(2x + 5)^{-3}$ d $-18(6x + 2)^{-3/2}$
   e $4x(x^2 - 2)$
   f $(2 - {}^2/x^2)(x - 1 + {}^1/x)$.

3. 8 Max T.P.

4. a Proof   b -2 Min. T.P.

5. a $-{}^3/(x - 5)^2$ b $y = -3x - 15$.

6. (1, -3) (-5, 3).

Exercise H15·5 Page 152

1. a $2cos2x$ b $5cos(5x + 1)$
   c $acos(ax + b)$ d ${}^1/_4cos{}^1/_4x$
   e $-2sin2x$ f $-6sin(6x - 2)$
   g $-mcos(mx + n)$ h $-{}^1/_3sin{}^1/_3x$
   i $2sinxcosx$ j $5sin^4xcosx$
   k $-2cosxsinx$ l $-7cos^6xsinx$
   m $4cos(4x - 8)$ n $10sin(9 - 10x)$
   o $-8sin4x$ p $18cos6x$
   q $-2sinx(1 + cosx)$
   r $2sinx(1 - cosx)$
   s $-4cos x/sin^2x$
   t 0.

2. a $(3 + 3cosx)(x + sinx)^2$
   b ${}^1/_2sinx(4 - cosx)^{-1/2}$
   c $-10cosx(5sinx - 2)^{-3}$
   d ${}^3/_4cosx(sinx)^{-1/4}$
   e ${}^1/_3(1 - cosx)(x - sinx)^{-2/3}$
   f $2cosxsinx$

2. g $8sin4xcos4x$
   h $-6cos3xsin3x$
   i $24xsin^2(4x^2)cos(4x^2)$
   j $-60x^2cos^3(5x^3)sin(5x^3)$

k $(2x + 2cos2x)(1 - 2sin2x)$

l $^1/_2(sin5x - x^2)^{-1/2}(5cos5x - 2x)$.

3. a $^\pi/_2$, $^{3\pi}/_2$ b $^\pi/_3$, π, $^{5\pi}/_3$.

4. a Proof b $x = \pi$.

Exercise H15·6 Page 153

1. a $^1/_5(x + 2)^5 + C$

b $^1/_{16}(2x + 5)^8 + C$

c $^1/_{6p}(px - q)^6 + C$

d $^{-1}/_{32}(1 - 8x)^4 + C$

e $-(x + 6)^{-1} + C$

f $^{-1}/_{21}(7x - 1)^{-3} + C$

g $^1/_6(4x - 9)^{3/2} + C$

h $^{-1}/_{10}(1 - 4x)^{5/2} + C$

i $^{-1}/_{x + 2} + C$

j $^{-2}/_{x + 4} + C$

k $-3(12 - x)^{1/3} + C$

l $(2x + 9)^{1/2} + C$

m $3(x - 4)^{1/3} + C$

n $(8x + 12)^{1/2} + C$.

2. a 30 b $^{32}/_5$ c $^{16}/_3$ d $^1/_{20}$

e $^{14}/_9$ f 2 g $136^2/_5$

h 6

3. a $-2cosx + C$ b $^1/_2sin2x + C$

c $-^1/_3cos3x + C$ d $^1/_4sin(4x - 1) + C$

e $-^1/_7sin7x + C$ f $-2cos^1/_2x + C$

g $-sin(2 - x) + C$ h $^1/_3x^3 - sin4x + C$

i $-2cos((2x + 1)/4) + C$

j $^2/_9sin(3x - 6) + C$

k $^3/_2x^4 + ^1/_6cos(6x - 5) + C$

l $^{16}/_5x^{5/2} - 16cos^1/_2x + C$.

4. a 0 b $^3/_8$ c $\sqrt{2}$ d $^1/_6$

e 1 f $-^1/_{24}$ g $^4/_3 - 3\sqrt{3}/_2$.

5. 1 sq. unit.

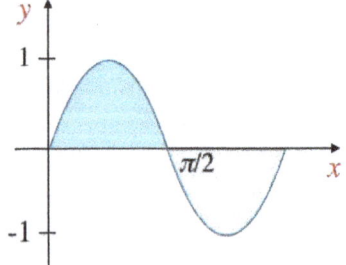

6. $^3/_2$ sq. units.

7. a $^1/_2x - ^1/_4sin2x + C$

b $^1/_2x + ^1/_4sin2x + C$

8. a $^1/_2$ sq. unit b $^{\sqrt{3}}/_8$ sq. units.

9. $^1/_6(1 + \sqrt{3})$ sq. units.

Exam Practice Ch 15 Page 154

1. a $^1/_{18}(3x - 8)^6 + C$

b $^1/_6(4x - 1)^{3/2} + C$

c $2sin(3x + 1) + C$

d $2x^4 - ^1/_8sin8x + C$

e $-^1/_2(1 - 4x)^{1/2} + C$.

2. $-18cos^5xsinx$.

3. 0.

4. $-8x^3(9 - 4x^4)^{-1/2}$.

5. $2xcos(x^2 - 7)$.

6. $2cos(4x - 5)^{1/2} \times (4x - 5)^{-1/2}$

7. $^x/\sqrt{(x^2 + 9)}$ $2(x^2 + 9)^{1/2} + C$

8. $p = 6$.

9. $b = ^\pi/_3$.

10. $^3/_4$ sq. units.

11. a Proof

b P(2, 0)

c $^4/_3$ sq. units.

12. a $a(t) = -20sin(2t - ^\pi/_2)$

b $a(^\pi/_3) < 0$, decreasing

13. a 0

b the sketch shows that between 90° and 270°, the areas cancel each other out

Answers to Chapter 16 Page 156

Exercise H16·1   Page 157

1. $13cos(x - 22·6)°$

2. a $10cos(x - 36·9)°$

b $\sqrt{17}cos(x - 14)°$

c $\sqrt{58}cos(x - 66·8)°$

d $\sqrt{7}cos(x - 49·1)°$

e $\sqrt{6}cos(x - 65·9)°$

f $\sqrt{29·5}cos(x - 77·2)°$

	Max	**Min**
3. a	(36·9°, 10)	(216·9°, -10)
b	(14°, √17)	(194°, -√17)
c	(66·8°, √58)	(246·8°, -√58)
d	(49·1°, √7)	(229·4°, -√7)
e	(65·9°, √6)	(245·9°, -√6)
f	(77·2°, √29·5)	(257·2°, -√29·5)

4. a $\sqrt{10}cos(x - 323·1)°$

b $\sqrt{17}cos(x - 346)°$

c $\sqrt{68}cos(x - 284)°$

d $\sqrt{8}cos(x - 324·7)°$

e $3cos(x - 298)°$

f $4·3cos(x - 303)°$

5. Max (36·9°, 10) Min (216·9°, -10)

6. $4\sqrt{2}sin(x + 135)°$

7. a $5sin(x + 143·1)°$

b $\sqrt{10}sin(x + 161·6)°$

c $\sqrt{61}sin(x + 140·2)°$

d $3\sqrt{2}sin(x + 160·5)°$

8. a $10sin(x - 306·9)°$

b $\sqrt{17}sin(x - 284)°$

c $\sqrt{58}sin(x - 336·8)°$

d $\sqrt{11}sin(x - 205)°$

9. Max (36·9°, 10) Min (216·9°, -10)

10. Proof

11. Proof

12. a $5sin(x - 323·1)°$

Max (53·1°, 5) Min (233·1°, -5)

b $\sqrt{53}sin(2x + 16)°$

Max (37°, √53) and Max (217°, √53)

Min (127°, -√53) and Min (307°, -√53)

c $\sqrt{3}sin(x - 215·3)°$

Max (305°, √3) Min (125·3°, -√3)

d $5·7cos(x - 282)°$

Max (78°, 5·7) Min (258°, -5·7)

13. a $25\sqrt{10}sin(t - 288·4)°$

b $25\sqrt{10}$

14. a $15\sqrt{13}sin(t + 33·7)°$

b No, will stop wave since $15\sqrt{13} = 54 < 55$

Exercise H16·2   Page 159

1. 22·6°

2. a 147·5°, 348·5°

b 60°

c 1·97, 6·16 radians

3. a 57°, 249·8°

b 61·4°, 279·7°

c 2·18, 5·67 radians

d 1·37 radians

4. $b = 36·9$

Capacitor is unsafe since 50 > 48.

5.

6. a Proof

b $\sqrt{2}sin(x + 45)°$

h = 41·4 cm

Exam Practice Page 160

1. a $5cos(x - 53·1)°$

b -5

2. a $41cos(x - 77·3)°$

b

c

3. a $2sin(x - 210)°$

b (44·5°, -1) and (195·5°, -1)

4. a $5cos(2x - 53·1)°$

b 26·5°, 206·6°

5. π and $^{3\pi}/_2$

Exercise H17·1 Page 161

1. a a^5 b a^4 c a^{12}
   d $10p^6$ e $8x^6$ f $2n^{10}$
   g $15t$ h m^{10} i $12a^3b^5$
   j $1000d^{12}e^{-6}$ k $2v^8$ l $1.5j^2h^4$

2. a 27 b $1/8$ c $1/5$
   d 1 e 6 f 5
   g 4 h 8 i $1/4$
   j $1/9$ k 8 l 7
   m 32 n 32 o 600

3. a $6x^5 + 10x^2$ b $x + 1$
   c $20x^3 - 4x$ d $x + 2 + x^{-1}$
   e $x - x^{-1}$ f $3x - 1$

4. a $\sqrt[3]{x^2}$ b $\sqrt[4]{x^3}$
   c $\sqrt[4]{x^5}$ d $\frac{1}{\sqrt[4]{x}}$
   e $\sqrt[5]{x^2}$ f $3\sqrt[3]{x^2}$

5. a $x^{4/3}$ b $x^{2/5}$
   c $x^{1/10}$ d $x^{-1/2}$
   e $2x^{-2/5}$ e $-3x^{-1/8}$

Exercise H17·2 Page 162

1. a $1/8, 1/4, 1/2, 1, 2, 4, 8$
   b/c/d
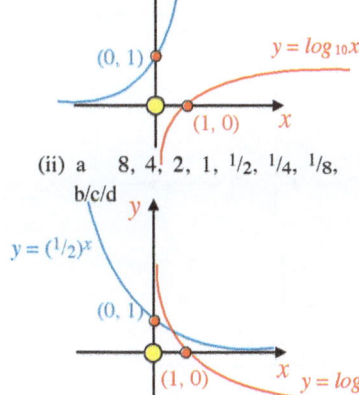

2. a $1/27, 1/9, 1/3, 1, 3, 9, 27$
   b/c/d

3. (i) a $1/1000, 1/100, 1/10, 1, 10, 100, 1000$
   b/c/d

   (ii) a $8, 4, 2, 1, 1/2, 1/4, 1/8,$
   b/c/d

Exercise H17·3 Page 163

1. a $log_2 16 = 4$ because $2^4 = 16$
   b $log_{10} 1000 = 3$ because $10^3 = 1000$
   c $log_3 27 = 3$ because $3^3 = 27$
   d $log_2 128 = 7$ because $2^7 = 128$

2. a 2 b 2 c 0
   d 1 e 3 f 5
   g 3 h 6 i 3

3. a $log_4 2 = 1/2$ because $4^{1/2} = \sqrt{4} = 2$
   b $log_8 2 = 1/3$ because $8^{1/3} = \sqrt[3]{8} = 2$
   c $log_{27} 9 = 2/3$ because $27^{2/3} = \sqrt[3]{27^2} = 2$
   d $log_{10} \sqrt{10} = 1/2$ because $10^{1/2} = \sqrt{10}$

4. a $1/2$ b $1/2$ c $2/3$
   d 1 e $3/4$ f $3/2$

5. a $log_2(1/8) = -3$ because $2^{-3} = 1/8$
   b $log_{10}(1/100) = -2$ because $10^{-2} = 1/100$
   c $log_5(1/125) = -3$ because $5^{-3} = 1/125$

6. a -2 b -4 c -5
   d -4 e $-1/2$ f $-2/3$

7. a $1\frac{1}{2}$ b -5

8. a 27 b 16 c 8
   d 125 e 100000 f 16

Exercise H17·4 Page 164

1. a 1 b 2 c 2
   d 2 e 2 f 0

2. a proof b proof

3. a 2 b 2 c $1/2$ d 0

4. a proof b proof

5. a 3 b 3 c 5
   d 5 e 5 f 3

6. a proof b (i) $log4$ (ii) $5/3$

7. a proof b proof

Exercise H17·5 Page 165

1.
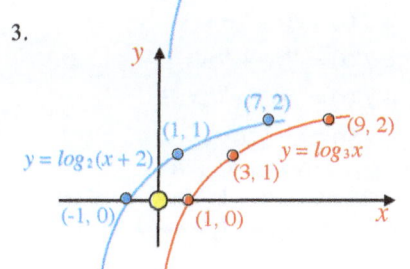

2.

3.

4.
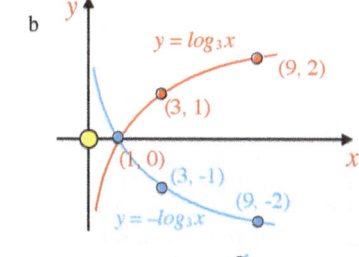

5 a
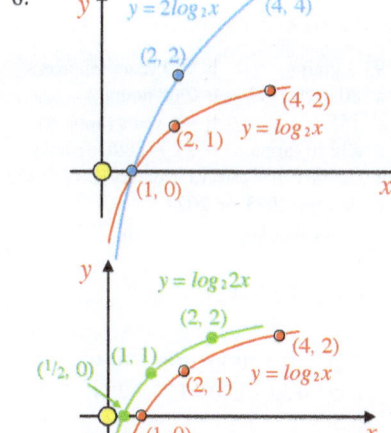

b

6.
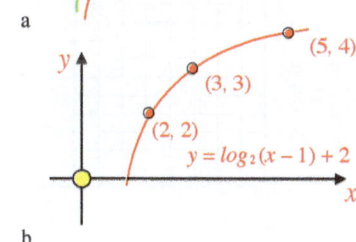

7. a
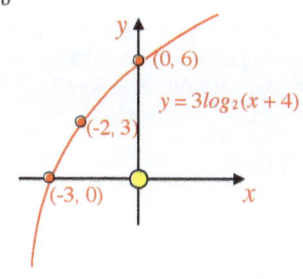

b

7. c

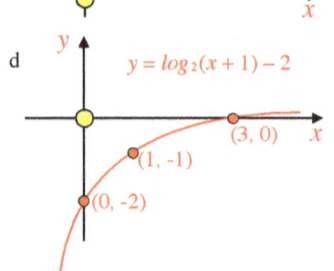

$y = 3 - \log_2 x$

(1, 3)
(2, 2)
(4, 1)

d

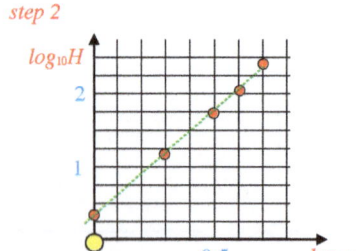

$y = \log_2(x + 1) - 2$

(3, 0)
(1, -1)
(0, -2)

8. a $y = \log_5 x$ b $y = \log_4(x + 2)$
   c $y = -\log_{10} x$ d $y = \log_2 x + 1$

Exercise H17·6 Page 166

1. 2·11
2. a 4·09   b 3·32   c 3·56
   d 3·32   e 0·699   f 3·71
3. 0·424
4. a -0·602 b 16·1   c 6·324

Exercise H17·7 Page 167

1. 93·5 grams   b 139 years (approx)
2. a 80   b 197   c 7·68 hours
3. a 155   b 9·6 years (approx)
4. a £1230 (approx) b 27·7 (28th birthday)
5. a Country A - 280713 Country B - 356452
   b Accept 2023 or 2024.
6. a Proof that $k = 0·15$ b 713

Exercise H17·8 Page 169

1. *step 1*

$\log x$	0	0·30	0·48	0·60	0·70
$\log H$	0·30	1·20	1·73	2·11	2·40

step 2

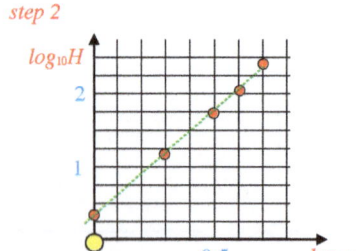

step 3

c from graph = 0·3 and m = 3 (approx)
=> $\log_{10} H = 3\log_{10} x + 0·3$
=> $\log_{10} H = \log_{10} x^3 + \log_{10} 2$
=> $\log_{10} H = \log_{10} 2x^3$
        $H = 2x^3$

2. $P = 3·16 v^{0·5}$
3. $D = 20 t^{-1·5}$

Exercise H17·9 Page 169

1. a $G = 3·16 p^{1·5}$ b $F = 1000 r^{-0·75}$
   c $L = 4h^{0·75}$ d $H = 40 d^{-0·5}$
   e $y = 3x^{-1/3}$

Exercise H17·10 Page 170

1. $y = 2 \times 3^x$
2. a $y = 10 \times 3·16^x$ b $T = 5 \times 4^n$
   c $P = 3^v$ d $F = 3 \times (0·05)^w$

Exam Practice Ch 17 Page 171

1. $x = {}^{13}/_7$
2. a $a = 3$, $b = 7$ b $\{x : x > 3, x \in R\}$
3. 82
4. a 300   b 10·46 hours
5. $x = 1$
6. $y = 32x^{1/3}$
7. a proof   b $x = 256$
8. $y = 16 \times 2^x$
9.

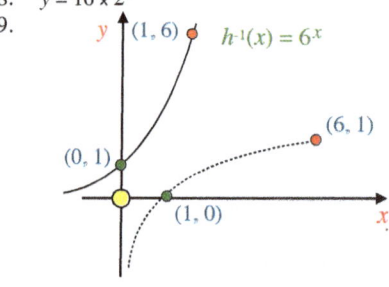

y (1, 6) $h^{-1}(x) = 6^x$
(6, 1)
(0, 1)
(1, 0)

10. a $k = 0·07$
    b $C_t = 0·87$ of C_0 => 13% drop

Answers to Chapter 18 Page 172

Higher Revision Page 172

Equations of Lines

1. a $x = -2$ b $y = {}^1/_2 x + 7$
   c $y = 3x + 12$
2. $y = {}^{-4}/_3 x + {}^1/_3$
3. $y = -{}^3/_2 x + {}^{17}/_2$
4. $y = -2x - 1$
5. a $y = {}^2/_3 x - {}^{14}/_3$
   b $y = {}^{-3}/_2 x + 17$, (10, 2)
6. a $y = 2x + 3$ b proof
7. a $y = 2x - 10$ and $y = {}^1/_4 x + {}^1/_2$
   b (6, 2)
8. 0·29

Differentiation

9. a $f'(x) = 10x - 3$
   b $f'(x) = 12x + {}^3/_{x^2}$
   c $f'(x) = -{}^{18}/_{x^3} + {}^3/_{2\sqrt{x}}$
   d $f'(x) = {}^9/_2 x^{1/2} - {}^9/_2 x^{-1/2}$
   e $f'(x) = 3 + {}^5/_{2x^2}$
10. $f'(x) = {}^1/_4 x^{-3/4} + {}^1/_4 x^{-5/4}$
11. a 36 m/s   b 0 m/s - top of arc
12. a $y = -x - 2$ b 2 and -1

13. a $m = 9$ b 35·5°
14.

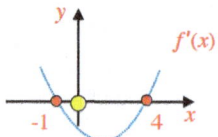

$f'(x)$
-1   4

15. $0 \le f(x) \le 32$
16.

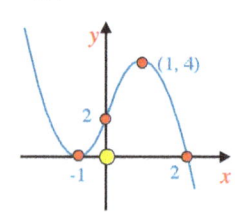

(1, 4)
2
-1   2

17. a $f'(x) = {}^3/_2\sqrt{x} - {}^3/_2\sqrt{x}$
    b $y = {}^9/_4 x - 7$ c $f'(1) = 0$

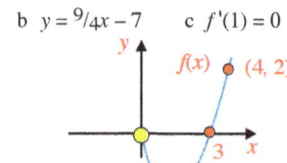

$f(x)$ (4, 2)
3
(1, -2)

Graphs and Functions

18. $f(g(2)) = 2$
19. $h(k(p)) - k(h(p)) = 2p$
20. a Can't find $\sqrt{}$ of a negative number
    b $y = {}^2/_{(1 - x)}$ $x \ne 1$
21. a

(0, 2)
(3, 1)
(-1, 1)
2

b

(-1, 2)
-2   2
(1, -1)

c

(2, 1)
-1   1   3
(0, -1)

d

(2, 1)
1   3   5
(4, -1)

e

(0, 2)
-1   1   3

f

(2, -2)
(2, 2)
(-1, 1)   (1, 1)   (3, 1)

22. $a = 2$ and $b = 2$
23. $c = 3$
24. a $s(x) = 1 - 2\,sin^2x°$ and $s(30) = {}^1/_2$
    c $r(x)$ has inverse $r^{-1}(x) = {}^1/_2(1 - x)$

Completing the Square

25. a $(x + 3)^2 - 9$ b $(x + 5)^2 - 24$
    c $-2(x - 1)^2 + 7$ d $2(x + {}^3/_2)^2 - {}^7/_2$
    e $-3(x - 1)^2 + 7$ f $-(x - {}^1/_2)^2 + {}^5/_4$
26. a min(-3, -9)   b min(-5, -24)
    c max(1, 7)   d min(-${}^3/_2$, -${}^7/_2$)
    e max(1, 7)   f max(${}^1/_2$, ${}^5/_4$)
27. a $-(x - 2)^2 + 6$ b (2, 2)

Trigonometry

28. a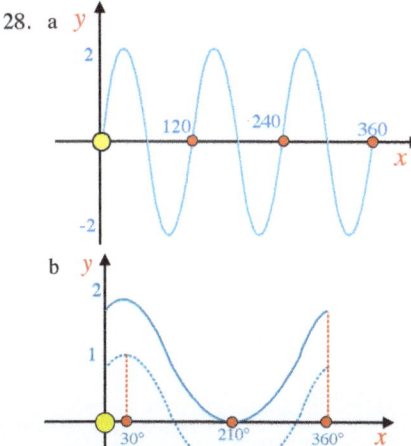

    b

29. a $\pi/_4, 3\pi/_4, 5\pi/_4, 7\pi/_4$
    b $0, \pi/_4, 3\pi/_4, \pi, 2\pi$
    c $4\pi/_3, 5\pi/_3$
    d $0, \pi/_3, \pi, 4\pi/_3$
30. a 0800 hrs   b 1600 hrs

Recurrence Relations

31. a $V_2 = 6.2$ b $n = 5$ c 15
32. 40.25%
33. $a = 1, b = -2$
34. Yes since limit is 21.7 kg
35. a proof
    b (i) 11000 (ii) 11800 (iii) 12440
    c 15000 to Rovers, 5000 to United

The Circle

36. Proof
37. $c = -116$
38. $y = 6x - 11$
39. a C(2, -1), $r = 10$
    b (8, 7) and (-8, -1) and M(0, 3)
40. C($pcos\theta, psin\theta$), $r = psin\theta$
    so just touches the x-axis
41. a proof and $y = {}^{12}/_5x$ b $m > {}^{12}/_5$
42. $r = \sqrt{2}t$

Trigonometric Formulae

43. 54.7°
44. ${}^{16}/_{65}$
45. 109.5° or 250.5°
46. 35° or 275°
47. a ${}^{24}/_{25}$ b ${}^{336}/_{625}$
48. a ${}^8/_{17}$ and ${}^{15}/_{17}$ b $90 - x$ c proof

Polynomials

49. Factorises to $(x + 2)^2(x - 1)^2$
    Only roots are at 1 and -2
50. Quotient $3x^2 + 5x + 2$, Remainder 0
51. $n = -19$, $(x - 3)(3x - 1)(x - 2)$
52. a (0, 0) Rising PI (-${}^1/_2$, -${}^1/_{16}$) Min T.P.
    b (0, 0) (-${}^2/_3$, 0)
    c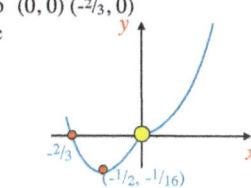
53. $k = 9$, $x = {}^3/_2$
54. a (0, 0) Min T.P. (2, $1{}^1/_3$) Max T.P.
    b (0, 0) (3, 0)
    c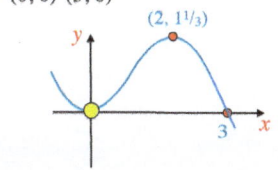
55. Proof

Quadratic Theory

56. $c = -1$ or $c = {}^{20}/_9$
57. $y = 5 - 4x - x^2$
58. $1 < t < 5$
59. Proof
60. $p \leq {}^1/_4$
61. $mc = 1$
62. a Proof   b $c = {}^9/_2$
    c (${}^1/_2$, -3)

Integration

63. a ${}^4/_5x^{5/4} - 3x + c$ b $2x^3 - 2x^2 + 2x + c$
    c $2{}^5/_8$ d $2\sqrt{3}$
64. a $6{}^1/_3$ sq units   b 13 sq units
65. $y = 4x + {}^1/_x + 1$
66. $1{}^1/_3$ sq units

Vectors

67. a Proof   b N(1, -9, -3)
68. 4
69. a 0   b perpendicular
70. $16 + 8\sqrt{2}$
71. 74°
72. a $\underline{p} + \underline{r}$ b ${}^1/_2\underline{q} + {}^1/_2\underline{r}$
    c Proof
73. M(5, 4, 9)
74. a Proof 5 : 3   b Proof

Further Calculus

75. $x(1 + x^2)^{-1/2}$
76. $-2cosxsinx + C$, $x = \pi/12$, $x = 5\pi/12$
77. $y = {}^1/_6x + 2$
78. $4cos2t - 3cos^2tsint$
79. a $x = 3\pi/4$
    b $x = 3\pi/4$ $x = 7\pi/4$ Values 0 and 2
80. $(\pi/3, 3\sqrt{3}/2)$ $(\pi, 0)$ $(5\pi/3, -3\sqrt{3}/2)$
81. a ${}^1/_{36}(6x - 5)^6$ b $4{}^1/_3$
    c ${}^2/_{21}$ d $-3cosx - cos2x + C$

The Wave Function

82. a $4\sqrt{5}sin(x - 63.4)°$
    b Max. $4\sqrt{5}$ at $x = 153.4°$
83. $2cos(x - 30)°$ $x = 66.9$ or $x = 353.1$
84. Proof $x = 40.2$ or $x = 252.4$
85. a $3cos2x + sin2x$
    b $\sqrt{10}cos(2x - 18.4)°$
    c Max. $\sqrt{10}$ Min. $-\sqrt{10}$
86. $20\sqrt{2}$ $\beta = \pi/16$ or $\beta = 9\pi/16$
87. a $A = 25\sqrt{5}$ $\alpha = 63.4$
    b $25\sqrt{5}$
    c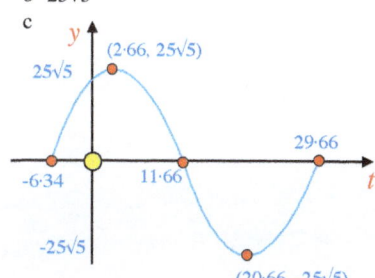

Logs and Exponentials

88. $x = 4$
89. $x = 2.89$
90. a 40   b 27.7 minutes
91. $B = 1000c^2$
92. $P = 100 \times ({}^1/_{10})^t$
93. $P = 3$,   R(4, 9.96)
94. a 3000   b $3{}^1/_2$ years